MW00658697

The Secret Life of Real Estate and Banking

The Secret Life of Real Estate and Banking

PHILLIP J. ANDERSON

SHEPHEARD-WALWYN (PUBLISHERS) LTD

© Phillip J. Anderson 2008

All rights reserved. No part of this book may be
reproduced in any form without the written permission
of the publisher, Shepheard-Walwyn (Publishers) Ltd

First published in 2008 as
The Secret Life of Real Estate by
Shepheard-Walwyn (Publishers) Ltd
Suite 107, Parkway House
Sheen Lane, London SW14 8LS
www.shepheardwalwyn.com
www.ethicaleconomics.org.uk

Reprinted 2009 under the new title
The Secret Life of Real Estate and Banking
Reprinted 2013, 2016, 2017, 2019, 2020
Reprinted 2021, 2022

British Library Cataloguing in Publication Data
A catalogue record of this book
is available from the British Library

ISBN: 978-0-85683-263-5

Typeset by Alacrity,
Sandford, Somerset
Printed and bound through
s|s|media limited, Rickmansworth, Hertfordshire

For Alan and MF

One day I hope they will understand

The water of life, wishing to make itself known on the face of the earth, bubbled up in an artesian well and flowed without effort or limit. People came to drink of the magic water and were nourished by it, since it was so clean and pure and invigorating. But humankind was not content to leave things in this Edenic state. Gradually they began to fence the well, charge admission, claim ownership of the property around it, make elaborate laws as to who could come to the well, put locks on the gate. Soon the well was the property of the powerful and the elite. The water was angry and offended; it stopped flowing and began to bubble up in another place. The people who owned the property around the first well were so engrossed in their power systems and ownership that they did not notice the water had vanished. They continued selling the non-existent water, and few people noticed that the true power was gone. But some dissatisfied people searched with great courage and found the new artesian well. Soon that well was under control of the property owners, and the same fate overtook it. The spring took itself to yet another place – and this has been going on throughout recorded history.

Said to be Dr Jung's favourite story, quoted in *Owning Your Own Shadow: Understanding the Dark Side of the Psyche*, Robert A. Johnson, p.vii

This book is dedicated to those very few brave souls who have searched with great courage to find that new artesian well and have seen what life could be like if we all agreed not to enclose it …

Every 18 Years ...

THE UNITED STATES began selling off its real estate, officially, under a set legal structure, on May 10, 1800. This marks a convenient starting point for our study of the secret life of real estate and banking, from which a remarkably regular pattern emerges.

In 1818 land sales peaked, followed by a downturn; in 1836 sales peaked again, ending in a depression; the next peak, in 1854, was followed by a depression; the 1869 peak was also followed by a depression; likewise in 1888. The downturn following the 1908 peak was cut short by the build-up to the First World War, and real estate peaked again in 1926, followed five years later by the world's worst ever depression. A construction-led boom (mainly government financed) peaked in 1944; the ensuing downturn was cut short by rebuilding after the destruction of the Second World War.

In other words, for the first 144 years of real estate enclosure in the US, land sales and/or real estate construction peaked consistently every 18 years.

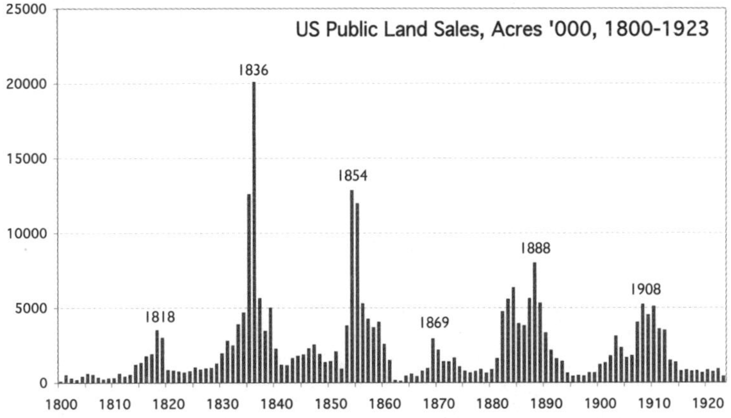

Since the US economy shrugged off the distorting effects of the Second World War, the average 18-year cycle reasserted itself with some vigour. The final years of the first decade of the 21st century will mark the passage of another cycle, 18 years from the trough of the previous one in 1992. So far there is little evidence that anything has changed to prevent yet another housing-related downturn, then recession. Should history repeat itself, we can expect the next trough around 2010.

This book is the story of those 18-year real estate cycles: why they happen, and why you can be assured they will repeat. A little knowledge of which could be exceedingly profitable ...

Contents

Author's note xi

PART I THE PRESENT

We've Been Here Before: The Subprime Recession of 2008-10 3

PART II THE HISTORY

1 In the Beginning: Land of the Endless Naughts 21
1792: The First panic 30
The Power of Credit 37
2 The Great American Barbeque 45
3 Mad Cash Disease 61
4 G.T.T. – Gone To Texas 69
5 US Banking History to 1860 97
6 The Western Blizzard 105
7 Solidarity and Permanence 133
8 Hell on Wheels 139
9 160 Acres, or 6 Feet 171
10 The Temple 197
11 Land of Oranges and Speculators 203
12 Hydrocarbon Man 239
13 Ask Not What Your Bank Can Do for You... 269
14 Life, Liberty and the Pursuit of a Mortgage 291

PART III THE FUTURE

(Understanding the Past and Predicting the Future)

15	Knowledge We Gained Along the Way	323
16	Why the Repeat?	333
17	Why 18 Years?	339
18	The Reliability of the Real Estate Cycle Repeating	343
19	What Time Is It?	351
20	Help with Telling the Time	363
21	They Say It Can't Be Done	375
22	The Secret Life of Real Estate and Banking	379
	Appendixes	385
	Acknowledgements	441
	Index	443

Author's Note

CONGRATULATIONS! You have just picked up the best book you will ever read about real estate cycles. This book will show you how the real estate cycle works and why it will continue to repeat. Properly understood, this knowledge will prove of immense value to you as an investor.

Whilst the book deals primarily with the American real estate cycle, it should be noted that the same principles apply to any nation that has enclosed its rent of natural resources, the largest of which is the capitalised ground rent. As more and more developing nations join the Western world in enclosing this ground rent (China and Russia being the latest two) the real estate cycle can only strengthen and globalise. For the 21st century, this will mean even bigger and more violent global (synchronised) booms, then busts.

Imagine knowing how to take advantage of that.

To explain: Part I of the book highlights the present situation in which the US finds itself. Part II of the book, Chapters 1 through 14, detail the clear historical repetition of the real estate cycle – necessary to go through as you probably wouldn't believe it otherwise. Economists deny it, but history clearly repeats. Only after that can the banking system that facilitates this repetition, and the enclosure of the commons that actually causes it, be fully explained. Part III of the book brings all the information together in order that we might work out how the current real estate cycle will play out into 2010, leading to the next real estate cycle boom, then bust, towards the end of the 2020s.

Me? I run Economic Indicator Services Ltd, a company I have directed since the very early 1990s. EIS is the world's foremost authority on business, real estate and commodity cycles; we have been teaching our subscribers for years how to profit substantially from this knowledge. EIS intentionally does this quietly and with little fanfare. You can see all of that on the website: www.businesscycles.biz (note especially the testimonials).

In this book I have tried properly to attribute all sourced material and hope I have not missed any. There has, over the years, been plenty written about each major US downturn but this is the first time anyone has put all the information together coherently and been able to tell you *why* the cycle repeats as it does.

Most of the chapters were written progressively between 1998 and 2004 and posted to the website for subscribers as they were completed, or used in classes run over those years. The original version of each chapter is still on the website. Our 18-hour real estate clock,* as pictured on page 360 of this book, represents the crystallisation of all this knowledge.

You are in good hands here. I guarantee that, if you read all the US land history, go on to read the further chapters explaining the cause of the cycle, and then go back to re-read the history with a new-found knowledge of the 18-year real estate cycle, a whole new world of understanding will open up before you. The information here is timeless and will stand you in good stead for the next US real estate cycle, 2010 to 2028 or so.

But hey, don't believe me – study it for yourself!

PHILLIP J. ANDERSON
September 7, 2008

The title of the book required a slight amendment – based on some feedback. This book is as much about the credit creation process as it is about real estate, so it has been changed to *The Secret Life of Real Estate and Banking*. This is an improvement and more reflective of what the book is all about. Do not fall into the trap, though, of blaming the banks for the recent 'Great Recession', as almost everyone seems to have done this year. It is easy to blame the banks for all the troubles: they are an easy scapegoat, especially for the politicians. As you will read, however, it has been the same every previous real estate cycle: blame the banks for the collapse, then change the banking laws 'to ensure it won't happen again'; 2009 is not proving any different. The recent changes to the current banking structures will, in fact, guarantee us yet another cycle.

PHILLIP J. ANDERSON
August 21, 2009

* Feedback from subscribers and readers of the first printing of the book suggests that it would have been clearer to call our clock 'the 18-year real estate clock', rather than 'the 24-hour real estate clock', the name given to it originally. So for this second printing and onwards, this is what we have done. A definite improvement. Thank you.

PART I

THE PRESENT

Those who cannot remember the past are condemned to repeat it.

George Santayana, *The Life of Reason*

We've Been Here Before

The Subprime Recession of 2008-10

Subprime mortgages do not pose a huge danger to the economy, and it's unlikely that this factor will trigger anything of a massive nature in the general economy.

Warren Buffett, 2007[1]

The US housing market [is] showing clear signs of stability.

US Deputy Treasury Secretary, Robert J. Kimmitt, at the World Economic Forum, Davos, Switzerland, January 2007

A summary of the views of all the key participants at this forum went on to say:

The global economic outlook for 2007 is full of hope. Things are generally expected to go 'fantastically well'.

The world economy is in good condition.

The German Chancellor, Angela Merkel, at the June 2007 annual G8 meeting[2]

THE WORLD ECONOMY, especially that of the US, did not seem to be in quite as good a shape as it looked. What goes up, comes down: all to do with that damned land price – *again*. We've been here before. The process remains just as Homer Hoyt described it all those years ago: 'A tight money market that limits new construction also curtails the demand for land and tends to lower its price.'[3] As is always the case, those in charge do not study history. Nor do they have any idea how the economy actually works.

The new 'new era'

BY 2004, it has become accepted wisdom that the US economy is functioning better than in the past: the economic expansions are lasting longer, the recessions are much shorter; there is no inflation to speak of and, with the new ways of spreading risk that the banks have found (securitising their loans), the odds of a serious financial crisis or economic downturn seem

1 Dominic Rushe, 'Crowds Flock to Omaha Sage', *Sunday Times*, May 4, 2008, p.8. Despite Buffett's comment, the subsequent subprime events proved of little consequence to Berkshire's results.
2 Quoted in *Barrons*, June 11, 2007.
3 *According to Hoyt: Market Value versus Speculative Value*, reprinted by Urban Land Institute, October 1967, p.795.

remote. One of the Fed's governors, Ben Bernanke, even gives a name to the new-found confidence: 'the great moderation'.[4] Greatly improved monetary policy, economic 'structural' changes and perhaps a small bit of old-fashioned good luck have been responsible for it, he argues forcefully.

The Bankers take Bernanke's confidence to heart, congratulating themselves once again on their successful efforts to achieve economic stability. This time things really are different, they say; the nature of banking has changed fundamentally and forever. Thanks to securitisation and derivatives, banks are no longer taking the excessive risks they once used to: banks are now 'spreading' the risk, not storing it. There is no shortage of money to play with either. Between February 1996 and October 1999, the money supply increases by approximately $1.6 trillion, almost 20 per cent of GDP.[5] At this rate, the supply will double in just the next eight years.

Before long we will not be able to work out what is happening with the money supply, however. By 2006 the Fed is going to deem the measure unimportant and stop calculating it.

New banks are starting up everywhere, but in particular around developing suburbs in areas like Southwest Florida, Atlanta and parts of California. To cater for the increased demand for mortgages, 630 new banks are established between 2003 and 2007, raising $8.9bn in capital.[6] Throughout 2005 the strong housing market creates a large number of vacancies at lending institutions. Thousands take the opportunity to change profession and become a mortgage broker. Countrywide financial CEO Angelo Mozilo proclaims loudly that his company will maintain a strong focus on growing market share, with the aim of achieving a 30 per cent market share by 2008. A profusion of real estate books argue that there has never been a better time to buy property, or to start a real estate career. None of the books makes even a passing reference to the possible existence of a real estate cycle.

In 2005 hurricane Katrina, the sixth strongest Atlantic hurricane ever recorded and the third strongest to make the US coastline, slams into New Orleans. Fears are raised for the US economy. However those who know their economic history know that, as the event is not credit-related, its effect on the economy will not be long-lasting – the Chicago 1871 fire and the 1907 San Francisco earthquake taught us this. For everyone else, the juggernaut US economy takes on the appearance of invincibility, immune to anything nature can throw at it.

In 2006 US stock markets reach all-time highs, continuing the repetition of past cycles. President George W. Bush continues with his tax cutting initiatives and tries to make them permanent. We know the effect this will have on land price – an effect policymakers are simply unaware of.

4 Speech given to the Eastern Economic Association, Washington DC, February 20, 2004.
5 Fleckenstein, *Greenspan's Bubbles*, p.74.
6 Figures from SNL Financial LC.

Into the Peak

US HOMEOWNERS are not the only persons demanding mortgages. The CEOs of the Wall Street investment banks are increasing their companies' trading risks, diversifying into hedge funds and the world of leveraged buyouts, and, of course, vastly expanding all manner of lending practices – even buying mortgage companies when they have to. As the decade progresses, the amount of top-rated, triple A corporate debt begins to shrink. This may be due partly to corporations' enjoying better cash flow – not having to raise additional cash via the debt markets – but it may also signal the ease with which it is now possible to sell far more risky debt to investors. With returns on AAA-rated debt falling, many traditional buyers, the life assurance and pension funds, begin to seek new ways to lift returns, using derivatives or chasing higher risk – but higher return – debt. By mid-decade, the outlook is all roses. Business has never seen it so good. The community begins hailing Fed chief Dr Alan Greenspan as 'the greatest central banker that ever lived'.

A consortium led by the Royal Bank of Scotland agrees to buy the Dutch bank ABN Amro. The deal has an astronomical price tag, but a heap of credit-creation possibilities. In Las Vegas the Tropicana Casino and Resort gets an overhaul. Even by US standards this is grandiose. Scheduled for completion in 2010, the hotel will have 10,200 rooms, a convention centre, shopping mall and parking for more than 6,000 cars. 'It's like three mega-resorts at once,' enthused one of the leading architects. Cisco Systems chief executive John Chambers, echoing the feelings of just about every CEO, claims repeatedly that the global economy is stronger than he has ever seen it. The chief economist at the International Monetary Fund declares the world economic outlook to be the brightest since the 1960s, with the prospect of growth rates of more than 5 per cent continuing for years. 'Major dislocations still appear to be a low probability event,' he declares. The Spanish prime minister announces to the world that Spain has now joined the 'Champions League' of world economies and is growing 'so robustly, and creating so many jobs, [the country will] soon be richer than Germany'. In the UK an oft-quoted Hometrack economist exclaims: 'there is more chance of finding Elvis on the moon than house prices crashing in the next five years'.

At the end of February 2007 world stock markets take a bit of a tumble. After almost five years of unbroken gains, market participants turn to each other and say, 'Whoa, what was that?' Who can explain the moods of stock markets, but it seems that HSBC Finance Corp, in one of its little-read securities filings, had highlighted some larger than normal overdue accounts in its subprime mortgage book. This implies an increase in bad debts for the company, and a slowdown in lending. After just a few days, however, it is back to unfettered optimism among market traders. But wiser heads – Economic Indicator Services subscribers and those who have read their history – pause for thought.[7] A load of tall buildings are now on the drawing boards, or half built, with competition for the tallest really hotting up; the price of copper is reaching all-time highs – and the yield curve had just gone negative. Even more significantly, US land prices, which went into the stratosphere as the economy approached the fourteenth year from the previous 1992 cyclical low, are now, unnoticed by the market in general, beginning to decline.[8] 'When land came on the market, you competed against national homebuilders who were flush with money and speculators who were jumping into the market and trying to resell it immediately,' explained one regional builder in Alexandria, Virginia. 'The price was high and the supply became limited. Then the market stopped when you couldn't get people to buy because it exceeded their ability to pay. Now we see land that's been on the market for months.'[9] Past cycles have taught us that the land market is always the first to peak at the end of a cycle; it then leads the decline into ultimate recession. Nothing different is happening so far in this present cycle.

By mid 2007 a glut of homes for sale indicates a weakening housing market. Says the *Wall Street Journal*, 'the market started to cool in mid 2005 after a buying frenzy that drove up the average US home price nearly 60% in the first half of the decade and more than doubled prices in many areas near the East and West coasts.'[10] In April, New Century Financial Corp, a mortgage lender based in Irvine, California, files for bankruptcy protection: rising interest rates are placing pressure on mortgaged home owners, prospective borrowers, and the lenders too. Most of the financial news goes unnoticed by the public, however, as the nation is transfixed on whether Paris Hilton has justly been put behind bars for her probation violation.

In late June two Bear Stearns hedge funds collapse.[11] The funds had been holding a good deal of their assets in collateralised debt obligations (CDOs) backed by subprime mortgage loans – something that will be explained in the following pages. Worse, it appeared that a senior managing director at Bear Stearns was also managing more than $13 bn worth of CDOs that had been bought by money market funds and other investors. This was a problem because money market funds, established some years before to offer better returns than are available at a bank, and yet still offer good security for investors, are not insured by the US government since they rarely fail. What is more, hedge funds, which take in investors' money which they then re-invest, usually top up the total by borrowing heavily

7 See www.businesscycles.biz/chartsbusiness/dow1.htm for more information.
8 See the EIS September 2006 forecast, 'Raw land rush in the US; indicates US real estate peak has arrived' (available at www.businesscycles.biz/pastforecastsbusinesscycles.htm).
9 'Toll, Centrex, Lennar join "moron" speculators in land grab bust', *Bloomberg*, February 7, 2007.
10 June 9-10, 2007, p.A1.
11 The funds were the High-Grade Structured Credit Strategies Fund, which lost all but 9 per cent of its value, and the more souped-up High-Grade Structured Credit Strategies Enhanced Leveraged Fund, which lost its entire value.

from banks to maximise their asset-buying potential. A number of banks had lent a collective $6 bn to the highly leveraged Bear Stearns funds, now worth practically nothing.[12]

The risk of further financial stress from continued exposure to subprime mortgages can no longer be ignored.[13] Significantly, the investors in such debt begin to demand higher interest rates, on better terms, from borrowers. On July 21 Treasury Secretary Paulson assures markets that the US is 'about at the bottom of the housing slope'. He has to say that, but since he could not forecast the peak of the cycle it is unlikely he can forecast the low.

At the end of July 2007 the possible scale of the problem is revealed when IKB Deutsche Industriebank, a previously little-known German bank based in Dusseldorf, warns investors of probable market losses caused by its investment in the US subprime mortgage market. This seems to have come as a shock: just ten days before IKB had reassured German markets that the bank was 'in no respect affected' by the recent events. The Bundesbank (the equivalent of the US Fed) plays down the threat of these mortgage problems flowing through to other German banks, but then immediately offers a rescue package to bail out IKB. The German chief regulator makes reference to the Kredit-Anstalt bank collapse of 1931 that saw Germany enter depression, so disturbed is he by what he saw at the collapsed bank.

A day later another German bank, Sachsen LB, receives a similar emergency bailout. Sachsen LB's exposure to the US markets is a possible $80 bn, via Irish funds kept off-balance-sheet. (Both banks will eventually require credit guarantees of €25 bn to cover their liabilities and poor investment decisions.) Just what, exactly, was going on?

'Subprime' is a term used to describe borrowers with low credit scores or poor credit history, who represent a greater risk of default. Lending institutions, it seems, had been bundling all their loans and mortgages, including subprime ones, into a product that resembled a bond which other investors might be willing to buy. The whole process – called securitisation – expands the market for loans, enabling banks to improve their balance sheets and allowing other investors access to the credit risk – and hence to supposedly increased earnings power. By 2006 there is $28 trillion in outstanding securitised loans, representing just slightly less than 40 per cent of all loans, up from a mere 18 per cent in 1990.

To keep much of their investment off-balance-sheet, banks established what became known as SIVs (structured investment vehicles),[14] typically registered in off-shore tax havens, which happily bought into securitised

12 *Financial Times*, June 22, 2007, p.12.

13 For the rest of the market at least; as the two Bear Stearns funds implode, the top two Bear Stearns executives are away competing in a week-long national Bridge tournament in Nashville.

14 Repeat behaviour: the banking trusts of 1907, the investment trusts of the 1920s and the currency trading banks of the 1970s all kept off-balance-sheet investments.

debts, renamed CDOs (collateralised debt obligations), being the bundled mortgages or CLOs (collateralised loan obligations) which contain the bundled corporate loans. It really is more simple than it looks: the financial engineering simply gathered, say, 5,000 American home loans of perhaps $200,000 each, put them together into a 'security' that would then be worth $1 bn, that could now be bought, sold or traded by any investor, investment vehicle or other bank with the money – or ability to borrow the money – to do so. Wall Street banks found ways to boost profits yet further by 'slicing and dicing' them, as the saying went, accounting-speak for merely carving the $1 bn package into differently rated risk levels and hence different levels of return.

All fine when the real estate market is going up, which of course everybody under 42 believes will continue into eternity because they have never seen anything different. But the securitisation process was revealed for what it is – a structure built entirely on an escalating land price – when mortgage defaults begin to undermine the cash-flows, the earnings, and hence the structure itself. The rent is no longer affordable by productive activity. Every 18 years; or perhaps, more correctly, every 14 years from the low of the previous cycle. Readers may rest assured that this process will continue to repeat, sure as night follows day, as long as the ground rent remains privatised and permitted to capitalise into a tradable, government-granted licence. Underpinning this behaviour is the law of rent. The SIVs themselves are in effect borrowing short-term to then buy longer-term, higher yielding debt. In the downturn some of the SIVs lose so much money that bank owners are forced to put their own capital into the fund to preserve their reputation or stave off total collapse.

Anyway, back to the unfolding drama that a collapsing land price is bringing ...

The Turn

ON AUGUST 7TH 2007 BNP Paribas, a large French bank, comes clean on its investments in this area and freezes withdrawals on several of its managed funds (an unusual move in the investment funds industry, especially in the money markets area). The bank says it is having trouble valuing such CDOs since many, if not most, are rarely traded on any exchange. For those in the money markets, where safety and high liquidity are absolute necessities, this statement comes as something of a revelation. It suggests that any fund manager holding subprime mortgages as part of his portfolio may be in desperate trouble and likely to be punished by the rest of the market. Whilst BNP is freezing withdrawals, the American Home Mortgage Investment Corp files for bankruptcy. This is the second largest residential lender failure for the year so far. The company says it was pushed into bankruptcy partly by margin calls from banks that had been providing loan funds to originate the mortgages.

American Home Mortgage could just as easily have said, 'Borrowing short, to lend long.'

In mid-August KKR Financial Holdings (an affiliate of buyout specialists Kohlberg Kravis Roberts) announces huge losses as a result of 'eroding confidence in mortgage backed securities', and that it will no longer invest in residential real estate. The same day, First Magnus Financial Corp, one of America's largest privately held mortgage companies, files for chapter 11 bankruptcy protection. After closing its offices and disconnecting the phones, the company simply says, 'In light of the collapse of the secondary mortgage market, First Magnus will not fund any future mortgage loans ...'[15] First Magnus had not been involved in the subprime mortgage business; instead it was an originator of loans that were then bundled into the secondary loan market. More than $30bn in loans had been originated by the company and then sold on in this manner in 2006. Credit, once abundant, is suddenly becoming that much harder to get.

The same month, Goldman Sachs reports that its Global Alpha quant fund has lost 27 per cent of its value. Goldman says this is because its computers failed to predict a '25% standard deviation move', an event so rare that they have only ever seen it twice before in their entire trading history. Doh! That unlooked for event – perhaps better described these days as a 'black swan' moment. Funny, though, how such moments – such credit blow-ups – turn up regularly, and most commonly *only after land price has turned down first ...*

On August 22 Toll Brothers, the largest builder of luxury homes in the US, announces a fall in fiscal third-quarter profit of 85 per cent and a forced write-down of property values. Five of the largest US home builders have now reported combined losses of $1.85bn and taken charges of $2.9bn to write down land values and walk away from various property options.[16] Those who know Ricardo's Law of Rent (see Chapter 16, 'Why the Repeat?') and have studied Fred Harrison's accompanying thesis (explained in Chapter 15, 'Knowledge We Gained Along the Way') will see that this is how the land price downturn will slowly transmit itself to the wider economy. This development is a prelude to recession. (*Peaks in the building cycle follow the peak in land value, but precede the recession.*) Nothing is happening differently from past cycles here either.

In an attempt to alleviate the tightening supply of credit and the rising price of risk, Federal bankers announce a series of measures, mainly to inject liquidity, i.e. cash, into the banking system. The amounts pumped in are unprecedented. Is this the sound of helicopters starting up? The Fed's action pacifies global stock and bond markets for the moment, but the rate of US home repossessions continues to climb. So too do interest rates: the

15 *The Business Journal*, Phoenix, August 17, 2007.
16 *International Herald Tribune*, August 23, 2007, p.14.

cost of funds in the interbank money markets hits a ten-year peak as the credit squeeze begins to raise borrowing costs. (The interbank rate is significant since it is used by a number of banks and other financial institutions to fund their portfolio of assets and securities lending.) The banks begin hoarding any available cash.

Throughout the rest of the Western world, most housing markets are going the opposite way and cooling rapidly. In Spain, Astroc, a large local builder, sees its shares down 89 per cent from the high of just a few months prior, and grass begins to sprout from its many unfinished or unoccupied hotels and apartments. Lawsuits alleging share market manipulation are initiated.[17] Few, it seems, know anything about real estate cycles, or the effect rising interest rates have at the end of them. Spain reports that, for 2006, real estate activity accounted for slightly less than 20 per cent of its GDP.

Somewhat presciently, Bundesbank president Axel Weber states in early September that the present turmoil in markets has all the hallmarks of a classic bank run: 'What we are seeing is basically what we see underlying all banking crises,' he says, voicing the concerns of bankers everywhere who fear a good old fashioned bank run just like in the old days, where savers lose confidence in banks and queue to get their money out. Despite this – perhaps because of it – the mid-September announcement by Northern Rock, a large UK bank and the fifth biggest mortgage lender in the country, that it is seeking 'assistance' from the Bank of England takes depositors and markets by surprise (though the share price had been weakening for months, and was well off its highs of February 2007). Savers queue around the block at every Northern Rock branch to get their hands on their money before it's too late. 'I'm putting my money under the mattress,' says one saver.[18] To add to the public confusion, the top five UK banks had, only the month before, issued record first-half results, showing combined profits of almost £22bn. The subprime mess had just gone global.

Northern Rock was a pioneer in using mortgage-backed securities and other forms of wholesale funding to finance its UK banking expansion, rather than just tapping its depositor base. History reveals that such banks are *always* the first to capsize as rising interest rates into the final years of the land price cycle reveal the weakness of such a strategy (as the yield curve goes negative). History repeating. A few days later the Fed begins to cut interest rates.

An indication that few private investors have any understanding of the information presented in this book is that The Share Centre, a UK stock broker, can announce a 591% increase on the previous week's account openings as private investors open up facilities to snap up Northern Rock

17 *International Herald Tribune*, August 23, p.12.
18 *Evening Standard*, September 17, p.5.

shares.[19] At the end of a land price cycle such behaviour is financial suicide. Notably, most of the big hedge funds and professional investors continue to short the stock – so much so that the stock of shares available for this activity runs out: the first time that this has ever happened for a blue chip company in the history of the UK stock exchange.

Meanwhile, Stan O'Neal, the soon-to-be deposed boss of Merrill Lynch, spends most of the month of September working on his golf game; James Cayne, the CEO at Bear Stearns, remains at the bridge table. Neither recognises the gravity of the situation.[20]

In October housing starts in the US drop to a twelve-year low; the sale of new homes falls to its lowest level since records began in the early 1970s; so too their prices. The Mortgage Bankers Association releases figures suggesting that more than 14 per cent of subprime borrowers are defaulting. This, they say, is the worst foreclosure crisis since their records began in 1953. In some states, like Michigan, one in every one hundred homes is in a state of foreclosure. Higher interest rates are taking their toll, as would be expected but so few saw coming. The extent of the developing crisis is revealed by the world's banks as they unveil results showing possible bad debts of $30bn as a result of American homeowners defaulting on mortgages. But are they coming clean and revealing the true state of affairs? Nobody knows, though stock markets appear to be speculating that the worst may already be over for the banks and building companies: they hit new highs for the month.

Of all the so-called experts and economists, just one has been able to understand the turn in the land market (as distinct from the real estate market) and predict it before it happens – Fred Harrison. Others continue to foresee stable, or at worst subdued, conditions for 2008. This is not what the 18-year real estate clock indicates.

Market optimism proves short-lived. By November it is clear that banks will have serious work in front of them to rebuild their balance sheets and protect themselves against further losses – if they can survive the downturn. They will have to begin 'hoarding liquidity'. A whiff of real fear is seen in markets as it is realised the debt write-downs could approach $200bn, perhaps more. The previous year's banking profits were indeed built on sand.

In Britain some £40 to £50bn of taxpayers' money has been chanelled to the stricken Northern Rock, to keep the bank afloat. This is almost 5 per cent of the nation's GDP, an unprecedented figure. Central banks around the world are forced to co-ordinate their actions, and inject cash into their respective economies to the tune of $100bn in an effort to stabilise credit markets. There is talk of the US facing its worst recession since the 1930s. But memories are short. The same thing is said in every

19 *Financial Times*, September 21, 2007.
20 *The Business*, November 17, 2007, p.35.

land-price-led downturn. As further proof that few understand how the economy works, comparisons are made to credit squeezes after the dot-com bust of 2001/2, the Russian bond default of 1998 and Long Term Capital Management issues that year. Such credit crunches, however, did not come at the end of a real estate cycle, and they did not involve land value, so economic recovery was much easier. Urgent financial news still can't make it beyond the neglected financial pages; space elsewhere is gobbled up by rumours that the sister of Britney Spears may be pregnant.

In 2008 UK house prices begin to copy their US counterparts, just as the world's largest cruise ship, the *Independence of the Seas*, enters service and sails into Southampton. An even bigger ship is expected in 2009. In an effort to stem the developing crisis, the British prime minister announces measures to ensure greater transparency in the banking system, better oversight of the regulatory bodies and a review of credit-rating agencies. (Didn't we hear that last cycle, and the cycle before that, and the cycle before that?) Back in the US, President Bush announces an economic stimulus package to 'reward' each American household with an extra $1,600. Francis Everett Townsend would be pleased.

By February it seems that the selling price of some homes will fall below the value of the outstanding mortgage. This is not how it was meant to be. Don't house prices always go up? The online company Zillow reports on February 12 that some 30 per cent of US homeowners who bought in the previous two years now owe more on their mortgage than the house is worth. Moody's Economy.com puts the figure at 8.8 million homeowners, or one-tenth of the entire US homeowner market. It is at such a point that prices can go into a dangerous downward spiral. Borrowers go into foreclosure, forcing the sale of properties at discounted prices, while buyers wait for even lower prices. Nothing so quickly stops an upturn as the belief that a commodity can be bought next month or next year at the same or a lower price. In an effort to stabilise house prices, the Fed chairman asks banks to consider forgiving part of the loan for borrowers in distress.

True to form, the end of the real estate cycle hits first, and hardest, those with a high level of debt, those in the economy most dependent on the free flow of credit. Amongst them are the buyers of houses over the previous two years, and home builders, as the flow of cash dries up from lack of sales. Such is the 'winner's curse' phase of the cycle: the very worst time to be highly leveraged is the very time it looks safest to be so. The US Conference of Mayors tells America that the number of hungry and homeless persons in US cities rose dramatically in 2007.[21] The ghosts of Coxey's Army, struggling to afford the high land price. Extensive welfare handouts will keep today's ghosts compliant, and docile too.

Finally facing the gravity of the situation, economists realise that

21 23-city *Hunger and Homelessness Survey*, December 2007.

real estate values have now lost around $1 trillion. Worse, it seems possible that the insurance companies' mortgage-related risks may actually overwhelm their capital bases. New capital will be required to fix the problem. In a further attempt to ease the worsening crisis, the world's central banks, again in co-ordinated action, inject a further, unprecedented, $200bn into the global economy to prevent what some are now warning will be the worst recession in decades. Stock markets bounce on news of the cash injection, but not for long.

The Panic

> ***The Bank never 'goes broke'. If the Bank runs out of money it may issue as much more as may be needed by merely writing on any ordinary paper.***
>
> From the 'Rules of Monopoly', by Parker Brothers

PERHAPS THE BANKERS knew what was coming, perhaps not. Regardless, 180 days from the Northern Rock collapse, a run on the investment bank Bear Stearns brings to an end its 85-year history. Spooked by the firm's probable exposure to the subprime crisis and related mortgages, investors withdraw, in just a single day, more than $10bn from their accounts. The run prompts a Federal Reserve taxpayer-funded bailout, although the Fed gets to avoid the words 'taxpayer-funded' after J.P. Morgan Chase agrees to buy the company for $2 a share (later increased to $10) once the Fed has spent $29bn on taking over the other distressed assets. $236m for a company valued at $20bn the year before … Bear Stearns was America's fifth largest investment bank. The bank did not take deposits from the public, like a commercial bank, but funded its operations with borrowed money. History shows that, at the end of each land-price-induced downturn, at least one investment bank will fail – the one most leveraged at the worst possible time. Said former US Treasury Secretary Lawrence Summers: 'It was fortunate that a natural partner was available when Bear Stearns failed – we might not be so lucky next time.' Shades of Arthur Burns and the 1974 Franklin National Bank fiasco (Appendix 5).

The run on Bear Stearns comes just days after the new CEO publicly denied it faced serious problems. As usual, investors are assured that nothing is wrong right to the very end, such is the nature of banking in a rent-enclosed economy. So the Fed assumes the risk yet again for a failed bank. Said Bear Stearns CEO Alan Schwartz: 'Due to the stressed condition of the credit market as a whole and the unprecedented speed at which rumours and speculation travel and echo through the modern financial media environment, the rumours and speculation became a self-fulfilling prophecy.' No longer can we blame the telegraph; this time it's the internet. 'There was, simply put,' continued Schwartz, 'a run on the bank.' A repeat of history. Shortly thereafter, the Fed lowers interest rates from 3 per cent to 2.25 per cent, the sixth such emergency decrease since August 2007. The great moderation appears to be waning.

By April 2008 the cost to the economy of all the credit creation and lending by banks so that people can afford the price of land is becoming clearer: actual losses total $300bn. The figure may eventually be as high as $1 trillion, according to IMF estimates. Citigroup lead the pack with reported losses of $40.9bn, followed closely by UBS at $38bn, then Merrill Lynch with $31.7bn in write-offs. The real estate woes are turning up in all sorts of places. Lehman Brothers says in June that it expects to report a second quarter loss of $2.8bn, or $5 a share. An equity stake in the leveraged buyout of Archstone-Smith, an apartment developer, is to blame. 'Lehman's problems are due almost entirely to its mortgage and real estate exposure,' noted *Barron's*.[22] To recover the losses and rebuild their capital, banks resort either to requesting an investment in their business by the rapidly developing Sovereign Wealth Funds, taking up loans from the Fed, or to selling non-core associated businesses and/or the now not-so-essential branches.

In a further effort to alleviate the distressed housing sector, the US Senate passes a $300bn relief bill[23] (read 'bailout') that will allow an estimated 400,000 homeowners to avoid foreclosure by permitting refinancing of their existing subprime mortgages into fixed-rate home loans, supported by the federal government. After threatening to veto the legislation, the Bush administration does a U-turn when the two organisations at the very heart of the US home mortgage banking system, Fannie Mae and Freddie Mac,[24] suffer a sharp and very sudden share price fall, despite repeated assurances by Fed officials of the financial health of both.

Fannie Mae and Freddie Mac do not actually lend money or offer mortgages; what they do is buy mortgages from banks and other financial organisations and securitise those mortgages so that investors from around the world can buy them – a process that frees up bank capital to help such banks originate even more mortgages. It is a process deliberately created by Congress to facilitate home buying for American citizens. (A process required only because the land rent is permitted to capitalise into a freely tradable price in the first place, and a process that will assist, ultimately, in maintaining high land prices – though few have the vision to see this.)

Due to the downturn, these two organisations report combined losses of $11bn for the nine months to March 31, 2008, the fear being that any further mortgage-related losses may erode their combined capital of

22 June 16, 2008, p.19.

23 The bill includes a requirement for all future mortgage brokers to be fingerprinted, in an effort to prevent future fraudulent lending practices.

24 Fannie Mae is a creative abbreviation for the Federal National Mortgage Association, set up as part of the post-depression New Deal in 1938, and Freddie Mac is the Federal Home Loan Mortgage Corporation, created in 1970 to provide competition to Fannie Mae after President Johnson privatised the organisation to help pay for the Vietnam war.

just $81 bn, rendering them insolvent and worsening the housing slump, not to mention the prospect of an unimaginable world-wide financial melt-down.

The ebullience at the top of the cycle has now well and truly turned to fear. To control that fear, the Securities and Exchange Commission decide to restrict the ability of traders to short the shares of banks and financial companies on the US stock market. It's ironic really. Successive American administrations spent years chastising other governments for engaging in the sort of financial socialism that is now taking place in the US, laboured for years to undermine socialist nations around the world and denounced any scheme that limited a trader's ability to … well … trade.

'The US banking system is safe …'

AMERICA'S 'FREE MARKET' is tested yet again the same weekend as the Fannie Mae and Freddie Mac problems become clear when IndyMac Bancorp fails as depositors queue at its 33 branches – all come at once to get their money out, only to find it isn't there. This bank specialised in loans to borrowers who did not, or could not, properly document their ability to repay a mortgage. The failure of IndyMac Bancorp is the second biggest failure of a financial institution in US history, and the largest ever regulated Savings and Loan institution failure. The numbers just keep getting bigger. This time, though, the Office of Thrift Supervision is better prepared and knows what to do. It quickly transfers the bank's operations to the Federal Deposit Insurance Corporation (ensuring that deposits of $100,000 or less will automatically be repaid) by creating a successor institution, the IndyMac Federal Bank. Same old, same old … the banks most heavily exposed to real estate start collapsing as land price declines. This time the IndyMac failure will cost the FDIC a probable $8 bn. Authorities say merely that the bank had succumbed to 'huge losses from defaulted mortgages made at the height of the housing boom'. Nothing new here then either. The FDIC begins running its bank failure readiness exercises.

Meantime, the Treasury Secretary appears on 'Face the Nation' assuring viewers that America's banking system is 'safe and sound'. Funny thing this confidence – if the system really was safe and sound, everyone would know it and there'd be no need to say it. The secretary then goes on to list a further 90 troubled US banks, but ones with 'manageable situations'. No wonder depositors are voting with their feet and queuing for hours.

Many banks that began business in the newly developing suburbs around America are now in trouble. Bradenton, in Southwest Florida, serving Tampa and the surrounding area of about 687,000 residents, 'was a centre of real estate speculation. Three new banks, formed … since 2000 saw the activity as an opportunity for fast growth. Home prices surged

35% in 2005, and bankers eagerly made loans to finance houses, strip malls and condominiums. When the housing market stalled, defaults ballooned.'[25] Just like First Priority Bank, a bank which opened in 2003 and that has currently reported non-performing loans at 16 per cent of total assets, loans made against real estate being the problem.

The *San Francisco Business Times* reports that the FDIC is alarmed by bank reporting on internet blogs. 'They'd rather keep the banking system's troubles out of the news.' The UK authorities go a step further and actually prohibit such reporting, making the information a state secret. Policymakers begin to redress the now obvious deficiencies in the way banks lend to those who can least afford it. Tougher regulations are proposed. Even the Fed has second thoughts about its way of dealing with asset price bubbles. Perhaps, after all, they should be stopped before they begin? We can be sure that, in the short term at least, new laws will not ease the downturn. In the next upturn new ways will be found by the banks to circumvent any proposed regulations anyway.

Write-downs and write-offs for the world's banks and securities firms now stand at $468bn. It is certain that the numbers will rise and economic conditions will worsen before they get better. So much for the credit crisis. The real economic downturn should now be prepared for. As always, it will be land-price led. History reveals that land-price led recessions take time to recover from – at least four years, maybe more. The downturns usually lead to increased US overseas military escapades to divert attention from mounting problems at home.

The scams, the cons and the corruption

IT REMAINS ONLY for the scams and cons to come to light. When the cost of money places undue pressure on corporations to continue maximising their performance, and as land price softens with rising interest rates, poorly or fraudulently managed banks and other financial concerns will come under pressure. So it was with Countrywide, the banking wunderkind of the early 2000s, that by 2006 had become the largest mortgage lender in the US and, ultimately, the symbol of all the excesses that led to the subprime mortgage crisis in the first place.

Countrywide offered loans to high-risk borrowers. It financed itself in the classic way of borrowing short to lend long. Crucially, unlike many of its competitors, the company was not diversified: it focused purely on the mortgage business. When the economy boomed, house prices went up and lending standards came down; so, too, the regulatory oversight. As late as September 2007, Countrywide co-founder and CEO Angelo Mozilo was heard to say: 'We have plenty of liquidity. We're in very good shape.'[26] Alas, not at the end of a real estate cycle. In the end the

25 'Start-Up Banks: Hog-Wild to Humble', *Wall Street Journal*, July 8, 2008, p.C1.
26 *Bloomberg*, September 8.

company was put up for sale and bought by Bank of America in a deal that will probably not affect the company's borrowers and will help a no doubt very relieved FDIC. But it exemplifies the greed of the times. The legal liabilities arising from Countrywide's lending practices remain to be seen. It will be the banks that are saved, though, and if necessary the people ruined.

One way in which the people will be ruined is through commodity prices. The Fed knows (though it has no idea *why*) that in the present situation it has to do everything possible to stop the money supply from contracting. This it will attempt to do by printing dollars, injecting liquidity into the banking system, swapping bank assets for cash – anything that will enable banks to continue lending to one another and keep the mortgage markets functioning. This will create inflation, good for farmers, bad for consumers, especially anyone living on a fixed income. It also spells a few difficult years ahead for those stuck in poverty in third world nations unable to afford soaring food costs. The US banking system cannot be permitted to fail.

For their part in the two Bear Stearns hedge fund collapses, two managers were indicted in June 2008 and arrested by the FBI. The Securities and Exchange Commission will sue the two for fraud, claiming they falsely told investors the managed funds were in good condition. A slew of further lawsuits by investors claiming to have been misled can be expected. The real Bear Stearns scam, however, may have been on the stock market. Just days prior to the fall of the company, options exchanges granted a substantial number of requests to open March and April 2008 puts with exercise prices as low as $20, although the Bear Stearns share price was above $70 at the time. Observed one US equities strategist at the time: 'That's incredibly aggressive. Someone was intimately familiar with the timing.'[27]

The first packaging of home loans sold on Wall Street was in 1977.[28] Wall Street is creative when it comes to designing games for people to play. The packaging of home loans was merely another such game, which came back to haunt the economy exactly thirty years later. The securitisation process was taken to the level of an art form in 2004 when a small group of investment bankers began meeting to design a better product for the mortgage and investment markets, to provide increased transparency and liquidity – more products to trade, more fees for Wall Street, in other words. Derivatives contracts for trading, backed by loans for commercial buildings, or the CDOs highlighted earlier, were the result: securities backed by all sorts of debt. It is the same every real estate cycle: the higher the land price goes, the more debt that will be created.

27 Quoted on *Bloomberg*, March 15, 2008: 'VIX closes at highest since March 2003 on Bear Stearns bailout'.

28 It was done first by Lewis S. Ranieri, considered to be the father of securitisation, who was then working at Salomon Brothers, though as this book details elsewhere the process was nothing new.

History has repeated. At the end of another 18-year real estate cycle we are witness to yet another Federal-Reserve-engineered banking bailout, because of declining land prices, that will again cost the taxpayer hundreds of billions of dollars, reward risky lending behaviour and guarantee another boom, then bust. The blame game has already started: 'a result of too little regulation', lamented one Congressman. Nobel Prize-winning economist Joseph Stiglitz suggested that the Iraq war was a 'central cause' of the subprime banking crisis (this particular economist should know better). The former IMF chief economist thinks the problem is 'the vast bonuses bankers receive when they lend and borrow'. Blame anything except the government-granted licence that is land value, permitted to capitalise in price and then be used as collateral in the credit-creation process. That is the real cause. The UK government is even set to launch a national enquiry into whether 'the trillions of dollars that flowed through the secretive tax havens created the conditions for the current global financial instability'. We have indeed been here before …

FURTHER READING

Fleckenstein, William A. *Greenspan's Bubbles: The Age of Ignorance at the Federal Reserve*. McGraw Hill, 2008.

Hoyt, Homer. *According to Hoyt: 53 years of Homer Hoyt*. (Publisher not given.)

Hartcher, Peter. *Bubble Man: Alan Greenspan and the Missing 7 Trillion Dollars*. W.W. Norton & Company, 2006.

Kuttner, Robert. '1929 Redux: Heading for a Crash', *Alternet*, October 8, 2007 (available at www.alternet.org/workplace/64684/).

PART II

THE HISTORY

The only thing new in the world is history you don't know yet.

Harry S. Truman

I

In the Beginning

The Land of the Endless Naughts

I thank God we have no free schools or printing, and I hope we shall not have these in a hundred years; for learning has brought disobedience and heresy and sects into the world, and printing has divulged them and libels against the government. God keep us from both.

Governor of Virginia, Sir William Berkeley, 1671,
quoted in Alfred Chandler, *Land Title Origins*, p.65

America: discovery and conquest

THE UNITED STATES is now considered the world's most dominant power. Whatever one might think of that, the US economy affects all others. It is very definitely cyclical in its behaviour: busts have followed economic booms with great regularity. This chapter is designed to give some historical background, and a bit more depth and meaning, to the chapters that follow about the real estate cycles.

One should observe in particular the role the frontier has played in American history, and the real estate speculation that went on around it. To get land was the name of the game. Men fought over it, went to war because of it, corrupted governments with it; many travelled halfway around the world to get a piece of it. And, because the supply was ultimately limited, in the face of the increasing numbers of persons desirous of owning it, land increased in value. It is with this in mind that the following historical summary is given. The chapter is not intended to be a concise guide to US history.

Christopher Columbus returned to Barcelona in 1492. The response to his discoveries was immediate: the King of Spain sent an ambassador to Rome petitioning the Pope to grant to the King all the newly discovered real estate. Fortunately Pope Alexander VI was Spanish. He granted the Spanish monarch his wishes – possession of all lands discovered, or to be discovered on the Western Ocean. Any person disregarding such a grant faced excommunication.

The Portuguese monarch, incensed at the Pope's actions, negotiated a treaty with Spain in 1494 dividing the spoils, should there be any. The English throne supported the sailing of John Cabot across the Atlantic in 1497 to see what all the fuss was about.

The French, 23 years later, demanded of King Charles V of Spain what right he and the King of Portugal had to monopolise all the land on earth. Said the French:

> Had our first father Adam made them his sole heirs? If so, it would be more than proper for them to produce a copy of the will. Meanwhile he should feel at liberty to seize upon all the land he could get. Chandler, p.3.

So began the fight for the New World.

Throughout the 1500s numerous voyages of discovery and plunder were made to the newly re-discovered Americas. To prove they had indeed been there, many a ship's captain brought back Indians as slaves. By 1540 French fur traders were occupying the Hudson River. In 1592 they had built a fort on Manhattan Island. A mass of conflicting claims and squabbles (usually ending in war) arose between the British, French, Spanish, Dutch and Swedish to land claimed in the names of their reigning kings or queens.

These voyages of discovery took on a slight but important variance after 1578 with Queen Elizabeth's grant to Sir Humphrey Gilbert. The desire to profit from the direct ownership of land in the Americas made its first appearance. Elizabeth decreed the following:

> Elizabeth by Grace of God, Queen of England; to all people to whom these presents shall come, greeting: know ye that we give and grant to our trustie and well beloved servant Sir Humphrey Gilbert of Compton Devonshire, and to his heirs and assigns forever, free licence to discover remote lands not possessed by any Christian prince or people and the same to have and enjoy forever, paying unto us, our heirs and successors one-fifth of all gold and silver discovered.

Gilbert did indeed make it to Newfoundland in 1583, and proclaimed to the assembled fisherman there his ownership of the land granted to him by royal edict. He then proceeded to parcel out the land to those assembled 'to be held by them so long as they paid him the rent for the land'.[1] Gilbert's ship, with all aboard, was lost on its return voyage to England. The Queen re-issued the grant to Gilbert's half brother, Sir Walter Raleigh. This was the time of the Spanish Armada. Raleigh eventually cleared the North Atlantic of Spanish vessels, allowing uninterrupted settlement of the new Americas by other Europeans.

1 Chandler, p.8.

An attitude to speculation

THE ENGLISH called the Americas New England. The Dutch named it the New Netherlands. The French, Swedes and Spanish also took great interest in this New World, but it is the English history we shall concentrate on. A brief review of how they settled the US will be useful in understanding how the American attitude to speculation developed, particularly land speculation.

The English settled first at Jamestown, Virginia in 1607. *The Mayflower* settlers reached Plymouth in 1620. On the English throne at this time was James I, who issued an edict claiming all the American lands between where the French were settled in the St Lawrence region and where the Spanish were in Florida. These lands he considered his personal property, to do with as he pleased. And this he certainly did.

Historian Alfred Chandler notes that the first Virginia charter, issued by the King on April 10, 1606 was

> [g]ranted to Sir Thomas Gates and three others named, 'and any others whom they join with them, to be called the first colony, all the lands, woods, soil, havens, ports, rivers, mines, minerals, marshes, waters, fishings, commodities and hereditaments whatsoever for fifty miles north and fifty miles south from the seat of their first location in America, and directly into the main land for one hundred miles'...The grants cited 'they shall order the search for gold, silver and copper, giving to us our heirs and successors the one-fifth part of such gold and silver, and one-fifteenth part of all copper found. Authority is granted to capture any persons, ships or goods which shall be trafficking without licence within the limits of said plantations. Upon petition, we shall grant unto such persons and their heirs and assigns, as either council shall nominate, all the lands and tenements which shall be within that colony.' Chandler, p.48

James I actively supported the colonisation but made it clear that he did not want it to conflict with other powers, notably France and Spain. As in Elizabethan times, the Crown continued to issue charters to 'companies of adventurers', who put their own money at risk.

Upon receiving a charter, the grantees would begin planning how to finance the venture. The grantees of the first Virginia charter did this by marketing subscriptions to shares in the charter company at par value of £12 10s per share. More than one thousand persons subscribed. Many more inquired about emigration. Finally, three ships of the London Charter company set sail on January 1, 1607, with about one hundred people on board. Before the year was out, stockholders started clamouring for a distribution of profits. It could be argued that America was born as a speculation.

> The financing ... was right: this was a speculative company investment, in which individuals put their cash into a joint stock to furnish and equip the expedition, and reinforce it. The crown had nothing to do with the money

> side to begin with. Over the years, this method of financing the plantations turned out to be the best one and is one reason why the English colonies in America proved eventually so successful and created such a numerous and solidly based community: capitalism, financed by private individuals and the competitive money market, was there from the start. At Jamestown, in return for their investment, each stockholder received 100 acres in fee simple (in effect perpetual freehold) for each share owned, and another 100 acres when the grant was 'seated', that is actually taken up. Each shareholder also received a head right of 50 acres for each man he transported and paid for. That was the theory. But in practice the settlers, who were adventurers rather than farmers – most were actually company employees – did not know how to make the most of their acres.
>
> Paul Johnson, *A History of the American People*, p.14

Maybe. As we shall see, however, those already in control knew exactly how to get the most from their 'in fee simple': add people to increase the land value, plain and simple. Anything else was neither supported nor tolerated.

In 1609 the King expanded the area granted to the London Charter Company to more than one million square miles of the new land. In particular, the land was 'made over to the sole use of the company and their assigns for ever, with authority to distribute and assign the lands therein granted.'[2] It was a decree expressly designed to allow the aristocracy to add to their existing power base.

However, bad reports filtering back to England of deaths and starvation in the new colony caused many company subscribers to question the further installments due on their shares. Other ways to finance the continuing venture were sought, including a series of lotteries. What probably saved the day was the planting of tobacco. Demand in Europe for the weed became so great that colonists were soon growing little else.

It was a settler by the name of John Rolfe who first began experimenting with growing tobacco, apparently out of fear of a new law, promulgated in 1611, threatening to punish severely idleness within the colony. 'After trying various seeds, he produced a satisfactory crop, the first sweet-tasting Virginian tobacco.'[3] He was busy in other areas too. In 1614 he had married the Indian princess Pocahontas, who had apparently been venturing in and out of the colony almost from the beginning. The marriage did bring a sort of peace between the colony and local tribes.

And what of the natives? This is what Columbus said of them:

> 'They are', he reported, 'so ingenious and free with all they have, that no one would believe it who had not seen it; of anything they possess, if it be asked of them they never say no; on the contrary, they invite you to share it, and they show as much love as if their hearts went with it.'
>
> Chandler, p.23

2 Chandler, p.50.
3 Johnson, p.26.

In contrast, King Louis XIV of France ordered his Governor in Canada:

> To diminish as much as possible the number of Iroquois; and moreover, as the savages who are very strong and robust will serve usefully in my galleys, I will that you do everything in your power to make a great number of them prisoners of war and have them conveyed to France. Chandler, p.27

It is likely that many of the first American colonies would not have survived without the assistance of the native Indians, at least in the beginning. The Jamestown colonists were so busy planting tobacco that they even gave the natives guns so that they could supply the colonists with meat.

Most of the early settlers were given grants of land in fee simple. Others who had rendered effective service to the Charter Company were also granted land in fee simple as payment. The rent was payable in tobacco. Tobacco was, pretty much from the start, the currency of choice within the colony. There was little coin. Neither were there many womenfolk. As no colony was likely to prosper without them, the Charter Company made efforts to bring women over. It was a company expense, which the company passed on: each accepting suitor had to pay 120 pounds of tobacco for the privilege. Ninety maidens were sent over in 1619, and one hundred more the following year.[4]

The year 1619 was important for two other reasons. Firstly, the Charter Company gave the colonists 'rights as Englishmen', and on July 30 the first General Assembly of Virginia met in Jamestown Church, the meeting lasting about a week. This was an historic development: the General Assembly was modelled on the English Lords and Commons, the Governor acting as the House of Lords, with 22 elected men as the Commons. In time the colonists got used to such rights, especially voting to elect their leaders: a situation very different to the average worker in England. Secondly, a Dutch ship arrived with '20 negars' to sell to the colonists. The Governor bought fifteen of them and put them to work as indentured servants on his tobacco plantation. Not that tobacco planting was actively encouraged: His Majesty the King himself hated the weed, saying that it 'tended to general and new corruption both of men's bodies and manners'. However the economics of the crop was excellent, farmers reporting that, for the same application of labour, tobacco yielded up to six times more than anything else that could be grown.

By 1622 the colony had extended greatly into the upper reaches of the James River, causing the Indians to realise that the ever-increasing arrivals would push them further and further from their hunting and fishing grounds. They attacked the settlements along the river in March 1622 (those guns coming in handy no doubt), leading to white reprisals. The settlers were about to discover that the practice of granting land in large

4 Chandler, p.55.

tracts – often to absentee holders – was not ideal when it came to defending themselves. Protests against the policy were unsuccessful, however.

> The apparent policy of the company was to dispose of all the land possible to appease the demands of shareholders for land dividends, and to increase the land rents, regardless of the safety of the settlers. Chandler, p.58

This was a common early complaint in nearly every new settlement, but whatever else happened in those early days, the private land privilege was never surrendered. This is highly significant. A nation's land policy will eventually come to underpin the way an economic system develops. By 1624, factional differences and the growth of popular government in Virginia prompted King James to force an alteration (revocation) of the company charter.

> After a strongly waged contest in England, the Lord Chief Justice declared the charter null and void. Thereupon James appointed Sir Francis Wyatt royal governor with a council of eleven members [US states are still run by their governor]. James assured the company shareholders that their vested interest in land would not in the slightest respect be infringed; that his intention was to alter the charter only as to form a government, with the preservation of the land privilege of every holder. The following year he again so assured them. The land grantees included a great array of noblemen, guilds and bishops, including the Archbishop of Canterbury. To have revoked the land grant, which the company was attempting to monopolize while making use of only a very small area about Jamestown, would have been considered an outrage on the recently acquired vested rights of these nobles and bishops. They wanted to hold the territory for themselves and their heirs to use to exact ground rents from succeeding generations. Chandler, p.58

Before the company charter was altered, land rents were owed to the company. After the change, the rents were payable to the King, and were collected by designated persons.

Universal suffrage in the colony ended in 1670 when the Virginia Assembly introduced a property qualification. Only freeholders, landholders and housekeepers could then have a voice in the election of burgesses. This was when Governor Berkeley made the statement quoted at the beginning of this chapter.

In 1684 King Charles banned the use of printing presses; Virginia did not get a public school till 1728, the first newspaper was not published until 1745, and there were very few roads prior to 1750. Despite such backward social conditions, or perhaps because of them, 'land grabbing, land speculation and other forms of gambling [soon became the] diversions of the gentry'.[5]

Speculation became the national pastime. By 1700 land was generally being granted on payment of a fee, on land rent of 5s per fifty acres,

5 Chandler, p.70.

payable in coin or tobacco, with the rent to begin only after the end of the seventh year. The object of settlement was to dispose of land – the more the better since this would increase the revenue from land rents. Much land was granted to tobacco growers and speculators, whose main aim was to sell or rent it to others, and who, under the law of the land, had seven years to sit on it before any rent was due. The increasing population could make your newly acquired wealth more valuable within that time frame. The land office of Virginia soon became a sink of corruption, with all the governors owing their appointments to politics and intrigue.[6]

Later arrivals were now finding that land near rivers and waterways (in such heavily forested country these provided the only means of communication with the outside world) had already been bought up. The pressure to find cheaper or untitled land could only increase. 'Shut out from temporarily free land on which to supply their labor,' writes Chandler, 'newcomers were forced to become tenant farmers, share croppers, or laborers for others.'

Or they could move on. Which is what Robert Green did as early as 1653, leading a hundred pioneers from Virginia into the Carolinas. One Virginian historian, Robert Beverley, described the locals in 1705 as 'not minding anything but to be masters of great tracts of land – lords of vast territory'. Some three million acres of land had been granted to owners, often absentee owners, by 1718.

Even George Washington, considered by many to be the father of the US, was much involved in speculation and land-grabbing. In 1767, when he was 35, he wrote his friend and associate, William Crawford:

> 'Any person who neglects this opportunity of hunting out good lands and in some measure marking and distinguishing them for their own [in order to keep others from settling them], will never regain it; if therefore you will be at the trouble of seeking out the lands, I will take it upon me the part of securing them as soon as there is a possibility of doing it … By this time it may be easy for you to discover that my plan is to secure a good deal of land.' Washington carefully advised Crawford to carry on his operations 'snugly, under pretense of hunting game'. Chandler, p.71

We will revisit America's founding father and first president later in this chapter.

Such is the manner in which Virginia was settled and developed. Many other settlements were also established by the English and others, for example in Massachusetts, Maine, New Hampshire, Rhode Island, Pennsylvania, Maryland and, of course, New York. Settlement patterns were not the same everywhere, but the land speculator was always present. By 1700 the US frontier had become a physical reality, the overwhelming dynamic being the lust to own land.

6 Chandler, p.69.

> Now, for the first time in human history, cheap, good land was available to the multitude. This happy prospect was now open, and it remained so for the best part of the next two centuries; then it closed, forever. In the early 18th century, the movements to acquire land outside the original settlements and charters, and dot it with towns, was just getting into its stride, which was not to relax until the frontier ceased to exist in the 1890s. Johnson, p.85

The significance of the closing of the frontier will be discussed in later chapters.

Americans got used to dealing in large numbers: it was 'the land of the endless naughts'.[7] Large tracts of land, often millions of acres, swapped hands in a 'continuing process of buying and selling farms, estates, and virgin soil which … made British America the biggest theatre in land speculation in human history.'[8]

A Brief word, then, about Colony money

NATURALLY SPECULATION in land had to be financed, as did other transactions. In early America it was commodities that were first used when an exchange of goods and services was required: beaver fur and wampum (coloured beads) with the Indians (who did not consider gold or silver of any value), rice in the Carolinas and tobacco in Virginia (where warehouse receipts for the storage of tobacco started to circulate as currency). As towns grew, gold and silver coins minted in other countries came into use, simply as a matter of convenience. Since gold and silver had become recognised commodities the world over, any foreign coins containing such could circulate as acceptable currency until the government chose to outlaw them. The word 'dollar' came from 'thaler', a coin minted by the Count of Schlick in Joachimstal, Bohemia. Thalers were minted successfully for many years without becoming too debased, so use of the word stuck.

The issue of fiat – paper money not convertible at some nominal gold or silver (specie) value, and given its legitimacy simply through government decree – took place first in Massachusetts.

> Massachusetts was accustomed to launching plunder expeditions against the prosperous French colony in Quebec. Generally the expeditions were successful, and would return to Boston, sell their booty and pay off the soldiers with the proceeds. This time, however, the expedition was beaten back decisively, and the soldiers returned to Boston in ill humor, grumbling for their pay. Discontented soldiers are ripe for mutiny, so the Massachusetts government looked around in concern for a way to pay the soldiers … Finally, Massachusetts decided in December 1690 to print $7,000 in paper notes and to use them to pay the soldiers. Suspecting that the public would not accept irredeemable paper, the government made a two-fold pledge when it issued

7 Johnson, p.90.
8 Johnson, p.90.

> the notes: that it would redeem them in gold or silver out of tax revenue in a few years, and that absolutely no further paper notes would be issued.
>
> Murray N. Rothbard, *A History of Money and Banking in the United States*, p.51

Both pledges were quickly broken. The Massachusetts government went on to issue another £40,000 in notes. There are lessons to be learned here because the subject will come up again:

- As the government issues more and more paper, the value of the paper notes will depreciate against the silver or gold that the community is also accepting as payment for goods and services: it will take more and more notes to collect the same quantity of gold or silver. The depreciation will worsen once the public realise that the government will continue to print ever-increasing quantities of paper money to pay its debts.
- People will hoard gold and silver coins. Therefore they will soon go out of circulation.
- Prices will rise.
- If the paper money is not accepted outside the colony, merchants will have problems. They may be forced to accept payment from buyers in paper money but have to pay their suppliers in gold or silver coin, further hastening the outflow of specie.
- The outflow will continue despite government efforts to prevent it with laws, say, compelling acceptance of paper money for transactions, backed by fines, imprisonment, or confiscation of property.
- Debtors could make the most of this inflationary process. Those obtaining grants of land and arranging payment over time will be in a strong position if the price of the land rises and the contractual value of the debt remains the same.
- Under such a process, if the inflation is high enough creditors will seek to avoid their debtors (usually it is the other way around), or demand repayment of the debt in hard coin.

So what is the relevance of all this to us? The issue/contraction of paper money creates a boom/bust economy.

When paper money is issued, a boom develops; when the paper money supply is contracted, business activity slows down. (The colony of Maryland at one stage gave away its printed notes.) Debtors – most often farmers – tend to favour the issue of paper money; merchants and 'moneyed' men do not. This became a great source of friction, even rebellion, among the colonists.

The British government forbade the establishment of banks in the colonies, an indication of the power they believed was inherent in the banking process – something that will become self-evident in the following chapters.

1792: The First Panic

So vast is the territory of North America that it will require many ages to settle it fully; and till it is settled, labor will never be cheap here, where no man continues long a laborer for others, but gets a plantation of his own, no man continues long a journeyman to a trade, but goes among those new settlers and sets up for himself. Benjamin Franklin, *c.*1754

THE US WITNESSED its first monetary, credit-based, financial panic in March of 1792. What happened is instructive, though to understand it we need to look at some of the events that led up to it.

The new domain

THE AMERICAN War of Independence, fought between Britain and thirteen of her North American colonies, officially began on April 19, 1775 with the battles of Lexington and Concord in Massachusetts. On July 4, 1776 the Declaration of Independence was issued.

A spirit of independence had been building in America well before the 1770s, culminating in the Boston Tea Party riot of December 16, 1773. Britain's response was to pass what became known to the American settlers as the Intolerable Acts. The colonies then organised their first Continental Congress, a meeting of all thirteen colonies to decide what to do. The federal government of the United States, complete with its Declaration of Independence, federal laws, constitution and, later, Bill of Rights, was soon to be born – along with a large public debt after paying for the war.

The English-speaking world had seen a marked economic downturn in the very early 1770s, and crops in England were poor between 1765 and 1773. Reduced English purchasing power hit the colonies quite hard. Revolutions, if they are going to happen, are more likely in times of economic distress. When the economy is booming, citizens are usually too busy making money to worry about anything else. The move out of the 1770s UK downturn also kicked off the Industrial Revolution.

Once the American Revolution had begun, all the states took for themselves the land within their borders, at that time belonging to the British. By 1780 the Continental Congress resolved that seaboard states claiming land west of their existing boundaries should cede it to the newly created federal government. With a bit of horse trading and carrying on, this is eventually what happened.

It was a lot of land, much of it still unexplored. The new federal government found itself with a public domain, the nation's largest landholder. The eventual shape of the Union was determined largely by the forces of these vested interests – land speculators in the main. This was not necessarily in the best interests of all citizens of the new republic.

> Before Congress could legislate for the West, control of that hinterland must be secured. At the beginning of the Revolution, all the trans-Appalachian country was claimed by seven of the states on the basis of their original charters which had contained sea-to-sea rights. A demand that these landed states cede their western holdings to the national government had been raised at once by the other six states without large western holdings, with Maryland serving as their principal spokesman. The public utterances of Maryland's statesmen stressed the benefits that all the nation would enjoy through the surrender of this territory to the nation, but their stirring phrases concealed an actual conflict between two groups of land speculators, one convinced that they could secure grants most easily from the states already in possession, and the other believing that the national Congress would be more generous. In the end the latter group triumphed by convincing Maryland to refuse to ratify the Articles of Confederation, the nation's first constitution, until the landed states ceded.
>
> Ray Allen Billington, *The Westward Movement in the United States*, p.29

Britain was no longer an impediment to westward expansion. The peace treaty signed between Britain and America in Paris had doubled the size of the US and those establishing the new government were quick to spot that authority over this land would strengthen its power base. When the states were forced to hand over their claims to the new land, Congress was soon inundated with petitions for grants of land. *How that land was sold off laid the basis for the real estate cycles that followed.*

The debt

THE FIRST national debt was born in the War of Independence. It was a similar story with US government debt in the years to follow.

To get the inside story always identify the vested interests. Learning how the vested interests behaved in history enables us to forecast. Future vested interest groups will behave the same way because they are protecting similar interests – mostly, but not always, the rent derived from the value of the land.

To win the war, soldiers had to be paid, goods and munitions supplied; a whole army and navy was virtually built from scratch. The Continental Congress issued notes (continentals) to pay for it all. In procuring war supplies, Congress relied upon the experience of established merchants, who were at first paid a commission on the value of their purchases.

Supplying the revolutionary army would have been quite some feat, involving huge personal risk for the merchants, but the payment of the commission encouraged substantial abuses. Later in the war a contract system was introduced by Robert Morris. A lucrative business nevertheless, as it has been ever since.

As the war dragged on, more and more continentals were printed to pay for it. They depreciated so quickly that they probably cost more to print than they were worth, hence the expression 'not worth a continental'. This made supplies that much harder to procure. Alarmed, Congress in 1779 took steps to limit its note issue. Under Congress authority 'certificates of indebtedness' were then also issued to pay for the war: you loan the government your money, the government promises to pay you back, the certificate being the proof of its promise.

America of course succeeded in its Revolution. And here is where it starts to get interesting. The official history tells us something like this: that by 1790 the new United States was deeply in debt, with a poor credit rating, having some \$13.2m of foreign debt, \$40.7m of domestic debt, plus outstanding state government debts of \$18.3m.[9] To do something about this Alexander Hamilton, the first Secretary of the Treasury, submitted his *Report on the Public Credit* to Congress.

> He called for funding nearly all the government's obligations, including the state debts, into long-term federal securities payable in specie – that is, hard money. After considerable debate Hamilton's proposals were adopted in August 1790. The foreign debt was fully funded, as was most of the domestic debt, although interest payments were deferred on part of the latter and another portion carried interest rates below the market rate. Only the depreciated Continental bills, nearly valueless, were funded at less than face value; one hundred dollars of Continentals were accepted as payment for one dollar of the new bonds. The most controversial part of Hamilton's plan, because some states had paid off the bulk of their debts while others had not, was the assumption of remaining state debts by the federal government. (To gain the support of Thomas Jefferson and his followers for the plan, Hamilton and the Federalists agreed to a compromise that located the future capital of the nation on the banks of the Potomac.)
>
> Hamilton's refunding plan was generous to the government's creditors, who replaced securities selling for as little as fifteen cents on the dollar in 1789 with new federal bonds that soon rose toward par. How was such generosity justified? Hamilton argued in his report that his plan would restore faith in the government and public credit, attract foreign capital to the United States, and increase the effective stock of money, thereby stimulating the economy. Subsequent experience proved him correct. The US government was nearly bankrupt in the 1780s; in 1803 it had no trouble borrowing \$11.25 million on short notice, mostly from foreign subscribers, to finance the Louisiana Purchase, which doubled the size of the nation. By that time nearly 60 percent of the national debt had been purchased by foreigners,

9 See www.college.hmco.com/history/readerscomp/rcah/html/rc_063100_nationaldebt

> who in effect lent money to Americans in return for the government's promises to repay them in the future. Within the United States, debt owners could sell their federal securities for money or use them as collateral for bank loans. In retrospect, Hamilton's plan was a political and economic masterstroke for the new Republic.
>
> www.college.hmco.com/history/readerscomp/rcah/html/rc_063100_nationaldebt

A masterstroke? Depends on for whom. Remember how the Continental Congress paid for the war? The bills of credit, the loan certificates, the certificates of indebtedness? As the war dragged on, it would have seemed such credit instruments would never be honoured. Many suppliers and lenders of money to the revolutionary army, the farmers, the ordinary folk and soldiers, sold them at a fraction of their face value to get some ready cash to see them through the war, and afterwards. Many of the certificates of debt ended up in the hands of those who could afford to sit on them, if only as a speculative holding. If you were a large holder of such certificates, and within the new government, wouldn't you want these debts honoured at full value?

Such was the plan of Robert Morris, merchant and Philadelphia financier, and, by the end of the war, the nation's largest creditor. Morris backed Hamilton. As we have seen, Hamilton submitted his report on the public credit to Congress in 1790 and received support for the war debts to be re-scheduled as long-term securities, payable in gold. It was also decided that the new government would take over the debts of the thirteen states and re-schedule them in the same way. There would be a massive transfer of wealth from the landed interest, farmers and artisans, to the financiers if and when the debt could actually be paid. This action guaranteed support from the 'investor classes' who now had a vested interest in ensuring the success of the new federal government. The currency debt, however, was funded only to the amount of one hundred continentals to one dollar, backed by specie. In other words it was essentially repudiated.

So, how to repay the investor classes? The way it has always been done. Tax the people and establish a bank. Hamilton's further reports to Congress, his 'Report on the Excise', 'Report on the National Bank' and 'Report on Manufactures', revealing the plans for repayment, were about just that.

Once the state debt had been taken on by the federal government, a method for its repayment was needed. Hamilton and his followers, Federalists as they became known, represented the emerging power of American industrialists and merchants. As so often happens after a peace-induced economic slowdown, there was clamour for 'protection' for local industry hurt by the drop in sales or having a tougher time competing with cheap imports. In this instance, the war had stepped up demand for goods and army supplies, which could be filled only by local suppliers.

With the peace came a flood of imported goods,[10] hence the demand for protection.

The thirteen states had different import duties to raise revenue. They were rarely effective and competition from other states rendered them almost useless. They were often avoided by smugglers anyway. Some writers claim that 90 per cent of American merchants were actively engaged in smuggling. What better way to keep out foreign competitors than to have a federal government with the ability to levy uniform tariffs across the nation? This they did, at the same time ensuring unrestricted trade within and across the states. This was sheer delight for the Federalist northern industrialists. The first bill that was introduced into Congress was for import tariffs, to be set on thirty commodities.

To raise more revenue to pay off the debt, Hamilton introduced a tax on whiskey. Should this not immediately strike one as odd? The country which had just fought a bloody revolution, ostensibly over the British levying unjust 'internal' taxes, was now set to do the same thing itself. Had the Indian tribes combined to wage war for the return of their lands, it could not have been more provoking to the frontiersmen. The tax on whiskey led to frontier rebellion in 1794. To put down this so-called Whiskey Rebellion[11] Hamilton persuaded Washington to assemble an army of some 15,000 and have them march through the troubled areas. This set a precedent for federal government interference in state affairs and 'gave evidence of the possession of sufficient power to enforce the decrees of the central government'.[12]

The Classes

TWO MAJOR political parties developed: the Federalists, led by Hamilton, and the party of Thomas Jefferson, based on states' rights. The Federalists wanted central government to back industrialisation, on the English model. Jefferson saw America as a land of small farmers, strongly backing states' rights and individualism, selling their surplus production to the world. He went some way towards denouncing the new constitution as a centralising power that would eradicate American liberty and go against everything the revolution had been fought for. Jefferson lost.[13]

The Corruption

IT ALWAYS PAYS to have the inside running. On the refunding of the national debt, Jefferson observed:

10 Britain may have been deliberately dumping goods to undercut US producers, another way of keeping the former colonies dependent.

11 See www.businesscycles.biz/docs/whiskeyrebellion.htm for more on the Whiskey Rebellion. For an illustration of what life at the frontier must have been like at this time, going on as it was amidst all the continuing land speculation (see www.businesscycles.biz/docs/lifeatthefrontier.htm).

12 Algie Martin Simons, *Social Forces in American History*, p.117.

13 Thomas Jefferson is one of this author's most admired Americans (more about him can be found at www.businesscycles.biz/docs/thomasjefferson.htm).

> 'After the expedient of paper money had exhausted itself, certificates of debt were given to the individual creditors, with assurance of payment as soon as the United States should be able. But the distresses of these people often obliged them to part with these for the half, the fifth, and even a tenth of their value; and speculators had made a trade of cozening them from their holders, by the most fraudulent practices, and persuasion that they would never be paid. In the bill for funding and paying these Hamilton made no difference between the original holders and the fraudulent purchasers of this paper. Great and just repugnance arose at putting these two classes of creditors on the same footing, and great exertions were used to pay the former the full value and to the latter the price only which he had paid with interest. But this would have prevented the game which was to be played, and for which the minds of greedy members were already tutored and prepared. When the trial of strength on these several efforts had indicated the form in which the bill would finally pass, this being known within doors sooner than without and especially than to those who were in distant parts of the Union, the base scramble began.
>
> 'Couriers and relay horses by land, and swift sailing pilot boats by sea, were flying in all directions … and this paper was bought up at 5/- and even as low as 2/- in the pound, before the holder knew that Congress had already provided for its redemption at par. Immense sums were thus filched from the poor and ignorant, and fortunes accumulated by those who had been poor enough before. Men thus enriched by the dexterity of a leader would follow of course the chief who was leading them to fortune, and become the zealous instruments of all his enterprises.' Simons, p.113

It appears that Hamilton did not benefit personally in any material way from the legislation he introduced. History broadly shows him to have been of impeccable honesty, genuinely believing in the rule of the elite for the benefit of all. The same cannot be said of some of the men around him. He seems to have turned a blind eye to their exploits until things started to get out of hand around 1791.

The banks

ENTER ROBERT MORRIS again. One of the signatories to the Declaration of Independence, Morris is generally considered the financier of the American Revolution. A member of a number of committees in Congress, his mercantile interests are known to have profited greatly from the war. As Superintendent of Finance (1781-4), it was he who introduced a bill to create the first commercial bank in the new Republic, as well as the first central bank, to be headed by Morris himself. This was the Bank of North America, designed to operate as a fractional reserve commercial bank, privately owned and modelled on the Bank of England.

> The money system was to be grounded upon specie, but with a controlled monetary inflation pyramiding an expansion of money and credit upon a reserve of specie. The Bank … which quickly received a federal charter and

> opened its doors at the beginning of 1782, received the privilege from the government of its notes being receivable in all duties and taxes to all governments, at par with specie. In addition, no other banks were to be permitted to operate in the country. In return for its monopoly licence to issue paper money, the bank would graciously lend most of its newly created money to the federal government to purchase public debt and be reimbursed by the hapless taxpayer. The Bank of North America was made the depository for all congressional funds. The first central bank in America loaned $1.2 million to the congress, headed also by Robert Morris … When Morris failed to raise the legally required specie capital to launch the Bank of North America, Morris, in an act tantamount to embezzlement, simply appropriated specie loaned to the US by France, and invested it for the government in his own bank. In this way, the bulk of specie capital for his bank was appropriated by Morris out of government funds. A multiple of these funds was then borrowed back from Morris's bank by Morris as government financier for the pecuniary benefit of Morris as banker; and finally, Morris channelled most of the money into war contracts for his friends and business associates.
>
> Murray N. Rothbard, *A History of Money and Banking in the United States*, p.62

By the end of the war, with his political power slipping, Morris moved to end the bank's role as central bank, giving it the status of a private commercial bank chartered in Pennsylvania, where he was resident. Hamilton as good as copied what went before in his quest to establish his own concept of a central bank as the bank for the federal government, and fiscal agent. However, for our purposes *it is what happened next* that will explain why we took the trouble to detail all of the above …

The Power of Credit

William Duer, the panic of 1792 and the Bank of the United States

There is scarcely anything but noise and racket last night, and the night before we had a mob raised, and nothing would satisfy them but [to get at] the father of speculation, the great William Duer, who is confined in gaol at present …

Contemporary New York observer to the events of 1792

THE BANK Hamilton wanted was also to be a private concern, the shares to be privately owned but for one fifth to be held by the government. The notes of the bank were made redeemable in specie, on demand, and acceptable as payment of taxes. Congress gave it a charter for twenty years in February 1791.

With great skill, Hamilton allowed the bank a capital of \$10 m, of which the government took up \$2 m, receiving in return a loan from the bank for the same amount, and those good old certificates of debt could be accepted for up to 75 per cent of the value of any number of shares in the bank stock. Hamilton's master plan for the embryonic US clearly displayed an understanding of the banking process. Hamilton was for

> economic growth first and foremost, and viewed funding and banking as complementary pieces to the same financial puzzle. The strategy that the Secretary employed was therefore to utilise the synergy of funding and banking. [An example of such synergy was the upcoming Bank proposal.] Shares in the Bank were paid for mostly in government bonds and not specie. Thus, the bond prices would be supported as individuals bought securities to turn into the bank. Next, the bank would issue paper notes, all backed 100% by specie. These notes, in turn, became the nation's principal money supply. In this fashion, the banking and funding system were working together to produce growth. Hamilton, therefore, viewed these two components as integral and co-working parts of a financial system that would create a solid base for economic stimulus.
>
> David Jack Cowen, *The Origins and Economic Impact of the First Bank of the United States*, p.12

Economic stimulus is exactly what happens when a bank creates credit: the following chapters will explain this. But, before continuing with the story of the bank, we need to take a look at William Duer. The events of 1792 start with Duer. English-born and Eton-educated, he had moved to New York after managing family estates in the West Indies, and became a Continental Congress member and New York judge. He had made a good deal of money out of contracts to supply the Royal Navy with masts, in 1768 and again in 1773. Then perhaps he switched sides, if he took sides at all, and became one of the largest contractors supplying the Continental Army. It was to be a lucrative venture, occasionally at the expense of the soldiers. In 1791 Maj. Gen. Arthur St Clair was commissioned to establish a military outpost down Miami way as a defence against those troublesome Miami Indian tribes. Secretary of War Henry Knox appointed Duer to supply the troops. The soldiers noted later a serious deficit in the number of horses for the task at hand, and that the gun-powder supplied had been reprocessed or was damaged. One soldier even reported seeing his musket balls 'bouncing off the Indians'.[14]

Congressman Duer was also busy speculating in western lands. In the late 1780s he and his associates were granted 3.5 million acres of the Northwest Territory (southern Ohio) for settlement. One of the company's first acts was to begin selling land to French families wishing to emigrate. Upon Duer's instructions, in 1789 a salesman was sent to Europe to sell the lands through the Campagnie du Scioto. There was no shortage of French royalists (in fear of their lives at the start of the French Revolution) willing to move after reading the company's (false, as it turned out) advertising claims. Five hundred persons set sail the following year. The company had appointed two officials, William Playfair and his assistant Joel Barlow, to attend to the sales. Not living up to his name, Playfair promptly stole the money paid over by the French, which meant that the company was unable to pay Congress for the land – which it was selling before it was paid for.[15] Moreover, Barlow had misrepresented the company's claim to the land. The land sold actually belonged to the Ohio Company (of which more in the next chapter). Arriving in their new homeland, the French found they had been cheated. The US government did eventually grant them some land, but the episode contributed to Duer's future problems.

Nor was Duer above a bribe. The new United States needed coins to be minted for distribution, and had struck, amongst others, the Immunis Columbia copper coin of 1786/7. The Rahway Mills Mint believed it could supply the patterns and meet the demands for coinage but, unbeknownst to the Mills, Duer, as Secretary of the Treasury Board, had already awarded the contract for minting to one James Jarvis, in consideration of a $10,000 'inducement' paid to Duer. Jarvis could not meet the contract demands, having no source of copper, and promptly fled the country to avoid a court judgement against him.[16]

14 See www.earlyamerica.com/review/summer/battle.html
15 The practice was called 'dodging' – selling United States public domain land in Europe before it had been paid for in the US.
16 See www.coinfacts.com

In 1789 Hamilton appointed Duer Assistant Secretary of the Treasury. Hamilton's wife was a cousin of Duer's wife. Duer now had a position that would give him access to all government goings on before they were made public. He chose to quit soon after, however, when he learned that federal law did not permit Treasury officials to speculate in federal securities. Upon quitting, Duer promptly began using his inside knowledge and connections to engage in the sort of speculation he previously could not, borrowing heavily from banks and even close friends to do so. As circumstances would have it, Hamilton's developing federal program gave Duer increasing scope for speculation in the form of shares in the new bank chartered by Congress in 1791.

The Bank of the United States (or BUS as it was known) was authorised to issue 25,000 shares at $400 each to raise $10m in capital. The government was to retain 5,000 of the shares; the remainder were to be offered to the public in an Initial Public Offering (IPO) and paid for in four instalments over the next two years. On July 4, 1791 'credit hungry citizens gobbled up $8 million in Bank of United States stock with unprecedented alacrity.'[17] Many members of Congress were amongst the purchasers. The IPO was well over-subscribed, selling out within hours in all the largest US cities where the shares were on offer. Duer and other speculators were able to add to their original holdings – limited to thirty shares per individual at the IPO – by buying BUS scrip in the aftermarket.

By early August BUS scrip had gone from $25 to $250: a full $400 share was now worth $625, a 50 per cent profit in a month. This did not go unnoticed by New York locals; merchants began deserting their shops, 'shopkeepers sending their goods to auction, and not a few of our merchants neglecting their regular and profitable commerce of the city.'[18]

In Philadelphia prices for the scrip topped out between $312 and $325 on August 11. Shortly thereafter a minor panic developed when the bank and other lenders curtailed their lending. Share prices bottomed out over the course of the following week between $110 and $125, before rebounding.[19] The first liquidity crisis in the US – to which the Treasury Secretary knew the appropriate response: add cash to the system. Acting like a central bank might today, Hamilton[20] soothed markets by buying government securities. Bank scrip prices went sideways for the remainder of the year, between $130 and $170. Duer and his agents were still buying, though. By September 1791 he had acquired 1,200 of the shares.

17 Cowen, p.35.
18 Cowan, p.38.
19 Cowan, p.40.
20 These and the following months were not a good time for Hamilton: he was also dealing with the husband of his mistress who was blackmailing him.

On October 7 (90 days after the issue date) stockholders met in Philadelphia to propose a board of directors. Voting took place on October 21. Since it was the board of directors who determined the salaries of all the officers and clerks, and supervised the printing and supply of bank notes,[21] board seats were eagerly sought after. Board members also approved loan applications. 'Certainly one's loan application prospects improved when fellow board members were passing judgement.'[22]

The board also set the guidelines and procedures for making loans. Bank deposits were voted to be accepted without charge, and payable upon request. Deposits could take the form of gold or silver, or state bank notes. Each branch had a set of scales that measured coin to determine its value. But were the banks scales true?

> Ever cautious against impure metal, cashier Kean [at the Philadelphia branch] believed in a small edge for the house; 'it always ought to be remembered that the Bank ought to have some trifling and hardly perceptible difference in its favour to guard against base money'. Cowan, p.58

By late December 1791 Duer and Co were putting into effect their plan to corner the US securities market, in particular the fixed income segment. Why this area? Duer's focus would have been upon the 6 per cent securities due to the bank, since $6m in these outstanding bonds was due in four instalments, the first in January 1792, the remainder at six-month intervals.

> Therefore the BUS subscription process created a natural demand for US securities. Once prices had appreciated, the plotters dreamt of selling their holdings to foreign investors, as well as other speculators, who had sold the stock 'short' in anticipation of lower prices. Duer may have also dreamed of controlling the Bank of the United States. Alexander Macomb described his partner [Duer] as possessing a 'fertile head … genius at recourse … it astonished me. He thinks very little of raising in a few days some hundred thousand dollars.' Cowan, p.90

Buying bank shares also makes sense from another angle: obtaining a loan. Speculating on the scale Duer had in mind requires money. What better institution to control than a bank, whose deposits (read credit creation) 'could be used to finance other things'.[23]

Duer was not the only scheming market operator. A flood of new IPOs were coming to market. Between September 1791 and March 1792

21 Monthly wages at this time for an average labourer were approximately $22, with estimated expenses for a family of four being: food $14, rent $3.50, firewood $2.50, clothing $2. At the local market, to which a daily visit would have been necessary, a pound of meat cost 6 cents, a gallon of milk 24 cents and a gallon of rum $1. (See Tench Coxe, *A View of the United States*, and Billy G. Smith, *Life in Early Philadelphia*.) By contrast, a cashier's wage at the BUS, the most senior position underneath the board, was about $220 per month; tellers were paid about $100 a month.
22 Cowan, p.45.
23 Robert Sobel, *Panic on Wall Street*, p.21.

there were seventeen, the same number as in the previous seven years. Other asset prices were also rising: 'The rise in the value of land is astonishing.'[24]

The high point in securities prices appears to have been in January 1792; prices declined for five weeks thereafter. With securities prices going lower, Duer, heavily long, announced on March 9 (210 days from the August 11 high) that he could no longer meet his contracts for securities purchases. He was also at this time, it later came to light, fighting a pending law suit against the government for what it termed 'indiscretions' as Secretary of the Treasury Board in the previous decade. An audit had discovered $238,000 missing. Duer's failure created panic: the panic of 1792.

From our point of view, as will become evident in later chapters, the most important piece of the jigsaw has only recently surfaced.

> In all previous discussions of the panic, it was logically assumed that, when the crisis began, the national and state banks restricted credit to protect themselves from financial loss. New evidence demonstrates that the BUS-Philadelphia was restricting credit in February, well before the panic started.
>
> Cowen, p.92

This is a critical observation. It was the bank's tightening of credit that was the cause of the bank's share-price slide (and the slide of the market in general) in February, which in turn caused Duer and other 'longs' to get into financing difficulties despite their best attempts to prop up the price. 'Duer was the biggest long ... his failure in March triggered a snowball effect on other security holders.'[25]

Remember, the first instalment of the BUS initial public offering fell due on January 1 of that year, 1792. The BUS was lending for a variety of purposes, particularly to merchants in the course of their normal trading; however a good many loans were also made to finance the purchase of the bank's own IPO shares – 'accommodation loans', as they were called.

> Therefore it is logical to say that some of these borrowers bought debt securities with their loans in order to pay for the debt portion of their subscriptions to stock of the Bank, helping to push market prices higher in January.
>
> Cowan, p.96

Today one might call this a margin loan – bank credit to buy shares. Why the credit tightening in February? The BUS was worried about its note issue, having observed that its notes were, in some areas, no longer being accepted at par. This raised the distinct possibility that some of the bank notes might come back to the bank for redemption (a cash call) or

24 Alexander Macomb to William Constable, February 5, 1792, quoted by Cowen, p.121, n.33.
25 Cowan, p.92.

that there would be a request for the equivalent in specie. Acting out of self-interest, loans were curtailed; bank credit was restricted.

The creation of bank credit is a necessary and important feature of a modern economy. Even more important, however, in any economy that permits the capitalisation of government-granted licences into a tradable commodity, is what the banks take as security to cover the credit so created: in coming years this was to be more and more the value of the land.

Duer was the first in a long line of speculators to over-extend themselves at the peak. Detractors had much to say about Duer's extravagance. He and his wife Lady Kitty (the daughter of the exceedingly wealthy General William Alexander, she was given away at her wedding by George Washington himself) were in the habit of serving up to fifteen different wines with dinner. Duer subsequently died in prison on May 7, 1799, though it is doubtful that the prison sojourn itself killed him. He might have been in jail, but he had still been able to conduct his business affairs, write to all manner of acquaintances, entertain friends and even take lunch at the local tavern.[26] Jail may well have been the safest place for him: Duer spent the last part of his life attempting to put his financial affairs in order, but he never successfully paid off his debts.

Some important things to note about this episode

- PANIC IS NEVER without a cause: the tightening of credit. Note the order: expansive bank policy (easy credit); insiders load up; speculators pile in; momentum starts; boom; crescendo as the public gets a sniff; credit is tightened; loans are called in; bank policy goes into reverse; panic. If the land market is involved, the downturn will be severe and protracted. The panic of 1792 was not followed by any severe economic slowdown, though no doubt Duer's creditors had their own troubles.
- The notes of the BUS quickly became a ready target for counterfeiters. Bank branches were soon being warned to watch for unsound notes.
- The New York Stock Exchange was born in the remains of this panic, on May 2, 1792. The few surviving brokers wanted business only from the more reputable businessmen. (Transactions still took place on the curb outside for those not good enough to join the 'club'.) The fact that the New York legislature was considering an all-out ban on brokering shares and financial instruments may have hastened the arrangement. No need for government involvement, the brokers argued, we shall regulate ourselves. It was an argument the legislature must have accepted.
- After the fall of Duer in New York, only two banks remained in operation – not that there had been many before. Of new banks proposing to be floated the previous year, none got to open its doors.

26 Sobel, p.31.

Finally, back to the land (it's always back to the land)

WE HAVE DRAWN attention to the early land speculation. It is worth noting that 'speculation' is the term used in Chandler's history of settlement until he uses the term 'wildest speculation' to describe settlement around Pittsburgh after the coal mines were opened up and substantial improvements were projected, in 1785 and later.[27] Then the term 'wild land speculation' is used to describe events in Vermont in 1792.[28] So perhaps the speculative fever in land, financed mostly on credit, had been building for some time – interesting timing considering the real estate events to follow.

Why did the government sell off land in this fashion anyway? Why not just sell it to smallholders and willing farmers and get people settled and farming as quickly as possible? The answer is simple, though in modern times not quite so self-evident as it was back then.

> The rapid growth of manufactures was hindered by the unwillingness of men to work for wages, when a whole great continent of untrodden fertile land lay at the western doors of society ready to yield up its bounty to whomever could get upon it and use his labour. Benjamin Franklin had seen this fact and had expressed an opinion that, while free land existed, manufacturing would be impossible because no one would work for wages. This land was now in the hands of the national government, and we find this taking steps to limit settlement and thereby create a body of wageworkers. Simons, p.70

The land of Maryland, for example, tripled in price between 1730 and 1760. A good part of it was owned by just one family, the Carrolls.

The emotion and psychology of chasing this value takes us into the very heart of the real estate cycle, to which we shall now turn.

FURTHER READING

Billington, Ray Allen. *The Westward Movement in the United States*. D. Van Nostrand Co Inc., 1959.

Chandler, Alfred. *Land Title Origins: A Tale of Force and Fraud.* Beard Books, reprinted 2000.

Cowen, David Jack. *The Origins and Economic Impact of the First Bank of the United States 1791-1797*. Garland Publishing Inc., 2000.

Coxe, Tench. *A View of the United States.* 1794.

Gordon, John Steele. *The Great Game.* Simon & Schuster, 2000.

Johnson, Paul. *A History of the American People.* Harper Perennial, 1999.

Rothbard, Murray N. *A History of Money and Banking in the United States: The Colonial Era to World War II.* Ludwig von Mises Institute, 2002.

27 Chandler, p.429.
28 Chandler, p.161.

Sakolski, A.M. *The Great American Land Bubble: The Amazing Story of Land-grabbing, Speculations, and Booms from Colonial Days to the Present Time.* Harper & Brothers, 1932.

Sheldon, Garrett Ward. *The Political Philosophy of Thomas Jefferson.* Johns Hopkins University Press, 1991.

Simons, Algie Martin. *Social Forces in American History.* 1911 (available online at www.ku.edu/ carrie/texts/carrie_books/simons/index.html).

Slaughter, Thomas P. *The Whiskey Rebellion: Frontier Epilogue to the American Revolution.* Oxford University Press, 1986.

Smith, Billy G. *Life in Early Philadelphia.* 1995.

Sobel, Robert. *Panic on Wall Street: A History of America's Financial Disasters.* Macmillan, 1968.

www.buyandhold.com – Wall Street History.

2

The Great American Barbecue

The Land Boom of 1818

'There was a near approach to a crisis in 1819 as the result of a tremendous contraction of bank circulation. The previous increase of bank issues had prompted speculation, the contraction caused a serious fall in the prices of commodities and real estate.'

William Peter Harrison, *The Stock Market Barometer*, p.25, quoting one of the all-time great stock market observers, Charles Dow

'A deeper gloom hangs over us than was ever witnessed by the oldest man.' A newspaper of the time describing early 1819.

Samuel Rezneck, *Business Depressions and Financial Panics*, p.56

REAL ESTATE is where we begin. We have noted already that when the existing thirteen states ceded their lands to the newly formed central government in the 1780s the public domain was created. The government of the United States assumed the position of trustee, holding right of eminent domain and of ownership. The process then began of transferring title to private ownership. This process of dividing and selling off the federal government's newly acquired lands was done under the Ordinance of 1787, providing a legislative means by which new states could be carved out of the western lands and then, when ready, be admitted to the Union. Laws were passed to provide for orderly western settlement, specifying that when a territory contained 5,000 male settlers with the ability to vote it could elect a territory legislature; upon reaching a population of 60,000 it could enter the Union. Importantly, the new state was to be on equal standing with the previously existing states. Not less than three or more than five states were to be created out of the region. Five were eventually created.

The Ordinance, which guaranteed to all states and future states the ideals fought for during the Revolution – the right to trial by jury, freedom of worship and habeus corpus – also provided for the surveying of public lands. Surveyors were required to measure the lands into

36-square-mile sections, each township comprising 36 sections of 640 acres, a section being one mile square. Alternate townships were to be offered in tracts of not less than a section, at $1 per acre, later increased to $2.

However, no sooner had the Ordinance laws taken effect than the federal government began to ignore them and sell extensive tracts of western lands to eastern speculators at prices way below the minimum levels set. As landowner, the first and foremost thought of the federal government was to sell the land for revenue to pay off the public debt, rather than for settlement. Larger tracts made it easier to sell, 'and the only buyers for large tracts were speculators.[1]

One such company formed by speculators out of Boston to acquire lands from the government was the Ohio Company, subsequently joined by some Members of Congress.

> They lobbied through Congress in 1787, a bill authorizing the sale to them of approximately 1,700,000 acres of the public domain, along the Ohio River on both sides of the Muskingham River. The following year, two groups of people, one from Danvers, Massachusetts, and the other from Hartford, Connecticut, founded Marietta, named for Marie-Antoinette, at the junction of these rivers. Each of the first settlers at Marietta received an in lot 90 by 180 feet, and an out lot of 8 acres; the remaining land to be held for sale at a profit to the company. Chandler, p.477

Congress granted to the company a further 100,000 acres in 1792, to put some protective land between the town and the Indians.

Around the same time Congress granted several million acres to the Scioto Company. One of their prominent officials was William Duer – we saw in the last chapter how this speculation contributed to his downfall. A third grant was made to John Cleve Symmes, a Member of Congress from New Jersey (not to be confused with a later US scientist of the same name who immortalised himself by seeking funds to prove the earth was hollow). He bought from Congress a million or so acres along the Ohio River between the Miami Rivers, upon which Cincinnati was subsequently founded. Symmes had spent a good deal of his personal finances supporting the Continental army, and from such support had collected plenty of certificates of indebtedness. These he astutely turned into real estate. Apparently, though, the purchase was badly managed, particularly the surveying, souring the desire of Congress to continue to make such large grants.[2] Symmes did, however, note to his partners that he foresaw large profits 'for the lucky speculators who would buy land from Congress for 5s per acre and sell it to settlers at 20s'. Symmes got that right, though perhaps he sold too early. Over the next three decades, the price of the land in his purchased area levelled off at around $8 per acre – a 356 per

1 Alfred Chandler, *Land Title Origins*, p.476.
2 Reported in C. Albert White, *A History of the Rectangular Survey System*.

cent yearly rise. Thus began what came to be called the Great American Barbecue – the give-away of the government's best asset at knock-down, fire-sale prices.

The actual settlers were most unhappy. They saw huge areas of land being carved off by well connected speculators, hoarded, then resold later at higher prices – land they believed should have been going straight to other settlers like themselves for farms and homesteads. Eventually, after extensive congressional debates, the land sale laws were modified. On May 10, 1800 Congress adopted a liberal credit system, reducing the minimum lot size to 320 acres per buyer (lowered to 160 acres a little later), priced at $2 per acre, with four years to make payment. To put this into effect, local land offices were opened in various western towns.

> With the eighty dollars needed to buy a farm [now] within the reach of most of the indigent, the term 'doing a land office business' entered the nation's vocabulary. Ray Allen Billington, *The Westward Movement in the United States*, p.39

This is relevant to what happened next. The new lot sizes and liberal credit terms increased sales, but also created the conditions for rampant speculation in land by a far larger number of people, who 'bought on those terms with the idea of exacting higher prices of incoming settlers, before the four years of credit expired.'[3] And the purchase by settlers of lands upon which to settle (if they weren't already illegally squatting), was often made with the assistance of a bank.

An early bank story

JOHN KENNETH GALBRAITH noted that banks and their money were an even more compelling discovery for the citizens of the young republic than paper money had been for the early colonists.[4] You needed a state charter to open a bank (a licence from the state government), which was not always easy to procure. The story goes that, to get a bank in New York, one had to start a water company …

After the Duer speculation and collapse of 1792 there remained just two banks in New York, the Bank of New York and the local branch of the Bank of the United States (BUS), both Federalist institutions. Hamilton was effectively in control, though he was neither on the board nor a director of either bank. So any New York merchant who happened to be a Jefferson supporter could find credit hard to come by – and, for the merchant, credit is his lifeblood. Jefferson supporters did not want increased federal power, least of all a 'central' bank. Hamilton's supporters wanted sound finance, federally controlled. For the New York merchant and politician Aaron Burr, matters were intolerably worse since the Federalists controlled the state government as well. How to get a bank loan?

3 Chandler, p.483.
4 *Money: Whence it Came, Where it Went*, p.71.

Clean water in New York was in very short supply, surrounded as the city is by salt water. Those who could afford it bought water from street sellers, who brought it in from elsewhere. Others had to make do. Cholera and typhoid epidemics were a constant threat, and on the rise. Burr floated the idea of a company to supply piped water from upstate, and petitioned Congress to support it. Who could deny the benefit? After securing approval, Burr presided over the committee drafting the charter bill to go before the State Assembly. With masterful timing, just prior to adjournment after the final debate, Burr slipped in an additional statement:

> And be it further enacted that it shall and may be lawful for the said company to employ all such surplus capital as may belong or accrue to the said company in the purchase of public or other stock, or in any other monied transactions or operations … for the sole benefit of the company.

In other words, any activity the directors felt like pursuing. No one noticed – perhaps some had reason not to – and the charter was signed into law on April 7, 1799. New Yorkers never got the piped water, but they did get a bank. Within three years Burr, then director, had used his own account to borrow some $65,000 from the bank, but he decided to step down as director because his other new position, Vice President of the United States, was taking up his time. The bank went on to become Chase Manhattan. Burr went on to his next duel.

Behind the scenes Burr had been hatching plans with senators and other Massachusetts hardliners to get New England to leave the Union. They wanted New York to go as well, and the plan would be that much easier if Burr were to be elected governor of that state. Hamilton must have got a whiff of the scheme and taken steps to frustrate it. He believed Burr was not a man to be trusted to govern well, and his views must have got into print. Burr challenged Hamilton to a duel with pistols. Hamilton strongly opposed such behaviour, but felt, in this instance, that he could not with honour decline the challenge. Not having the conscience to shoot at his opponent, Hamilton was himself shot dead. Burr went into hiding and eventually faced charges of treason, though these may have been just for show because Burr continued in his attempts to get states to join what he was trying to found – a new country, his kingdom, way out west.

Early bank history

BANKS AND WHAT they do are important to the real estate cycle, *so understanding their development is crucial to forecasting the cycle.* A good historical summary can be found at www.college.hmco.com/history:

> Not banks but merchants were the sources of money and credit in the colonial period of American history (1607-1783). It was only after independence that the first commercial bank received a charter of incorporation – the Bank of North America, in 1781. British merchant banking houses stood at one

end of a long chain of credit that stretched to the American frontier. They gave short-term (less than a year) credits to American merchants who then extended them to wholesalers of their imports, and the wholesalers passed them on to both urban and rural retailers – country stores and wandering peddlers.

When the Constitution went into effect in 1789 the nation boasted three commercial banks, the Bank of North America, chartered by Congress at the behest of Robert Morris, the superintendent of finance, and two state banks, those of Massachusetts and New York. The primary function of these and later commercial banks was the making of short-term loans, which they did either by issuing their own bank notes or by creating a deposit in the name of the borrower (opening an account to the person's credit) and dispersing checks to draw against it. Since the bank notes were promises to pay specie (gold and silver) to the bearer on demand, banks had to maintain adequate reserves in order to do so. Defining adequacy, however, was no easy task, and numerous banks were forced into bankruptcy because they had over-expanded their loans and discounts.

Conservatism was the hallmark of the earliest commercial banks. The thinking of the time favored the establishment of a single quasi-governmental bank in each state that would operate in the public interest under private management. The overriding fear of political leaders was that excessive numbers of banks or loans too much in excess of specie reserves would hobble the taxing and spending functions of government by swamping the economy in depreciated paper. Political leaders also recalled very well the wild inflation resulting from unrestrained governmental issues of continental and state bills of credit (paper money) during the Revolution, and in the Constitution they barred the states from issuing them.

The management of the first Bank of the United States (BUS), chartered by Congress in 1791, reflected these concerns. Although the BUS was a large commercial bank providing loans to the private sector as well as to government, its board of directors managed the institution in a highly conservative manner. Balance sheets for the years 1792-1800 reveal a generally high degree of success in maintaining the Bank's specie reserves. The ratio between bank notes in circulation and specie holdings was quite small.

Growing population and trade, however, created a need for comparable growth in the volume of money and credit – for a policy of accommodation rather than restraint. Sharp increases in the number of state banks and in their authorized capital stock represented a response to this need. During the life of the first BUS (1791-1811) banks chartered by the states increased in number from 5 to 117, and their combined capital stock went from $4.6 million to almost $66.3 million.

For our purposes, note particularly the meaning of a bank note as legally issued by any bank at this time: a promise to pay to the holder (bearer) the equivalent worth in gold or silver, upon presentation to the bank (on demand). The subsequent chapters on banking explain further the importance of this.

The federal constitution prohibited state governments from issuing notes – a re-run of colonial state-issued fiat paper was not wanted. Banks granted a charter by the state were a different matter, however. Despite Jefferson's hostility to them, when he was elected President in 1800, after Washington, his party did little, if anything, to limit federal banking – or any banking. Murray N. Rothbard, who reports the chartering of 28 state banks by 1800, growing to 117 by 1811, quotes some interesting figures:

> In 1804 there were 64 state banks, of which we have data on 13, or 20% of the banks. These reporting banks had $0.98 million in specie, as against notes and demand deposits outstanding of $2.82 million, a reserve ratio of 0.35 (or, a notes plus deposits pyramiding on top of specie of 2.88 to 1). By 1811, 26 per cent of the 117 banks reported a total of $2.57 million (specie); but the two and a half fold increase in specie was more than matched by an emission of $10.95 million of notes and deposits, a nearly four-fold increase. This constituted a pyramiding of 4.26 to 1 on top of specie, or a reserve ratio of these banks of 0.23. As for the Bank of the United States, which acted in conjunction with the federal government and with the state banks, in January 1811 it had specie assets of $5.01 million, and notes and deposits outstanding of $12.87 million, a pyramid ratio of 2.57 to 1, or a reserve ratio of 0.39.
>
> *A History of Money and Banking in the United States*, p.70

The chart of bank specie reserves for several Boston banks (Graph 2.1 below) helps give us an idea of how specie fluctuated at the banks around

Graph 2.1: Bank Specie Reserves

in dollars, half yearly – Massachusetts, Boston and Union Banks, Boston

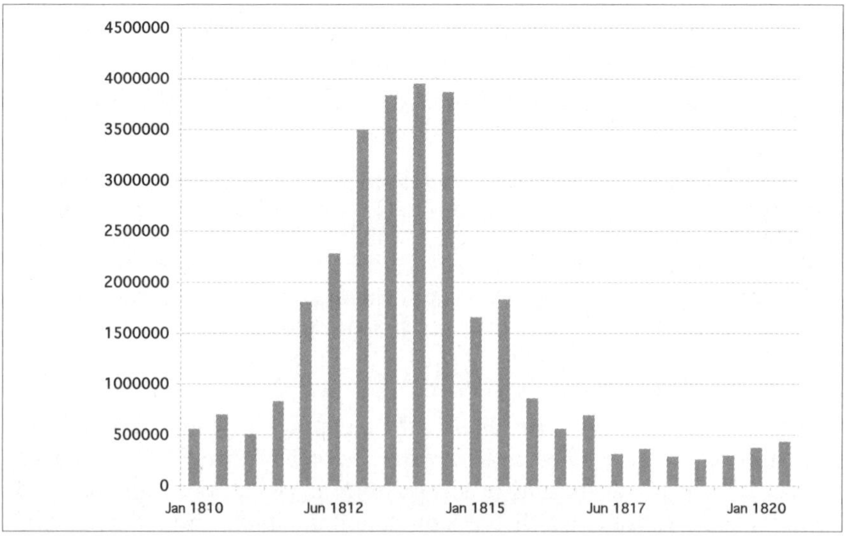

Source: Smith and Cole, *Fluctuations in American Business, 1790-1860*, Harvard University Press, 1935, p.28.

this time. Note particularly the expansion of bank credit after the war against the British of 1812-15. The lower the reserves of specie, the more expansionary and accommodating are the bank's lending policies.

It is likely that city banks would have created more credit as deposits but out at the frontier issuing newly printed notes was the order of the day: these were of more immediate need in day-to-day transactions. As will be further explained in the banking chapters that follow, there is nothing wrong with such banking activities – issuing notes and the like. The creation of credit will properly grease the wheels of commerce – provided two things happen:

- credit is created and lent for productive economic activities (*not* on land value); and
- banks are never permitted to renege on their contractual obligations to pay the holder of notes the equivalent value in specie if so demanded.

Banks' creating credit upon land value increases the violence of the real estate cycle. Subsequent chapters will expand upon the implications of this statement.

In 1811 the charter for the Bank of the United States came up for renewal and was defeated by one vote. Congress was still deeply divided on the usefulness of such a federal institution.

War – again – and its financing

THE US WENT to war again with the British in 1812. The war lasted just on two years. On December 24, 1814 the Treaty of Ghent was signed, bringing a lasting peace between the two sides. The US government paid for the war by issuing treasury notes, much of it in 1814, which were interest-bearing and redeemable in specie in one year. This was inflationary. The government also decided to accept its own paper as payment for debts and taxes, so it became a sort of tradable legal tender. The war also had a number of consequences for the monetary system, not least of which was an increase in the number of banks and an expansion of the money supply via an increase in bank notes.

> New England banks were more conservative than in other regions, and the region was strongly opposed to the war with England, so little public debt was purchased in New England. Yet imported goods, textile manufactures, and munitions had to be purchased in that region by the federal government. The government therefore encouraged the formation of new and recklessly inflationary banks in the Mid-Atlantic, Southern and Western states, which printed huge quantities of new notes to purchase government bonds. The federal government thereupon used these notes to purchase manufactured goods in New England.
>
> Rothbard, *A History of Money and Banking in the United States*, p.73

If you avoid death on the battlefield, or remain a politician, war can be good for career advancement: two generals from this time, Jackson and Harrison, went on to the presidency. Land greed was as important a factor as any other for the two sides going to war.[5]

By 1815 the number of banking establishments stood at 212. Most notably, there had also come into existence 35 private unincorporated banks, illegal in most states but their existence permitted under the needs of war. The reserve ratio of all the banks was at 0.17[6] – in other words, more and more notes and deposits backed by less and less gold and silver.

The federal government was now paying for manufactured goods from New England with bank notes created and printed outside the region. As the New England banks eventually began requesting the issuing banks to honour their contract and redeem the notes in gold or silver, the issuing banks found themselves in increasing difficulty. In August 1814 the federal government permitted all such banks to suspend their contractual obligation to honour their note issue in specie. (As a private debtor, your contract to repay your loan to the bank was still required, of course.) It was in 1815 that the private unincorporated banks sprang up. The suspension of obligations continued for two years after the war. Thus was established, for future American crises at least until the Civil War, the precedent of allowing banks to circumvent their obligations and suspend the paying of specie to customers who wanted to redeem their savings in gold or silver coin. As the decade progressed, the country was increasingly awash with paper – an expansion in the credit of the country.

Theoretically, in an economy that is justly and appropriately organised – that is, in an economy that does not permit the value of its government-granted licences and privileges to capitalise into tradable commodities – banking would be like any other business: if badly run it would be allowed to fail and go bust. However, we shall not dwell on this point at present.

The events described above did not happen in a vacuum. People soon noticed that some banks were issuing far more paper than others.

> From the 1814-1817 experience on, the notes of state banks circulated at varying rates of depreciation, depending on public expectations of how long they would be able to keep redeeming their obligations in specie. These expectations, in turn, were heavily influenced by the amount of notes and deposits issued by the bank as compared with the amount of specie held in its vaults. In that era of poor communications and high transportation costs, the tendency for a bank note was to depreciate in proportion to its distance from the home office. One effective, if time consuming, method of enforcing redemption on nominally specie-paying banks was the emergence of a class of professional 'money brokers'. These brokers would buy up a mass

5 Billington, *The Westward Movement in the United States*, p.37.
6 Rothbard's figures, p.73.

> of depreciated notes of nominally specie-paying banks, and then travel to the home office of the bank to demand redemption in specie. Merchants, money brokers, bankers, and the general public were aided in evaluating the various state bank notes by the development of monthly journals known as 'bank note detectors'. These 'detectors' were published by money brokers and periodically evaluated the market rate of various bank notes in relation to specie.
>
> 'Wildcat' banks were so named because in that age of poor transportation, banks hoping to inflate and not worry about redemption attempted to locate in 'wildcat' country where money brokers would find it difficult to travel … It can be imagined that the advent of the money broker was not precisely welcomed in the town of an errant bank, and it was easy for the townspeople to blame the resulting collapse of bank credit on the sinister stranger rather than on the friendly neighbourhood banker. During the panic of 1819, when banks collapsed after an inflationary boom lasting until 1817, obstacles and intimidation were often the lot of those who attempted to press the banks to fulfil their contractual obligation to pay in specie.
>
> Rothbard, p.78

The actions of people were soon speaking for themselves: pay your expenses in notes, hoard the gold and silver which keeps its value in inflationary times. An example of Gresham's law of bad money driving out the good. (An easier way than war for a nation to defeat its enemies would be to flood the enemy country with fake notes. But then how would all those merchants make money without government contracts to supply weapons and supplies?)

The nation's finances emerged from the war chaotic, and remained so for several years after 1814. The number of banks was continually expanding, each with its own note issue, and the value of the respective denominations fluctuated continually against its specie backing. The government treasury would not have been happy about continually having to accept depreciated bank notes from western areas as payment for land the government was selling, whilst having far more expenses to pay in less depreciated money in areas closer to the east. The government had two options to change the situation. Firstly, it could compel all banks to redeem in specie, under threat of closure, and so eliminate all the fiat paper. Eventually the specie would re-emerge from those hoarding it, putting an end to inflation. Secondly, it could establish a new central bank to oversee the existing behaviour. Political expediency probably drove the latter course, and so it was that the Second Bank of the United States was born in 1816, pushed again by wealthy individuals heavily invested in the war debt. In addition, there were so many influential people interested in the state banks as stockholders that it was probably not advisable to give offence by demanding payment in specie. Condy Raguet, Philadelphia state senator, economist and merchant, wrote to fellow economist David Ricardo on April 18, 1821:

> You state in your letter that you find it difficult to comprehend, why persons who had a right to demand coin from the Banks in payment of their notes, so long forebode to exercise it. This no doubt appears paradoxical to one who resides in a country where an act of parliament was necessary to protect a bank, but the difficulty is easily solved. The whole of our population are either stock-holders of banks or in debt to them. It is not the interest of the first to press the banks and the rest are afraid. This is the whole secret. An independent man, who was neither a stock-holder or debtor, who would have ventured to compel the banks to do a justice, would have been persecuted as an enemy of society …
>
> David Ricardo, *Minor Papers on the Currency Question, 1809-23*, quoted in Rothbard, *The Panic of 1819*, p.10

As Rothbard comments, 'Borrowers were anxious to keep the banks in the humor to lend'.[7]

Monetary expansion: farmers and settlers buy on credit

MONETARY EXPANSION continued, recovering from the British capture of Washington DC in 1814 and from the initial suspension of specie payments by the banks. It continued despite what looked like a fragile banking system in the chaos after the war. A feeling of American invincibility may well have taken hold at this time. They did, after all, thrash the British. Today one might label it a buy-the-dips mentality (or, it's still really cheap, let's buy more) – regardless, the monetary expansion went on.

The number of chartered state banks rose to 338 by 1818, most from the western states.

> *Prices rose greatly in real estate*, land, farm improvement projects, and slaves, *much of it fueled by the use of bank credit* for speculation in urban and rural real estate. There was a boom in turnpike construction, furthered by vast federal expenditures on turnpikes. Freight rates rose on steamboats, and shipbuilding shared in the general prosperity.
>
> Rothbard, *A History of Money and Banking in the United States*, p.88 (emphasis added)

Population

ANOTHER IMPORTANT factor at this time was population growth. There is no point speculating in land value unless there is a growing population to increase demand, and hence increase value. Between 1800 and 1820 the population of the US doubled to almost ten million, a flood of immigrants arriving after 1815. In this period America was achieving birth rates, in terms of children reaching adulthood, that were astonishing Europeans. What's more, the offspring were on average a good two inches taller.[8] The immigrants after 1815 simply wanted out of Europe after the Battle of

7 Rothbard, *The Panic of 1819*, p.86.

8 Evidence of the link between health and freely available land is well documented by George Miller in *On Fairness and Efficiency*.

Waterloo, the crippling taxes foisted on them by royalty and the dire winter of 1816 (the year without a summer, with sleet and snow in July and August, and no harvest). Attracted by tales of 'free' land, and without the need for visas, health certificates or passports, they began moving, en masse, to the frontiers of the US. You just needed ten quid. If you wanted to go to Canada, the British would send you gratis, courtesy of His Majesty. Just bring your own food for the voyage.

Panic

THE GOOD TIMES stopped rolling in 1819. It is worth quoting from Paul Johnson's *A History of the American People* for an initial explanation of the panic:

> From 1815 the price of American cotton rose rapidly and that in turn fed the land boom. At the time public land was sold primarily to raise revenue rather than to encourage settlers, who needed no encouragement anyway. Each was charged $2 an acre in minimum blocks of 160 acres. But they only had to put 20 percent down, borrowing the rest from the banks on the security of the property. The $2 was a minimum; in the South potential cotton land was sold at $100 an acre in the boom years. The Second Bank of the United States (SBUS), fuelling the boom by easy credit, allowed purchasers to pay even the second instalment on credit, again raised on the security of the land, like a second mortgage. Jones [William Jones, first president of the SBUS], whose only concern seems to have been to pay high dividends, based on the total lent by his bank, ran this federal central bank like a bucket-shop. He actually allowed the SBUS to deal in 'racers', short for Race Horse Bills. These were bills of exchange paid for by other bills of exchange, which thus raced around rapidly from one debtor to another, accumulating interest charges and yielding less and less of their face value. It was a typical bit of 19th-century ruin-finance …
>
> Jones' easy-credit policy was further undermined by the activities of the SBUS's branch offices, some of which were run by crooks. In Baltimore the branch was run by two land speculators, James A. Buchanan and James W. McCulloch, who financed their speculations by taking out unsecured loans from their own bank ($429,049 and $244,212 respectively, with the First Teller borrowing a further $50,000). In effect, this was to put their hand in the till. Here was a typical example of the general credit expansion Jones encouraged, raising the debt on public land from $3 million in 1815 to over five times that amount ($16.8 million) three years later. p.285

The publisher of *Niles Register*, Ezekiah Niles, wrote that between 1815 and 1819 all one needed to found a bank was a printing press, a set of plates, and paper. 'It was enough to drive genuine counterfeiters out of business.'[9] Niles reported, too, that by 1819 counterfeit notes from at least a hundred banks were freely circulating. Forges, inns and even churches were converted to banks.

9 Johnson, p.286.

The debt of public lands now stood at $22m, just as the price of cotton saw Liverpool UK buyers start shipping in cheaper Indian cotton to replace it. Suddenly the US cotton price fell, the price in fact halving in December to January of 1819. This in turn caused land prices to fall, which caused banks to discover they had much collateral in land now worth far less than what they had loaned against it. Bank failures mounted.

The Second BUS president, Jones,

> compounded his earlier errors of inflation by abruptly switching to savage deflation, ordering the branches of the SBUS to accept only its own notes, to insist on immediate repayments of capital as well as interest, and by calling in loans. This immediately doubled and trebled the number of state-chartered banks going bust, and the SBUS, their main creditor, secured their assets – the land deeds of hundreds of thousands of farmers. Johnson, p.285

Congress forced the replacement of the president with a more conservative rival, Langdon Cheves, who promptly intensified the banks' calling-in of loans so that the Second BUS did not fail. As one contemporary expert, William Goude, put it, 'The Bank was saved but the people were ruined.'

Always watch in the economy the relationship between the availability of credit and the level of speculation.

> John Kenneth Galbraith writes of a real estate bubble that grew wildly in the years after the War of 1812. State chartered banks, with few assets to back their aggressive note printing, made credit cheap and plentiful. The banks were housed in churches, taverns or blacksmith shops. In fact, they were set up in any place that was large enough to do business. The credit boom led to a major bull market in property. Ron Insana, *Trendwatching*, p.134

Alfred Chandler notes the same thing when writing about the public domain:

> Many state banks were organised in Ohio to facilitate creating credit for speculative purchases of land: during the five years just preceding the financial crash of 1819, about 5,500,000 acres were bought, and the indebtedness of the speculators to the government for land purchased increased from $3,000,000 to $17,000,000. *Land Title Origins: A Tale of Force and Fraud*, p.486

Another historian writing about this period, Murray Rothbard, notes:

> The federal government facilitated large-scale speculation in public lands by opening up for sale large tracts in the Southwest and Northwest, and granting liberal credit terms to purchasers. Public land sales, which had averaged $2 million to $4 million per annum in 1815 and 1816, rose to a peak of $13.6 million in 1818. Speculation in urban and rural lands and real estate, using bank credit, was a common phenomenon which sharply raised property values … Federal construction expenditures also helped to further the boom: they rose from $700 thousand in 1816 to over $14 million in 1818.
> *The Panic of 1819*, p.9

Graph 2.2: US Federal Government Public Land Sales
'000 acres, 1800-22

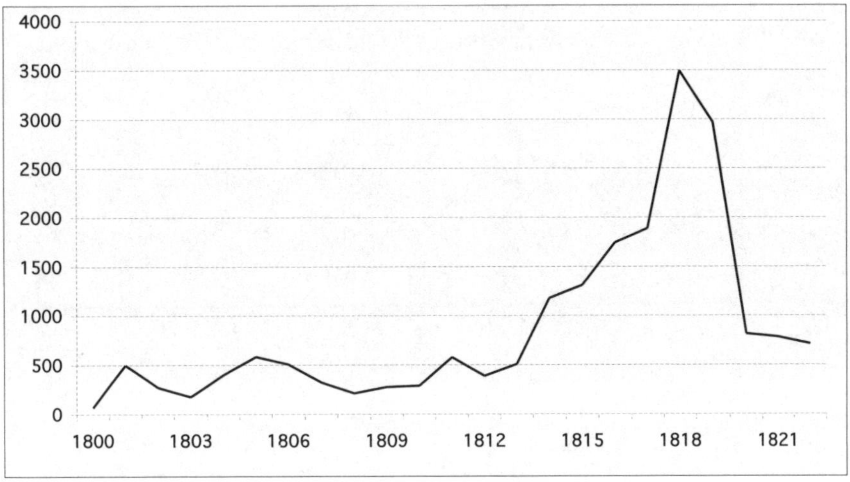

Source: Smith and Cole, *Fluctuations in American Business, 1790-1860*, Harvard University Press, 1935, Appendix D.

Purchasers of the western lands were required to pay only a quarter of the total amount within forty days, and the rest over five years – liberal credit terms indeed. Graph 2.2 shows the quantity of US government land sales in these years.

The sale of the public domain

SO THERE IT IS, the first serious US economic downturn, brought about by the decline in land prices. We shall see the same pattern emerging again and again. It begins with easy credit, used to facilitate speculation in government-granted licences and privileges (land value being the largest), leading to a boom. A sudden shock, unforeseen by the many, comes out of the blue – but appears blindingly obvious in hindsight (in this cycle it was the bursting of the cotton land bubble) – followed by a contraction of credit. Things will get worse for the banks if the land value falls below the value of the outstanding credit so created, forcing the curtailment of loans. A bust is the end result. Banks then have to find ways to rebuild their balance sheets, assuming they survive the economic stagnation/collapse.

It can be seen in the US federal government public land sales data for 1800-22 that land sales peaked in the fourth quarter of 1818. Bank stock prices (at least those in the Smith and Cole Index) peaked in 1818 also (Graph 2.3, page 58), although the bank stock index peak was in the context of an overall downtrend for the whole of the previous decade. Statistics and their interpretation must be relevant to the times, however.

Graph 2.3: Index of Bank Stock Prices
1802-21

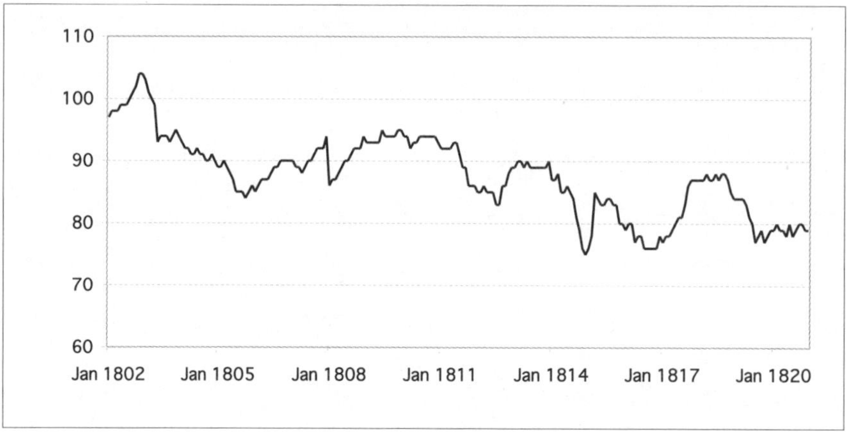

Source: Smith and Cole, *Fluctuations in American Business, 1790-1860*, Harvard University Press, 1935, Appendix C, Table 61.

Speculation in stocks was not as active then as it is now; securities speculation did not really get underway until the advent of railroad stocks – 'the rails' – in the early 1830s. So the relevance of the bank stock index at this time to speculative activity may be limited. Also at this time banks curtailed their loan books, not by charging higher interest rates, but by a process of rationing (often at directors' discretion). Thus responsible directors kept a close watch on specie levels. For the Boston banks measured in Graph 2.1 back on page 50, these levels bottomed in the first half of 1819. There does not appear to have been a specific panic day of highly charged emotion and tension in the severe downturn of 1819.

Scandals

IT REMAINED only for the scandals to come to light, typically exposed as the downturn proceeded. Simons writes of the Second Bank of the United States:

> The earliest beginnings of this bank, that was to be such an important factor in the financial, industrial, and political life of this country, were tainted with fraud. The provisions for a paid-in capital, which had been a part of the law creating it, were evaded. The first subscribers were allowed to borrow money upon their stock with which to purchase more stock, and so on until a most unsteady pyramid was built with no genuine assets at bottom. The operations of the bank were then manipulated to the benefit of the board of directors and stockholders. Among the latter, it was alleged by Niles, who was by no means an enemy of the bank, were forty members of Congress. The scandals were so great that a Congressional committee

> was appointed to investigate the bank, and when this committee reported, January 16, 1819, the bank stock fell from near 140 (at which point it had been accepted as collateral for loans up to almost its full market value) to 93. Yet the report was largely a whitewash, and its main effect was to frighten the president of the bank into fleeing from the country. Three years later a report was forced from the institution that showed that it was absolutely bankrupt at the time of the Congressional investigation, and that it had been guilty of nearly all the acts of crooked finance that such a still unsophisticated age knew.
>
> *Social Forces in American History*, p.163

The US experienced a new phenomenon in the 1819 – the first of many:

> The result of the contraction was a massive rash of defaults, bankruptcies of business and manufactures, and liquidation of unsound investments during the boom. *There was a vast drop in real estate values* and rents and in the prices of freight rates and slaves. Public land sales dropped greatly as a result of the contraction, declining from $13.6 million to $1.7 million in 1820. Prices in general plummeted … the great fall in prices aggravated the burden of money debts, reinforced by the contraction of credit. Bankruptcies abounded, and one observer estimated that $100 million of mercantile debts to Europe were liquidated by bankruptcy during the crisis. Western areas, shorn of money by the collapse of the previously swollen debt, often returned to barter conditions, and grain and whisky were used as media of exchange.
>
> Rothbard, *A History of Money and Banking in the United States*, p.89 (emphasis added)

Real estate speculation funded by bank credit has become a repeating phenomenon – a bankable pattern. This is what Charles Dow, quoted at the beginning of this chapter was trying to say: the economic contraction caused by a fall in the price of real estate (land). So, before we go any further, we should explain bank credit and fractional reserve banking.

FURTHER READING

Galbraith, John Kenneth. *Money: Whence it Came, Where it Went*. Andre Deutch, 1975.

Hammond, Bray. *Banks and Politics in America: From the Revolution to the Civil War*. Princeton University Press, 1957.

Harrison, William Peter. *The Stock Market Barometer*. John Wiley & Sons, originally published 1922.

Rezneck, Samuel. *Business Depressions and Financial Panics*. Greenwood Press, 1969.

Rothbard, Murray N. *A History of Money and Banking in the United States: The Colonial Era to World War II*. Ludwig von Mises Institute, 2002.

— *The Panic of 1819*. Columbia University Press, 1962.

Robbins, Roy M. *Our Landed Heritage: The Public Domain 1776-1936*. University of Nebraska Press, 1962 edn.

Smith, W. B. and A.H. Cole. *Fluctuations in American Business, 1790-1860*. Harvard University Press, 1935.

3

Mad Cash Disease

Fractional Reserve Banking

The modern banking system manufactures money out of nothing. The process is perhaps the most astounding piece of sleight of hand that was ever invented.

Lord Josiah Charles Stamp (1880-1941), 1st Baron Stamp of Shortlands, and Bank of England director 1928 to 1941, in a public speech at Central Hall, Westminster, England, 1937

'THE PROCESS by which banks create money is so simple that the mind is repelled,' wrote John Kenneth Galbraith, arguably one of the world's most knowledgeable economists.[1] 'Where something so important is involved', he went on, 'a deeper mystery seems only decent.'

Let us have a look at this process and attempt an explanation, for it is indeed simple – so simple, in fact, that it is the very reason you yourself are forbidden, by law, to establish a bank and then go ahead and print your own notes. Such an activity today requires a government-granted licence.

So here is a question. If I owed you $100, would you accept from me a signed IOU as settlement of the debt? And, if you did, could you pass this signed IOU on to someone else as payment of your own debt? Probably not. Hence metal was fashioned into coin to operate as some sort of medium of exchange to assist us in swapping or trading our goods with one another, and to pay off our accounts. Out of convenience, notes eventually followed. We accepted this because everybody else did, and it still works because of continued community confidence and trust.

Picture yourself as a businessperson in London some five hundred years ago. As you ply your trade and sell your goods, you are paid for your wares in gold and silver coin. What do you do with all these coins – place them under the mattress? Aside from disturbing your sleep, this could be risky. Fortunately at this time one could use the facilities of the nearby goldsmith, who would accept your coins for safekeeping. In exchange, and to prove your ownership of the coin so deposited, he would give you a receipt. We should understand the importance of these receipts. They held

1 *Money, Whence it Came, Where it Went*, p.18.

the signature of a man who had acquired considerable stature and reputation within the city and it was unthinkable that such a man, a goldsmith, would dare cheat a client. The receipt of a goldsmith came to be regarded, in fact, as something as good as gold. (Now, of course, greed being what it is, there were isolated instances over the years of bad behaviour from a goldsmith or two – clipping of gold coin, filing of the edges and other tactics calculated to add to his supply of gold in the vault. Such acts were rare, however, and carried considerable penalties, usually death.)

In the continuing course of business, you, the merchant, might have a large invoice to pay. You can trek down to the goldsmith, take out some of your coin, and then pay the invoice by delivering your gold to the relevant person. Or you might instead hand over your receipt, signing (endorsing) it to the new owner as payment of the invoice. He can then claim the amount of the receipt, in gold, from the goldsmith. A considerable saving of time and effort.

Time passes. Out of ease and business convenience, the paper receipts begin to circulate more freely. For even greater convenience, the receipts come to be marked simply 'pay to bearer', obviating the need for endorsement at every exchange. These receipts, backed by the good standing of the goldsmiths, are now being treated in the same manner as coin: they are money in their own right. Daily, any goldsmith might be presented with a 'pay to bearer' receipt, and not necessarily one of his own. He will without argument pay gold out to the bearer of the receipt to the full face value, when so requested.

More time passes. So much gold lying idle in the vaults of the goldsmiths gives them plenty to think about. Who is the real owner? Why is so much left uncollected? Since it is never all claimed at once, perhaps some of it could be put to better use?

Your son – for much time has passed – needs to buy some equipment, but does not yet have the coin to do so (in your day one had to save hard). He heads down to your goldsmith to ask for some credit. The goldsmith thinks: well, his business is growing, he has a good name … the risk is small; it could be good for business. The goldsmith could, of course, lend your son some gold coin; but why not simply write out a receipt for the amount asked for, 'pay to bearer'? The goldsmith does this and passes it to your son, who promptly uses the credit so obtained to pay for his new equipment. The receipt has gone into circulation as money. Nobody questions the receipt, for it has the backing, the signature, of a reputable goldsmith. Eventually, as the son puts the equipment to use, he will pay back the amount 'loaned', plus that bit extra the goldsmith asks for as recompense for the risk. (Just a little interest, you understand.)

Think about this for a minute. The merchant's son wanted credit to expand his trade; the goldsmith issued him a receipt for the gold that he had not yet in fact deposited, but would eventually, the goldsmith demanding just a little extra for his help. As trade grew, so did the demand for these receipts, now called 'notes' or 'bills'.

The goldsmith continues to observe that not everyone comes to collect his gold at once. How much, therefore, of the gold might he 'loan out' to inquiring customers? There is no shortage of them at any time. After a while it was established, at least by the more reputable goldsmiths, that, for every $100 worth of gold held, $1,000 worth of notes could be issued. Merchants were now being paid for their goods not just in coin but, more often, in goldsmiths' receipts, issued increasingly by the goldsmith turned banker as bank notes.

Thus the process of fractional reserve banking arose: the creation of credit for customers out of something that does not exist. In other words, banks issue loans and advances to customers that ultimately create their own deposits. Money from nothing. Riches out of thin air. Such a simple process, it is impossible to believe. Our mind is indeed repelled, is it not?

The accounting process

PERHAPS, THEN, we can come at this from another angle. Returning to the era of the goldsmiths for a moment, they are issuing receipts for the gold that clients choose to store on their premises. Eventually the owners of the receipts find it more convenient to pay for their goods by handing over a receipt rather than gold or silver coin. The new owner of the receipt can, when he wishes, present it to the goldsmith and demand 'his' gold. For the most part, though, the receipts continue in circulation.

The goldsmith eventually discovers he can issue a note (receipt) instead of gold itself to customers wanting credit – a loan or an advance of money, call it what you will. The borrower will eventually repay the loan, not with the original note but, most likely, with other notes issued by other goldsmiths, received from other businessmen in payment for goods the trader is supplying.

Business grows. Demand for the notes increases. The goldsmith-turned-banker, instead of issuing receipts, now prints (bank) notes, which for convenience have fixed denominations – $5, $10, $20 and so on. The balance sheet of the banker undertaking this activity will look something like this:

ASSETS	LIABILITIES
Gold in safe 100	(Goldsmith's) notes in circulation 1,000

Double-entry book-keeping demands the books be balanced, assets to equal liabilities, so we would get:

ASSETS	LIABILITIES
Gold in safe 100	(Goldsmith's) notes in circulation 1,000
Advances to customers 900	

By printing their own notes the bankers, it should be noticed, have actually enlarged their own asset base, namely 'advances to customers'.

Kings and queens are quick to take note. A process soon develops whereby the monarch asks the banker for a loan to help run the monarchy – or, more likely, to finance the latest plundering of a neighbour – promising to pay it back at a later date. The banker uses some of his printed notes to buy the promises to pay, the government securities. The government immediately spends the money into the economy, on whatever has been decided (building warships is a favourite), and, since it has the power to tax, it does so to pay back the loans. The banker's balance sheet now looks like this:

ASSETS	LIABILITIES
Gold in safe 100	Notes in circulation 1,000
Government securities 200	
Advances to customers 700	

Soon the banks' customers are depositing not just gold, but other banks' notes as well. So the balance sheet can be drawn up as follows:

ASSETS	LIABILITIES
Gold in safe 100	Deposits 1,000
Government securities 200	
Advances to customers 700	

Bank deposits are created by the banks themselves, not by you and me as customers. Nor has the bank 'lent' money: there isn't actually any to lend. The bank has created credit, actually out of nothing but the original capital in the vault. (In early US banking history, sometimes there wasn't even capital in the vault.) This is fractional reserve banking.

The early banks were very familiar with this process. The word 'bank' derives from the Italian *banco*, which described the old merchants' benches set up in medieval marketplaces. The Lombardy money traders preferred to set up their own dealing benches rather than have a permanent stall or shop. The breaking of a money merchant's bench was the signal of his failure – even then banks went out of business! An account of the early banking houses of Venice relates:

> Banks of deposit to the number of a hundred or more came into existence in Venice in the 13th, 14th and 15th centuries. A very considerable number also failed with varying degrees of resonance. Numerous efforts were made by the Senate at regulation, including such details as the hours that banks were required to be open and their obligation to count out the depositor's cash in his full view. The results of the regulation were less than perfect. A 16th-century Senator, one Tommaso Contarini, told in a speech of the difficulties. He noted that a banker can accommodate his friends without the payment of money, merely by writing a brief entry of credit. The banker can justify his own desires for fine furniture and jewels by merely writing

two lines in his books, and can buy estates or endow a child without any actual disbursement.

'The Bank of Venice', *Quarterly Journal of Economics*, Vol. VI, No. 3, April 1892, quoted in Galbraith

For such early European bankers, the best borrowers soon proved to be the kings and princes, of which there were dozens in Europe at that time. A king or prince would borrow by issuing securities – debt acknowledged by the principality or government – which were then bought by the banks in exchange for their bank notes. The notes were spent by the government and the debt to the bank paid out of future tax revenue. So the ruler's ambitions were easily financed. It has been suggested that the great Rothschild banking concern's Paris office lent generously to Napoleon whilst its English office was providing funds for Wellington, and that just one condition attached: loans were approved to either side on the understanding that the victor assume responsibility for the loser's debts!

The system is little different today. The fractional reserve process was used actively by the United States government to pay for its recent foray into Iraq: some $80-100bn worth of credit was initially created. The US treasury simply issued bonds, which were snapped up eagerly by banks, pension and insurance funds (mostly foreign) for the interest payable thereon. Risk free, or at least as good as the solvency of the government, they were considered as good as gold.

Early US bankers were keenly aware of where their profits came from. 'The profit,' said Senator George Cabot, a board member of the First Bank of the United States, in 1792, 'depended upon the circulation of credit instead of specie.' The president of this same bank, Thomas Willing, expressed a similar sentiment, suggesting to his New York board members that 'the bank's profits [depended] essentially upon its ability to keep in constant circulation its own credits instead of specie'.[2]

Today few individual banks issue their own banknotes – at least in the Western world. It is a function governments and central banks have taken over, providing a standard legal tender for the nation. Recently a new currency, the euro, with its own central bank, was introduced in parts of the European Union. It wasn't always this way. The US had as many different styles of notes as there were banks in the mid-19th century.

Notes now represent 10 per cent or less of the debt in circulation in any country, a debt no longer backed by gold, but instead by the production of the country: that is what the credit issued by banks is loaned against. This is a far more substantial backing than mere gold.

The process of fractional reserve banking is a good one; it works well if left to its own proper devices. And it is very important, for it greases the wheels of economic activity and exchange. A bank, like any business, is entitled to a reasonable profit from its work.

There are four problems, however. Perhaps also a fifth.

2 David Jack Cowen, *The Origins and Impact of the First Bank of the United States*, p.85, n.180.

Banks, now more than ever before, lend not only against the production of the country but also against government-granted licences and privileges, the largest of which is land value. Banks do not make this distinction, of course, but it is important for us to understand. The value of these government-granted licences and privileges is *not* one that is actually produced, or 'manufactured', by labour and capital; it is created by government in the awarding of the licence. It is a value that also comes out of nothing. This is explained further in the section on government-granted licences and privileges (Chapter 16). The process of credit creation is a worthwhile one; it is vital to business and helps boost trade. But the process will fail if credit is created on a value not backed by the productive enterprise of the nation. The situation becomes critical when the value of the asset mortgaged to obtain the loan falls below the value of the loan currently outstanding. Here is the crux of the issue; it is why we get real estate cycles of boom and bust. Banks create not only credit, but a mortgage and indebtedness as well. They end up owning the world, so to speak – or at least we the people end up mortgaging the world to them. When this happens, society works for the banks. It should be the other way round.

The second problem flows from the first. Were all the depositors to come to the bank at the same time, for whatever reason, and demand what is owed to them, their money wouldn't actually be there. (This is illustrated repeatedly in the chapters describing each real estate cycle.) The first problem intensifies the second, of course. It is only when the ability of any bank to continue paying depositors is questioned – mostly in a downturn – that depositors will all come to the bank at the same time. This was one reason for the development of a central bank which could act as banker to other banks in time of trouble.

Theoretically, if banks are doing their job properly, in a society where government-granted licences are not permitted to capitalise in price into tradable commodities, defaults would not be damaging to the economy. The trouble starts when credit is created and backed not by produced wealth but by the price of the licences – the capitalised rent. The inevitable downturn often sees the price of the licence (a mortgage as far as the bank is concerned) fall below the outstanding level of the credit so created. If this happens on a large scale, banks fail. Roughly every 18 years, it seems.

The third problem is one of debt. Most banks no longer issue their own notes, and our notes are not backed by gold, but the fractional reserve banking process still operates through the use of demand deposits, the creation of overdrafts and cheque facilities. Today's credit still comes into existence and is spent into the economy as a debt. Every dollar in circulation has at some time in the past been borrowed into existence. It could probably be said that, if everyone decided to pay off his or her loan, no one would have a bank deposit.

The debt problem is not our concern here, though it continues to escalate out of all proportion to what it could be if society chose to organise its banking in a different way – for example, allowing only the government to print and issue notes. Such notes would still be spent into the economy, but, significantly, they would be debt-free. Abraham Lincoln made this process work in 1862. This would not, however, solve the riddle of the real estate and other trade cycles, since speculation could still take place in those all-important government-granted licences.

The fourth problem is one of inflation (or deflation). The credit-creation process would be a good one if it was mostly backed by the production of the nation. When a loan is taken out, it is paid back out of the future income stream. If, however, the bank creates credit not backed by production, too much money will be produced, chasing the existing quantity of the nation's goods and services, and prices will rise. This is called inflation. The reverse may also occur, though in practice less often: if the banks cease to grant credit, trade and industry will be stifled, resulting in deflation.

Now more than ever, governments are some of the biggest borrowers from banks. They borrow vast sums of money not backed by the productive wealth of the country, being secured instead against future tax revenues. This is also inflationary. Banks are willing lenders to governments. Such lending – read credit-creation – is now international in its scope.

A fifth problem is perhaps one of financing for war. Fractional reserve banking makes it too easy to pay for war through government-issued bonds. A history of any country's debt shows this to be the case. In the US federal government debt has increased most in wartime, being slowly reduced afterwards. Only once has the debt been paid off completely, in 1836-7. Again, this issue is not our story, but it is worth noting in passing. Future generations will be burdened with heavier taxes on their labour and enterprise to pay back the borrowing.

So much for the problems of banking. They are highlighted further in each of the real estate cycle chapters. It is important at this stage simply to remember two facts:

- Bank deposits are created by the banks themselves, not by you the customer.
- Banks create credit; they do not lend money.

The basis upon which that credit is created, whether backed by government-granted licences or the production of the nation, is the critical difference. To view the real estate cycle in this fashion is to see something few others will ever see. Money may not have sex, but it sure can reproduce.

FURTHER READING

Galbraith, John Kenneth. *Money: Whence it Came, Where it Went.* Andre Deutsch, 1975.

Rowbothom, Michael. *The Grip of Death: A Study of Modern Money, Debt Slavery and Destructive Economics.* Jon Carpenter Publishing, second printing, 2000.

Acres USA: acresusa.com/magazines/archives/0204newsletter.htm.

4

G.T.T. – Gone To Texas

The Land Boom of 1836

After the war of 1812 the American social mind became introspective. Henceforth it was not to be concerned primarily with treaties, commercial bounties, impressment, embargoes, and matters of open sea and distant lands, but with turnpikes and canals, tariffs and manufactures, public lands, currency, banks, crises, poverty, state sovereignty and chattel slavery.

Algie Martin Simons, *Social Forces*, p.151

Speculation! Speculation!! Speculation!!! Verily the people are mad.

Headlines, *Niles Register*, May 9, 1835

IN NOVEMBER 1820 President Monroe was heard advising Congress of the 'prosperous and happy' condition of the country. He continued that it was 'impossible to behold so gratifying, so glorious a spectacle, without being penetrated with the most profound and grateful acknowledgments to the Supreme Author of All Good for such manifold and inestimable blessings.' Well that's not quite how things were. The country was still reeling from the previous year's economic collapse, including the mad scramble that took place for a cash position (a pattern to be repeated) and the availability of commercial goods at sometimes ruinous prices. The contraction of credit had seen *the value of land sales drop sharply*, and heated debate arose about the plight of 'poor' debtors – those owing money on past purchases who could no longer afford to pay.

The largest groups of debtors were those that had purchased public land (on credit) from the government, at what now looked like ludicrous prices, and still owed payment. The terms had been liberal enough: one-fourth of the land price due within 40 days, the remainder in three installments, but if not paid in full by the fifth year the land would be forfeit. By 1819 this class of debtor owed the government a collective \$23m,[1] and its

1 *Annals of Congress*, 16th Congress, 2nd session, p.15.

collection looked doubtful. What to do? Interestingly, most of the 'men of influence' were, even in the midst of the downturn, reluctant to see government interference in the running of the economy. The President himself was largely indifferent to the panic and unmoved for any government assistance to alleviate it, especially in the case of private contracts made between individuals, such were the ideological beliefs of the time. Except, however, for the land debt. This required a solution – therefore government interference.

A good many within the government were themselves debtors, or represented constituents who were, especially out west. The argument was that they had incurred their debts whilst prices were high but had to repay when prices were low and, what was worse, with the purchasing power of the dollar at a record high. Various suggestions were made to government: they might permit debtors to hand back to the government a portion of their land to cover what they had failed to pay; there might be complete forgiveness of any interest due, or an extension of time for payment. It was all the banks' fault, was it not? In their expansion during the boom

> [they] had liberally furnished money to the purchasers of public lands, inducing them to bid up the prices of the land to great heights. During the crisis, bank facilities were withdrawn, and banks were becoming bankrupt, their notes no longer receivable. The resulting destitution of the debtors (argued one Senator) required government relief.
>
> Murray N. Rothbard, *The Panic of 1819*, p.26

The fact that the government, if it did not get its money, would get the land back and so lose nothing seemed lost on all the senators save Allen of mid-Tennessee, such is the power of vested interests. The suggested relief was duly passed.

The land credit system itself was repealed in 1820. The minimum size of tracts to be sold after that date was reduced to 80 acres, and the price lowered from $2 to $1.25 per acre, payable in cash. (The reduction in the minimum size may or may not have been a reaction to the downturn and reduced government income. History does not make this clear, though it became a repeating pattern after each downturn whilst the government had a public domain to sell.) A writer in 1820 said:

> 'It has become common to see men after getting land, to maintain themselves in the first year without further resources than a gun, a net and a few tools, living from these like Indians and afterwards from their land. In a few years they were able to maintain themselves and their families comfortably …'
>
> Alfred Chandler, *Land Title Origins*, p.486

The widespread, popular feeling in the early 19th century was that the public domain was inexhaustible. The Secretary of the Treasury, Richard Rush, reported in 1827 that it would take no less than five hundred years to dispose of and settle the land of the public domain. As we know, most of it was sold off within the next fifty.

The fact that the frontier was seen as unlimited probably helped to restore confidence after the 1819 collapse. What's more, because land was available, those unemployed or down on their luck could simply move to the frontier, squat and hunt: this is of great significance to our study of real estate cycles. John Steinbeck's 'Okies' did not have this option. In all downturns up until the Great Depression, the availability of 'free' land at least somewhere meant that the downturn did not have a *prolonged* devastating effect in the face of a government and body of economists who believed that these things were pre-ordained and not to be fiddled with. By 1900 the frontier had closed. This fact is overlooked by most historians and economists who seek to explain why the 1930s depression was so acutely felt by all concerned.

Daniel Brush and a small group of Vermonters settled in Greene County, Illinois in the spring of 1820. 'A prairie of the richest soil,' Brush wrote, 'stretched out about four miles in length and one mile wide … complete with pure springs of cold water in abundance.' Once a cabin, 16 by 24 feet, had been built, they began the hard task of breaking up the prairie. This done, Brush wrote: 'no weeds or grass sprung up upon such ground the first year and the corn needed no attention with the plough or hoe. If got in early, good crops were yielded, of corn and fodder.' He added: 'provisions in abundance was the rule … no one needed to go supperless to bed.'[2] Such a lifestyle would have been one of genuine self-sufficiency, with very few commercial transactions in a market or business sense. Financial downturns would not have meant much to such settlers busy working their land so as to survive the next winter.

By 1828 two thirds of the population of Illinois were squatters: they had simply got there first and paid over some money to the land office after surveying but before the land was sectionalised and ready to be sold officially. They risked challenges to their title by those more knowledgeable of the law – speculators in particular – but squatters banded together for protection, which often worked.

Rapid settlement of the western lands was everywhere. The first building in a new settlement was usually a Protestant church, and this quickly became the focus and rallying point for surrounding farmers. In true US fashion, a newspaper would then begin publication; then came a bank, and then the lawyers, who would do their rounds and dispense justice on horseback until a courthouse was built. Growth was fast as more and more settlers poured in. Once there, however, getting about was another story.

2 Paul Johnson, *A History of the American People*, p.290.

Transportation

JOHN STEELE GORDON notes in his book, *The Great Game* (about the emergence of Wall Street as a great power):

> The cost of transportation made it extremely costly to ship produce back over the mountains to eastern markets. Instead the farmers had to either consume the produce themselves in a subsistence economy or ship it by one of two routes. The first, via the Great Lakes, the St Lawrence River, and Montreal, required a portage around Niagara Falls. It also wasn't available in winter, and passed through British territory. The other, via the Mississippi River and New Orleans, passed through Spanish territory. In the 1790s, the transportation of western produce was one of the major concerns of the new nation's leaders. Washington himself remarked that the loyalty of the western settlers was 'hanging by a thread' because their economic interests lay more with New Orleans and Montreal than with the eastern seaboard. Jefferson's purchase of Louisiana (from the French – sold by Napoleon for $11 million in cash) removed the threat of a foreign power closing the Mississippi to American commerce, but did nothing to solve the transportation problem.

That problem was solved by the New York Governor, De Witt Clinton. Clinton noticed the gap in the Appalachians near Albany, on the Hudson River. From Albany, through this gap to Lake Erie, the land does not rise above 600 feet. Why not build a canal? The idea, first put forward by Gouverneur Morris, was laughed at and dismissed as impossible but Clinton, as Governor, had the political ability and determination to build it. Started on July 4, 1817, the canal had 83 locks over its 363 miles and was dug entirely by hand. It was ceremonially opened on November 7, 1825, kicking off a wild mania in canal stocks.

Ron Insana describes the developing canal fever this way:

> The first mania for canals and their financing vehicles, canal bonds, began in 1825 with the proposal of the Erie Canal … Its development … would 'require tools not even invented yet. And its structure needed material that science said couldn't be developed (like cement that could be poured and cured under 4 feet of water).' The 400 miles of canal, cut through mountains, swamps, and forests, cost the then sizeable sum of $7 million … Thomas Jefferson referred to the project as 'sheer madness'. But the effort proved quite successful, helping to enhance New York City's status as a centre of commerce. Bondholders who had financed this 'sheer madness' were fully repaid in 11 years. The success of this issue led to a wave of speculation in canal building – The ebullience created by this endeavour led to one of the early bouts of market euphoria in the United States. *Trendwatching*, p.113

The Erie was not the first canal to be built. That honour went to the Middlesex canal in Massachusetts, started in 1789 and completed 1808. These canals, which were large providers of employment, not only speeded up transportation but also lowered actual transportation costs, while at the same time keeping the owners happy as the tolls levied tended to rise. The population of the towns alongside the canals often doubled or trebled – which was also good for business, not to mention the surrounding land value.

The new issues (IPOs), such as Blackstone Canal and the Morris Canal of New Jersey, were heavily oversubscribed. Few made profits; some were simply fraudulent, others ran into overwhelming technical obstacles rendering the building of the canal uneconomic.

But if the IPO couldn't make you money, perhaps beating the news could. Overstating the case for lack of transportation in early America as a limiting factor to development would be difficult. Development became, quite rightly, a national obsession. Up until this time, to get news from Boston to New York could take a week. It was possible to outrun the news: Philadelphia brokers at their exchange learnt to 'dread the sudden appearance of a stagecoach full of Wall Streeters because it meant that they were in possession of important news from London that might make them a small fortune.'[3] Small wonder that, in the early 1830s, a semaphore line was put in place: men with flags and telescopes were stationed on tall buildings and hills every few miles to signal Wall Street opening prices. They could get news to Philadelphia in thirty minutes. (One wonders about the speculative value of that last semaphore position just before the Boston exchange ...)

It was not just canal companies that increased speculation during booms. Turnpike corporations were the most common type of business established in the north eastern United States between 1800 and 1830. (To be followed by railroads.) Turnpikes, however, developed a poor reputation for return on capital, plagued as they were by

> ... expensive maintenance, and the widespread practice of 'shun-piking': travellers would simply walk or ride around the toll-gates, so often, in fact, that new paths appeared in adjacent fields, circumventing the only means turnpike companies had for collecting revenue. Insana, p.54

Cotton

AMERICAN GROWTH in the 1820s and '30s came in no small measure from another field as well, the cotton industry. This quote from Johnson puts things into better context for today's reader:

> Until the end of the 18th century, the human race had always been unsuitably clothed in garments which were difficult to wash and therefore filthy. Cotton offered an escape from this misery, worn next to the skin in cold countries, as a complete garment in hot ones. The trouble with cotton was its expense. Until the industrialisation of the cotton industry, to produce a

3 Gordon, p.78.

> pound of cotton thread took twelve to fourteen man days, as against six for silk, two to five for linen, and one to two for wool. With fine cotton muslin, the most sought after, the value added multiple from raw material to finished product was as high as 900. This acted as a spur to mechanical invention. The arrival of the Arkwright spinning machine and the Hargreaves jenny in the England of the 1770s meant that, whereas in 1765 half a million pounds of cotton had been spun in England, all of it by hand, by 1784 the total was 12 million, all by machine. Next year the big Boulton and Watt steam engines were introduced to power the cotton-spinning machines. This was the big bang of the first industrial revolution. By 1812 the cost of cotton yarn had fallen by 90%. Then came a second wave of mechanical innovation. By the early 1860s, the price of cotton cloth, in terms of gold bullion, was less than 1% of what it had been in 1784, when the industry was already mechanised. There is no previous instance in world history of the price of a product in potentially universal demand coming down so fast. As a result, hundreds of millions of people, all over the world, were able to dress comfortably and cleanly at last ... The new British cotton industry was ravenous for raw cotton. As the demand grew, the American south first began to grow cotton for export in the 1780s. The first American cotton bale arrived in Liverpool in 1784. Then, abruptly, at the turn of the century, American exports were transformed by the widespread introduction of the cotton gin. This was the invention of Eli Whitney ... The supreme virtue of this simple but brilliant idea, was that the machine was so simple to make and easy to operate. A slave on a plantation, using a gin, could produce fifty pounds of cotton a day, instead of one ... by 1800-1810 his gins had made the United States the chief supplier of cotton to the British manufacturing industry's rapidly rising demand. In 1810 Britain was consuming 79 million pounds of raw cotton, of which 48 percent came from the American south. Twenty years later, imports were 248 million, 70% coming from the South. In 1860 the total was over 1,000 million pounds, 92 percent from Southern plantations. During the same period, the cost (in Liverpool landing prices) fell from 45 cents a pound to as low as 28 cents.
>
> *A History of the American People*, p.307

There are important things to note here. As will be shown in later chapters, ultimately the benefit of all human progress will inflate the purchase price of government-granted licences and privileges, the largest of which is land value. Cotton was no exception. Land price captured the huge gains to be made in cotton, ultimately putting the south in permanent debt to the northern banks. Also, a further huge slave trade grew up around the cotton industry, greater than in tobacco, though the slave trade is not our story here.

The other essential thing to understand is that, where land is not enclosed, where it is still free, or at least still available without a fence around it and not yet owned by someone else, wages will be high.

> America was a place where an industrial worker could save up enough in three years to buy a farm, and no immigrant would stay in the manufacturing

> industry if he could become an independent, landowning farmer. So the thrust to reduce the industrial headcount was enormous, and Whitney showed the way ahead.
> Johnson, p.309

R.C. McGrane gives the example, in his *Panic of 1837*, of women workers in Massachusetts shops receiving wages as high as $5 or $6 a week while few of their sisters in Europe could earn more than 20 cents a day. Wages were high in 1830s America due to the open frontier. Cheap land and high wages versus high land prices and a surplus workforce on low wages was a common vested interest debate in Congress throughout the 1820s. This was one factor, of many, which brought General Jackson to the presidency in 1828 – of which we will learn more shortly.

This situation explains the radical difference in attitude between workers in the US and their brothers in Europe and the UK. The introduction of new technology was not feared by US workers as something that would reduce their wages or even take away their jobs. They embraced new inventions as labour-saving devices which also improved their working conditions. In Europe and Britain, because land had long been enclosed, limiting opportunities, labour-saving devices were viewed with great suspicion, if not downright contempt; they were not wanted by the working classes and this led to revolts, especially in the UK. Most historians overlook this fact; they do not understand the relationship between wages and a land value permitted to capitalise into a tradable commodity. An understanding of this relationship will improve one's economic forecasting ability. This is another subject that we will tackle in later chapters.

Where flows the benefit?

THE IMPORTANT question to ask is, 'Where does the benefit flow, and to whom?' With cotton, the consumer in one sense definitely benefited – from cheaper prices and better clothing. And the inventor saw a bit of money … but, as history shows, few brilliant inventors have ended up wealthy. (Unless, of course, they convert their idea into a company and sell it to Wall Street, retaining enough shares for themselves.) Ultimately, the gain to society manifests as land value.[4] By 1857 almost every single cotton plantation owner in the US was deeply in debt to the banks, loans to buy land at ever-escalating prices being the problem. Slavery is usually seen as the cause of the Civil War, but behind the scenes was a mounting debt problem. More on this in the following chapter.

4 For a great mathematical discussion of how this eventuates, see Chapter 3, 'Rent and the Dysfunctional Economy', in George Miller's *On Fairness and Efficiency: The Privatization of the Public Income over the Past Millennium*. For an even better, but less mathematical, discussion see *The Wonderful Wealth Machine* by Phil Grant.

Politics

AT THIS TIME in the US a strong religious revival of all sorts was taking place. So too in politics. About the politics of the 1820s, Johnson says:

> The Monroe presidency has been described, at the time and since, as the Era of Good Feelings, the last time in American history when the government of the country was not envenomed by party politics. But a case can also be made for describing the Monroe presidency, and the rule of John Quincy Adams which formed its appendage, as the first great era of corruption in American politics. Many Americans came seriously to believe, during it, that their government, both Administration and Congress, was corrupt, and this at a time when in Britain the traditional corruption of the 18th century system was being slowly but surely extruded. By corruption, America of the 1820s did not simply mean bribes and stealing from the public purse. They also meant the undermining of constitutional integrity by secret deals, the use of public office to acquire power of higher office, and the giving of private interests' priority over public welfare. p.326

So American citizens of the 1820s had good reason to believe their congressmen and senators received fees and retainers from various sources for services performed. Well, laws are made on Capitol Hill, so if you want the law changed to your advantage... The very wealthy J.J. Astor had Senator Thomas Hart Benton on a retainer. It was Benton who had the government's war department 'factory' system abolished, a system in direct competition with Astor's business interests. Congressman Webster was paid by the Second Bank of the United States (the Second BUS, as it was known) for services from time to time.

> Astor seems to have had dealings with other men high in private life; indeed he even loaned \$5000 to Monroe himself, this was eventually repaid though not for fifteen years. He lent the enormous sum of \$20,000 to [Congressman] Clay during the panic year of 1819 when credit was impossible to come by. Clay, like Webster, served the Bank for money whilst speaker.
>
> Johnson, p.327

Such visible corruption, coinciding as it did with the aftermath of the 1819 panic, brought one General Andrew Jackson into the political fray. He campaigned in the 1824 election on the issue of corruption in government. General Jackson is credited with being the first US politician to believe in the democratic will, and his proposals laid the foundations of the Democratic Party: that residence was adequate qualification for the vote; that, since all were subject to the nation's laws, every free man should have such a vote; and that voting power, when used well, could be the remedy against authoritarianism and corruption in government.

There were five contenders for the presidency in 1824. Jackson won the popular vote, but less than 50 per cent against his closest opponent, Adams; Jackson also won more electoral college votes and carried a greater number of states, but he did not win a *majority* of the electoral votes. The House of Representatives was therefore required to choose the president from the top three candidates. There was talk of a deal between several of the powerbrokers, Clay and Adams in particular. Adams was handed the presidency, and Clay became Secretary of State in the Adams administration. Jackson, however, had been the real winner of the 1824 election, and he knew that the people knew. He began immediately to prepare for the 1828 elections, to be fought on the same issues: federal government corruption and the fact that government land sales did not put land into the hands of those who would use it best, the actual settlers.

Jackson is important to our real estate story. He began what was to become the 'endless election campaign'. A popular party was formed after 1824 to campaign for a Jackson presidency: thus began what turned into the two-party system still in operation today, complete with much that we would recognise: electioneering, slogans, party organisation and general election razzmatazz. Jackson won a decisive victory in 1828 and went to Washington with a clear mandate for change, doubtless changing US politics for ever. His views – and he had plenty of them – ruled America right up to the Civil War of the 1860s. What is relevant to us is that General Jackson hated banks. Well, perhaps not banks *per se*, but how they operated at the time (and still do), by means of fractional reserve banking. He believed this process was corrupting the very soul of America and set about achieving its destruction. His eight presidential years were a showdown: the Jacksonians versus the banks. He and many of his followers were 'hard money men' – they believed banks should operate on 100 per cent reserves, backed fully by gold and silver. It began this way:

> Jackson was the first president not to come from a privileged background. Born in poverty and orphaned as a boy during the revolution, Jackson studied law and, in 1788, emigrated to Nashville, Tennessee, then little more than a collection of cabins. He soon prospered as a lawyer and began acquiring huge tracts of land, whose value rose quickly as settlers poured into the lush country of middle Tennessee. But when one land deal with complicated financing went awry, Jackson found himself responsible for another man's notes. It would take Jackson more than a decade to settle this matter, and as a result, he developed a lifelong horror of speculation, debt, and paper money.
>
> Gordon, *The Great Game*, p.62

Now, do note here that at this time the US did not have a uniform national currency, the circulating medium instead consisting of specie (gold and silver) and all the paper notes issued by all the local banks, as well as the Second Bank of the United States.

> Throughout the country there was a fervently held belief that privately issued paper money was an explicit device by which capitalists and bankers could control prices and the money supply. This, in turn, it was argued, gave these special citizens enormous political and economic power and made

> a mockery of a society that emphasized equal rights for all and special privileges for none. James Roger Sharp, *The Jacksonians versus the Banks*, p.8

So General Jackson was not alone in his belief.

The banks of course did not take Jackson's hatred lying down, especially the Second Bank of the United States. Though the Second BUS was at first incompetently managed, as John Steele Gordon reminds us:

> When Philadelphia banker Nicholas Biddle took control in 1823, it quickly developed into the largest and most powerful bank in the country. Because it was nationally chartered, it was the only bank able to operate across state lines. As the federal government's fiscal agent, with a branch in every major city, its notes were accepted without question throughout the country. Biddle was an extraordinary man, one of the greatest bankers this country has ever produced. He completed all the work necessary to earn a degree at the University of Pennsylvania by the time he was thirteen, but the university refused to grant it because of his age. So he went to Princeton, earned a B.A. there in two years, and at the age of 15 was class valedictorian. By the time Jackson became President, Biddle was probably the second most powerful man in the country… *The Great Game*, p.63

Biddle commissioned leading architects to design all Second BUS buildings in Greek revival granite and marble. As already noted, over the years bank design was conceived on an ever-grander scale. Perhaps there was an unconscious desire by bankers to solidify a process (credit-creation backed by lending on government-granted licences and privileges) built on sand. Things are rarely what they seem.

Battle lines were drawn. Jackson won the 1832 election by a landslide – the first landslide in US political history. The people seemed to like his minimalist approach to government – 'no frills and no pretensions to world greatness'.[5] More significantly for Jackson, as Bill Clinton was also to find to his benefit, he was governing at a time of vastly increasing national wealth, albeit some of it built on sand. The people were making money, who cared about anything else? The 1837 panic started here.

John Steel Gordon notes:

> At the heart of national prosperity was a land boom developing in the West, financed by new state-chartered banks. In 1829, only 329 banks existed in the entire country. Just eight years later there were 788. But while the number of banks more than doubled, the face value of the notes these banks had issued more than tripled, from $48.2 million to $149.2 million. And the loans outstanding almost quadrupled, from $137 million to $525.1 million. Many of the states had slapdash banking laws, and many of these new banks were badly – if not fraudulently – managed, undercapitalized, under-regulated and overly sanguine about the future. *The Great Game*, p.65

We will come back to the subject of banking and bank fraud later in the chapter.

5 Johnson, p.345.

Land speculation

IN THE 1830s the mania that was affecting almost all persons within the nation was connected with the occupation and sale of the public domain.

> All classes and all sections of the country were guilty of the same offense, all were impelled by the same craze for speculation. The farmer, the manufacturer, and the merchant, instead of paying their debts, bought land and speculated in land. The conservative eastern capitalist, the reckless easy-going southern planter, and the wary, doubtful western farmer joined hands in their efforts to purchase land. Villages and cities sprang up overnight in every direction, lots increased at the rate of 200 and 300 per cent per year, fortunes were made and lost in a few moments. All who had money or credit plunged headlong into the stream. Companies were formed, and through the generosity of the banks the mad rush to destruction was facilitated. The face of the country was checkered with new, well-mapped boom cities. The sale of the public land for 1834 was 4,658,000 acres; for 1835, 12,564,000 acres, and for 1836, 20,074,000 acres. Naturally the increase in sales enlarged the amount of public deposit, and this in turn stimulated the banks to extend still further their issues. The public deposits, by the close of 1836, amounted to $49,000,000, while the deposit banks, with an aggregate capital of $77,000,000 showed discounts to the sum of $115,000,000. But in this transaction, as Jackson pointed out, the government received little more than credit on the books of the bank. 'The receipts from the public lands were', as the president stated, 'nothing more than credits on the bank. The banks lent out their notes to speculators, they were paid to the receivers, and immediately returned to the banks to be sent out again and again, being merely instruments to transfer to the speculator the most valuable public lands. Indeed, each speculation furnished means for another.' Public men, representing both parties, reiterated and strengthened Jackson's contentions. Representatives and senators from the West called attention to the hardship the connection between the banks and the speculators necessarily had upon the settlers. The land office report substantiated these charges of connivance between certain of the land offices and the land grabbers. Unquestionably, speculation and bank juggling often went hand in hand.' McGrane, p.43[6]

Nor was the feverish speculation confined solely to the frontier areas and western lands. It is estimated that the value of New York real estate increased from $250m in 1830 to $403m by 1835, an increase of 50 per cent in just five years. 'The eagerness for land, declared Miss Martineau, is extraordinary.'[7]

6 I have quoted liberally from various works to show that all the US economic downturns have been extensively studied, though most authors have specialised in just one or two of them and not gone on to analyse common themes. None has offered the thesis that the cause of each downturn is bank credit, created out of nothing and loaned against the value of government-granted licences and privileges, also created out of nothing. Any downturn preceded by a land boom financed by bank credit will be more severe and consequently harder to recover from.

7 McGrane, p.45. Miss Martineau was one of the historians of the time, unusual for the era in being female.

Sound familiar? Speculators were having a field day. The process went something like this, the example being a Mississippi land sale of the 1830s:

> On the morning of the second and third days of the sales, a short time before the sales were open, R.J. Walker called the attention of the people before the tavern door about thirty yards from the land office, and read an arrangement, announcing that a company was formed to buy the land, and that settlers as would comply with the terms proposed by the company should be protected; the settlers were to abstain from bidding; were to give into the company of speculators the number of the land, and one-eighth of the land, including the settler's improvement, was to be transferred to the settler on his paying on the day it might be sold, the amount to be paid to the United States; and if one-eighth of a section would not cover the improvement, then the settler was to have one-fourth section. In general, people deemed it best 'to close with the terms offered to them'. A few persons refused, and some of these were forced to pay as high as $10 per acre. After the company had finished its purchases, the settlers were disposed of: the settlers' lands were portioned off to them, agreeably to the first and main designs of the company, and the residue was then put up at public sale, and was sold to the highest bidder, without any fixed price other than the first cost of the same … For the lands sold the company received various prices, from one dollar and a quarter up to six and seven dollars per acre, and in one instance of a supposed town site, $20 per acre.
>
> McGrane, p.50

In this one instance, noted McGrane, the actions of the speculators lowered the return to the government of the sale of the public domain by some $65,000.

The fever to speculate was everywhere. One visitor to the US, the French economist Michael Chevalier, wrote:

> Everybody is speculating … the whole country is an immense Rue Quincampoix. Thus far, everyone has made money, as is always the case when speculation is in the ascendant.
>
> *Society, Manners and Politics in the United States*,1839, p.305

Sakolski noted:

> When, in the early thirties, the speculative fever raged throughout the country, and government lands, as well as other property, could be purchased with 'rag money', created by 'wild-cat banks', then 'the land office business' began in earnest. The auctions were attended by veritable mobs. They were scenes of great excitement. Premiums were paid for choice locations near the auctioneers, and bribery and corruption in the process of receiving and registering bids were common.
>
> *The Great American Land Bubble*, p.234

And Roy Robbins:

> From a Wisconsin newspaper came the estimate that in the newer sections of the country, real estate investment for the ten years between 1825 and 1835, paid a 20 to 30 per cent return per annum … 'The speculators in Maine

> nearly beggared the state. Men left their warehouses, counting-rooms and stores and rushed off to buy townships, village lots or mill privileges.' In Milwaukee, it was being reported that speculators went to bed at night hugging themselves with delight over the prospect that the succeeding morning would double their wealth. *Our Landed Heritage*, p.60

It was around this time, 1825 to 1840, that 'the Texas Fever' raged. Moses Austin was the man who, having lost a fortune in Missouri, trekked all the way to Texas in 1820, where Spain ruled, to press for a grant of land that he had heard was being offered to colonisers in the territory. It was a long story, but eventually his eldest son Stephen received the grant and undertook to colonise the family's holdings by advertising for settlers to take up plots. His eventual success encouraged others, as did persistent rumours after 1827 that Mexico might sell Texas to the United States. Soon the US government did indeed pursue the purchase and an offer of $5m was subsequently made. Speculators moved in and land was grabbed.

> From 1820 to 1840 the Texas wilderness was the lure of land-hungry, adventurous Americans. From the swamps of Florida and Louisiana to the hills of Kentucky and Ohio, the sign 'G.T.T.' (gone to Texas) could be found on many cabin doors. Some went to find new homes, but many went to get land grants, and to form Texas land companies. Sakolski, p.219

Texas and a fair chunk of California, some 522,568 square miles, was eventually annexed by the US after a war with Mexico and payment of a bit of cash, in 1845.

One of the best states to study for the working of this land mania, noted McGrane, was Illinois.

> The large amount of refuse land in the state afforded abundant occasion for investments, while the ever increasing stream of migration westward stimulated the desire to possess land. By 1835 Illinois was in a most prosperous and flourishing condition. p.53

Luckily we have a clear picture of the Illinois of the time, Chicago in fact, thanks to Homer Hoyt's fascinating studies for his thesis, subsequently turned into a must-read book, *One Hundred Years of Land Values in Chicago*. There follows a summary of the events that led to the panic of 1837, and a bit about local geography, but first let's go back to the subject of banks.

Banking

WE HAVE SEEN how, from the 1819 downturn and panic, there emerged a movement for banking reform. The hard-money men, libertarian in outlook, wanted the eradication of fractional reserve banking and of the only federally chartered bank, the Second BUS. They managed to take their ideas right to the top in 1928 but, where speculation in government-granted licences and privileges was concerned, they were bound to be defeated. Their programme of reform ultimately added fuel to the speculation, though they may not have seen it at the time.

Once the first BUS had been dealt with, state governments simply chartered as many banks as they could, to facilitate their aggressive development of transportation, kicking off the so-called era of free banking. State governments, banks and the individuals behind them were often one and the same, or at least closely connected. Of these banks, noted Robert Sobel, few could be classified as conservative. In Pennsylvania they were issuing ten paper dollars for each one of silver in their vaults, some acknowledging the ratio to be as high as thirty to one. New banking laws in Michigan state meant that almost anyone could open a bank.

> During the last months of 1837, forty-nine banks were opened in the state, with a nominal capital of $3.9 million, but with actual reserves of less than $1.8 million. Some of the banks in the West did business, transacted loans and printed currency with no initial reserves.
> Sobel, *Panic on Wall Street*, p.38

Rothbard noted one further significant development in the early 1830s, 'the enormous increase in specie' which 'was the result of two factors: first and foremost, a large influx of silver coin from Mexico, and second, the sharp cut in the usual export of silver to the Orient.'[8] It seems China was finding more interest in opium than in silver. More important, the Mexican government was financing its deficits by minting highly debased copper coins.

> Since the debased copper grossly overvalued copper and undervalued gold and silver, both of the latter metals proceeded to flow rapidly out of Mexico … the Mexican government was forced to rescind its actions in 1837 by shifting the copper coinage to its proper ratio. The inflow of Mexican silver promptly ceased.
> Sobel, p.39

Note the year. Increasing flows of specie were coming into the country; there was easy access to banks and more of them than ever before were printing currency as economic expansion continued. Opportunities were sought everywhere. 'Canals and railroads appeared interesting,' noted Sobel, 'but much of the money went into that favorite American speculative vehicle: land.' Land companies were being created in all parts of the US to facilitate the speculation. 'Banks accepted land as collateral for loans, issued paper money based on land, which was then used to buy more land, repeating the cycle again and again.'[9]

8 Murray N. Rothbard, *A History of Money and Banking in the United States*, p.98.
9 Sobel, p.40.

Chicago

NOW BACK to that review of Chicago. The geography first.

> The reason for the fortunate position of Chicago could be traced back a million years to the Ice Age when the glaciers scoured out Lake Michigan but did not cut a channel deep enough to turn the waters of the Great Lakes permanently into the Mississippi Valley. The St Lawrence River and the chain of Great Lakes formed the first highway into the heart of America from the East. The great network of rivers that emptied into the Mississippi was the first road to penetrate the interior of America from the south. Taken together, the two systems formed a huge arc around the English settlements on the Atlantic seaboard, and, if properly fortified, would have formed an insuperable barrier to westward expansion. At one point these two great waterways almost joined, and the land barrier was so slight that it was the route most frequently used for portage between them. This vital spot was Chicago. Homer Hoyt, *One Hundred Years of Land Values in Chicago*, p.7

Of course, any invading army would have to pass that way as well. So the first thing to be built after the US had bought six square miles of territory from the native Indians around the mouth of the Chicago River was a fort, Fort Dearborn. Around it a few rudimentary huts were built – mostly for fur traders and trappers. It had already been recognised that a continuous waterway for boats would be useful, so in 1816 more land was acquired from the Indians. The state of Illinois was admitted to the Union in 1818 with slightly adjusted boundaries, to take account of a new canal to be built from Chicago to La Salle. In 1825 the Illinois legislature incorporated a private company to dig it. Once Congress extended a land grant to the state, land sales could be used to help finance the digging. Even so, by 1830 there were still only twelve cabins in what might by this time be called Chicago. However, the way west to Chicago was becoming easier, and events occurred that put the city on a direct route to New York. Once the US army had defeated the Black Hawk Indian 'menace', around 1832, an increasing flow of settlers were attracted to the area and growth exploded. By 1833 the rise in population was reflected in a sharp increase in land values in the developing town. A lot bought for $42 in September 1830 was sold for $800 in November 1833. The fever was on, described in this way by Hoyt:

> At first the purchases were what might be termed legitimate, a lot sold for cash on which the purchaser would erect a building or store. The legitimate demand soon absorbed the floating supply and prices began to rise under the competition of anxious buyers. Lots purchased one day for $50 were sold the next for $60 and resold the next month for $100. It did not take long under such circumstances to develop a strong speculative fever, which infected every resident of the town and was caught by every newcomer. At the close of the year 1834 the disease had become fairly seated. p.26

The rise in land value gained momentum in 1834.

> The entire United States was beginning to engage in feverish land speculation, and people were coming to Chicago with visions of the future city at the mouth of the Illinois and Michigan canal. In June 1834, the corner of South Water and Clark Street, 80 by 180 feet, sold for $3500, thirty-five times as much as had been paid for it two years before. A year later it sold for $15,000.
>
> Hoyt, p.27

The speculation climbed still further when, in 1835, digging actually started on the canal, the State Bank of Illinois was chartered with a capital of $1.5 m to be re-loaned on Illinois real estate, and a government land office opened in the town on May 5. Hoyt had already noted, regarding new banks opening up, that 'one of the most potent devices for raising land values, liberal credit to land buyers, was thereby created.' The land office was now putting these buyers, flush with credit, into close proximity with the original seller.

> The fame of Chicago real estate was so great in New York City that Chicago lots were sold there at public auction. The high prices paid for these lots in the eastern city astonished the local speculators and stimulated fresh advances when the news finally reached the West. The report of a sale by Mr Hubbard of a half interest in a tract of eighty acres at the corner of Halsted and Chicago Avenue for $80,000 in New York in 1835, which represented a profit of $77,500 made in a few months, was at first not believed to be true. When confirmed ... local landowners revised upward their opinion as to the value of their holdings ... the bills of the state banks of Michigan, Indiana, and even Wisconsin were even more numerous in Chicago than the bills of the state bank of Illinois. New batches of Michigan bills could be secured almost at will by a law which authorized such notes to be issued in exchange for private obligations secured by mortgages on the lands of that state.
>
> Hoyt, p.27

News of further land sales and auctions was brought to the Chicagoans themselves by messengers riding on horseback through the streets. The story goes that a prominent physician, busying himself in his office selling town lots, was called away to a lady in urgent need of his professional services. Reluctantly leaving, he promptly diagnosed her ailment and made haste to return to his office. 'Why Doctor,' the woman called, 'you don't say here how to take the medicine.' 'Ah yes,' shouted back the doctor, 'Canal terms: one quarter down, with the balance in one, two and three years.'

There was much speculation in subdivided lots. McGrane quotes numerous examples, such as: 'Paper towns were laid out and advertised in the east as being at the "head of navigation" or the "handsomest location for a city in the world".'[10] One wag suggested to his speculator friends that,

10 McGrane, p.54.

as so many towns were being planned, it might be an idea to reserve a plot or two for farming.

So much for Chicago's very first boom. By 1839 most land values had plummeted 90 to 95 per cent. Very few speculators were not ruined.

Such rampant speculation in the sale of public lands, and such obvious losses of revenue to the government, begs the question why the government failed to put a stop to it. As speculation in the sale of the public domain intensified, it is probable that the government must have felt under increasing pressure to do something, even if some in the government were among the most active speculators.

> The people of the West thought they had just cause in protesting against the methods employed in disposing of the public lands. The speculator with his ready cash, his advance knowledge of good lands acquired by shrewd agents, his connivance with the registrars and the banks, and the pressure he could bring to bear on the legislatures, had every advantage over the poor settler. The country people [quoting correspondence between politicians at this point] 'waking or sleeping, eating or working', never thought of anything but land, and how to procure their equitable rights. To them the whole land-office system was odious, and as they formed a large portion of the new states, they were able to turn the scale of public opinion in many an election when they united. Their protests had to be listened to …
>
> McGrane, p.61

John Steele Gordon put it this way:

> Sales by the government's General Land Office had totaled a mere $2.5 million in 1832. By 1836 sales totaled $25 million and in the summer of that year were running at the rate of nearly $5 million a month … Jackson understood perfectly well what was happening … typically, Jackson resolved to stop this speculation in its tracks. He proposed to his cabinet that the Land Office accept only specie – gold and silver – in payment for land. But the cabinet, many of whose members were deeply embroiled in the speculation themselves, strongly opposed him. Congress, equally involved, would also have nothing to do with the plan. So Jackson simply waited until July 11 [1836], after congress had adjourned for the year, and then issued the so-called specie circular as an executive order. It required, with a few exceptions, payment in gold or silver after August 15. *The Great Game,* p.66

The downturn

THE WORSENING business conditions were not immediately obvious to all; things did not change overnight, it was a gradual process. In the 1836 November elections Van Buren, a follower of Jackson, just managed to win the presidency. In response to the specie circular, bank notes were being returned to issuing banks, especially those out west, to be redeemed for gold. Britain had been raising its discount rate to keep its gold in the country and was about to suffer the failure of several of its banks. Complicating matters further, the price of cotton was falling, bringing the failure of several US mercantile houses that traded in that commodity. The failures in the cotton region were contagious, soon spreading to New York, where by March 1837 a panic looked imminent. John Steele Gordon summed it up this way:

> Jackson had hoped that his action would dampen speculation in land, but it did more than that, bringing it to a screeching halt. As the demand for specie soared, holders began turning in bank notes and demanding gold and silver. Banks, to raise the needed money, called in loans as fast as they could. Western banks drained gold and silver from eastern banks, but they then held on to the metal as best they could, because of yet another government program. With the federal government running large surpluses and having no debt, money tended to pile up uselessly in the Treasury and was deposited in the pet banks. But in 1836, Congress decided to give much of this surplus money to the various state governments to use as they saw fit. It directed the Treasury to withdraw $9 million every quarter, beginning in January 1837, from its bank deposits and divvy it up among the states according to population. The banks had to be ready to absorb this considerable shrinking of their deposit bases. The weaker ones, with small gold reserves and large note issues, began to fail. The country's businessmen, who needed bank credit to operate, were crippled … the *New York Herald* reported on January 2, 1837, the day the first $9 million was transferred from mostly eastern banks to the state governments, that interest rates that had been 7 percent a year had risen to 2 or even 3 percent a month. Bankruptcies began to spread. When the Bank of England raised interest rates to prevent gold from flowing out of that country, British cotton purchases declined, further injuring the American economy. With higher interest rates at home, British capitalists were less inclined to invest in American securities, and prices on Wall Street plummeted still further … By the end of the next month every bank in the nation, at least those that had not already failed, suspended gold payments. Government revenues, which had reached $50.8 million in 1836, plunged to a mere $24.9 million the following year, and Andrew Jackson's vision of a debt-free federal government vanished, never to be seen again. By the early fall of 1837, about 90 percent of the country's factories had closed, and the country's first (and still its longest) great depression was underway. Given the depth and extent of the depression of 1837, it was fortunate that the vast majority of the American population still lived on farms and outside what economists call the cash economy. They could make do, providing for themselves, until better times returned. Those in the cash economy, the factory workers and owners, the merchants, and of course the brokers on Wall Street, suffered far worse. p.67

A severe contraction of bank credit was now well underway. Short selling, the art of selling a share you do not yet own, was invented at this time by Jacob Little, the first great Wall Street bear. This was probably indicative of the volatility in the market that was available to be exploited by speculators.[11]

11 The EIS website (www.businesscycles.biz/docs/jacoblittle.htm) has more about Little's exploits and subsequent wipe-out.

The poor crops had reduced the tolls collected by canal operators. States which for some years had been building all sorts of transport infrastructure, with money loaned by banks both local and overseas, were forced to scale down the building work, if not cancel projects entirely, as revenue declined. The state of North Carolina reported a decline of 50 per cent in its active and tangible property, and on land yet more, with many lots realising the cost of improvements only. Thus the action of credit in reverse.

The website www.campusprogram.com gives May 10 as the panic day of 1837 (nine months after the specie circular). This was the day New York banks suspended specie payments, though things had been worsening for months. Business failures had continued through April and several Wall Street offices like that of Hicks, Lawrence & Co closed as well. The unemployed held protest meetings, one in Greenwich Village attracting 50,000 workers. Riots broke out in Boston and Philadelphia. 'Stock prices on Wall Street fell sharply as gold seemed to vanish.'[12] Lightner, quoting excerpts from New York newspapers, says that John Fleming, President of Merchants Bank, 'fell dead from excessive anxiety with regards to the affairs of the bank May 4th, from which a run set in on all banks. The failures grew worse over the next two days, and US Bank stock fell below the issue price for the first time. On May 9th there was a "furious run on all banks", May 10th, "chaos".'[13]

Graph 4.1: Public Land Sales
acres '000, 1800-42

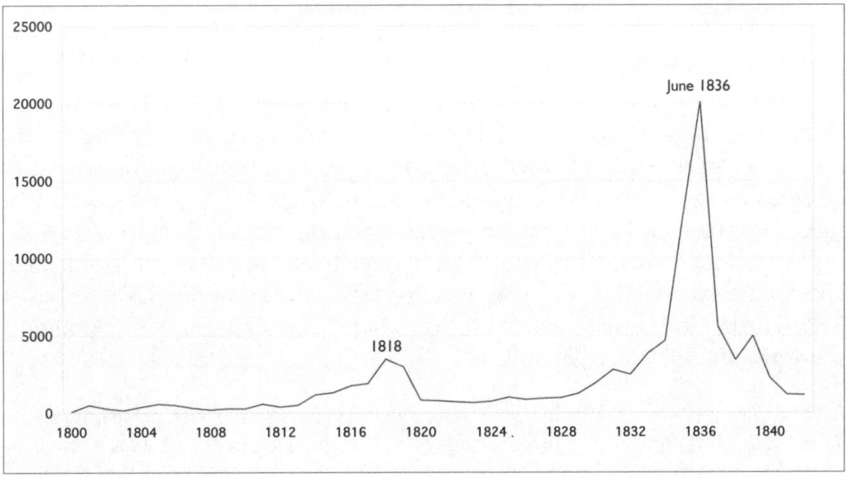

Sources: Annual Reports, Commissioner of the General Land Office, and Smith and Cole, *Fluctuations in American Business, 1790-1860*, Harvard University Press, Appendix D.

12 Sobel, p.67.
13 *History of Business Depressions*, p.135.

Graph 4.2: Public Land Sales
Quarterly Receipts to US Government, $000, 1830-40

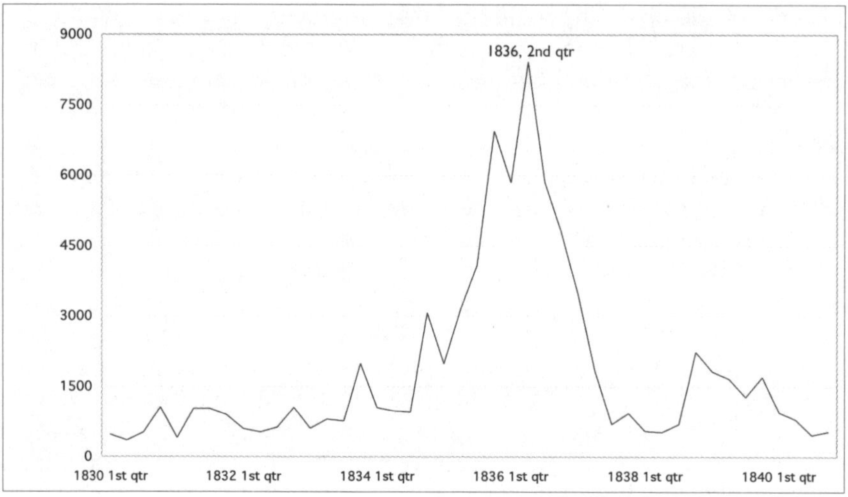

Source: Smith and Cole, *Fluctuations in American Business, 1790-1860*, Harvard University Press, 1935, Appendix D.

Land sales peaked in 1836, the dollar value of federal government receipts indicating that the peak was in the second quarter, April to June (Graphs 4.1 and 4.2). Hoyt identifies July as the top month for Chicago land transfers. Smith and Cole specifically rule out the land sales peak being attributable to immigration, going on to state that 'peaks in the sale of public lands uniformly preceded the outbreaks of the several crises … and frequently recovery in the volume of land sales preceded that of general business.'[14] This is an important observation.

Interestingly, railroad stocks peaked in 1835 (Graph 4.3). It seems that even back then stocks were doing what they do best, discounting future business activity so that stock prices are lower well before a downturn is obvious to the public. (One would actually expect this to have been even more pronounced back then. In the absence of any stock market regulation whatsoever, insider activity would have been rampant – as later cycles spectacularly reveal – and it is the insiders who know their stock best.) The railroad index also appears to have bottomed first, in 1842, heralding the forthcoming business upturn.

> The characteristic relationship among these three curves [stock prices, interest rates and commodity prices] may be said to be a sequence in which stock prices moved first, commodity prices second, and discount rates last. Thus in the culmination of the cyclical movement surrounding 1837, railroad stocks attained their maximum in May 1835, and broke precipitously after

14 W.B. Smith and A.H. Cole, *Fluctuations in American Business*, p.54.

Graph 4.3: Railroad Stock-Price Index 1834-44 (8 selected stocks, base 1834-42)

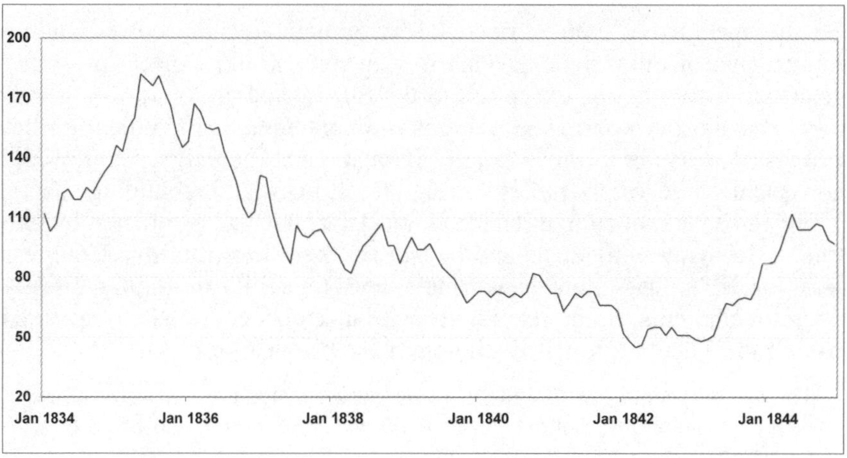

Source: Smith and Cole, *Fluctuations in American Business, 1790-1860*, Harvard University Press, 1935, Table 64, p.179.

Graph 4.4: Condition of the Banks in 4 states (for which data are available), October to December, annually, 1830-44, % ratio of specie to combined note circulation and deposits (Massachusetts, Rhode Island, New York and Pennsylvania)

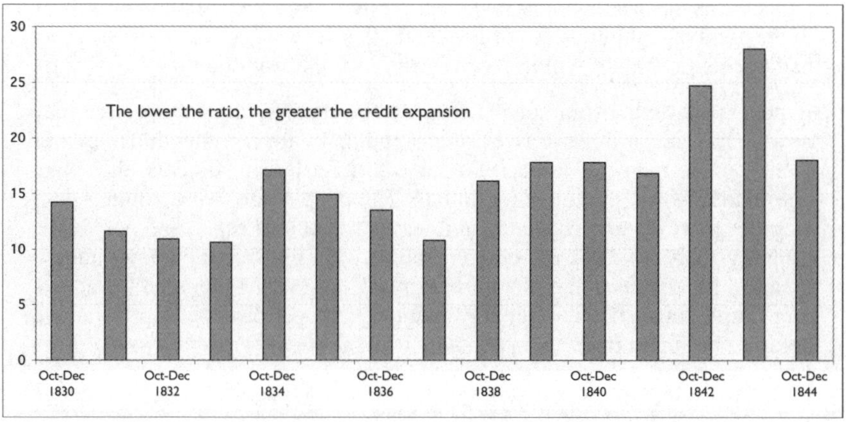

Source: Smith and Cole, *Fluctuations in American Business, 1790-1860*, Harvard University Press, 1935, Table 64, p.179.

> June 1836; commodity prices continued to rise until February 1837; and interest rates did not begin to fall decisively until after May of the latter year. Smith and Cole, p.83

So the speculative indices moved first, anticipating the corresponding movements of other indices. This is what one would expect; any other sequence would be the exception to the rule. Banking policy was generally expansionary up to 1833; there was a tightening in 1834, then further expansion of credit through to 1837 (Graph 4.4). Thereafter it followed a consistent conservatory policy of reigning in loans and rebuilding specie.

By 1840 the money in circulation, mostly notes, had contracted by two thirds. So many individuals and businesses were bankrupt that Congress was forced to pass new bankruptcy laws to avoid swamping already overcrowded jails. Some forty thousand bankrupts consequently avoided paying their debts. Crowd psychology played its part too:

> The instant people saw that the government suspected the reliability of the banking institutions, distrust seized upon the public mind, and like fire in the great prairies, nothing could stop it. McGrane, p.63

Some further quotes

WE CAN round out the study of this particular cycle with the following quotes, illustrating the extent of the reversal from boom to bust.

McGrane describes the Mississippi region:

> The currency of the state was in a terrible condition, as the banks refused to pay coin, and proposed to shave their paper. By 1839 extensive plantations were thrown out of cultivation and lying waste for want of hands to till them, the slaves having been seized under execution and carried off by the sheriff. The greatest embarrassments … were mostly confined to the old counties, as the new counties had been created and settled too late to embark in the extravagant purchases of land and Negroes at twice their value which had been so common within recent years in the lower counties. p.117

> Lands … that once commanded from twenty to fifty dollars per acre may now be bought for three or five dollars, and that with considerable improvements, while many have been sold at sheriff sales at 50 cents, that were considered worth ten to twenty dollars. The people, too, were running their Negroes to Texas and Alabama, and leaving their real estate and perishable property to be sold, or rather sacrificed … So great is the panic, and so dreadful the distress, that there are a great many farms prepared to receive crops, and some of them actually planted, and yet deserted, not a human being to be found upon them. p.118

In Illinois, the once prosperous public were now reduced to barter in order to carry on trading, the notes sometimes drawn as payable in a cow or a horse, or other farm products.[15]

15 McGrane, p.127.

> The hardships among the laboring classes were intense. One-half to two-thirds of the clerks and salesmen in large commercial houses in Philadelphia were without work by June 1837. Mothers were begging in the streets of New York for their children by the close of that year. The almshouses and poorhouses were full to the brim, while hundreds unable to gain admittance suffered from cold and starvation. As the cold months came on the suffering of the poor became so aggravated, and the number of unemployed increased to such a degree, that the ordinary means were inadequate to relieve even those who were destitute of every one of the necessitates of life. Some died of starvation. Some were frozen to death. Many, through exposure and privation, contracted fatal diseases. A large number who had never before known want were reduced to beg. McGrane, p.131

McGrane goes on to observe: 'It was upon the well-to-do land operators in the West and the eastern capitalist who had invested so heavily in lands that the panic fell with the greatest force.[16]

We might also include a few salient points about this episode noted by Charles Kindleberger in his classic study of business cycles, *Manias, Panics and Crashes.* Monetary expansion, he observed, had been underway since the 1830s, particularly as a result of the English textile boom. In the US so-called 'wildcat banking' and the importation of silver fed speculation in cotton and land, especially land used for cotton production. In the UK joint stock banks, a new creation, assisted further speculation in cotton, cotton textiles and railroads. At the height of the speculation in the US, French banks were assisting Nicholas Biddle of the Bank of the United States in his attempt to corner the cotton market. Kindleberger dates the speculative peak in the UK to April 1836, and the panic to December; the speculative peak in the US was November 1836, and the panic June 1837.

In *The Stock Market Barometer* William Peter Harrison quotes Charles Dow:

> 'The year 1837 brought a great commercial panic, for which there was abundant cause. There had been rapid industrial and commercial growth, with a multitude of enterprises established ahead of time. Crops were deficient, and breadstuffs were imported. The refusal of the government to extend the charter of the United States Bank had caused a radical change in the banking business of the country, while the withdrawal of public deposits and their lodgment with state banks had given the foundation for abnormal speculation.' p.26

Other writers reported similarly:

> Many of those who had experienced the distress of the collapsed land boom and panic of 1819 having passed away, and affairs being guided by a newer generation, all classes and in all sections of the country were, in the 1830s, infected with another land gambling mania. Chandler, *Land Title Origins*, p.489

16 p.133.

It was reported that, by 1836,[17] of the 13 million acres sold during the past year, 8 million had been bought for speculation. It seems a fair proportion of the settlers out west ended up as squatters by the early 1830s.

The banking frauds

THE SEVERE downturn brought into the open what had probably been going on for years – banking cover-ups, counterfeiting and embezzlement by bank officers. Stories were told that in Maine the bank commissioners discovered that in some instances loans had been made to shareholders before the capital had been paid in; in New York, bank capital had been paid in only to be borrowed immediately by stockholders under pledge of stock.[18]

Concealment was a feature of the banking process in Mississippi:

> Often the capital stocks of the banks … were paid in the notes of the stockholders. Charters gave an opportunity for this in using the words 'secured to be paid'. The issues of the banks were consequently not issued upon what the stock holders had paid into the bank, but on what they owed to the bank, thus making their indebtedness, and not their actual capital, the basis of their circulation. In many instances the directors borrowed nearly the entire capital of their respective institutions, while all the banks gave heavy discounts to their officers. By 1840 the bank commissioner could definitely state that he knew for certain individuals were indebted to the banks of Mississippi for sums of from one-half million to one million dollars, who, a few years previous, were not worth one dollar, but by virtue of the credit system they had been able to secure loans from the banks to purchase property. This property gave them additional credit, and from one bank they proceeded to another, extending their credit and increasing their property …
>
> McGrane, p.25

In Georgia, where the bank charter was to be granted, the incorporated gentlemen,

> to comply with the precautionary regulations of the legislature, borrowed, for a few days, the amount of specie required to be placed in the vaults before operations could be commenced. The bank would open under these auspices, the specie would be returned to its proper owner, and the notes of the stock holders would be substituted for it. McGrane, p.27

Banking is a highly privileged sector in any modern economy, wielding enormous power. Referring to Pennsylvania, McGrane reported that the members of the state legislature proved 'most pliable to outside pressure' when offered tempting internal improvements to their districts; 'Nicholas Biddle was to find this an efficient means for securing desirable

17 Chandler, p.489.
18 See McGrane, p.14.

legislation.'[19] When Biddle's bank, the Second BUS, collapsed in 1841 after a failed speculation in cotton, one of the bad debts listed was an amount of $114,000 owed by Congressman Daniel Webster, Secretary of State and outspoken supporter of the bank. McGrane also lists some of the vast number of thefts perpetrated by bank officers and reported in the newspapers of the time.[20]

What the newspapers were saying...

EBULLIENCE at the top:

> On whatever side we turn our eyes, we are greeted by the gratifying evidence of universal prosperity. *New Yorker*, October 1836

Politicians have other agendas:

> 'I leave this great people prosperous and happy.'
> *New York American*, February 21, 1837, quoting outgoing President Andrew Jackson

– when clearly they weren't. So too the bankers:

> Our banks are all pretty safe. *Bicknell's Reporter*, Philadelphia, March 28, 1837

– when clearly they weren't either.

The reversal to fear:

> The United States were never in such a perilous condition as they are at this moment. *New York Herald*, March 30, 1837

> The present commercial revulsion is without a parallel in our history. The distress pervades all classes – the prudent and the foolhardy, the regular merchant and the speculator, the manufacturer, tradesman, laborer, banker – all are involved in one general calamity. *New York Evening Post*, May 1, 1837

Blame the government:

> What good has the administration done us with all its experiments upon us? Eight years of experiment has brought us to the verge of bankruptcy, where the country stands now. *New York Daily Express*, April 18, 1837

> The cause of our calamities is traced mainly to misgovernment.
> *Washington DC Daily National Intelligencer*, May 13, 1837

> The great danger to our system lies in the tendency to an excess of power in executive hands, a system fast yielding to dispositions which are favorable to despotism. *New York Tribune*, October 11, 1841

19 McGrane, p.13.
20 McGrane, p.137, Table I, seemingly taken from the Illinois Senate House Reports, II, 1842. A copy can be found on the EIS site at www.businesscycles.biz/docs/bankthefts.htm and makes intriguing viewing.

Blame anything, except the speculation in government-granted licences and privileges:

> The present evils which afflict the country have been produced by over-banking, overtrading, overspending, overliving, overdashing, overdriving, overreaching, overcheating, overborrowing, overeating, overdrinking, over-praying, oversinning, overthinking, overplaying, overriding, overstepping, overfiddling, and overacting of every kind and description, except over-ploughing.
>
> *New York Herald*, May 3, 1837

To sum up, 1820 to 1837

AN EXPANSION of bank credit – it doesn't matter how this happens, just note that it happens – fuels an increase in speculative activity in government-granted licences and privileges. As more people pile into this activity, the action feeds on itself. The creation of credit to finance the buying and selling of these government-granted licences cannot, however, go on forever. At some point an event or combination of events will force a contraction. If this event is enough to erode public confidence, especially if it involves land value, a recession, perhaps even a panic, is inevitable. Sure as night follows day.

Such an event or combination of events does not have to be out of the ordinary. It is just that, towards the peak, the economy is less able to withstand the shock, built as it is upon that notoriously sandy idea of the creation of bank credit to finance the speculative buying and selling of government-granted licences and privileges – the largest of which is land value.

> Loans for land speculation defy any estimate as to their quantity, but probably constituted a large percentage of total assets during the entire period – larger than the percentage assigned to business loans, and in the years 1834-39, they possibly exceeded all other loans combined.
>
> Sharp, *The Jacksonians versus the Banks*, p.34

History will show us that the greatest speculation always takes place into the final years of the real estate cycle. In the 1837 cycle, after the Second BUS was put out of business, the federal government still needed to put its own collected revenues somewhere – formerly they had been deposited with the BUS. The decision was to divvy them up amongst selected state banks. Such banks could thereby extend their own lending, and did so. Many new state banks were chartered largely in the hope of gaining a share of such government deposits. The sale of public lands far exceeded what might have been expected as the cycle developed. Soon the federal government actually had no debt outstanding, further building up the surplus that was eventually handed back to the states.

Speculation in all sorts of things developed – reckless over-investment as it turned out. An inflow of specie from Mexico allowed banks further licence to print money. Distributing the federal surplus funds on deposit with selected banks, and transferring them to the states, put pressure on the reserve holdings of the banks involved. Poor crops from the previous year – apparently the result of the Hessian fly – saw the US importing more the following year, bringing pressure from English banks to settle payment. The Bank of England, for its own reasons, was increasing interest rates, shifting the flow of capital back in the direction of Britain. Suddenly credit, once abundant, was that much harder to get …

FURTHER READING

Grant, Phil. *The Wonderful Wealth Machine*. 1959.

Insana, Ron. *Trendwatching: Don't be Fooled by the Next Investment Fad, Mania or Bubble.* HarperCollins, 2002.

Lightner, Otto C. *The History of Business Depressions*. Northeastern Press, 1922.

McGrane, Reginald Charles. *The Panic of 1837*. University of Chicago Press, Phoenix edn, 1965.

Miller, George. *On Fairness and Efficiency: The Privatization of the Public Income over the Past Millennium*. The Policy Press, 2000.

Sakolski, A.M. *The Great American Land Bubble: The Amazing Story of Landgrabbing, Speculations, and Booms from Colonial Days to the Present Time.* Harper & Brothers, 1932. Chapters X and XI in particular.

Sharp, James Roger. *The Jacksonians versus the Banks*. Columbia University Press, 1970.

Smith W.B. and A.H. Cole. *Fluctuations in American Business, 1790-1860*. Harvard University Press, 1935.

Sobel, Robert. *Panic on Wall Street: A History of America's Financial Disasters.* Macmillan, 1968.

ARTICLES OF INTEREST

American Heritage, May 2001, Vol. 52, No. 3, 'Perils of the Surplus'.

American Heritage, August/September 2002, Vol. 53, No. 4, 'The Man Who Invented the Newspaper'.

5

US Banking History to 1860

A Précis

When I was young, people called me a gambler. As the scale of my operations increased, I became known as a speculator. Now I am called a banker. But I have been doing the same thing all the time.

Sir Ernest Cassel, British financier

PRIOR TO 1776 the British Crown had not permitted the establishment of banking facilities within its American territories. Various American colonies had proceeded to issue notes and paper – fiat money backed by government legislation and decree rather than gold or silver – but that is not our story here. The lack of banking, or, more correctly, credit facilities within the colonies was as strong a grievance as any that led to the War of Independence.

After 1788 the states surrendered their right to print notes to the new federal power and Alexander Hamilton established the First Bank of the United States. All states, however, maintained the right to charter banks by issuing licences, and proceeded to do so with remarkable dexterity.

The history of US banking can be divided into clear eras:

1791-1811	The First Bank of the United States, acting as a central bank.
1811-1816	Banking is in the hands of state-chartered banks.
1816-1836	The Second Bank of the United States again adopts a quasi-central-bank role.
1836-1913	No central bank of any kind: 1836 – Civil War, the so-called 'free banking' era; 1863-1913 National banking (with federal bank charters).
1913-present	The Federal Reserve System.

Each of the cycle chapters includes a discussion of the relevant banking era, to which the following could be added.

Banking before 1836

THE FIRST US banks were established in major ports such as Boston and New York. This was where commercial need was initially greatest. As settlement extended westwards, banks were never far behind, assisting farmers to buy land and equipment. Especially land.

By 1820 most town folk would have been familiar with the process of banking and the use of bank credit in the form of coin, notes and deposits. Until about 1860, if you went to a bank and succeeded in gaining a loan, the bank would give you bank notes, which it printed, equal to the amount of the loan. In reality, these notes were nothing more than IOUs, though at the time you may not have thought of them in this way. You then spent these notes on what you wanted, putting them into circulation.

If you preferred to hold gold and silver in the form of coin, rather than printed bank notes, the law allowed you to go to the bank which issued the note and exchange it for coins to the equivalent value. Under normal conditions the bank could not refuse your demand, but, as the various chapters show, times were not always normal. Generally the notes issued by a bank did represent an enforceable contract between the holder and the issuing bank, so that you could swap them for gold or silver coin, but a bank note's value was only ever as good as the assets of the bank.

It was a profitable activity for banks to issue notes as loans. Early on it was realised that notes could be printed and issued in excess of the quantity of gold and silver coin (specie) held in the vaults (fractional reserve banking). The leverage was about ten to one. In addition, interest could be earned on such loans at 6 to 7 per cent per annum. Individual banks jealously guarded and continually fought for the right to print their own notes against insistent demands by the federal government (and many presidents' suspicious of the banks and their power) to exert some sort of control over US banking activities. This is a constant theme throughout 19th-century US banking history.

Within a local community there were soon in circulation as many varied and colourful notes as there were banks. They were not necessarily of standard denominations, as we are used to today. The system rested on confidence: an unfamiliar bank note might not be acceptable in settlement of a transaction, so bank notes usually circulated within their own state of issue only, though there were exceptions. Most state charters, as distinct from a federal charter, allowed for the establishment of just one bank per charter, prohibiting banks from opening branches in other towns or operating across state lines. (This limitation on banking – a development that occurred only in the United States – was to have dramatic consequences in later years.)

Several problems could arise. Firstly, would Bank A accept notes from Bank B as a deposit? If it did, this raised questions of inter-bank dealing and note-redemption, matters handled today by Federal Reserve cheque-clearing services. Back then, if Bank A accepted Bank B's notes, it would then need to return them to Bank B and request the equivalent specie (note redemption). In practice, because returning the notes involved a cost, Bank B's notes were often just put back into circulation by Bank A. No bank appreciated having its notes returned for redemption, preferring to have them remain in circulation for as long as possible. Note redemption lowered reserves and forced a contraction in lending.

Another problem was that banks earn their profit by lending (creating credit). A loan was effected by the printing and issuing of notes to the borrower, hence the temptation to over-issue.

Yet another problem arose in a downturn of business activity. If it was feared that a bank would not be able to convert its bank notes into gold or silver on demand, a 'run' on the bank might result. Customers wanting to be first to get to the bank before the gold ran out would escalate the rush. As all banks were independent and there was no central bank, if the gold in the vaults did run out a bank would be out of business if it could not convert its assets quickly enough into the gold sought by its depositors.

Most banking required a charter and those who got one naturally sought to protect themselves from additional competition. A vested interest was created. But states generally also received a revenue stream from the banks as they prospered, in the form of dividends if the state took an investment

Graph 5.1: Bank Numbers and Loans Outstanding 1820-60

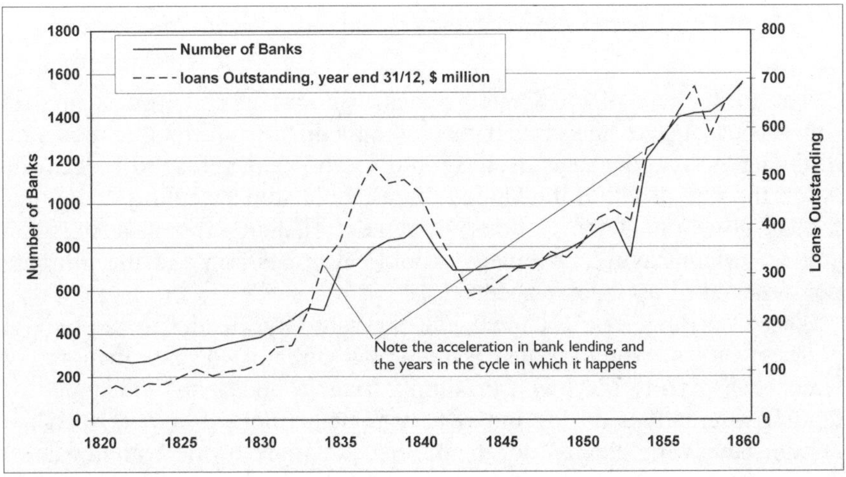

Source: Bodenhorn, Howard, 'Antebellum Banking in the United States'. EH.Net Encyclopedia, edited by Robert Whaples, September 5 2001 (www.eh.net/encyclopedia/contents/bodenhorn.banking.antebellum.php).

in part of the stock of the bank, or in the form of a tax on the capital of the bank, which some states levied. So there was pressure to issue more charters. The state-chartered banks were generally incorporated concerns.

States granting bank charters did not always have the public welfare in mind. Often it had more to do with the personal gain of the promoter and his ability to sway the legislature through political connections. A bribe was often helpful – a precedent established by the Philadelphia Bank which got its charter from the Pennsylvania legislature with the help of a $135,000 'donation'.[1] So states earned revenue in that way as well.

There were many requests for state banking charters – always more than were granted. Charters were often rejected or delayed in the legislature, especially where this would have resulted in competition for an existing bank. One outcome was the rise of 'private' or unincorporated banks. Not much is known about these establishments. Some states sought to restrict their activities, passing laws against them or prohibiting their note issues. For a bank that was chartered, once the charter was obtained it could open for business. The paid-up capital that was required was accumulated by the issue of shares, for which there were usually plenty of buyers – insurance companies, other savings banks and wealthier individuals. Historian Naomi Lamoreaux described the raising of capital by promoters in New England this way:

> By securing a charter for a bank, [the promoters] obtained a vehicle that, almost as if by magic, could assist them in raising funds. First, the incorporators subscribed for a controlling interest in the new bank's stock; then, when payment for the stock became due, they borrowed the requisite sum from another institution ... As soon as the state's examiners had satisfied themselves that the new bank's capital had actually been deposited, the investors could borrow back the money they had tendered for their stock (using the stock itself as security for the loan) and repay the original debt...
>
> *Insider Lending*, p.19

The First Bank of the United States was able to carry out a modest supervision of state-chartered banks by immediately returning to them any of their notes deposited with it. Should a state bank refuse to redeem its notes, the First Bank of the United States could stop accepting such notes for US government transactions – payment of duties for instance. Such activity might have contributed to political opposition and the ultimate non-renewal of its federal licence.

The First Bank of the United States was a large lender to the federal government: it would either issue notes directly to the government treasury, as to any borrower, or simply make a book entry. This lack of lending alternatives during the 1812 war with England helped ripen the circumstances for the creation of the Second Bank of the United States. Raising taxes was never popular, and the floating of bonds was not very

1 Howard Bodenhorn, *Antibellum Banking in the United States*.

successful at this time, so the state banks had to be approached for loans. The federal power base soon wanted its own bank. The Second Bank of the United States was therefore created and lasted from 1816 until 1836. Its demise led to the era of free banking in which anyone could open a bank and issue bank notes as long as adequate capital could be provided.

Free banking, 1836 to the Civil War

THE STATES OF Michigan and New York were first to adopt some changes to the established banking laws, around 1837. Up to 1836 any incorporated entity (of limited liability) could issue notes as a bank if it had gained government (generally state government) approval via a charter. After the 1837 panic those same incorporated entities no longer required the approval of an increasing number of state legislatures if they wanted to open a bank. With the demise of the Second Bank of the United States there was also no effective oversight by a federal body, hence the term 'free banking'. This did not mean complete freedom for bank-creation, or that the laws pertaining to banks were the same laws that pertained to other incorporated entities. There was still in existence legislation applicable only to banks, it was just that anyone could set up a bank as long as he adhered to such laws. The charters were in effect done away with. One of the main reasons states moved into free banking was so that banking would be less politicised and bank-note issue would be safeguarded by better laws. However, as we see in the relevant cycle chapters, this did not change the underlying system: bank lending (credit creation) on government-granted licences, based mostly on land value. It was never likely to achieve what it was meant to: the elimination of the business cycle and a banking panic in the downturn.

In states where free banking came into operation, the relevant legislation involved the following:

- A minimum subscription capital was generally required (as paid in).
- Banks were required to deposit with the state government bonds to the value of bank notes issued. The government signed the notes and handed them back to the bank for use. As the bonds to be deposited had to be well recognised, actively traded bonds, this would establish the worth of the bank and its notes, improving public confidence. It also meant that, if the bank failed, the bonds could be sold off and the proceeds paid to creditors, the note-holders and depositors.
- The law of convertibility of notes into specie still applied, so banks continued to hold reserves. But they still operated on a fractional reserve basis, so liquidity in the event of a run was still a problem.
- States reserved the right to inspect each bank, and also required for the first time that information about their activities be made public.

- A bank was permitted one location only; branch banking as we know it was still unavailable. 'Wildcat banks' did spring up, operating in hard-to-find locations (though obviously there had to be customers), making it that much harder to have their notes redeemed.

So many notes came to be issued by different banks in this free-banking era, and so many counterfeits of those notes, that it became essential for businesses to keep at hand guides to note identification. These were called 'Bank Note Reporters'. Although most of the banking system operated in an honest fashion, there are many colourful stories about rogue banks and the ease with which such a proliferation of bank notes could be counterfeited.

The Federal Reserve Board of San Francisco suggests in historical articles on its website that there were more than 30,000 different notes in circulation towards the end of this era, one third of which might have been counterfeit. The Bank of Battle Creek in Michigan had its teller, Tolman W. Hall, leave via the back door if a note-holder ever entered the bank. The Farmers' Bank of Sandstone lived up to its name by offering to redeem its notes in local commodities should any note-holder come to the bank: one sandstone whetstone for each one dollar note presented. And, the story goes, the Jackson County Bank vault contained boxes with silver coin visible at the top, but, further down, coloured glass, lead and nails.

The era of free banking was taxed out of existence when, after the Civil War, the federal government put a 10 per cent tax on all state bank notes, to improve the operation of its newly designed national banking system.

One further development in the 1850s should also be noted: the connection between banking and securities markets. To facilitate redemption in active port cities, and provide local currency for merchant clients, banks elsewhere would keep cash on deposit with banks in these port cities. New York evolved into the most important city in this regard. New York banks could afford to pay interest to other banks that kept deposits with them because those same deposits were lent to customers wanting loans for investment in the developing New York stock and bond markets – loans that could be called in by the bank at a moment's notice. The call – or margin – loan became an attractive business proposition for such banks,[2] progressively making stock markets more and more responsive to the fluctuations in interest rates.

2 Margaret Myers, *The New York Money Market*.

FURTHER READING

Bodenhorn, Howard. *Antebellum Banking in the United States*. EH.Net Encyclopedia, edited by Robert Whaples, September 5, 2001 (www.eh.net/encyclopedia/contents/bodenhorn.banking.antebellum.php).

Dwyer, Gerald P. Jr, *Wildcat Banking, Banking Panics, and Free Banking in the United States*, Economic Review, Federal Reserve Bank of Atlanta, December 1996.

Lamoreaux, Naomi. *Insider Lending: Banks, Personal Connections and Economic Development in Industrial New England*. Cambridge University Press, 1994.

Myers, Margaret. *The New York Money Market: Origins and Development*. Columbia University Press, 1931.

Rolnick, Arthur J., and Warren E. Weber, *Free Banking, Wildcat Banking and Shinplasters*. Research Department, Federal Reserve Bank of Minneapolis.

Sylla, Richard. *US Securities Markets and the Banking System, 1790-1840*. Economic Review, Federal Reserve Bank of St Louis, May/June 1998.

6

The Western Blizzard

The Land Boom of 1854

No nation has ever before been embarrassed from too large a surplus in the Treasury.

President Buchanan, in his inaugural address, March 1857[1]

O Posterity, Posterity, you can't think how bothered, bedeviled, careworn, and weary were your enlightened ancestors in their counting-rooms and offices and bank parlors during these bright days of September, A.D. 1857.

Diary entry of George Templeton Strong, September 1857, lamenting the panic gripping the nation

'THE GOLD RUSH and the boom in railroad shares ended in a spectacular bust known as the Blizzard of 1857', wrote Ron Insana. He says further:

> The gold rush and railroad mania created a nearly insatiable appetite for shares in both those endeavours. Of course, investment houses and the firms themselves were more than willing to accommodate the demand. Banks also got in on the act, following the path of miners into the Western states. The banks … issued a steady supply of notes, reflecting the ever-increasing supply of gold. The printing of paper money, which was not controlled by a national central bank at that time, caused inflation, which created the *appearance of even more prosperity*. As is often the case, excessive credit finances uneconomic ventures that, in turn, go bust when credit conditions tighten or economic conditions deteriorate. A case in point is the failure of the Ohio Life Insurance and Trust Company in 1857, whose collapse touched off a panic in American financial markets that ended the speculative interest in gold and rail shares. *Trendwatching*, p.116 (emphasis added)

Sound familiar? Let's dig a little deeper. From the previous peak of 1837, it had taken five long years for the economy to bottom out. And even then things did not really recover until the end of the Mexican war

1 He goes on to suggest that the nation ought to extinguish its debt, strengthen the armed forces, expand its boundaries and build a rail line to the Pacific.

in 1848. In Chicago, writes Homer Hoyt, discussing previous speculation in the canal and the lots the canal company had put up for sale,

> the buyers of canal lots, unable to meet their payments in 1837, had their time of payment extended by special act of the legislature … as this was of little avail by the time land values had declined drastically, the legislature again came to their relief in 1841, first by deducting one-third from the price they had agreed to pay in 1836, and, second, by allowing them to apply all the money they had paid in toward the full payment of one lot or one portion of a lot, so they received a clear title to at least one piece of land in return of what they had spent. *One Hundred Years of Land Values in Chicago.*, p.41.

It was one small step on the road to recovery. We return to the Chicago story later in the chapter.

The followers of Jackson, who still had the White House with Van Buren, continued their banking reform. They succeeded in divorcing federal government from banking entirely with an act, passed in 1840, that established an independent treasury. The 1837 panic, which turned into full-scale depression after the land-price decline, focused attention on banking, and speculation in general. Many Americans blamed the banks, and sometimes land speculators too, for their misfortune. One ardent Jacksonian and hard-money politician, Senator Thomas Hart Benton, said ruefully:

> I did not join in putting down the Bank of the United States to put up a wilderness of local banks. I did not join in putting down the paper currency of a national bank, to put up a national paper currency of a thousand local banks. I did not strike Caesar to make Antony master of Rome.

Yet that is precisely what had happened.

President Van Buren supported the idea of pricing land sales according to value rather than size, and giving preference to those making actual improvements. Eventually Congress settled on a bill granting right of pre-emption, passed only after intense and heated debate, and with many amendments, in 1841. Any individual could then legally venture forth upon public, surveyed but unclaimed land and stake a claim. The limit to the claim was still 160 acres, payable at $1.25 per acre. You had to be a US citizen (or to have filed a declaration to become one), the head of a family, a widow or, if single, over the age of 21. This was a solid attempt to get land into the hands of genuine settlers, though ingenious speculators found ways around it, as we shall see.

In banking, we saw how the destruction of the Second Bank of the United States (Second BUS) had removed any influence a central bank might possibly have had over the state banks. Once the Second BUS was eliminated, the federal government passed the Deposit Act in 1836, increasing the number of banks authorised to receive and hold funds the federal government paid out and collected. The deposit bank system was in part an attempt to regulate these state banks and ensure their stability. So by 1840 the US had an independent treasury for the management of its revenue.

To solve perceived banking problems, other suggestions were also put forward: a federal bank prohibited from issuing notes or discounting paper, with branches in each state; properly regulated local banks – or indeed a new national bank. The ongoing war of ideas about banks is a major part of US history. *The context is an economic system that allows the capitalisation of government-granted licences and privileges into tradable commodities* – otherwise such arguments would not arise. Importantly, once the independent treasury came into being, the regulation of the banks, if there was to be any, was left to the then 26 states.

So bad was the downturn, every state was prepared at least to attempt some banking reform to avoid another panic. Some thought forbidding the issue of small-denomination notes might help, by forcing the use of gold and silver coins which ought not to depreciate. Others introduced legislation to control banks' reserve ratios, compelling them to maintain a certain level of specie to support the notes issued. Some states went so far as to control the banks through state (public) ownership. There were even suggestions to do away with banks completely as those distraught by what they saw as an utterly corrupt system took a fervent, almost religious, stand. Some states, like New York, went for 'free-banking'.

The predominant view among the Jacksonians was that the banking establishment represented a power base that threatened a free, democratic society. They especially denounced the exclusive, monopolistic contracts, or charters, that states had been granting them. The Jacksonian sentiment was manifested in two ways: firstly, it was proposed that states have the power to alter charters awarded to banks at any time in the public interest; secondly that there should be free banking, where anyone could open a bank provided the requirements laid down by state statute were met. No longer were banks to have a privileged status enforced by state charter. They were, after all, the most important corporate institutions in the newly developing nation. By the peak year, 1856, Wall Street played host to some 360 rail stocks and 75 insurance stocks, but 985 bank stocks.

> A flood of legislation was enacted … to remedy many of the abuses of the preceding years. These laws generally called for the appointment of bank commissioners by the governor of the state, with power to investigate the books of the institution, limitations of circulation, investments, and liabilities; penalties for failure to pay in specie, restrictions of officers, directors, or stockholders becoming indebted to the bank, or borrowing from it on the pledge of their stock.
>
> R.C. McGrane, *The Panic of 1837*, p.121

But ingenious bank directors found ways around the laws, just like the land speculators.

Graph 6.1: Railroad Stock-Price (all-inclusive) Index monthly, 1841-62 (base 1853)

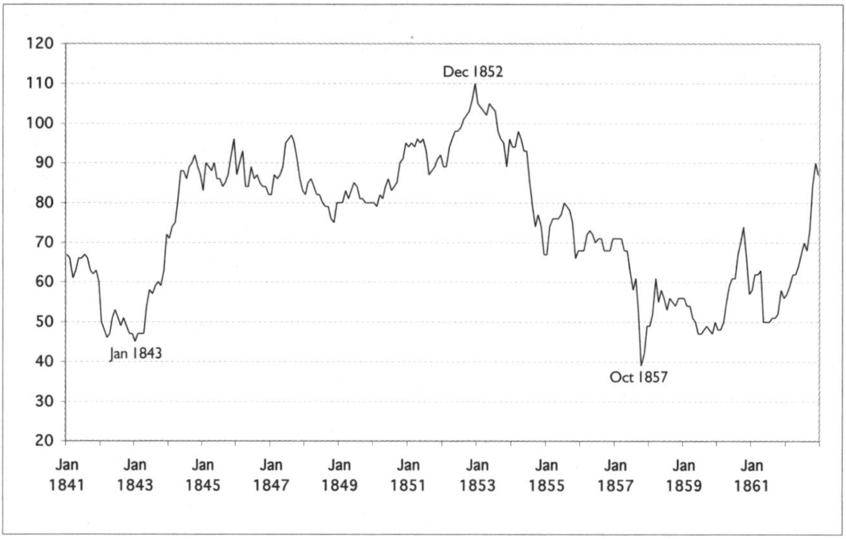

Source: Smith and Cole, *Fluctuations in American Business, 1790-1860*, Harvard University Press, 1935, Table 70, p.184.

A review of interest rates and stock prices for the early 1840s is instructive. Rail stocks underwent a substantial re-weighting in 1843; prices on the Smith and Cole index more than doubled from the low point in January of that year (Graph 6.1). Smith and Cole themselves highlighted the reappearance of cheap money in 1843, a return of public confidence after the banks resumed their contractual obligations to back note issues with specie, and 'possibly other factors', such as the growing realisation of the highly promising outlook for railroads in general, as reasons for the rise in price of rail stocks. The chart of interest rates (Graph 6.2) confirms the low price of money in 1843, at least as offered by the New York banking establishments.

> By 1843, the number of banks had declined to a low of 691, and in the same year the amount of notes in circulation had dropped almost two-thirds, from the 1837 high to 58 million dollars. The boom figures were not reached again until the decade of the 1850s … the period after 1837 was characterised by an increasing interest in the liquidity of banks. It was recognised that the older mercantilist ideas of a capital-circulation ratio or a bond backed circulation were not adequate to insure a bank's solvency and liquidity. Thus, in the years after the depression, banking became more and more based upon specie, with some states requiring each bank to maintain a certain ratio between specie on hand and notes in circulation.
>
> James Roger Sharp, *The Jacksonians versus the Banks*, p.28

Graph 6.2: Discount Rate, New York City
monthly average 1841-62

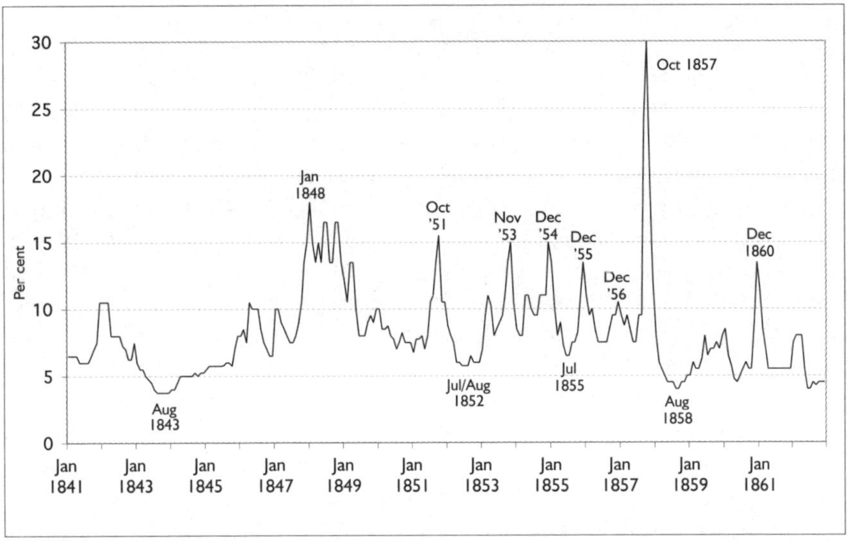

Source: Smith and Cole, *Fluctuations in American Business, 1790-1860*, Harvard University Press, 1935, Table 74, p.192.

Now it is indeed ironic – that banking became more and more based upon specie – given the events of January 24, 1848, the California gold strike. James Marshall had been inspecting a millrace he had just constructed on the American River, not far from Sacramento. A millrace carries water from a stream to the top of a waterwheel. Marshall had just

> turned the water into his new apparatus the night before to clear the debris. Now something 'about the size and shape of a pea glinted in the water.' 'It made my heart thump', he remembered later, 'for I was certain it was gold.' 'Boys', he said to his workmen, 'by God, I believe I have found a gold mine.'
>
> John Steele Gordon, *The Great Game*, p.84

He had indeed. And within a very short time the event was transforming the whole country.

Marshall's find was not exactly in US territory at the time. But, in one of those fateful quirks of history, the area surrounding the find, as well as what is now Nevada, Utah, New Mexico, Wyoming and Colorado, was ceded to the US for $15m plus claims of US citizens against that country, as part of the Mexican War treaty of February 2, 1848, ending a war fought ostensibly over the territory of Texas. In those days California was so isolated from the rest of the US that news of the gold strike took several months to work its way east. When it got there, the result, says John Steele Gordon, was mass hysteria. Actually a brief report of Marshall's find had been published in a San Francisco newspaper in March, but incredibly it seemed to go unnoticed. It was not until a Mormon elder, Sam Brannan, walked through the streets of San Francisco with a bottle of the yellow stuff, shouting 'Gold! Gold from the American River!' in an effort to lure customers to his supply store, that people sat up and took notice. The rest, as they say, is history. Marshall, for reasons that are unclear, was never able to secure legal recognition of his own claims. He watched his saw-mill fail for want of workers, as they went off panning for gold, and died poor, tending a small garden in a home-steaders cabin, in 1885.

Francisco Lopez, the story goes, discovered gold in the roots of an onion he dug up for lunch, which set off a local rush to the site at San Feliciano, near Los Angeles, though news of this particular discovery was ignored elsewhere.[2] The next year, 1849, the 'forty-niners', some 80,000 people, travelled to California from all parts of the country, indeed the world, expanding greatly the network of cross-country trails and tracks.

Now take note of the times. Gold ruled. The financial system, particularly in Britain, was backed by gold. The Bank of England had been on a gold standard since 1821, and bought gold from anyone at the rate of £3 17s 10d per ounce. The US government did not issue bank notes – that was in the hands of the states – but it did issue gold coins, $20.66 to the ounce. This started as a Jacksonian initiative for the federal government to mint its own low-denomination coins from the small amounts of gold coming from the North Carolina and Georgia mines (another scheme to get the public using coin instead of depreciating notes). The gold rush kick-started a major spurt of investment and speculation. President Polk took time during his congressional message of December 5, 1848 to speak of the gold strike, displaying for effect a twenty-pound gold nugget. 'The whole nation went suddenly, deliriously mad.'[3]

> The influx of gold, spurred a major economic boom as it expanded the money supply and greatly increased the backing of the dollar. Foreign investors, who had shunned American securities in the 1840s, now flocked back into American railroad and government bonds … Railroad mileage increased by nearly 150 percent as the railroads rushed westward to the Mississippi, the jumping off point for wagon trains to California. Pig iron production in turn soared from only 63,000 tons in 1850 to 883,000 tons in 1856. Coal production more than doubled as well … This swelling economic activity was, of course, reflected on Wall Street. Mining shares, many of them of highly dubious value, traded briskly on the curb, and a Mining Exchange was soon established to handle the business in a more formal manner. Gordon, p.86

One enthusiast, Count Agoston Haraszthy, did find his fortune in gold, though not by digging for it. Forced to flee Hungary after being caught in an uprising of workers against the monarchy, the Count arrived in

2 Quoted by pbs.org.
3 Ray Allen Billington, *The Westward Movement in the United States*, p.66.

America and wound up in politics on the Republican side. So good were his services that he was appointed director of the new Federal Mint which opened in San Francisco in 1854. Within the year the Count was approached by federal investigators searching for gold bars missing from the mint, worth around $140,000.

> 'Easily explained,' said the Count. 'In the process of the mint smelting the gold, slivers did sometimes inadvertently escape through the flue of the furnace, only to disappear into the air.' Dana L. Thomas, *Lords of the Land*, p.63

With his new found wealth the Count went on to buy a bit of real estate in the Sonoma Valley, planted a few grapevines and fathered the California wine industry.

And, to prove the adage that there is more money in selling shovels to miners than in digging for gold, there is the story of Levi Strauss who in 1850 started making his now famous heavyweight trousers (called 'genes' in France) from twilled cotton cloth. His original, less successful, idea had been the manufacture of tents for the miners.

Suddenly, the US economy was back in full swing. And it was big, helped along by some rapidly developing new technologies: plank roads, railroads and the telegraph.

Plank roads

RON INSANA describes the plank roads best, so let's quote a few words of what he writes about this early invention:

> Plank roads are, as they sound, roads made of wooden planks, instead of gravel or dirt, which were popular in the early days of this country. A Russian innovation, plank roads were used more aggressively in Canada and then copied here in the United States. *Trendwatching*, p.56

The planks were laid by plank-road companies who issued securities to the public, promising dividends of 10 to 40 per cent per annum, according to the literature of the day, says Insana.

> Very few … ever even paid 10 percent. And yet, between 1847 and 1857, some 1,388 plank road companies incorporated in the 17 states, [of which] 340 alone were incorporated in New York. In New York, those companies built 3,000 miles of plank roads. And at least 1,000 plank roads were chartered nationwide.

They went public by the hundred. It was a full-blown fever.

> The effort was helped by aggressive pamphleteering on the part of self-styled plank road promoters, who made dubious claims about a number of attributes of their projects. They claimed that plank roads had unusual durability, ten to fifteen years, as opposed to their real shelf lives, if you will, which was closer to four. They overestimated rates of return on invested

> capital and over-hyped the roads' utilitarian values, often leaving out such niggling concerns as the fact that horses riding over the planks would sometimes slip through the planking and break their legs, a rather substantial deterrent to use among horse owners who either rode them or used them to pull wagons or carriages.

So much for the plank roads, a little known but important contributor to the speculative fever of the times.

Railroads

> I've heard of the call of the wild, the call of the law, the call of the church. There is also the call of the railroads.
>
> Reed Richardson, *The Locomotive Engineer*, p.102

NOW HERE was a truly revolutionary invention. It must have been astonishing for a mid-19th-century local to see for the first time a large 'iron horse' steam into town. The railroads changed everything, even time itself.

> The great railroad boom in the United States took a while to reach a crescendo. In fact, a railroad boom in Great Britain was fully under way just as the U.S. boom began. It started rather inauspiciously in the summer of 1831. The Mohawk and Hudson Railroad began its Albany and Schenectady service in an unexpectedly smoky manner … the passengers on the first rocky ride were deluged with smoke and ash from the engine up front because there were no windows to let in fresh air. Despite its discomfort, the journey successfully promoted the railroad and led to many more trips before the transcontinental railroad was completed in 1869. The Mohawk and Hudson was listed on the New York Stock Exchange that year. Many railroads would follow until a full-blown mania in railroad securities took hold.
>
> Insana, p.58

Railroads – 'the rails' – looked decidedly like they were going to change for ever the way business had been done and the way humanity had lived for centuries. Remember General Jackson? To get to his own inauguration in Washington in 1828 from his home state of Tennessee took him thirty days. Yet within the life of this 1857 cycle the journey time would come down to just three days. Travelling for purely social reasons became an option. (In Scotland rail travel had become so popular on the people's free day, Sunday, that the church tried to ban it because the flock had stopped going to church.)

What brought the railroads into such sharp focus in America was the vast give-away of the public domain that went with their development. Much American history for the remainder of the 19th century is about how the country chose to distribute the enormous wealth the rails created. More about that in the next cycle.

The telegraph

THE TELEGRAPH was the other great transforming invention of the time. It certainly put an end to Wall Streeters' outpacing the news to other stock exchanges. It was Samuel Morse who assembled all the existing bits and pieces into a workable apparatus; adding to it the code he had devised was the really smart bit. In 1844, after he successfully demonstrated his project to the government, who were footing the bill, the clear benefits for the country were seen.

> That same year, 1844, Morse and partners formed the Magnetic Telegraph Company to run a line between New York and Philadelphia. By 1846 the company was profitable and paying dividends. Within ten years, twenty-three thousand miles of telegraph wires tied together most major American cities, and by 1861, a telegraph line stretched all the way to San Francisco.
>
> Gordon, p.80

In the beginning, the telegraph companies, like the railroads, developed as strictly local businesses. But in the 1850s one of them, Western Union, began buying out the independents and in the process put together a nation-wide system that would come to dominate American communications until the arrival of the telephone.

Alexander Bell in fact offered to sell Western Union the patent for his new device, the telephone, but Western Union turned him down. They did, however, offer a sweetener: 'we'll stay out of the phone business, if you stay away from the telegraph'.

Railroad companies were quick to realise that telegraph lines could be run along their ready-made rights of way. It also became possible for the railroads to develop a system of telegraph signals which allowed trains to run safely at much higher speeds. And the new telegraph medium found many users from the ever-increasing stock market business, with brokers quick to put the telegraph to use.

Chicago

TO SEE HOW these inventions combined to further the speculative fever we can study the development of the city of Chicago. Hoyt reports that, by 1845, after a lot of haggling, construction of the canal did finally get underway again; it was completed two years later. This enhanced Chicago's good location as a meeting place for wagon-hauled and lake-travelling commerce and trade. Importantly, the canal helped re-establish the business confidence of merchants. The flow of goods and services continued to increase, so too the people passing over and through, including farmers trading their wheat and hauling the vast timber supplies out of the forests of Michigan. Despite all the movement, though, Chicago still had no paved streets or bricked sidewalks, and no sewerage system – surface drainage was the only way to get rid of the waste (the stench must at times have been quite something).

The first telegraph line, from Chicago to Milwaukee, was connected on January 15, 1848; the first gas lights were lit in September 1850. Soon the city was at the centre of four intersecting telegraph lines: wheat buyers and sellers could now effectively communicate with world markets. New plank roads were built, connecting outlying areas to central districts, and were heavily used by the wagon trains. Some of these plank roads did actually pay a dividend to investors. The canal, the plank roads and the telegraph connections together created a strong incentive for railroad companies to invest in the city; their 'importance in making Chicago a great wholesale and manufacturing centre and in causing a tremendous rise in its land values far transcended any other single factor.' Hoyt explains further:

> The railroads finally became an interlocking network of lines covering the entire United States, but in the beginning they were conceived of as merely connecting links between waterways, and hence a city with a large existing canal and lake commerce provided a magnet that was sure to draw them to it … Each state was planning its own railroad system with little regard for its junction with the railroad systems of other states, and hundreds of private companies were planning small lines between neighbouring towns … there was at first no conception of a great western railroad system with its centre at Chicago. The influence of astute eastern capitalists, however, who foresaw the possibilities of Chicago in 1851, compelled the Rock Island to make Chicago its terminus. What had not even been dreamed of before 1848 had become an accomplished fact six years later. Chicago, without a single mile of railroad in January 1848, was the railroad centre of the west in 1854.

The next year Chicago boasted the largest rail system in the world. By 1856/7 it was the focus of ten trunk lines with connections to all parts of the country, running 58 passenger trains and 38 freight trains in and out every day. Revenue from these lines was $18.5 m for the year, up from just $170,000 in 1851. Chicago to New York was now just a 36-hour trip.

This development couldn't have happened without the banks. In fact, a virtually new financial system had been created to service the frenetic expansion.

> In 1851, a new banking law was passed authorizing the organization of banks in Illinois which were allowed to issue their own notes against bonds deposited with the state auditor. A feature of this law, which afterwards became of great significance, was the requirement allowing notes to be issued to the full amount of the bonds only in the case of those obligations that regularly paid 6 percent interest per annum. This induced the banks to invest largely in the bonds of the southern states, whose 6 percent bonds were not above par. The effect of this new law, under which nine banks were organized in Chicago by January, 1854, was greatly to increase the ease of

> borrowing money and, beginning in 1852, this was a pronounced factor in real estate speculation.
> Hoyt, p.59

Fortuitous timing, given the low interest rates of 1852 – something we will come to shortly.

Land could be bought on easy instalments. Requirements for rail terminals, timber yards, hotels, grain sites and everything else an expanding population requires added to the demand, and values rose. Prices were now quoted per foot rather than by size of lot. Land just a couple of miles out of town, offered at $200 an acre in 1845, was commanding up to $150 a foot ($20,000 an acre) in 1856. No longer were riders on horseback shouting out the latest land news, prospective buyers were being taken to suburban real estate and auction sites in omnibuses. Hoyt measured the land value of the then city limits of Chicago as being $126m in 1856, an eighty fold increase in just 14 years, from a value of $1.4m at the 1842 bottom. The railroads just kept opening up more and more territory, No limits could be seen on the horizon…

Banks

EASY CREDIT policies from banks around the country were again in evidence after 1851. We have seen how the discovery of gold was giving a lift to the economy and providing banks with specie to back the increasing issue of notes. (Graph 6.3 also reveals the extent of the credit expansion.)

Graph 6.3: Eastern Banks
Ratio of Specie to Deposits plus Circulation
Massachusetts, Rhode Island, New York and Pennsylvania banks

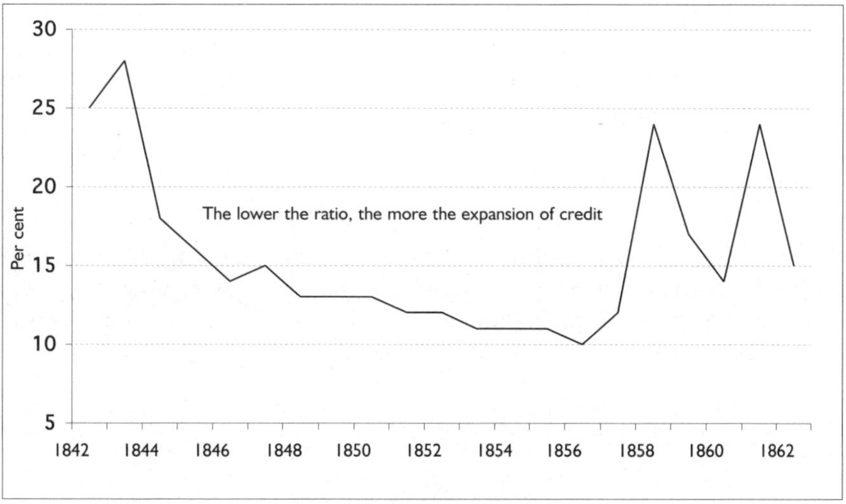

Source: Smith and Cole, *Fluctuations in American Business, 1790-1860*, Harvard University Press, 1935, Table 32, p.120.

And there were plenty of notes. J.K. Galbraith reports[4] that about 7,000 different bank notes were in circulation at this time, the issue of some 1,600 existing or defunct state banks. And 'since paper and printing were cheap and the right of note issue was defended as a human right, individuals had gone into business on their own behalf.' Some 5,000 counterfeit issues were also estimated to be in circulation.[5]

Banking procedures in general had also evolved, it seems. In *A History of Money and Banking in the United States*, Rothbard noted that now:

> The expansion of bank notes and deposits was directly tied to the amount of state government securities that the bank had invested in and posted as bond with the state. In effect, then, state government bonds became the reserve base upon which banks were allowed to pyramid a multiple expansion of bank notes and deposits. Not only did this system provide … for fractional reserve banking, but the pyramid was tied rigidly to the amount of government bonds purchased by the banks. This provision deliberately tied banks and bank credit expansion to the public debt; it meant that the more public debt that the bank purchased, the more they could create and lend out new money. Banks, in short, were encouraged to monetise the public debt, state governments were thereby encouraged to go into debt, and hence, government and bank inflation were intimately linked. p.113

This is not very different from today, except it is now done by banks under more central control, and they cannot issue their own notes as part of the process.

The 'flood of legislation' and state banking laws to 'remedy many of the abuses of past years' were often flouted, or more 'creative' procedures were invented by the bankers to get around them. The story goes that the banking commissioner in Michigan was always closely watched so that, if need be, gold or silver could be transported from one bank to another, depending on the schedule of visits which required him, under Michigan state banking laws, to confirm each bank's specie holding. Bags of gold and silver might pass the commissioner on the road or, if they arrived late at a bank being inspected, they might be handed in around the back.[6]

Corruption

ONE THING that stands out when you read US economic and banking history is the extent of political corruption, which can only be described as utterly rampant. Today's African dictator has nothing on a few of yesterday's US politicians. Much, though by no means all, of the corruption was connected to real estate, railroads and banking.

4 *Money, Whence it Came, Where it Went*, p.89.

5 Counterfeiting of US coin had also become common, particularly in Beaver County, western Pennsylvania. See Kenneth M. Stampp, *America in 1857*, p.39. An essential part of running a business was now to have a 'Bank Note Reporter' or 'Counterfeit Detector', so as to be able to detect 'the wholesome notes from the less good, the orphaned and the bad' (Galbraith).

6 Otto C. Lightner, *History of Business Depressions*, p.144.

> Most of the financial corruption resulted from the temptations dangled before politicians by land speculators, railroad promoters, government contractors, and seekers after bank charters or street railway franchises. Often the politicians were themselves investors in western lands, town properties, railroad projects, or banking enterprises, and the distinction between the public good and private interests could easily become blurred in their minds … in New Jersey, during the legislature's winter session, wine seemed to be the lubricant used effectively by the banking and railroad lobbyists to expedite passage of bills beneficial to their clients. According to one reporter, the flow increased in proportion to the importance of the interests at stake. During a dinner for legislatures at the Trenton House, agents for the Camden and Amboy Railroad saw that wine was served copiously. Later, when the legislature reassembled, there were not a few dizzy-headed members among them, and … bills were carelessly rushed through on their final passage.
>
> Kenneth M. Stampp, *America in 1857*, p.28

Stampp gives some additional examples of the prevailing political corruption. In the state of Wisconsin, Milwaukee Democrats Byron Kilbourne and Moses Strong were found to have been granted by the legislature of which they were a part several million acres of federal land for their own railroad, the La Crosse and Milwaukee. Discovered only after the line failed and was declared bankrupt was the wholesale bribery of the legislature, important politicians and newspaper editors.

> When an interest payment on Ohio's bonded debt was about to fall due, the Republican state treasurer, William H. Gibson, revealed that his Democratic predecessor and brother-in-law, John G. Breslin, had embezzled $550,000 in state funds. Because Gibson had kept the theft secret for six months, Governor Salmon P. Chase forced him to resign. Breslin, after being indicted by a grand jury, fled to Canada.
>
> Stampp, p.29

A good deal more corruption resulted from the Federal Lands Act. In 1850, the federal government passed its Swamp Land Act, granting to each state any 'swamp or overflowed' land inside its borders. This meant that any forty-acre tract that was underwater and traversable only by boat, either at harvest or planting, could be sold and the proceeds put towards reclamation and drainage if the new owner promised to drain the land. Later investigations in California found that plenty of irrigation work had been carried out on so-called 'swamp' land.

Henry Miller, a German immigrant who arrived in San Francisco in the year the Federal Lands Act was passed, with just six dollars in his pocket, amassed 14 million acres of land by the time he died. Realising that water would become far more valuable than gold in California, Miller bought land along the rivers of California's central valleys. Irrigating his land by means of ditches, he was able to give his cattle better grass on which to feed. The fact that landowners and homesteaders further from the river would lose their water supply did not worry him – it meant he could buy up their land at lower prices. The story is told that one day Miller saw some land he coveted. Hitching a rowing boat to the back of one of his wagons, he had a team of horses drag him and his boat across the desired land. The government then received a map of the area from Miller, with a sworn statement that he had rowed across it in a boat. The land became his.[7]

How much has changed?

THE NEWSPAPERS of 1857 were full of talk of an increase in crime and lawlessness. July 4 saw street riots in New York, the Dead Rabbit and Bowery Boys gangs, amongst others, battling it out from behind barricades with rocks, brickbats and pistols. The Germans in the city joined in, protesting against the closing of the beer halls on Sundays.

A San Francisco editor[8] deplored the high divorce rate in that young state, indicating a 'terrible amount of family difficulties and domestic quarrels'. Immigration having continued to increase up to 1857, especially of Irish Catholics (between 1850 and 1860 2.5 million people emigrated to the US), talk was of a papal plot to subvert the country to Catholicism. It had to be stopped! A Protestant crusade began, with a variety of secret societies, the largest of which was the Order of the Star Spangled Banner. Since the members of this order were sworn to secrecy, and refused to talk about their activities, they were labelled 'know nothings'. Their 1856 presidential candidate gained 22 per cent of the votes cast.

With the bad weather came an increase in colds, pneumonia and other respiratory ailments, for which there were no shortage of remedies. You could try Holloway's Pills and Ointment (to disinfect the blood and secretions), Dr Shallenberger's Fever and Ague Antidote (for an immediate cure), Dr Duponco's French Golden Periodical Pills, or Helmbold's Highly Concentrated Compound Fluid Extract (guaranteed to cure all diseases of the bladder, kidneys, and urinary and sexual organs).

Then, as now, the dramatic turns of the weather were an oft cited concern of farmers and growers, 'sometimes the rest of the population as well'.[9]

The year 1857 also saw a new fashion, the hoop skirt. 'After women overcame their initial prejudice, the new style vied with many of the more noted methods for improving the exterior contour of the female form.'[10] Fashion tends to outdo itself in the extravagant years leading up to a speculative peak.

7 Peter Barnes, *The Great American Land Grab.*
8 *Evening Bulletin*, January 2nd 1857.
9 Stampp, p.33.
10 Stampp, p.34.

Into the peak

HAVE ANOTHER look at the chart showing rates of discount in New York City over the years 1841 to 1862 (Chart 6.2, page 109). You will notice a sharp drop in interest rates in 1852. Charles Kindleberger[11] blames the glut of gold that year. Deposits at city banks surged after 1849 and peaked in 1853.[12] The credit base of the US was being enlarged, leading directly to an explosion of land speculation (Graph 6.4: Public Land Sales 1800-60)..

> Bank management had been conservative and wise in the ten years, 1843-1853, notably in the eastern cities. Few new banks were established, loans were extended with caution, and the issue of notes was kept within reasonable limits. The $100,000,000 worth of gold sent to the mints from California mines furnished a sufficient specie basis for bank currency. Credit agencies kept pace with the normal business development of the country. But in 1853 a speculative mania took possession of the financial world …
>
> Lightner, *History of Business Depressions*, p.145

Graph 6.4: Public Land Sales 1800-60

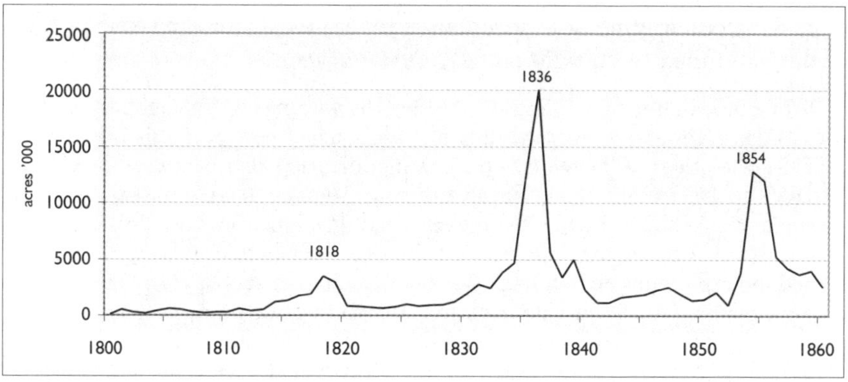

Sources: Annual Reports, Commissioner of the General Land Office, and Smith and Cole, *Fluctuations in American Business, 1790-1860*, Harvard University Press, 1935, Appendix D.

Stampp says of 1857:

> Nearly the whole West swarms with speculators … who neither intend to cultivate the soil nor settle there, but who expect to realize fortunes without labour out of the *bona fide* settlers. Land speculation, observed a Wisconsin editor, had become a mania. 'Merchants have shut up their shops, lawyers have left the bar, farmers have laid down the shovel and the hoe, manufacturers have abandoned their business to turn land agents and real estate dealers.' In Minnesota, complained a territorial politician, people were

11 *Manias, Panics and Crashes*, p.63.
12 Smith and Cole, Chart 41, p.122.

> 'so engrossed in speculating', that they had no time for politics. In May, when the Minnesota railroad land grants were put up for sale, 'the cormorants were gathered there from all quarters … all engaged in a general scramble for the spoils.' Lots on the best street in Omaha, which had sold for $500 in the spring of 1856, went for $5,000 a year later. In a Kansas land sale, reported a correspondent, five-eighths of the land went to eastern speculators.
> p.218

And Lightner:

> The previous year, 1856, 3,642 miles of railway had been constructed. At that time America had seven-ninths of the railroad trackage of the world. Development was far beyond the needs of the time. People apparently invested purely in their imagination of the future. The number of banks had increased rapidly…
> p.141

By 1857, notes John Steel Gordon, the mood on the street was exuberant. The dark days of the late thirties and early forties were forgotten, or rather unknown to the new traders now flocking to Wall Street in search of wealth. Of the old speculators, says Sobel, only Jacob Little was still around from previous bull markets, and even he was not as active as he had been.

It's a peculiar thing how speculative fever gives way to a sense of foreboding and then to outright panic. *Sauve qui peut.*

> While the volume of building in Chicago, the earnings of Chicago railroads, and the grain and lumber receipts had all reached new peaks in 1856 and 1857, the prices of the main staple commodities had been falling from May, 1855, to December, 1856, wheat dropping from $2 to $1 a bushel. In the summer of 1857 a financial stringency had developed in New York which was blamed by eastern interests on the over-speculation in western lands and too rapid railroad building. The suspension of specie payments by New York banks forced a private bank in Chicago to close on August 11, 1857, and with their eastern bills protested two more private banks in Chicago closed on September 30, 1857. Many railroads had been built in advance of traffic and during October, 1857, fifteen railroads with obligations of $181,700,000, including the Illinois Central with $24,000,000 in debts, the Michigan Southern with $18,000,000, and the Michigan Central with $14,000,000, were forced to make assignments for the benefit of creditors. The prices of railway shares broke sharply on the New York Stock Exchange during 1857, Galena stock falling from 119 on December 15, 1856, to 54 on October 12, 1857, and during the same period New York central shares fell from 93 to 53, Erie from 61 to 8, and Michigan Southern from 88 to 9.
> Hoyt, p.74

John Steel Gordon quotes the *New York Herald* of June 27, from the pen of its editor, James Gordon Bennett:

> 'Government spoilation, public defaulters, paper bubbles of all descriptions, a general scramble for western lands and town and city sites, millions of

> dollars, made or borrowed, expended in fine houses and gaudy furniture; hundreds of thousands in silly rivalries of fashionable parvenus, in silks, laces, diamonds and every variety of costly frippery are only a few among the many crying evils of the day …'
> *The Great Game*, p.88

New York Herald editor James Bennett was a long-time critic of Wall Street, believing that America's prosperity was better served by workers and farmers than by bankers and stock market speculators. Despite this, Bennett was by June 1857 in league with Leonard Jerome, a known Wall Street bear who did not mind seeing stock prices fall, especially if he was actively 'shorting' them – hence the bearish tone of the above quote.[13] Such a practice became quite common as the 19th century wore on, Jesse Livermore perfecting the art in the first three decades of the 20th century.

On August 11 the oldest flour company in New York, N.H. Wolfe & Co, a conservatively run business, announced its failure. This shook the confidence of Wall Street. On August 19 Edwin C. Litchfield, President of Michigan Central Railroad, resigned, 'in order to spend more time on personal matters'. Even in 1857 such a statement was taken to mean the company was in big trouble. The Michigan Central was soon in receivership (one of Leonard Jerome's shorts).

On August 24 the New York branch of the Ohio Life Insurance and Trust Company, a bank, informed the public of some internal disorders. This was a Cincinnati operation but its New York branch was perhaps *the* most respected bank in the city. It did not issue its own notes, merely accepting deposits which were then used to make secured advances to businesses and other commercial interests, often in the west. The Ohio's activities reached into all areas of US commerce. 'No bank was favoured with more deposits, nor was there any which was abler to loan on adequate security than the New York branch of the Ohio Life Insurance and Trust Company.'[14]

The president Charles Stetson announced on August 24 that the bank was to suspend payments. (A chart of the share price would be most interesting to study …) Apparently 'certain parties', unspecified, had failed to repay loans, though the president assured anxious shareholders and depositors that the company's assets and capital were 'sound and reliable'. Four days later the stock price was down 85 per cent, the market having made its own judgement. Depositors queued outside, waiting to withdraw their money, but the bank never did re-open. The question now was whether all the other banks could continue to collect their loan repayments, and, given their no doubt low reserves of gold and silver, continue to meet the demands of depositors wanting their money back – in coin not paper. Our economy, built as it is on sand, works only as long as it has the confidence of the players. Exuberance can quickly turn to fear, fear to panic.

13 Sobel, *Panic on Wall Street*, p.96.
14 Bray Hammond, *Banks and Politics*, p.710.

Panic

CONFIDENCE WAS undermined further by two not uncommon disasters that September. On September 5, 1857 there was a collision of a passenger train and a wood train just outside Philadelphia. On September 12 the steamer *Central America*, bound for New York, sank in a hurricane off Cape Hatteras, taking with her 400 passengers and $1.6m in California gold. It was the loss of the uninsured gold that upset the market.[15] Here is demonstrated the psychology of the crowd. If the trend in markets is up, bad news tends to be shrugged off; in a downturn it is seized upon by the public mind and any glimmer of light is overlooked. In a situation where speculation, especially in land value, is out of control, a disaster takes on a vivid significance.

To stem the panic, and raise banks' specie holdings, the Secretary of the Treasury ordered the minting of $4m in gold coin; to no discernible effect.

On September 25, thirty days after the failure of the Trust Company of Ohio, another leading financial institution, the Bank of Pennsylvania in Philadelphia, closed its doors. Panic. Newspapers reported 'the wildest excitement' in the city as queues of depositors formed outside other banks, everyone demanding their money *now!* A nation-wide specie suspension followed in early October, reversing the obligation of banks to redeem their notes from deposit-holders and thus giving them time to improve their financial health. It did not shorten the eventual economic downturn.

> *The West suffered from the drastic decline in land values* and commodity prices and from a shortage of credit. For a time the Illinois Central tried to help those who were buying its land on credit by postponing instalment payments or accepting payment in produce, but eventually both farmers and railroad were caught up in the general ruin of panic and recession … in rural Wisconsin money was so scarce that many of the small transactions of daily life were carried on by barter. Stampp, p.225 (emphsis added)

The situation was aggravated by activities such as those of the Milwaukee and Mississippi and other Wisconsin rail lines which, with the promise of high dividends, had persuaded thousands of farmers living along the right-of-way to buy railroad stock with personal notes secured by mortgages on their farms. 'The railroads then sold the mortgages to eastern bankers to obtain a portion of the funds required for construction and the purchase of rolling stock.'[16] The expansion of credit, and the securitisation of so many of the mortgages, was unravelling.

Back in Chicago, Hoyt reports that the effects of the 1857 panic were felt the following year when the earnings of railroad companies fell, as did the amount of lumber being moved. A lot of men were out of work.

15 Kindleberger, p.94.
16 Stampp, p.225.

However, 'Most of the holders of real estate held firmly during 1858 to the peak prices of 1856. Those who were able to hold, would not sell.' This is a common phenomenon as a cycle turns down: people hold on and hope. But it was just a matter of time for those who had bought too late. Hoyt continues:

> The depreciation in the price of corner lots was great in the winter of 1857, but it was much greater in 1858 and 1859, as payments matured which could not be met. A large portion of the real estate in the city had been bought on canal time; they had depended upon a continual advance in quoted values to meet those payments and found they could not sell even at a ruinous sacrifice.

There had been the occasional warning and perceptive comment as the speculation in railroad securities and land went over the top, but at a peak no one is listening. 'This was an age', fretted a Philadelphia editor, 'in which men sought to grow rich without labour, and speculation was their favourite means ...'[17] Another editor feared because

> 'Western land speculators held more land than could be settled in 20 years. Many of them were men of modest means, who had borrowed at high interest rates and would be ruined if declining commodity prices should cause land values to fall.'
>
> Stampp, p.219, quoting Philadelphia *Public Ledger*, April 14, 1857

The causal link

FROM THE LATE 1840s, particularly after the business downturn of 1847, and with the discovery of California gold, New York banks increased in number from 24 to 60. The issuing of a cheque or bill involves two parties, the paying bank and the receiving bank; even if these are the same bank, there are two sides to the transaction. To settle between banks, runners (or porters) were used to move these negotiable instruments and carry out the financial business of their clients. As the number of banks increased, their activities became unmanageable. A better method of inter-bank exchange was needed. Eventually a 'clearing-house' was established and began operations on October 1, 1853.

Clearing-house procedures are of interest to us because the statements banks had to issue reveal the rise and fall of New York banking credit, i.e. banks loans, deposits and specie on hand.

J.S. Gibbons, in *The Banks of New York, Their Dealers, The Clearing House, and The Panic of 1857*, gives clearing-house figures for 1854 to 1858 and it is from this source that the following analysis is drawn. It is clear the 1857 October panic was a direct result of banks' curtailing credit after the August collapse of the Ohio. *But activity in the land market fell first.*

17 Philadelphia *North American*, June 20, 1857.

Graph 6.5: New York Clearing House Bank Credits
weekly averages, 1854-58

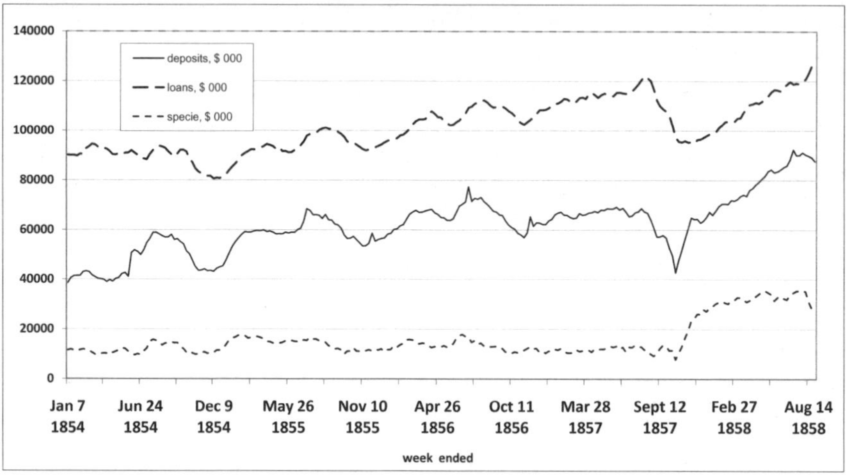

Source: Gibbons, J.S., *The Banks of New York ... and the Panic of 1857*, Greenwood Press, 1968, pp.330-6.

The clearing-house figures (Graph 6.5) show a seasonal loan contraction each year around August. Loans reached their highest point of expansion in the first week of August in 1853 and 1854, the third week of August in 1855, and once again the first week of August in 1856. This was not coincidental; it was the by-product of an agricultural economy – which America still was at this time. Ron Insana sees it this way:

> ... the harvest period was one of notable volatility both in market terms and in terms of liquidity or money available in the nation's banks. As the harvest neared, farmers routinely pulled their money out of big-city banks to finance the labour needed to harvest crops. That put a drain on available cash in the nation's money centres. Stock prices typically fell from August to October, owing to the lack of available funds. But stock prices bottomed in October when farmers, flush with cash from the sale of their crops, re-deposited the proceeds in the New York banks. *Trendwatching*, p.167

Insana goes on to remark that some market experts believe this to be the principal reason why the stock market has historically had a tendency to crash and bottom out in the month of October. The August loan contraction would then proceed in a fairly orderly fashion till about mid-November. Smith and Cole also note this seasonal loan contraction (and another small decline sometimes in late March/early April).[18] Rail statistics confirm the phenomenon. Rail employment tended to rise sharply in the autumn when the transport of agricultural produce reached its peak;

18 Smith and Cole, p.127.

employment then declined into the winter months.[19] Rail companies would have added to the autumn currency requirements in order to pay workers, and their needs must have grown over the following decades.

In the four years of data here, the largest decline prior to October 1857 came in October 1854. In 1857 credit contraction began on August 8, continuing in the normal seasonal manner for the next two weeks. There were a couple of reports of company failures and a large-scale misuse of funds in a leading rail company in these weeks, but this was not considered much out of the ordinary.

The Ohio bank failure of August 24 was not in itself an immediate cause for concern: the main branch in Cincinnati was reported by telegraph to be open for business as usual. However it was soon revealed that practically thc cntire capital base of the bank, some $2m, had been embezzled. Most New York banks were creditors of the Ohio. Suddenly the city's merchants found their banks a little less accommodating with credit. The next week's clearing-house report confirms that banking policy had changed substantially. Credit was contracting. Between September 5 and 19 bank loans were reduced by $3,443,944 despite an *increase* in deposits of nearly $600,000. 'There can be no escape from these figures', says Gibbons.[20] 'They show beyond [doubt] that the banks, not the depositors, took the lead in forcing liquidation.' It was a credit squeeze initiated by the banks to restore their balance sheets. Up to September 26 depositors had not been alarmed; it was after October 3 that their trust was reversed. Clearing-house data suggest that the panic was a direct result of the marked contraction of credit after August 24. However the situation had been set up by the substantial lift in bank credit in the four years prior to 1857, facilitating the concomitant rise in land speculation.

Scams

IT REMAINED only for the scams, cons and frauds to come to light. More than a few persons at more than a few companies were discovered with their hands deep in the till. At the Ohio Bank there had been embezzlement by the cashier (apparently to sustain his stock market operations)[21] in addition to the bank's souring investments in highly speculative railroad bonds.

In another case in New York Robert Schuyler (grandson of Alexander Hamilton's nephew), president of both the Harlem and the New Haven railroads, was found to have secretly printed twenty thousand shares of New Haven stock and sold it quietly on the market. By the time of the discovery Schuyler was already well on his way to the Canadian border with proceeds of about $2m. He was never caught.

19 See, for example, Walter Licht, *Working for the Railroad.*
20 *The Banks of New York* ..., p.354.
21 Kindleberger, p.71.

An assistant of Schuyler's, secretary of the Harlem Railroad Alexander Kyle Jr, admitted to having forged some five thousand shares of Harlem stock and swapped them for securities in the New Haven line (which were also forgeries). Kyle had had a hand in picking an apartment for Schuyler's mistress, though this revelation was eclipsed when the New York social set learned that Schuyler had in fact been leading a double life, fathering a second family under the assumed name of Spicer.[22]

The board of directors of Parker Vein Coal Company were found to have issued five times as much stock as had been authorised and gone on to sell it, pocketing the proceeds. A teller at the Ocean bank paid himself some $50,000 of the bank's funds; a teller at the National grabbed $70,000. The bookkeeper of the Union Bank stole $200,000 and promptly fled with the loot after it was discovered he had been forging balances for months.

The Bank of Sandstone, it was later discovered, never had any specie or any assets to cover its liabilities at the time it was being reported upon by the commissioners of Michigan state. The Exchange Bank of Shiawasee was found by the same commissioners to have a mere seven coppers and a small amount of paper in its vaults, though it had bills in circulation amounting to $22,267. The Jackson County Bank had many large, full boxes in its own vaults, but whilst the tops of each showed silver dollars, they covered little but nails and glass.[23]

That blizzard

THE WINTER of 1856/7 was more brutally cold than usual, but with a general lack of snow until, between January 16 and 19, the east coast was struck by a 'monster blizzard' that would be long remembered for its intensity and howling winds. The weekend of the 17th and 18th was particularly extreme: record winds and temperatures as low as –20° F were recorded in places. Warmer weather intervened, but the severe cold returned on January 23, 'cold Friday', and it was even colder the next day when a low of –55° F was recorded in northern New England.[24]

In *Panic on Wall Street: A History of America's Financial Disasters* Robert Sobel lists the Western Blizzard of 1857 as one of the twelve most harrowing moments in American financial history between 1792 and 1962. One review of the book notes that Sobel chose these particular twelve moments to demonstrate the complexity and variety of events that have led to financial panics, and to show that we can make only the vaguest generalisations about panic as a phenomenon.

Hopefully you can see through such an argument. There does not have to be land and real estate speculation to bring on a panic but, if real estate is involved, the collapse will be more prolonged and harder to get out of.

22 Sobel, p.90.
23 Lightner, Chapter XIV.
24 See www.geocities.com/donsutherland1/1857blizzard2.html for an interesting description of events.

There is order amidst the chaos of boom and bust, and liberal credit is always at the heart of it, but economic collapse will require something else as well…

February 21, 1854 also saw great storms hit the east coast. 'The most tremendous snow storm ever known here commenced last night,' it was proclaimed in the February 22 issue of the *New York Daily Times*. But no panic followed. The economic sandcastle that is land price had not yet been built high enough to enable that 'un-looked for' (credit created) event to shatter public confidence.

After-effects of the downturn

THE DOWNTURN gave the south yet another reason for despising the north; it deepened the divide that led to the Civil War in 1861. The downturn in the south proved not as severe as that in the north as cotton exports held up relatively well. In the south wealth was in farming, not in 'land and stock jobbing'. Southerners genuinely feared their economic welfare was at the mercy of reckless northern bankers. Funny how war has often followed an economic downturn…

As might be expected, the newspapers of the day expounded all sorts of reasons for the decline in economic activity. A new era of self-criticism dawned.

> The puzzling question repeatedly asked was how a country with a rapidly growing population, rich in fertile soils and natural resources, producing food in abundance, busily engaged in manufacturing and commerce, could get itself into such a predicament. Stampp, p.31

Indeed. Another bewildered observer wrote:

> 'It seems indeed very strange that in the very midst of apparent health and strength … the whole country … should suddenly come to a dead stop and be unable to move a step forward – and that we should suddenly wake up from our dreams of wealth and happiness, and find ourselves poor and bankrupt.' Stampp, p.231, quoting Nashville *Republican Banner*, October 18, 1857

The answer is, 'You're standing on it.' But this would have to wait another two cycles, for the writings of Henry George, whose ideas shook the US to its foundations.

Some relevant observations

IN *MANIAS, Panics and Crashes* Charles Kindleberger has interesting observations to make about 1857. It was probably the first truly world-wide panic and downturn. The discovery of gold in California in 1849 and in Australia in 1851 vastly increased the credit/money base of the US and parts of Europe, especially Britain, feeding existing railroad and banking booms. The banks lent vast sums to further finance trade and industry.

Speculation was rampant: in the US in railroads and public lands; in the UK in railways and wheat; on the Continent in railways and heavy industry. The speculative peak in the US and Britain was the end of 1856; the panic came in August 1857 in the US, in October 1857 in the UK. The speculative peak on the Continent was in March 1857, the panic in November. The collapse was worsened by the ending of the Crimean War and the subsequent collapse of wheat prices. Financing the war had fed the huge expansion of credit in the first place. At the peak, UK banks had lifted interest rates to between 12 and 15 per cent. In the downturn few banks could be found to honour or accept any bills of exchange.

Alfred Chandler makes an important observation:

> With each recurring land boom there has been a new crop of speculators, with similar endings in each succeeding panic – occurring about every twenty years. But land values on the crest of every land boom are always higher than they were on the crest of the preceding boom – and that is the backlog which keeps the fires of land speculation for ever going.
>
> *Land Title Origins*, p.491

Chandler notes further:

> Huge sales of land from the public domain to speculators, on credit, just previous to 1857, brought on another financial crisis, as similar speculation had brought on previous panics and years of depression … There followed in the same pattern the panics of 1819 and 1837, and this one, which began with the failure of the Ohio Life Insurance and Trust Company. Millions of dollars of its depositors' and policy-holders' money had been loaned by it to holders of idle land, and to promoters, to build railroads through unproductive regions and to attract buyers of land. p.499

What the newspapers were saying …

EBULLIENCE at the top:

> 'Cincinnati presented to the world a picture of progress heretofore unknown to the history of cities. Its solidity and continued prosperity had become matters of special wonder.'
>
> *Cincinnati Enquirer*, June 3, 1857, quoted in Stampp, p.213

The reversal to fear:

> It is a gloomy moment in history. Not for many years – not in the lifetime of most men who read this paper – has there been so much grave and deep apprehension; never has the future seemed so incalculable as at this time. In our own country there is universal commercial prostration and panic, and thousands of our poorest fellow citizens are turned out against the approaching winter without employment, and without the prospect of it. In France the political cauldron seethes and bubbles with uncertainty; Russia hangs, as usual, like a cloud, dark and silent upon the horizon of Europe; while all

> the energies, resources and infancies of the British Empire are sorely tried, and are yet to be tried more sorely.
>
> *Harper's Weekly*, Vol. I, p.642, October 10, 1857

> All the panics previously experienced are as nothing compared with that of today. If there is a much lower depth for some stocks, they will go completely out of sight. *New York Herald*, October 3, 1857

> Several of the clergy preached hard times sermons yesterday enjoining patience under adversity. The parsons might well have preached to the winds. Money is the thing that is wanted – money! money! money! – not homilies from the Book of Job. *Newark Daily Advertiser*, October 7, 1857

> The financial condition of our country is unprecedented. Business of all kinds is more completely suspended than if a hostile fleet had anchored in our harbor. *New York Evening Post*, October 9, 1857

> Like a star of the night, darting out of the skies and losing itself in the sea, the whole country has suddenly, and while in the enjoyment of unparalleled prosperity, plunged headlong down into universal bankruptcy. Now no one is any longer known to be rich. *New York Evening Post*, October, 14, 1857

Blame the government:

> Had we had more statesmen and fewer politicians, the country would not have been reduced to its present distressing and humiliating condition.
>
> *Philadelphia Pennsylvanian*, September 12, 1857

> The Democratic Party is responsible for all these troubles …
>
> *North American and United States Gazette*, Philadelphia, September 24, 1857

Blame anything except the speculation in government-granted licences and privileges:

> Men speak of overstocking the market, or of over manufacturing, or over-importations, and of extravagance of various kinds.
>
> *The Independent*, October 8, 1857

> The great men of the exchange, to whom we bowed with a selfish idolatry, are proving to be but wooden images.
>
> Kansas *Leavenworth City Herald*, October 17, 1857

> The cause of our present [distress is] that our dry goods merchants have over-imported … Letter to the editor, *Newark Daily Advertiser*, September 25, 1857

> Our present disorders have been provoked by the extravagance of our women. Crinoline and moiré, gloves and feathers, fans and furbelows, kickshaws and gewgaws, these have ruined us. These have drained us of our western wheat and our Californian gold, to give us in return only hotel flirtations and watering place polkas. *New York Weekly Times*, October 17, 1857

> What caused trade thus to topple over, almost without a struggle? What hurled to the dust so many stately fabrics of industry, skill and enterprise? The answer is plain enough – we have been living too fast.
>
> *Philadelphia Press*, October 12, 1857

Hunt's Merchants' Magazine listed one of the causes as the telegraph disseminating bad news 'too quickly'. And, finally:

> The *Herald* lays it to wine, women, cards and [wait for it] fast horses.
>
> *Washington Evening Star*, August 28, 1857

To sum up

> After a brief but sharp contraction in 1854, the prosperity of the 1850s reached its peak in the middle of the decade. Immigration declined after 1854, and by the end of 1856, government land sales, bank loans and discounts, and domestic trade were falling off. During the previous two years the Crimean war, which deprived Western Europe of Russian wheat, had provided an expanded international market for American cereals at a time when production was rising faster than demand at home. When, early in 1856, peace was restored, American farmers lost a large part of their foreign market, and American shippers soon found themselves in a recession. By the spring of 1857, imports had begun to diminish; earnings of the Erie, New York Central, and other railroads were disappointing; and New England textile mills had substantial inventories but few buyers. In July the Mills of Manchester, New Hampshire, suspended operations; others in Lowell and elsewhere soon followed. Meanwhile, a significant change had occurred in the international financial markets. The Bank of France, weakened by the loss of specie during and after the Crimean war, was obliged repeatedly, in a period of economic expansion, to draw specie from the Bank of England. This, in turn, led to substantially increased interest rates in London, which tempted British investors to sell off American securities and put their money in less speculative and often more remunerative domestic securities. The result was a decline in the price of shares on the New York Stock Exchange. The decline of security values weakened the American banking system by reducing the value of assets supporting it. In short, an economic recession had already overtaken the economy before … [that] … 'unlooked for incident' [in this case the Ohio failure] brought on a crash.
>
> Stampp, p.221, summarising George W. Van Vleck, *The Panic of 1857*

The charts also tell us a little more. Railroad stocks peaked some years before the panic, in December 1852 (Graph 6.1, page 108). This suggests that railroad earnings had not improved for some years prior to 1857, something insiders may have known but would not have admitted in public. (Compare Graph 6.2, page 109, to Graph 6.1 and observe that interest rates moved higher after the 1852 lows, a direct influence on railroad costs.) Land sales peaked in 1854 in acreage sold, and in the fourth quarter of 1855, if the dollar value of receipts is used as the reference

Graph 6.6: Public Land Sales
Quarterly Receipts, 1849-60

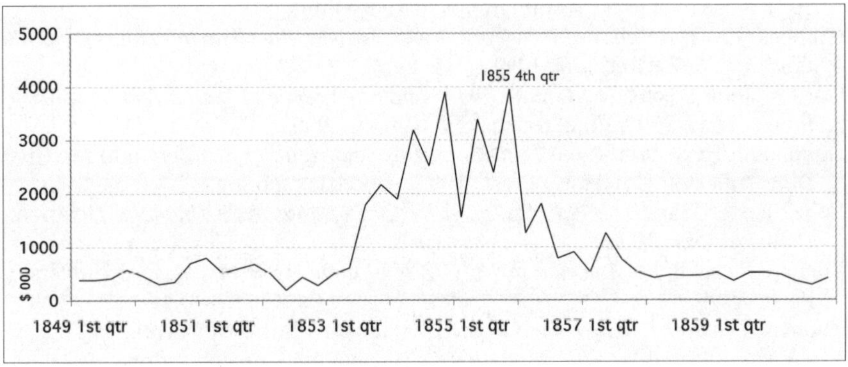

Sources: Annual Reports, Commissioner of the General Land Office, and Smith and Cole, *Fluctuations in American Business, 1790-1860*, Harvard University Press, 1935, Appendix D.

(Graph 6.6). A repeating pattern. The speculative indices will generally pick up the future economic trend well before this is obvious to the public at large. The chart of quarterly receipts of land sales to the federal government clearly shows the speculative frenzy in land that resulted from the massive expansion in credit after the gold strikes and corresponding lower interest rates of the early 1850s.

The panic once again created a buying opportunity, but since emotions practically force us to be in the market the wrong way at a peak – our credit over-extended like everyone else's – it can be difficult to take advantage of. One must go through a cycle and be actively engaged in it before the emotions can be understood. Unless a study of history is undertaken…

In this cycle rail stocks ran up 119 months, January 1843 to December 1852, then down for 58 months to October 1857 (Graph 6.1). Discount rates in New York cycled 15 years exactly – 180 months low to low, August 1843 to August 1858 (Graph 6.2).

The days of most intense emotion would have been around October 5 to 13. Said Gibbons: 'Such is the outline of the most extraordinary, violent, and destructive financial panic ever experienced in this country.'[25]

Until the next one, not quite eighteen years later, in 1873.

25 p.346.

FURTHER READING

Barnes, Peter. 'The Great American Land Grab', *The New Republic* magazine, 1971 (see www.progress.org/archive.barnes3.htm).

Gibbons, J.S. *The Banks of New York, their Dealers, the Clearing House, and the Panic of 1857*. Greenwood Press, 1968.

Gordon, John Steele. *The Great Game: The Emergence of Wall Street as a World Power, 1653-2000*. First Touchstone edition, 2000.

Hammond, Bray. *Banks and Politics in America from the Revolution to the Civil War*. Princeton University Press, 1991, paperback edition.

Sobel, Robert. *Panic on Wall Street: A History of America's Financial Disasters*. Collier Books, 1972.

Stampp, Kenneth M. *America in 1857: A Nation on the Brink*. Oxford University Press, 1990.

Thomas, Dana L. *Lords of the Land*. G.P. Putnam's Sons, New York, 1977.

Van Vleck, George W. *The Panic of 1857*. Columbia University Press, 1943.

7

Solidarity and Permanence

National Banking 1863-1913

> ***My agency in promoting the passage of the National Bank Act was the greatest financial mistake of my life. It has built up a monopoly which affects every interest in the country. It should be repealed, but before that can be accomplished, the people will be arrayed on one side and the banks on the other, in a contest such as we have never before seen in this country.***
>
> Salmon P. Chase, Secretary of State and Chief Justice of the Supreme Court, quoted in Sheldon Emry, *Famous Quotations on Money*

IT COULD WELL be imagined that, by the Civil War, the profusion of bank and other notes circulating within the US was more than a little chaotic. The war added yet another dimension to the problem. To pay for it, the north began to issue 'greenbacks', so called because of the colour of the ink on the back of the note. Significantly, these greenbacks were printed and issued by the government, not the banks (about which President Lincoln had a lot more to say). This meant the currency (paper money or fiat) was backed only by government say-so and enforcement. The dual problems of free banking and how to pay for the Civil War led to the creation of a new banking system, the result of the National Banking Act of 1864.

This attempted to do the following:

- provide a uniform note issue to the whole country that was responsive to the seasonal demands of business (for example when the farmers of the west required currency to pay for the harvest);
- reduce, if not eliminate, the excess of notes (effectively achieved with the 10 per cent tax on state notes); and
- (most significantly) create a market for government debt.

As the Civil War dragged unexpectantly on, more and more money was required to pay for it. So the government again went into debt to the bankers.

In theory, under this new national banking system anyone could still open a bank. You had to include the word 'National' in its name, apply for a charter from the new federal agency, the Comptroller of the Currency, and then deposit with the Treasury government bonds to the value of one third of the capital. Hence the creation of a demand for government-issued securities. A national bank could then issue notes up to 90 per cent of either the par or market value of its securities, whichever was lower. All national banks had to accept the notes of other national banks at par.

So, after 1863, national banks bought government securities (bonds), deposited them immediately with the (federally controlled) Comptroller of the Currency and received (national) bank notes in return. The notes went into circulation as they were lent to those who were granted loans.

> National bank notes were produced and distributed through an involved process. Once the basic engraving and printing was done (at first by private printers, later by the US Bureau of Engraving and Printing), the notes were entered on the books of the Office of the Comptroller of the Currency, then returned to the printer where the seal of the Treasury Department was stamped on each. Next, the notes were shipped to the bank whose name appeared on them, where they were signed by two senior bank officers. The notes were then ready for circulation. National bank notes were the mainstay of the nation's money supply until the Federal Reserve note appeared in 1914.
>
> www.factmonster.com

The complexity of design of the notes was deliberate and intended to foil counterfeiters.

Because of the war effort, during and immediately after the Civil War metal coins disappeared from circulation. 'Paper coins' were introduced to replace them, to help with small payments. Paper notes of 3, 5, 10, 15, 25 and 50 cent denominations were circulated. The Superintendent of the National Currency Bureau, Spencer Clark, in search of a design for the 5 cent note, decided to use his own portrait. Congress, upset, promptly banned the portrait of any living person on a US note from that time on.

The national banks, interestingly, were initially not permitted to accept real estate as collateral for loans, nor were they permitted to lend in excess of 10 per cent of their capital base to any one borrower. The Comptroller of the Currency also required a financial report from each national bank, which was subject to possible audit. As the coming chapters show, this still did not stop future bank crises.

Neither did the new pyramid structure.

> At the bottom of the pyramid were the numerous national country banks. These were national banks located anywhere in the country outside certain designated cities. Country banks were required by law to hold reserves equal to 15% of outstanding bank notes. Up to 60% of these reserves could be held as deposits in reserve city banks. All remaining reserves were required to be held as cash. The next level of the pyramid consisted of the reserve

> city banks. Reserve cities were specified by an act of Congress and consisted of large cities such as Boston, Philadelphia, and Kansas City. Reserve city banks were required to have reserves equal to 25% of outstanding bank notes. Half of these reserves could be held as deposits at banks in central reserve cities and half were required to be held as cash. Thus reserve city banks held deposits from country banks and could place deposits with central reserve city banks.
>
> Mark Carlson, *Causes of Bank Suspensions in the Panic of 1893*, p.6

Carlson noted further that:

> In practice reserve city banks acted as pass-through banks, most of the interbank deposits they received from country banks were placed as deposits at central reserve city banks. New York City, and later Chicago and St. Louis, were designated as central reserve cities. Throughout the National Banking Era, New York was the primary central reserve city, holding a vast majority of the central reserve cities' interbank deposits.

The chapters describing the real estate cycles after 1860 give further details of some of the effects this had.

Graph 7.1: Number of National and State Banks 1863-1913

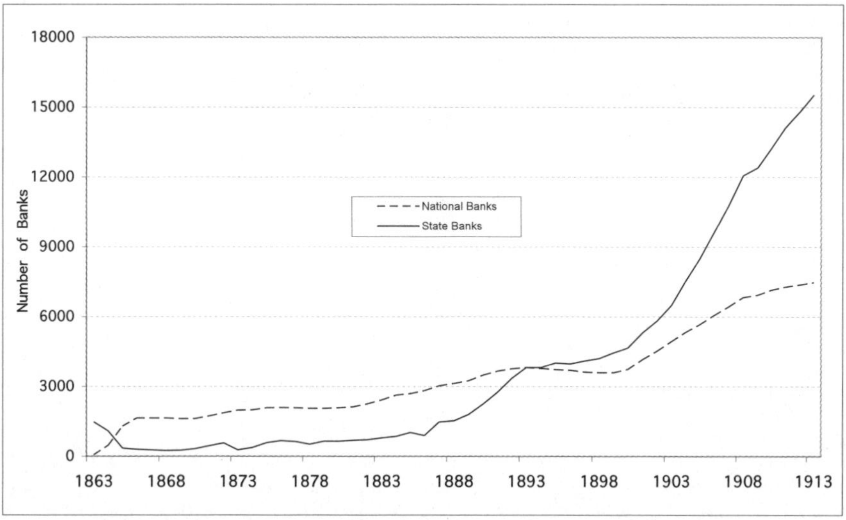

Source: Richard S Grossman, 'US Banking History, Civil War to World War II', EH.Net Encyclopedia, edited by Robert Whaples, www.eh.net/encyclopedia/contents/grossman.banking.history.us.civil.war.wwii.php

The number of national banks expanded rapidly after 1863, and the number of state banks declined. They were not eliminated, however, and those that remained coexisted with the national system, albeit without the ability to print their own notes. Another method of credit creation was soon found through the use of demand deposits: a loan to the customer would be credited to an account created for the purpose rather than being issued directly as notes. Credit could thus be created with the stroke of a pen rather than the printing press. State banks were back in business. The number of state banks rose rapidly after 1885.

The increasing abundance of banks meant the industry became a much more obvious and visible feature of the developing US economy. Edwin Green points out:

> By 1900 the head offices and branches of banks were landmarks of city centres … market towns, staging posts and smaller settlements. The appearance of these buildings was often grand and elaborate, as the architecture of banks was one of the few ways in which banks were prepared to advertise themselves. At corner sites of main streets these edifices could rival town halls and other public buildings in terms of their prominence and prestige, and some of the larger banks were already employing architects who specialized in bank design … At the outset of the 20th century these buildings reflected bankers' eagerness to give a public impression of solidarity and permanence. *Banking: An Illustrated History*, p.87

It was as well bankers did try for the *impression* of 'solidarity and permanence'. The way we have allowed them to develop the fractional reserve banking process, creating credit on government-granted licences and privileges, means the reality is exactly the opposite.

Graph 7.2: National and State Bank Assets 1863-1913

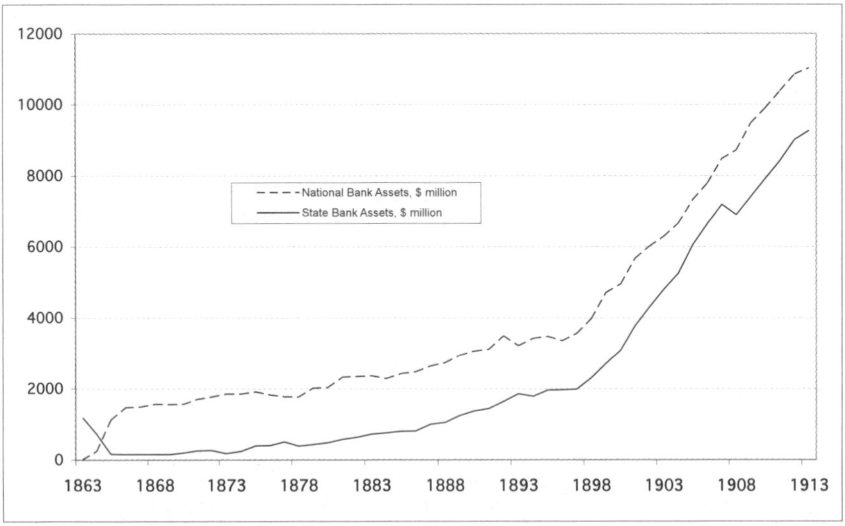

Source: Richard S Grossman, 'US Banking History, Civil War to World War II', EH.Net Encyclopedia, edited by Robert Whaples, www.eh.net/encyclopedia/contents/grossman.banking.history.us.civil.war.wwii.php

FURTHER READING

Carlson, Mark. *Causes of Bank Suspensions in the Panic of 1893*. Paper provided by the Board of Governors of the Federal Reserve System (US) in its Finance and Economic Discussion Series, No. 2002-11.

Grossman, Richard S. *US Banking History, Civil War to World War II*. EH.Net Encyclopedia, edited by Robert Whaples (www.eh.net/encyclopedia/contents/grossman.banking.history.us.civil.war.wwii.php).

8

Hell on Wheels

The Land Boom of 1869

One who when bought, stays bought.

Commodore Vanderbilt, describing,
in the politics of his day, an honest politician

Along with ordinary happenings, we fellows in Wall Street had the fortunes of war to speculate about and that makes great doings on a stock exchange. It's good fishing in troubled waters.

Daniel Drew, quoted in Matthew Josephson,
The Robber Barons, p.59

THE YEARS from 1858 to 1873 were all about railroads – many of which were listed on the New York Stock Exchange – and about the men who fought to control them. The age, of which 1857 to 1873 was a large part, came to be called the Gilded Age, and for good reason. What happened – the wealth that was created and then lost, the speculation and the corruption – was astonishing. Did I say railroads? Yes, well this is true, but underlying the rails was a land give-away and, as we shall see, the railroad speculation was often more about collecting the value of what the railroads ran over rather than the railway itself.

Charles Dow, in his studies on business conditions, observes about the 1860s:

> 'The London panic in 1866, precipitated by the failure of Overend, Gurney & Co., was followed by a heavy fall in prices in the Stock Exchange here. In April there had been a corner in Michigan Southern and rampant speculation generally, from which the relapse was rather more than normal.'
>
> William Peter Harrison, *The Stock Market Barometer*, p.26

Our mid-cycle slowdown, an established feature in the property cycle by this era.

About the 1873 panic, Harrison quotes Dow as saying:

> 'The panic of September, 1873, was a commercial as well as a Stock Exchange panic. It was the outcome of an enormous conversion of floating

> into fixed capital. Business had been expanded on an enormous scale, and the supply of money became insufficient for the demands made upon it. Credit collapsed, and the depression was extremely serious.

Let's carry out a repeat analysis. What is it that Dow is attempting to explain and in the end can't quite manage to?

The 1857 downturn ushered in a good deal of soul-searching, leading to a marked religious revival in most of the country, especially the towns and cities. Clergymen were heard warning their flocks that the autumn panic was a well-deserved punishment for the ostentatious display and 'criminal extravagance' of the time. Prayer meetings in New York were attended by clerks, merchants, lawyers, bankers and even the brokers themselves. The 'Businessmen's revival' it was termed, the meetings taking place at lunchtimes. When earthly hopes have been ruined, where else should one turn? And besides, since it appeared mere mortals were incapable of ending the depression, perhaps one should trust God to do it. The newly found piety led one Massachusetts editor to muse: 'If the pressure should be lifted, we fear Wall Street will lose its interest in the noon prayer meeting, and return to its old modes of preying.'[1] The brokers did not have long to practice singing the Lord's praises. Civil war broke out on April 12, 1861, though tensions had been building for years. Long lines formed at the White House, all hoping to receive a lucrative military supply contract.

In 1860 the government finally declared itself in favour of free homesteads for settlers. The Homestead Act, duly passed after Lincoln won the presidency, offered, totally free, a quarter section (160 acres) of government land to any adult US citizen prepared to live on the land for five years. Within three years one hundred thousand people had taken up the offer. Another small kick-start out of recession. We have run out of unclaimed land with which to do this nowadays – unless you want to go to the Amazon. The homesteading idea actually went back to 1832, the days of Jackson; it was pushed by many who were weary of the land speculation going on around them and the increasing concentration of land ownership in fewer hands, resulting in larger estates. Opposition to the Act was continual, however. Astor and other big fur-trading companies didn't like it: the settlers were making it harder for them to trap animals. Landowners in the east didn't like it because it drew people out west, and population was required to maintain eastern land values. Southern members of Congress were determined the Act should never see the light of day as it would immediately threaten the slavery system.

In the early days of Congress, the numbers of states had been balanced: thirteen slave states and thirteen free. But new states were being added to the Union every decade and, under the strongly held principle of state sovereignty, each had the right to choose its destiny, slave or free.

1 *Springfield Republican*, November 7, quoted in Kenneth M. Stampp, *America in 1857*, p.238.

Encouraging even more settlers to the west would add to the numbers demanding free and not slave states, and threaten the very survival of the south's plantation system. It was this question, and the violence that erupted in Kansas because of it – complete with our fellow John Brown – that brought on the Civil War. This war was as much about land ownership as it was about slaves.

> 'If the Homestead Act for free land had been adopted in 1832, as suggested by President Jackson, instead of thirty years later, after the war began, slavery would have died a natural death, as the Homestead Act would break up land monopoly in the south.' Roy M. Robbins, *Our Landed Heritage*, quoted in Alfred Chandler, *Land Title Origins*, p.502

Conjecture of course – but southern opposition to homesteading never wavered. Once the south ceded from the Union, after Lincoln's pledge to pass the bill and his further pledge to oppose the spread of slavery, numbers were more favourable for the Act's passage.

Non-settlers still found ways to accumulate more land than was allowed under the Act, however. By means of dummy entries at the land office, movable cabins built on wheels, or homestead living quarters placed at the intersection of adjoining quarter section lines, the Homestead Act was circumvented and land was still accumulated by speculators.

Civil war

THE CIVIL WAR (1861-5) saw the biggest era of speculation experienced up to that time in the US. It started slowly but expanded as the decade progressed. Younger men had come to replace older, more conservative brokers on Wall Street wiped out by the 1857 panic. Markets were initially undecided about the possible effects of the north-south conflict, and nervous. There was a stock market decline in the lead-up to war, and after the events at Fort Sumter a bit of a sell-off. But in 1862, once the Union decided to pay for their side of the fighting by issuing $150m worth of paper – the new 'greenbacks' – and by the selling of bonds, markets started climbing. Not dissimilar to the events of 2003, though the Bush administration did not issue paper in the form of currency to pay costs, but rather bonds. The selling of bonds is an expansion of the money supply, and inflationary in tendency. Markets are quick to figure this out, and the lessons of history are never lost on the remaining older players. Cause and effect repeat. Government spends to pay for the war, buying armaments, clothing, food, rations, paying railroads, iron mills, textile manufacturers – the list is endless; profits most likely increase; the financing needs are significant. 'Good fishing in troubled waters', Daniel Drew called it. The previous downturn was fast becoming history.

Markets are also quick to set up systems to gather relevant information. The 1860s gold market was usually the first to hear war news, before even the President himself, having developed extensive spy networks in both Union and Confederate camps.

Call loans

TAKING A LOAN from the bank and offering your shares as security was not a new idea; it had been going on since the days of the markets in Amsterdam back in the 1600s. But it was not that common in the US until the 1850s, at which time such loans started to dominate the New York exchanges. If you wanted to play the markets, it was becoming much easier to get a loan from your broker, with money (credit) supplied to him from the banks; the shares so bought were security for the loan. The effect was to make Wall Street more susceptible to monetary conditions and the prevailing movement of interest rates. It also attracted a lot more people to the market.

Increasing speculation

IT WAS ALL ABOUT access to and control of the rent, as it has always been. Edward Chancellor, in his excellent review of this era, notes:

> America's vast wilderness invited speculation. Many of the country's founding fathers were land speculators: George Washington started his own Mississippi company to purchase lands in the west; Benjamin Franklin was involved in an Illinois land speculation of sixty-three million acres; Patrick Henry, the fiery revolutionary, was among the investors in the 'Yazoo Company', which attempted to purchase ten million acres in Georgia; even Thomas Jefferson and Alexander Hamilton were occasional 'land-jobbers'. For a century after independence, the country was in a constant ferment of land speculation. In the late eighteenth century, millions of acres in large blocks were exchanged in Maine, Georgia, and New York State. The developing towns and cities were also the objects of speculation. Fittingly, the capital city, Washington, D.C., was founded by land speculators. Forty years later, Chicago was the new boomtown. Later still, the railroads opened up the western part of the country to the national pastime, the railroads themselves, established with federal land grants that exceeded 170 million acres, were primarily vehicles for land speculation. *Devil Take the Hindmost*, p.155

This brings us to the railroad story, which involves the stock market and government land grants. There were many other 'boomlets' over the course of the cycle, which we will take note of further into the chapter. However, the big guns were operating in the stock market because federal lands so granted were usually transferred to a land company organised and owned by the promoters and railroad company shareholders. And it was a lot of land, so it is on the rails that we will concentrate our study of this cycle. The story to 1873 goes like this.

Historians seem in agreement that the Civil War, despite the atrocious loss of life, created a speculative mania the likes of which had not been seen before.

> Almost every man who had money at all employed a part of his capital in the purchase of stocks or of gold, of copper, of petroleum, or of domestic produce, in the hope of a raise in prices, or staked money on the expectation of a fall.
> Chancellor, p.165

Not that the federal government always approved. President Lincoln tried to ban the trading of gold, considering it unpatriotic as it was based on events in the war – the price tended to rise with Confederate victories and fall with Union wins. But he did not succeed. Gold trading reached a climax in early 1864 with the opening of a new gold exchange, but panic hit on April 18 with the failure of the speculator Anthony Morse.

Exuberance revived in 1865 with trading in the new black gold – petroleum – a substance hailed as a vermin killer, 'hair oil, boot grease and a cure of kidney stones'.[2] The product was so new nobody knew what it could best be used for. It was easy for the brokers though. They simply discarded the gold samples from their offices, replaced them with petroleum phials and oil barrels, and advised the buyers of the pros and cons of the next certain winner.

The Union government borrowed heavily to finance its war operations. (There are only three ways to pay for a war: raise taxes, print money, or borrow.) Perhaps concluding that existing Wall Street methods of raising bond finance might be insufficient, they turned to a new banker, Jay Cooke of Jay Cooke and Co (who was well connected to the government via friends) to raise additional finance. He hit upon the novel idea of advertising government bonds in local newspapers and flyers. People were coerced into thinking it was their patriotic duty to buy the bonds, and buy them they did. 'Mums and dads' bondholders were successfully introduced to the intricacies of the Wall Street markets.

The advent of the telegraph and railways meant that even remote places in the country had daily contact with 'the markets'. Out went the sedate, closely connected brokers who went home for lunch; in came the 'counter lunch' and an influx of new brokers, operating in the new exchanges or 'on the curb'. 'By 1863 they may well have been trading as much as a million shares a day on the street.'[3] By 1865 volume was reckoned at \$6bn a year, some brokers earning up to \$10,000 a day in commissions – at a time when \$1,000 a year was a decent wage.[4] And, if still one had not had enough action in the day, there were night markets conducted in local hotels. In these war years, 24/7 trading was just about do-able.

While the public were being reminded of their patriotic duty to support the war effort by buying bonds, war contractors were busy filling government contracts.

2 Chancellor, p.170.
3 John Steele Gordon, *The Great Game*, p.97.
4 James K. Medbury, *Men and Mysteries of Wall Street*.

> Cornelius Vanderbilt furnished the navy with unseaworthy vessels, the young Pierpont Morgan sold faulty carbines to the army, and other contractors supplied goods to the government that were equally 'shoddy' (the word derived from a material made from shredded rags used for union soldiers' coats).
>
> Chancellor, p.174

Profiteering flourished under the Secretary of War, Simon Cameron, who continually issued military supply contracts without competitive bidding. (Sounds familiar.) President Lincoln did eventually replace him, but not before Union soldiers had received 'knapsacks that came unglued in the rain, uniforms that fell apart, and guns that blew the thumbs off the soldiers firing them.'[5] The defective rifles were supplied by one J.P. Morgan, who financed the deal to purchase five thousand from a Union Army depot in New York at \$3.50 each and sell them on to soldiers in Virginia for \$22, Morgan taking 25 per cent commission.[6] Soldiers were issued with boots made largely of paper and meat from diseased cattle and hogs.[7] Most of the contractors had already made their initial war investment by paying substitutes \$300 so that they themselves could dodge the draft. A modest investment.

Never aspire to be a part of 'the public'. The public's ignorance condemns it to perpetual slaughter.

In 1867, after the war, came 'the ticker', a new invention using existing technology to communicate the very latest stock prices to the observer, without his having to be anywhere near the exchange. Truly a revolution. (The ticker created a bit of a paper glut, which New Yorkers solved by inventing the ticker tape parade.) The first stock market 'bucket shop' followed soon after. Stock markets were now big business for little people. But any regulation to protect them against unfair business practices and market scams had not yet been given any consideration. Government ethics were possibly even worse.

The stock ticker had followed hard on the heels of the successful laying of the transatlantic cable in 1866. New York was 'talking' to London. This was also the year Jesse James launched his criminal career with a bank hold-up in Liberty, Missouri, in February. Takings were about \$57,000. Their first train hold-up came on July 21, 1873, when the Chicago and Rock Island express was stopped near Adair, Iowa, the outlaws having removed part of the track. In 1875 Pinkerton agents (forerunners of the FBI) tried to firebomb the James family farm and kill the outlaws, but succeeded only in raising sympathy for the gang, seen by many as robbers of the rich – banks and railroad companies – who were exploiting those who could least afford it.

Soon it seemed the whole nation was copying outlaw Jesse and trying to get rich quick – not by robbing banks but by trading markets. 'The

5 See www.hnn.us/articles/880.html
6 *Washington Post*, February 10, 2002, p.F01.
7 Stewart H. Holbrook, *The Age of the Moguls*, p.20.

mania seemed to possess everybody', *Fraser's* magazine told its readers in 1869.

> Old-fashioned merchants abandoned the principles of a lifetime and 'took a flyer', or, in other words, bought a few hundred shares of Erie. Professional men, tired of the slow gains; clerks, sick of starvation salaries; clergymen, dissatisfied with a niggardly stipend, followed fast in the same course. Even the fair sex, practically asserting women's rights under the cover of a broker, dabbled in Erie shares.
>
> John Steele Gordon, *The Great Game*, p.109

It was in 1869 that Jay Gould, with Jim Fiske as his agent, sought to corner the gold market.

> Success for these notable scoundrels depended on the government's not selling gold, which Gould thought he had ensured by buying Grant's brother-in-law (and thus the President) and also a minor official or two. His men couldn't, as it happened, deliver Grant.
>
> J.K. Galbraith, *Money: Whence it Came, Where it Went*, p.105

The corner fell over. The collapse and ensuing gold market panic occurred on September 23 and 24. That speculators and the general public believed that those in power might actually go along with such a scheme shows the low opinion of politicians at this time. And not just politicians. *Fraser's* magazine was at pains to explain to its English readers that in New York there was a custom among litigants 'of retaining a judge, as well as a lawyer'.[8] At later Congressional hearings Gould and Fiske were asked what had happened to the profits. Fiske responded that they had gone 'where the woodbine twineth', a phrase that immediately captured the imagination of the country. Woodbine, or honeysuckle, was often planted around outhouses to mask unpleasant odours.[9]

The collapse of the attempted gold corner did not lead to a severe downturn. Land prices had not yet risen to levels high enough to threaten the banking sector.

In these years government was seen as part of the problem for efficient markets, not as part of the solution. Nor was the regulation of any market seen as a government responsibility. It was left to participants, and did eventually take place when enough brokers tired of the shenanigans. Railroads were the main game and it was here (as well as in banking, of course) that the big operators were found – the colourful characters collectively known as the Robber Barons.

These included Daniel Drew (known as 'the Great Bear', 'the Old Bear', 'Ursa Major', 'the Sphinx of Wall Street' or just plain 'Uncle Daniel') and Jay Gould. Gould would print share certificates of the Erie Railroad and award himself the stock, selling the shares into the stock market to raise cash as he needed it. The exchange outlawed this practice

8 *Fraser's*, May 1869.
9 Gordon, p.135.

in 1869 by demanding the declaration of issued shares. There were also John W. Tobin, Henry Keep ('Henry the Silent'), 'Commodore' Vanderbilt, Hetty Green ('the Witch of Wall Street', who ended up the richest woman in the US), Addison Jerome and his brother Leonard (grandfather of Winston Churchill), Anthony Morse ('the Lightning Calculator'), Thomas Durant and Oakes Ames ('the King of Spades'), J.P. Morgan, John 'Bet-a-Million' Gates, Jim Fiske ('Prince Erie', 'Jim Jubilee', or Admiral James Fiske, Jr) and many others. Much has been written about the exploits of the barons.[10] But our study has a different perspective from the others, so we will stick to the land side of things.

Railroads and land grants

> 'We'll buy the lands on long time, backed by the notes of good men; and then mortgage them for money enough to get the road well on. Then get the towns on the line to issue their bonds for stock … we can then sell the rest of the stock on the prospect of the business of the road … and also sell the lands at a big advance, on the strength of the road.'
>
> Samuel L. Clemens and Charles Dudley Warner, *The Gilded Age: A Tale of Today*[11]

ASSISTANCE FROM the government to build the country's railway network began in the form of land grants. The first was in 1850 when the state of Illinois was given 2.5 million acres of prime public domain to help with the construction of the Illinois Central. By 1857 railroad projects in the west and south had received 22 million acres of land.

> The grants proved to be a stimulus not only to the railroads but to land speculation and to a considerable amount of corruption growing out of the competition of rival promoters for a share of the land at the state's disposal.
>
> Kenneth M. Stampp, *America in 1857*, p.215

Stephen A. Douglas, Senator for Illinois, in 1853 convinced the federal government, which already accepted the need for an east-west railroad link, that it could best be built by private enterprise, with just a little assistance from government in the form of land grants. Odd then (or perhaps not so odd in the light of how much the value of government-granted licences depends on the government) that, during the long years of the previous economic downturn, when calls were made by public officials and citizens for the government to 'appropriate funds to feed the hungry through a program of public employment', such arguments were virulently attacked by the ruling politicians and newspapers of the day as being anti-American.

10 Gordon's *The Great Game* (Chapters 5, 6 and 7) and Chancellor's *Devil Take the Hindmost* (Chapter 6) make great reading, to name just two of the many books.

11 A novel about eastern railroad promoter Mr Bigler and his plan to build the Tunkhannock, Rattlesnake and Youngwomenstown railroad, which would not only be a great highway to the west, but would also open to the market the nearby inexhaustible coalfields and untold millions of lumber.

> Honest citizens would be unjustly taxed for 'extravagant and unnecessary' public works, and the 'thriftless and disorderly' would be taught to look for government support.
>
> Stampp, p.228

It was suggested that the unemployed might instead head west; that self-help was the American way: such was the laissez-faire attitude of the ruling class at this time. Except for funding the railroad interests.

Southern interests originally opposed the building of a railway to the Pacific coast that did not follow a southern route, but, the south having now ceded from the Union, bills granting the promoter's right of way were passed in 1862 and 1864. The lines were named the Union Pacific and the Central Pacific and they were to be built along the 42nd parallel. In addition to rights of way, Congress granted the lines 19.5 m acres of land, and two loans of United States Government 6 per cent bonds, the accrued interest on the loans for the thirty-year period to be paid semi-annually.

The rail company would sell off the granted land as and when the building of the line made it more valuable. The promoters also chose, naturally, to issue both bonds and shares to the public via the stock market, to raise much needed revenue, which kicked off wild manias and pitched battles in the stock market for control of these enterprises. And, as we noted in the previous chapter, farmers near to the rail lines were 'enticed' to part with their hard-earned cash, or indeed money borrowed on the security of their land, to buy railway shares. The railway company would then bundle up the mortgages – securitising them – and sell them on to eastern bankers. (A process bankers will rediscover in later cycles to help further reduce risk and expand profits.) A further expansion of credit backed by land value.

It is not hard to imagine settlers along the way fighting to get the line built through their villages, or have a station strategically placed to bring in new business. Perhaps a little 'inducement' could be offered?

Between 1850 and 1871, the year the final land grant to a railroad was made, promoters of 72 railroads received some 94 m acres of land. Another 36 m or so acres of federally controlled land had been granted to the states to further railroad building. It was specified by Congress that these should be only agricultural, coal or iron lands, but it was not uncommon for the railroads to appropriate 'other valuable mineral lands … with all the gold, silver, copper and oil under them, and all the timber and stone above them, with all harbor rights and franchises' through fraudulent surveys carried out by dishonest public officials.[12] There was no lack of interest from powerful quarters in rail stock.

Insider promoters were a step ahead of mere investors in other ways too. The behaviour of Union Pacific insiders gave rise to the most highly publicised fraud of the era, the Credit Mobilier scandal.

12 Chandler, p.504.

> The construction [of the line] was subsidized by granting the railroad millions of acres of land along the route, land that would become much more valuable once it was accessible by the railroad. To feather their own nests, the management of the Union Pacific set up a construction company with the fancy French name of Credit Mobilier, then hired this company to construct the railroad. Credit Mobilier wildly overcharged the railroad to do so, making the shareholders of Credit Mobilier millions while draining Union Pacific, and thus its stockholders, dry. To make sure there was no interference from Washington, management bribed many members of the Grant administration (including his first Vice President, Schulyer Colfax) and Congress. Rather than cash, the Union Pacific executives gave them sweetheart deals, allowing them to buy stock in Credit Mobilier and pay for it out of the enormous dividends.
>
> Gordon, p.137

The story of the scandal starts with Thomas Durant, who believed there was more money in building a railway than in operating one. Having already had some involvement in running other western area railroads, one of which he used to smuggle illegal cotton shipments from the south to the north during the Civil War, he set about lobbying Congress to grant land and bonds to the Union Pacific company (UP, of which he was now Vice President) to build a transcontinental line. Once granted, Durant had an associate supply a construction bid to the UP, which, when accepted, Durant transferred to his own company, styled for just that purpose, the Credit Mobilier. It proved a neat bit of corporate organisation. The UP received government subsidies for every mile of track built. Credit Mobilier charged UP for the actual construction but UP bore all the risks (and was the company in which the public was invited to invest). Credit Mobilier took all the profit. As it substantially overcharged for the cost of building, there was a good deal of profit. For Credit Mobilier it was irrelevant whether the line would eventually be profitable, or indeed how much it would cost, as it had no liability in the project. The profit, once earned, could not be taken back – and the more the line cost, the more money these guys made. Durant had effectively hired himself to build the railway, paying Credit Mobilier with money given to UP by the government. Construction got off to a great start out of Omaha, a few extra bends adding nine unnecessary but profitable miles to the railroad.

It appears that, after the Civil War, Oakes Ames, a member of Congress but now also a rail man, had ousted Durant from the UP in a boardroom tussle. Ames, 'the King of Spades', had made his money supplying shovels to miners; the business founded by his father had became very profitable after the discovery of gold in California. To ensure continued government goodwill towards the UP, Ames distributed Credit Mobilier stock to 'strategic' legislative members. To give an idea of the profitability of this stock, in 1867 the Mobilier declared a dividend worth as much as its entire capital. In this way Ames and his 'group' made off with profits that some estimated at $44m, though the real figure was probably a bit less.

Importantly for our story, it left the UP with very large debts (at the mercy of prevailing interest rates), to be serviced out of future profits. The scandal broke in January 1873. In his enthusiasm for the project, Ames had

> unwisely solicited some members of Congress to buy stock in the Credit Mobilier … not from need of any small capital thus obtained, but to secure their support in Congress of any future desired legislation concerning the undertaking.
> Chandler, p.505

For this Ames was expelled from Congress, though many members later apologised to him for having voted him out merely to satisfy the public clamour. No charges for the looting were ever laid.

This was not the only scam to come to light with the building of the railroads. Over level desert and prairie lands in the west, 'tracks were not always laid straight as one might have anticipated, but meandrically' to increase track mileage and therefore land grants 'and an increased amount of railroad company bonds – which were issued to the promoters' construction companies at from $15,000 to $25,000 for each mile of road constructed.' Not too many years later most of the railroads went bust through high operational costs due to poor construction and high interest charges on the bonded debts.

> Thousands of miles of road had to be straightened, shortened or rebuilt. The operations were carried out through receiverships and financial reorganisations, at great loss to the bondholders. But the land companies continued to be profitable.
> Chandler, p.508

Some rail trivia

RAILROADS HAD a huge impact on just about everything. There was now a year-round cheaper, quicker and safer carriage of goods and people, vastly extending the market economy. Markets for iron, steel, wood, coal and machine-building tools all exploded. Practically everything about the rails was new, or required re-inventing.

The railroads quickly replaced stagecoach services between Missouri (the rail terminus at the time) and San Francisco, and the pony express that took US mail across the continent. Passengers happily exchanged twenty-five sleepless nights in a coach for a more luxurious week in a steam-driven carriage.

Railroads were pretty much the first 'corporate' employers: previously few had worked in an employee hierarchy. In the early days of rail, employment was seen as a 'calling': it was common, for example, to see engine-men on a Sunday, their only day off, back at work shining the brass on their steam locomotives. Engine-men were a proud lot. Some got together with conductors to run a line to suit themselves; if they lived near one another they'd make every effort to be home at night, train and all, and lay over until next morning. At least in the beginning. Spare a thought for the early pioneer locomotive drivers and cabmen: they drove in open cabs, without protection from the weather, sparks and smoke. The travelling public simply would not permit covered cabs in order that the driver's alertness and constant attention to the task at hand could be monitored. Engine-men could earn an extra twenty dollars or so for being first to drive across a new bridge, testing its safety. A safer way to increase their earnings was through small gratuities if the train carried important dignitaries, politicians or wealthy stockholders.

Train conductors became men of some importance; theirs was a sought-after job bringing swift elevation up the social ladder. They often wore top hats, fancy gloves and elegant pocket watches. So important did they become that train journeys were often identified by conductor name rather than number or destination: Smith to meet Jones at La Salle, for example. Conductors were at first also responsible for printing and issuing journey tickets, a fact not lost on some of the conductors as a source of occasional additional income. The Philadelphia and Reading Railroad eventually discovered that they were losing 32 per cent of ticket revenue (18 cents per mile) to conductors after an audit by Pinkerton's National Detective Agency.[13] Early conductors also supplied potable water at a penny a cup, and were known to accept bribes from male passengers wanting entrance to the ladies' compartment.

The rail builders came to employ a large number of Chinese labourers – the Chinese would happily work for less, $32 a month rather than $52. It was perhaps no coincidence that the Senate in 1868 passed a treaty permitting unrestricted immigration from China. In later cycles many labour disputes arose with the Chinese immigrants, from feelings that 'white' jobs were being pinched.

Most worked a ten- to twelve-hour day, from 7am to as late as 7pm – perhaps an hour less on Saturdays. It was commonly a seventy-hour working week, though there was no contract as such. If work was available, one was 'called'; if not, the saloon was the only other 'employer'. Payment was not always guaranteed every week either: there were stories of workers going without wages for up to six months, or of receiving scrip in lieu of wages; even, in states where it was permitted, of being paid in railway bank notes.

The workers were of course men, female labour being almost unheard of in those days – though there was the occasional exception. A Miss Minnie Rockwell was taken on by the Chicago, Burlington and Quincy line as a station telegraph operator, the line's controller Robert Harris being known as a champion of feminism. Alas, Miss Rockwell became something of a 'curiosity', attracting the attention of a 'rowdy element' that disrupted station routine.[14] Whether Miss Rockwell quit or was fired has

13 Walter Licht, *Working for the Railroad*, p.96.
14 Licht, p.216.

been lost to time, but the policy of hiring women had to wait a few more years.

The god-fearing, church-going citizens of the western states saw depravity as well as benefits following the railroads. A heady brew of whisky, guns, gambling and vice fermented in the boom-towns that mushroomed ahead of the rail line to house grade crews and line workers, and which served as jumping-off points for hardy souls venturing even further west. This was a particular problem on the Union Pacific, the railway built to connect east and west. The Rector of St Mark's Episcopal Church, the Reverend J.W. Cook, reported on his arrival in 1868 in Cheyenne, one of the new towns:

> 'The activity of the place is surprising and the wickedness unimaginable and appalling. This is a great centre for gamblers of all shadcs, and roughs and troops of lewd women, and bullwhackers. Almost every other house is a drinking saloon, gambling house, restaurant or bawdy.'
>
> www.wyomingtalesandtrails.com/sherman3.html

More rail workers died in brawls in such towns than were killed in railway accidents. Some of the towns, notably those that serviced railway junctions, stayed and prospered, others simply disappeared or were relocated as construction teams moved steadily westwards – hence the term 'hell on wheels' to describe the relentless and continual movement forwards. It was said that, during the brief existence of the town of Benton, more than a hundred died in gunfights. When the Echo Canyon saloon was torn down seven human skeletons were found under the floorboards. When the Union Pacific reached Utah, the local Mormons were mortified by the immorality of those escorting its advance.

The railroads were changing everything: 'The printed train schedule, the conductor's gold timepiece … the pace of life had quickened and become more ordered.'[15]

> 'They come and go with such regulated precision, and their whistles can be heard so far, that the farmers set their clocks by them … Have men not improved somewhat in punctuality since the railroad was invented? Do they not talk and think faster in the depot than in the stage-office?'
>
> Stewart J. Holbrook, *The Story of American Railroads*, p.15, quoting Thoreau

As regards land, it was becoming obvious to everyone by the mid to late 1860s that railways were a huge 'loot' of the public domain, as noted by many historians, in particular Gustavus Myers in *History of the Great Fortunes*. A rush began to get in before there was no more land to hand out. Although the government tried to pre-empt land-grabbing speculators by releasing land to railways in alternate sections, rather than contiguous to the line itself, this was easily countered. The alternate sections were not

15 Licht, *Working for the Railroad*, p.79.

always marked as such, so homesteaders could not determine which land was government and which belonged to the railway company; if a section was marked, railway workers simply pulled up the markers. Rail companies knew the land was going up in value, so why rush to sell something that would be worth twice as much tomorrow? Besides, the 'even' sections retained by the government could, if necessary, be gained for the railroad by dummy entry-men at the local land office.

In this manner the rails, a speculative land gamble, brought down the financial genius of Jay Cooke – that 'unlooked for' event of 1873.

Jay Cooke and the Northern Pacific – Part I

THE NORTHERN PACIFIC railroad was chartered by Josiah Perham, a Boston wool merchant, and his associates. Perham lost his first fortune in an unwise land speculation in 1837, but made another selling cheap day excursions to Boston. The Northern Pacific (NP) had been granted 43 m acres of the public domain (in alternate sections of land ten miles wide, on both sides of the track) to build a line connecting Duluth on Lake Superior to Puget Sound. Not initially successful, the line came into the hands of Jay Cooke in 1869 and he proceeded to put all his energy into running it. It eventually bankrupted him. But before telling this story we need to understand the profound changes he brought to the US banking system, and also take another look at Chicago.

Banking

THE BANKS were not in great shape after the downturn of 1857 and the Civil War, and were hindered by the many different bank notes in circulation. Recovery took some years. For example, Hoyt puts the state of Illinois bank note circulation at around $12 m in the late 1850s, backed by deposits of $14 m in bonds, about two thirds of which were southern state bonds – a weakening security base which was destroyed completely once the south was defeated. By 1864 only 23 Chicago banks were still in business.

> A situation in which there was circulating in the United States 7,000 genuine notes of 1,600 different state banks of issue which were at varying rates of discount, mingled with which were 5,500 varieties of altered and counterfeit notes, was a serious handicap to every type of business.
>
> Homer Hoyt, *One Hundred Years of Land Values in Chicago*, p.76

This situation was reversed by the National Banking Act drafted in 1863 by the federal government under Lincoln. It was Jay Cooke's baby.

The following summary is drawn largely from Murray N. Rothbard's *A History of Money and Banking in the United States*,[16] but we start with a quote from Galbraith.

16 Rothbard has passed on now, but there is a book about him entitled *An Enemy of the State: The Life of Murray N. Rothbard*. The title suggests he might have written a few interesting words …

> The exigencies of war could be urged against the disorder and confusion of the state banks and their notes. A new central bank could not be contemplated but a new system of banks, chartered and regulated by the federal government, was a possibility. In 1863, at the strong behest of the Secretary of the Treasury [Salmon P.] Chase and the Congress, the National Bank Act was passed establishing a new system of national banks. First attention, as might be expected, was given to the regulation of their note issue. Notes could be issued but only to the extent of 90 percent of the value of federal bonds purchased by the issuing bank and deposited in the Treasury. The safety of the arrangement will be evident; if a bank capsized, the bonds could be sold and the notes redeemed with, under all ordinary circumstances, a comfortable margin to spare. It was also a useful way of ensuring a wartime market for government bonds. *Money, Whence it Came, Where it Went*, p.91

That is a general history one might read in any textbook about the change. But why go to all that trouble? In whose interest was it? What was to be the effect on the economy? Such questions must be answered if one is to forecast the future result. Let us look a bit deeper.

In 1860 a new government with a new agenda had taken over. The Democrat hard-money, state's-rights men were out; men who believed in a federally controlled national bank system were in. There was also a war to be won and paid for. Both north and south were trying to do this of course, but the north had 'the markets' to back them. The south was trying to defend the indefensible – slavery. As already noted, there are only three ways to finance a war. Taxes being unpopular, both north and south began printing notes to pay for supplies. Then the north turned to borrowing by issuing bonds.

Jay Cooke suggested to Senator Salmon P. Chase that the government appoint his firm, Jay Cooke and Company, sole agent for these bond sales (a government-granted licence). The appointment was made. The contract Cooke got was a total monopoly on the underwriting of the public debt.

> With enormous energy Cooke hurled himself into the task of persuading the mass of public to buy US government bonds. In doing so, Cooke perhaps invented the art of public relations and of mass propaganda; certainly, he did so in the realm of bonds. With characteristic optimism, he flung himself into a bond crusade. He recruited a small army of 2500 sub-agents among bankers, insurance men and community leaders and kept them inspired and informed by mail and telegraph. He taught the American people to buy bonds, using lavish advertising in newspapers, broadsides, and posters. God, destiny, duty, courage, patriotism – all summoned 'Farmers, Mechanics, Capitalists' to invest in loans. Loans which of course they had to purchase from Jay Cooke. And purchase the loans they did, for Cooke's bond sales soon reached the enormous figure of $1 million to $2 million a day.
>
> Rothbard, p.134

Cooke ended the war a millionaire. 'To be as rich as Jay Cooke' was an expression of the era.

After the successful bond issues, Cooke again teamed up with Chase, and Senator John Sherman, to push through Congress a national banking system. This provided for the federal chartering of banks, to be called national banks; anyone could open one provided the substantial reserve specie requirements could be met. Three types of bank would be permitted, New York banks, reserve city banks, and country banks. New York banks had to keep 25 per cent of their notes and deposits in gold, silver or government-issued paper (greenbacks) – this was their 'reserve' requirement. Reserve city banks could keep half their reserves in gold, silver or notes and half on deposit with New York banks. Country banks were required only to maintain their reserve ratio at 15 per cent notes and deposits, of which 40 per cent could be in gold, silver or greenbacks, and 60 per cent as deposits with the national banks above them. So now, instead of individual, decentralised state banks lending and holding on to their own specie reserves, there was in operation an inverted pyramid system. Country banks could lend (expand) on top of reserve city banks, which were expanding on top of New York banks, at the base of which was a reserve of specie and greenbacks.

To get rid of the myriad state bank notes, the federal government put a 10 per cent tax on each (the power to tax is indeed the power to destroy). A national bank could issue notes only

> if it deposited an equivalent of US securities as collateral at the US treasury, so that national banks could only expand their notes to the extent that they purchased US government bonds. This provision tied the national banking system intimately to the federal government, and, more particularly, to its expansion of public debt. The federal government had an assured, built in market for its debt, and the more that banks purchased that debt, the more the banking system could inflate.
>
> Rothbard, p.142

Many state banks disappeared, as was intended, under the weight of the tax on their notes, but those remaining accepted their subordinate role (if they did not renew themselves with a federal charter).

> In order to survive, the state banks had to keep deposit accounts at national banks, from whom they could 'buy' national bank notes in order to redeem their deposits.
>
> Rothbard, p.144

State banks became another layer of the banking pyramid on top of the country banks, and soon began to multiply.

Such a system brings us closer to today's structure, of which more later. Under the guise of wartime commitment, it was structured so as to

> necessarily purchase large amounts of US government bonds … [it] tied the nation's banks with the federal government and the public debt in a close symbiotic relationship.
>
> Rothbard, p.135

There was no longer an independent government treasury. Treasury funds were now 'on deposit' with respected national banks. A federal-government-controlled 'centralised' banking system could inflate the supply of credit uniformly. And government spending came into the economy as a debt.

This did not change the fact that banks create credit out of nothing. Only the structure of control had changed, and the way some loans were issued. If you were granted a bank loan now, instead of taking it in the form of your bank's own printed notes, it would be credited to your account as a deposit. The loan is an asset to the bank, an amount you owe the bank. The bank is still creating its own asset, backed by the security (probably land) you are prepared to offer, in a deal binding you to future interest payments. Your spending, like the government's, comes into the economy as a debt. Most people still believe banks lend you money from funds other people have deposited with that bank. Nothing could be further from the truth.

The vested interest and government-granted licence

> Beautiful credit! The foundation of modern society. Who shall say this is not the age of mutual trust, of unlimited reliance on human promise? That is a peculiar condition of modern society which enables a whole country to instantly recognize point and meaning to the familiar newspaper anecdote, which puts into the speculator in lands and mines this remark: 'I wasn't worth a cent two years ago, and now I owe two million dollars.'
>
> Samuel L. Clemens and Charles Dudley Warner, *The Gilded Age*, p.263

IT WAS NOT coincidental that the US got the banking system it did after the end of the Civil War.

> The Cooke-Chase connection with the new national banking system was simple. As secretary of the treasury, Chase wanted an assured market for the government bonds that were being issued so heavily during the civil war. And as the monopoly underwriter of US government bonds for every year except one from 1862 to 1873, Jay Cooke was even more directly interested in an assured and expanding market for his bonds. What better method for obtaining such a market than creating an entirely new banking system, the expansion of which was directly tied to the bank's purchase of government bonds – from Jay Cooke. Rothbard, p.145

The creation of the new banking system was quite deliberate. Cooke's father, writing of Henry, Jay's brother, in a letter to Jay, said:

> I took up my pen principally to say that H.S.'s plan in getting Chase into the Cabinet and [John] Sherman into the Senate is accomplished, and that now is the time for making money, by honest contracts out of the government. Rothbard, p.133

Henry wrote to his brother Jay:

> It will be a great triumph, Jay, and one to which we have contributed more than any other living man. The bank had been repudiated by the House, and was without a sponsor in the Senate, and was thus virtually dead and buried when I induced Sherman to take hold of it, and we went to work with the newspapers.
>
> Rothbard, p.145

The 'work with the newspapers' meant this:

> As monopoly underwriter of government bonds, Cooke was paying the newspapers large sums for advertising, and so the Cookes thought – as it turned out correctly – that they could induce the newspapers to grant them an enormous amount of free space in which to set forth the merits of the new national banking system. Such space meant not only publicity and articles, but even more important, the fervent editorial support of most of the nation's press. And so the press, implicitly bought for the occasion, kept up a drumfire of propaganda for the new national banking system. As Cooke himself related, 'for six weeks or more nearly all the newspapers in the country were filled with our editorials [written by the Cooke brothers] condemning the state bank system and explaining the great benefits to be derived from the national banking system now proposed.' And every day the indefatigable Cookes put on the desks of every member of Congress the relevant editorial from newspapers in their respective districts.
>
> Rothbard, p.145

Jay Cooke was now selling bonds to all the national banks. His agents set up new national banks in small towns that would have to buy the bonds he was marketing. He also established a very big New York bank, the 4th National Bank of New York, in order to help stabilise the base of the system. It was in place by 1866. By 1870

> State banks began to boom as deposit creation institutions. With lower requirements and fewer restrictions, they could pyramid on top of national banks … Total state and national bank notes and deposits rose from $835 million in 1865 to $1.964 billion in 1873, an increase of 135.2 percent or an increase of 16.9 percent per year.
>
> Rothbard, p.153

An expansion of credit.

The house of Jay Cooke was also expanding, so it was only natural to move into the area of railroad bond finance, and perhaps outright ownership. To quote Cooke directly:

> 'Why should this grand and glorious country be stunted and dwarfed – its activities chilled and its very life blood curdled by these miserable "hard coin" theories – the musty theories of a bygone age – These men who are urging on premature resumption know nothing of the great growing west which would grow twice as fast if it was not cramped for the means necessary to build railroads and improve farms and convey the produce to market.'
>
> Rothbard, p.156

By the late 1860s the Northern Pacific Railroad was in the hands of Jay Cooke and Company after it had been agreed

> that a company shall be organised for the purpose of purchasing lands, improvement of town sites, or other purposes, and the same shall be divided in the same proportion; that is, the original interests shall have one-half, and Jay Cooke & Company shall have one-half.
>
> Sakolski, *The Great American Land Bubble*, p.293

In other words it was a land grab.

Chicago real estate

ONE OF the reasons Hoyt was able to put together such a phenomenal study of Chicago was because of the efforts of George C. Olcott and his Blue Book of Chicago land values, meticulously recording the value of practically every lot in Chicago from 1910 onwards. From 1868 *The Chicago Tribune* recorded a good deal of useful information, and prior to that the extracts of land titles of the Chicago Titles and Trust Company were used by Hoyt to obtain land sales data. Of course one cannot take Chicago real estate as an exact proxy for real estate throughout the US in any cycle. There were events in Chicago that were unique to that city, one being the great fire of 1871. Nevertheless, Hoyt's is a very well documented case study. What was going on in Chicago was mirrored in other developing US cities, as is evident from the literature of the time. This summary of Chicago conditions comes from Chapter III of Hoyt's *One Hundred Years of Land Values in Chicago*.

For Chicago, the onset of civil war at first intensified the depression which followed the panic of 1857, especially for the banks, until at least 1862. Then the benefits of the war kicked in. The Chicago rail lines were soon busy with the profitable business of transporting men and munitions. Local firms adjusted to supplying war necessities like food, uniforms and wagons, and the war caused quite an inflation in the currency. Business profits leapt to levels 'hitherto unknown'.[17] The city was also a mecca for draft dodgers and war profiteers. New national banks were opening up too. Land prices had not yet moved, however; the speculator focus was elsewhere, in particular on the lucrative military contracts.

Other developments were taking place. Refrigerated rail cars were a great boon to the city's meat industry. Grain markets were transformed by the needs of war to resemble what we know today: traders dealing in the transfer of ownership rights by means of warehouse receipts and futures contracts rather than actual inspection and delivery. Expanding markets attracted manufacturing industries, in turn attracting workers, often with wives and families in tow. The Union Pacific, completed in 1869, put Chicago in touch with California, and trade with the Orient. Between 1865 and 1871 the population of Chicago doubled.

17 Hoyt, p.82.

Times and needs were changing. 'When an increase in the volume of sewage and the industrial wastes poured into the stagnant Chicago River made the stench almost intolerable',[18] public works were undertaken to remedy it. Plank roads began to be rebuilt with wooden or stone blocks; plank sidewalks were put in, and bridges were built over the river.

> The precipitous rise in Chicago land values which began in 1865, after reaching a peak in certain downtown sections in 1869, gained a fresh impetus near the parks and boulevards in 1870 and 1871. After a check and decline caused by the great fire on October 9, 1871, the rise again continued during 1872 and the spring of 1873 in certain spots until the record altitude was reached just before the panic of 1873.
>
> Hoyt, p.88

This begs the question, which few ask, why Chicago land prices could recover after the great fire but not after the collapse of Jay Cooke (the story which will follow shortly). Both were 'unlooked for' events. The answer has to do with land prices, banking and interest rates, and whether the productive sector of the economy can afford the increased rents high land prices cause.

Hoyt tells[19] how Potter Palmer, who made a fortune speculating in cotton during the Civil War, bought almost a mile of frontage in State Street. He knew what he was doing. He proceeded to give the street a completely new character by moving back the houses on his lots to widen it. He then built an attractive hotel and enticed merchants and businessmen to the area, gaining cash flow from the rentals. So rapid was the gain in land values in downtown areas in 1868 and 1869 that it was said to be possible to buy one day and sell the next.

The politicians probably also knew what they were doing. They combined with groups of promoters 'to secure such public improvements as sewers, water pipes, and wooden-block pavements on the streets they had selected for development as fashionable sections.'[20] (Farthest removed, one might note, from the river – an open sewer, with tanneries, slaughterhouses and distilleries on either side.)

> The working population was barred from these exclusive centres by the price of land, the annual wages of a labourer being insufficient to pay even the interest charges on one of the vacant lots, not to mention the taxes.
>
> Hoyt, p.91

Meanwhile, in one of the areas where workers were crowded,

> 'the street may be singled out of a thousand by the peculiar, intensive stench that arises from pools of thick and inky compound which in many cases is several feet deep and occasionally expands to the width of a small lake.'
>
> *Chicago Tribune*, June 19, 1893, quoted by Hoyt, p.97

18 Hoyt, p.86.
19 p.90.
20 Hoyt, p.91.

Perhaps it was not surprising that the fame of Haussman's Park and the boulevard system in Paris were quick to reach a city that was seeking new outlets for its fashionable expenditure. Reports of the rapid rise of land values in the vicinity of Central Park in New York no doubt also inspired real estate operators, adding to the general boom. Public participation in land buying began about 1868 when 'many cases of large profits made in real estate since 1861 had become common knowledge'. By 1871 'every other man and every fourth woman in Chicago had an investment in lots'.[21] This ferment was no doubt added to by immigrants from Europe who could hardly believe the opportunities Chicago must have presented, having been used to the domination of landlords back home.

Jay Cooke and the Northern Pacific – Part II

CONSTRUCTION OF the Northern Pacific (NP) railroad started in July 1870, after Jay Cooke had raised $30m selling NP bonds the same way he had sold government bonds. He put many leading politicians and government officials on the NP payroll. He hired writers and pamphleteers to proclaim the benefits of the north-west – its Mediterranean climate, its forest mountains and plains where bumper crops of grain and fruit could be grown, a vast wilderness 'waiting like a rich heiress to be appropriated and enjoyed'. The fact that Cooke himself owned 40,000 acres of land in and around Duluth no doubt helped him understand such climatic attractions, not to mention the fact that twenty feet of snow is not uncommon in winter. But, as time went on, as fast as Cooke could raise the finance for the line, the money was spent building it. Probably Cooke and Coy overestimated its possibilities. In the lead-up to 1873, when Cooke was considered the nation's most prestigious, rock-solid banker, this would prove disastrous.

Into the peak

HOYT RECORDS that in the ten years autumn 1862 to spring 1873 Chicago land values as a whole increased 500 per cent, and values were 360 per cent higher on average compared to the 1856 peak. 'If speculators could find unlimited credit, one can't tell what crises would ensue.'[22] On the city outskirts gains of 1,000 per cent were not uncommon, such was the combined effect of the rails, horse-car lines and parks. Still, there was as yet 'no fear of a collapse of the structure of land values that had been reared so high during the last ten years'[23] – only a deflation brought on by yet another catastrophe like the panic of 1857, the Civil War or great fire could do that. Or so it was thought.

21 Hoyt, p.100.
22 Baron James de Rothschild, testifying before the 1865 French Enquete (inquiry) into monetary circulation, acknowledging that rising interest rates could be relied upon to reduce speculation in commodities and public funds. Quoted in Kindleberger, *Manias, Panics and Crashes*, p.126.
23 Hoyt, p.117.

Developments that had previously been regarded as normal – bridge building, paving and all the improvements – had one thing in common: all had been built at high cost on borrowed money. Much real estate business was now being done on small initial downpayments – again that illusion of wealth, and optimism at the top. Real estate men were forecasting Chicago would be the largest city in the world.

Reading the tea leaves

WHENEVER BUSINESS is looking brisk and busy one should always note who are the heaviest borrowers of capital. Such businesses will be impacted materially by the movement of interest rates. The biggest borrowers of capital at this time were the railroads. But not far behind were the land speculators and those paying for landed improvements, the municipal governments. Signs of distress before a panic will be there, though rarely obvious: it is not in the interests of too many people to have them pointed out.

By early 1873 the NP line was paying its workers in scrip rather than cash, and Jay Cooke and Coy was probably deeply overdrawn as regards its own financial obligations to other banks. But such a condition will of course never be advertised to the market; in fact a company will make its best efforts to conceal it. However, business owners and market insiders will know and be acting on the information without informing others, which will eventually cause stock prices to move accordingly. Astute observers at this time should have been able to notice that a lot of capital was being tied up in ventures yielding, at least initially, very little income, and subject to escalating interest costs, both in railroads and land speculation. The interest bill for the rail lines alone was estimated at $80m even in 1868.[24] This could not go on for ever. To add to these troubles, the railroads were coming under attack from the so-called Granger movement – groups of farmers who banded together to counter what they saw as predatory pricing and monopoly control of commodity movements by rail. The Grangers sought, and often got, state legislative restrictions on what rail companies could charge for freight. This did not help railroad companies cover their debt repayments. (Remember, the profits from land sales alongside the lines often flowed to a different company set up for the purpose.)

Production statistics, if any could have been gathered (we have the benefit of hindsight), and most other things about the year 1873 would have given the appearance of the utmost prosperity. There was plenty of money around and plenty of things to spend it on; everyone was busy. But appearances can be deceptive. It is earnings that have to be watched, or more correctly the anticipated future earnings of the main sectors of the economy. The stock market can tell you this, if you can correctly read a chart, because stock markets always successfully manage to discount

24 Otto C. Lightner, *History of Business Depressions*, p.160.

future earnings. This is how the chart-reading skills of legendary trader W.D. Gann, or of Charles Dow, would be developed – but we are getting ahead of ourselves by a cycle or two.

The panic

ON SEPTEMBER 8, 1873 The New York Warehouse and Security Company suspended operations, admitting it was insolvent, having lent to railway construction companies and individual rail builders who were themselves now insolvent. This was a sign of trouble. Then on the 13th, a Saturday, Daniel Drew's firm of Kenyon, Cox & Co admitted difficulties and closed its doors. Drew had lent $1.5m to the Canada Southern Railway and the loan now looked doubtful. The Street had the rest of the weekend to think about the solvency of other railway corporations.

Monday was quiet. Tuesday saw further failures, but of minor companies only. The first signs of a possible panic appeared on the morning of Wednesday 17th.

> *The Herald* reported that market insiders seemed to expect a major news item to shake the market and were unloading so as to be prepared to pick up bargains later on. Robert Sobel, *Panic on Wall Street*, p.177

Short selling was on the rise.

In the summer, May to September 1873, Hoyt reported a decline in the cash resources of intending real estate buyers. When this seemed to halt rising land values, 'the desire to purchase land fell off sharply, for nothing so quickly stops an upturn as the belief that a commodity can be bought next month or next year at the same price.'[25] A revival of the property market was anticipated in the autumn, but the September 18th announcement in New York of the failure of Jay Cooke and Company startled investors. The initial reaction to the collapse of America's most prestigious banking concern was disbelief. In Pittsburgh a paper boy was arrested for shouting out the news because it was something the police had not yet heard and they suspected the boy was making it up to garner more sales. 'Incredulity soon gave way to panic, as the stock market collapsed and daily call rates rose to 5 percent.'[26] Chancellor goes on to describe events this way:

> The next day, crowds thronged the financial district to witness the unravelling of the speculative drama that had entranced the nation for the past decade and a half ... Vanderbilt's son-in-law, Horace Clark, was found dead after the failure of the Union Trust Bank, from which he had borrowed heavily to finance his margin speculations. Daniel Drew, the Old Man of the Street, took his final curtain call as his brokerage, Kenyon, Cox and Co, was swept away in the panic. Declared bankrupt, Drew retreated to his bed ...

25 p.118.
26 Chancellor, *Devil Take the Hindmost*, p.185.

> he died a year later. When the panic continued into Saturday, the President of the New York Stock Exchange announced that for the first time in its history the exchange would close until further notice. p.185

Historian Alfred Chandler writes about September 18th:

> On the day of the Jay Cooke failure, these shares dropped in price so suddenly and sharply that banks and prominent brokerage houses collapsed like pins in a game of ten-pins. On the street, within the shadow of the stock exchange, some men wept and some attempted suicide at the realization of their financial ruin. I saw all this, as I was in the midst of it and it made a lasting impression. *Land Title Origins*, p.506

The stock exchange was shut down; no one knew when it might re-open. Money could almost not be had; 1.5 per cent per day was the going rate for a bank loan – if you could get one.[27] Banks, like everyone else, began hoarding cash.

Back in Chicago there was no immediate serious drop in land values. Any lot holder hard pressed for cash could find a ready market for his land at some 20 per cent below previously prevailing prices. A continued abundance of loan funds was being offered to renew mortgages. But time was putting things into reverse. Unemployment was growing, reducing pressure on the need for rental space. For property owners facing lower rental receipts, their fixed interest charges and building costs were still the same. The legendary reserve powers of property owners were being slowly whittled away.

Banking unrest, cash withdrawal suspensions, sometimes the closure of the bank itself, spread selectively down the eastern seaboard, then to the middle of the country. Some serious bank runs developed in Chicago.[28]

The New York Stock Exchange did eventually re-open, ten days after it had closed. 'Unofficial' trading had meanwhile continued on the streets, on New Street in particular, despite warnings that such behaviour was punishable by expulsion from the Exchange. The panic was over, but the depression had only just started – a depression second only to that of the 1930s.

> Throughout the following winter factories closed down, railroads discharged employees, banks failed, wages were cut, and money was hoarded. By the end of 1873, over five thousand commercial failures had been announced, among them the Northern Pacific Railroad and nearly fifty New York brokerages. In January, a crowd of unemployed protesters rioted in Tompkins Square, New York, and were charged by mounted police … By 1877 it was estimated that only a fifth of the labour force was in regular employment. Strikes and unrest became frequent … in New York a religious revival movement thrived in response to the apparent endlessness of the depression.
> Chancellor, p.186

27 Lightner, p.161.
28 Elmus Wicker, *Banking Panics of the Gilded Age*, p.21.

In Chicago,

> the bank failures that had followed in the wake of the panic of 1873 culminated in 1877 with the failure of the largest savings bank in the city … Serious labour riots broke out all over the United States, and on July 5th 1877, a pitched battle was fought between the police and a great mob … in which twenty were killed and seventy injured. In this period, when capitalists were frightened by the industrial disturbances, twelve thousand loans for a total of $50 million that had been made by local property owners to finance the rebuilding after the fire, fell due. Scant capital was available for refunding these maturing obligations or for buying property at any price. Wealthy men were hoarding their money because currency was constantly appreciating in terms of gold, while lands and commodities had been constantly declining in terms of currency. Hoyt, p.123

The action of credit in reverse.

One speculator, Samuel H. Walker, worth $15m in 1873, had lost the lot by 1877. In that year it was being frankly admitted that a return to pre-1874 property prices was highly unlikely, that the values then were probably the result of an hallucination. The decline in some Chicago land values was 90 per cent, the average about 50 per cent. Jay Cooke went on to extricate himself from the bankruptcy of his firm by judicious selling of his land holdings around Duluth, but never fully recovered his pre-1873 status (the vacuum he left was filled by J.P. Morgan). Cooke's Northern Pacific line was reconstituted and construction began once again, falling into the hands of Henry Villard in 1881; the land side of the company going on to employ some 800 land agents to assist immigration from all corners of the globe to add value to its land not already sold. Another cycle, same result.

An international perspective

THE 1873 panic and downturn was not just an American phenomenon. Railroad expansion was occurring everywhere, so too credit creation by the banks that financed it. There had been a number of European building booms: the opening of the Suez Canal in 1869 (which wrought huge economies of scale in shipping) and the excitement of German unification under Bismarck fed further extensive speculation by Europeans, the Germans in particular. The Vienna Stock Exchange experienced a panic on May 9, 1873, which spread to Germany, Italy, Holland and Belgium. The US September panic spread in a contagious fashion to England, France and finally Russia. A protracted economic slowdown followed for some years, extending into the 1890s. In 1875 Baron Carl Meyer von Rothschild was heard lamenting to friends the low stock prices everywhere: 'The whole world has become a city.'[29]

29 Kindleberger, p.121.

Scandals

THIS TIME swindles and frauds had been coming to light thick and fast before the peak year, and as usual continued well into the downturn. These are just some of them.

- *The Indian trading post scandal.* In 1875 William W. Belknap, Secretary of War, was impeached by Congress for allegedly accepting bribes from employees in the government Indian service in his role as seller of government trading posts in the west.
- *The whisky ring.* Exposed in 1875, it sold US-made whisky without excise tax, thereby defrauding the government of revenue. The gains, starting in about 1870, were estimated at over $2 m. An association of government revenue agents, politicians, grain dealers and distillers in St Louis, Milwaukee, Cincinnati and other cities were implicated, as was the President's private secretary, Orville E. Babcock. Two hundred men were indicted. The distillers would bribe government officials so that the taxes collected could be retained. The money was used to finance various political activities, thwart investigations and buy off investigating journalists.
- *The Dominican Republic fiasco.* In 1870 Buenaventura Baez, the dictator of this small republic, sought to sell his country to the United States. The President liked the idea, sending his private secretary to have a treaty signed. This actually took place but the Senate never ratified the treaty.
- *The New York customs rent scam.* A corrupt system whereby the customs house was granted a monopoly for the storage of imports, allowing the controller, Colonel Leet (personally appointed by the President), to charge one month's rent for just a day's storage on the wharf, surplus funds accruing to the Colonel.
- *The New York 'tweed ring'.* Busted on July 8, 1871.

  > William 'Boss' Tweed is exposed in a series of articles published in the *New York Times*. Tweed will be brought up on trial and held responsible for taking up to $200 million in fraudulent contracts, kickbacks and other corrupt practices which brought New York City to the verge of bankruptcy in six short years.
  >
  > www.pinzler.com/ushistory/timeline7.html

The administration of President Grant continued from one scandal to the next until the election of 1876 (itself the most corrupt in US history until recent events in 2000) replaced Grant with Rutherford Hayes.

The Deputy State Treasurer of New York, Charles Phelps, took off after the panic with $300,000 of the Treasury's funds. E.J. Blake, president of the Mercantile Bank of New York, was not so lucky. He was caught with the stolen bank funds still in his possession.

But there was some public morality remaining. By 1870 a good deal of gold coin circulated daily around Wall Street and central New York, carried by runners going to and from the clearing house to settle inter-bank debts. If a bag was accidentally dropped and fell open on the street, a crowd would form a circle round the runner so that he could recover all the coin – typically around $5,000 – and continue on his way.

One scandal in particular captivated the nation and reflected the age: the Henry Ward Beecher adultery trial of 1875. Beecher was a charismatic American preacher and reformer, born in Connecticut in 1813. By 1847 he was pastor of the new (Congregational) Plymouth Church in Brooklyn, where he drew large crowds speaking passionately about the causes of the day, such as slavery, taking mainly the middle ground. He was an advocate of women's suffrage and a believer in Darwin's theory of evolution. His political involvement was first with the Free-Soil Movement, then the Republican Party, though he was in general a man of liberal ideas. At the outbreak of the Civil War he helped raise funds for rifles to be sent to the Union front, the guns becoming known as Beecher's Bibles. After the war, so popular was he that the boats used to ferry his congregation over to Brooklyn came to be known as Beecher Boats. Beecher was not averse to appearing in newspaper advertisements endorsing the latest cure-all. So it came as a shock when, early in 1875, his protégé Theodore Tildon accused Beecher of having an affair with his wife, Elizabeth. The rumour mill and gossip columns went wild. Tildon, expelled from the church and denounced by its members, filed criminal charges. As the case came to court that summer hardly a dinner table in the country did not discuss the latest reports. Both sides engaged expensive lawyers, scalpers commanded the unheard of sum of five dollars for tickets to the trial and thousands were turned away daily from the court house.

Gossip about his sex life had in fact trailed Beecher for years. It seems probable he was guilty.

> When Beecher wooed Elizabeth Tildon, he assured her that their pure affection and high religious love would not damage her virtue as long as she kept it secret from outsiders who were not spiritually evolved enough to understand their relationship.
>
> Gail Collins, *Scorpion Tongues*, p.67

However, were the court to find him guilty, it would bring untold misery to the people of America and joy to 'every quarter where the wicked classes make their meetings and hold their gossips with a sneer and a smile.' The jury deadlocked nine to three for acquittal, ending the trial of the century without a verdict. Beecher held on to his pulpit and fame; Tildon emigrated to France while Elizabeth kept going to the church in Brooklyn as she had always done.

The focus of society is different at different times in the real estate cycle. In a downturn it is less likely to accept bad moral behaviour. During the upswing people are too busy making money to worry about anything else.

The Gilded Age

THE DECADE of the 1860s kicked off America's Gilded Age. Saul K. Padover described it this way:

> It was, and for the next half-century continued to be, an era of unrestrained capitalist enterprise and of ruthless exploitation of natural and human resources for private profit. It was an age of vast individual fortunes, piled up by a handful of entrepreneurs through the use of means and methods that shocked people accustomed to an earlier protestant ethic. Politicians on all levels were openly bought or controlled by the aggressive new capitalists who operated either as predatory speculators, as did Jim Fiske and Daniel Drew, or through monopolistic trusts and corporations, such as John D. Rockefeller's Standard Oil company ... The plutocracy, which controlled government as well as educational institutions and the media of opinion formation, lacked the characteristics of older aristocracies – personal taste and a sense of public responsibility. The magnates of whisky and sugar and cattle and timber and land despised politics and, except for personal charities, showed a monumental indifference to the social problems created by the industrial age they dominated. They equated politician with crook and, as a matter of course, acted accordingly. *The Genius of America*, p.221

Creative opportunity in this era was abundant, and it was everywhere. Though there was much corruption in business, there was much that was good too. Andrew Carnegie built his steel empire and farmers began to see the advantages of new machinery that would save them huge amounts of labour. Robber barons could be identified more in government than in business. Nowhere was this more true than in land grants. Some historians claim that the grants, a deliberate government subsidy, were the only way to get the lines built quickly, but the success of J.J. Hill's Great Northern Railway proves the fallacy of this argument. Hill's line received no grants, and never went bankrupt; there was no corruption. Many eminent authors have noted the connection between land and railroads. The English novelist Anthony Trollope, visiting at the time of the Civil War, wrote:

> Railroads are in fact companies combined for the purchase of land. They purchased land, looking to increase the value of it fivefold by opening of the railroad ... in this way ... thousands of miles of railroads in America have been opened. *North America*, Vol. I, p.143

Then, as soon as the location of the railroad had been determined:

> a town would be plotted, streets laid out and named for the heroes of the Civil War, and lots put on sale. Sakolski, *The Great American Land Bubble*, p.293

Government land grant subsidies went to those with the best political 'savvy', rarely to those with the best business acumen. This led to subsidies flowing into the lavishly styled mansions and prestigious expenditure that so characterised the gilded age. And there was worse to come. The grants fostered a government-granted licence, creating a monopoly railway line which might run from anywhere to nowhere. Feeder lines were discouraged for fear they might rake off the surrounding land value. A monopoly permits no competition, so freight rates were as high as the market could bear. Vanderbilt had control of the rail routes into and out of New York. Fiske and Gould used the Erie as their own personal treasury. The response was of course public pressure demanding that government do something about it; the result was yet more legislation and government interference in a market that could have operated well enough, as markets will do if ruled by the free interplay of supply and demand. Meanwhile profits mounted in companies that controlled the land. The over-building of railroad lines was the inevitable outcome – all part of the boom and subsequent bust. Said the now ageing Commodore: 'Building railroads from nowhere to nowhere is not a legitimate business.'[30]

Ernest Ray McCartney put it this way:

> Immediately following the close of the civil war, the United States suffered a short post-war depression which began in May 1865 and extended into April 1866 … After 1870 there was an upward turn in industrial activity … extended into the early part of 1873 … After the first quarter of 1873, industrial activity began to decline, cumulative financial difficulties appeared, followed by a panic in the middle of September, when a number of financial agents for railroads were forced into bankruptcy. A serious breakdown of the whole financial machinery resulted in New York. The influence of this crash spread to all of the important markets of the United States finally leaving practically no business or industry untouched. *The Crisis of 1873*, p.113

Why September this time? We have already noted the seasonal tendency towards monetary tightness in the late summer and early fall that was a characteristic of the economy at this stage. It appears the harvest may have been earlier than usual in 1873.

Land sales peaked in 1869. Railroad stocks, according to McCartney's index of data, peaked in May 1871, the month *before* interest rates on prime commercial paper bottomed in New York, at 4.85 per cent, in June 1871, the stock market correctly discounting lower earnings in future years, pricing in the information beforehand. (Graphs 8.1 and 8.2, page 168.)

Interest rates peaked with the panic in October 1873. This was thirty years (362 months actually) from the August 1843 interest rate low, the halfway point between them being the 1858 low.

As a result of the panic of 1873, a bitter antagonism developed between workers and the leaders of banking, railroads and industry. Labour unrest, with mass strikes, was the general rule for several decades. On occasions federal troops were brought in to break the strikes. A land and rail monopoly was acceptable; striking workers were not.

30 Holbrook, *The Age of the Moguls*, p.55.

Graph 8.1: Public Land Sales 1800-80

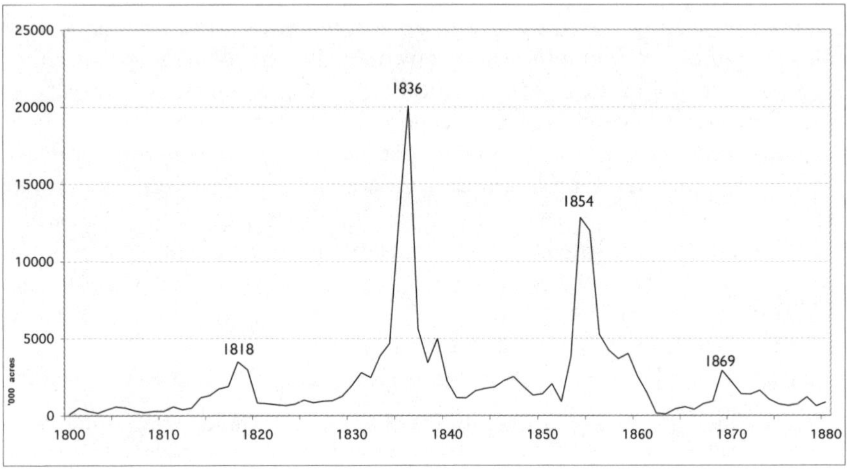

Sources: Smith and Cole, *Fluctuations in American Business, 1790-1860*, Harvard University Press, 1935, Appendix D. After 1860 from McCartney, *Crisis of 1873*, Table XXV, p.131.

Graph 8.2: Interest Rates prime commercial paper in New York, and US railroads stock index 1866-81

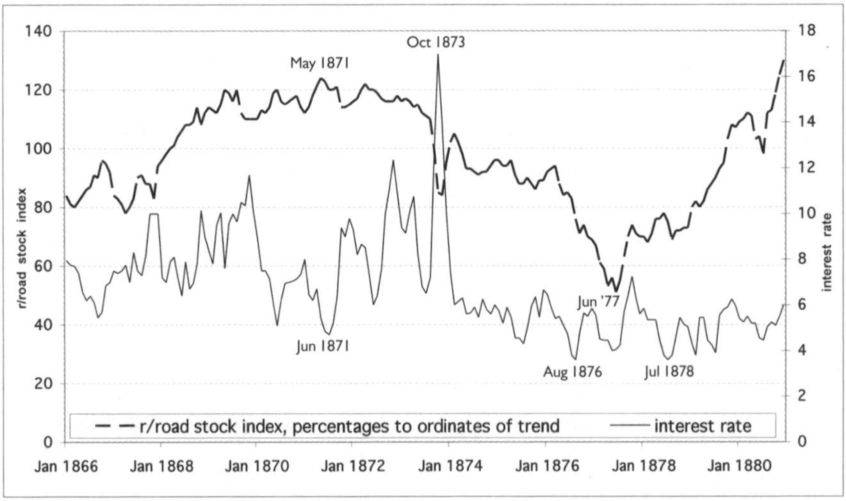

Source: McCartney, *Crisis of 1873*, Tables xxxvi, lviii

'Nothing in the nineteenth century is more remarkable', wrote Galbraith, 'than the way men forgot the last railroad debacle and proceeded to lose money in the next.'[31] But perhaps it made sense at the time. The largess extended to rail companies by both state and federal governments was stupendous in anyone's language. US citizens desirous of a piece of their country's real estate to call home had to pay around $1.25 per acre. The rails received some 100m acres for free. At $20 an acre, to which a good deal of the land rose quickly once the lines were laid, it grew into a half-million-dollar grant per mile of track built. For Jay Cooke's Northern Pacific that represented a return of $1.1bn on an outlay of about $100m,[32] which the bondholders paid anyway. That's enough to dull anyone's memory.

What the newspapers were saying…

> Only a few months ago we were promised abundance of prosperity and good times, and it has turned out just the opposite.
>
> *New York Commercial Advertiser*, October 7, 1873

The fear:

> Famine and bankruptcy stare the nation in the face. Want is beginning to press all classes, and will come more threateningly as the winter closes.
>
> *Albany New York Argus*, October 28, 1873

Politicians have other agendas:

> 'Our manufacturers are increasing with wonderful rapidity. They give employment and support to hundreds of thousands of people.'
>
> President Grant, quoted in *New York World*, December 1, 1873

Blame the government:

> Under the policy of this administration the financial world is in a state of disorganization and bankruptcy. These are the promised blessings which were to flow from the President's re-election. How do you like it?
>
> *Albany New York Argus*, November 4, 1873

> Republican misgovernment and misrule have brought upon us the financial troubles that now afflict so terribly all parts of the country.
>
> *Baltimore Gazette*, November 4, 1873

> The Democratic Party caused these hard times.
>
> *New York Daily Graphic*, October 27, 1876

Blame anything except the speculation in government-granted licences and privileges:

> The financial disturbance has been brought about by the trade unionists.
>
> *New York Journal of Commerce*, December 29, 1873

31 *Money: Whence it Came, Where it Went*, p.105.
32 Henry George, *Our Land and Land Policy*, p.9.

> Women's extravagance bears a large portion of the responsibility.
>
> *Carthage Illinois Gazette*, January 26, 1874

Spare a thought for the fairer sex:

> The present crisis is having a most disastrous effect upon the nervous system of the ladies. Something can be done to alleviate their lot. Let the press omit the fashion department.
>
> Letter to the editor, *New York Daily Graphic*, October, 20 1873

> Mrs. Jones says that a woman should have two husbands 'these times', for one man can't keep a woman respectably. *New York Star*, August 3, 1874

FURTHER READING

Chancellor, Edward. *Devil Take the Hindmost: A History of Financial Speculation*. Papermac edition, 2000.

Foldvary, Prof. Fred E. *Ground Rent Seeking in US Economic History* (available at www.foldvary.net/works/seeking.html).

George, Henry. *Our Land and Land Policy*. National and State, White and Hauer, 1871.

Licht, Walter. *Working for the Railroad*. Princeton University Press, 1983.

McCartney, Ernest Ray. *The Crisis of 1873*. UMI books on demand (originally published 1935).

Medbury, James K. *Men and Mysteries of Wall Street*. Ann Arbor: University Microfilms (reprint based on 1878 edition published in New York by R. Worthington).

Padover, Saul K. *The Genius of America: Men Whose Ideas Shaped our Civilisation*. McGraw-Hill Book Company, Inc.

Raimondo, Justin. *An Enemy of the State: The life of Murray N. Rothbard*. Prometheus Books, 2000.

Robbins, Roy M. *Our Landed Heritage, The Public Domain 1776-1936*. University of Nebraska Press, 1962 edition.

Sobel, Robert. *Panic on Wall Street: A History of America's Financial Disasters*. Collier Books edition, 1972.

Wicker, Elmus. *Banking Panics of the Gilded Age*. Cambridge University Press, 2000.

NOTE

Readers may like to consider the following link to a policy statement from Abraham Lincoln detailing his view about the effectiveness of government creation of money: www.businesscycles.biz/docs/lincolnpolicy.htm. Lincoln wrote it after the Civil War and just a few weeks before his assassination on April 14, 1865. Some say this was not coincidence.

9

160 Acres or 6 Feet

The Land Boom of 1888

There has never been a time in our history when work was so abundant, or when wages were as high, whether measured by the currency in which they are paid, or by the power to supply the necessaries and comforts of life.

Outgoing President Benjamin Harrison,
in his final message to Congress, January 1893

THE 1873 DOWNTURN lasted four to five years; it probably felt like a lifetime to those hardest hit – the workers, the poor and those who came late to the party, between 1870 and 1873. But the cycle always turns – eventually.

> The prices of raw materials, the wages of labour, the rents of houses and stores, and the interest rates for capital advances having been reduced to an extremely low level by 1877, it became a favourable time to expand manufacturing operations to replenish depleted stocks.
>
> Homer Hoyt, *One Hundred Years of Land Values in Chicago*, p.128

In Chicago the interest rate on loans, if you offered good security, had roughly halved, favouring the building of dwellings.

> Population was about to catch up with the supply of houses, the resumption of specie payments was not far away, and the motive for hoarding money was disappearing. The telephone had been invented and Edison was about to demonstrate his electric light.
>
> Hoyt, p.127

It was in 1881 that electricity was introduced to New York. Not everyone was at first taken with the idea of an invisible and deadly power source, and when electric light bulbs went on sale the *New York Times* warned that they might cause blindness.[1] Edison maintained a winter home and additional laboratory at Fort Myers, Florida. The story goes that, as electric light began gaining popularity, he offered his assistance in

1 *The Economist*, November 10, 2001.

introducing a street lighting system to the town. The locals declined his offer, however, believing that the lights would keep the citizens – and the livestock – awake all night.[2]

Table 9.1: Business Failures

Year	Per 10,000 firms	Year	Per 10,000 firms
1870	83	1876	142
1871	64	1877	139
1872	81	1878	158
1873	105	1879	95
1874	104	1880	63
1875	128		

In Chicago, a good harvest in 1878 and the confidence engendered by the resumption of specie payments in 1879 gave the rise in land values its initial impetus.

> Rising prices and profit margins speeded up production, increased employment, and furnished the funds for a brief era of speculation that culminated in 1883.
>
> Hoyt, p.128

The years 1883/4 – our mid-cycle slowdown once again. About 1884, Charles Dow, in his studies on business conditions, reported:

> The year 1884 brought a Stock Exchange smash but not a commercial crisis. The failure of the Marine Bank, Metropolitan Bank and Grant & Ward in May was accompanied by a large fall in prices and a general check which was felt throughout the year. The Trunk Line war [a battle between two of the largest railroads for supremacy of the region they served], which had lasted for several years, was one of the factors in this period.
>
> William Peter Harrison, *The Stock Market Barometer*, p.27

Grant and Ward was a stockbroking concern that closed its doors on May 6, 1884 as a result of a failed Ponzi-type fraud by one of its directors, Ferdinand Ward, who later received a ten-year jail sentence. The firm had been prestigious; Grant was the son of former President Ulysses S. Grant. The failure pulled down an associated bank, the Marine National, which had been lending to Ward. A week later John C. Eno, the president of another bank, the Second National, made off with some $4m of the bank's money. He fled to Canada, a popular destination for such runners at the time. A wave of stock-selling resulted, culminating in a panic sell-off on May 14, but a rescue operation mounted by a consortium of banks at the New York Clearing House successfully reversed the situation. The panic did not get further than Wall Street.

2 Stephen J. Flynn, *Florida: Land of Fortune*, Van Rees Press, New York, 1962.

Public land sales continued strongly throughout 1884 and further into the decade (see the chart on public land sales, 1800-1900, page 193). When a loss of confidence in a downturn does not involve bank credit, created and loaned against land value, a stock market sell-off is easier to 'manage' by the appropriate authorities. In the meantime John Eno's father mounted a rescue operation of his own and repaid his son's stolen millions.

We might note in passing that the 19th century was generally a century of deflation. Prices in 1896 were lower than half a century before. Inflation is not the prime cause of business cycles.

The New York Stock Exchange had its first million-share day on May 5, 1886, two years after the events of 1884. During these years big changes were being forced on the travelling public as railroad companies attempted to get time standardised. Previously every town had kept its own time. When it was noon in New York City it was 11.35am in Pittsburgh, making train scheduling difficult. A train sometimes arrived at a station earlier than it had left the previous one. Since 1872 there had been attempts to find a solution. On November 18, 1883 the railroads adopted the idea of William F. Allen for four time zones: Eastern, Central, Mountain and Pacific, assuming that the prime meridian ran through Greenwich in England. The Attorney General ruled that congressional approval would be required to change time, and clergymen were furious because they felt the prime meridian ought to run through Bethlehem – 'God's time, not Vanderbilt's.' The French were livid. But the rail companies stuck to their decision and Congress settled the matter the following year.[3]

Another change was taking place: men were shaving. Beards were out, clean-shaven faces were in.

Chicago

IN CHICAGO, recovery was underway:

> With the return of a more prosperous time after 1879 ... a large number of labourers, employed full time, began to accumulate small amounts of capital. Thus in all ranks of society surplus funds were accumulating or were being made available for investment. To attract this surplus, Chicago real estate was in an advantageous position. As compared with other forms of investment in 1879 it seemed to offer the highest rate of return compatible with safety ... the failure of practically all the savings banks in Chicago by 1877 had caused labourers to avoid them as places for depositing their savings.
>
> Hoyt, p.130

A real estate broker of the time said:

> 'Good crops and business activity call for larger stores and warehouses and the rise in rents of such buildings increases their value. The men engaged

3 *American Heritage*, July/August, 2001.

> in business want, as they make money, to live better, to move from small houses in downtown streets into their own houses in more fashionable locations. This makes a demand first for small uptown residences, then for larger ones, then for palaces. This starts the builders and their demand for vacant land increases the price for vacant land where the street improvements are completed, and this finally starts the value of land not yet ready for building, and speculation follows.' Hoyt, p.132

Of course it was not the same for all sites in Chicago: some did better than others. And in this cycle there were some features relevant only to Chicago:

- *George Pullman* decided to locate his huge 'carworks' (making railroad sleeper carriages) on the outskirts of Chicago. Just where he would choose was a burning question: huge crowds of brokers and newspapermen followed him round to see if they could find out. Wisely, Pullman publicly inspected one area but secretly bought in another. When the works were completed in 1883, nearby land rose in value by 500 to 1,000 per cent.
- *'Flat fever.'* The building of apartments became popular, 'flat fever' being the name given to the new craze. The new apartments appealed to many housewives: the family could now live on just one floor, requiring fewer servents and less furniture, with the added bonus of having heating requirements taken care of by the janitor. So here is a more intensive use of residential land, increasing its value. Some of the apartments even had porcelain bathtubs. Other cities soon caught on.
- *The World's Fair*, celebrating the 400th anniversary of Columbus's voyage, came to Chicago in 1893. Its effect on land values was like today's Olympics – one reason such events are sought. The impact of the fair should not be underestimated. It was promoted as the biggest event of its type in history. Every day of the two years prior, two or three thousand promotional packages were mailed to all parts of the globe inviting participation. Posters could be seen at almost every European railway station. Water treatment plants with a capacity of 64 million gallons a day were built to handle drainage and the needs of 6,500 toilets. A steam plant generating 24,000 horsepower was constructed to supply electricity.[4] Ebullience peaked during a massive building programme, which included a moving sidewalk and a Ferris wheel (erected by George Ferris). And it was at this fair that the hamburger was introduced to America.

The Chicago 'wire store' fraud was uncovered around this time. The wire store was the place where a suitably connected con man could bet on a winning horse, secure in the knowledge that the result of the race, delivered by Western Union wire, was being delayed. The film *The Sting* made the operation famous, though the movie was set in the 1930s.

4 See www.users.vnet.net/schulman/Columbian/Columbian.html

The story elsewhere

IN 1874 another sort of wire was patented: barbed wire, invented by Joseph Glidden. Cheap and long-lasting, it was proving great fencing material; eventually it fenced off much of the plains as wild buffalo were being hunted to extinction (led by Buffalo Bill, ostensibly to kill off Indian food supplies). Agriculture and ranching took over; free-range land was quickly turned into private pasture. Within a couple of years Glidden was selling 80 million pounds of wire a year with the slogan 'As light as air, stronger than whisky and cheaper than dirt'.[5]

In 1877 Congress passed the Desert Land Act, legislation not dissimilar to that passed at the comparable point in each previous cycle. This Act, though, had a special history. The bill was promoted by California's Senator Sargent, acting on behalf of Haggin and Tevis, two wealthy San Francisco tycoons.

> Congress approved the Desert Land Act, the bill signed by President Grant in the last days of his administration. The law removed several hundred thousand acres from settlement under the Homestead Act. These lands, alleged to be worthless desert, were to be sold in 640-acre sections to any individual who promised to provide irrigation. The price was 25 cents per acre down, with an additional $1 per acre to be paid after reclamation.
>
> Fred E. Foldvary, *Ground Rent Seeking in US Economic History*, p.11

A good deal of this land, located close to the Kern River and already partially settled, was being eyed by Haggin and Tevis. A *San Francisco Chronicle* story of 1877 describes what happened next:

> The President's signature was not dry on the cunningly devised enactment before Boss Carr [Haggin and Tevis's agent in the valley] and his confederates were advised from Washington that the breach was open. It was Saturday, the 31st of March. The applications were in readiness, sworn and subscribed by proxies – All that Saturday night and the following Sunday, the clerks in the Land Office were busy recording and filing the bundles of applications dumped upon them by Boss Carr, although it was not until several days after that the office was formally notified of the approval of the Desert Land Act.

By hiring a swag of dummy entry-men and vagabonds to make phoney claims for 640 acres, and then

> by transferring those claims to themselves, Haggin and Tevis were able to acquire title to approximately 150 square miles of valley land before anybody else in California had even heard of the Desert Land Act. In the process, they dislodged settlers who had not yet perfected their titles under old laws and who were caught unawares by the new one. *The Chronicle*

5 Stewart H. Holbrook, *The Age of the Moguls*, p.145.

called the whole manoeuvre an 'atrocious villainy' and demanded return of the stolen lands. A federal investigation followed, but Haggin and Tevis, as usual, emerged triumphant... Peter Barnes, *The Great American Land Grab*, Part 4

Rothbard reports[6] that the 1880s went on to become the most prosperous decade of any in the US, before or since (but possibly eclipsed by the 1990s, another deflationary era). It may have been prosperous, but amongst whom were the spoils divided? The working conditions of the poor remained arduous. Prices were generally falling, however, and wages increasing. The trend on long-term interest rates had been down since the 1870s, but with prices falling the real rate of return was higher, benefiting savers and lenders and helping to maintain capital investment. The country was very busy making money – except perhaps the farmers.

Underlying apparent prosperity was the same set of circumstances: expansion of the money supply and cheap credit, some of which, as always, was finding its way into the purchase of government-granted licences and privileges. Plus, of course, that old US standard, the legislative demands of vested interests, round which the US political system seems uniquely built.

Falling prices are not necessarily either good or bad, but they have different consequences for different social classes, in particular for those who owe and those who have money. Where land price is permitted to capitalise into a tradable commodity, farmers will almost always be owers of money. Before they can start farming they will usually have been to the bank for a loan to buy land or seed and equipment, or both. In a deflationary era there is no price inflation to help chip away at what you owe. Falling prices for farm produce would not have helped either, though this does not have to mean farming was unprofitable. Farmers' actions during this era, however, betray their feelings. They were keen agitators for inflationary policies, as debtors always are. By about 1890 they aligned themselves with the growing force of the silver miners to demand the remonetisation of silver. This had important implications for the 1893 panic. But first we need some background about the so-called 'Crime of 1873', which impacted heavily on the economics and politics of the time.

Silver: the Crime of 1873

IT COULD BE said that economic history is the story of the debtor class versus the creditor class. The creditor class will always win. Once you borrow money you surrender a degree of your autonomy to the lender. A loan must be repaid.

The US has used both silver and gold to back its dollar currency (when specie backing was not suspended) and minted both, though gold

6 Murray N. Rothbard, *History of Money and Banking in the United States*.

had become more important. All nations were doing this, backing their currencies with specie, but in 1867 leading European states met in Paris and agreed to ditch silver and rely only on gold. In 1871 France and Germany were at war. As victors the Germans proceeded to inflict upon France extraordinarily heavy war reparations. The French did actually pay the bill – in gold – and this the Germans used to finance a new gold standard for themselves. Neighbouring countries feared what might happen; a few smart bankers in the US *knew* what would happen, and acted accordingly. Eastern industrialists and US bankers wanted a continued gold standard: it was solid and good for business. The flood of European silver was certain to make silver much cheaper on the market than at the mint – where anyone could take their silver and have it minted at 371 pure grains and receive back one silver dollar. You could do the same with gold, 23.5 grains getting you one gold dollar. This meant a legally defined ratio of gold to silver of 16 to 1. If the US government held that ratio and the price of silver was cheaper on the market than at the mint, one would naturally mint one's silver and buy and hoard gold. The supply of gold coins would disappear.

Gold and silver had uses other than just being minted into coin; there was also an industrial market for these metals. If the market ratio of gold to silver changed, as it did occasionally, either more silver or more gold would end up in the mint. This is what was about to happen, but on a much larger scale than ever before. Another classic example of how national politics is susceptible to the influence of vested interests at the expense of far better economics.

In 1873, the year of the previous downturn, it became apparent to those in the US who were watching that silver was about to undergo a radical revaluation downwards. But, as circumstance would have it, large silver deposits had just been uncovered (mostly on land set aside for Indian reservations) in Nevada and other areas out west, increasing supply. To avoid silver piling up at the mint and gold flowing out to be hoarded, an Act of Congress was quietly passed to stop the minting of silver dollars; another ruled that silver coins above five dollars in value would not be legal tender. A crime? Those who wanted to retain silver as legal tender thought so and called it 'the Crime of 1873'.

J.K. Galbraith states[7] that it was the English financier Ernest Seyd who bribed Congress to pass this legislation and that the crime was soon taken to be the result of a (notably Jewish) bankers' conspiracy. If you plug the name Seyd into Google you will find a whole swathe of Jewish banking conspiracy theories. Most of this stems from a complete ignorance of the capitalisation of land rent into a tradable government-granted licence; being a value used by credit creation agencies to then lend against. Conspiracy theorists will tell you that banks deliberately expand and

7 *Money, Whence it Came, Where it Went*, p.98.

contract loans to bring on the cycle, but clearly banks themselves do better in boom times and would, if they could, have the upside of the cycle continue indefinitely.

There is a monetary consideration that needs to be grasped here too. The silver forces saw a 'hard money' way of increasing the US money supply and reserve against which banks might lend, with the US government maintaining the 16 to 1 silver/gold ratio – a policy of currency inflation. They agitated for retention of this ratio at government level. And this is precisely what the US got, first in 1878 with the Bland-Allison Act. This mandated the US government to purchase a minimum of $2m per month of silver from the silver mining corporations, to be minted into silver coin and such silver coin to be restored as legal tender. The victory was only partial, however, as paper notes were still to be backed by gold only. This was an attempt by government to prop up the price of silver artificially (at the 16 to 1 ratio price of $1.29 per ounce), against free market forces. As hard as a government might try, and many do, it is a battle a government cannot win. Market forces always triumph in the end.

With increasing prosperity through the 1880s, little more was heard about silver until the storms and droughts at the end of the decade reversed farmers' accumulation of profits (or their ability to pay off the mortgage). To recover lost profits, a farmer did what seemed sensible and increased production the following year, as his neighbour was doing, putting further downward pressure on prices. Silver miners found ready allies in indebted farmers and pushed for relief. Congress didn't fail them. The Sherman Silver Purchase Act of 1890 required the Treasury Department to purchase 4.5 million ounces of silver per month (that's 281,250 pounds, which just happened to approximate the entire monthly production of the silver mines). The Treasury would not this time coin it, but would issue new treasury notes, redeemable in either gold or silver at the discretion of the Treasury Secretary. This policy would lead to the probable expansion of bank credit. The Act was a trade-off: the silver forces declared their support for the import tariff demanded by eastern manufacturers in return for relief on the silver question. US economic history reveals the levying of one protective tariff after another, mostly by Republican administrations, designed to shield US manufacturers from overseas competition in home markets. They are still at it.

A comment in *The Farmers' Alliance* of August 23, 1890 sums up what indebted farmers would have been feeling:

> 'There are three great crops raised in Nebraska. One is a crop of corn, one a crop of freight rates and one a crop of interest. One is produced by the farmers, who by sweat and toil farm the land. The other two are produced by men who sit in their offices and behind their bank counter and farm the farmers.'
>
> Quoted in John D. Hicks, *The Populist Revolt*, p.85

We will come back to the silver question soon, but note in passing that popular remedies to economic problems are rarely remedies, merely ideas to satisfy vested interest groups whose problems are often a land question.

Westward expansion

EXPANSION WESTWARDS continued apace. The propaganda campaign by railroad companies in Europe and new farming equipment coming onto the market brought the largest ever mass movement of people and goods in the history of frontier settlement between 1870 and 1890. In this twenty-year period 225 million additional acres was put under cultivation for the first time.[8] Windmills were improved, allowing plains winds to bring water to the surface for livestock and irrigation. Grain drills, cord binders and the steam thresher meant one farmer could plant and harvest 135 acres of wheat instead of a mere 7 acres. One must remember that such productivity gains feed ultimately into the value of government-granted licences, especially land value. Some gain may flow to the inventor (McCormack and his farm equipment is an excellent example, though his profit had much to do with his business acumen), but never into higher wages for the labourer. In a land-enclosed society wages will tend to the least workers are prepared to accept.

By 1880 Kansas and Nebraska were fully settled; westward movement was into the central and northern Great Plains areas of the Dakota Territory, then into Wyoming and Montana. This left just one region remaining to be settled: Oklahoma, known as the Indian Territory.

Into the peak

MANY US cities, including Los Angeles, Seattle, Kansas City, Omaha, Duluth and Minneapolis, were now experiencing land booms, most reaching their peak in 1887 or just after. Often they were in anticipation of the arrival of the railroad, always expected to bring lasting prosperity. What a town got, of course, was massive land speculation, then a spectacular bust. Chicago's land boom continued a little longer for special reasons including railroad and manufacturing growth, the World's Fair, the growth of department stores and the advent of the skyscraper.

The use of steel frames in buildings made what came to be called skyscrapers possible, the development being a huge boost to building and real estate generally. At first, at least in Chicago, the upper floors of nine-story buildings were avoided by tenants, but after a thirteen-story building went up, demonstrating the 'advantages' of abundant air and light, popularity increased with the height of the building. Not everyone was happy though. Speculators wanting to see the city expand horizontally rather than vertically pushed for height limits but, as we have seen since, 'in spite of

8 R.A. Billington, *The Westward Movement in the United States*, p.82.

[the] apparent lack of need for more office space, great structures were erected.'[9] Businesses sought to enhance their prestige

> by having an office in these popular skyscrapers. Doctors and dentists found that it paid to have an office in high buildings near the State Street stores. Department stores discovered that people preferred to ascend in elevators rather than walk a block to a side street. Hoyt, p.152

Chicago was enjoying a boom, captured in all its glory in 'bizarre and grandiose conceptions' on drawing-boards for the upcoming World's Fair. Ebullience was at a peak. Hoyt reports that, as the land boom in the aforementioned cities started to peter out, 'veteran operators' moved in on Chicago in expectation of the forthcoming fair. Optimism prevailed.

> Tales of profits in real estate already made by their neighbours circulated amongst the residents of local communities and aroused their desire to use these accumulating funds for the purchase of Chicago land. Hoyt, p.162

A desire cultivated and enhanced by professional promoters. When one particular sale of a city lot smashed all previous records, the effect was to convince other Chicago real estate owners that they had 'hitherto undervalued their property'. Hoyt has some wonderful descriptions of the Chicago crowd of the late 1880s as their emotions carried them away.

> The majority of buyers … ran in crowds to the spot where the most rapid rises were taking place and where land values were highest – they were influenced by rumours that were circulating everywhere. p.164

> A majority of the purchases were made with a down payment of not over one-fourth of the total price, the buyer expecting to sell before he was called on for his second payment. p.164

> Again it was pointed out that it was a dangerous game to pay for more than the intrinsic value of the property in the expectation that someone else could be found who would pay still more. p.165

> Early in 1889, thousands of labourers and clerks pooled their savings and formed syndicates to purchase suburban acre tracts. Even servant girls, seamstresses and women clerks have caught the fever, put their savings into a lump sum and become joint owners of suburban property. Kindled by stories of large profits, they believe it is impossible to pay too much. p.165

Who says history doesn't repeat? The secret in forecasting, however, is to know not whether it repeats, but how. The repeat can never be exactly the same of course, but repeat it will, within the context of the times. A simple example is to compare the Chicago boom of 1836, when riders went on horseback through the streets shouting out the news of land sales, with 1853, when buyers were taken to the new subdivisions in omnibuses,

9 Hoyt, p.151.

and 1890, when trains were being used for the purpose. By this time real estate agents and newspaper advertising were spreading the message of impending sales and subdivisions. A mere decade later one enterprising real estate salesman put the recently introduced telephone directory to good use. Soon women were being employed to 'go diligently through stores, shops and factories' to 'tell wonderful stories about [land] values.'[10] In Florida by 1926 the women would not be walking through stores but reclining semi-naked on beaches. But the message was always the same, only the medium was different.

As the US headed into the 1890s, a number of problems were stirring beneath the seeming prosperity. Though railroad construction and expansion was continuing, often frenetically, it was still mostly financed by bankers underwriting and issuing bonds – i.e. debt financed. There is nothing wrong with this, it can be a profitable use of money; however construction was not always undertaken with revenue in mind. Railroads were the first major listed enterprises that saw ownership – by shareholders – divorced from those involved in day-to-day operations – the directors. So the operations were not always in the owner's best interests, even less in the interests of bondholders. There were no reporting requirements, and no accounting in some instances. The Central Pacific, that ran through California to connect with the Union Pacific and join east to west, was built by the Contract and Finance Company in the manner of the Credit Mobilier: they 'lost' their books just prior to a government enquiry into their activity.[11]

It was not unusual for lines to be built in areas already well served, solely to allow a buyout by the other line and so preserve the monopoly. Some directors were busier planning their next on-market manipulation rather than tending to earnings and profitability (some might say no different to what happens today). Commodore Vanderbilt's son, who ran the railway empire left to him by his father and successfully doubled its value to $200m, was asked by a reporter whether he ought to take more interest in his customers and the travelling public. 'The public be damned,' was his reply.

Railroad companies found plenty of ways to remain influential, the issue of free passes being one of them. Newspaper editors, public officials and their families, members of state legislatures and even the judges hearing cases against the rail companies often travelled on free passes.[12]

Rail lines were known to have been built in wilderness areas merely to secure the land for promoters, or additional track laid to win a federal subsidy in land. By 1890 rate wars were eating into earnings on some trunk lines and railroad debts were once again building. The Northern Pacific – Jay Cooke's old line – was finally completed in 1883 at a cost of some

10 Hoyt, p.443.
11 Holbrook, p.122.
12 Frank B. Latham, *The Panic of 1893*, p.14.

$70m, construction being financed by the sale of bonds. By 1930 sales of land given it by the government amounted to around $136m, money that went to the promoters and shareholders. Even in 1939, 15.8 million acres of its land grant remained to be sold.

The US government found itself with a continuing surplus of funds after a prosperous decade and rising tariff receipts. Congress in 1890, under the Harrison administration, found plenty of ways to spend it. The 'Billion Dollar Congress', as it was dubbed, sanctioned additional spending on extensive internal improvements, military hardware to build up the navy, and pensions for Civil War veterans unable to work on account of war injuries (and there were many, the Civil War being renowned for the sometimes needless amputation of injured limbs). The Harrison administration was elected in 1888 after vast sums of money had been spent to buy votes, particularly in states where a close contest had been anticipated, such as Indiana and New York. It has been suggested that the government giveaways were thinly disguised programmes to further enrich wealthy industrialists. Whatever the truth, fifteen or more years into the cycle the surplus was being distributed.

By 1890, 29 per cent of US farms were mortgaged – even more in the mid-western plains. Kansas lands were mortgaged to 45 per cent of value, Minnesota 44 per cent, Montana 41 per cent.[13] Only in good times is such an interest burden supportable.

The 1890 US census revealed that, for the first time, the majority of Americans no longer lived or worked on the farm, they were in towns and cities. Around this time Frederick Jackson Turner made a soon-to-be-famous speech on 'The Significance of the Frontier in American History'. He pointed out that the US western land frontier was now almost closed. The government give-away of land was about to cease.

> Throughout the 1860s, 1870s and 1880s, the frontier had been advancing westward. It was not just a name but a specific geographical definition. It means land occupied by two or more but less than six persons, on average, per square mile. By 1890 it was gone – there were no more areas which corresponded to this definition.
>
> Paul Johnson, *A History of the American People*, p.523

Those seeking land and a fortune could not but have been aware of this. It would have added to the desperation of those hoping to get a bit of what was left to call their own. The 'Sooners' were massing.

Towards the end of the 1880s, Commissioner Sparks of the United States Public Land Office (one of very few incorruptible commissioners according to historian Alfred Chandler) reported:

> 'The near approach of a time when the United States will have no land to dispose of has stimulated the exertions of speculators and promoters to

13 See www.eh.net/encyclopedia

> acquire outlying regions of public lands in mass, by whatever means, legal or illegal.'
> Chandler, p.510

Speculators made great efforts to have the incorruptible Sparks removed from office; they eventually succeeded.

The 'Sooners'

APRIL 22, 1889 dawned bright and clear upon the hordes of people that had massed at the 300-mile perimeter of the Indian lands of Oklahoma, lands now being opened up to white settlement for the first time. At the stroke of noon, by presidential decree, any US citizen would be permitted to enter the territory and seek a 160-acre lot of unclaimed land. Twelve thousand plots had been made available. You just had to be the first there and then register your ownership at the nearest federal land office. Fifty thousand people waited impatiently at the Arkansas and Texas borders of the Indian Territory to do just that.

Since the Civil War the land had been used to create a reservation for the Plains Indians and other tribes displaced from their ancestral homes. The region was now considered the best 'unoccupied' land in the nation. Crowds had been gathering for weeks along the border; towns had sprung up overnight as people camped out at strategic entry points. '160 acres or 6 feet, and I don't give a damn which,' was the cry of those demanding land, and best sums up the lawlessness of the days and nights that led into April 22. At noon buglers stationed at intervals along the border sounded reveille and all hell broke loose. There was a great surge forward as men on horseback, families in covered wagons and passengers in trains packed to absolute capacity (ordered to go no faster than 15 miles per hour, considered to be the average speed of a man on horseback) hastened to claim the best site they could find before someone else did. The first great Oklahoma land rush was on.

In theory the entry of all citizens was to have been supervised by US cavalry forces, but by nightfall it was clear that more than a few had jumped the gun and were already settled in the region. Such persons earned the name 'Sooners'. Many were to challenge these claim-jumpers, but without great success as often the 'Sooners' were there legally as persons put in charge to supervise the rush.

There were more land rushes in the years following – 1891, 1893, 1901 and 1911 – though in the last two a lottery system was used. On the eve of the first rush the *New York Herald* had observed: 'men will fight harder for $500 worth of land than they will for $10,000 in money'. As the sun set on April 22, Oklahoma station, a previously isolated rail stop, had become a tent city of some ten thousand new inhabitants. The outpost of Guthrie, previously just a few huts housing soldiers and rail staff, was now a town of 15,000 citizens.

Shocks into the peak

THERE WERE a number of shocks in the lead-up to 1893. (Just possibly this gave false comfort to those who believed the US economy could take anything, helping to entrench a 'buy the dips' mentality.) On November 20, 1890 Baring Brothers Bank stunned the English market by suspending operations. The 1st Baron Revelstoke, Edward (Ned) Baring, had promoted and bought a few too many Argentine bonds in a declining market. This was a tad embarrassing for the English as it was in this bank that the Queen had deposited all her money and a good many of the family jewels. Only a vast shipment of gold from French banks saved Barings (and the Royal family) from complete ruin. (Nick Leeson will make a better demolition effort a century later.) Other British investors began selling good US stocks to carry bad Latin American loans, resulting in some financial stress in New York, short of a banking panic. It did mean, though, that finance for further railroad expansion was now harder to procure.

A downturn seemed imminent, but nature (or was it God?) came to the rescue. A much better US wheat crop proved handy as the grain crop in Russia failed. US wheat exports to this region greatly improved the gold position of the US in 1891/2, a buoyancy in which England and Europe did not participate. (Famine in Russia was to cost hundreds of thousands of lives.) However, the boost to the US economy proved short-lived.

Events led to a 'money stringency' (a phrase used by historians to describe the time) – in other words a sharp curtailment of credit, though nothing like earlier banking panics. Interestingly, the stock market had been declining between May and October 1890, a decline that was greater than the disturbance the news of the Barings collapse brought on. Insiders must already have been aware of other problems looming.

We can now return to the silver question. The history books tell us something about the impact of the Silver Acts, especially after 1890. The country's silver and paper circulation increased dramatically between 1879 and 1894. O.M.W. Sprague notes that between January 1891 and June 1893 there was an increase of $68m in the estimated amount of money in circulation. 'The low rates for loans were a clear indication that the banks would have been glad to lend more than the demand of borrowers made possible.'[14] In other words credit was easy and there were plenty of funds for speculation. Unemployment was low and the country seemed prosperous, as it always will when awash with paper money. To take advantage of the credit expansion 163 new national banks were founded in 1892. On the last day of the year, R.G. Dun & Company's *Weekly Review* noted: 'The most prosperous year ever known in business closes today with strongly favourable indications for the future.'[15] The outgoing President, Benjamin Harrison told Congress in January 1893: 'There has never been

14 Sprague, *History of Crises under the National Banking System*, p.158.
15 Quoted in Otto C. Lightner, *The History of Business Depressions*, p.188.

a time in our history when work was so abundant, or when wages were as high.'[16] 'The sun shines brightest at midday,' said W.D. Gann.

We have seen how the US government, under pressure from vested interests, had mandated by law that the silver to gold ratio was to stay at 16 to 1, despite the fact that Mr Market indicated otherwise: that the value of silver was declining relative to gold, the ratio by 1893 being almost 32 to 1. The buying power of silver had in fact halved. If you owned silver, you could take it to the mint and receive the equivalent face value in treasury notes, which you could then immediately redeem in gold. Thus silver flowed into the treasury, gold flowed out. The US government was advertising its notes as redeemable in gold. How long would the government's store of gold last? That was the question on Wall Street.

You were on a certain winner if you had a contracted debt payable in 'coin', not specifying gold. The government was giving its official imprimatur to a silver coin containing 371¼ grains of silver being worth one dollar when the market was saying it was worth just over fifty cents.

Government support in buying silver created a glut of the commodity. Such policies are still practised today: there are both European and US farm subsidies, and Asian governments tried the artificial pegging of their currencies to the US dollar. The final day of reckoning can be delayed, but never put off indefinitely. Market forces must in the end prevail. If the distortion lasts long enough, the end will be accompanied by drama. How long would US gold reserves last? The markets had focused (as they are wont to do) on the magic number of $100m. If gold reserves at Fort Knox dipped below that figure, the US would no longer be obliged to redeem notes. The number was purely symbolic, of course. The real worry was that the US might default on its debt. The potential implications for interest rates were alarming: it would send them up much higher.

Banks were cautious and *started quietly calling in loans*. Loan growth declined some 10 per cent between February and May 1893.[17] On February 20 the Philadelphia and Reading Railroad declared bankruptcy. This was probably a shock as only the month before the stock had paid its usual dividend, but the company's assets were subsequently found to be practically zero. The financial condition of other railroads was now open to question. On April 22 (some say 21), that magic number $100m was triggered. There was not enough gold left to guarantee the value of the notes the treasury was issuing. This hastened the contraction of credit and banks called in loans even faster to preserve the gold in their own vaults.[18] Pennsylvania Steel announced its failure at this time and rail lines such as Missouri Pacific and Manhattan Elevated suffered heavy falls of their stock price.

16 Quoted in Robert Sobel, *Panic on Wall Street*, p.243.
17 Charles Hoffman, *The Depression of the Nineties*, p.56.
18 'Banks were frightened and began calling in loans at a frantic pace.' Reed, *The Silver Panic of 1893*, p.58, quoting Fels, *American Business Cycles*, p.186.

The Panic

ON MAY 3, 1893, for no obvious reason, a wave of selling hit the New York Stock Exchange. 'Not since 1884 had the stock market had such a break in prices as occurred yesterday,' claimed the *New York Times* a day later, 'few days in its history were more exciting.' The next day, May 4, National Cordage, manufacturers of rope and cord, failed, endorsing the previous day's heavy selling. This was big. National Cordage was the darling of Wall Street, a new 'industrial' stock widely held and actively traded. In the Cordage Trust circle of the New York Stock Exchange

> hats were being smashed, coats torn, cravats ruined. Here was an agony that meant financial life or death to many. Cordage common had gone off 18 points. The preferred had lost 22. Suddenly howls went up from the floor. Those who could distinguish the words, heard the ominous cry: Nineteen for Cordage! The shares, a few moments later, went down to $12.
>
> Charles Albert Collman, *Our Mysterious Panics*, p.164

The stock, down to $12 from $140, was now quite possibly worthless. The stock market panic was on.[19] In June 128 banks failed (Graph 9.1).

Graph 9.1: Bank Failures 1865-1900

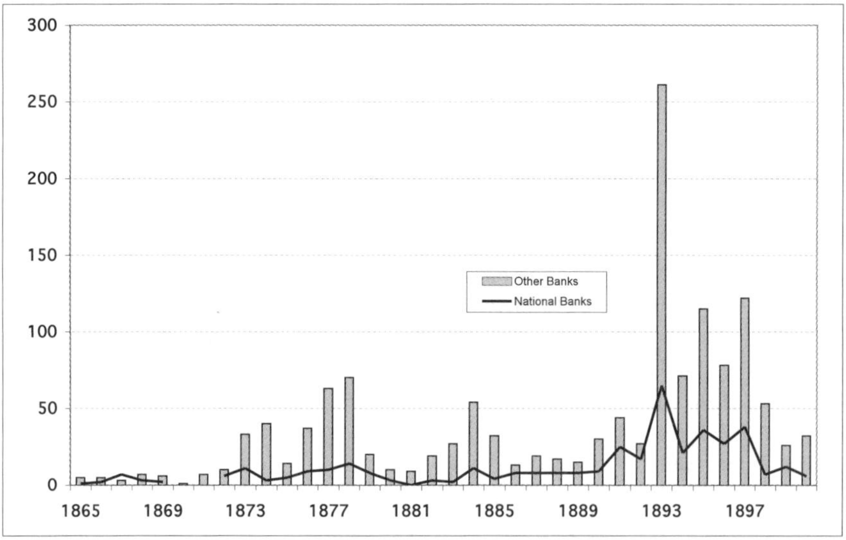

Source: Richard S. Grossman, 'US Banking History, Civil War to World War II', EH.Net Encyclopedia, edited by Robert Whaples, eh.net/encyclopedia/contents/grossman.banking.history.us.civil.war.wwii.php.

19 This was thirty days after a *New York Times* report of April 5 which read: 'There was an entire change of sentiment in Stock Exchange orders today, and it was accomplished by what appeared to be a pre-concerted movement to cover outstanding short contracts all along the line. It is too soon to say that a bull market is upon us, but the figures show that the tendency is toward higher prices.' (Quoted in John Steele Gordon, *The Great Game*, p.164.)

Seven weeks later, on June 26, US markets heard that India was no longer to coin silver. India had been the world's second largest buyer. There was panic in the silver market. Within twenty-four hours most silver mining companies were out of business. At the end of July the Erie appointed receivers. It was the turn of the Northern Pacific in August and the Union Pacific in October; on December 23 the Atchison, Topeka and Santa Fe Line declared bankruptcy.

Graph 9.2: Percentage of Railroad Mileage put into Receivership

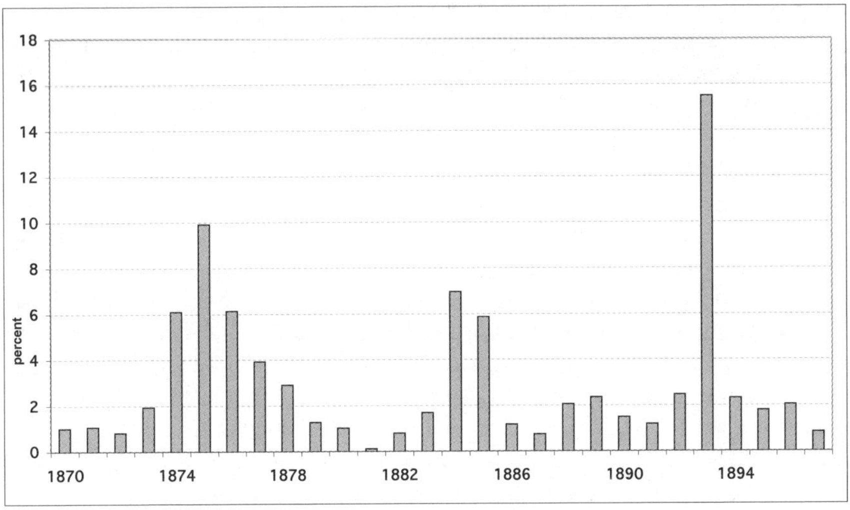

Source: Swain, H.H., 'Economic Aspects of Railroad Receiverships', *Economic Studies* 3, 1898.

The banking panic began this time in the interior of the country – in Chicago. On May 8, without prior warning (to the public and its depositors at least), the Chemical National Bank of Chicago failed to open for business. Its doors were never to reopen. Depositors were faced with the prospect of losing a collective $1.6m. The failure did not apparently come as a surprise to Chicago bankers, however. They considered that the bank had not been competently managed. 'Excessive loans had been made to the bank's directors and to some of the shareholders.'[20] No support was offered to the bank. The timing is interesting in view of what Hoyt says about land speculation and the World's Fair, which was opened on May 1 by the President himself. By this time it might have become obvious to enough market operators that the city was way overbuilt, resulting in a rapid change in speculator sentiment, especially after the previous week's stock market events. Whether this led to a bank run is conjecture, but it

20 Elmus Wicker, *Banking Panics of the Gilded Age*, p.60, quoting F.C. James, *The Growth of Chicago Banks*, Vol. 1, p.581.

is interesting that the bank panic started in Chicago, where real estate speculation had become concentrated as a result of the World's Fair.

In Indianapolis the Capital National Bank, closely associated with the Chemical National, failed three days later on May 11 and depositors lost $1.1 m. The next day, May 12, the Columbia National Bank of Chicago failed (as a result of rumours after the Chemical National failure), with the loss of $1.5 m of depositors' cash. This was more serious as the Columbia's deposits were mostly deposits from other banks. This might have been the catalyst for spreading the banking disturbance to other states, but the next three weeks were relatively calm, with no real loss of confidence by depositors in other Chicago banks.

June 3 saw a renewal of unrest, however. The largest commercial paper house in Chicago, Herman Schaffner & Co, closed its doors, taking with it depositors' money to the tune of $850,000. A private bank, Schaffner & Co had been speculating in railway bonds, which, as a result of the stock market collapse, were now worth far less. The bank's president was last seen renting a boat, rowing far out into the waters of Lake Michigan and is presumed to have jumped overboard, never to return. The panic was on.

No longer could it be said that panics were a result of monetary stringency in the fall when farmers needed cash for the harvest. June 5 has been described as 'the most exciting day in Chicago's financial affairs in a decade'.[21] Runs spread to Spokane (Washington) on June 5 and 6, then to Cleveland, Kansas City (Missouri), Omaha and Detroit. Californian cities saw runs in the third week of June. These accelerated in the second week of July, affecting western and mid-western states, the farm belt where farmers were heavily mortgaged. Most stocks reached their lows on Wall Street in this month. On July 19 one mortgage broker in Boston 'was forced to sell a $220,000 mortgage for $9,000 in gold as a result of the sharp decline in real estate values and the increase in the gold price.'[22] Therein lies the difference between this downturn and previous downturns in 1884 and 1890. The downturn of 1893 saw land price deflation.

In the middle of the panic it was discovered that President Cleveland had cancer of the mouth and required immediate surgery. On June 30, under the pretext of a fishing trip, the operation was carried out on a yacht belonging to a friend. It was feared that informing the market would add to the panic.

On August 3 New York banks started to restrict, though they did not stop, shipments of currency to banks in the interior. Although bank runs had by this time slowed down, a scarcity of money for day-to-day transactions developed. Banks and depositors were hoarding the cash. Contemporaries spoke of a currency famine the further west one went. An economic depression had begun, eighteen years after the previous one. It was to prove worse than any that had occurred previously.

21 Wicker, p. 63.
22 Sobel, p.253.

Currency shipments probably had to be restricted for another reason. As we have seen, under the national banking system New York banks held the reserves of smaller reserve city banks, many of which were in the interior. The New York banks did not leave these deposits sitting idle, they lent them out – at call – to stock market investors. A call for those deposits would necessitate calling in the loans, which would probably lead to forced sales of stocks in an already declining market. Any default by the borrower, the stock speculator, would make repayment of the deposits that much harder. The unsound condition of the banks and their lending practices was now obvious.

> It became evident during the crisis that the banks had been carrying a large amount of loans which should have been long since written off or at least written down. These loans had been made in many instancces beforc ... 1890, and in part they had been made more recently, serving to bolster up weak enterprises and to make an already unhealthy situation more unsound.
>
> Sprague, p.161

After-effects of the downturn

THE CAUSES of the 1893 depression are generally given as follows: deflation since the Civil War; under-consumption (i.e. the production of goods and services at a rate higher than could be consumed, resulting in producers having to cut back on production and employment); government overspending and extravagance; government purchases of a commodity (silver) for which it had no use.

Farmers blamed the bankers; bankers blamed the Sherman Silver Purchase Act. The speculation in government-granted licences is rarely mentioned.

Hoyt reports that the land boom peaked in Chicago in June, July and August 1890, 'when the volume of weekly and monthly sales broke all past records'.[23] At this time Chicagoans regarded anyone a traitor to the city who questioned 'any part of the process that was making so many people rich'.[24] Screaming 'Fire!' in the theatre will not win one friends, even if there really is smoke in the stalls. When news of the failure of Baring Brothers reached Chicago, a 'serious financial stringency'[25] developed. Banks suddenly refused further loans on real estate, though not for other purposes. No real panic resulted; indeed an air of confidence remained during the spring of 1891 on account of the forthcoming World's Fair of 1893. But, by the time the crowds had departed, the overbuilt condition of the city had become obvious.

23 Hoyt, p.173. On June 15, 1890, the *Chicago Tribune* reported one salesman, a Mr S.E. Gross, selling as many as five hundred lots per week. On one of the free excursions offered to his subdivisions at Grossdale, west of Chicago, 27 coaches pulled by two engines were required to cater for the three thousand eager buyers (Hoyt, p.171).
24 Hoyt, p.173.
25 Hoyt, p.173.

> The termination of the World's Fair projects and the contraction of firms into smaller quarters reduced the demand for office space at the very time when its supply was being greatly increased by the completion of a number of new skyscrapers. Hoyt, p.179

Seattle had its problems too.

> The Panic of 1893 thundered west from Wall Street, first clobbering San Francisco, then spreading its carnage up the West Coast. In Washington State, as elsewhere, a run on banks ensued. Depositors withdrew their savings, converted them into gold when possible, and just buried or otherwise hid them when they couldn't. Credit became impossible to procure. Construction came to a dead stop. Banks tried to collect mortgage payments, foreclosed on those who couldn't pay, then went bankrupt themselves. Within a year, 11 Seattle banks had bolted their doors. After the Panic, local land values sank by as much as 80 percent. Some people fled the area with only their last savings in their pockets, hoping to protect what little they had. Others vanished with other people's life savings in their pockets. In September 1893, Seattle city treasurer Adolph Krug hopped an early morning train to Canada, taking with him about $225,000 in public funds. At the end of November, the president and cashier at Buckley State Bank of Tacoma skipped with $30,000 … So precious was cash in Everett, that at one point the Merchants' Protective Association actually began publishing the names of people who spent their money in Seattle. The *Everett Times* endorsed running those 'traitors' out of town. www.historylink.org/output.cfm?file_id=2030

It is the sinking of land values that will differentiate the decade cycle downturn from the property cycle downturn. The deflating of land values is inevitable if they are permitted to inflate in the first place. This takes place roughly every eighteen years, subject only to the influence of world wars. There is more about this in Chapter 15, 'Knowledge We Gained Along the Way'.

Meanwhile in Utah:

> Even before the panic, Utah had experienced hard times. During the territorial boom of 1889-90, the value of land and of business and residential property had skyrocketed to as much as ten times pre-1889 prices. Speculators reaped enormous paper profits, and real estate transactions in Salt Lake City alone reached an unprecedented $100,000 daily. To meet voracious demands for credit, nine new banks opened in the city. Then, in December 1890, shock waves from the collapse of London's Baring Brothers bank burst Utah's speculative bubble, and Utahns numbly reaped the harvest from their craze: depressed prices, lowered profits, overextended credit, and tight money … Thus, when the Panic of 1893 reached Utah, it found – and worsened – an already precarious situation. By the end of June, Utah businessmen began to lay off workers and reduce wages. A half-dozen prominent citizens were bankrupt and many more were on the verge. 'I have never witnessed a greater stagnation in business enterprises than has manifested itself during the last month,' wrote a prominent Utahn. 'Money is not

> to be had, confidence seems to have disappeared, and credit is denied by nearly all tradesmen. www.media.utah.edu/UHE/p/PANIC1893.html

And in Wisconsin:

> The panic of 1893 flooded the mid-West with misfortune. The failure of the Wisconsin Marine and Fire Insurance Bank involved the financial ruin of David Ferguson, its cashier and also the Treasurer of the Diocesan Missionary Funds. With the collapse of this bank about a half million dollars of diocesan money was lost, about $25,000 of which belonged to the endowment fund of the diocese and the remainder to Nashotah House. Using his experience as a banker, Bishop Nicholson took the situation into his own hands. The fund had been wiped out. Mr. Ferguson offered the diocese his only asset, his home, which the bishop administered. So well was this done that it subsequently began to make small returns to the diocesan loss.
> www.justus.anglican.org/resources/pc/usa/ilnicholson/wagner.html

The next year, 1894, proved a tough year:

> Jacob Sechler Coxey leads 400 people, known as Coxey's Army, from Ohio to Washington, D.C. The marchers protest unemployment. Underlying their protests is their sense that the government refuses to legislate in favour of working people. Coxey is arrested for trespassing, and the 'army' melts away. The Pullman Strike erupts. Workers at the Pullman Palace Car Company protest the fact that the management has reduced its payroll and substantially reduced wages without reducing rents in its model workers homes, nor prices in its company stores. Eugene V. Debs calls a sympathy strike of all railway workers. The Railway Managers Association refuses to negotiate and hires 3,600 deputy marshals to break the strike. The U.S. Government issues an injunction against the striking railway workers on the grounds of 'interference with interstate commerce and postal service.' The injunction orders Debs to call off the strike. That the Pullman cars do not carry mail is disregarded by Cleveland. Federal troops are sent to enforce the injunction, and several months later, Debs is sent to prison for his part in the railway strike. www.pinzler.com/ushistory/timeline7.html

Striking workers were not permitted. Property rights to collect the rent? Never in doubt from the government.

What the newspapers were saying ...

EBULLIENCE at the top (see President Harrison's comments in January 1893 at the start of this chapter) soon turned to fear:

> There is depression, distrust and gloom on every hand.
> *New York Herald*, April 30, 1893

> There will be few regrets in Wall Street at the passing away of the old year. The net losses in commercial, industrial and financial circles have been the severest ever met. At the moment the outlook is as discouraging and forbidding as ever. *New York Commercial Advertiser*, December 30, 1893

Blame the government:

> The president had depreciated the currency, looted the national vaults. At this rate the peculiar pyrotechnic methods of the Administration will have nothing left upon which to experiment. *Colorado Sun* (Denver), May 9, 1893

> It is all plainly the result of the wild profligacy and reckless management of Republican control. *New Orleans Daily Picayune*, June 28, 1893

Blame anything, except the speculation in government-granted licences and privileges:

> The theories as to causes of panics range from that of the late Professor, who imagined that the periodicity of panics might be connected with that of spots on the sun, to that of the writer who recently informed us that they are intimately related to the prophecies of the Hebrew scriptures.
> *New York Times*, June 19, 1893

> Wall Street is not liked. It has not only to bear the odium that has rested on money lenders from time immemorial, but, in addition, it suffers from the reputation it has gained of selling goods at more than their true value, of floating doubtful enterprises, of listing securities of notorious swindlers, of fleecing trustful investors, of doing in a large way and without suffering the appropriate penalty that which when done in a small way is rightly called swindling. *New York World*, July 24, 1893

Graph 9.3: Index of American Railroad Stocks (weighted by the number of shares outstanding at the start of each year)

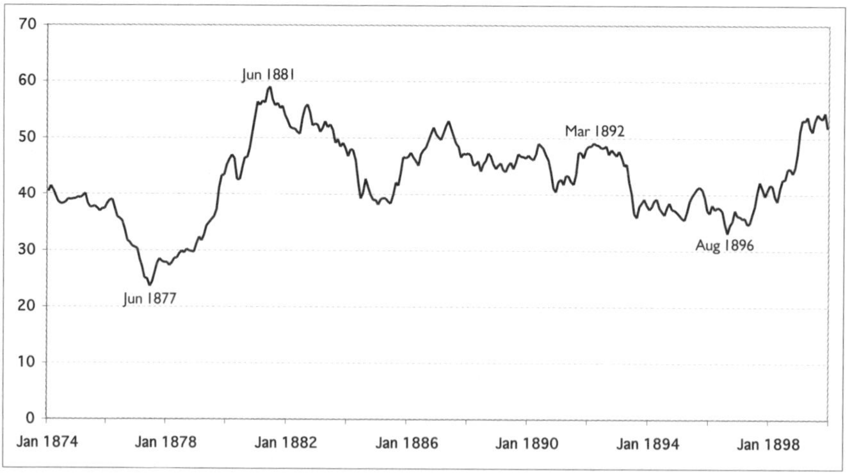

Source: Macauley, Frederick R., *Some Theoretical Problems Suggested by the Movements of Interest Rates, Bond Yields and Stock Prices in the United States Since 1856*, NBER Inc., No.33, 1938.

To sum up

NO HISTORIAN has linked the credit-creation process used to finance speculation in government-granted licences and privileges (the largest and most important of which is land value) to the sharp periodic booms and slumps in the economy. We are out on a bit of a limb here. However, not one historian has ever managed to forecast with precision the next downturn. This you will now learn to do.

Everything plays a part in the unfolding drama of a downturn. Under normal circumstances an economy will weather problems, but when it is weighed down by heavy debts to purchase land, or to speculate in its value, any shock, and more particularly a shock to the related credit-creation process, will expose the weak foundations. Economists consider land purchase to be wealth production. It isn't – unless you can time it just right. One of the secrets, in the final stages of a cycle, is to watch for a contraction in credit. A downturn is yet to happen without one.

Graph 9.4: Public Land Sales 1800-1900

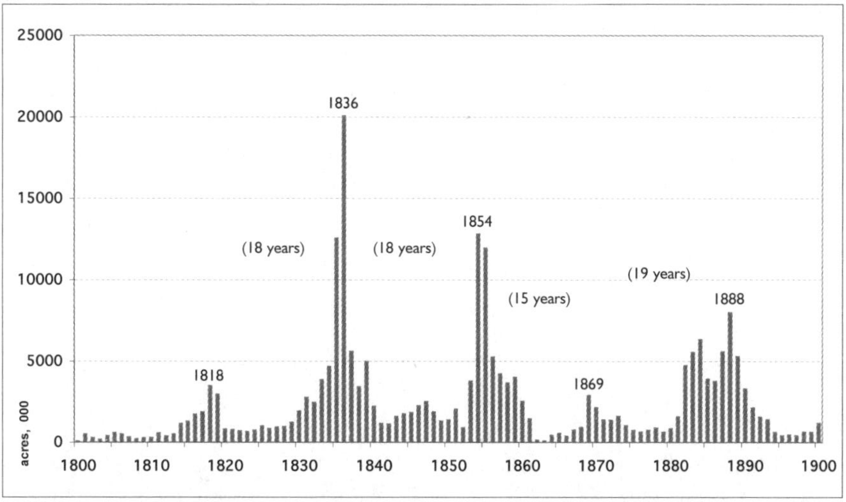

Source: Smith and Cole, *Fluctuations in American Business, 1790-1860*, Harvard University Press, 1935, Appendix D. After 1860 from McCartney, *Crisis of 1873*, Table XXV, p.131. After 1875 from Hibbard, *A History of the Public Land Policies*, p.114.

Land sales peaked in 1888, as usual well before the months of panic, and fell markedly after 1890 (Graph 9.4). Railroad stocks never quite managed to rise above their peak in June 1881 (probably because of increased government regulation, increased competition and the clout of the Granger movement), though they did reach a lower high in March 1892 after an overall decline in the 1880s (Graph 9.3). Interestingly, rail stocks bottomed in August 1896, fifteen years from the high. The March 1892 high came fifteen years after the June 1877 low.[26]

Interest rates on New York commercial paper peaked in July and August 1893, in line with the final crisis in New York at the end of the panic. This was twenty years (238 months actually) from the October 1873 panic high, and exactly fifteen years from the 1878 low (Graph 9.5).

The government ran budget surpluses for all the years 1866 to 1893. Despite this, business boom and bust was *still* in evidence and a major downturn had *still* taken place some twenty years after the last one.

In years past, depressions had occurred in economies without electric light, without telephones, fax machines or any other fast means of communication, and in conditions that seem less than civilised to today's onlookers. Whether the US economy was operating under a central bank, a national banking system, paper money issues or fixed ratios of gold to silver, whether it was a time of inflation or of deflation, whether there was a budget surplus or a deficit, severe downturns – depressions, in fact – were occurring every eighteen to twenty years.

All of this had been taking place within an ever-expanding frontier of settlement, a frontier that was now rapidly closing. It was dawning on more and more Americans that in the future they would have to face an expansion-less existence for the first time in their history.

Graph 9.5: Interest Rates
1874-1900

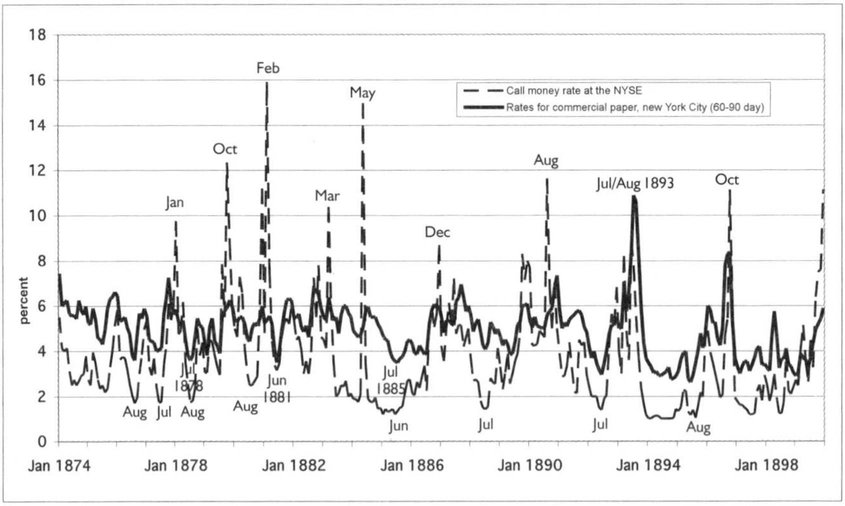

Source: Macauley, Frederick R., *Some Theoretical Problems Suggested by the Movements of Interest Rates, Bond Yields and Stock Prices in the United States Since 1856*, NBER Inc., No.33, 1938.

26 Both McCartney and Macauley's index figures, two different sources, post the June 1877 low.

FURTHER READING

Fels, Rendigs. *American Business Cycles: 1865-1897*. University of North Carolina Press, 1959; reprinted Greenwood Press, 1973.

Hoffman, Charles. *The Depression of the Nineties: An Economic History.* Greenwood Press, 1970.

Holbrook, Stewart H. *The Age of the Moguls*. Doubleday & Co, 1954.

Lauck, W. Jett. *The Causes of the Panic of 1893*.

Noyes, A.D. 'The Banks and The Panic of 1893', *Political Science Quarterly* 9, No.1, p.15.

Reed, Lawrence W. *A Lesson from the Past: The Silver Panic of 1893*. The Foundation for Economic Education Inc., 1993.

Sobel, Robert. *Panic on Wall Street: A History of America's Financial Disasters.* Collier Books, 1972.

Sprague, O.M.W. *History of Crises Under the National Banking System*. Washington, Government Printing Office, 1910.

Wicker, Elmus. *Banking Panics of the Gilded Age*. Cambridge University Press, 2000.

10
The Temple
The Federal Reserve
1913 to the Great Depression

I believe … that the Federal Reserve System will materially check undue expansion by making banks conservative as to their loans, because of the knowledge that any departure from strictly commercial transactions will take away their ability to liquidate such investments by rediscounting in the Federal Reserve Banks …

Charles Hamilton, delivering his initial address as Governor of the newly created Federal Reserve Bank, December 1914

THE PANIC of 1893, and the land price collapse that brought it on, ushered in the worst depression the US had so far experienced. The banking system was accorded much of the blame, but there was of course more to it than that.

Nevertheless, the national banking system had its problems. It was successful in providing a national uniform currency but it did not prove 'elastic' enough to meet the seasonal demands of the nation. A national bank could only issue notes to the value of the bonds it deposited with the Comptroller. Once this limit was hit, no further note issue could be undertaken. This meant that the supply of currency remained constant throughout the year. This was unhelpful as currency requirements were seasonal. Variations in interest rates reflected this problem and can be seen in the charts of interest rates after 1860 and up to 1913. Rates generally increased in the fall, often peaking in December/January (Graph 10.1, page 199).

A second problem arose from the way in which reserves were pyramided. Country banks placed reserves with reserve city banks, who put reserves into central reserve city banks. This worked until a nation-wide bank run was a possibility, then banks acted self-interestedly, calling on reserves, compounding liquidity problems at the very time liquidity in the system was required. In addition, most of the reserves that found their way to New York central reserve banks were put to work for profit, often as call loans for stock-market investment. The system proved unstable in a downturn.

Said one bank historian, Edwin W. Kemmerer, in his banking study for the National Monetary Commission of 1910:

> It has been found that the two periods of the year in which the money market is most likely to be strained are the periods of the 'spring revival', about March, April and early May, and that of the crop-moving demand in the fall; and the two periods of easiest money market are the 'readjustment' period, extending from about the middle of January to nearly the 1st of March, and the period of the summer depression, extending through the three summer months. Of the eight [banking panics of the era], four occurred in the fall or early winter … and these four included two of the three really severe panics of the period [i.e., those of 1873 and 1907]; three occurred in May … and one … probably the least important … extended from March until well along in November. The evidence accordingly points to a tendency for panics to occur during seasons normally characterized by stringent money markets. This does not mean that the seasonal stringencies are the causes of the panics; it does mean that the months in which they occur are the weakest links in the seasonal chain, and that in periods of extraordinary tension the chain breaks at these links.
>
> *Seasonal Variations in the Relative Demand for Money and Capital in the United States*

The panic of 1907 provoked calls for banking reform to provide financial stability and a more elastic currency. The Aldrich-Freeland Act of 1908 established a line of enquiry to find the solution. Wrote one economist, Franklin MacVeagh, a little later, in 1911:

> It is … extravagant and inefficient to live under a banking and currency system which in the most ordinary and quiet times saturates everybody concerned with a sense of financial uncertainty – a condition that constantly hampers not only the bankers themselves but business in all its branches and forms … This apprehension – this habitual looking forward, especially to the autumn – this customary wondering how the market is going to be one or two or three or four months hence – and this calculation as to how one's own bank is going to be fixed to meet the situations and fluctuations that ought to be immaterial – are all incorporated into the very nerves of bankers and more or less into the nerves of business men in general.
>
> 'Banking and Currency Reform', *Journal of Political Economy*

After some years of debate, Congress passed the Federal Reserve Act in December 1913, 'An Act to provide for the establishment of Federal Reserve Banks, to furnish an elastic currency, to afford means of rediscounting commercial paper, to establish a more effective supervision of banking in the United States, and for other purposes.' A key plank of this reform was the creation of a central bank to supply currency to business whenever it was demanded, avoiding the seasonal spikes in short-term interest rates. The new system of note issue was to be based not on bonds but on commercial assets.

Thus developed the Fed's rediscounting responsibilities. If a member bank of the reserve system ran into difficulties, it could on-sell (rediscount) part of its loan (asset) base to the Fed, in return for immediate cash to satisfy depositors. The assets had to be normal business loans and not loans to purchase stocks, bonds or real estate. This meant the currency represented real transactions, a sounder basis for the future. W. Randolph Burgess, a long-time official at the Federal Reserve Bank of New York, noted:

> The fundamental change which the Federal Reserve had made … is to shift much of the burden of meeting fluctuations in the demand for credit from the reserves of the member banks in New York City to the twelve Reserve Banks, which through the strength of their holding of pooled reserves and through their power of note issue and deposit expansion can provide almost any extra funds required.
>
> *The Reserve Banks and the Money Market*, revised edn, 1936

The interest (discount) rate used to do this is set by the Fed.

Graph 10.1: New York Interest Rates 1894-1936

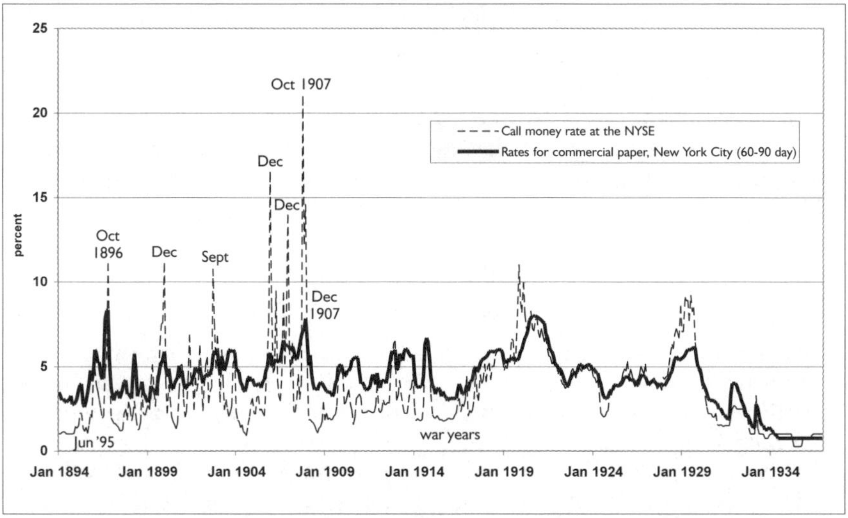

Source: Macauley, Frederick R., *Some Theoretical Problems Suggested by the Movements of Interest Rates, Bond Yields and Stock Prices in the United States Since 1856*, NBER Inc., No.33, 1938.

Once the Fed got going, it was clearly successful in one of its stated objectives: supplying a more elastic currency to the markets (Graph 10.1). There was a dramatic change in the behaviour of short-term interest rates after 1914 (allowing for the uncertainties of the First World War). Said Burgess:

> In the old days there were rigid and not far distant limits to the reserves available; now the mechanism of the Reserve System provides for a much larger possible expansion. It gives much greater elasticity …
>
> 1st edn, 1927, p.122

Importantly, Burgess noted further that:

> The presence of the Reserve System gives greater elasticity to the supply of funds and stability of the money market and *removes the fear of money panics.*
>
> 1st edn, p.125 (emphasis added)

There are two interesting things here. Again it was believed, at very senior banking levels, that a system had been found which would eliminate monetary panics. What psychological effect would this have had in the 1920s? There is a clue in the fact that, in Burgess's second edition, the one published in 1936 *after* another banking panic, the above passages were amended, the quote from page 125 now reading:

> The presence of the Reserve System gives greater elasticity to the supply of funds – and the control of that elasticity is the central problem of Federal Reserve policy.

The second interesting thing is that the Fed could command a 'much larger possible expansion' in the money supply. This was almost limitless, resulting in unprecedented inflation rates in subsequent decades and a continuing decline in the purchasing power of the dollar relative to 1913 values.

Anyway, by the early to mid-1920s, many professional and business people had come to believe that the creation of the Fed had 'tamed the business cycle'. The Fed now had control of the money supply, control of the creation of money and control of the gold supply, and it could regulate its member banks. The Fed chairman had said as much. In an address to students of the Graduate College, Harvard University on November 28, 1922, Benjamin Strong described the panics of the national banking era:

> These extreme credit conditions arose because there was no stretch. When the period of surplus reserves arose, those funds poured into the speculative markets. When the period of deficient reserves arrived, all the banks sought to contract their loans to make good their reserves and we witnessed the extremes of speculation and of business embarrassment. There was neither control of the volume of credit, nor moderating influence as to rates of interest. And, finally, there was no control over the movements of gold in and out of the country.

The Fed had solved the problem of seasonal interest rate spikes, but the continued failure of central bankers to recognise the fatal flaw in the fractional reserve system guarantees the return of periodic *land-induced,* economic downturns. *Land-induced, economic downturns are beyond the control of the Fed.* Understand this and you are halfway to making much greater profits from the real estate cycle.

FURTHER READING

Kemmerer, Edwin W. *Seasonal Variations in the Relative Demand for Money and Capital in the United States*, National Monetary Commission, Senate Document No. 588, 61st Congress, 2nd Session, Washington, Government Printing Office, 1910.

MacVeagh, Franklin. 'Banking and Currency Reform', *Journal of Political Economy*, 19, 10, pp.809-18.

Strong, Benjamin. *Federal Reserve Control of Credit*. Federal Reserve Bank of New York, Quarterly Review Special Issue, 75th Anniversary.

Wheelock, David C. *Seasonal Accommodation and the Financial Crises of the Great Depression: Did the Fed Furnish an Elastic Currency?* Research Department, Federal Reserve Bank of St Louis.

11

Land of Oranges and Speculators

The Land Booms of 1908 and 1926

There is no possibility of a panic in the foreseeable future.
Joseph Stagg Lawrence, economist, writing from Princeton University, 1929

Stock prices have reached what looks like a permanently high plateau.
Irving Fisher, another famous economist of the era, September 1929

I do not think there can be any question about the safety of call loans at this time, and of their liquidity.
Roy Young, Federal Reserve Chairman 1927-1930

IF UNEMPLOYMENT STATISTICS are a fair guide to the depth of a depression, the downturn of 1893 must have been serious. It was described as the worst depression up to that time, though the same had been said about every depression up until then.

> It is probably safe to say that in no civilized country in this century, not actually in the throes of war or open insurrection, has society been so disorganized as it was in the United States during the first half of 1894; never was human life held so cheap; never did the constituted authorities appear so incompetent to enforce the respect for law.
>
> H.P. Robinson, editor of *The Railroad Age*, writing later

Wages collapsed, as did the prices of wheat and cotton.

> Hungry, jobless men roamed the land, begging food and sometimes stealing ... Ragged, shivering men in Chicago insulted policemen or smashed store windows in order to be put in jail where it was warm and where they would be given food.
>
> Frank B. Latham, *The Panic of 1893*

Unemployment was persistently above 10 per cent for the five years 1894-8. Statistics become scarcer the further back one looks, but it does appear that this was the first time that had happened. It is significant in that the option for those without work of simply taking up a plot and living at a subsistence level was no longer available. There was little unclaimed land left of farmable quality – though this does not mean that it was all under cultivation.

Table 11.1: Unemployment Estimates 1890s

Year	% unemployed	Year	% unemployed
1890	4.0	1896	12.0
1891	4.8	1897	12.4
1892	3.7	1898	11.6
1893	8.1	1899	8.7
1894	12.3	1900	5.0
1895	11.1		

Source: Romer, Christina, 'Spurious Volatility in Historical Unemployment Data', *Journal of Political Economy*, No.1, 1987, pp.1-27.

In Chicago there were no more excursions taking prospective lot-buyers out to the subdivisions. By the mid-1890s

> the demand for vacant property [was] at the lowest ebb in the history of the city … By this time a majority of the buyers of lots on easy payments had lost their holdings and had nothing to show for their investment. Other real estate dealers said that in some localities two thirds and perhaps three-fourths of the lots sold in good times had been sold on foreclosure and that nine-tenths of the cheap lots sold on easy payments had been sold for taxes and special assessments.
>
> Homer Hoyt, *One Hundred Years of Land Values in Chicago*, p.180

The taxes of which Hoyt speaks were levied to pay for improvements such as sidewalks and lighting in the city, but many such improvements had been made in unnecessary places, often at the whim of developers, such as boulevard lamps in the swamps of the Calumet region. By 1896 'real estate was in such a dull and disorganized condition that land values were difficult, if not impossible to determine.' The worst point in the depression for Chicago came in 1897, when real estate was said to be 'a liability instead of an asset'.[1] Not all areas were affected the same way, but the 'wild speculative boom of 1889 and 1890' was definitely over.

The 19th century in America had produced some awesome booms and busts, the regularity of which could not have been lost upon those whose business it was to study such things. That the 1893 downturn affected far more citizens than previous downturns is clear from the efforts of vested interests to prevent a repeat:

> The banking and monetary arrangements of the [19th] century … were admirably designed to respond to euphoria, finance it, enhance it and then add force to the ensuing collapse. Banks and money could be created, without effective constraint, to finance the expansion and speculation. Failure,

1 Hoyt, p.181.

> or fear of failure, the contraction of loans and deposits then made the day of contrition worse ... The decisive thing was to have possession of property, and this the banks provided. So, while the banking system was manifestly designed to accommodate expansion and speculation, there was also a powerful incentive sending people to the banks.
>
> J.K. Galbraith, *Money: Whence it Came, Where it Went*, p.114

A desire was developing amongst the wealthier bankers and financiers for a central bank to moderate the effects of downturns, especially runs on banks that couldn't pay out.

Recovery

ONCE AGAIN, slowly, the cycle was turning. The Sherman Silver Purchase Act was repealed in November 1893 and a few well-timed government gold purchases eventually restored market confidence. The silver question came up again at the 1896 election but never regained its earlier momentum. The miners were not as prosperous, and farmers were now a declining percentage of the voting population as city laborers grew in number.[2]

Graph 11.1: Index of American Railroad Stocks
(weighted by the number of shares outstanding at the start of each year)

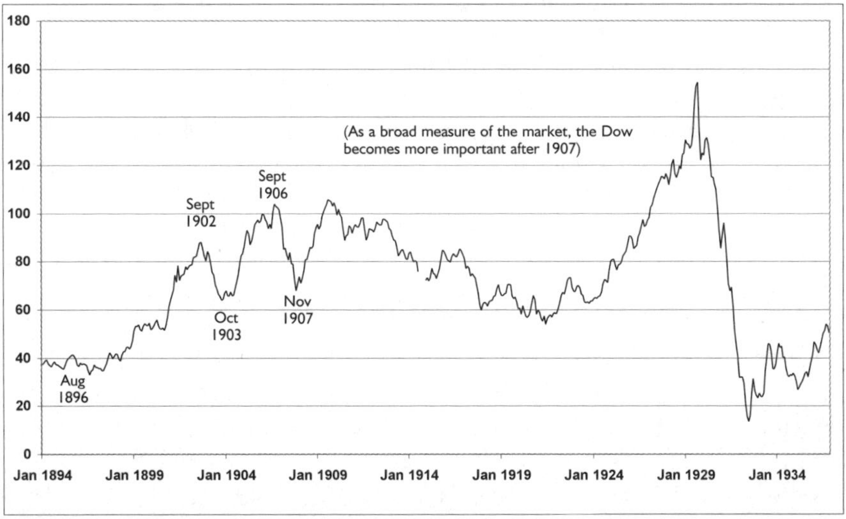

Source: Macauley, Frederick R., *Some Theoretical Problems Suggested by the Movements of Interest Rates, Bond Yields and Stock Prices in the United States Since 1856*, NBER Inc., No.33, 1938.

2 The whole silver episode is believed to have inspired *The Wonderful Wizard of Oz*, though author Frank Baum never explicitly said so. The tin woodsman was the labourer, the alienated worker; the scarecrow was the western farmer with no brain, trying to comprehend monetary theories; the lion was William Jennings Bryan, a gifted public speaker but politically on the losing side three times; the Emerald City was Washington DC; following the yellow brick road was sticking to the gold standard; and Dorothy had silver shoes and kicked her heels three times.

In his memoirs, one of the great speculators of the period, Bernard Baruch, described the panic of 1893, the first he had experienced directly, as having closed many mills and mines and put into receivership a large number of railroads in the country. But by 1895 'One could detect the first promises of better financial weather',[3] though this may have been easier to write with hindsight. In the charts we see that stocks measured by the rails index bottomed in August 1896 (Graph 11.1, page 205). The silver question was finally put to rest, just as the parties were again lining up for battle, after huge gold strikes in the Klondike, Australia and South Africa, at a time when a more efficient extraction process using cyanide had been developed. The fact that gold would be in good supply solved at a stroke the seemingly intractable money problem. Sound money men could be placated and the gold standard maintained. Those pressing for more coinage (and hence inflation to make debt-repayment easier) were pleased that gold would flow to the banks, expanding the reserve base. Recovery was at hand, helped in the latter part of 1896 when it became clear that European and Indian wheat crops were poor, giving US farmers a better year. Government borrowing in 1898 to pay for the war against Spain (a manufactured war if ever there was one) increased the amount of money in circulation that year and the next.

As the cycle turned further, recovery became rapid expansion. The new century was looking to be prosperous. By 1900 the US was the world's pre-eminent industrial power, ahead of the UK. J.P. Morgan's reorganisation of Andrew Carnegie's steel works into United States Steel, making Carnegie the richest man in the world, proved it. The deal was enormous. The newly floated US Steel hit the markets with a capitalisation of $1.4 bn, at a time when the value of the entire US manufacturing industry was $9 bn. US Steel was producing more steel after 1900 than the whole of the UK industry combined. Carnegie himself made $480 m, retired and had given it all away, as he believed a man should do, by the time he died in 1919.

Chicago real estate

IN CHICAGO foreclosures had been mounting for several years. Rents, subdivisions and sales were low and there was an oversupply of office buildings in the central business district. Landlords were even being forced to accede to the demands of tenants for extensive repairs and improvements.[4] Could things get any worse?

> Interest rates of mortgages in the central business district had declined to 4 and even 3½ percent, with the result that long-term leaseholds were capitalized on a 4 instead of a 5 percent basis. This alone would tend to raise downtown land values 25 percent, and although its effect did not immediately

3 *My Own Story*.
4 Hoyt, p.208.

show itself in such a blanket increase, the lowering of the capitalization rate was now operating to increase valuations. Hoyt, p.208

There was a further improvement in general outlook and business conditions in Chicago in 1899. Real estate foreclosure sales began to attract some interest. In about 1900 the city's elevated train loop, simply called 'the Loop', was completed, attracting more people to the central area, increasing business and rents. That year Chicagoans legally consumed almost 153.5 million gallons of intoxicating liquor.[5] Soon, however, the Anti-Saloon League (founded in 1893 and dedicated to the eradication of every saloon in the nation) were to have some big political wins in Ohio and go on to distribute 40 tons of anti-alcohol literature every month. They succeeded in having the US voted dry on January 17, 1920. Drinking anything alcoholic after that date would be illegal.

Chicago's business potential kept on improving. Steel industries sprang up at the tip of the lake around East Chicago and Gary. Oil refineries were built to refine oil now being piped in from Kansas and Oklahoma. As electricity supplanted steam, Chicago became the focal point of power generation for the area. The city became a centre for the manufacture of telephone equipment as the phone ceased to be regarded as a luxury toy. The Sears Roebuck mail-order distribution business was located in Chicago, and the advent of the automobile, aeroplane and radio speeded up development. Between 1890 and 1930 the population of the city tripled.

By 1902, with few new buildings having been built since the 1893 depression, the previously large supply of vacant office space was fast disappearing. The building of CBD office space was now profitable, and height restrictions were being eased. Between 1896 and 1915 the value of Chicago manufacturing tripled. So did the number of passengers on trains. Automobile ownership jumped from 5,000 to 86,000, the number of telephones installed from 12,000 to half a million. Electricity generation increased 34 fold.[6] Despite all this, land prices were showing only moderate and steady increases. On average land values doubled, but the growth was gradual; 'the painful remembrance of the aftermath of the boom of 1890' checked reckless speculation. This is an important observation.

Other cities, though, for various local reasons, did see land booms as the new century dawned, notably St Louis, New York and Seattle. It was the discovery of gold at Klondike in the Canadian north-west, and the ensuing gold rush, that kicked off the boom in Seattle, and into Canada, after 1896. Perhaps the timing was not coincidental. One would expect there to have been a few more gold diggers after 1893. Who goes prospecting for gold in the midst of a land boom?

Behind the scenes, extraordinary changes were taking place in the way

5 Hoyt, p.205, quoting *Chicago Tribune*6 Hoyt, p.205., September 8, 1900.
6 Hoyt, p.205.

US business organised itself. The 1890s saw the arrival of genuinely big business. At the time of the Civil War, only railroads could be said to be big business. Slowly other businesses were growing in size: iron and then steel works, munitions factories, manufacturers of nails from wire instead of the old metal plates. Between 1895 and 1905 an explosion of business mergers took place, establishing many names familiar today, such as General Electric and Westinghouse. Whole new industries were built up in meat packing, electricity generation, tobacco (cigarette-making machines replacing hand-rolling) and photography (Eastman and Kodak). Huge new industrial concerns arose: International Harvester, Singer, United Fruit and more, which totally dominated their fields. The industries that did best were those in which the barriers to entry were high, or could be artificially created and maintained, for example through advertising.

But it didn't happen without substantial opposition to the ruthless exploitation some big corporations were practicing, the opposition coming from many quarters including the labour movement, various land reformers and the general populist revolt against the huge fortunes amassed by the relatively few who formed the great trusts, holding companies and industrial concerns. Some of the opposition was at great personal risk. Upton Sinclair exposed the dastardly processes of the meat packers and Ida Tarbell the methods of Standard Oil; Mary Elizabeth Lease incited farmers to raise hell instead of corn; Marie Van Vorst revealed the plight of working women and John Spargo the abuses of child labour; Louis D. Brandeis exposed how 'they', the bankers, used other people's money; and Henry George pointed out where real political control was to be found.

This was also the time of the Anarchists, whose two major original writers were Pierre Proudhon of France and Michael Bakunin, a Russian exile. Proudhon proclaimed defiantly: 'Whoever lays his hand on me to govern me is a usurper and a tyrant; I declare him to be my enemy.' The highest perfection for which society ought to aim, he believed, was no government, *An-archy*. To be governed is to be

> 'watched, inspected, spied on, regulated, indoctrinated, preached at, controlled, ruled, censored, by persons who have neither wisdom nor virtue. It is in every action and transaction to be registered, stamped, taxed, patented, licensed, assessed, measured, reprimanded, corrected, frustrated. Under pretext of the public good it is to be exploited, monopolized, embezzled, robbed and then, at the least protest of word or complaint, to be fined, harassed, vilified, beaten up, bludgeoned, disarmed, judged, condemned, imprisoned, shot, garroted, deported, sold, betrayed, swindled, deceived, outraged, dishonored. That's government, that's its justice, that's its morality.'
>
> Quoted in Barbara Tuchman, *The Proud Tower*, p.72

In the army of downtrodden and poor he found a lot of followers.

> So enchanting was the vision of a stateless society, without government, without law, without ownership of property, in which, corrupt institutions having been swept away, man would be free to be as good as God intended him …
>
> Tuchman, p.72

so enchanting that six heads of state were assassinated in the twenty years leading up to 1914.[7] The anarchists proved an unusual and difficult foe; committed to being stateless, they were an enemy for which the state's standing armies were unprepared. In these years European cafes were places where one's time drinking coffee was likely to be disrupted by a strategically placed bomb.

The 1890s also saw the rise of the industrial securities market on Wall Street. Before 1890 railroad stocks and bonds accounted for most investment options; the few industrial stocks were new, and considered risky. In the 1890s all this changed. Industrial shares gained wider acceptance, making it easier to raise finance, merge companies or float new ones. The era of 'frenzied finance' as the new twentieth century began. This led to another, brief, panic.

The 1907 panic

FROM OCTOBER 16 to November 6, 1907, the US, chiefly New York, witnessed yet another banking panic. The cause? Well, you could say it was just that too many people came to the banks all at once, demanding their deposits in cash, because of doubts about the solvency of banks. Of course, why so many should do so all at once is the real story. And the fact that Jesse Livermore made his first three million trading the short side of the market shows that at least one person foresaw the possibility of panic. Livermore gained the title 'Boy Plunger'. His shorts of 1929 would eventually dwarf his 1907 profits. We will get to that later.

The panic was triggered by the failure of both the Knickerbocker Trust Company and the Trust Company of America. Behind the Knickerbocker was F. Augustus Heinze. And attached to Heinze is quite a story about copper, a metal in increasingly heavy demand with the advent of electricity. Heinze had made his money out-foxing the copper trust Amalgamated Copper in the mining areas of Montana. He did this by using an obscure mining law of Montana state that permitted miners to follow a seam of copper ore from their own property even if it ran under the property of someone else, which such seams are wont to do. (The Montana legislature had thought such a law would increase production, but underground warfare was the result.) Heinze struck a seam of copper so rich it was practically pure, a seam that ran right into the property of Amalgamated Copper next door. Sitting on the board of Amalgamated was a veritable

7 President Carnot of France, 1894; Premier Carnovas of Spain, 1897; Empress Elizabeth of Austria, 1989; King Humbert of Italy, 1900; President McKinley of the US, 1901; and another Premier of Spain, Canalejas, 1912.

Who's Who of American business, including H.H. Rogers, William Rockefeller, brother of J.D., and J.P. Morgan himself. To reduce the bloodshed, Amalgamated Copper eventually settled out of court with Heinze for the princely sum of \$10m. With his new money and confidence, Heinze went to Wall Street to play the market.

And the markets were in a decidedly bullish mood. Said the President in his message to Congress on December 3, 1906: 'We still continue to enjoy a literally unprecedented prosperity.' Wall Street had no doubt about the President's perceived wisdom:

> It had for many years been a cardinal doctrine, in American banking circles, that a panic like those of 1873 and 1893 would never again be witnessed in this country. The ground for this belief lay in the phenomenal increase of our economic strength, the coordination of American industry since 1899, the establishment of the gold standard of currency, and, more particularly, the great and concentrated resources of our banks.
>
> A.D. Noyes, *Forty Years of American Finance*

But there was one other reason for acceptance of the President's views: belief in a now obvious twenty-year cycle in panics. There had been unprecedented growth since 1897, which had continued with two brief interruptions in 1901 (eight years from 1893) and 1903 (ten years from 1893). A further few years of growth was expected. Such a belief should put us forecasters on our guard. Markets rarely do what the majority believe they will – usually just the opposite.

The creation of credit, too, had been playing its part. After 1896, the volume of money in circulation rose from \$1.5bn to \$2.7bn by the time of the President's December 1906 message, with deposits at the banks rising from \$1.6bn to \$4.3bn. And the assets of American financial institutions had more or less tripled.[8] So banks were having no trouble making loans. Until 1906.

> '[G]old sales enabled prices to rise, industry to expand, and prosperity to return after the long depression of the early 1890s. But then industrial output began to outpace gold ... This slowing of the growth rate of gold [production], as demands for investment funds increased, rapidly caused a capital shortage.
>
> Sobel

Bank reserves were now lower than they had been, causing bankers to adjust loan rates upwards in an effort to reduce lending and recover reserves, but the demand for funds continued even at these higher rates. The UK interest rate was lifted 1 per cent to 5 per cent on October 11, 1906, then just a week later a further 1 per cent to 6 per cent. There was even talk of the rate going to 7 per cent, a level not experienced in more than one hundred years. Into this scenario came Heinze.

Heinze set up his own brokerage firm, bought a seat on the exchange,

8 Robert Sobel, *Panic on Wall Street*, p.301.

listed his new company, called United Copper, then hatched a plot to corner its stock himself by purchasing shares and call options, 'running up the price and inducing other speculators into going short'.[9] Once he had a corner, Heinze could exercise his call options and trap the opposing shorts in a classic bear squeeze.

Along the way, Heinze acquired a partner, Charles W. Morse, and together they began accumulating a number of banks as sources of funds to aid the plan. 'Chain banking,' said Noyes, of what was a growing play, a process watched by conservative financiers with increasing unease. Eventually the Bank of North America was bought, Heinze using its money to gain control of Mercantile National Bank, the assets of which, in turn, allowed the pair to gain control of the Knickerbocker Trust Company, one of the largest banks in the city. The trust banks were themselves exploiting a loophole in New York laws allowing them to operate without material reserves. (Anything to increase profits. This was later outlawed.) The United Copper play began in February 1907.

That year the Dow had a peak at 86.53 on March 12, followed by a sharp sell-off. We will assume one could not reasonably have known it was a high exactly on the day, but the Dow was off 12 per cent over the next few days, dropping 8.3 per cent on March 14.[10] Apparently no startling event precipitated the fall, but it took place when the listed corporations were reporting record earnings.[11] As abruptly as it began, the sell-off ended. The low for the month was on March 25.

Throughout the year, stocks were under pressure, declining steadily from the March high. In October there was a marked downturn, led by copper stocks. On Monday October 14, however, as other copper stocks declined, United shot up from 37 to 60. 'Heinze was sure that triumph was at hand and sent word to his various brokers to exercise his call options.' But for some reason the brokers were not acting as quickly as Heinze would have liked.

> Stories began appearing in the papers about United Copper, questioning its finances … Non Heinze and Morse banks began to call in loans the pair had taken, forcing them to sell stock at the worst possible time. On Tuesday morning [October 15] United sank under the weight of these problems and sank further as large blocks of stock from an unknown source – but rumored throughout Wall Street to be H.H. Rogers – were thrown onto the floor. By the end of Tuesday, United had lost all the gains of the previous day, closing at 36. On Wednesday it sank to 10. Gordon, p.191

The corner was finished. Almost simultaneously, there was a run on the Mercantile Bank. Normally the New York clearing house might have assisted a bank under such a run, but this time, influenced by Rockefeller

9 John Steele Gordon, *The Great Game*, p.189.
10 See www.buyandhold.com, Wall Street History, Heinze and Morse story.
11 Sobel, p.303.

and Standard Oil it is said, it refused to do so unless Heinze and Morse resigned as directors. They did so on October 18.

Such an event cannot reduce markets to a panic unless the conditions are ready for it, and unless the event exposes the lack of reserves in banks. Such was the case this time. 'The once solid banking institutions were like fully blown balloons,' writes Sobel, 'solid to the sight but easily destroyed with a single pinprick.'[12]

The following Monday, October 21, the bank runs continued, including one on the Knickerbocker, where depositors fought all day to get to a teller in scenes of utter chaos. The next day the Knickerbocker's president chose to open the doors at the regular hour, hoping the gesture would give confidence to the depositors. It didn't. 'Within a few hours they had withdrawn $8 million. By the afternoon the Knickerbocker Trust Company announced its insolvency and closed its doors.[13] Heinze and Morse were finished. Some weeks later the bank's president, Charles Barney, shot himself. So too, apparently, did a few of the banks unpaid depositors.[14] On October 23 queues of depositors formed outside other New York banks. A telephone call could spread the word pretty quickly these days. The situation was deteriorating.

Recognising its gravity, the Secretary of the Treasury arranged to deposit $35m of its surplus with the banks. The understanding was that it would then be lent to the trusts (the government could not legally deposit its funds directly into these trusts) to meet the demands of depositors to withdraw their money in cash. But it was not enough. The runs on the trusts continued for a further fourteen days. Account holders kept their places in queues at night so as to secure access next morning. On October 24 panic swept the exchange. Credit restrictions were so severe it was feared the exchange itself might collapse into insolvency.

At this point the panic was successfully stemmed, in the main by a group of bankers, headed by J.P. Morgan, who combined to extend liquidity (for a fee) to those trusts and other banks sustaining the largest runs. This is exactly the sort of thing a central bank is designed to do – to increase the supply of available money. Morgan also encouraged his associates to release optimistic statements to the press; then he summoned the city's religious leaders and demanded that they deliver upbeat sermons to their flocks on the Sunday.

The Dow bottomed for the year 1907 at 53 on November 15 (the equivalent drop today would be about 11,000 to 6,800). The legendary Wall Street trader W.D. Gann learnt his trade over the course of this decade, which culminated in his famous Ticker Tape Review article of 1909. The dates would not have been lost on him.[15] October 24 proved the

12 p,305.
13 Gordon, p.191.
14 See www.buyandhold.com, Wall Street History section, J.P. Morgan story.
15 The EIS website has a lot more information about Gann.

most difficult day for the exchange, still under pressure from margin selling, sending its president, Ransom Thomas (known for some reason as 'Pay Me'), to plead with J.P. Morgan for help in keeping the exchange open.

> When the support package was announced, pandemonium broke out on the exchange. Morgan heard a thunder of noise at his office across the street. It was the members of the NYSE giving him an ovation. www.buyandhold.com

The events of 1907 came after a steady rise in interest rates the year before. The collapse of the Dow in 1907 was followed in 1908 by an impressive 46 per cent return: it was a year in which credit conditions eased markedly.

> The restoration of credit at the beginning of 1908 was widely regarded as the catalyst for the ensuing bull market ... although credit conditions began to improve early in the year, the stock market ran well ahead of the economic recovery. Martin S. Fridson, *It Was a Very Good Year*, p.27

Such is the stock market in action, discounting future economic conditions six to twelve months in advance.

In 1908 William Jennings Bryan stood again for president on a Democrat ticket, and called for 'mandatory disclosure of campaign contributions above $100, as well as [the] prohibition of contributions in excess of $10,000.[16] Such calls are still being made (though the amounts to be prohibited have increased) and continue to fall on deaf ears. How otherwise could government be bought?

Significantly, Chicago land prices did not suffer greatly in 1907/8: Hoyt's data shows that prices plateaued but did not decline.[17]

> In this period sub-dividers could only sell vacant lots by building houses or apartments on them and selling land and buildings together. Although seventeen years had passed since the peak of 1890, there was no general boom in 1907, as there [had] been at seventeen-year intervals prior to 1890.
>
> Hoyt, p.219

Land value will not substantially increase until there is a manufacturing and/or population boom. This is why real estate is last on the investment clock (see Chapter 19, 'What Time Is It?'). Government-granted licences like real estate take all the productivity gains ultimately, but the gains have to present themselves first. 'Either the excesses of the boom of 1890 had produced an unusually long aftermath', continues Hoyt, 'or else land values had not kept pace with the growth of the city.'

Demand for the public domain continued right through this period also. Indeed, sales of public land were higher in 1908 than in 1907, but they did peak in 1908, twenty years from the previous peak in 1888. Rail stocks,

16 Fridson, p.16.
17 *Per Capita Land Values*, Fig. 98, p.410. See also Hoyt's Fig. 99, reproduced here as Graph 11.2, p.216.

as might be expected, peaked well before the crisis, in September 1906, ten years (121 months) from their low of August 1896, and were well off the highs of September by the time of the actual panic in 1907. The panic was in fact the low point for stocks, which bottomed in November.

Interest rates, in particular call loan rates, spiked during the panic. Banks called in these loans first and money could not be had, almost at any price. This was an 'elasticity' problem that the soon-to-be-created Federal Reserve Bank would solve with some success, as can be seen from the chart of New York interest rates (1894 to 1936) in the previous chapter (see page 199).

What the newspapers were saying about the panic of 1907 has been included as Appendix I.

The Federal Reserve

THE 1907 PANIC again highlighted the weaknesses of the national banking system. As already noted, country banks were keeping their reserves in reserve city banks; reserve city banks were keeping theirs in central reserve banks (mostly in New York) – a deliberate pyramiding of reserves. The New York banks at the base of the pyramid were not holding their reserves as currency or cash, they were putting them to other uses – such as call loans for stock market speculation. Satisfying a need for currency by banks at the top of the pyramid could mean stock-selling at the base as loans were called – at the very time when stocks would be worth least.

Once a run on one bank was underway, other banks, fearing they could be next, would hardly offer assistance. At the height of the 1907 panic,

> [e]verywhere the banks suddenly found themselves confronted with demands for money by frightened depositors; everywhere, also, the banks manifested a lack of confidence in each other. O.M.W. Sprague, *History of Crises Under the National Banking System*, p.259

After the panic, even the most ardent opposition to a US central bank was quietened. Over the next six years details were hammered out to create one.

The bill creating the new US institution commonly called 'the Fed' was signed into law by the President on December 23, 1913. Hundreds of thousands of hours of political manoeuvring had gone into its establishment. Twelve banks were created, one in New York, the others in designated cities around the country, reflecting probably a genuine desire for decentralised banking and a fear of control by Wall Street. The Fed is a private concern; it is not owned by the government (as is, say, Australia's Reserve Bank), though top officials are government-appointed. The Fed is run for the profit of its owners, the member banks.

All US national banks were required to belong to the new system; state banks were all invited to join but for them it was not mandatory. Member banks were required to contribute 3 per cent of capital stock to the Federal Reserve Bank in its district, and a further 3 per cent was to be on call. The member banks 'investment' became the capital base of each federal bank. Member banks also had to keep a specified minimum of reserves against their deposits, and one third of it was to be kept on deposit at the federal bank. These reserves became the deposits of the twelve federal banks. Against these deposits, the federal banks had to keep 35 per cent in cash or gold. This replaced the system of national bank bonds by which note issues had been secured; national banks were invited to surrender such bonds progressively.

Membership was to have its reward: the ability to borrow money from the Fed in times of need, perhaps when depositors came all at once to withdraw their money. For some banks, however, there were things the Fed could not cover. The continuing lawlessness in parts of the wild west prompted one Wyoming bank in the early 1900s to lampoon itself with this proclamation, issued after a series of shooting incidents:

> Patrons thinking an error has been made are requested not to shoot the cashier before making investigation. Strangers must enter the bank holding their hands above their heads or they will be fired upon by staff. Deposits of persons killed on the premises remain the property of the bank. The bank will not be responsible for lost guns or bowie knives. Persons desirous of transacting business quickly will please remember that shooting out the lights tends to delay rather than to expedite the work of the staff. This bank will not be responsible for the funeral charges of persons killed on the premises of the bank.
>
> Edwin Green, *Banking: An Illustrated History*, p.80

There does seem to have been a genuine desire on the part of most market players to do something about the terrible depressions and banking panics that had become a regular feature of US economic life. The downturns affected everybody. This, then, was what the Fed was set up to do: to stem the banking panics, regulate the money supply, and control the economic levers. In other words it had to control bank lending in good times and act as lender of last resort in times of panic. It was fervently believed, even by many of the best economic minds in the country, that a system had been found which would rid the country of the terrible panics.

War again

THOUGH LITTLE noted at the time in the US, Serbian terrorists assassinated the Archduke of Austria, Franz Ferdinand, on June 28, 1914. The threat of war was already in the air, especially after the decision in 1912 by Bulgaria, Serbia and Montenegro to declare war on Turkey. The Balkan War saw British consols (bonds) fall in price as English and European banks lifted interest rates. The English rate went from 4 to 5 per cent. European nations prepared for the possibility of hostilities. Thirty days after the shooting, on July 28, Austria declared war on Serbia, effectively drawing in friends and belligerents on all sides. The world was at war. The war is not our story, but it is relevant to the real estate cycle.

Of particular interest are Hoyt's Chicago real estate and subdivision statistics for this time. They show increased levels of building activity right up until 1917, a peak of property transfers in 1916, and a peak in subdivision activity in 1914, just prior to the entry of the US into World War I, though, 'compared with 1890, these were only minor peaks.'[18] The effects of the war, Hoyt noted, 'turned world demand away from housing to the production of munitions and foodstuffs to supply the armies in the field … and had cut short [the] land booms in the cities of the Canadian northwest and in New York city.'[19]

So, after substantial rises in real estate activity in 1913 and 1914, peaking some twenty years after the previous depression, the outbreak of war focused economic activity elsewhere: it became more profitable for US business to supply the world with instruments of war than to develop real estate. That is where economic activity now flowed (Graph 11.2).[20]

Graph 11.2: The Chicago Land Value and Building Cycles Compared with General Business Activity in the United States 1830-1933

(The business activity index is by Leonard P. Ayres of the Cleveland Trust Co.)

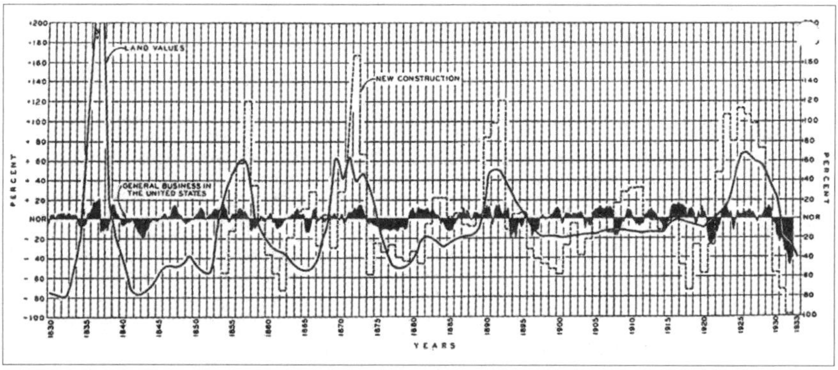

Source: Hoyt, Homer, *One Hundred Years of Land Values in Chicago*, Fig. 99

Although in the sixteen years from 1900 to 1916 land values had doubled, there was 'no wild excitement and no widespread public participation in the real estate market.'[21] Perhaps the 1893 downturn had been of such magnitude that its memory lasted a lifetime for those who went through it. Never again would they squander their hard-earned cash

18 Hoyt, p.219.
19 p.233.
20 Hoyt, Fig. 99.
21 Hoyt, p. 206, and see Fig. 99 above, extracted from Hoyt's research.

dabbling in real estate. It would take a further 18-year cycle for the memory to pass and another generation to take over.

When a European war was looming in 1914, American economists had been unanimous in forecasting disaster. European nations would, it was feared, sell their $5bn in US securities to pay for the war, resulting in a catastrophe for US interests. Partly in response to this, all US exchanges were closed on July 31, the day after hostilities began, and trading was suspended until further notice. Economist Irving Fisher, chief among the forecasters, wrote in August: 'This general depreciation of investment securities will doubtless lead to many bankruptcies, if not to a general crisis.'[22]

There was an active conversion of stock into gold, but the dire forecasts of economists proved spectacularly wrong. Britain and the European powers ended up selling gold to pay for armaments, and the US was flooded with the yellow metal. The exchange reopened – first for the trading of bonds – on November 28, 120 days after the closure. Trading hit its lowest volume in many a year on December 30, 1914; a mere fifty thousand shares were sold. Henry Ford must have been feeling bullish too, for it was in this year that he increased the daily wage of his auto workers from $2.34 to $5, an unheard of rate, and reduced the working day by one hour to eight hours. The *Wall Street Journal* denounced the new wage rate as an economic crime. The news from Ford roused more interest than the outbreak of war.[23] Within 48 hours ten thousand men had gathered at the Ford plant gates in Highland Park to sign up. Said Ford: 'Industry must manage to keep wages high and prices low.' His workers made a quarter of a million Model Ts that year – and sold every one of them.

For the market 1915 was a most profitable year, one of the ten most profitable ever, according to Fridson. Restoration of credit was again the catalyst that launched the 1915 bull market.[24] War contracts also assisted US profitability. Bethlehem Steel was supplying guns, shells and submarines to the UK whilst Du Pont ended up supplying 40 per cent of the Allies' munitions, increasing business from pre-war levels 276 times. The Morgan Bank purchased over $3bn worth of supplies for Britain, and at a 1 per cent commission booked profits of $30m.[25] The Bethlehem Steel stock price went from $47 to $460, with a high at $600 during the year. The American military-industrial complex was born. It is still with us.

Stocks in general had a short-term peak on January 23, 1915, then between March 15 and April 15 the Dow Industrials lifted 19 per cent (Graph 11.5, page 229). 'Fueling the furious speculation was a reduction in bank reserve requirements under the legislation creating the Federal

22 Quoted in Sobel, p.338.
23 Stewart H. Holbrook, *The Age of the Moguls*, p.207.
24 Fridson, p.32.
25 Gordon, p.203.

Reserve System.'[26] There was a brief reaction in stocks from May 6 to 10, in response to the German sinking of the *Lusitania*, but the following months saw the Dow continue its relentless upward move, jumping a hefty 13 per cent between September 15 and October 15 (180 days after the March jump).

> Easy credit was further facilitated by European monetary expansion as a means of financing the war. Through a variety of forces, including prosperity arising from war orders, deposits at New York clearing institutions increased by approximately 65 percent. That unprecedented rise helped banks to increase their outstanding loans by roughly 46 percent.
>
> Fridson, p.48

By the end of 1915, six-month money was available in New York at the highly attractive rate of just 2¾ per cent. Easy money!

Graph 11.3: New York Interest Rates 1912-19

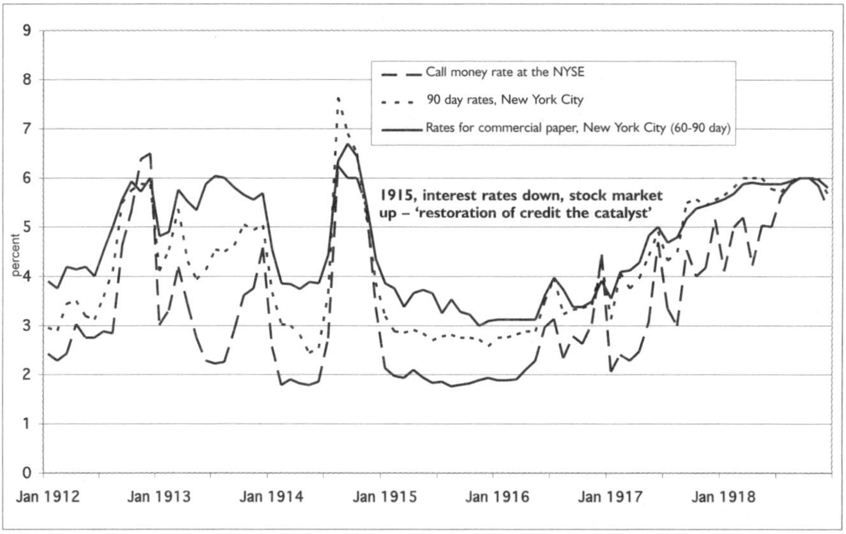

Source: Macauley, Frederick R., *Some Theoretical Problems Suggested by the Movements of Interest Rates, Bond Yields and Stock Prices in the United States Since 1856*, NBER Inc., No.33, 1938.

The market was pricing in what was becoming evident: that Europeans were slowly selling their gold and stock holdings to pay for armaments manufactured in the US. This meant higher earnings, and therefore higher stock prices in New York.

There was talk of a new era unfolding as the Dow climbed some 80 per cent in 1915. And, now that the Fed was in control, a belief grew that

26 Fridson, p.37.

banking panics and economic depressions could be eliminated. The first governor of the Federal Reserve, Charles Hamilton, himself hinted at this in one of his first speeches.

> If in the future business expands unduly under the spirit of speculation, the day of reckoning will come in the future as in the past. Undue expansion will correct itself just as the air bubble will ultimately bust. I believe, however, that the Federal Reserve system will materially check undue expansion by making banks conservative as to their loans, because of the knowledge that any departure from strictly commercial transactions will take away their ability to liquidate such investments by rediscounting in the Federal Reserve Banks…

Markets went on to experience the largest ever expansion seen to date, fuelled by easy money. Hamilton concluded his speech by saying that banking panics generated by distrust of the US banking system would be relegated to 'the museum of antiquities'.

The US was eventually dragged into the war, in support of Britain and France, in 1917, but not before making it plain to its allies that gaining access to new supplies of raw materials, especially oil, was on the agenda for negotiation. As W.D. Gann has made plain, past tops and bottoms help to determine one's future highs and lows, so it's worth noting that in February 1919 Sir Arthur Hirtzel, a top British colonial officer and head of the British government's India Office, pointed out to his superiors (though not publicly): 'It should be borne in mind that the Standard Oil Co is very anxious to take over Iraq.' At the end of the war Iraq's oil was divided amongst the victors, Britain, France, Holland and the US. Part of the spoils of war.[27]

The high prices paid for farm produce during the war produced an inflation of farmland prices. US farmers had never had it so good. The winning formula of the day was: 'Buy more land, to raise more corn, to fatten more hogs, to get more money in Chicago to buy more land.'[28] But in 1920 the end of the war saw a downturn: 'A boom, based on a scramble to replace inventories exhausted by war, collapsed simultaneously everywhere'.[29] On September 16 that year a huge bomb was detonated outside the Morgan Bank office on Wall Street, injuring hundreds and killing forty. Timed for two minutes before midday, it was calculated to upset the movement of nine tenths of a billion dollars worth of gold from one section of the US Treasury across the road to another. But the workers shifting the gold bars had broken for lunch a few minutes early that day. Just seconds before, the heavily guarded doors to the building had closed, thwarting what might have been the biggest bank heist in US history.

27 An analysis of the oil market using W.D. Gann's time-scale can be found on the EIS website (www.businesscycles.biz/subscriber/oil.htm).
28 Chandler, p.513.
29 Charles Kindleberger, *Manias, Panics and Crashes*, p.123.

The authorities tried valiantly to lay the blame on the Anarchists or the newly developing Communist Party, but no person or group was ever charged.

The downturn at the end of the war should not be lightly dismissed. It ushered in profound changes for 1920s America. Some five million returning US soldiers, and further immigration into the country, caused a housing shortage, particularly as, for the past five years or so, all production efforts had gone into war supplies. Hoyt notes that housing rents doubled between 1919 and 1924. Rent theory is interesting here. Returns to owners of existing buildings increased; the capitalised rate of return went up, which encouraged others to build and take advantage of the higher rents on offer, pushing up urban land values as demand for building lots increased. Hoyt notes that by 1926 US urban land values were double what they had been at the end of the war, and Chicago land values were up 150 per cent from 1918 values.

Graph 11.4: Wholesale Price Index
1866-1927 (1913=100)

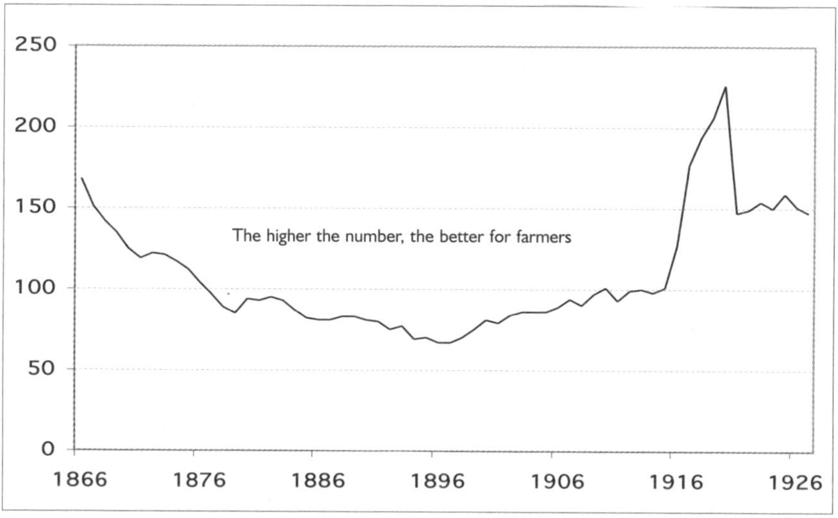

Source: Fisher, I., *The Theory of Interest*, Appendix to Chapter XIX, citing United States Bureau of Labor Statistics, Index Numbers of Wholesale Prices on a Pre-War Basis, 1890-1927.

On the other hand, agricultural America went into decline after the boom of wartime demand (Graph 11.4). Australian and Argentinean wheat was again available for European consumption and the few souls who survived the trenches and gas of Verdun could go back to farming in Europe themselves. It was discovered, also, that a large surplus of commodities had been stockpiled by the US during the war, causing a sharp decline in prices once this was realised. Farmland values dropped, of course. Hoyt says they halved. As the 1920s wore on, more and more country banks were suspending operations and closing. If this was noticed in Wall Street, it was ignored in the rush to get rich.

Another consequence of the Great War for our story of boom and bust was that it awakened the US public to the virtues of investing in liberty bonds, which were put out during the war. A whole new class of investors was created, 'people who had never before owned a bond or a share of stock in anything'.[30] And, come the 1920s, there arose plenty of men willing to sell the public all the bonds and stock they wanted.

The roaring twenties

THE YEARS 1921 to 1929, and the Great Depression which followed, have been intensively scrutinised. It is a history well known to most. There are a few misconceptions, however, that require clearing up, and a few points that need to be highlighted.

The 1920 downturn promptly reversed itself the following year. That all-important lending rate had much to do with it.

> In the fall of 1921 the national economic picture reversed itself in sixty days. The postwar depression promptly ended, and a new and more durable boom replaced it ... The recovery was officially smiled upon and encouraged by the Federal Reserve System, which, beginning in 1921, progressively reduced its discount rate from the postwar peak of 7 percent all the way to 3 percent by 1924.
>
> John Brooks, *Once in Golconda*, p.41

The discount rate set by the Fed was flashing easy credit conditions once again. Pretty much simultaneously, the new Treasury Secretary, Andrew Mellon (the Philadelphia banker who was possibly America's wealthiest citizen, who resigned as director of more than fifty corporations to accept his new government position), embarked upon one of the most systematic and vigorous tax-reduction programmes yet seen. As President Coolidge famously expressed it, 'the business of America is business'. Mellon agreed:

> ... government existed mainly to facilitate business; indeed it was no more than a business itself. Mellon set about improving the conditions for business by reducing the top rate of income tax from 65 to 32 percent, cutting corporate taxes to 2 and a half percent, and slashing capital gains taxes. As a result of these tax cuts the rich had more money to invest in stocks, companies reported higher after tax earnings, and more of the profits of speculation could be retained by the players.
>
> Edward Chancellor, *Devil Take the Hindmost*, p.197

What no historian ever picks up about such tax cuts, of course, is the

30 Holbrook, p.235.

effect on land value. The dramatic savings in income tax were quickly capitalised into higher land values.[31]

> The Revenue Act (1924) gave taxpayers a 25 percent reduction retroactive to 1923 income, increased personal and surtax exemptions, and brought the top rate (which had stood at 73 percent in 1921) down to 46 percent in 1924. This coincided perfectly with the land boom in 1924/25.
>
> Fred Harrison, *The Power in the Land*, p.134, n.17

The land boom was fed further by the easy credit policies of the banks.

> A particularly ominous development was the expansion of the banking system itself for the specific purpose of financing real estate promotion and development. Real estate dominated the policies of many banks, and thousands of new banks were organized and chartered for the specific purpose of providing credit facilities for proposed real estate promotions. The greater portion of these were state banks and trust companies, many of them were located in the outlying sections of the larger cities or in suburban regions not fully occupied by older and more established banking institutions.
>
> Herbert D. Simpson, *Real Estate Speculation and the Depression*, p.164, quoted by Hoyt, p.385 n.10

It is the rise of the stock market and its subsequent collapse that everyone remembers about the 1920s, but there was also a big, if not bigger, boom in real estate. As we have already noted, the price of urban land doubled between 1920 and 1926.[32] Such an increase would have left land and house owners feeling much wealthier than before.

The 1920s land boom

OKLAHOMA, OSTENSIBLY the last of the US frontier, had been settled within twenty-four hours on that memorable April day in 1889. There was, however, found to be just a little frontier left – in Florida – though part of it spent time underwater.

In the 1850s the state of Florida bought from the federal government millions of acres of land classified within the state as swamp under the Federal Swamp and Submerged Lands Act. For a while development was hindered by legal and debt problems, but by 1881 the way was clear for land reclamation and agriculture. This created a need for railroads to carry freight and farm produce.

It could be said that the story of Florida land speculation started with the railroads. There were three in the early days, though it was Henry Flagler's East Coast line into Miami, opened in April 1896, that really got the ball rolling, establishing a direct connection to New York. Soon the small Miami business community was going nation-wide, promoting

31 An excellent proof of why this is so is to be found in Chapter 3, 'Rent and the Dysfunctional Economy', of George Miller's *On Fairness and Efficiency: The Privatization of the Public Income over the past Millennium*.
32 Hoyt, p.234.

Miami as the place 'where summer spends winter',[33] though until 1913 one needed a boat to get to the beaches, before the Collins bridge allowed the motor car all the way into the city. After that wealthy northerners began building winter residences in Miami as Henry Ford's 'tin lizzies', Model Ts, started rolling south.

Early southern farmers had considered Florida land too sandy for profitable farming, but as the railroad carried more and more crops this belief was proved wrong. Soon

> people across the farm belts of the United States were heard sprouting the railroad promotion slogans, 'below the frost line' and 'ten acres and independence'. www.mcbobleonard.hypermart.net/railroads.htm.

In 1910 $1,000 could get you a piece of Florida acreage and a cottage, and such an investment could yield $3,400 from tomatoes in one year. 'Despite the need of huge doses of fertilizer and heavy labor, southern farmers [now] considered Florida an agricultural paradise.'[34] The railroad owners built massive hotels at their railroad heads and other strategic sites along the way, kicking off the winter hotel resort industry. The Spanish-American war of 1896, fought over Cuba, also focused attention on Florida, particularly the city of Tampa. A construction boom followed as many US soldiers returned to Florida to find cheap land to start farming.

By the early 1900s, developers were crying out for more land in Florida. In 1906 began the serious work of dredging canals to remove some of the water from the Everglade areas. The feasibility of complete drainage was discussed in a federal government report, though some were pressing for their preservation. One report, the Wright Report of 1909, claimed that 'approximately two million acres of Everglades land could be reclaimed by digging eight canals from Lake Okeechobee southeast through the Everglades, at a cost of about one dollar per acre.'[35] Land sales boomed. Real estate men lost no time in promoting the benefits of such land investment, auctioning off large swathes of undrained swamp. Said one buyer in 1911: 'I have bought land by the acre, I have bought land by the foot, but by God I have never before bought land by the gallon.' In 1912, however, the Wright Report was shown to be flawed – water from nearby lakes was flowing into unfinished canals. Florida's first land boom was over. Twenty thousand purchasers of land were demanding their money back.

World War I brought benefits to Florida, Europe being no longer a vacation destination for wealthy Americans. In 1915 Florida state instituted a substantial road-building programme. Four years later, when the Dixie Highway was completed, one road linked Michigan state all the way south

33 *Miami Herald*, September 15, 2002.
34 See www.floridahistory.org
35 See www.everglades.fiu.edu/reclaim/timeline/timeline6.html

to Florida. As highway construction increased in earnest, Florida was opened to the middle classes as well.

The economic impact of the automobile was recognised early in Florida, which benefited from the 'tin can tourists'.

> With the arrival of the twentieth century, Americans continued in the pioneering spirit of their forebears and looked upon the automobile as a new way to explore the unknown. Throwing a tent in the back of the car, thousands of Americans set out to enjoy the back roads of the United States. Carrying the extra gasoline in five-gallon cans, plenty of canned food, and extra tires strapped to the fenders, these intrepid souls began an exploration of the North American continent with a thoroughness that put Lewis and Clark to shame. These tourists became the symbol of another 'new generation' of Americans, restless, adventuresome and filled with boundless curiosity.
>
> Nick Wynne, *Tin Can Tourists in Florida*

These mostly northern travellers took their name from their b.y.o. tin-can cuisine carried in the car.

> [W]ith the postwar drop-off in industrial production in the north, many laid-off workers still had a cushion of money – and a Ford Model T. Instead of despairing, they decided 'Let's take a vacation'.
>
> www.tincantourist.com/ tidbits.html

En mass they headed to Florida, sometimes several families piled into one auto.

> 'What started with chilly Northerners seeking a slice of America's newly civilized frontier on which to vacation or to retire, soon turned into one of the greatest social and economic movements of population and capital in the history of the world.'
>
> *Smithsonian Magazine*, January 2001, quoting a promoter of the time

The kings of this movement were the land developers.

> If the railroad barons dominated the Gilded Era, the great land developers dominated the Florida of the land boom. These people didn't just design developments; [they] created entire cities. These architects and engineers did more than build houses; they created a way of life that became known throughout the world as the Florida lifestyle.
>
> www.floridahistory.org/ floridians/1920s.html

Developer Dave Davis dredged two mud islands in Tampa Bay and built Davis Islands, complete with yacht clubs, hotels and tennis courts. Barron Collier, who made his fortune from streetcar advertising, put together 1.3 million acres of the state after visiting Florida in 1911, then built the city of Naples and Marco Island into winter resorts that proved wildly popular. (It was Collier who pressed for the drainage of the Everglades.) Carl Fisher built Miami Beach, investing in it his substantial fortune from the manufacture of automobile headlamps. Locals literally gasped as Fisher proceeded to fill hundreds of acres of swamp with sand dredged from the bay, top it with thousands of tons of Everglade topsoil, then build hotels, golf courses, yacht clubs and polo grounds.

A born promoter, Fisher had started his working life at the age of 12, selling newspapers on the railway. Sales soared when he started flashing a photo of a naked woman from underneath his jumper. This time, to draw attention to his Miami Beach development, Fisher 'brought in a circus elephant, imported a polo team from England, dressed young women in risqué bathing suits, and started taking pictures.'[36] The press loved it. Soon, every paper in the country was carrying pictures of suitably un-clad women on the beach in Florida. All of a sudden, Florida was the place to be. Fisher's promotions sparked a national hysteria for Florida real estate.

> Fisher was the first man to discover that there was sand under the water... that could hold up a real estate sign. He made the dredge the national symbol of Florida. www.theledger.com/static/top50/pages/fisher.html

By 1925 Florida was known for wide avenues, golf courses, palm trees and sun-drenched beaches. Southern Florida became the American Riviera: 'a place to vacation, a place to be seen, a place to make money'. Could Florida real estate be anything else but a sure thing?

Sea-front lots were offered to investors, especially wealthy northern investors, with just 10 per cent down. It was implied that, by the time your second installment was due, your investment could have doubled in value. Lots forty miles from Miami were going for $20,000, a beachfront lot for $75,000.[37] Most of the real estate activity took place in the hundred-mile stretch from Palm Beach to Miami. By early 1925, those who had bought in '23 had seen gains of 600 per cent or more.[38] Lots were being sold and re-sold many times over. Real estate men lined the railroad stations, waiting for their buyers, or had students, 'binder boys', stand at the lot sites in the blazing midday sun to take bids. 1925 saw $1 bn flow into Florida construction: Wall-Streeters bought up, small town America converted its savings into Florida lots, even wealthy Europeans came to Florida to invest.

So many citizens were now pushing Florida real estate that the municipal authorities had trouble finding essential staff – policemen, firemen and other employees were quitting to buy and sell land. The Miami authorities resorted to grabbing sharecroppers from the hills of Georgia to put into uniform, despite the fact that most had never before worn shoes. The desired improvement in law and order was not achieved.

Towns north of Florida reported a severe slump in the movie business because so many theatre-goers were travelling south. Warehouse managers as far away as New York were running out of space because of all the

36 See www.pbs.org Mr Miami Beach.
37 See www.digitalhistory.uh.edu
38 See www.buyandhold.com, Florida land boom.

furniture they had in store from those selling up and travelling south. Said the *Indianapolis Times*: 'Literally thousands of people are leaving our state in search of something for nothing in the land of oranges and speculators.'[39] The Massachusetts Savings Bank Association complained that more than a hundred thousand depositors had taken their money out of the state's banks and headed to Florida to buy land.

Readers of history might have seen such a story before. Prosperity that depends solely on ever-rising prices will not last. Minor difficulties arose late in 1925. In that year new federal income tax laws required officials to study real estate records for understated or unstated profits. Anti-Florida propaganda mounted up north. That October a nation-wide rail strike halted deliveries of building materials to Florida. Then, early in 1926, the *Prins Valdemer*, filled with lumber, overturned in Miami harbour, delaying shipments of further building supplies for additional weeks. Further bad news followed in March when the US stock market took a dive. The Dow fell from 162 to 135, bottoming on March 29 and 30, though it went on to recover strongly by June.

Perhaps this gave some pause for thought. Money and credit were starting to thin out too. The flow of speculators along the Dixie Highway began to reverse a little as a few prospective buyers headed back north. Those who did so avoided the hurricane that hit Miami on September 18, 1926, killing almost four hundred and injuring thousands. There had been nothing like it since 1910, but back then there was little man-made to destroy. As the 125 mph winds swept in from the Atlantic and moved counterclockwise over Lake Okeechobee, the southern end of the lake dried up. As the storm passed, it brought a wall of water to the towns of Belle Glade and Moore Haven, drowning three hundred. The news of people drowning in a wave thirty miles from the Atlantic stunned the world.[40]

Reconstruction began immediately, but another hurricane struck in 1928, ending the Florida land mania for decades to come. Said historian and former St Petersburg, Florida realtor, Walter Fuller: 'The 1925 Florida land boom just ran out of fuel in the late fall of 1925 and quit – we just ran out of suckers, that's all.' All the major real estate players went bust and lost every cent. The Marx Brothers parodied the whole Florida episode in their 1929 production of *The Cocoanuts*: opening a hotel, auctioning off plenty of land (naturally), thwarting a jewel heist and generally carrying on as only the Marx brothers could do.

Meanwhile in Chicago the cycle played out in pretty much the same way as in previous Chicago booms – only this time the public was contacted by telephone. Land promoters called everyone listed in the newly available telephone directory to arrange an appointment with real estate sales representatives.

39 Dana L. Thomas, *Lords of the Land*, p.198.
40 See www.floridahistory.org/floridians/1920s.htm

> Free train rides and free lunches lured the prospect to the property where promises of a safe investment coupled with a great speculative profit led many people of small means to invest their life savings. Hoyt, p.257

Lambs to the slaughter…

The increasing speed of transport and communications, including the advent of the automobile, was massively changing urban landscapes, not just in Chicago. A surge of population outwards from city centres had begun (which continued in earnest after 1945), to places where new homes could be built with impressive modern amenities such as bathrooms. There was a huge demand for the new way of suburban living, much of it funded by credit.

> Credit expansion always concentrates its booms in titles to capital, in particular stocks and real estate, and in the late 1920s, bank credit propelled a massive real estate boom in New York City, in Florida, and throughout the country. These included excessive mortgage loans and construction from farms to Manhattan office buildings. Murray N. Rothbard, *A History of Money and Banking in the United States*, p.418

As a self-confessed libertarian Rothbard was unable to see that the capitalisation of government-granted licences and privileges into tradable commodities is the true cause of the real estate cycle. Nevertheless, libertarians remain good at analysing credit and the role played by banks.

The new era

NO DOUBT the mid-1920s income-tax cuts, courtesy of Treasury Secretary Mellon, influenced the stock market too. And continuing credit expansion brought forth imaginative ways in which to spend such cuts. Gaining leverage was the key. Call loans were already a common feature of the market by this stage. Buying stocks on margin was not new in this era, but the activity came to be practised far more widely. And no longer just for stocks. Call loans were available for many other consumer items as well. A Model T Ford could be had with, say, $100 down and the balance, perhaps another $300, financed through the dealer and paid off month by month, the car being the collateral for the loan. Listed corporations saw the benefits of leverage – borrowing – to increase earnings and hence stock prices. Investment trusts used the process extensively. A new trust company might float on the exchange, raise money, and invest the proceeds immediately back into the market with the purchase of listed stocks, also on margin. Certainly by 1927 it was conceivable that a margined individual buyer of a share in a listed investment trust was buying a trust that owned stocks that were margined, and that possibly even owned shares in other investment trusts. Leveraged trusts were buying other leveraged trusts. A small movement of the price could increase one's wealth substantially – provided that prices went up…

And prices did go up, all decade. Another new era was truly believed to be underway. President Coolidge, in his 1925 inaugural address, said, 'We appear to be entering an era of prosperity which is gradually reaching into every part of the nation.' The public had no reason to doubt him. The Fed had solved the business cycle once and for all: management was learning to operate at lower levels of inventory; leaders of industry were better educated than ever; mergers were promising greater economies of scale; and investment trusts could be seen to be ameliorating speculative fluctuations (according to Irving Fisher at least). One professor, Paul Nystrom of Columbia, even concluded that the nation, now 'dry', could increase the efficiency of its workers by switching demand from alcohol to 'home furnishings, automobiles, musical instruments, radio, travel, amusements, insurance, education, books and magazines.' Said John Moody, founder of the Rating's Agency that bears his name: 'No one can examine the panorama of business and finance in America during the past half dozen years without realizing we are living in a new era.'

Banks were of course very much involved in what was happening, and the 1920s saw a number of developments in their systems of handling payments and in their record-keeping; there were huge increases in efficiency.

> Telephones and typewriters, calculating machines and addressing machines had of course made their banking debut well before the First World War but this equipment was rarely found outside headquarters. Record keeping in small banks had been dominated by hand written ledgers and registers of securities; the only mechanical aides were coin weighing scales and the cumbersome hand presses used for wet-copying manuscript documents. In the interwar period by contrast, banks introduced ledger posting machines, dictaphones, loose-leaf binders and card indexes, not only at their head offices but branches as well. Edwin Green, *Banking: An Illustrated History*, p.108

And it was women who were mainly recruited to operate the new machinery, giving many a new-found independence, and spending money.

This was not the first time a new era had been seen on the horizon. As far back as 1825 Disraeli had asserted that the boom of 1825 in Britain would not turn to bust, the era being so different from times past because of superior commercial knowledge.[41] In 1928 the outgoing US President, President Coolidge, took the unprecedented step of publicly stating that he did not believe brokerage loans were out of hand: 'The rise in outstandings simply paralleled increases in bank deposits and the amount of securities on the market.' Privately though, he told a journalist: 'If I were to give my personal opinion about it, I should say that any loan made for gambling in stocks was an excessive loan.'[42] The incoming President, Herbert Hoover, declared in his 1928 acceptance speech that the end of poverty was in sight.

41 Chancellor, p.191.
42 Fridson, p.69.

Politicians and their speeches … Why *do* we vote them in? Any public announcement will usually have an underlying agenda. It may not be obvious at the time, and it is rarely what you, the investor, need to hear.

Graph 11.5: Dow Jones Index, 1920s Boom

But perhaps this time things really were a bit different. For the first time in the US, woman was exercising her innate speculative talents. For the newly independent, freedom-loving gal, there was no better expression of her status than to while away her time watching the ticker in one of the special rooms set aside in the hotels of Upper Broadway: '…gum-chewing blondes [and] shrinking spinsters who looked as if they belonged in a missionary-society meeting,'[43] could be found watching the market all day. Some figures were suggesting women now owned more than 40 per cent of the nation's wealth and that 35 per cent of market turnover was attributable to them. They held about one-third of the stock of US Steel and General Motors, and perhaps half of the stock of Pennsylvania Railroad, dubbed the 'petticoat line'.

At the end of a day's trading, the girls could relax out on the road in a newly bought – and paid for out of profit – Ford, Buick or Studebaker. (Not everyone approved. Preachers lamented the auto as nothing more than a 'house of prostitution on wheels'.) The Lady Bulls spent the household money, why shouldn't they know better than hubby which shares to buy? They were said to be sporting losers, too. One lady speculator, upon

43 Chancellor, p.204, quoting the *North American Review*, 1929.

losing a million, insisted, 'I had a perfectly stunning time while it lasted.'[44]

The speculative bandwagon hit a minor bump in the road in October 1929. Writing in *Forbes Magazine* as early as 1928, Richard Schabacker perceived a tightening of credit as the main threat to a continuing bull market. 'There can be little doubt', he declared, regarding the steep rise in stock prices since 1921, 'that the underlying cause for such advances has been easy money.'[45] A healthy business climate and benign government policies had contributed, said Schabacker, but only as background factors.

The Peak

> At first it seemed as though the market rise was a once-in-lifetime chance to make money with little or no risk. But as stock market prices continued to rise, many began to believe that the rise would be permanent, that the growth curve would be unending. In prospect, this conclusion was reasonable, for the nation was engaged in a great expansion, profits were rising, and conditions seemed sound.
>
> Sobel, *The Great Bull Market*

CONDITIONS ALWAYS do seem at their best right at the top. This is everyone's most bullish moment. And the '20s were not called 'roaring' for nothing. Frederick Lewis Allen, who lived through the '20s and wrote his account of it in *Only Yesterday*, described the decade thus:

> The rich man's chauffeur drove with his ears laid back to catch the news of an impending move in Bethlehem Steel; he held fifty shares himself on a twenty point margin. The window cleaner at the broker's office paused to watch the ticker for he was thinking of converting his laboriously accumulated savings into a few shares of Simmons

Allen continued with stories of a broker's valet who made nearly a quarter of a million dollars in the market, and of a nurse who cleaned up thirty thousand following tips from grateful patients. It was claimed in a new book published in August 1929, *New Levels in the Stock Market*:

> We have seen our country as it has grown at a tremendous rate in population; in wealth; and in the desire for finer things. Each generation has been thrilled by the rapidity of the progress which it has experienced in its lifetime. An optimistic psychology is in the air.
>
> Charles Amos Dice

The decade had indeed been one of optimism and crowds: 'An era celebrated for excesses and exhibitionism in every facet of human behavior.'[46] Men hung suspended from aeroplanes, walked tightropes between the highest buildings, or escaped from strait-jackets suspended above city streets. Women sought to emulate the swim of Trudy Ederle across the

44 Chancellor, p.205, quoting journalist Edwin Lefevre.
45 Fridson, p.68.
46 J.P. Chaplin, *Rumor, Fear and the Madness of Crowds*.

English Channel. Mid decade, August 24, 1926, saw one of the worst crowd riots in New York's history when around seventy thousand people took to Broadway, near 66th Street. Hundreds were injured, many trampled underfoot, as the crowd, mostly women, jostled to view their recently departed heart-throb Rudolph Valentino, the movie hero of the '20s, lying in state in a funeral parlour.

> The idol of the hour … his movie love-making gave his female fans high voltage emotional jolts … men too came under his spell, and many copied his oiled back hair-do, gaucho style side-burns and broad bottomed trousers.
>
> J.P. Chaplin, quoted in Robert Menschel, *Markets, Mobs and Mayhem*, p.111

As it was with Rudolph, so it is with the economy: there comes a time in the life of every boom when the taps must be turned off. 'Faced with the growth of speculation, the Fed changed tack and from February 1928 successively raised the discount rate until it reached 6 percent in August 1929.'[47] Rising interest rates are almost guaranteed to bring on a contraction in credit, as banks and/or monetary authorities attempt to curb speculation.

There were a few Cassandras warning that expansion would not go on forever, that what went up had an ugly tendency to come down. Roger Babson was one. A market forecaster and economist, he repeated his assertion in early September that a crash was imminent; he had been saying that for several years. This time the market responded and the slight selloff after September 3 was termed the 'Babson Break'.

The Turn

IN THE middle of September 1929 word was received from London that the business empire of Clarence Hatry had collapsed amidst revelations of fraud. (It eventually transpired that Hatry had been creating and issuing false securities to finance his business dealings, eventually drowning in $65 m worth of debt to the banks.) 'The bank of England reacted by raising interest rates, causing British investors to start selling their American investments and repatriating their capital.'[48] Why this collapse led directly to an interest rate rise is not all that clear. Nevertheless, it may have been enough to have investors re-think their belief in future prosperity. The celebrated economic historian Charles Kindleberger wrote of the Hatry revelations:

> [The Hatry empire] consisted of a series of investment trusts and operating companies in photographic supplies, cameras, slot machines, and small loans, all of which Clarence Hatry was trying to parlay into a larger operation in steel. He was caught using fraudulent collateral in an attempt to borrow £8 million to buy United Steel, and his failure led to tightening of

47 Chancellor, p.198.
48 Chancellor, p.214.

> the British money market, withdrawal of call loans from the New York market, a topping out of the stock market, and the October crash.
>
> *Manias, Panics and Crashes*, p.71

Again, that un-looked for event at the peak, or just after, that reveals the economic show for what it is: a show built on sand – on credit. It was the land price that had peaked first, however.

Graph 11.6: Dow Jones Index, 1929

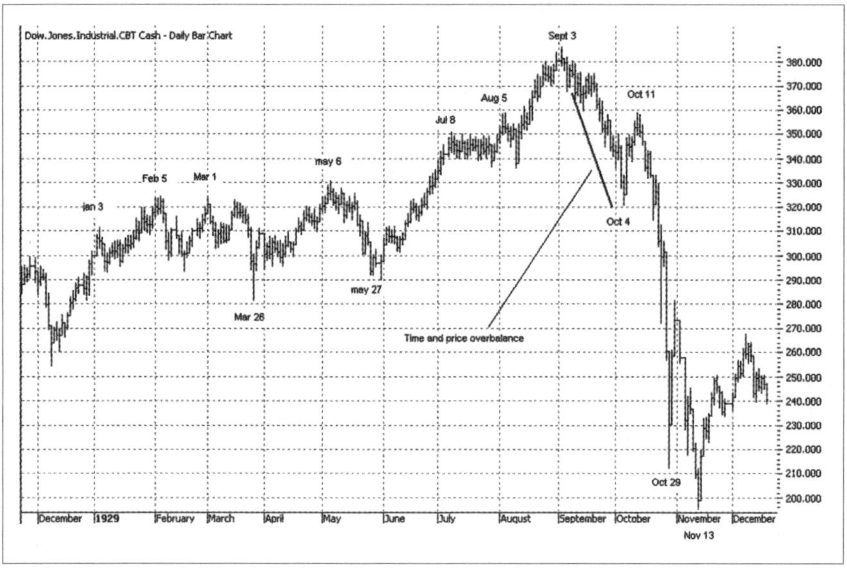

On October 4 (30 days from the market top) Alfred Sloan, the head of General Motors, observed a sudden dip in car sales and announced that the end of the expansion was at hand. Markets seemed to have anticipated the news. The announcement marked a short-term low from which the Dow, as usual, bounced back by half, highlighting an overbalance of time and price. After that market players began accentuating bad news and ignoring good – the reverse of what had gone on before. This emotional aspect of markets can never be ignored. Gann believes market psychology unfolds according to time frames, which repeat – something I have come to accept, having seen it so often now. Time frames of 180 – days, weeks or months – can be especially important. A more scientific assessment might call this process 'cognitive dissonance': it is a process of selectively filtering information so that it accords with one's own beliefs. Anything found to be in disagreement is ignored, is actively avoided – until the pain of avoidance becomes greater than the pain of recognising the truth. This is why markets trend. Spot the trend early and one is well on the way to solid profits, as the great stock market trader Jesse Livermore pointed out. Livermore ought to know. A biography sourced from Livermore family records shows that the trader had taken profit to the tune of $100m by the October 1929 low.[49] A mere six years later his wife had spent the lot.

The Dow achieved a new record high on November 28, 1928, after which a marked sell-off began, down to the low of December 7. The absolute top for the Dow came on September 3, 1929, 270 days later. The subsequent crash was on October 29, 1929, on volume of 16.4 million shares, a record that was not exceeded for forty years. On that day the ticker stopped, overwhelmed; only hours afterwards were the day's records completed. Telephone lines were overloaded with inquiries; the telegraph system could not process the number of margin calls made and the transatlantic cable broke. September 3 plus 52 days indicated October 24 as the day to watch in advance. It came to be called Black Thursday, due to the unprecedented selling. On October 24 the Dow dropped 9 per cent on volume of 12.8 million shares, only to be eclipsed four days later on the 29th when the Dow dropped 17.3 per cent.

On the night of the crash Groucho Marx paused on stage, in an unscripted moment in the Broadway version of the Marx Brothers' comedy *Animal Crackers*, to lament the plunge in stock prices – a line the New York crowd of October 1929 would have instantly recognised. 'Living with your folks, the beginning of the end,' said Groucho, commenting on the possibility of marrying his usual foil, actress Margaret Dumont. 'Drab dead yesterdays shutting out beautiful tomorrows. Hideous, stumbling footsteps creaking along the misty corridors of time. And in those corridors I see figures, strange figures, weird figures, Steel 186, Anaconda 74, American Can 138…'[50] Groucho had good reason to know the figures; it is believed he too had been speculating heavily.

On October 24 the president of the Stock Exchange, Richard Whitney, attempted some theatrics of his own. After a hastily arranged meeting of wealthy bankers had broken up shortly after lunch – a meeting he was desperate to show was not a panic meeting – Whitney (J.P. Morgan's own broker) strode to the post where trading in US Steel took place and yelled an order, showman-like, for ten thousand shares of the company at 205, even though the most recent sale price and current offer was below 200. It was 'the most celebrated single order in Stock Exchange history'[51] and a clear demonstration of organised support for the market. The bankers committed some $240m to buying, according to some later reports, but the market continued down anyway. Indeed, so ferocious was the further selling that some of the bankers present at the meeting were later that day forced to deny that the group had reversed their position and were now selling.

49 Richard Smitten, *Jesse Livermore: World's Greatest Stock Trader*, John Wiley & Sons, 2001, p.147.
50 Quoted in Insana, *Trendwatching*, p.2.
51 Brooks, p.125.

And it was sell at any price. The story went that White Sewing Machine Company stock, having fallen from 50 to 10, could not find any buyers after lunch on the day of the crash, at which point someone, said to be one of the exchange runners, put in an order to buy a heap of shares at just one dollar. In the absence of any other bids he got all the stock he wanted.

Claud Cockburn, a visiting English journalist who happened to have been invited to lunch at the home of a prominent Wall Street banker, Sir Edgar Speyer, on the day of the crash, told of a sudden disturbance in the kitchen as the butler and footman were serving the main course of lamb. Four or five maidservants of various ages had been standing behind the door, looking agitated and angry. The butler begged Sir Edgar to come into the kitchen for a moment to sort things out. The staff, it was explained to the visitor, had their own ticker-tape in the kitchen and were all heavily engaged in the market…[52]

The glamour stock of the era had been Radio Corporation of America (RCA). From $1.50 a share in 1921, the stock went to $574 in 1929, such was the speculative frenzy in the new radio technology. Neither profits nor dividends had supported the rise. Those who tuned in late and bought in 1929 would not break even on the investment until the mid-1960s.

In the end, the number of suicides told the story of woe. Legend has it that the most popular exit was jumping from the window of a skyscraper, but most, like the speculator J.J. Riordon, simply took a gun and shot themselves – Riordon having to go first to his bank on November 8 to get his pistol. The comedian Eddie Cantor gave strength to the suicide legends. Had he not seen two speculators jumping off the Brooklyn Bridge holding hands because they shared a joint account? Had he not overheard a hotel receptionist questioning guests checking in whether they came to sleep or to jump?

The scams

After the downturn had well and truly begun, the usual scams came to light – only this time on a hitherto unimaginable scale. What goes up…

The Vans – brothers Oris and Mantis Van Sweringen

The Van brothers were born two years apart but did everything together; one was seldom seen without the other. They lived in a huge Cleveland mansion but employed no servants, living in just a few rooms and sleeping in twin beds.[53] They were successful property developers. One of their projects had been to connect Shaker Heights to downtown Cleveland by rail. In this the Vans had made use of a holding company, a new development for the era, the Nickel Plate Securities Coy, which sold stock to the public to raise the finance. The Vans must have liked it, for they then embarked full time upon buying and selling rail companies, floating stock

52 Brooks, p.118.
53 See www.buyandhold.com, Wall Street history section.

and selling bonds. A complicated web of companies resulted, which the crash exposed as one huge pyramid scheme, the holding company (the Allegheny Corporation) being used to manipulate earnings. The whole put-together was sponsored by the bank of J.P. Morgan. (Not so different from subsequent events at Enron.)

Albert Wiggin

> 'I think it is highly desirable that the officers of the bank should be interested in the stock of the bank.'

Albert Wiggin was Chairman of Chase National Bank. At the Pecora Commission of 1933, set up to look at the circumstances of the 1929 crash, it was revealed that he had established his own private corporation to bet on the shares of the bank (not illegal in his day). Beginning on September 23, 1929, Wiggin began to short his own Chase Bank stock (financed by a bank loan – from his own bank), which he bought back on December 11 for a profit of some $4m. Canadian registered companies were used to hide the gains. After the details became public at one of the many inquiries held to explain the depression, Wiggin was forced to settle with a group of disgruntled Chase shareholders for $2m.

Sunshine Charlie – Charles Mitchell

> 'Securities are manufactured, like so many pounds of coffee.'

In 1921 Mitchell was CEO of National City Bank, a step up from his previous position, president of National City Coy, the securities arm of the bank. Banks did not have a charter to deal in shares but got round this by owning subsidiaries to do it for them. Mitchell built up a sales force to market shares and bonds to the rising middle class, eventually coming to underwrite over 150 bond issues, raising $10bn. By 1928 he was director of the Federal Reserve Bank of New York – a position of some influence and prestige – whilst still flogging his bonds, many now of dubious quality. One raising, for the Brazilian state of Minas Gervais, went ahead despite the bank's internal report denigrating the ability of the state to pay any interest, let alone the principal. Ever the bull, Mitchell borrowed several million from his bank on the day of the crash in an attempt to support the share price – which did not work. He was forced to resign his position in 1933 and faced tax-evasion charges; he was acquitted, despite admitting he hadn't paid taxes in years. The bank's stock price eventually hit bottom at just 4 per cent of its 1929 peak.

The Swedish Match King – Ivar Kreuger

The Kreuger Group (Kreuger and Toll) grew during the 1920s through a whole string of acquisitions by its owner, Ivar Kreuger. By 1929 it controlled three-quarters of the world's match production, built largely on debt to finance the buy-out of competitors. Kreuger and Toll attracted a large following of small United States investors with the payment of regular and quite large dividends. It was discovered later, however, that much of the money to pay the dividends had been borrowed from various banks. The story goes that Kreuger himself would draft the accounting statements, then have his accountants prepare the books to agree with what he had calculated the profit ought to be. Not surprisingly, the structure eventually collapsed, early in March 1932, under the weight of debts and Kreuger's own fraudulent activities. The collapse shook Wall Street to its foundations, and the ensuing scandal led to the passage of laws mandating the audit of the books of all companies listed on the exchange. Kreuger and Toll was one of the most widely held stocks and this was the largest bankruptcy of the time – until, that is, the Insull Empire fell. Upon discovery of the fraud, the Match King committed suicide in a Paris hotel on March 12. There were rumours that it was murder.

Samuel Insull

> 'Bankers will lend you umbrellas only when it doesn't look like rain.'

The empire Insull built collapsed owing some $700m. It was the largest corporate failure to date. Insull worked originally under Thomas Edison, helping to build and run the first electric power plant in New York in 1881. Moving west, to Chicago, he built Middle West Utilities into a company that came to supply 12 per cent of US power by 1912. It was one of Insull's companies that had helped light the 1893 World's Fair so brilliantly at night with the new wonder of electricity. Soon Insull was acquiring or merging the interests of his and other electric concerns into one listed vehicle, proving adept at issuing stocks and bonds to pay for it all. It was Insull who introduced the turbine into electricity generation, facilitating the transmission of this new power source. Turbines drove ships so why not electricity? By this time Insull had become known as the Aladdin of Power. And it was he who suggested power plants operate around the clock, to offset the high cost of operation; that US homes go all-electric; that US firms gear up for 'massing production' (later shortened to 'mass-production').[54] It was worth a million dollars, so it was said, to any man seen chatting with Sam Insull in front of his bank.[55]

By the 1920s US power supply was in the hands of just three entities, one of which Insull owned. The bribing of legislatures to get favourable laws passed was common, as were generous political contributions to those in power. Constant expansion involved ever-increasing amounts of debt. Elaborate networks of cross-company shareholdings were in place to fend off the constant threat of takeover. In 1928 investment bankers advised the formation of a new company, an investment trust, to own large blocks of

54 Robert Menschell, *Markets, Mobs and Mayhem*, p.7.
55 Holbrook, *The Age of the Moguls*, p.236.

shares in all the companies Insull operated. The IPO of the new company, Insull Utility Investments, offered at $12, hit the board at $30; soon it was at $150. The investment trust became the owner of numerous cross-shareholdings in all the Insull utilities, each highly leveraged so that any small rise in earnings had a disproportionately large effect on holding company profits. Insull was not averse to seeing subsidiaries sell assets to each other at 'manufactured' prices either.

Insull's mighty corporation at first weathered the depression in reasonable shape. He even managed to have his company loan the City of Chicago $50m to fund its payroll for teachers and police.[56] However, continued low cash flow as the depression wore on brought down the interconnected network in 1934; the debt could no longer be serviced. Insull was charged with mail fraud and embezzlement, and fled to Greece, a country with which the US had no extradition treaty. He did, however, return to face the charges and was exonerated on all counts, the court ruling that a holding company could not be held accountable for the actions of subsidiaries. But fleeing had not won him public acceptance; it destroyed his reputation. Insull died of a heart attack, penniless, in a Paris Metro station, though it was reported that he had reimbursed some of the investment losses of his employees, of which there were plenty, out of his own pocket. His investors were to get nothing, and were mighty unhappy at the prospect: thirty-six personal bodyguards were employed to protect the Insull family day and night from the threats of shareholders.

Richard Whitney

Acting president of the NYSE in 1929, while the president E.H.H. Simmons was enjoying an extended honeymoon in Hawaii, Whitney was officially elected president in 1930. It was discovered later that he had been living a lifestyle he could not afford, borrowing heavily and then stealing to cover heavy 1929 stock losses. His thieving had climaxed in 1937 with the embezzlement of $1m from the NYSE itself – much resented since the theft was from the Exchange Gratuity Fund (of which Whitney was a trustee) set up to pay the estates of exchange members $20,000 upon death. Whitney went to jail for his crime, the only character of his era to do so.

56 Menschell, p.7.

FURTHER READING

Baruch, Bernard M. *My Own Story*. Henry Holt & Co, 1957.
Brooks, John. *Once in Golconda*. Harper & Row, 1969.
Chancellor, Edward. *Devil Take the Hindmost*. Papermac edn, 2000. (Chapter 7 in particular.)
Fridson, Martin S. *It Was a Very Good Year*. John Wiley & Sons Inc., 1998.
Gordon, John Steele. *The Great Game*. Simon & Schuster, 2000. (Chapters 10, 11 and 12 in particular.)
Green, Edwin. *Banking: An Illustrated History*. Rizzoli International Publications Inc., 1989.
Harrison, Fred. *The Power in the Land*. Shepheard-Walwyn, 1983.
Hoyt, Homer. *According to Hoyt: 53 Years of Homer Hoyt, 1916 to 1969*. (Collected works, published by author.)
Latham, Frank B. *The Panic of 1893: A Time of Strikes, Riots, Hobo Camps, Coxey's Army, Starvation, Withering Droughts and Fears of Revolution*. Franklin Watts, Inc., 1971.
Menschell, Robert. *Markets, Mobs and Mayhem: A Modern Look at the Madness of Crowds*. John Wiley & Sons Inc., 2002.
Noyes A.D. *Forty Years of American Finance*. G.P. Putnam & Sons, 1909.
Porter, Glenn. *The Rise of Big Business*. American History series, Harlan Davidson Inc., 1973.
Simpson, Herbert D. 'Real Estate Speculation and the Depression', *American Economic Review*, XXIII, No. 1, March 1933.
Sobel, Robert. *Panic on Wall Street: A History of America's Financial Disasters*. Collier Books, 1972. (Chapter 9 in particular.)
— *The Great Bull Market: Wall Street in the 1920s*. W.W. Norton & Co Inc., 1968.
Sprague, O.M.W. *History of Crises Under the National Banking System*. Washington, Government Printing Office, 1910.
Tuchman, Barbara. *The Proud Tower: A Portrait of the World Before the War, 1890-1914*. Bantam Matrix, 1972.
Wicker, Elmus. *Banking Panics of the Gilded Age*. Cambridge University Press, 2000.
www.buyandhold.com, Wall Street History section. (Plenty of very good reading.)

12

Hydrocarbon Man

The Land (real estate) Boom into 1973

The free land had been for a hundred years the outlet for restlessness, the field of ambition. When that came to an end, restlessness turned in upon itself and fermented into something a little bitter ... so long as there was free land, every man had the opportunity to create new wealth for himself by the simplest and oldest means known to mankind. With the end of free land, American men for the first time had occasion to look with envy upon the wealth of others, or with jealous scrutiny upon how they had acquired it. The end of free land was the beginning of those political issues which had to do, in one way or another with 'dividing up', or with curbing those who had much...

Mark Sullivan, *Our Times*, 1926

Never try to sell a man a larger lot than his wife can mow.

Bible talk for Real Estate Salesmen of the 1950s

SO THE FED had not solved the riddle of the business cycle after all. That periodic, land-induced slump was back, worse than ever. By July 8, 1932 the Dow was at 41, down 90 per cent from the '29 peak and only a little above its all-time low of 28 on August 8, 1896, 36 years before.[1] Things must have felt grim at this time, no matter where in the US one was; a lot of wealth had been created between 1896 and 1932, but there was little to show for it, at least in the Dow averages.

The market crash of 1929 was large, but not at the time catastrophic. There had been falls of similar magnitude before – in 1926, for example, with most market players expecting another one at some time in the future. Early 1930 saw a rally – the market was back by half. Stock markets have a habit of doing this, of course – of retracing by half (often exactly half) the prior move in the opposite direction. There are good reasons why the market should have done this in early 1930. The Hoover administration

1 The Dow averages, then twelve stocks, was introduced on May 26, 1896. Calculated each day by Charles Dow, it appeared in the paper he edited, *The Wall Street Journal*.

did several things after the crash in an attempt to maintain economic order and stability. The President urged business leaders not to cut wages, so that demand would not fall, and he suggested that firms might bring forward any construction plans on the books; and Treasury Secretary Mellon announced a further small tax cut.

Graph 12.1: Dow 1930s Crash

Several listed companies, US Steel and General Motors among them, announced dividend increases. Several corporations promised to guarantee employee margin accounts if necessary. Most importantly, banking authorities acted reasonably, if not predictably, by reducing interest rates. The Fed lowered the discount rate to 5 per cent on October 31, 1929, and to 4½ per cent several weeks later. As corporations withdrew funds from previously profitable call loan businesses, banks stepped in to stabilise the situation by placing funds in this area. In 1929, in contrast to previous panics, interest rates did not spike upwards as was expected. And there were very few bank failures immediately after that fateful October day, although the Industrial Bank in Michigan failed when it was discovered that several employees had 'created' $3 m to play the market, and lost.

Robert Sobel describes conditions just after the panic:

> The Federal Reserve Bank of New York … immediately contracted for an additional $160 million worth of short-term notes, followed by more purchases in the next few weeks. By the end of November, the Bank had

> accumulated some $370 million of such securities. These funds were used to maintain interest rates which, in previous panics, had risen sharply and then led to further difficulties … as many expected they would. Instead the New York Federal Reserve lowered its discount rate so as to make for an easy money policy. The rate went to 4 and a half percent on November 14, and to 4 percent on January 20, 1930; by mid-March it reached 3 and a half percent. The easy money policy was instrumental in restoring a measure of confidence and helped lead to the correction of December 1929-April 1930.
>
> *Panic on Wall Street*, p.387

The banking structure had been preserved with the bag of tricks we have come to expect from the Fed, in this instance inflating the money supply and lowering the cost of credit. And so the stock market rallied back by half.

Sobel, like most other historians of this period, gives a sadly superficial account of what happened next, failing to investigate the events which did bring on the depression: the continued collapse of land values, putting further pressure on bank loans. It went like this.

As already noted, US farmers had been having a tough time since well before the 1929 stock market crash. The boom for farmers had ended in mid-1920, when post-war commodity prices fell. An illuminating study of Kansas and the bank failures in that state throughout the 1920s, published by the Federal Reserve Bank of St Louis, illustrates this. Citing US Bureau of the Census figures, the study notes:

> Like most agricultural states, Kansas prospered from increased demand for farm output during World War I and immediately thereafter. The increase in output prices was accompanied by higher land prices and the expansion of agriculture into new areas. In Kansas, land value per acre increased 54% between 1910 and 1920, while in some states the increase was over 100% … [M]uch of the increase in land value … was financed with borrowed money from banks, and from 1910 to 1920 the number of banks operating in Kansas rose 30%.
>
> *Regulation and Bank Failures: New Evidence from the Agricultural Collapse of the 1920s*, pp.2, 3

Therein lies the issue, of course. Banks were doing what they do best – supplying credit to help businesses expand. But, as history is teaching those who study it carefully, the system we have inherited is a cyclical system built on sand. The farmers' terms of trade worsened as the decade progressed, and farm income declined (see Note 1 at the end of this chapter).

> … farmers found it increasingly difficult to repay their debts, and the consequent increase in farm loan defaults resulted in bank failures. Across the United States, areas which had enjoyed the greatest agricultural boom seemed to suffer the worst downturn, having the highest rates of farm and bank failure.
>
> *Regulation and Bank Failures*, p.3

Other studies confirm this observation.[2] Real net farm income declined some 60 per cent between 1929 and 1932.[3]

Table 12.1: Real Prices of Agricultural Commodities and Real Farm Income 1925-32

Year	Wheat	Cotton	Corn	Beef steers	Net income to farmers
1925	100	100	100	100	100
1926	90	74	106	93	90
1927	84	76	123	114	88
1928	80	86	121	138	91
1929	71	82	115	134	94
1930	57	60	90	113	70
1931	43	43	54	94	62
1932	39	36	59	86	43

Source: Rockoff, Hugh, *Deflation, Silent Runs and the Great Contraction*, Rutgers University, 2001, p.21.

The bank failures themselves occurred in part for a different (though related) reason: the profoundly poor structure of the US banking system at this time. This was due mainly to seemingly absurd government regulations, the prohibition of branch banking, often within states but in particular across state lines. Most state-licensed banks at the time, and for many years afterwards, were not permitted to establish branch operations in the way, say, an Australian or Canadian depositor would have been used to. It meant individual US banks were more vulnerable than they would otherwise have been to local economic shocks such as a land-price collapse. For our purposes this is of course incredibly fortunate for it highlights in the most obvious way the inherent flaw in the capitalist system that guarantees the real estate cycle.

Agricultural distress because of land-price declines, and the inability of farmers to repay mortgages due to commodity price declines, were the most important causes of bank suspensions and failures throughout the 1920s, while urban areas were enjoying the boom of a lifetime. Things got really serious when urban real estate declines brought similar conditions to city centres. This became evident late in 1930.

In early November the banking empire of Rogers Caldwell, centred on Nashville, Tennessee, collapsed (see Appendix 2 for a more in-depth study). Caldwell controlled the largest network of banks in the southern regions of the US and was heavily invested in real estate. On December 11, 1930, the New York based Bank of the United States (a misleading

2 See Alston, Lee J., 'Farm Foreclosures in the United States During the Interwar Period', for example, or Alston, Grove and Wheelock, *Why Do Banks Fail?* (See Further Reading.)
3 Hugh Rockoff, *Deflation, Silent Runs and the Great Contraction*.

name since it was not connected with the government in any way) went bust. This, it is said, was due not only to the stock market losses of its affiliates but also to an over-exposure to declining property prices.[4]

> It was one of the most disastrous failures in the banking history of the country … men wept as they tried to rush past the police guards and pounded on the closed doors; women screamed as they held up their bank books. Crowds refused to disperse and stayed outside the doors for days, hoping that their savings were not lost.
>
> James D. Horan, *The Desperate Hours*

It would appear also that a degree of mismanagement and director fraud was involved in the downfall.[5] The bank's investment in real estate had been excessive.[6] Curiously, the Fed literally stood by and watched the bank fail. It was at this point and not before that real concern about the safety of the banking system began.[7]

The Bank of the United States had some sixty offices in New York and depositors had been withdrawing money extensively over the preceding eight weeks – 25 per cent of its deposits, in fact. Reports of the bank's weakness had been suppressed since November 1929,[8] though it seems word was now trickling out. Although the bank went bust, it did eventually pay out a little over 80 per cent of its liabilities, indicating that it was probably solvent at the time of its collapse, just short of cash. Although this failure did not touch off a further liquidity crisis in New York – no other banks went down with it – the psychological effect of its closing was immense. Interestingly, the Dow broke below its 1929 November low in the week of October 10, 1930 – the market discounting bad news to follow. The Dow lowed in December for a two-month rise after that (see Graph 12.1, page 240).

Between April and August 1931 a banking crisis developed in northern Ohio and Chicago suburban regions, where small banks had established themselves and multiplied with the real estate boom between 1922 and 1926.[9] Collapsing real estate prices, this time in the mid-west, again brought on the crisis. These banks had been made more vulnerable to this occasional inevitability by a Chicago law, passed in 1923 by the Illinois legislature, outlawing bank branches within the state. It prevented existing banks from establishing offices in the fast-growing outlying suburbs, allowing only new banks to open there. These new banks were then highly dependent on a narrow asset base (although in the 1920s real estate promoters and developers loved it).

4 Edward Chancellor, *Devil Take the Hindmost*, p.223.
5 Susan E. Kennedy, *The Banking Crisis of 1933*, pp.1-5.
6 Elmus Wicker, *Banking Panics of the Great Depression*, p.36.
7 Rockoff, citing evidence using the deposit-currency ratio, a measure of the confidence of the public in its banking system.
8 See www.futurecasts.com website, 'Great Depression Chronology'.
9 F.C.James, *The Growth of Chicago Banks*, p.953.

> Promoters of real estate developments needed a source of funds to finance mortgages which they found in the chartering of new and independent banks. During the real estate boom land values had soared, and mortgages became valued securities in the portfolio of earning assets ... By the end of 1930 many of these banks in outlying areas were in dire distress ... The value of real estate assets plummeted ...
>
> Elmus Wicker, *Banking Panics of the Great Depression*, p.70

The Chicago banks that failed held fewer secondary reserves, had a higher percentage of real estate loans, owned more fixed assets and showed lower levels of earned capital than the Chicago banks that did not fail.[10]

In June 1932 yet another rash of bank failures occurred in Chicago, again because of declining asset values. 'Failures during the panic reflected relative weakness in the face of common asset value shock rather than contagion.'[11] In other words, falling land values against the loans outstanding. Again, the Chicago banks in trouble initially were the small neighbourhood banks in the outer regions. Then on June 24, a Friday, depositor fear spread to two banks in downtown Chicago, within the Loop, the Continental Illinois and the First Union Trust.

> In the case of earlier runs, the crowds had been drawn from a particular locality or a special group: this time people from all parts of the city seemed to converge on the Loop in hysterical fear and anxiety.
>
> F.C. James, *The Growth of Chicago Banks,* p.103

The fear continued into Saturday. It was only after the president of the First National Bank, Melvin Taylor, climbed up onto one of the marble pillars inside his bank to talk to his depositors that the fear began to subside – in Chicago at least. The toll, however, was mounting. By the end of July 1932, Chicago had just 60 banks left out of the 225 that had been in business in 1929.

A short time later, several Detroit banks failed in quick succession for the same reason: too many non-performing loans to the real estate sector. These failures triggered a wider and more general banking crisis in February 1933. The incident that precipitated the 1933 panic was a decision by the Governor of Michigan, on February 14, to close all his state's banks in an effort to protect the (Ford family) Guardian Group of Banks in Detroit. These were also heavily invested in real estate, the weakest bank in the chain being the Union Guardian Trust. 'The source of its problems was an unusually heavy commitment to real estate financing,' noted Wicker.[12] In fact more than 70 per cent of this bank's total assets were illiquid real estate mortgages.

So depositors maintained their distrust of banks with good reason,

10 M. Esbitt, 'Bank Portfolios and Bank Failures During the Great Depression'.
11 Charles W. Calomiris and Joseph R. Mason, 'Consequences of Bank Distress during the Great Depression'.
12 p.118.

revealing a marked lack of confidence in the system. Consequently banks just kept on going bust.

> It would seem that we can safely say this much, that real estate, real estate securities, and real estate affiliations in some form have been the largest single factor in the failure of the 4,800 banks that have closed their doors in the last three years and in the 'frozen' conditions of a large proportion of the banks that still remain open. Herbert D. Simpson[13]

Government decisions up to the beginning of 1933 had not been helping either. The Smoot-Hawley Tariff was passed by Congress in June 1930, raising tariffs on imports even higher. This prompted practically every US trading partner to do the same, exactly as the thousand economists who signed a letter of protest to the President said would happen. This law was one of the greatest government policy blunders of all time. Economists got that one right, but little else. Academic opinion at the time still called for no government action to alleviate downturns since they were pretty much ordained by God. John Maynard Keynes proved them wrong,[14] though his economics has been shown to be fallible too, as became obvious in the next land-price-induced downturn.

This economic belief, one of total laissez-faire,[15] may also explain the actions, or rather inactions, of the Fed as social conditions got worse. Basically the Fed did nothing. Interest rates were lowered, and declined to record low levels of around 1 per cent, but so did prices; in fact prices declined in some years by as much as 25 per cent. This left the real rate of interest – the true cost of borrowing money – at extremely high levels, a fact that seemed to escape the attention of monetary authorities. Credit conditions remained tight. One doubts this could ever escape attention again. The money supply contracted drastically too, by almost one-third. On this the Fed took no action either.

In 1931 the Kredit-Anstalt, one of Austria's biggest banks, collapsed, badly shaking confidence in Europe and adding to the nervousness of US bank depositors. At the same time some major US corporations were collapsing, including the Kreuger and Insull empires.

> The first [shock] was the suicide, in Paris, of Ivar Kreuger, which exposed an undreamed of web of fantastic speculative pyramiding in international finance. The second was the collapse of the Insull Empire in the Middle

13 *Real Estate Speculation and the Depression*, 1933, p.165, quoted by Homer Hoyt, *One Hundred Years of Land Values in Chicago*, p.401 n.26

14 In a system where the rent of government-granted licences is permitted to capitalise into tradable privileges at least.

15 The term *laissez-faire* originated with the Physiocrats of France around 1770. Conveniently though, English-speaking economists overlook the full expression, which is *laissez faire, laissez aller*, a loose translation of which would be, 'a fair field with no favours'. Today, whilst we accept the *laissez-faire* bit – to let go, to allow market forces to rule (the invisible hand) – we conveniently forget to level the playing field and continue to allow government to grant massive privileges and licences, doled out gleefully to those well connected or rich enough to bribe the politicians.

> West. By wiping out tens of thousands of small investors in America, and by further assaulting public confidence in banks and investment, these two financial crashes carried the country once more to the very brink of a general money panic.
>
> Lawrence Sullivan, *Prelude to Panic*, p.4

Overall, however, it was the decline in urban US property prices (a non-monetary cause) that was the real killer, because of credit-creation and poor real estate lending.

> As real estate investment was one of the principle means by which the assets of the banks had become frozen and as liquidity is of extreme importance during an epidemic of bank runs, the banks that remain[ed] open [were] extremely cautious.
>
> Homer Hoyt, *One Hundred Years of Land Values in Chicago*, p.401

> Real estate loans, not failed stock broker accounts, were the largest single element in the failure of 4800 banks in the years from 1930 to 1933.
>
> Charles Kindleberger, *Manias, Panics and Crashes*, p.103, paraphrasing Hoyt

Graph 12.2: Bank Lending
1921-40

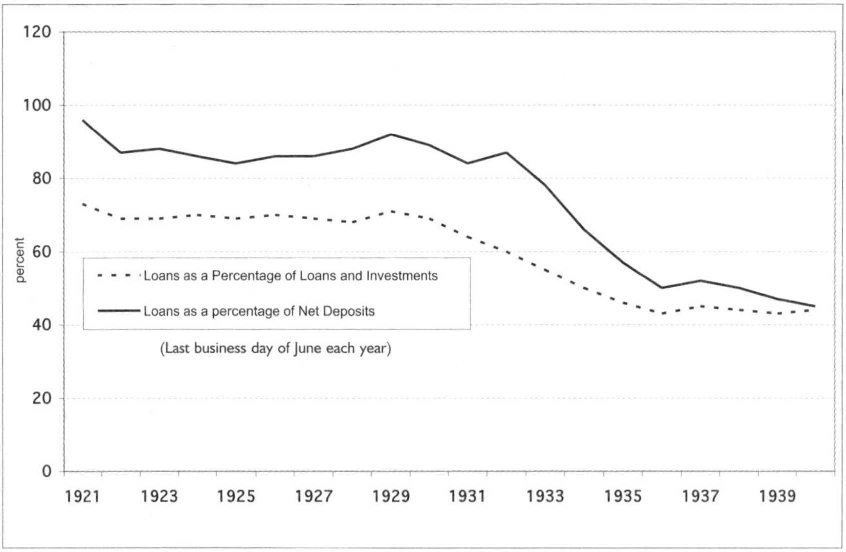

Source: Butkiewicz, James, 'Reconstruction Finance Corporation'. EH.Net Encyclopdia, edited by Robert Whaples (www.eh.net/encyclopdia/contents/butkiewicz.finance.corp.reconstruction.php), citing Banking and Monetary Statistics, 1914-41.

So the public continued right on hoarding their money. Who could trust a bank when so many were closing? There were some banks that found a way round the panics. Apparently the president of the Baker Boyer Bank in Washington state stopped a run on his bank by surreptitiously dividing what cash was left in the vaults amongst several close friends and relatives, who were then instructed to wave 'their' money about and noisily make a deposit, as they forced their way through the hordes of other depositors wanting to take their money out.

The causes and effects of the 1920s stock market boom and bust are still much debated today. Was it a bubble? Did that cause the subsequent depression? Historians and market forecasters would do better to turn their attention to the concomitant real estate boom and bust. The story goes that, in 1915, a Greek physician arrived in Chicago with little but a flare for understanding the workings of the real estate and rental markets. With a small investment, he acquired a number of vacant lots strategically located on business corners. By 1928, 87 such corners had been bought, most still subject to mortgage, with an estimated total equity of $6m. Blocks that had sold for $14,000 in 1905 were being sold in 1926 for more than $1m.[16] The new purchaser no doubt used the bank's money to buy. Could one call that a bubble? Historians fail to discuss it. 'Thousands of stories of sudden profits accruing to the owners of land could be cited for this period.'[17]

Is it any wonder Chicago banks were in trouble after the city's land prices collapsed? A land price collapse has far wider implications than a mere stock market crash. They are not in the same league.

The 1930s downturn wrought other changes too – women's hemlines for starters.

> The skirt length had come down with stock prices. Dresses for daytime wear were longer, if only by a few inches; evening dresses swept the ground … Frills, ruffles and flounces were coming in again, and the corset manufacturers were once more learning to smile … No longer was it the American woman's dearest ambition to simulate a flat breasted, spindle-legged, carefree, knowing adolescent in a long-waisted child's frock.
>
> Frederick Lewis Allen, *Only Yesterday*

Books and conversations about sex were out; decorum and romance were in. Woolworth's reported some of its best profits ever as people sought to buy cheap. Mini-golf was the new recreation: this now prosperous industry saw increased investment of some $125m, with some courses earning 300 per cent a month return on investment.

Recovery

THE MOST SERIOUS of the four banking crises developed in mid-February 1933. One by one, states were declaring local bank holidays as bank runs got worse. As one state declared a 'holiday', pressure was put on neighboring states as people sought access to cash elsewhere.

16 Hoyt, p.388, n.16.
17 Hoyt, p.388, in concluding his note 16.

> The final dissolution of the banking system was ushered in by the holiday declared in Michigan in mid-February. Most of the larger Michigan banks belonged to one of two holding companies. The smaller, the Guardian Detroit Union Group, was teetering on the edge of bankruptcy. A desperate effort was launched to save this group through a Reconstruction Finance Corporation loan combined with aid from the Ford interests. But the plan foundered on demands that the Reconstruction Finance Corporation hold adequate collateral for its loan and the unwillingness of Henry Ford to take part.
>
> Hugh Rockoff, *Deflation, Silent Runs and the Great Contraction*

This was at the time of the inauguration of the new Democrat President, F.D. Roosevelt, who immediately instituted a national bank holiday, closing all banks in the country. No re-opening date was set. Now, whatever one might think today of such an unprecedented action – every single bank in the entire country shut down – in 1933 it came as quite a relief to the public.

> 'That penniless springtime of 1933 revealed the people of Detroit to one another. It broke down the barriers of class. It ended whatever talk there might have been of Communism, Fascism or social conflict. Folk realized that ahead of them was a long, hard pull, and quietly they made up their minds to pull together.'
>
> Barrons, describing the event three years later, quoted in Martin Fridson, *It Was a Very Good Year*, p.103.

Editor's hyperbole perhaps. There was plenty of turmoil to follow, but now the people realised the government was finally in the mood to act. On March 13 the secretary of the treasury began granting licences to any bank wishing to re-open for business. About 75 per cent of banks within the Federal Reserve System re-opened after the imposed holiday, and within a month had an extra $1 bn to play with as hoarded currency and gold was re-deposited with them. The immediate crisis was over. Confidence is a fickle thing.

There were other government initiatives to further economic recovery. These included:

The Reconstruction Finance Corporation (RFC), which was set up by President Hoover to promote economic activity by lending money. Loans were made at first only to financial, industrial and agricultural institutions. In particular, the RFC was to help banks by easing the pressure for cash that forced them to remain highly liquid for fear of a run on deposits. (This of course begs the question why the government felt the need to usurp what should have been the Fed's role.) Roosevelt's New Deal expanded operations even to foreign governments.

But in the beginning the RFC lent particularly to railroads. Railroads were singled out because so many banks owned a good deal of their bonds, now worth far less than when originally bought since so much railroad business had disappeared. Improving the financial condition of railroads, it was believed, would ease the financial condition of their bondholders.

> The theory was that railroad bonds must be protected, since many of these securities were held by savings banks and insurance companies, alleged agents of the small investor. In practice, the bulk of these RFC railroad loans went to repaying debt. About a third of these loans went to repaying railroad debts to banks. Thus, one of the first RFC loans was $5.75 million to the Missouri Pacific Railroad to repay its debt to J.P. Morgan and Company, and an $8 million loan to the B and O Railroad to repay its debt to Kuhn, Loeb and Company.
>
> Murray N. Rothbard, *A History of Money and Banking in the United States*, p.292

This, of course, is a shifting of the debt from private to public interests, a bailing out of the banks at taxpayers' expense. These two banking concerns, in particular, were well connected to government. As soon as the Missouri Pacific had undertaken the task of repaying its banker, 'it was gently allowed to go into bankruptcy.'[18]

There was also direct lending to banks, which in return pledged part of their loans as collateral. This was a way for banks to raise cash to pay depositors without calling in loans. Nevertheless, the chart of bank lending reveals that it took a long time to recover during the 1930s (Graph 12.2).

The RFC also loaned directly to farmers, with one RFC subsidiary, the Commodity Credit Corporation, empowered to buy certain farm products at guaranteed prices, mostly above market, thereby setting a floor price for the product. This had the pleasant side-effect of underwriting farmland value – a value that many banks had created credit against.

The Agricultural Adjustment Act, designed to boost farm prices and provide subsidies to farmers in need. Under the Act a lot of existing crops and livestock were destroyed to reduce surpluses – at a time when many were starving – on the erroneous belief that over-production is the cause of depression and that limiting production and fixing higher prices would help lift the country out of depression.

Many of these subsidies have since been vastly increased and widened in scope, distorting today's world trade and causing needless third-world misery – but that's another story. Such subsidies, because they capitalise into land price, go on to create a vested interest in their maintenance. Take for example the sugar industry, based mainly in Florida. The Sugar Act of 1934, intended to stabilise the price of sugar in the face of what was considered at the time to be ruinous overproduction, is still in force today and has been expanded to include heavy quotas and controls on imports. To maintain its profitable protection, the sugar industry, though small by US standards compared to other agricultural industries, has become the largest agricultural donor to political campaigns. It rigorously promotes its

18 Rothbard, p.292.

product to make sure Americans eat vast quantities of it, despite health and obesity warnings. So important are its connections to top office that in 1996 President Bill Clinton is said to have interrupted an office tryst with Ms Lewinsky to receive a call from his biggest political donor in the industry.[19]

A new *Securities and Exchange Commission* (SEC) was created to oversee banking and markets, including a new federally controlled bank deposit insurance scheme. All bank deposits would now be protected by the government up to a value of $5,000 (since adjusted). There have been few bank runs since, but the scheme has created what some have called a situation of moral hazard for banking: if deposits are guaranteed, who cares about the risk?[20] The 1920s speculator Joe Kennedy, father of JFK, was put in charge of the new SEC. Many considered it an astonishing appointment. Speculator Joe had made his money in organised pools, insider-trading rings and any other scheme that was going. He had begun his market days in partnership with Bernard Smith, a renowned bear operator. Together they would secretly obtain access to highly confidential bank loan data in order to identify a heavily margined investor. Smith and Kennedy would then institute a savage bear raid on the portfolio of the unsuspecting stock owner and later, when the investor's bank had demanded further margin coverage, show up with an offer to buy all the stock – at a cheaper price, naturally.[21] Said the new President Roosevelt, however: 'It takes a thief to catch a thief.' And sure enough, Kennedy set about efficiently outlawing all the practices that had made him so rich.

The federal government continued with other schemes as well. *The Civilian Conservation Corp* was set up to aid the unemployed and conserve scarce natural resources. *The National Industrial Recovery Act* was an attempt to get voluntary acceptance by business of a minimum wage of between 20 and 40 cents an hour, a maximum working week of 40 hours, and no more child labour. Note how low wages were. And they were going lower – a direct result of the now fully enclosed land frontier.

These schemes, and many others, came to be known collectively as the New Deal, and were put into place against what was often a concerted attack from professional quarters and conservative opinion. The ruling economic ideology stated that the deflation that was now occurring was the natural result of prior inflation (as in some ways it was) and must be allowed to run its course. The speculation in assets and inventories during the inflation must naturally 'liquidate' in the deflation: prices and wages

19 Edward Alden and Neil Buckley, 'Big Sugar fights to maintain the status quo', *Financial Times*, February 26, 2004.
20 The issue of moral hazard pushed the banking system to the limits sixty years later, in the 1980s – a tale taken up in the next chapter.
21 Fridson, p.128.

must find their 'natural' level. This was considered quite in order, and a process not to be meddled with by government. But the general public approved of the New Deal, and voted Roosevelt back into office, when the time came, in a re-election landslide. 'The only thing to fear is fear itself,' said the President. His policies did not end the depression, however. And, since government spending had not yet been admitted to be legitimate (governments are expected to balance budgets at all times) things were still depressed as World War II approached.

Other plans from individuals and groups were put forward in the 1930s to lift the economic depression. One that drew many supporters was the Townsend Plan. Francis Everett Townsend, a Californian doctor, suggested a monthly payment of $200 to every person aged 60 or over, on condition that the money was spent within the month, and only within the United States. Roosevelt stole the plan as a means of frustrating Townsend's wild popularity with seniors and called it Social Security.

Banking

BANKS ARE important. Therefore, if in any economy those government-granted licences, especially land value, are permitted to capitalise in price and be traded as a commodity, then the credit-creation process undertaken by the banks for their profit (fractional reserve banking) will become the linchpin of the economy. Academic studies do occasionally point this out, though not in these words. One examination of the effects of banking distress on the economy during the Great Depression notes:

> Microeconomic evidence suggests that reductions in the value of bank assets were an important source of variation for bank loan supply … adverse shocks to banks' asset values, combined with depositor preferences for liquidity and low risk, caused banks to contract the supply of loans in the 1930s. That evidence suggests that exogenous variation in loan supply was driven in large part by bank distress. Bank distress raised funding costs and reduced deposits, leading banks to reallocate assets toward cash and curtail loan supply.
>
> Calomiris and Mason, *Consequences of Bank Distress During the Great Depression*, p.8

That is probably rather obvious, though it is good to have it statistically verified through some very detailed research. They also note a link between the bank-induced contraction of credit and state level income growth during the Depression. In their words, depending on certain variables, a '17.9 percent decrease in loan supply (over 1931 and 1932) produced roughly a 7 percent decline in income over the same period.' The effect on building permits was even more pronounced.

> At the sample mean, a loan-supply shock producing a one standard deviation (23.4 percent) decline in deposits results in a 67.7 percent decline in the county-level value of building permits. The fact that the size of the

> loan-supply effect is so much larger for building permits likely reflects the high cyclical volatility of the construction sector and its sensitivity to conditions in local credit markets.
>
> Calomiris and Mason, p.8

Clearly the creation or contraction of credit by the banking industry is of major importance to the economy.

In this regard, the Glass-Steagall Act of 1932 finally allowed a substantial expansion of bank credit. The Act widened the type of assets that could be re-discounted by banks at the Fed, and lowered interest rates.

> The Fed promptly went into an enormous binge of buying government securities, unprecedented at the time. The Fed purchased $1.1 billion of government securities from the end of February to the end of July [1932], raising its holdings to $1.8 billion. Part of the reason for these vast open market operations was to help finance the then huge federal deficit of $3 billion during fiscal year 1932.
>
> Rothbard, p.294

Perhaps markets picked up on what was happening, for the Dow lowed in July 1932, effectively anticipating, as markets do, the likely improvement in economic activity. In 1932 the public, however, were yet to be convinced of the soundness of the banking system and, despite the attempted credit expansion by monetary authorities, kept right on taking gold out of the banks and withdrawing deposits to hold as cash.

Markets respond to the creation of credit

AS IT TURNED out, 1933 was a big year for the stock market (as was 1935), though it might not have seemed likely at the start. By the end of 1933 the market was up 54 per cent (by 1935 a further 48 per cent), though it had been a big fall from 1929, of course. It was the Roosevelt administration's inflationary measures that were providing the economic stimulus. 'The market surged on the strength of restored confidence in the banking system, abundant credit, and an economic rebound led by the automotive sector.' [22] Easier credit in other words.

Both times the market correctly anticipated the favourable impact of credit expansion on economic and industrial activity. Bank deposits grew quickly in 1934. The re-inflating of the economy was of course a deliberate government policy initiative. The President was determined to reduce the gold value of the dollar, and even outlawed the holding of gold by US citizens. Through the RFC, gold was purchased at progressively higher prices: it rose from $20.67 per ounce to $35, at which price it was eventually fixed. Relative to other currencies still backed by gold, the US dollar was now worth 60 per cent less. It was deliberate inflation. Under such a policy, the only thing to do if one could not buy gold to maintain one's purchasing power was to buy stocks.

22 Fridson, Introduction, p.x.

Speculators had anticipated such an action from the Roosevelt administration as early as January 1933 (before Roosevelt was sworn in) and had been actively buying and hoarding gold – which worsened the February/March banking panic (Note 3, page 268). The hoarding drained the banks of their reserves upon which credit is expanded. In order to re-establish their reserves, the banks either reduced overall lending or called in loans.

Well before March 1933,

> [m]en recognized as being high in the councils of the Democratic Party converted large sums into gold, or purchased substantial interests in gold mines at home and abroad ... Trade advices in Wall Street – which were privately confirmed in official Washington – told of large gold operations by men close to the president-elect. Lawrence Sullivan, pp.71, 77

A deliberate inflation policy had not been publicly advocated by Roosevelt in the lead-up to his election. He had in fact been calling for a steady dollar, non-inflationary policies and a dramatic reduction in government expenditure to balance the budget.

The general public is always the last to know…

As for the real estate market, Hoyt notes:

> After the bank moratorium in March 1933, there was a rapid rise in the price of wheat, corn, and securities in the United States, and a marked improvement in general business conditions. While the influence of inflation had been but faintly reflected in real estate values if at all by the summer of 1933, there was a decline in vacancy rates for apartment buildings in many sections of the city, which is usually the first step in the recovery. p.275

So the real estate cycle starts out from the bottom once more. Hoyt's study of Chicago land values was first published shortly thereafter – perceptive comments in light of the Dow low the year before, in 1932.

The 1930s were tough years. Said historians and prodigious business cycle analysts, Edward R. Dewey and Edwin F. Dakin:

> The 18-year rhythm, falling from 1925, reached its low around 1933, and left such a wake of foreclosures in the nation that, in the depths of the depression, incipient rebellion was abroad in the land. In parts of the Middle West, for instance, farmers actually banded together to use force against sheriffs entering with writs. Auction sales of foreclosed properties had their purpose defeated by the refusal of attending visitors to bid. Refusals to pay taxes were common. Before such rebellion could become a challenge even to federal authority, there was organized a series of credit aids to save farmers and defaulting homeowners, together with the banks and insurance companies which had invested heavily in mortgages… The upturn in building and real estate activity was kicked off on the strength of large government funds made available for lending to the building of homes … and the home building activity … was largely under government control. *Cycles*, p.124

Vast public works programmes were instituted and government activity in these markets went even further after the outbreak of European hostilities again, 20 years and 65 days after the peace agreement signed in 1919 ended the First World War.

> As a result of such measures, government funds invested in industrial plant facilities from 1940 through 1943 amounted to a total of some 25 billion dollars. When the United States actually became involved in war at the end of 1941, building of homes and farm structures had to cease almost entirely, under government decree – the famous L41 regulation of the War Production Board ... But the continuing boom in industrial construction carried total American building activity steadily forward into new highs.
>
> Dewey and Dakin, p.125

Dewey and Dakin reported a peak in real estate building activity in the third quarter of 1942. *Cycles: The Science of Prediction*, published in 1947, contained some prescient observations about the real estate market, one suggesting that the sheer size of recent government activities in this sector did not necessarily indicate that the real estate cycle would be altered much. The comment may have been in reference to J.M. Keynes's contention that government could do far more to 'iron-out' the terrible ups and downs in the cycle.

> The pattern of our recurrent building booms has been so similar for many years that its repetition seems almost routine. The entrance of government into building activity has not discernibly changed the pattern.
>
> Dewey and Dakin, p.124

As we know now, some sixty years later, it didn't.

Continuing the usual pattern, the world's largest building (though this time not in height), The Pentagon, opened for business in early 1943, right at the peak of construction activity. It was built, of course, by government to house the developing US military machine.

Roy Wenzlick, in another prescient publication, *The Coming Boom in Real Estate and What to Do About It* (1936), shows the historical relationship between the real estate cycles. He was the only person apart from Hoyt to do so up to that time. Analysing the simple repetition, Wenzlick predicted that US construction was likely to peak in 1943, a recession following in 1955. We revisit Wenzlick's work in Chapter 21.

There is one final subject to discuss before moving on: the Bretton Woods Agreement and the dollar reserve system. Towards the end of World War II, the Allied powers and their best economists assembled at the Mount Washington Hotel in the New Hampshire resort town of Bretton Woods to discuss a way forward after the destruction of the war. The US, one of the few countries not materially affected by the war, and the world's largest creditor – with most of the world's gold supply in its vaults to prove it – maintained a US dollar that, by default as much as anything else, was considered 'as good as gold'. The Allied powers therefore agreed to give the US dollar official status as the only currency to be convertible into gold at an international level. The Bretton Woods agreement was signed in July 1944. In inter-governmental transactions and as a reserve asset for nations to hold, the dollar would in future take precedence. Signing nations agreed to a fixed exchange rate (plus or minus 1 per cent) based on gold. The agreement was to unravel in 1971, a subject to which we shall return shortly.

1955

IT IS HERE that we must bid farewell to Hoyt's great study of Chicago land values. (Remarkably, Hoyt went on to claim that the 18-year rhythm which he had so assiduously studied in the Chicago market was not likely to repeat. He considered it a pattern to be found only in young and vibrant cities, not older, more developed ones.) Fortunately, we have an even better study to move on to, that of Fred Harrison in *The Power in the Land.* In a most helpful piece of economic detective work, Harrison shows that, after the 1930s depression, land prices in the US (as distinct from building construction) bottomed in 1955.

> On March 28, 1978, Emanuel Melichar, an economist on the staff of the Board of Governors of the Federal Reserve System, presented the results of his analysis of the income received by the agricultural industry. From the aggregate data, he deducted the returns to labour, management and the imputed income derived from the investment in dwellings, to disclose the residual return to production assets. This showed a downward movement which terminated in 1955-56... Harrison, p.122

Although these returns were to capital assets as well as land, a little further empirical evidence showed that

> the residual return to agricultural production assets was declining until 1954. So it would have paid investors to sink their funds into other investments – capital equipment – rather than land. From the mid 1950s, however, once the economy had shaken off the distorting influences of the Second World War and the Korean War, and begun to pick up its growth rhythm, it became increasingly prudent to switch from investment in capital to the hoarding of land. p.124

Easy in hindsight, of course (see Note 4).

This establishes for us a general land price low, after the 1930s depression, at 1955. Before that higher profits were to be had manufacturing consumer items to meet pent-up demand after the war. Few were developing land. In Chicago at this time, real estate men were despondent, particularly about development within the city itself. Things appeared so bad, it was said, that the Loop 'might as well be returned to the Indians'.[23]

23 Carl W. Condit, *Chicago 1930-1970*, quoted in Harrison, p.120.

It was also in 1955 that Al Gore Sr challenged Congress to build a nation-wide highway system connecting one side of the country to the other, to lift development potential. Echoes of the railroad men – increasing the speculative potential of the land and its value is what such a development is all about. (China is currently doing the same, and claims that its highway system will be more extensive than that of the existing US system by 2015. It remains to be seen how much the next real estate downturn will affect this goal.)

It was around this time, too, that American banks pioneered the principle of personal loans, in which 'lending was related to an individual's ability to pay, rather than to the security which he or she could offer'.[24] This was in marked contrast to banks' previous credit-creation practices and became an important factor in credit growth in the years following the 1950s.

Loan maturities changed too. In the 1920s, a house buyer faced a loan repayment date about five years hence, with the lender normally requiring at least a third of the property value as a downpayment. In some cases limited repayment was required over the period so that at the end it was necessary to renew the mortgage. If money happened to be tight at that time, renewal could prove difficult. (This may have made downturns worse than they already were.) Longer maturities on smaller downpayments now became the norm. By the end of 1955, real estate loans at commercial banks represented about 10 per cent of total assets and 16 per cent of total mortgage debt.[25]

Increases in federal taxes also brought changes after the war. For the first time tax avoidance became an important dynamic in real estate investment.[26]

Stocks

On November 17, 1954 the Dow, after a wait of 302 months (25 years) regained its 1929 peak. The depression had not been forgotten, however, and the government announced an enquiry into the market's rise. Significantly, in June 1954 the Fed had responded to pleas from business and manufacturing interests and retreated from their hard money policy. 'A feeling set in,' reported Martin Fridson, 'that thanks to wise monetary and fiscal policies, periodic depressions were no longer inevitable.'[27]

The 1950s were not plain sailing for stocks, however. October 4, 1957 (30 years prior to 1987) saw the start of a sharp fall in prices as the Russians launched Sputnik I, an event that caught the US by surprise. The month's low, on October 21, saw the Dow down 10 per cent. 1958 was better, one of the very good years according to Fridson, as 'the biggest

24 Edwin Green, *Banking: An Illustrated History*, p.124.
25 Alan Rabinowitz, *The Real Estate Gamble*, p.91.
26 Rabinowitz, 167.
27 *It Was a Very Good Year*, p.150.

public works project of all time', the interstate 41,000-mile highway system and associated federal road networks, expected to cost $27bn over the next 13 years, got underway. Paving materials, dynamite, bridge steel and other supplies were thought likely to add $2bn to 1958 demand. Added to this was an easing of credit in November 1957. Then in July 1958 the US sent its marines into Lebanon, a venture the market thought expansionary. A stock-buying frenzy resulted.[28]

Oil

IF THERE IS one commodity that could be said to have changed the world, it is oil.

> The inexorable flow of oil transformed anything in its path. Nowhere was that transformation more dramatic than in the American landscape. The abundance of oil begat the proliferation of the automobile, which begat a completely new way of life. This was indeed the era of Hydrocarbon Man. The bands of public transportation, primarily rail, which had bound Americans to the relatively high-density central city, snapped in the face of the automotive onslaught, and a great wave of suburbanization spread across the land.
>
> Daniel Yergin, *The Prize*, p.550

Suburbanisation, says Yergin, may well have begun in 1946 when a family of builders named Levitt built a whole row of houses at exactly sixty-foot intervals on a former patch of potato farms in Hempstead, Long Island. This was the prototype of the post-war suburb. 'No man who owns his own house and lot can be a Communist', declared William Levitt. 'He has too much to do.' By 1950, housing starts were running at 1.7 million a year. Within ten years of the end of the war nine million Americans had moved to 'the suburbs'. The auto – and oil – was vital to this new way of life.

To service the needs of these new suburbs, new-style industries grew up around and in them, including shopping centres and malls (the first one built in Raleigh, North Carolina in 1949) and motels. Starting as clusters of cabins near gasoline stations, motels were refined a bit when a couple of entrepreneurs put up a sign in green outside their Memphis motel in 1952 reading, 'Holiday Inn'. There followed drive-in restaurants, drive-in Churches, and of course drive-in cinemas. What this was worth to society – the economic gain – has manifest in the price of land; which is why we still have to work a 40-hour week and take on bank-assisted debt to buy into it.

The 1960s

ATTEMPTS TO boost manufacturing were taken up by the Kennedy administration with calls for a cut in corporate taxation. This accorded with the now entrenched economic philosophy of John Maynard Keynes, who was

28 Fridson, p.160.

confident that he had demonstrated how government, through better use of the economic levers at its disposal, could smooth out the ups and downs of boom and bust. Keynes also thought that government could deliberately choose growth policies, like tax cuts, to achieve full employment. The tax cuts, at a cost of some $14bn in government revenues, were enacted in 1964, but not before the stock market underwent a fast and substantial correction in May 1962, reflecting fears that the Democratic Party administration elected in 1960 might after all be anti-business. Sobel called it the 'Kennedy slide'. Stocks fell on very heavy volume on May 21 and 22. Noted one broker: 'People have been sitting around praying all day.'[29] Stocks tanked on the 28th, recovered slightly, then lowed on June 25 and 27. The May emotion, the sharpest market drop since the Crash of '29, was 18 months prior to the events of November 23, 1963.

A little earlier, 1961 had seen the introduction of the Real Estate Investment Trust Act. Under this Act, investors could exempt themselves from federal taxes on income derived from real estate at the corporate level – a new incentive to channel money through the REITs into property. Initially the REITs bought into existing property for a steady income flow.

In 1963 the Fed celebrated its 50th birthday with the re-publication of a booklet defining its purposes – 'to foster growth at high levels of employment, with a stable dollar…' The economy celebrated by going on to record its highest ever inflation levels, and serving up higher unemployment for dessert. Far from there being a stable dollar, its purchasing power continues to decline as ever more quantities are printed.

A decade later, Sherman J. Maisel noted:

> Before my appointment to the Board of Governors of the Federal Reserve System in 1965, I had spent nearly 20 years studying and teaching monetary economics. I thought I understood what the Fed did and how it affected the economy. I soon discovered how little I knew. I also found that the Fed itself, while it had a definite philosophy, had no clear concept of how monetary policy worked. I searched for an official statement of doctrine or an outline of operating procedures. None existed, except at the most general level.
>
> *Managing the Dollar*, p.ix

Yes it's true.

In 1964 the now infamous Tonkin Gulf incident up-scaled the Vietnam conflict into a wider war. Early in August the US destroyer *Maddox*, which was in the Tonkin Gulf, off the east coast of North Vietnam, on an espionage mission, reported that she was under attack, and returned fire. Screamed the newspapers next day: 'American Planes Hit North Vietnam after Second Attack on our Destroyers'. It transpired much later that there had been no attack on the *Maddox*. The ship's captain, John Herrick, had after some hours reported by cable that the earlier scare was perhaps due to 'freak weather effects and an over-eager sonar-man' and recommended

29 Sobel, p.414.

no further action be taken until a complete evaluation in daylight.[30] But this was not what Congress got to hear over coming days. After listening to top secret testimony from Secretary of Defence McNamara and Secretary of State Dean Rusk, it went on to pass the Tonkin Gulf Resolution (with only two dissenters) authorising the President, Lynden B. Johnson, to take 'all necessary measures to repel armed attack against the forces of the United States and to prevent further aggression'.

Because of a lie (some claim a pretext certain persons in the military were actually looking for) the US increased its commitment to South Vietnam to stall the spread of the communist hydra (events echoed in Iraq forty years later). The President announced air strikes against North Vietnam (using plans already drawn up), thereby dramatically escalating the war. At its peak in 1969 some 543,000 troops were committed, dropping 400 tons of bombs a day, contributing markedly to later inflation, as the US printed money to pay for the war, and to substantial rises in commodity prices in the early 1970s. On average, one US soldier was using one ton of copper per year in Vietnam.[31] In the de-foliage of Vietnam, 44 million litres of Agent Orange was dumped on forests to deny the enemy cover.

Into the peak

> 'I can feel it coming, S.E.C. or not, a whole new round of disastrous speculation, with all the familiar stages in order: blue-chip boom, then a fad for secondary issues, then an over-the-counter play, then another garbage market in new issues, and finally the inevitable crash. I don't know when it will come, but I can feel it coming, and damn it, I don't know what to do about it.'
>
> Bernard J. Lasker, Chairman, New York Stock Exchange, 1970, quoted in John Brooks, *The Go-Go Years*, p.xv

US GROWTH RATES halved in 1967/8 as the economy went into minor recession in the last quarter of 1966, the tax cuts having pushed up land values. This was something different, or so it seemed. Since the end of the Second World War, economic growth had continued uninterrupted.

> The twenty years from 1948 through 1967 may well be celebrated by historians as the most benign era in the history of the industrial economy. The two decades were without panic, crisis, depression or more than minor recession.
>
> Galbraith, *Money: Whence it Came, Where it Went*, p.253

Unemployment was low and there was no inflation to speak of, although prices did increase from time to time. All this appeared to confirm what the new generation of Keynesian economists had been saying: that government really could be proactive in the economy and affect the level of output and growth, releasing these things from the vagaries of the dreaded business cycle. Add to this the better quantitative measurement of all

30 Ellsberg, *International Herald Tribune*, February 27, 2004.
31 *Counterpunch*, October 20, 2003.

things growth-related – calculations of national income, gross domestic product etc – and the boom and bust scenario was now considered to have been mastered. Said the President's economists in 1968:

> 'During these last years of achievement, it was far more than a coincidence that fiscal and monetary policy have been actively and consciously employed to promote prosperity ... no longer does Federal economic policy ... wait for a recession or serious inflation to occur before measures are taken.'
>
> Economic Report of the President, 1968, p.7, quoted by Galbraith, p.269

Circumstances had confirmed, too, the inability of simple monetary policy to extricate the economy quickly out of depression, as was revealed by the 1930s depression. Noted Keynes and his followers: yes, in a slump money could be made available and indeed interest rates could be aggressively lowered, but this did not ensure that the money *would* actually be borrowed, or *would* actually be spent. Trying to enforce that would be like pushing at a piece of string to move it forward. Hence government and its budgetary policy were a necessary addition to the economic tool kit.

As it happened, such an economic policy did not much affect the status quo. The owners of the means of production, and the owners of the *ground* upon which that means stood, would not be disturbed by the new economics. In fact, things proved positively delightful when it could be shown through the new theoretical modelling that government tax cuts, a Keynesian initiative, could be used to improve growth rates, and that, if such cuts were slanted slightly in favour of those paying higher taxes, the effect would 'trickle down' to those underneath and make everybody richer. Almost, a free lunch. Who could deny the effectiveness of such a policy?

All of this did not guarantee that stock markets would remain stable, neither did it make redundant the Fed and its use of monetary policy. The Dow in 1966 retraced half its prior run up, falling back to past tops. Economic growth continued, though, and then picked up pace, land prices are reported to have doubled between 1970 to 1974.[32] In past cycles land prices increased fastest towards the end of the 18 years, and the 1974 cycle was not proving to be exceptional in this regard. Finding finance to buy land was not difficult. Developers and builders were having money thrown at them by the Real Estate Investment Trusts (REITs), which by this time had discovered the advantages of short-term bank loans at rates sufficiently below their lending rate to provide them with attractive profit margins. The assets of these REITs went from $1 bn in 1969 to $20 bn by 1974. Soon banks were launching trusts, with an IPO in which the public could invest, and extensive lines of credit available. An innovative new method had been found to finance continual growth.

32 Harrison, p.130.

Though the growth hit a few bumps along the way. Strongly rising prices into the early 1970s – something no one could remember experiencing before – were worrying economists and the establishment generally. In mid-1970 the long boom in the stock market came to an end, halted by the sharply increased interest rates of 1969, introduced by the incoming Nixon administration in preference to other forms of economic control, such as price controls, to curb increasing prices and wages.

In the stock market Penn Central Transportation Company collapsed on June 21, 1970, marking the stock market low that year. Penn Central was the world's largest privately owned railroad, with assets of more than $6 bn – an American institution 'just behind hot dogs'.[33] Appendix 3 has more about the Penn Central collapse.

Graph 12.3: Dow Jones Index, 1952-77

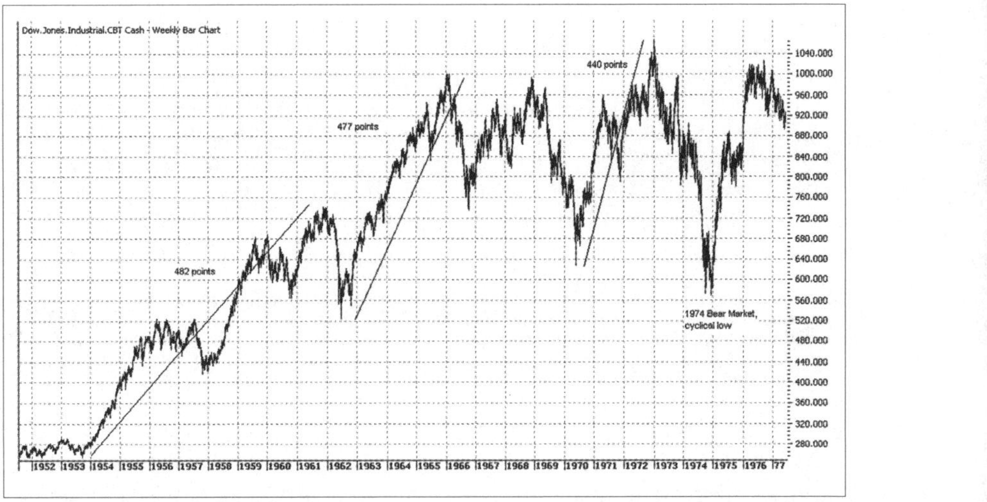

By July 1971, with a presidential election just one and a half years away, political expediency had prompted price controls (subsequently ineffectively administered), a relaxation of monetary policy, a request for tax cuts and a more liberal budget. Easier credit conditions rallied the markets to a final high in January 1973 (to be followed by a two-year bear market). The rally was helped along by the Fed, which had obligingly eased monetary policy in the spring of 1970 to shore up the collapse of a stock market in free fall since early 1969. The early 1970s saw an unlikely stock market bubble develop around a group of stocks called the Nifty Fifty, 'a glamorous group that promised eternal growth during an unusually erratic period [of US] economic history.'[34] Born in a period of rapid

33 Alan Lechner, *Street Games*, p.156.
34 Ron Insana, *Trendwatching*, p.139.

technological advancement, companies like IBM, Polaroid, and Xerox were at the forefront of the 1960s innovations. The bubble soon went the way of all others, and deflated.

We can now return to the Bretton Woods agreement and the dollar reserve system. The agreement was historic; it helped avoid what happened after World War I. After World War II the defeated nations, Germany and Japan, recovered strongly, assisted without prejudice by the Allied powers, the US in particular. This was by historical standards a generous concession; had they so wished, the Allies could have inflicted heavy repayment terms on the losers for war damage. As the '50s and '60s wore on, both Germany and Japan, not permitted to re-arm, invested their growing surpluses in modern plant and equipment and went on to produce goods and services at much lower cost than the rest of the world.

It soon become obvious that it was expedient to buy in Germany and Japan, and sell in the US.

> [F]oreign corporations, beginning in the late 1950s, accumulated dollars from their flush sales in the United States. These were not absorbed by the much smaller purchases from the United States. In the hands of the recipient firms or deposited with them in European banks, the dollars became the newest mystery of the monetary cognoscenti – the Euro-dollars. And when borrowed or loaned they became the Euro-dollar market … numerous of the dollars so assembled, not surprisingly, were turned into gold.
>
> Galbraith, p.295

The huge stockpile of gold built up by the US after 1914 (mainly from selling weapons to Europe) began to disappear. And what was the US doing? She was bogged down in Vietnam and running a large trade deficit because of it. Rivers of gold were now leaving the US for what seemed to be the safer haven of Switzerland.

By the late 1960s the US stopped supplying gold to holders of dollars. It confined itself to providing gold only to central banks in settlement of claims. By August 1971 the game was up. The US dollar ceased to be convertible into gold. The US currency became – and remains – fiat (paper money not convertible into gold or silver). The ramifications of this will be returned to in the next cycle and the one following that. By 1971/2 the dollar had become way overvalued. In expectation of its devaluation, a movement out of dollars and into other currencies ensued. Currency instability became the order of the day, acknowledged eventually by the established order as a currency 'float'. Exchange rates were no longer fixed.

Meanwhile an oil crisis was developing – slowly in the beginning, but it had everybody worried by late 1972 when it was believed that the world was running out of oil (so said the Club of Rome). To protect reserves (and profits) in a newly inflationist world, OPEC on October 16, 1973 lifted prices by 70 per cent to $5.11 a barrel, thereby bringing prices into line with the oil spot market.[35] OPEC enjoyed a huge windfall of dollars that could not immediately be spent. They accumulated in massive Arab bank balances. These Petro-dollars were added to already large Euro-dollar balances. After the 1971 Nixon gold decision, banks went international and competed vigorously for these Euro-dollar and Petro-dollar accounts. New York banks were now 'chock-a-block with liquidity'.[36] Looking around for profitable outlets and inspired by the idea that nation states were safe from bankruptcy, they recycled these dollars into credit-hungry developing countries, especially those in Latin America.[37] This ignored one of the most obvious lessons of banking history. The almost totally unregulated lending (and further extensive credit creation) returned to haunt the banks later, as one third-world nation after another defaulted on its debts – as had always happened in the past (in roughly 60-year cycles, noted author Christian Suter).

In the midst of all this, on November 15, 1971, the world changed forever, though no one noticed on the day. Intel, a small start-up two and a bit years old, released its Intel 4004, a microprocessor. The technical description read: '4 bit microprocessor, operating speed 0.1 MHz, for sale at $US 200, with 2300 transistors to process (an astounding) sixty thousand instructions per second.' This invention kicked off the digital age and went on to re-shape the world, in particular the world of finance – a topic to be taken up next cycle.

It would also add to the price of land.

None of this was affecting the REITs, though.

> During the 1969-70 period of tight money, which affected the orthodox financial institutions – commercial banks and savings and loans associations – the REITs forged ahead: loans for construction and development rose from $260 million to $2.5 billion, a staggering increase of 890%. [Developers] agreed to pay hugely inflated prices for land because the trusts were pouring funds into their pockets. Money was no obstacle to any deal which appeared – on paper – to offer bonanza profits. The easy money period which followed in 1971 aggravated the speculative fever which gripped the economy. Commercial banks increased their construction loans by nearly $3 billion in that year alone. Prestigious banks, like Chase Manhattan, set up REITs, using their names to sell stocks and debentures to the public.
>
> Harrison, p.115

The real estate market

A FEW NOTED what was happening, but not many. The autumn 1974 *Real Estate Review* reported:

> In many suburban areas, speculators are outbidding developers. Outlying land of dubious use potential is trading briskly. The professionals are

35 Daniel Yergin, *The Prize*, p.606.
36 Kindleberger, p.32.
37 Green, *Banking: An Illustrated History*, pp.137, 145.

> applauding this activity and proclaiming their faith in its eternal life. Most alarming is the obvious effort made to bring outsiders into the land market. Vigorous syndication efforts and even the current popularity of obvious land development purchases are hailed as innovative and exciting applications of marketing 'technology' to the 'backward' field of real estate marketing...
>
> J.B. Lindeman, *Is the Real Estate Market Coming to an End?*

Shades of Chicago there.

The full real estate story goes back to the 1950s, when a couple of larger firms began marketing lots mainly in Florida and remote desert areas of California. Soon they created a nation-wide market for real estate sold by installment, often sight unseen.[38]

> This type of land development soon became a national phenomenon; raw or partially developed acreage was subdivided into small parcels and offered for sale on liberal terms ... By the late 1960s rural land was being subdivided at an unprecedented rate. Widespread growth continued until 1973 ...
>
> Hubert B. Stroud and William S. Spikowski, 'Planning in the Wake of Florida Land Scams', p.3

Land hustling was becoming as much a part of contemporary America as superhighways and rock concerts.[39]

The turn

ONLY A MAJOR bank failure was needed to hasten the economic turn. One came in October 1973. The collapse of the US National Bank of San Diego was the biggest in forty years. The bank collapsed 'because of the activities of its major shareholder, C. Arnholt Smith',[40] a close friend of Richard Nixon and a major real estate speculator in southern California. Smith's bank had loaned heavily to one of his conglomerates, the Westgate-California Corporation, which between 1967 and 1971 had relied on property deals for most of its reported pre-tax profits. In 1979 Smith was sentenced to three years in prison for tax evasion, fraud and theft – something to do with the company he was keeping, perhaps, though the President managed to avoid jail. More information about C. Arnholt Smith, his Westgate-California Corporation and, more importantly, his United States National Bank of San Diego, is contained in Appendix 4.

An even bigger bank failure, that of the Franklin National Bank of New York, followed twelve months later, in October 1974, despite a rescue package from the Fed worth an unprecedented $1.7bn. Property loans were a feature of this failure as well, though they were not the only factor. The owner of the bank, Michele Sindona, was charged with 65 counts of fraud and got 25 years. The incredible story of Franklin and Sindona is recounted in Appendix 5.

38 Leslie Allan, Beryl Kuder and Sarah L. Oakes, *Promised Lands*, p.4.
39 Morton C. Paulson, *The Great Land Hustle*, Introduction.
40 Harrison, p.131.

The first major difficulty for the REITs came in December 1974, with the failure of Walter J. Kassuba Realty, a Florida building corporation which had $550m invested in nearly 120 properties. A few REITs now found themselves with bad loans. The cycle had turned. It was later found that more than a few trusts had been using dubious accounting tricks to hide a few shenanigans. (Appendix 6, Walter J. Kassuba Realty and the REITs, has more on the tricks used.)

The scams and cons

THESE ARE NOT peculiar to the peak of the cycle; they go on all the time, as evidenced by the huge 'salad-oil' swindle of 1963[41] or Bernie Cornfield's Investors Overseas Services scam of 1970. The majority of scams, however, will tend to reveal themselves to the public when the cost of money is placing undue pressure on corporations to continue maximising their performance. As land prices soften with rising interest rates, poorly or fraudulently managed banks or other financial concerns will come under pressure.

So it was with the US Financial Corporation, the real estate wonder of 1973. The man in charge, R.H. Walter, had loudly declared his corporation's objective: 'To make housing happen'. But, as his houses went up, behind the scenes Walter was furiously creating sham transactions using a raft of subsidiaries and affiliated companies to create phony profits and inflate earnings per share, and hence underwrite the stock price. Following the money, government agencies uncovered the accounting tricks. When US Financial filed for Chapter 11 bankruptcy protection in January 1974 it became the largest bankruptcy recorded up to that time. (Appendix 7, US Financial and its Land Office Business, has more information.)

Nor was the stock market immune from the swindlers. In March 1973 Raymond L. Dirks, a securities analyst at Delafield Childs, took a call from an unhappy Equity Funding employee, Ronald Secrist. Secrist complained to Dirks that his Christmas bonus was not enough. As a result he had a story to tell about his employer. He revealed a tangled web of false insurance policies that Equity Funding Corp was repackaging to other re-insurers, pocketing the cash received. This had been going on for ten years, it was later discovered, and involved many hundreds of employees. The cash, augmenting profits, was used to help drive higher the company share price. Of the $3bn in life insurance written by Equity Funding Corp, an unbelievable $2bn eventually proved completely fictitious. Appendix 8 has the story.

41 The story can be found on the EIS site at www.businesscycles.biz/docs/saladoil.htm

To sum up

IN THE EARLY 1970s commodity prices were running wild. Steep increases in price, especially of what was now the most central commodity, oil, took the blame for pushing the US economy into recession. Everything plays its part, but the commotion over oil conveniently disguised the real problem: deflating land prices – which had been permitted to inflate in the first place. Oil prices later collapsed, of course (as higher prices brought forth better technology to recover more oil), just as much as land prices later recovered, though supply and demand does not operate the same way in the land market. Speculation at the peak of this cycle ran rampant and covered not only the usual stocks, office buildings and land but also tankers, other ships, and even Boeing 747s.

FURTHER READING

Allan, Leslie, Beryl Kuder and Sarah L. Oakes, *Promised Lands*. New York: Inform Inc., 1976.

Alston, Lee J. 'Farm Foreclosures in the United States During the Interwar Period', *Federal Reserve Bank of St Louis*, 43, December 1983, pp.885-903.

Alston, Lee J., Wayne A. Grove and David C. Wheelock. *Why Do Banks Fail? Evidence from the 1920s*. Federal Reserve Bank of St Louis, 1991.

Brooks, John. *Once in Golconda*. Harper & Row, 1969.

Calomiris, Charles W and Joseph R. Mason. *Contagion and Bank Failures during the Great Depression: The June 1932 Chicago Banking Panic*. NBER Working Paper No. W4934, November 1994.

Calomiris, Charles W and Joseph R. Mason. 'Consequences of Bank Distress during the Great Depression', *American Economic Review*, Vol. 93, June 2003, pp.937-47.

Chancellor, Edward. *Devil Take the Hindmost*. Papermac edn, 2000.

Esbitt, M. 'Bank Portfolios and Bank Failures During the Great Depression', Chicago, *Journal of European History* 46, June 1986, pp.455-62.

Federal Reserve Bank of St Louis. *Regulation and Bank Failures: New Evidence from the Agricultural Collapse of the 1920s*. 1991.

Fridson, Martin S. *It Was a Very Good Year.* John Wiley & Sons Inc., 1998.

Harrison, Fred. *The Power in the Land*. Shepheard-Walwyn, 1983.

James, F.C. *The Growth of Chicago Banks*. Harper & Brothers, 1939.

Kennedy, Susan E. *The Banking Crisis of 1933*. University of Kentucky Press, 1973.

Lechner, Alan. *Street Games*. Harper & Row, 1980.

Maisel, Sherman J. *Managing the Dollar*. W.W. Norton & Company, New York, 1973.

Montgomery, David. 'The Monetarist Explanation of the Great Contraction: Fact or Fiction?' (www.members.aol.com/profdavidmont/monetary.htm).

Paulson, Morton C. *The Great Land Hustle*. Chicago, Henry Regnery, 1972.

Rabinowitz, Alan. *The Real Estate Gamble: Lessons from 50 Years of Boom and Bust*. AMACOM, 1980.
Rockoff, Hugh. *Deflation, Silent Runs and the Great Contraction*. Rutgers University, 2001.
Shughart, William F. II. 'A Public Choice Perceptive of the Banking Act of 1933', *Cato Journal*, Vol. 7, No. 3, Winter 1988 (www.cato.org/pubs/journal/cj7n3/cj7n3-3.pdf).
Simpson, Herbert D. 'Real Estate Speculation and the Depression', *American Economic Review*, XXIII, No. 1, March 1933.
Sobel, Robert. *Panic on Wall Street: A History of America's Financial Disasters*. Collier Books, 1972.
Stroud, Hubert B. and William S. Spikowski. 'Planning in the Wake of Florida Land Scams', *Journal of Planning Education and Research*, Association of Collegiate Schools of Planning, 1998 (www.spkowski.com/landscam.htm).
Sullivan, Lawrence. *Prelude to Panic*. Statesman Press, 1936.
Temzelides, Ted. 'Are Bank Runs Contagious?' *Business Review*, Federal Reserve Bank of Philadelphia, November/December 1997, pp.3-14.
Ways, M. *Land: The Boom that Really Hurts*. Fortune, June 1973.
Wheelock, David C. *Regulation and Bank Failures: New Evidence from the Agricultural Collapse of the 1920s*, Federal Reserve Bank of St Louis, Working Paper 1991-006 (www.research.stloiusfed.org/wp/1991/91-006.pdf).
Wicker, Elmus. *The Banking Panics of the Great Depression*. Cambridge University Press, paperback edn, 2000.

NOTE I

Farmers' troubles after World War I arose in part because of the activities of the War Finance Corporation (WFC). The WFC was instituted, in wartime conditions, in May 1918 by Secretary of the Treasury McAdoo. Its aim was to help finance industries deemed essential to the war effort. Its two functions in providing this assistance were to support the market for US government bonds and to subsidise, bail out or otherwise support 'essential' US industries in difficulty due to the war. The initial focus was on utilities, railroads and banks. The banks were deemed to be in difficulty because helping to finance the government deficit due to war spending had put their assets under strain.

After the war, despite changed conditions, the WFC was continued. It was approached by big business for even more government assistance to maintain high prices in the expectation of a post-war recession and to provide credit to a war-torn Europe so that the Europeans might continue to buy US-made goods. As recession followed the war in 1920, Congress, acting on the advice of Eugene Meyer and others, revived the WFC, but this time simply as an agricultural relief agency. The new WFC established by the Agricultural Credits Act of 1921 would lend directly to farmers, amongst others.

And lend it did, heavily, allowing farmers to buy and store crops, increasing farm prices.

> By the summer of 1923 the WFC had loaned $172 million to farm co-ops and another $182 million to rural banks, which in turn loaned money to farmers. The WFC, working closely with farm block leaders, appointed a Corn Belt Advisory Committee of

> farm leaders to pressure Midwestern rural bankers into lending more heavily to farmers in that region.
>
> Rothbard, p.285

Further Acts followed in 1923, again focused on farm lending.

It is easy to see the potential after-effects, should farm commodity prices drop, which they began to do as the 1920s wore on. More and more farmers, with progressively lower incomes, had difficulty paying back their loans – which lowered farm land prices, which affected outstanding bankers' loans. Slowly, trouble was brewing.

NOTE 2

Economics professors spend their academic lives telling anyone who will listen that stock markets are efficient. But, as any active stock market trader comes to learn, markets will usually have priced in news before it is public knowledge; the issuing of news is the culmination of a (short-term) trend, not the beginning. Markets are more efficient for some than for others.

NOTE 3

It could be argued that the 1933 banking panic ended up worse than it might have been due to the political vacuum between the election of November 9, 1932 and the inauguration of the new President on March 4, 1933. During these 120 days the political situation was in a state of limbo. Neither the outgoing Hoover nor the incoming Roosevelt were willing to offer clear, decisive leadership in the absence of approved joint action.

Perhaps the incoming administration was content to maintain a low profile and to be seen to be taking over the situation at the lowest point of crisis. Sullivan argues for this possibility (*Prelude to Panic*, p.104). Politics can be like that.

NOTE 4

It's always easy in hindsight. We may note, however, that Harrison used Hoyt's 18-year thesis in his *Power in the Land*, published in 1983, to forecast, to the year, the UK property market peak of 1989, and its bust. Harrison went on to forecast in 1997 (www.businesscycles.biz/chartsbusiness/chaos1997.htm) and again in 2005 (www.businesscycles.biz/chartsbusiness/boom.htm) the next 18-year cycle, this time predicting the eventual UK peak not just to the year but to the quarter (the final quarter of 1997). This is impressive in anyone's language.

13

Ask Not What Your Bank Can Do for You ...

The Land (real estate) Boom into 1989

I think that the banking and savings and loan community in this country is probably as solid as one could get in any type of institution.

Alan Greenspan[1]

'Greed is all right by the way – I want you to know that,' said Ivan Boesky in May of 1986, at a commencement speech at University of California at Berkeley's School of Business Administration, just prior to his arrest on charges of insider trading. 'I think greed is healthy. You can be greedy and still feel good about yourself.'

We built thick vaults; we have cameras; we have time clocks on the vaults; we have dual control – all these controls were to protect against somebody stealing the cash. Well, you can steal far more money and take it out the back door. The best way to rob a bank is to own one.

A former Commissioner to the California Department of Savings and Loans[2]

AFTER THE 1973/4 collapse, land values recovered strongly, reaching their 1973 speculative peak within just five years. Here we have a change from all past cycles.

In the past banks went under, land values halved and a general readjustment took place that eventually put business on a sounder footing from which to launch its recovery. And the cycle turned. This time, just about all western governments launched 'rescue operations' to keep the shakier lenders of money from collapsing. The policy developed from a profound change in the way we view government.

1 'Nightline' programme at the time of the Ohio and Maryland S&L shutdown, 1985, quoted in *The Nation*, November 19th, 1990.
2 To a 1988 Congressional Committee. (US Congress, House Committee on Government Operations 1988:34).

Economists since John Maynard Keynes, after the terrible depression of the 1930s, came to accept that, in times of weak business and consumer spending, governments should step in to 'take up the slack', to better manage the economy. Since the Second World War government spending has become progressively larger and is now a significant part of the economy. (What the government is doing and in whose interests it operates has not changed, however.)

After 1974 we saw government action on a hitherto unprecedented scale to try to stop economies going into recession. (It becomes an effort to support land price, but it is never marketed to us that way.) About the UK market Fred Harrison noted:

> The land market was set to collapse by early 1974 in the way that it had traditionally done after a speculative orgy. But the Bank of England, towing along the main High Street banks, floated a £1.3 billion 'lifeboat' operation to support the fringe banks that had helped to fuel the speculation. Twenty-six fringe (or secondary) banks were thrown financial lifelines, and subsequently only eight of them went into liquidation. Had they all gone bust, many more property companies would have sunk with them. The market would have been flooded, and land values would have been depressed to economically realistic levels ... The politicians played their part too. Harold Wilson's government spent millions of pounds of taxpayer money on the inner cities, which inflated the expectations of landowners – both private individuals and public corporations – and encouraged the hope that land prices would rapidly recover. *The Power in the Land*, p.250

Which they proceeded to do.

A similar rescue operation was mounted in the US. Alan Rabinowitz[3] noted that, at the bottom of the market in 1974, REITs had lost on average 80 per cent of their stock price, with over half of all mortgages in default. The Fed gave support to the REITs and encouraged other banks to do the same. This meant that the distressed property of the REITs did not have to be put on the market in a disorderly fashion but could instead, because of the additional bank support, be held back to await recovery and higher prices.

> The business of unloading and buying distressed properties is being conducted in the most discreet way possible. Like a family which refuses to admit that one of its members has died and keeps the corpse embalmed in the living room rouged by a make-up specialist, so the trusts and the banks who are unloading their properties are pretending that nothing out of the way is happening... Dana L. Thomas, *Lords of the Land*, p.289

In support of the vested interests, in 1976 Congress passed the Tax Reform Act, offering further incentives to the REITs as tax shelters. Slowly (but faster than in the previous cycle), the real estate market turned.

3 *The Real Estate Gamble*, p.207.

Stock markets

IN ANOTHER expected repeat of history, the stock market rebounded in 1975 from the low of December 6, 1974. It was another of those very good years, remarked Martin S. Fridson. 'The 1975 rebound rally began with a steep drop in interest rates.'[4] The Fed had good reason to ease up on the brakes too. Sharply rising unemployment and the collapse of the Franklin National Bank (one of the largest banking failures of the time) were causing notable angst. Another loan loss, \$30m at the Beverly Hills Bancorp, caused it to fail. After the Bank of San Diego farce, 'hundreds of southern Californians were reportedly so unnerved by these events that they withdrew their savings from local banks and secreted the funds in cookie jars and beneath potted plants.'[5] Confidence in American banks was at its lowest ebb in forty years.

Taking its cue from the interest rate decline, the Dow climbed 14 per cent in January 1975 alone, the largest one-month rise in 35 years, and with it the 1973-5 land-price-induced recession passed into history. That March, Congress voted for a \$22.8bn tax cut (we know the effect that would have on land price) and the Dow went on to finish almost 40 per cent higher for the year.

Further tax reform followed. Tax shelter provisions were tightened in an effort to stop a few rorts:

> The 1976 Tax Reform Act specifically limited the amount of loss from oil and gas tax shelters, cattle feeding, equipment leasing and film-making and from partnerships *other than those in real estate*. The 1978 Tax Revision went further and limited losses in any trade or business *other than real estate*.
>
> Harrison, p.144 (emphasis added)

Needless to say, real estate became the hottest buy for anyone wanting to offset 'losses' against other income.

There was another item in the 1978 Act as well: it reduced the tax rate on capital gains from around 50 per cent to 28 per cent. The effect for the venture capital industry was almost immediate. The Great Depression had seen a change in the tax treatment of capital gains. Prior to that, capital gains or losses were just part of income, and taxed as such. After 1931, many wealthy US citizens found themselves, whilst still fortunate enough to be earning something, sitting on large stock losses. It was soon realised that they could sell the shares, create a 'capital' loss, deduct this from their income and so pay no taxes for the year – though they would buy back the shares immediately after the sale. Laws were changed to stop the practice. By 1977, with capital gains taxes approaching 50 per cent, fewer Americans were taking business risks, especially as any prospective loss could only be offset against a far from certain future gain. In that year only

4 *It was a very Good Year*, p.177.
5 Fridson, p.178, quoting *Business Week*.

$39m was raised by venture capitalists for risky ventures. By 1981, the figure was $1.3bn.[6] The development of the internet owes much to this Act and reveals the utter stupidity of taxes on income and profits.

The tax cuts had an immediate effect on land price: it climbed steeply after 1978.[7] As a result, most Western economies ended up with a marked period of stagnation and worker dis-satisfaction. Rents stayed high, unemployment stayed high and prices kept rising.

> The banking industry was reeling from soured loans to troubled Latin American nations, and a malaise gripped the nation that was nearly unshakable. Unemployment and inflation rates topped 13 percent. The nation's prime lending rate exceeded 20 percent! Home and car purchases collapsed under the unusually heavy financing burden. Gold and oil prices soared, drawing money away from financial assets. Indeed, US Treasury bonds were nicknamed 'certificates of confiscation' since their yields failed to keep pace with the soaring inflation rate. Financial instruments were universally loathed, leading *Business Week* magazine to declare 'the death of equities' in the summer of '82.
>
> Ron Insana, *Trendwatching*, p.139

The lead in to 1982

Monetarism

FROM A Keynesian perspective it was not possible to have at the same time a recession and rising unemployment on one hand, and rising interest rates and consumer prices on the other. So, with unemployment, interest rates and inflation measurements all well into double figures, the '70s was not a showcase decade for Keynesian economic theory. In recognition of the shock this delivered to mainstream economists, an answer for the economic malaise was sought elsewhere.

For the owners of the economy, the answer was easily found: the economist they turned to was Milton Friedman.

> For two decades, Milton Friedman, an economics professor at the University of Chicago, had been battling against Keynesian orthodoxy. Resurrecting the economic liberalism of the nineteenth century under the new guise of 'monetarism,' he argued that the market was fundamentally a self-correcting mechanism, and that government attempts to interfere with its operation – whether by introducing price controls to curb inflation or by compelling management to influence the level of unemployment – were doomed to failure. In *Free to Choose*, a popular introduction to free-market ideology that Friedman wrote with his wife Rose, he contended that all government intervention, however well-intentioned, had harmful side effects. For Friedman, markets were the best way to distribute information and provide incentives, regardless of the inequities that might emerge. In a 1973 interview with *Playboy* magazine, Friedman boldly asserted that all

6 John Steele Gordon, 'The Business of America', *American Heritage*, April 2000.
7 Harrison, p.147.

> societies were structured on greed: 'The problem of social organization,' he claimed, 'is how to set up an arrangement under which greed will do the least harm; capitalism is that kind of system.'
>
> Edward Chancellor, *Devil Take the Hindmost*, p.241

Friedman's work contributed to a revival of economic liberalism, particularly in the area of financial markets. The Friedman thesis defended the role of the speculator, proclaiming that market speculators were essential to the well-being of markets and to the efficient distribution of the economy's scarce resources. It was the speculator that was uniquely situated to take on the investment risk of the capitalist process.

Building upon the work of Friedman, other economists began an intensive study of the operation of the financial markets. Practically overnight a new body of thought, the Efficient Market Hypothesis (EMH) was born.[8] In the 1970s this theory spread quickly through US universities and was soon the working gospel of all finance graduates.

At the same time, another attack upon the prevailing economic paradigm was taking place.

> In the early 1970s Ronald McKinnon led an intellectual attack against what he called 'financial repression', that is, the segmentation of financial markets in developing countries that favoured (1) loans to government, (2) foreign trade, and (3) large firms at the expense of everyone else. The message appealed particularly to Latin American countries already influenced by Chicago doctrines of liberalism. [Financial] deregulation was adopted in a number of countries …
>
> Charles Kindleberger, *Manias, Panics and Crashes*, p.33

Astute readers of history would have seen this before, of course, with predictable results: explosive bank formation, a huge increase in the creation of credit, inflation, and an asset price boom most notably in land price – followed by bank collapse. But we are ahead of ourselves.

On October 6, 1979 the newly ensconced Fed chairman, Paul Volcker, in an effort to bring inflation under control, announced that no longer would the country's money supply be permitted to fluctuate. The supply of money to the economy would for the time being remained fixed; instead, interest rates would be permitted to rise. This was a marked shift in Federal Reserve monetary policy. It was now possible for interest rates to swing rapidly. One well placed bond trader of the time, Michael Lewis, described it this way:

> Bond prices move inversely, lock step, to rates of interest. Allowing interest rates to swing wildly meant allowing bond prices to swing wildly. Before

8 In 1965 Eugene Fama published his now famous thesis attempting to show beyond doubt that markets are completely efficient in processing information. If this were so, it would not be possible for any investor, through extra effort and knowledge, to outperform the market in the long run. But, as Warren Buffett once pointed out, believing the market to be efficient does not prove that it *is* always efficient.

> Volcker's speech bonds had been conservative investments, into which investors put their savings when they didn't fancy a gamble in the stock market. After Volcker's speech, bonds became objects of speculation, a means of creating wealth rather than merely storing it. Overnight the bond market was transformed from a backwater into a casino. *Liar's Poker*, p.39

Derivatives

With the US dollar now fiat, with Friedman's economic liberalism being accepted into mainstream economic thinking (replacing the now discredited Keynesian theory) and with the rise of computing power, a financial revolution began. This revolution showed itself in the creation of derivatives markets. A derivative is nothing complicated; it is simply a security created from a contract between two parties. The contract derives its value from the underlying asset, for example a share. When trading a derivative, such as an option contract, a smaller downpayment is required than if one were to purchase the real share upon which the option is based. A leveraged position, in other words. Such leverage, it had been believed, encouraged more speculation than was good for the economy. Friedman's work put an end to that belief.

> If markets were efficient and in constant equilibrium, and if price movements were always random, then the activities of speculators could be neither irrational in motivation nor destabilizing in effect.
>
> Chancellor, p.243

Derivatives markets for gold opened in 1975, for mortgages in 1976 and for oil in 1978. Currency futures markets followed in 1982, index futures thereafter.

In 1982, however, the country was still in an officially defined recession from the year before (what looked suspiciously like the usual mid-cycle slowdown). Volcker's latest Federal Reserve policy manoeuver had in fact deliberately attempted to engineer it.

> [J]ust as the entire investing population began to believe that stocks and bonds would go down forever, and gold and oil would soar, a strange phenomenon occurred. Latin American nations, specifically Mexico, threatened to declare a moratorium on the tens of billions of dollars in debt they owed to struggling US Banks... In order to prevent a wholesale financial catastrophe, the Federal Reserve promised to backstop the banks, providing billions of dollars in bailout assistance. The Fed slashed interest rates and turned on the monetary spigot, ballooning the nation's money supply in an effort to 're-liquefy' the banking system and stimulate the stagnant economy.
>
> Insana, p.139

The old credit-creation trick of the bankers again.

> The trick worked marvelously well... At the same time, the federal government, under President Ronald Reagan's direction, cut tax rates aggressively

> … Government spending also increased dramatically on defense programs (which created countless jobs) and on a whole host of programs that stimulated state, local, and national economic activity. The trillion-dollar defense buildup, a variety of make-work, pork-barrel projects, along with huge increases in entitlement spending, 'primed the pump,' as economist John Maynard Keynes liked to say. That added gas to an economy that was already being fueled by the Fed's new easy money policies. Insana, p.139

There was one more stimulus added: an acceptance by the Group of Five (which is now Eight) industrialised nations to weaken what was considered an overvalued US dollar. A seven per cent reduction in the dollar's value, some economists suggest, is like a full percentage point reduction in interest rates.[9] The lower dollar was wanted to boost US growth rates. The monetary spigots once again turned recession into boom times.

The rise of the trader

The ability of the financial revolution to sustain itself was completed by the coming to power of Margaret Thatcher in the UK and Ronald Reagan in the US. Both were products of economic liberalism, the free-market ideology sweeping the world. In 1981 President Mitterrand took up the cause in France, followed by Chancellor Kohl in Germany and then Prime Minister Hawke – leading a Labour Party – in Australia. The ideas even extended to China and Deng Xiaoping. As political adviser to republican presidential candidates Nixon and then Reagan himself, Friedman had a hand in all of this as well.

> A powerful alliance had emerged between economic liberals and Reagan Republicans; both agreed that government intervention in economic affairs was undesirable and that the judgment of the market was paramount.
>
> Chancellor, p.250

The government granting of licences and privileges went on unhindered, of course. Government has since become larger than ever, having been forced to re-regulate the entrepreneurial abuses of the licences and economic privileges so granted.

The pursuit of self-interest was now paramount. Ayn Rand was finally to have her time in the sun. Taxes were reduced, for both individuals and corporations; the entrepreneur's role was eulogised. Derivative traders working for large institutions and banks, and private traders with hedge funds, using the latest advances in communications, were quick to see the potential profits in exploiting the new-found leverage.

The most successful hedge fund, the Quantum Fund founded by George Soros in 1977, produced annual returns on its leveraged positions in bond and currency markets in excess of 25 per cent. Ivan Boesky developed techniques in risk arbitrage and Michael Milken made himself famous and

9 Insana, p.143.

the highest paid man on Wall Street ($550m in one year alone, his federal and state taxes weighing in at $205.9m) with junk bonds (debt) to effect leveraged buyouts (LBO's) and takeovers of listed public companies. Suddenly the trader was hip. It was an international phenomenon. Everyone wanted to be one.

It was the boom in LBOs and easy credit that pushed the 1980s bull market to such heights.

> The boom in leveraged buyouts became the driving force behind the bull market of the mid-1980s. Conventional measures of value gave way to LBO valuations, known as 'private market value', which were calculated by examining how much cash (free cash flow) a company generated and how much debt it could support. Professional 'risk arbitrageurs', on the lookout for the next takeover, became the medium through which private market value was established in the stock market. Acting in unofficial collusion, arbitrageurs searched for vulnerable companies and took large stakes in them, thus putting them 'in play.' Members of the public followed the arbs' operations and imitated them, just as their forebears had followed stock market pools in the 1920s.
>
> Chancellor, p.262

The stock market party ended in October 1987 with a crash on Monday October 19. It was not, however, followed by an economic crisis; for that we had to wait for the Savings and Loans debacle, brought to a climax, eventually, by the next land price downturn – 18 years after the last one.

The Savings and Loans farce

JUST AFTER the peak of this cycle, in 1989, the US underwent the biggest bailout ever seen of banks and banking institutions generally, the so-called Savings and Loan (S&L) scandal of the 1980s.

> Thrifts had been established originally to help homeowners obtain mortgages. But in the 1970s inflation undermined the stability of the industry, sticking the thrifts with low interest mortgages arranged years before when inflation was slight. To help the thrifts survive Congress deregulated the industry, lifting restrictions on the kinds of loans they could make. Swindlers immediately took over the industry. As the saying went, 'Why rob a bank when you can own one.' By the end of the 1980s the thrifts were in danger of collapsing after approving billions in insider loans for worthless projects. Congress eventually bailed out the industry at taxpayer expense.
>
> www.hnn.us/articles/880.html

Despite the prodigious amount of information available about this banking scandal, most commentators miss the causal connection between easy credit and a land-price boom – leading eventually, as it must, to bust. But the historical repetition is clear. Let's take a closer look. A little history is required.

The first S&L association, The Oxford Provident Building Association, was founded in Frankford, Pennsylvania in 1831. A few locals decided to pool their resources so that they might be able to buy their own homes, the banks having turned down their requests for credit. The idea had originated in England. Following the Great Depression of the 1930s,

> [large] commercial banks had abandoned housing lending in favor of more lucrative corporate and state lending, or had charged interest rates that made home mortgages inaccessible to Americans on a moderate income. Congress facilitated the creation of 'thrift' depository institutions (S&L banks and mutual savings banks) to fill this void. The S&L branch of the banking industry was created to supply affordable mortgages to working class families, so that the American Dream of home ownership would not slip beyond their grasp … This regulation of banking created a structure of institutional distinctions within the industry: commercial banks were allowed to invest in a broad variety of instruments (including corporate, governmental, and mortgage lending; stocks and bonds investments; and real estate speculation), to charge market-based interest on loans, and to pay competitive interest rates on deposits. S&L institutions, on the other hand, operated within restrictions not placed on the commercial banks, including a narrow definition of their business activities to home mortgages offered at lower interest rates and for longer maturities than commercial banks; prohibitions against paying out high interest rates on deposits; and restrictions against investing in high-yield but risky investment instruments like real estate speculation and junk bonds. US Congress: House, 1989a

The federal government encouraged the thrifts to stick to home mortgages. Thrifts were consequently required by law to provide a safe 'deposit' institution for household savings, then invest such savings in thirty-year, fixed-rate mortgages (secured by the property) within a fifty-mile radius of the head office. Such deposits, as those of other banks, would now be federally insured against loss through possible collapse of the institution. With economic recovery after World War II, the thrifts prospered as the US went from a nation of tenants to a nation of home-owners. Said the US Savings and Loan League's Executive Vice President Norman Strunk in 1954:

> 'We love the guy who walks in with 50 bucks to start a savings account, because we know that in five years he'll probably have several times that in his account – and in the meantime the chances are good that he may have taken out a loan with us.' Quoted in *Time*, November 1954

By 1963 S&Ls were making 46 per cent of all home mortgage loans in the US, three times the number made by the commercial banks.[10] They prospered most where house prices went up the fastest. S&Ls had a slight (government decreed) edge over banks in that they were permitted to lend up to 90 per cent of the price of a house and the land on a 30-year mortgage; banks had to observe the Fed's mandated 75 per cent lending

10 *Time*, August 30, 1963.

valuation policy spread over 20 years. So successful was this government policy that, by the mid-1960s, S&Ls were having trouble finding lenders for all the new deposits being lodged. Thrift managers took the motto '3-6-3': offer savings at 3 per cent, lend at 6 per cent, hit the golf course by 3.

Ironically, however, the prosperous times contained the seeds of trouble, undermining what seemed in the 1930s, at the time of drafting, pretty safe laws. The legislation ensured that the thrifts were borrowing short (paying interest on deposits) and lending long (receiving interest on long-term mortgages). Normally the long interest rate stays above the short rate, presenting little problem to the thrifts. In addition, houses are often sold prior to the end of a 30-year mortgage, reducing further any risk. But in the late 1960s and early '70s things were anything but normal. Interest rates went up and up. So did inflation.

A squeeze began within the S&L industry as depositors, in a high-inflation environment, took their money out of the thrifts and sought higher interest rates from other institutions not hindered by laws and regulations – money market accounts and mutual funds for example. Remember that thrifts had been prohibited from paying high interest rates on deposits – to protect them from high funding costs. Neither could they adjust the rate on 30-year mortgages once issued to borrowers; the mortgage rate was fixed for the life of the loan.

Worse was to come as interest rates continued to rise into the late 1970s. The thrifts were now paying more to depositors than they were earning on mortgage loans – not an effective business model. In part, this trouble arose from deliberate Federal Reserve policy.

> Paul Volcker had made his historic speech on 6 October 1979. Short-term interest rates had skyrocketed. For a thrift manager to make a thirty year home loan, he had to accept a rate of interest of 10 percent. Meanwhile, to get the money, he was paying 12 percent. He ceased, therefore, to make new loans, which suited the purpose of the Federal Reserve which was trying to slow the economy.
>
> Lewis, *Liar's Poker*, p.117

Housing starts collapsed as a result, dropping to record post-war lows. Prior to the Fed's move, only 7 per cent of thrifts were losing money. After Volcker's actions, 85 per cent of the thrifts were in trouble.[11] The monetarist theories of Friedman, as put into practice by Chairman Paul Volcker at the Fed, were packing quite a punch.

The Carter administration, with an eye to re-election (he was subsequently defeated) made some changes that took effect in March 1980. The Depository Institutions Deregulation and Monetary Control Act (DIDMCA) aimed at, in the words of the Federal Deposit Insurance Corporation (FDIC):

11 *Washington Monthly*, May 1995.

> … eliminating many of the distinctions among different types of depository institutions and ultimately removing [the] interest rate ceiling on deposit accounts. Authority for federal S&Ls to make ADC [acquisition, development and construction] loans [was] expanded.
>
> www.fdic.gov/bank/historical/s&l/

Oddly, though, at the very last moment and without debate, the deposit insurance limit was raised from $40,000 to $100,000, a crucial development. More on that shortly.

The new Reagan administration (Reagan took office in 1980), under the now direct influence of Friedman's economic liberalism, went further with the deregulation of the industry, permitting the Federal Home Loan Bank Board (FHLBB) to allow any thrift in difficulty to issue Income Capital Certificates. As these could be purchased by the Federal Savings and Loans Insurance Corporation (FSLIC), they were regarded as capital by the issuing thrift, which would therefore not be seen to be insolvent. This accounting sleight of hand helped the troubled thrifts present accounts that gave an immediate impression that the industry was returning to better health.

In January 1982 the FHLBB reduced the net worth requirement for insured thrifts from 4 to 3 per cent of total deposits.

> Additionally S&Ls [were] allowed to meet the low net worth standard not in terms of generally accepted accounting principles (GAAP), but with the even more liberal regulatory accounting principles (RAP).
>
> www.fdic.gov/bank/historical/s&l/

Incredibly, this meant for example that, if one thrift took over another with assets of, say, $4 bn but liabilities of $5 bn, the difference, a billion dollars, could be counted as goodwill and the goodwill treated as capital in the accounts of the buying thrift. Noted Bert Ely, a respected author of the S&L crisis:

> Therefore, just as [thrifts], encouraged by deregulation, took on more risk, they had a smaller capital cushion to fall back on.
>
> www.econlib.org/library/Enc/Savingandloancrisis.html

In April 1982 the FHLBB lifted restrictions on the minimum number of shareholders a thrift had to maintain. Up to that time there had to be at least 400, of which 125 were required to be local citizens. Previously one person could not own more than a tenth of the shares and no single group could control more than a quarter. Now there could be a single owner. And the new purchaser could, if he wished, put up real estate as collateral, making the purchase of a thrift much easier.

Meanwhile the Tax Reform Act (1981) came into force, providing, in the words of the FDIC, 'powerful tax incentives for real estate investment by individuals'. Readers of history would have had no trouble forecasting the results: an increase in land value, and over-building. Said Steven Wilmsen about the Act, when writing about the Silverado S&L in Denver: 'Nobody could lose because property values went through the roof as speculators nearly went hysterical bidding for prairie acreage-cum-office parks.'[12]

The 1981 Act also included a further tax break for thrifts, well explained by Michael Lewis, who saw the effect this had from the inside:

> The tax break allowed thrifts to sell all their mortgage loans and put their cash to work for higher returns – often by purchasing the cheap loans disgorged by other thrifts ... The huge losses on the sale (they were selling loans for sixty-five cents on the dollar they had originally made at par, or a hundred cents on the dollar) could now be hidden. A new accounting standard allowed thrifts to amortize the losses over the life of the loans ... But what was even better is that the loss could be offset against any taxes the thrift had paid over the previous ten years. Shown losses, the Internal Revenue Service returned old tax dollars to the thrifts. p.121

For the thrifts, the idea was now to generate losses – any losses. The vast surge in trading brought a massive windfall to Wall Street bond-trading corporations (like Salomon Brothers). 'The most irresponsible period in the history of capital markets,' said one partner of the Blackstone Group.[13]

To complete the reflating of the thrift industry, the Reagan Administration passed the Garn-St Germain Depository Institutions Act in December 1982. This, noted the FDIC, was designed to

> complete the process of giving expanded powers to federally chartered S&Ls and enable them to diversify their activities with the view of increasing profits. Major provisions included: elimination of deposit interest rate ceilings; elimination of the previous statutory limit on loan to value ratio; and expansion of the asset powers of federal S&Ls by permitting up to 40% of assets in commercial mortgages, up to 30% of assets in consumer loans, up to 10% of assets in commercial loans, and up to 10% of assets in commercial leases.

'All in all', said President Reagan, as he signed the Garn-St Germain bill into law in front of over two hundred S&L executives, bankers and Congressmen, 'I think we hit the jackpot.'[14]

Now thrifts were no longer required to lend only within their own communities – that fifty-mile radius; 100 per cent financing had become a reality and a thrift could now be owned by just about anybody, who could then use the thrift to lend money to themselves. It is said that Mafia lawyers and accountants spent a good deal of time following the passage of the Garn-St Germain bill through Congress.

12 *Silverado: Neil Bush and the S&L Scandal*, p.75.
13 Lewis, p.124.
14 See www.presidency.ucsb.edu/ws/index.php?pid=41872

To politicians within the Reagan administration, the response to the crisis in the thrift industry no doubt appeared quite logical at the time. Government legislation had got the thrifts into a mess in the first place, so give them more freedom, with less government oversight, so that they could trade out of it. Writer Catherine England at the Cato Institute put it succinctly:

> Imagine a fifty-year-old owner/manager of an S&L opened by his father. It is 1980, and he has helplessly watched his institution's capital erode. The housing market has slowed to a virtual standstill, and his customers have moved their savings to money market mutual funds. He is unhappy with general economic conditions and the regulatory constraints that have caused his problems, and he wants his congressman and senators to know about it. In addition, he expresses the strongly held conviction that it would be wrong to close hundreds of S&Ls with financial problems not of their making. Then Congress acts, granting him permission to make loans and investments other than mortgages. In addition, the phase out of interest rate ceilings is begun.
>
> *Lessons from the Savings and Loan Debacle*

Michael Lewis explains further:

> The Savings and Loan industry made the majority of home loans to average Americans and received layers of government support and protection. The breaks given to Savings and Loans, such as deposit insurance and tax loopholes, indirectly lowered the interest cost on mortgages, by lowering the cost of funds to the Savings and Loans. The Savings and Loans lobby in Washington invoked democracy, the flag, and apple pie when shepherding one of these breaks through Congress. They stood for homeownership, they'd say, and homeownership was the American way. To stand up in Congress and speak against homeownership would have been as politically astute as to campaign against motherhood. Nudged by a friendly public policy, Savings and Loans grew, and the volume of outstanding mortgage loans swelled from 55 billion dollars in 1950 to 700 billion dollars in 1976. In January 1980 that figure became 1.2 trillion dollars, and the mortgage market surpassed the combined United States stock markets as the largest capital market in the world. p.97

There were two further changes. As already noted, part of the early 1980s legislative response to the thrifts' difficulties was to lift the level of deposit insurance to $100,000 – despite the fact that up to that time the average thrift deposit rarely amounted to more than $10,000. Since deposits were now insured, depositors did not have to worry whether a thrift was sound or well managed. And the thrift could afford to offer rates marginally, and continually, above market to attract funds. Got more than $100k to invest? Just spread it round more than one thrift. Here, then, the government had, with one quick stroke of the pen, disproved the market maxim that high yield equalled high risk. So much for deregulation.

The second change was the computerisation of the industry. Any depositor could now access markets nation-wide. Intermediaries – deposit brokers – began gathering deposits from individual savers and funnelling the total proceeds, broken down into $100k bundles, to thrifts (or other institutions) that offered the highest rates. More deposits, more lending creates more deposits. With restrictions virtually eliminated, a liberally inclined government and ever-decreasing supervision of the industry, the only controls left were the thrifts own management integrity and risk-management practices. And these were effective in some and ignored in others. Ironically, a more favourable interest rate climate through 1983-5 saw the circumstances of most thrifts ease considerably.

In response to a rash of state-chartered thrifts defecting to the federal system, which offered more potentially lucrative opportunities, various states, including California, Texas and Florida, passed liberal laws allowing their thrifts to invest 100 per cent of their deposits in activities of any nature. State thrifts converting to a federal charter also meant the loss of a lucrative source of campaign funding for state politicians.

After all the regulatory changes, thrifts began lending heavily to real estate developers, builders and construction companies. There was no shortage of investors – people queued up to take advantage of the 1981 federal tax law changes that generously rewarded investment in construction. The federal government had acted. The thrifts had begun to lend themselves out of trouble and into potentially more profitable areas … or so the government thought…

Easy credit

IN ACTUALITY, more than a few financially savvy Savings and Loans managers quickly proceeded to rip the 'thrift' out of the thrifts. As they were no longer dependent upon funds from local borrowers, but were permitted to borrow wholesale from virtually anywhere, were also officially encouraged to diversify their loan portfolios away from 30-year mortgages into other property areas, were allowed to lend on almost any speculative venture, the loans being up to 100 per cent of appraised value, and with accounting changes to help it all look good, this proved rather easy to do.

Former house builder and real estate developer David Paul bought into Dade Savings and Loan. Regulators were happy at the time that someone wanted to take over the faltering thrift, which had been caught like many others in the interest rate squeeze of the early 1980s. He renamed it Centrust Savings Bank of Miami and used the deposits he brought into the bank through loan brokers to buy $1.4bn worth of Michael Milkin's so-called junk bonds and other related Milkin issues.

> [Paul] paid himself $16 million, took an apartment at the Carlyle Hotel in Manhattan, and spent $1.4 million a year on a corporate jet, $13 million on a painting by Rubens and $8 million on a yacht.
>
> Chancellor, *Devil Take the Hindmost*, p.274

With gold-leaf ceilings and a jacuzzi in the master bedroom, the thrift's yacht *Le Grand Cru* added to the bank's balance sheet and made quite an impression on visiting dignitaries and politicians. The losses on the junk bonds went unreported.

Thomas Spiegel, a former Milkin associate and bond salesman, bought into Columbia Savings and Loan, Milkin taking part of the business. Using the plentiful supply of deposits now available to the thrifts (when they wanted more they had only to lift the interest rate a percentage point or two), Spiegel easily moved the bank balance sheet totals up to \$13bn by 1987, from just \$400m five years earlier. One third of the deposits entering Columbia found their way into Milkin's junk bonds. For all the hard work, Spiegel travelled in the bank's recently bought corporate jets for all the deal-making and paid himself around \$9m a year.

A number of thrifts were soon expanding at the rate of 1,200 per cent a year or more simply by taking in deposits from the growing legion of deposit brokers – who would, for a fee, match thrifts with savers like pension funds and other institutions wanting to put their money to work at the highest interest rate available. The thrift would then loan out the funds, '*mostly on speculative property deals*'.[15] Under the new accounting rules, the thrift could then report a profit from the fees charged. More deposits, more loans, more profits (at least on paper) … pretty soon the young thrift was reporting solid growth. Or so it appeared.

All the hard work did not prevent thrift owners and managers from enjoying the finer things in life.

> … Don Ray Dixon of Vernon Savings took his wife by private jet and Rolls-Royce on a 'market study' of French Michelin three-star restaurants … He also bought half a dozen jets, a vintage car dealership, and the sister ship to President Roosevelt's yacht. Edwin 'fast Eddy' McBirny of Sunbelt Savings, fed his guests at his north Dallas home on lion meat and antelope, while presiding over the festivities dressed as Henry VIII with dry ice billowing around him. At another party at his penthouse suite in Las Vegas, McBirney allegedly diverted his bank's clients with an 'enthusiastic lesbian romp'…
>
> Chancellor, p.274

Thomas Spiegel and his family made at least four trips to Europe; he bought guns and accessories totalling \$91,000, resort villas and other real estate, and spent \$1,900 on silverware, \$8,600 on towels and \$11,840 on music concerts – all paid for by federally insured Columbia thrift deposits.[16] Said Tom Gaubert, former Texas real estate developer and new owner of Independent Savings Association: 'I'm tired of playing Monopoly with my money. This way [through owning a deregulated thrift] we can use the depositor's money.'[17]

15 Chancellor, p.274 (emphasis added).
16 K. Calavita *et al*, *Big Money Crime*, p.59.
17 Calavita *et al*, p.103.

Graph 13.1: Thrifts, Percentage of Real Estate Loans 1980-2000

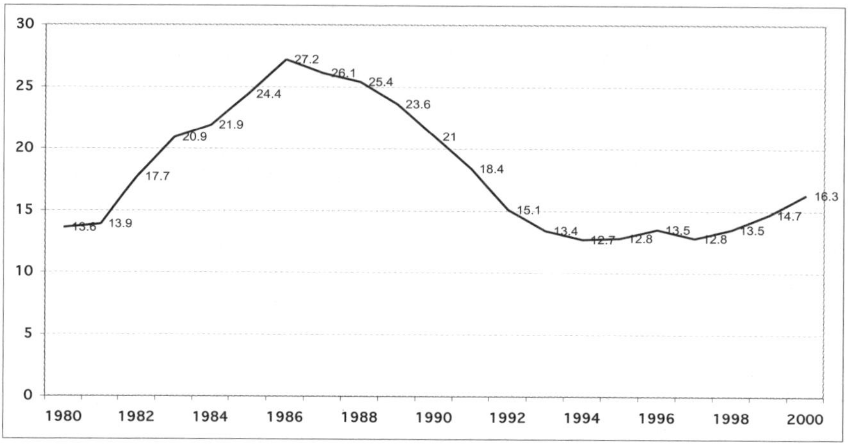

Source: *Bank Failures in Mature Economies*, Bank for International Settlements, Table 3, p.59 (available on-line at www.bis.org/publ/ bcbs_wp13.pdf).

As word spread and conferences were organised to discuss the huge window of opportunity the government had opened, the thrift rorting reached epidemic proportions. Any reader of *Business Week* knew what to do:

> Start an S&L. Offer a premium interest rate and watch the deposits roll in. Your depositors are insured by Uncle Sam, so they don't care what you do with their money. And in states like California, you can do almost anything you want with it. Add enormous leverage – you can pile $100 of assets on every $3 of capital – and you've built a speculators' dream machine.
>
> 'Casino Society', *Business Week*, 1985

The list of thrifts looted was practically endless, as were the deposits available from deposit brokers with which to finance it. Some examples of the looting are given in Appendix 9 – it is worth reading that before you continue with this chapter as it includes a run-down on many of the real-estate-based schemes. What took place this cycle practically defies belief.[18] Each cycle the bad real estate loans eventually having to be written off have grown larger – which suggests figures for the 2010 cycle will be astronomical. The authorities are going to have to be inventive in their rescue plans and socialisation of the losses.

In 1988 the comptroller of the currency, having surveyed all the recent banking and thrift failures, reported that less than 10 per cent of the failures had been caused solely by economic factors. Most were attributable

18 For a more succinct list of the (known) banks robbed, 1991 style see www.businesscycles.biz/docs/banksrobbed1991style.pdf

to faulty lending practices or outright fraud. (The FHLBB had by this time referred more than 11,000 S&L cases to the Justice Department for possible criminal prosecution.) At this time the FSLIC reported that it would have $20bn available for bailing out any thrift in the industry in difficulty, an amount it had deemed 'adequate for the bank *provided there is no economic downturn*'.[19]

It was not just the thrifts but banks in general that went on an acquisition and real estate lending spree in the 1980s. The Boston-based Bank of New England (BNE) had by the mid-1980s become quite a large regional bank after acquiring Connecticut Bank and Trust, Maine National Bank and other smaller local institutions. BNE then went aggressively into real estate lending. By the late 1980s over 30 per cent of its loan portfolio was in commercial real estate.[20] This was shortly to prove disastrous.

Into the peak

IN THE SPRING of 1989 one of the San Fernando Valley's hottest real estate moguls, Mike Glickman, made the bold prediction that Southern California real estate values would never fall.

> Glickman, who at age 15 delivered real estate tear sheets for a local broker, became one of the most successful real estate agents by the time he was in his early twenties. By age 30, he owned the fastest-growing real estate brokerage in the region. He was frequently billed as one of the best young entrepreneurs in Los Angeles. He paid above-average commissions, gave generous perks and bonuses, and expanded his operations with a speed unheard of in the real estate business.
>
> Insana, p.136

Glickman's prediction marked the top of the cycle. In several landmark real estate transactions that set new records as Glickman was delivering his forecast, Minoru Isutani, a Japanese real estate developer, paid $841m – or rather his banks did – for the hallowed greens of Pebble Beach Golf Course, further stoking fears that Japan was set to take over America. (The Japanese had already bought New York's Rockefeller Centre.) A consortium of American golfing enthusiasts, including Clint Eastwood, bought it back some years later, for less.

The quality of the S&Ls', indeed all banks', credit risk had of course become dependent on the quality of their lending, and the value of the security supporting it. These 'risk-factors' for credit providers are always the same: property values, rental income and occupancy rates. Everything looks good as property prices (land values in reality) rise, but should prices ever start to fall… And, when some of the loans are never designed to be repaid, or loans are simply stolen, there will be major trouble ahead.

After 1987 land values stopped rising. Remember those 1981 tax law changes that promoted real estate over-building? They were tightened in

19 *Time*, June 20, 1988 (emphasis added).
20 BIS, p.63.

1986, affecting the value of much that had just been built. Falling prices began to undermine thrift assets all over the US. Although thrifts had been failing throughout the decade (due to local conditions or outright fraud), the failure rate reached fever pitch in 1989, just as President Bush took office. Predictably, though, the massive S&L problems did not form any part of the 1988 election debate: the Democratic contender's running mate Lloyd Benson owned a thrift or two, and so also did the Republican candidate's son, Neil.

Given the growing size of the failing thrifts, and the amounts of money involved, Congress in 1989 began adopting legislation for taxpayers to foot the bill and bail out the industry, whilst at the same time moving ahead with plans to deregulate the 14,000 federally insured banks. But not before a number of scams and crimes on a hitherto unimagined scale came to light. Falling land values meant that the S&L scandals could no longer be hidden from public view: a lot more real estate loans were now worth less than the value of the real estate itself. As a result a lot more banking institutions and thrifts were in trouble.

The scams

TWO THRIFT frauds in particular had America enthralled and angry: Charles Keating and Lincoln Savings and Loan, and Neil Bush and Silverado S&L. Both typified the prevailing mood, as detailed in Appendix 10.

It was not just the thrifts that had gone on a real estate lending spree. Bankers had also turned to real estate, 'expanding those credits by threefold in the 1980s, to $750 billion from $248 billion.'[21] Between 1984 and the middle of 1990 some 72 per cent of all loan growth at commercial banks was provided by real estate. 'By late 1990, the concentration of real estate assets on the balance sheets of banks of all sizes had reached alarming proportions.'[22]

For the Bank of New England (BNE) the collapse of real estate values brought difficulties in the form of non-performing loans, which by the end of 1989 were running at approximately 2.2 per cent of total loans.[23] As the real estate situation grew worse, so too did their loan portfolio. A mere one year later, BNE's non-performing loans on real estate stood at 20 per cent of all loans. By early January 1991, the bank announced a probable fourth quarter loss that would technically render the bank insolvent. Nervous depositors withdrew over a billion dollars, a good deal of it over the weekend from the new automated teller machines. (No need now to wait until Monday for the doors to open.) The taxpayer-funded bailout would ultimately cost $2.3bn after the FDIC and Reserve Bank decided the bank was simply 'too big to fail'.

21 James Grant, *The Trouble with Prosperity*, pp.171-2.
22 Grant, pp.171-2.
23 BIS, p.63.

Credit created out of nothing, on the back of a government-granted licence in land value that inflates such land value, will at some point lead to a bust. In this style of economy that operates today – and is being taken up by more and more countries around the world – such a bust is inevitable. This is discussed further in Chapter 16, the chapter about those all-important government-granted licences.

In England the publishing empire of Robert Maxwell collapsed after it had become obvious that Maxwell Communications had paid inflated prices for its media assets – bought on credit, financed by friendly banks. (Media assets usually require a government licence to operate, generating for the owner a capitalised rental value.) It was soon discovered that Maxwell had also looted $1.4bn from the company, including some $800m from the employee pension scheme.

The Bank for Commerce and Credit International (BCCI) scandal came to light after the downturn in 1991, when it was revealed that it was being used to launder drug money, and as a haven for the ill-gotten gains of various dictators from around the world, President Ferdinand Marcos of the Philippines in particular. Marcos used the bank to launder his gains to his family's Swiss account. BCCI (since dubbed the Bank for Crooks and Criminals Inc.) was Pakistani-managed and Middle-East financed, with branches in more than sixty countries. This was, and remains, the largest banking and land heist in history. In July 1991, $20bn was found to have been stolen, lost or swindled.

At the height of the crisis, *The Nation* of July 9, 1990 suggested that a study of the 'catastrophe' that overtook the thrift and banking industries might offer a unique insight into institutional corruption and decay. The Justice Department, it said, had run out of staff to investigate and prosecute the officers of thrifts who had run off with money; the FBI reported too few agents for the task; the Treasury Department raised daily its estimate of the eventual cost to the taxpayer; and Congress refused to investigate, let alone discipline, any of its members for accepting campaign contributions and honoraria (read bribes).

Two symbols of the era, right at the top of the real estate market, were completed at this time. David Paul's 48-storey Centrust Tower and Charlie Keating's Phoenician Hotel.

> In March of 1989, when [Glickman] made his bold assertion that the market would never go down, he was riding the wave of a 15-year bull market in real estate. The bubble had been inflating with great vigor for at least the preceding five years … When interest rates started to go up in 1989, leveraged transactions in the stock market and the real estate market were hit hard. Within a year, Glickman's operations were severely constrained. He eventually went personally and professionally bankrupt, the victim of overexpansion and the undying belief that prices only go in one direction: up. Real estate prices in Southern California crashed. Those who bought at the top watched the value of their homes plunge by 25 percent or more. The

> bear market in real estate would last close to eight years. It would be a decade before prices returned to their pre-crash levels. The entire real estate bubble, while driven by the changing demographics of the region and a huge population influx, was financed by very easy money. The implosion of that bubble, along with a huge bear market in commercial real estate, would saddle the nation's biggest banks with uncollectable debt. The subsequent banking crisis in 1990 and 1991 led the Federal Reserve to embark on another dramatic lowering of interest rates. That repetitive cycle led to the new bull market in stocks and, ultimately, a new bubble in financial assets.
>
> Insana, p.136

Which leads us into the next real estate cycle.

FURTHER READING

Chancellor, Edward. *Devil Take the Hindmost: A History of Financial Speculation*. Papermac edn, 2000.

Grant, James. *The Trouble with Prosperity: A Contrarian's Tale of Boom, Bust and Speculation*. Random House, 1996.

Lachman, Leann. 'Demographics: The Key to Successful Real Estate Projects in the 1990s', *Real Estate Finance Journal*, 6, 1990, pp.16-21.

Lewis, Michael, *Liar's Poker*. Coronet Books, 1989.

Stroud, Hubert B. and William S. Spikowski. 'Planning in the Wake of Florida Land Scams, *Journal of Planning Education and Research*, 1998, Association of Collegiate Schools of Planning (www.spikowski.com/landscam.htm).

Stroud, Hubert B. *The Promise of Paradise: Recreational and Retirement Communities in the United States since 1950*. John Hopkins University Press, 1995.

www.buyandhold.com – Wall Street history section.

S&L Crisis

Bank for International Settlements (BIS). *Bank Failures in Mature Economies* (www.bis.org/publ/bcbs_wp13.pdf).

Calavita, K., Henry Pontell and Robert Tillman. *Big Money Crime: Fraud and Politics in the Savings and Loan Crisis*. University of California Press, 1997.

England, Catherine. 'Lessons from the Savings and Loan Debacle: The Case for Further Financial Deregulation', *Regulation, The Cato Review of Business and Government*, Cato Institute.

Ely, Bert. *Savings and Loan Crisis*. The Library of Economics and Liberty (www.econlib.org/library/Enc/SavingsandLoanCrisis.html).

Georges, Christopher. 'Egads! The S&L Scandal Lives!', *Washington Monthly*, January/February 1992.

Glasberg, Davita Silfen. 'The Dialectics of White-Collar Crime: The Anatomy of the Savings and Loan Crisis and the Case of Silverado Banking, Savings and Loan Association', in 'Money, Trust, Speculation and Social Justice – Part 1: Trust, Confidence, and Crime', *American Journal of Economics and Sociology*, October 1998.

Lowy, Martin. *High Rollers: Inside the Savings and Loan Debacle*. Praeger, 1991.
Pizzo, Stephen. *Inside Job: The Looting of America's Savings and Loans*. McGraw Hill Publishing Co, 1989.
Simons, Teresa. 'Banking on Secrecy', *Washington Monthly*, Vol. 22, Issue 11, December 1990.
Time magazine:
'Savings and Loan Men Teach Bankers a Lesson', November 29, 1954.
'The Twelve-fold Increase', August 30, 1963.
'A Program for a Banking Free-for-all', August 13, 1973.
'Earthquake Dangers for S&Ls', March 2, 1981.
'Another Time Bomb Goes Off', Stephen Koepp, May 27, 1985.
'Troubled Temples of Thrift', George Russell, May 18, 1987'
'Too Far Gone to Bring Back', June 20, 1988.
'How to Rob Banks without a Gun', Gordon Bock, August 15, 1988.
'Gold Among the Ruins', Christine Gorman, September 19, 1988.
'Who Will Pick up the Check?', November 7, 1988.
'Dad Would Make a Deal with the Devil', Richard Woodbury, February 20, 1989.
'Help Your Country and Help Yourself', S.C. Gwynne, February 20, 1989.
'His Personal Piggy Bank', March 12, 1990.
'Good Ole Bad Boy', John E. Gallagher, June 25, 1990.
'Spooky S&L Stories', Richard Zoglin, December 3, 1990.
US Congress: House, 1989a. *The Other Side of the Savings and Loan Industry.* Committee on Banking, Finance and Urban Affairs, Subcommittee on Financial Institutions Supervision, Regulation and Insurance, 101st Congress, 1st session, Washington, DC: Government Printing Office.
US Congress: House Committee on Government Operations, 1988. *Combating Fraud, Abuse and Misconduct on the Nation's Financial Institutions: Current Federal Efforts are Inadequate.* HR 100-1088.
Wilmsen, Steven. *Silverado: Neil Bush and the Savings and Loan Scandal.* National Press Books, 1991.

14

Life, Liberty and the Pursuit of a Mortgage

The Land (real estate) Boom of 2006[1]

... such imbalances and dislocations as we see in the economy today probably do not suggest anything more than a temporary hesitation in the continuing expansion of the economy.

Fed Chairman Alan Greenspan, summing up at his appearance before the Joint Economic Committee, January, 1990

I think the real estate market, with the exception of Northern New Jersey, is probably not going to be any significant drag in terms of the over-all national picture of the real estate sector.

Gerald Corrigan, President of the Federal Reserve Bank of New York (and Fed Vice-Chairman), to a closed meeting of the Federal Open Market Committee, February 1990

There are several things that we can stipulate with some degree of certainty: namely, that those who argue that we are already in recession ... are reasonably certain to be wrong.[2]

Fed Chairman Alan Greenspan again, this time to the Federal Open Market Committee, August 21, 1990

'Neither the market nor the regulators had anticipated the adjustment of asset values or the drop in US real estate values.'

James Grant, *The Trouble with Prosperity*, p.180, quoting Citicorp's 1990 Annual Report, which was suggesting the downturn was really nobody's fault as the bank reported more and more non-performing real estate loans

1 **This chapter formed the basis of classes presented to subscribers in 2005, and was posted to the EIS website in March 2006.** Save for a few minor editing amendments for clarity, the chapter has been reprinted here without change so that the reader can see that the timing of the present US housing-led difficulties was eminently forecastable. The original chapter can be seen here: www.businesscycles.biz/docs/2010.htm

2 The National Bureau of Economic Research subsequently went on to date the start of that year's recession at July, with Greenspan's Fed going on to cut short-term rates 24 times in succession in a desperate bid to shore up market confidence, stop the recession, save the banking system from collapse and reflate the economy.

The issue is very, very serious. We cannot allow ... a loss of faith in the deposit insurance system ... Confidence is at the root of everything because if we lose the confidence of the people, no system will stand up to that.

Congressman Henry Gonzalez, Chair of the House Committee on Banking, warning FBI director William Sessions of the urgency of dealing with the thrift crime[3]

Perhaps the most significant financial crisis in this nation's history.

GAO director Harold Valentine, describing the bank and thrift fraud to a Senate Committee on Banking, Finance and Urban Affairs, Sub-committee on Consumer and Regulatory Affairs[4]

'This industry is very close to the heart of the American economy. We teetered on the edge of a major, major problem here ... we teetered on the edge of a major collapse ... You know, all these [financial] industries could bring down the whole economy!'

Senior staff member of the Senate Banking Committee, personal interview[5]

PLUS ÇA CHANGE, plus c'est la même chose. Another boom, another real-estate-led bust 18 years after the last one. As the newly elected President, George Herbert Walker Bush, took office in 1989, his most pressing first problem is the thrift industry, or rather its impending implosion. Some $100-$150bn worth of assets is threatening the entire US economy – all because land prices are now deflating. The thrift industry will not be unfamiliar to the President; one of his first tasks as Vice-President in the Reagan Administration's first term was to chair the Task Force on Regulation of Financial Services.

The changed economic conditions of the late 1980s exposed and then deepened the thrift crisis. First, in Texas, the fall of previously high energy prices – reflected soon thereafter in real estate values – revealed for all to see the poor loans the S&Ls had been making in oil and real estate. Fewer loan repayments and rising defaults compounded the problem. Real estate prices nation-wide began falling after that, made worse by the 1986 Tax Act that took away some of the favourable treatment previously offered for real estate investment. Thrifts (and banks) were left with more non-performing loans since the loans were secured by the real estate now worth significantly less than the loan balance.

In June of 1989, Integrated Resources, a real estate syndication company with a large load of debt, failed. The company had suddenly found

3 *Effectiveness of Law Enforcement against Financial Crime*, Pt 2, p.15, House Committee on Banking, Finance and Urban Affairs. 101st Congress, 2d session, April 1990.
4 *Effort to Combat Criminal Financial Institution Fraud*, p.19. 102nd Congress, 2d session, February 1992.
5 Quoted K. Calavita *et al*, *Big Money Crime: Fraud and Politics in the Savings and Loan Crisis*, 1997, p.135.

itself unable to renew its commercial-paper borrowings. In October of 1989 the junk bond market collapsed (the proposed buyout of United Airlines had hit a snag and did not proceed, the market reacting badly with the Dow falling 6 per cent) rendering the junk bond portfolios of many a thrift practically worthless overnight. Again, a problem compounded when all the thrifts tried to offload all the bonds all at once. Shortly thereafter, several previous junk-bond-financed leveraged buyouts failed, with the companies seeking bankruptcy protection. On February 13, 1990, Drexel Burnham itself, the firm that had started it all, joined fellow clients in bankruptcy. Thomas Spiegel's Columbia Savings and Loan failed shortly after that, leaving depositors short billions of dollars. The thrift industry was in a fine mess.

So too were the banks. The FDIC reported that its fund for guaranteeing bank deposits was under 'very substantial stress' because of the rising number of bank failures. FDIC chairman, L. William Siedman, noted that the thrift crisis had clearly had an effect on real estate markets, 'by lowering property values and making mortgage loans harder to get'. Siedman added further that: 'Real estate markets have an effect on bank results. So there is a relationship between the two. And the effect has not been good.'[6]

On April 18, 1990 the government put the Seamen's Bank for Savings into receivership: the continued rise in short-term interest rates was putting heavy pressure on the market value of the bank's securities.[7] This bank's failure was going to cost the FDIC $400 m. Even Citicorp seemed to be in difficulty. Indeed, as shown by James Grant[8] the state of the top New York banks, including Citicorp, was actually worse in 1990 than it had been at the bottom of the Great Depression in 1932. 'If a panic had actually occurred, no journalist or historian would have been at a loss to explain why,' Grant explained.

> The existence of government guarantees inspired the bankers to take greater risks than their unsocialized forebears could have afforded to take. When some of those risks turned out badly, the depositors were calmed by the knowledge that the government and the biggest banks were partners in all but name.

Swiftly, Congress sought a bailout of the bankrupt institutions with the help of Joe the Taxpayer, raising $50 bn over three years through the sale of government bonds to be paid back over the next forty. After the Columbia failure, it looked like the cost of the bailout might approach half a trillion dollars if interest was added to the bill. (A subsequent July 1996 General Accounting Office calculation confirmed this figure to be about right.) To put that figure into some sort of perspective, it was noted by various authors that at the average house price then of about $85,000 the

6 *Time*, August 13, 1990.
7 James Grant, *The Trouble with Prosperity*, p.106.
8 p.64.

government could, with the same amount of funds, have built a new house for every family living in the nine largest cities in the US. Instead, \$12.5 bn will be repaid to banks every year for the next forty years. The fact that part of the funds for the bailout were going to come from borrowings and the issue of government bonds – keeping the monies off budget – helped maintain a Bush campaign pledge: 'Read my lips, no new taxes.'

Under the 1989 Financial Institutions Reform, Recovery and Enforcement Act (FIRREA), signed by the President into law in August 1990, the FSLIC was dissolved and the FDIC made the insurer for both the thrifts and all other bank deposits. The FHLBB was also dissolved, with its authority transferred to the newly created Office of Thrift Supervision (OTS), to be run by the secretary of the treasury. Bank holding companies would now be permitted to buy S&Ls, requiring a change to the earlier Bank Holding Company Act of 1956. Thrift operating rules were strengthened, accounting rules amended and new lending standards imposed. Ironically, these actions probably for a short time worsened the crisis since the stricter lending standards caused a brief credit crunch in early 1990.[9] The primary objective of the bill was of course to restore confidence to the thrift industry and its depositors, some of whom were now actively withdrawing their savings from the system in fear of its insolvency. Indeed, *Time* magazine[10] reported that such was the fear in the new administration of the possibility that its plan to bail out the thrifts might start a run on deposits, that senior administration officials met with the Fed Chairman, Alan Greenspan, in the Roosevelt Room of the White House the night before the plan was made public, with Greenspan assuring officials that the Fed stood ready to pump whatever cash was needed into the thrifts, if required, to make sure a panic didn't happen.

Anyone following the yield curve will have noted that the curve inverted in late 1988, warning of potential trouble ahead, especially for any banks heavily dependent on short-term borrowings to finance longer-term lending (as the Seamen's Bank was), and especially since the inversion was happening at the tail-end of what has proved a remarkably consistent 18-year land price cycle.

In order to facilitate the smooth selling of all the assets of the failed (and yet to fail) thrifts, the Resolution Trust Corporation (RTC) was created as a further provision of the 1989 bill. The RTC discovered it was now the proud owner of billions of dollars worth of all kinds of real estate and other assets, including *objects d'art*, yachts, planes, windmill farms, mushroom farms, golf courses, shopping malls, junk bonds and even a sperm bank. The RTC became the nation's largest employer of property managers, appraisers, accountants, lawyers and real estate agents as it engaged people to sell off what it had recently acquired. 'The biggest liquidation in the history of the world,' noted the FDIC chief.

9 *Time*, August 13, 1990.
10 February 20, 1989.

By 1995, the RTC has collected some $350bn as proceeds from the property sales, effectively reducing the ultimate net cost to the taxpayer and the administration of the bailout. Though this is in dollar terms, of course, and ignores the social costs of job losses and the wasted capital allocated to massively over-building real estate that could have gone into other more socially beneficial projects or new businesses. Not to mention the fact that a good many of the criminals are never chased and get away with their loan proceeds. In 1996 the RTC itself is dissolved, having completed its task of selling off all the real estate. The administration also recovers various sums from accounting and law firms caught up in the scandal. Ernst and Young, for example, admits that it, as auditor of some of the nation's largest thrift failures, including Lincoln, Silverado and Vernon, failed in its duty as auditor. The accounting firm settles for $400m, with $300m coming from insurance syndicates associated with Lloyd's of London, and $100m from partners spread through the company's operations over the next four years. 'This would not have a significant impact on the yearly earnings of the company's partners,' said one partner.[11] No wonder the firm settled.

The orderly sell-off of the troubled real estate, and the recapitalising of the banks (effectively nationalising the failed institutions and 'socializing the losses'), helps ameliorate the nasty side-effects of the property collapse. Land values do not collapse as previously, though some areas fare far worse than others. Pyhrr (1999) reports for Texas that office properties selling for $100 to $120 per square foot in 1985 sold for $25 to $35 per square foot in 1992; apartment buildings that sold for $25,000 to $30,000 per unit in 1985 were selling for $7,000 to $10,000 per unit in 1991, and zoned office land that sold in 1985 for $25 to $30 per building square foot (with approved site development permits) sold for only $4 to $5 per square foot in 1992/3. The city of Boston suffered its 'worst commercial real estate crash' in that city's entire history.[12]

More important, however, no depositor lost his or her savings, since the other responsibility taken over by the RTC was to mail out the reimbursement (bailout) cheques to depositors. In this, the federal bankers have learnt from history: in a stock-market-led downturn, lowering interest rates as low and as fast as possible will protect asset values (lower interest rates must ultimately lift capital values, or at least mitigate the fall). In a real-estate-led downturn, back-stop the banks, bail out the ones worth saving, or, if 'too big to fail', collect all the real estate collateral and keep as much as possible off the market until it can be re-sold when things improve. *And make sure depositors don't lose their money.*

Bankers have realised the government will bail them out if the system is threatened, so who cares where the credit creation ends up? The

11 *LA Times*, November 24, 1992.

12 Richard Herring and Susan Wachter, *Real Estate Booms and Banking Busts: An International Perspective*, University of Pennsylvania Working Paper No. 99-27, July 1999.

situation is made worse with government insuring deposits, resulting in a situation of 'moral hazard', as it has come to be called. It guarantees us another banking crisis at some point in the future. Government cannot ultimately substitute for market behaviour in controlling the risk in lending. The government did though, in 1991, move to pass the Federal Deposit Insurance Corporation Improvement Act (FDICIA), requiring the FDIC to close any future failing bank promptly, by the least costly method.

In an ironic twist to the orderly real estate sell-off, some former owners of once high-flying but now defunct thrifts were keen bidders for the very properties their thrifts had once owned or loaned money on. Amongst private investor groups trying to buy what the RTC was selling was Charles Knapp, of Financial Corporation fame (he cost the taxpayer \$4 bn), and Joe Russo from Ameriway Savings in Houston (who cost the taxpayer \$170 m). Russo was bidding on a \$3.8 m four-acre tract next door to the Houstonian hotel complex (which Russo owned), the hotel of choice of President Bush when not at home or in the White House – 'his home away from home'.[13] One wag quickly labelled the private investor groups scooping up the sometimes heavily discounted real estate offerings 'PIGS'.

The public attention to (and anger at) such matters did not last long, however. In what became, with hindsight, quite a prophetic comment, as the clean-up bill for the S&L scandal mounted, Paul Horvitz, a finance professor at the University of Houston, declared, 'the government needs a sideshow to shift focus from the cost of dealing with the problem.'[14] The government got one in August of that year when Saddam Hussein invaded Kuwait, the US response in January of 1991 proving rather bullish for markets.

So where did all the money go? In testimony before the Senate Banking Committee in February 1989, Attorney General Richard Thornburgh said most of the money was long gone.

> 'In many cases, the assets have been dissipated through laundering schemes or taken out of the country, and are beyond the reach of federal authorities. We'd be fooling ourselves to think that any substantial portion of these assets is going to be recovered. Besides the money that was simply stolen, billions of dollars were lost on high-risk investments and frittered away by paying excessively high interest rates to attract depositors.'
>
> Quoted in *Time*, February 20, 1989

In some respects, though, this may have been a cover; government was far more interested in making sure the system did not break down than in pursuing justice by prosecuting all the fraud. Government, after all, depends more for its existence upon the relatively smooth functioning of its government-granted licences and privileges (monopoly capitalism) and future tax receipts than it does on satisfying citizens' demands that crooks

13 *The Nation*, July 30, 1990.
14 *Time*, June 25, 1990.

be put in jail. Especially if one or two of those crooks are in government. Not even 15 per cent of suspected criminals in Texas are ever likely to face prosecution. On average, less than 3 per cent of borrowers in any state who receive loans fraudulently are likely to face indictment.[15] For those unfortunate enough to be caught, the jail time is far less than had they attempted to do the same thing – rob the bank – with a balaclava and a gun.

Fortune magazine[16] also tried to find out where all the money went. In a graph it listed a $25 bn cost due to the original mismatch of the government's mandated borrowing short and lending long during the inflation of the 1970s; $28 bn on real estate losses made possible by the 1982 deregulation; $14 bn in excessive operating costs fuelled by brokered deposits and protected by insurance (read lavish living); $14 bn paid by thrifts in excessive interest to get the brokered deposits in the first place; $5 bn in crime and the cost of crooks; a further $6 bn on other real estate investments, junk bonds and insider lending; $12 bn in government inefficiency (though this hides the fact that, in closing down a thrift, regulators had rules to follow, 'careful, measured' rules, says Stephen Pizzo,[17] so that it could be done 'calmly, quietly and secretly … so the public wouldn't *panic*'); and $43 bn in government delay in shutting down the industry. Shutting it down in 1982, when it should have been done, would have reduced all other costs. But of course back then the real estate market was in full swing. In the state of Texas, of more than 400 thrifts in 1982, all but 16 failed.

Whilst the whole S&L episode does not immediately look as if it involved the creation of credit (it seemed to be merely thrifts grabbing deposits from other institutions so that they could lend them out as they saw fit), it was ultimately a very effective credit-creation process since in the end the government borrowed (from banks) what had to be paid back to insured depositors, by issuing bonds. Plus interest. The thrifts' owners just spent it before the government had paid for it.

Rough final calculations were eventually made of the final bailout bill, which the FDIC Banking Review in December 2000 put at $153 bn, of which the US taxpayer will pay $124 bn. The most costly banking crisis the world has ever seen, though, as we have noted already, in every cyclical land-price-led downturn the collapse has been the same, just the numbers grow larger.

One further banking cost that *Fortune* magazine could have added to the bill, had it known about it, is the alleged $5 bn in loans supplied, some suggest, by the Bush and Reagan administrations, and perhaps other Western powers, to Iraq between 1985 and 1989, through the Atlanta branch of the Banco Nationale Lavoro (BNL), allowing Saddam to secretly re-arm. It is not known what happened to all the money.

15 Calavita *et al*, pp.147, 154.
16 September 10, 1990.
17 *Inside Job*, p.71.

The turn

FOLLOWING A SET economic and political routine, in 1990, with the recession really beginning to bite, real estate industry trade associations united to try to recover the federal income tax subsidies that were lost in the 1986 Tax Act.[18] Real estate needs a stimulus, they argue, to get the economy moving again and out of recession.

The real stimulus comes, however, from an unanticipated source – the stock market – though it is still ultimately a repeat of past behaviour. Whilst the boys are away at Desert Storm, the market quietly begins its absorption of the collateralised real estate, with the banks beginning the arduous task of rebuilding their balance sheets, ably assisted by the banking authorities.

Engineered by the Fed, short-term interest rates fall from 8 per cent in 1990 (actually 10 per cent in late 1989) to 3 per cent in 1992 (then do not move for the whole of 1993) – it's the lowest rates have been since 1960 or so. In January 1991, as the US goes into Iraq to push Saddam out of Kuwait, it becomes likely the market low has been seen. The January low for the Dow is higher than the October low, and war is mostly bullish for markets. More important, markets tip to the bullish side as it becomes clear the government and the Fed will not permit a system-wide bank run (Citicorp had a severe credit scare on October 24, 1990), the non-performing real estate loans at the banks are stabilising and, besides, not all can be lost since the real estate involved is most likely worth something in a market that has now readjusted its values. If the banks can lift their earnings from here, then their shares are in fact cheap.

We have seen it before.

> In the late 1980s, speculative-grade debtors had promised to pay very high interest rates, but the collateral values and the income streams on which the promises depended sometimes fell short. The result in those cases was a period of adjustment that took the form of bankruptcies …
>
> James Grant, *The Trouble with Prosperity*, p.184

The fall in short-term interest rates puts the yield curve back into its usual territory, short rates below the long bond. Borrowing short to lend long puts the US banks back into profit.

> Borrowing at a low rate, an investor was able to earn a slightly higher rate … For $10 million down, a well-to-do speculator was able to purchase $500 million of two year Treasury notes. His or her bank would lend the $490 million difference. The cost of the loan was 5.125 percent. The yield on the notes was 5.89 percent. The difference between the yield and the cost worked out to approximately $4 million per annum. Thus, the rate of return on the speculator's down payment amounted to approximately 40 percent.
>
> Grant, p.189

18 Marc A. Weiss, 'The Politics of Real Estate Cycles', *Business and Economic History*, Second Series, Vol. 20, 1991.

All built on the yield curve. The exact process that killed off the S&Ls in the late 1970s. It is indeed all in the timing.

The true money-making schemes are never marketed to the public.

This time around, though, the numbers for the players get even better as the bond market goes into 1992 and '93. The buying of government securities by the banks in these years, borrowing short to lend long, breaks all records, until the party stops on February 4, 1994. Twenty-four times in succession the Fed eases short-term rates, keeping the yield curve in positive territory and sometimes even widening the gap (steepening the curve). The profits rebuild the bankers' balance sheets. But on February 4 the Fed lifts rates – albeit by a mere quarter of one percentage point, but it causes the speculators to reverse positions and sell, which causes more selling, which eventually unmasks those late to the party – Orange County, California being one. The county had continued to bet, using derivatives, that interest rates would go lower – or at least not go higher.[19]

Gradually, the financial improvement spills over into other economic activity, finally moving the prices of commercial real estate upwards once again. 'The stock market assisted recapitalisation of the banking system', as the Fed Chairman puts it, is in full swing. Naturally the banks only pass on the lower rates to customers slowly. Profits are boosted because the rates banks charge for loans fall less quickly than the rates paid for deposits.

Along the way, the Fed has instigated one additional move as regards credit. In December 1990 it reduced or eliminated reserve requirements on certain bank liabilities. Fed watchers knew what this meant: an accommodating stance in monetary policy. The Dow, staying above the October 1989 lows, was reflecting the buying support of professional investors prepared to back their view with their capital.

The stock market move out of its October 1990 and January 1991 lows is not without a few jitters – but higher lows nevertheless. Midlantic Bank in Edison, New Jersey warned on January 24, 1991 that, without an improvement in general operating conditions, the bank (a 'real estate-bedecked bank'),[20] might shortly have losses approaching $4bn. 'There is a nervousness out there that I haven't seen in my 25 years in the organization', said Nicholas J. Ketcha, Director of Supervision for the New York region of the FDIC, in March. 'We are running our businesses on the assumption that next year will be difficult,' the Chairman of Citicorp stated to the market in April.[21] In June the Chairman of the FDIC chipped in with a very downbeat forecast on the future of the banking system. In July the firm of Keefe, Bruyette & Woods declared that, 'This year could shape up as the grimmest for dividend cuts since the Great Depression by major banks'. The Dow however, hardly moved, remaining in a tight range just

19 Frank Partnoy, *F.I.A.S.C.O. Guns, Booze and Blood-lust: The Truth about High Finance*, Chapter 8.
20 James Grant, *The Trouble with Prosperity*, p.205.
21 Grant, p.205.

under past all-time highs. W.D. Gann would have approved. It was happening just as he says it does: the passing of dividends marks the passing of the lows.

In October Donald Trump warned of a 'deep recession – slash – depression' if real estate moguls like him were refused tax breaks.[22] Of course he would say that. Each time an impending warning came out, however, it seemed as if the Fed was there to lower rates yet again. In 1993 the Fed lifts its portfolio of government securities by 11.7 per cent.[23] The Fed buying Treasuries is credit-creation plain and simple. The nation was being reflated.

Wall Street is able to help with the reflation one final time, through the vehicle of the REITs – the real estate investment trusts, those same structures that sent the markets over the top in the early 1970s. This time around, with markets improving and credit expanding, Wall Street and the REITs allow the banks to reprice, refinance or indeed offload their non-performing collateral.

> Banks and insurance companies could sell the properties they had acquired in bankruptcy proceedings. Developers could sell their buildings before they lost them in bankruptcy proceedings. Fully half of the public money raised for REITs in 1993 was equity capital, and this $9 billion represented no less than 22 percent of all the initial public offerings floated in the United States in that year ... In need of funds, leveraged corporations and real estate-clogged banks successfully turned to investors. Grant, p.241

With that, the 1991 land-price-induced recession passed into history and investors found new things to worry about.

The acceleration

1994 SEES a reversal in Fed policy somewhat, as interest rates are put back up. Stock markets go sideways or retrace the 1993 gains. The Fed policy shift lifts short-term rates by 2½ per cent over the year; 30-year bond yields rise also. Mexico defaults on its bonds, only to have the new US President, William Jefferson Clinton, argue – successfully – that the US ought to bail them out. Some ripple effects spill over into 1995 when Chemical Bank discloses a thumping pre-tax loss on what it calls 'unauthorised Peso trading'. Nick Leeson sends Baring's Bank to the wall with $1.4bn in derivatives losses. Baring's blames its rogue trader; the Bank of England concludes a serious failure of controls. The directors still get their bonuses.[24]

22 Grant, p.206.
23 Grant, p.239.
24 For an inside account of all the derivatives manufacturing going on at this time, *F.I.A.S.C.O.* by Frank Partnoy is an entertaining and lively read. About the Mexican bailout, Partnoy says (p.214): 'The US had agreed to lend $20 billion to Mexico to help it support the Peso and repay other debts. By doing so, the Clinton administration saved Wall Street a fortune and secured many of [Morgan Stanley's] risky positions.'

The S&L scandal comes up again in 1994 with the $73m bailout of Madison Guaranty Savings and Loan, owned by President Clinton's close associates Jim and Susan McDougal, and the bank's alleged questionable land deals and/or diversion of funds to help with the then Governor Clinton's campaign expenses – the Whitewater deals. All up though, any alleged wrongdoings are chicken-feed compared to the 1980s deals and bailouts – but ultimately an effective political football for Republicans, who use this material far better than the wealth of evidence available to the Democrats in 1988. The material available at that time went begging – the Democrat presidential candidate's running mate, Lloyd Bentson, was himself an S&L owner.[25] Whitewater cleverly diverts attention and media resources away from the earlier looting.

Midway through 1995 the Fed yet again reverses interest rate policy, lowering rates and easing monetary conditions. As it happens, 1995 proves, according to Martin Fridson,[26] yet another 'very good year' for stocks, with the S&P ending the year up 37 per cent. The markets tenth best year since 1900 in fact. A sharp reversal of Fed policy has again provided the initial impetus, reports Fridson.[27] Liquidity to the banking system is being quietly provided in response to the Orange County and Mexican debt debacles. Business and the public in general seem unperturbed by the news, however, and celebrate the loose monetary policy: mergers and acquisitions set a new record in 1995; so too the inflows into Mutual Funds. A bull market is in full swing, just a couple of years into the new land price cycle.

The Fed had been busy last cycle; after all, a lot of bad loans had to be shifted to the public. Between 1982 and 1986 the Fed backed up the US government in bailing out Mexico, Argentina and Brazil when each country defaulted on its bonds. The Fed bailed out the Continental Bank in 1984, after it was deemed too big to fail. (Similar problems to the thrifts.) The Fed supported panicking stock market investors after the 1987 crash with liquidity and lower rates, then contrived supportive conditions again for the Savings and Loan institutions that could be brought back to life, quietly killing off the others, between 1989 and 1992. The Fed also found time to rescue the Bank of New England, then Citibank, after the tanking of the real estate market. This new cycle is not proving much different as far as bailouts are concerned, the Fed helping to prop up the Mexican peso in 1994/5 in its need to help all the US banks and pension funds that have bet the other way.

Despite it all, however, US markets just keep going up, defying all the odds except one – easy money.

In March 1997 the Fed Chairman mentions to Congress, in one of his bi-annual addresses: 'We are now in a position where we have to move

25 *The Nation*, January 25, 1993.
26 *It Was a Very Good Year*, p.215.
27 p.196.

ahead of the curve.' Markets take this as a sign the Fed might start a round of tightening. Several events intervene to prevent it, however: the Asian economic flu, a Russian bond default, the Long Term Capital Management hedge fund collapse, and Y2K. All in a day's work for the Fed, but it keeps interest rates low and liquidity high, and fuels a NASDAQ stock market bubble.

It is worth a brief digression to study a little of the 1997 Asian economic downturn and the 1998 Russian bond default. Both are instructive of what will continue to occur around the globe in the future as the world progresses into the 21st century with the system of fractional reserve banking used to finance the purchase of locational value underpinning world economic activity.

The Asian economic flu

AT THE G7 Naples summit in 1994, leading nations resolved to have a look at and update, if necessary, the post-World War II international financial institutions (IMF and World Bank) to enable them to better address the present huge – and growing – private capital flows. The Mexican peso crisis brought the resolve into focus at the next year's G7 meeting in June 1995 in Halifax, Nova Scotia. Here, leaders decided that prevention of a future crisis would be helped by increasing the IMF's surveillance of countries' policies and at the same time demanding better and more timely numbers from their central banks and respective governments.[28] An effort was also started to ensure the IMF and other relevant international institutions had enough capital on hand to provide liquidity to member nations should it be required.

The Asian crisis of July 1997 caught both plans by surprise. Did the global community of economists see the crisis coming? Nope, not a single one. Just prior to the Thai economic collapse, both the World Bank and IMF had issued glowing economic reports for its 'Asian Tiger' economies, including that of Thailand. Thailand's savings rate was high, the government budget in surplus, the foreign debt low, its growth rate between 7 and 8 per cent. Notably, Thailand had achieved everything asked of it by the IMF: acceptable inflation policies, improved growth policies and better reporting of its numbers. As for Korea, in a report released that summer the IMF 'welcomed Korea's continued impressive macroeconomic performance and praised the authorities for their enviable fiscal record.' Only months later that same IMF was putting together a $56bn relief package to bail out South Korean banks from their disastrous property loans and poor business lending.

At a meeting several months before the Thai crisis hit the headlines, the Pacific Economic Co-operation Council (PECC) had taken the opportunity to congratulate themselves on their forecasting accuracy, and current

28 *Australian Financial Review*, June 19, 1995.

forecast of 'slightly better growth and stability' for Thailand.[29] 'Nor were there grounds,' continued the PECC at the meeting, 'for expecting immediate financial collapse.'

Alas, the IMF and others do not measure land price. Both residential and commercial South East Asian real estate prices had escalated sharply in the several years just prior to the 1997 economic downturn.[30]

The countdown and events leading up to the crisis went something like this:

March 1997. The Thai central bank reports that 10 lending institutions are 'cash strapped'.

Mid-May, 1997. The Thai Baht remains fixed to currencies led by the US dollar. The Thai economy has been slowing for twelve months, as measured by its GDP. The banks, it has been noticed, are suffering from an excess of property loans and the current account deficit is rising. Currency speculators take an interest in events as they begin to see the Baht might be ripe for devaluation. Hedge funds see the opening and also take positions. They borrow massive quantities of Baht, with the intention of buying it back later at the cheaper – devalued – price. (Hedge funds have the ability to borrow many times their capital base.)

End of May. Central Banks unite to bail out Thailand and defend the Baht's fixed rate to the US dollar. They respond to the currency speculators by imposing currency controls, to prevent the free flow of Baht overseas, and by lifting interest rates, to make the borrowing of Baht prohibitively expensive.

Early June. The Thai property slump worsens. The raising of interest rates does further damage. Even more empty buildings are now visible on the streets of Bangkok. The Thai government bans all media from printing negative reports about the economy.

June 11. The Central Bank defence of the Baht backfires. Selling on the Thai Stock Exchange begins in earnest as foreign controlled funds take advantage of the government-defended currency value to sell out of local stocks and redeem their Baht for dollars (taking advantage of the artificially high currency rate).

June 25. It is reported that Thailand's current account deficit has worsened. The high interest rates needed to attract overseas investment have slowed the economy even further. Thai officials continue to oppose any devaluation, suggesting this would push up inflation and hurt companies

29 *Australian Financial Review*, September 21, 1997.

30 A chart of these land prices was highlighted by Fred Harrison in his 1997 introductory chapter to Frederic J. Jones's *The Chaos Makers* (Tables 4 and 5, pp.31, 32, viewable also on the EIS website at www.businesscycles.biz/docs/asian.htm).

with US$ denominated debts, many of which are well connected to, or owned by, Thai politicians.

June 30. The Bank of Thailand intervenes in the economy to protect the integrity of the Thai financial system by forcing sixteen of the worst affected banks to close or merge. The six finance companies and ten security firms, with combined assets of US $18bn, 'have for some time been struggling under bad loans to the chronically over-supplied property sector', says the Bank.

July 1. Thailand's Prime Minister states firmly: 'The Baht will never be devalued' as 'we would then all become poor'. He blames over-consumption for the crisis. 'This can be seen from the fact that each family has many cars. This has led to a trade deficit and to speculative attacks on the currency.'

July 3. Two days later, the Baht is floated – effectively a devaluation. The Central Bank abandons its previous defence of the currency through high interest rates (which were crippling local companies) and the use of its own reserves (which was proving expensive). The currency float is intended to breathe life back into the economy by reducing interest rates and boosting exports. The risk is inflation and hurting companies with US dollar denominated debts.

Mid-July. It is realised that international aid may be required to help Thailand stabilise its economy, as per the Mexican crisis. The difference here is that most of the debt in Thailand is held by private companies, not the Government, as was the case in Mexico. The international aid will be required to avert a liquidity crisis, as banks stop lending, hurt by the bad property loans, and as the cost of financing previously incurred debt soars for all borrowing in non-Thai currency. These borrowings would have been undertaken because, at the time, overseas interest rates were much lower than Thai rates, especially in the preceding twelve months and since the currency was pegged – effectively government guaranteed. Why hedge the risk? Welcome to monopoly capitalism.

Into 1997, the heightened speculation is fed even further by European, American and Japanese banks aggressively seeking to expand their balance sheets. As the process reverses, these same banks begin pulling out, worsening the credit contraction. Thailand's troubles cascade to other South East Asian nations in late 1997, including Malaysia, Indonesia, the Philippines, Hong Kong and South Korea.

By early 1998 both the Fed Chairman and Treasury Secretary Robert Rubin are telling Congress that the US is yet to feel the worst flow-on effects of the Asian downturn, and asking Congress to increase the borrowing authority of the IMF so it has the resources to stem the collapse. If not, a global panic is possible, they reason.[31]

What these two gentlemen were pointing out, but did not say, is related to what is called a bank's 'credit risk' – a bank's exposure to a counter-party's inability or unwillingness to repay its debt. And plenty of US banks had quite a bit of credit risk exposure to these Asian countries now in economic meltdown. Frank Partnoy puts it this way:

> Asian banks had been feasting, like the fat Mexican banks of the early 1990s, making leveraged bets on their own markets and currencies using equity swaps, total return swaps, options, futures, forwards and more complex derivatives. Now, they faced annihilation. Within months, the foreign currency value of investments in East Asia dropped by 50 percent or more … Most of the derivatives causing the pain were 'over-the-counter' rather than traded on any exchange. That means, for example, that Asian banks engaging in swaps had a counter-party, typically a US or European bank, who expected repayment in this swap … In other words, the Asian banks and companies hadn't lost money to any centralized exchange; they had lost money to other companies, primarily western banks. *F.I.A.S.C.O.*, p.276

Therefore, if the Asian banks defaulted, the counter-parties stood to lose what they were owed. (An exposure of more than $20bn to South Korea alone, said banking regulators.) So the IMF bailed out the Asian economies so that western banks and Wall Street could be repaid.

The US could now expect slower growth as exports to the region slowed (16 per cent of all US farm products go to Asia, reported the secretary). 'A likely slower economy, no need to lift interest rates,' admitted the Fed chairman, suggesting further that 'economic policymakers still did not fully understand today's global financial system'.

The authors of an enlightening review of the area published by the Queensland University of Technology documented over 300 pages of commentary from various market players, bank directors and heads of legal and accounting firms in the region. They were staggered by the admissions of interviewees:

> We had very senior bankers – I mean heads of banks, local and foreign – saying to us unhesitatingly that more than half the banks in Indonesia were technically insolvent, but that the then President Suharto wouldn't let them go down. The banks had finished non-viable projects and were not calling up loans from borrowers connected to the right families.

Notably, the world's tallest building, the Petronas Towers, was completed in Malaysia just prior to the crisis, overshadowing Thailand's attempt at seizing the world height record with the Baiyoke Sky Tower, then still under construction. (The tower eventually opened in early 1998,

31 *Australian Financial Review*, May 23, 1998.

much of it still an incomplete shell.) In August of 1997, just prior to the unfolding of the crisis in Indonesia, its government announced plans to build the world's longest bridge, linking itself to Malaysia across the Malacca Straits – a 42 kilometre bridge to be built by a construction consortium headed by President Suharto's second daughter. Also, plans were announced by a private group to build a 558 metre tower, the Jakarta Tower, the world's tallest, on the site of the old airport near the centre of the capital – this time by the President's brother-in-law.

In Hong Kong the property investor Wong Kwan paid US $70 m in March 1997 for the Hong Kong mansion 'Genesis', overlooking the city, the most money ever paid anywhere for a house. By 2001 Kwan was having trouble paying the household bills.[32]

Eventually, once the Thai government stopped fudging the figures, it was revealed by the Bank of Thailand that its country's non-performing real estate loans for 1998 stood at almost half of the total lending by the financial sector for that year. Nearly US $30 bn will be required for the banks to recapitalise.[33] It was later discovered that the Bank of Thailand had squandered hundreds of millions of dollars from its Financial Institution Development Fund, using it like an ATM to take out cash in an effort to support ailing property development companies throughout 1996 and 1997. Some 430 bn Baht (US $10 bn) was lent (unauthorised) to 56 now failed finance companies. In what soon became a national scandal, dozens of politicians and senior bank staff were implicated. Taxpayers eventually bore the cost of the gigantic losses.

In Singapore Lee Kwan Yew is quoted as saying his nation was now facing its worst crisis since the withdrawal of British Armed Forces in 1968, thirty year before.

In Indonesia the severity of the downturn brought a leadership change to the nation on May 19, 1998 when, under substantial pressure from the crisis, the corrupt regime of Suharto collapsed. This was the same day prices for bread, oil and other essentials peaked, from policies widely viewed as deliberately instigated by the regime in response to the tough economic times. (Petrol prices were lifted 71 per cent, for example; electricity price rises of 60 per cent were foreshadowed, amidst growing fears of an impending rice shortage and rumours that International Monetary Fund relief packages were helping bail out the president's family connections first, before anyone else.) Exactly 180 days later the new regime brought out the troops to quell rioting and looting in the capital, Jakarta. The recapitalisation of Indonesian banks will eventually top US $35 bn.

The previous South East Asian downturn had occurred in 1985/6, ten years prior to this latest one – about the upper limit for a decade business cycle. The value of the respective currencies fell then as well, but

32 *Australian Financial Review*, June 26, 2001.
33 *Australian Financial Review*, March 5, 1999.

devaluations soon improved the region's export competitiveness, allowing eventual re-growth within the group of nations affected.

What happened in South East Asia is worth studying because something similar could replay in the United States towards the end of this decade. But note the order of events. Declining real estate prices came first, placing increased pressure on banks over-exposed to this area of lending. Only after that was there a crisis of the currency.

Russia's bond default

ANOTHER FINANCIAL crisis spread through the use of derivatives. After the fall of the Berlin Wall, Moscow began, slowly, its move towards what some might call a free market, though it more aptly represents monopoly capitalism. Yeltsin, amidst furious opposition, moved to start the privatisation process in the land market in the early 1990s, backed finally by the Duma in 2001, ably supported by the World Bank. Mikhail Gorbechev had already pronounced commercial banks legal way back in 1988, but banks cannot create their credit effectively without a government-granted licence in land.

New Russian power centres formed quickly, built on the two newly created government-granted privileges, banking and natural resource (land) companies, the rent of which the government gave away at fire-sale prices. This is where Russia's newly created oligarchs come from, as does their wealth – from the economic rent of land.

Unexpectedly, Russia defaulted on its bond payments in late August 1998. The collapse of the market exposed the strategies of the highly leveraged Long Term Capital Management (LTCM) hedge fund, which had been attempting to exploit such bond markets for profit. For every $5 of their own capital, the fund had borrowed $50 from banks and was now exposed to derivative positions of nearly $2 trillion. The Basle Committee of Banking Supervisors reported a couple of months later that 'banks and securities houses had compromised credit standards in their eagerness to do business with the fund'. The Fed bailed them out anyway, restraining interest rates from going any higher in the US to help with the process. Coming right after the Asian economic flu, interest rates in the US stayed lower than they otherwise might have, leaving it that much easier for a bubble to form in the NASDAQ, as the Fed fought the economic fires elsewhere.

As a result of all the chaos in currency markets in late 1998 from the Russian bond default and LTCM farce, the Group of Seven (G7) leading economic nations set up a new body, the Financial Stability Forum, in an effort to anticipate future financial market crises. But again, since the forum is not likely to measure land price, it is unlikely to be successful in its goal.

Pssst ... wanna buy some air?

AMIDST ALL the Asian flu and Russian bond defaults, US corporations start buying air – as much of it as they can fund. In 1993 the Federal Communications Commission starts auctioning off in earnest more wireless communications rights – another government-granted licence. Corporations (or others who can afford it) are asked to bid for these rights, and are then permitted to retain ownership. To access the licences, buyers usually borrow – the money raised either from stock market investors or from banks. These government-granted licences again capitalise into a tradable commodity, financed (if from a bank) by credit created for that purpose. Between 1994 and 1996 the federal government auction of the frequency allocation (air rights) for personal communication services nets $18bn. The NASDAQ rise is built in part on these communication rights as corporations roll out their networks (MCI, WorldCom, Vodafone, Global Crossing ...) or facilitate trading by creating their own (like Enron).

The 1996 Telecommunications Act goes even further, practically giving away the public wealth contained in the air waves. A new industry is founded virtually overnight. Things could have been done a little differently, and all the eventual wasted capital and bankruptcies avoided, had these frequency allocations been leased to buyers instead of sold. The wealth would then have been kept in the public coffers to facilitate, say, lower taxes in other areas. But that's another story.

BRW magazine[34] calls the whole process 'the beach-front property bonanza of the information age'. Inevitably, start-ups are formed amongst venture capitalists for the express purpose of acquiring what the government is selling. Alliances both old and new are formed to control the newly created space, or to ensure existing licences (e.g. TV broadcasting) do not come under threat. Government influence is, as ever, bought to protect the new licences. Repeating history, just applied to a new space.

Describing the government bonanza in Australia, the Australian Communication Authority's manager of spectrum marketing says, 'This is better than selling sand to the Arabs or ice to the Eskimos ... we are selling nothing here,' as he delivers $1.33bn from the sales into the pockets of the government.

Eventually it is realised that the telcos have overbid for the licences and may now be caught in a web (no pun intended) of debt and have trouble building their networks as a result. This realisation helps deflate the NASDAQ very early in 2000, just after the yield curve goes negative. Telcos go on to fail in record numbers in 2001, crippled by their debt load.[35]

34 August 12, 1996.
35 *Wall Street Journal*, May 11, 2001.

True to form, the actual real estate takes a good deal of the digital real estate gains. Online companies very quickly discover that a physical presence is just as important – if not more so – than an online presence. Rents go through the roof in select areas of the US, especially the warehouse districts of San Francisco and Chicago, and in Silicon Valley. Such realisations regarding the rent also hit home in late 1999.[36]

Thewave.com

THE SCIENTISTS who created the World Wide Web in 1991 did not provide click-on pictures, images or sounds for their new baby. It takes a 23-year-old programmer at the University of Illinois, Marc Andreesen to do that. His Mosaic program makes it easier to view documents on the web and click between them. The internet is away, and the battle for its control has begun. New businesses spawn everywhere as the space is put to all sorts of new uses.

Since readers more than likely have lived through the whole NASDAQ explosion, then implosion, we need not cover the whole story here – just give a few pointers.

As interest rates stay low and the Fed pursues an accommodative monetary policy, by early 1997, in the excitement of all the new business growth, pundits are claiming an end – yet again – to the business cycle as we know it. The venerable *Wall Street Journal* reports on November 15, 1996: 'From board rooms to living rooms and from government offices to trading floors, a new consensus is emerging: the big, bad business cycle has been tamed.' The *Washington Post* adds its voice several weeks later, exclaiming: 'The economy appears to have entered a new period of stability in which recessions no longer seem inevitable and both inflation and joblessness remain relatively low.' Opinions of the Fed and its handling of the economy lift with the stock market. Bankers move back en masse into real estate lending. The FDIC reports banks now have $316bn of real estate on their books at the end of 1996, up from $299bn one year ago.

The July 1997 edition of *Wired* magazine screams on its front cover: 'We're facing 25 years of prosperity ... You got a problem with that?' A mania develops in collectables, particularly in Beanies. The child's toy becomes eBay's hottest selling item. Wave Systems, a small technology outfit in Massachusetts, attracts a devoted following calling themselves 'Wavoids'. Each devotee puts all his money on the stock; the company touts a security chip that is soon expected to be in every computer in every part of the world. An absolute certainty to go to $500. The next Microsoft, say all the chat sites. The wave turns into a bubble, inflating on easy money.

In April of 1998, the Department of Commerce issues a report revealing a new internet law: internet traffic doubles every 100 days, a claim

36 See *Fortune* magazine, *The Age*, and *Australian Financial Review* articles amongst many others.

WorldCom takes to repeating every chance it gets.[37] The claim is later traced to UUNET, WorldCom's internet subsidiary. To carry the expected surge in traffic, telcos build even more furiously.

In 1999, as internet floats lift off into the stratosphere, two analysts, James Glassman and Kevin Hassett, scholars at the American Enterprise Institute, suggest that a Dow at 36,000 is entirely reasonable since the usual market valuation models are now out of date. Also in this year, to compensate for historically depressed prices, Congress passes a rescue package for farmers. The package capitalises straight into land price, of course. (All the available literature on this point agrees with the contention that support for agricultural production is readily capitalised, with the owners of land being the main beneficiaries. These owners may not necessarily be the actual farmers.)

In the backwaters of Melbourne, Australia, a little known company begins advertising land for sale on Mars for $45 per plot, including defined boundaries. The response is overwhelming. Back in the US, NetJ.com is currently trading at $4.68 a share, with turnover averaging just under 100,000 shares a week. NetJ's business model reads: 'The Company is not currently engaged in any substantial business activity and has no plans to engage in any such activity in the forecastable future.' A recent 5 for 1 stock split sees the shares surge from 32 cents a few months prior.[38] On November 16, 1999, the Fed lifts interest rates a quarter point for the third successive time. The yield curve is now negative, though few notice amidst the bubble fever.

History shows the stock market bubble deflated. Our usual mid land-price cycle slowdown was underway. Notably though, the US economy, after a stock market peak and collapse, has been far easier to reflate with the orthodox toolbox available to the Fed than has been the deflation of the real estate market, though it can also make a difference at what time in the real estate 18-year cycle the stock market crash occurs. The later in the real estate cycle, the longer it takes to recover. At least that is what history teaches us.

The usual scams and cons

WHEN THE stock market collapses mid land-price cycle (or any time really) the usual stock-market-related scams and cons come to light as it deflates. This one is no exception. It is revealed that executives at Qwest Communications International Inc. made almost $500 m selling stock from 1999 to 2001, during which time the company was reporting profits that it said later were 'exaggerated and based on improper accounting'.[39] Ken Lay at Enron grossed $247 m in pay and remuneration from 1999 to 2002, whilst leading the company into the largest bankruptcy ever seen – until the

37 *The Economist*, July 20, 2002.
38 *Australian Financial Review*, February 17, 2000.
39 *International Herald Tribune*, July 31, 2002.

WorldCom debt and accounting farce just a few months later. Global Crossing CEO Gary Winnick took home $512m in the couple of years prior to this company's collapse. Having incorporated in Bermuda, Global Crossing had made notable savings in its tax bill. In total, executives at the biggest bankruptcies (almost all of them telcos with ownership rights to that all-important public air space), made $3.3bn.[40]

The telcos themselves ran up debts of approximately $1 trillion,[41] much of it bank-created credit. As the debts increased, some companies began resorting to finance and accounting tricks to conceal the problems; WorldCom, for example, classifying $3.8bn of its network maintenance costs as capital rather than an expense, inflating profits and hence the stock price. One of the simplest accounting tricks available. (What *were* the auditors thinking?) Much of CEO Bernie Ebbers' wealth was of course tied up in WorldCom stock. By early June of 2002, WorldCom's stock value had deflated from a high of $120bn in June 1999 to just $300m, a value that was less than the quantum of personal loans ($408m) the company had kindly extended to Mr Ebbers. The more appropriate business name as things turned out might have been WorldCon. The company went under with more than $30bn of debt outstanding.[42] Fears of a credit crunch in the bond market surfaced.

At Enron, both its bankers, J.P. Morgan and Citigroup, facilitated the hiding of losses in dummy accounts.[43] In subsequent settlements, liability by the bankers was neither admitted nor denied. It was also later disclosed that Enron had given the White House and senior Bush officials early warning of its financial troubles,[44] confirming once again that key insiders practically always know these things well before the public does, which is why the market is so effective in its discounting of future news.

As the London *Financial Times* ably pointed out,[45] Kenneth Lay and Bernie Ebbers had now successfully done more damage to America's wealth than Osama bin Laden and Mohammed Atta. Bank-created credit financing government-granted licences permitted to trade as a commodity – a process built on sand, inherently unstable. Global Crossing discovered that laying fibre-optic cable from nowhere to nowhere still did not make a viable business model.

All remaining telco entrepreneurs came under 'duress' as their stock prices plummeted. Craig McCaw sold down his holdings in Lucent and Nextel, and then performed a bit of house cleaning with the sales of several island resorts, ranch and waterfront properties, a Gulfstream G-5,

40 *Financial Times Europe*, July 31, 2002, p.1.
41 *The Economist*, July 20, 2002.
42 *Financial Times*, June 27, 2002.
43 *CNN*, July 22, 2002, and *Wall Street Journal Europe*, June 25, 2002.
44 *International Herald Tribune*, January 11, 2002.
45 June 27, 2002, p.13.

Boeing 737 and 300-foot yacht that housed two helicopters, speedboat, sailboat and swimming pool.[46] The telco crisis of 2002 continued when Adelphia Communications, owned by the Rigas family, defaulted on a $96m bond payment in late June and was declared bankrupt. The SEC would later be investigating the intermingling of family and company business where loans of up to $3.1bn were used to finance luxury apartments, golf club membership, golf courses, the buying of forests and even a professional ice hockey team.

The mid-cycle banking and economy bailout

OFFICIALLY THE RECESSION is dated from March 2001 to November 2001, nine months. The average since World War II has been eleven months. Prior to that the recessions lasted longer, but government is much more pro-active these days and economists no longer argue that recessions are ordained by God – though they do believe them to be a 'natural' and inevitable part of capitalism, which they are not. They are, however, an inherent feature of monopoly capitalism in which land prices are commoditised – that is what the real estate cycle is all about.

So the Fed dived back into its tried and tested toolbox of economic quick fixes, lowering interest rates in quick succession, again opening the monetary spigots somewhat, and then waits to see what will happen. This time the stock market does not respond so quickly (the NASDAQ has a long way to fall) and the capital spending of business doesn't seem to move. (A good deal of it has been speculated away on those air rights and the occasional luxury resort and yacht or three.) As the stock market deflates further, in particular the NASDAQ, every time it bounces a little there is talk that the Fed is quietly intervening. With rates so low, the Fed has exhausted one of its tools of reflation. (Could rates go to zero?) But the intervention stays just that – talk – and can be neither proved nor disproved, although the Fed's January 2002 minutes do speak of 'unconventional policy measures' as something that 'could not be dismissed altogether'. The fear? If interest rates go to zero, and the US stays in recession, can anything else be done to rescue the situation?

House prices (more correctly land prices) do respond, however: prices go up. Housing starts increase and hit a 16-year high the first quarter of 2003. As interest rates fall, capital is freed up for home-owners as they take advantage of the lower rates to refinance existing mortgages. An estimated extra $100bn in spending power for consumers,[47] who promptly do what is required and go out and spend it.

In May of 2002, the US Congress, in a move to ensure continued support for Republicans in the up-coming November mid-term elections, votes to extend US farm subsidies to a record total of $173bn, spread over

46 *International Herald Tribune*, September 29-30, 2001.
47 *Wall Street Journal*, May 2003.

the following ten years. This dollar amount is now larger than the output of 158 of the world's 180 measured economies. The government is now paying farmers a 60 cent subsidy for every one dollar of output.[48] The amount of the subsidy, as we know, capitalises immediately into land price at the prevailing interest rate (Ricardo's Law of Rent). Between them, the US and the EU now spend more than $1 bn *a day* supporting their farmers – money that could be far better spent elsewhere. Perhaps the farmers should just plant dollars.

The Fed is also worried about Latin American prospects in 2002. In August the IMF is forced to loan Brazil $30 bn, its biggest loan ever, to stem a regional economic breakdown when it looks like the country could again default on its debt as the Brazilian currency, the Real, plumbs new lows on fears leftists may actually win the approaching election. This comes just three days after the US gives Uruguay $1.5 bn for essentially the same reason. The US can ill afford their neighbours collapsing at such a crucial time for itself.

In June 2003 the Fed drops rates to just 1 per cent. Adjusted for the current inflation measured at 2.1 per cent, it makes the real interest rate for borrowing actually negative – cheaper to borrow than if it were free. A possible new bubble is forming – in housing. But it saves the stock market for the time being, and the economy too. Fed intervention has again removed the threat of a deflating economy and saved the banks from themselves; and we move on – to yet another war. It begins in the March, at the start of which the Dow forms a higher low, the same as in 1991. The surge in military spending becomes a big contributor to second quarter growth for 2003. 'Blessed are the young,' said Herbert Hoover some time ago, 'for they shall inherit the national debt.'

History shows the pattern of US national debt has always expanded during war time. The debt tripled between 1812 and 1816; quadrupled between 1845 and 1851 (the Mexican War); increased 42 times during the Civil War; increased 50 per cent between 1893 and 1899 (the Spanish-American War); rose 21 times during World War I; and lifted sixfold between 1939 and 1946.[49] With the assistance of today's central banks, the issuing of debt is simple, and the marketing has become virtually continuous: newly created money (credit expansion) for federal government debt. It is a convenient way for nation states to finance their wars against one another.

The President, George W. Bush, also has an election to think about. He needs unemployment lower, a growing economy and a happy populace – otherwise they won't vote for him. As his father found out in 1992. The year before (early 2002) the President had already announced economic measures to his people that he hoped would 're-invigorate' the economy,

48 US Department of Agriculture and Congressional Budget Office.
49 *Reader's Companion to American History.*

including extending unemployment benefits by 13 weeks, a variety of tax breaks and a stimulus package to 'pump' $51 bn into the economy in 2002, $43 bn in 2003 and $29 bn in 2004.

The monetary spigots of the Fed, combined with federal government pump-priming, once again turn recession (our mid-cycle slowdown) into boom times. In late 2003, the pace of new home construction hits an 18-year high. The Fed says growth rates, now the fastest since 1986, are 'excellent'.[50] Interest rates, at 1 per cent, are at 45-year lows. Tom Beyer, president of Home Builders Financial Network Inc., is quoted as saying: 'Builders almost unanimously believe this market is real, is strong and that the supply absolutely does not meet demand … they are more optimistic than ever.'[51]

However, the gain has not been without some pain. In July of 2004 it becomes clear from IRS figures that overall incomes Americans have reported to the government 'shrank for two consecutive years after the internet stock market bubble burst in 2000'.[52] It's the first time this has happened since the tax system enabled record keeping after World War II. Quite a mid-real-estate-cycle slowdown this time. This may have something to do with so many more pay packets being dependent upon stock option performance than ever before. American industrial production has fallen for 13 consecutive months, also the first time for such a continuous decline since the Second World War. Significantly, though, the recession has not been land-price induced, as can be anticipated for the next one due later in the decade.

A lead-in for the second half of the real estate cycle

Credit standards

DESPITE THE TELCO and internet bubble and the deflating of much paper wealth, a good deal of actual real wealth has been produced. With the lower rates and repayment of debt by surviving companies, business does eventually improve and a new (decade) business cycle commences, what has historically been the second half of the 18-year real estate cycle. After almost a year of rates at 1 per cent, the Fed reverses policy once again, and starts on a tightening cycle, in July of 2004. (The Fed will eventually lift rates in small increments to around 5 per cent, which is about half way back from the point at which they fell, a balance point, and a point from which they are unlikely to move higher in the short term: 4 to 5 per cent is about the historical norm.) The behaviour of the yield curve will be important to observe as the economy turns further through the real estate cycle. An inversion of the curve becomes more critical the further the land price cycle runs.

50 Bloomberg, Nov 19, 2003.
51 Bloomberg, November 19.
52 *New York Times*, July 29, 2004.

As US interest rates have progressed back to more normal levels, credit standards have been dropping, not just in the US, but everywhere. Mortgages approved in the UK without proof of income account for just under 30 per cent of new lending for the second half of 2003.[53] These are being called in the UK 'self-certified' mortgages, in Australia 'low documentation (low-doc) loans'. This is never a problem whilst land values are on the up. There are even suggestions that banks may start approving 'zero-interest equity finance loans' – in other words borrowing a set percentage of any property without interest payable, in exchange for giving up some percentage of the capital appreciation. Again, such schemes look attractive whilst house (land) prices are rising …

For the US itself, the National Association of Realtors is reporting that the number of loans issued to persons of higher credit risk, or with no downpayment, or both, is on the increase.[54] This is of course very much a part of the real estate cycle, especially since 1945, and will occur as house prices (in reality the land underneath) increase. The borrowers are taking on debt that previously might have been beyond them. At lower interest rates a larger loan – more debt – can be afforded, pushing land prices ever higher. Such borrowers will remain confident that house prices will continue to go up, as they have in the immediate past. Indeed, this is most likely the only take on the housing market that such buyers will have experienced. By now few home owners anywhere in the world under 40 will have had any direct experience of a land-price-induced recession. They will only ever have seen 'house' prices go up. The yield curve will at some point in the future test the soundness of such a belief and of the credit-creation practices that cause it. The memory home owners will have is of the 2002 downturn, one induced by a stock market collapse after interest rate increases. This is not the same as a downturn induced by declining land prices.

Watch the currency

The US is likely to pay for its war by printing dollars, as it has done for every other war it was engaged in. A study of past currency crises is appropriate: 1893 in the US, the UK in the mid-1960s and again in 1992, Mexico in 1994 and South East Asia in 1997. If the bond-holders lose confidence in the US for whatever reason, the US government may have to offer a higher rate of interest to entice the buyers back. The effect could be a slower growth economy, even some sort of currency crisis if investors lose faith and stampede out of dollars. A currency crisis is often preceded by a land price downturn, which brings on banking difficulties, leading to a loss of confidence in the economy.[55] The land price downturn is likely

53 *Australian Financial Review*, May 28, 2004.
54 *International Herald Tribune*, June 25, 2004, quoting the National Association of Realtors Mortgage Statistical Annual, March 2004.
55 See the discussion in Herring for further information on this subject.

to begin, however, before a currency crisis in the US is possible. The land price, or real estate cycle, is usually marked at the top by the collapse of a major financial institution. The spark that could then ignite the currency crisis is the ensuing loss of faith by investors in the US government's ability to finance its external deficit and overseas borrowings.

History has most certainly repeated so far ...

In the study of past land price cycles we have observed that, without exception, the turn of the real estate cycle has been marked either by a deliberate contraction of credit by monetary authorities or by the collapse of a major financial institution, or both, after a sustained period of land speculation. In **1792**, after wild speculation, the Bank of the United States contracted the supply of credit; in **1819** the bursting of the cotton price and its effect on land prices saw the Second Bank of the United States way overdo the calling in of loans; in **1837** the President's specie circular – issued to cut short the land speculation – made the public begin to suspect the reliability of the nation's banks, then freely establishable by just about anybody; in **1857** the Ohio Bank collapse of August 24 came after wild land speculation in the several years before it; on September 18, **1873** the failure of Jay Cooke and Company was announced in New York – due to overexposure to railroad bonds backed by government real estate give-aways; in early **1893** banks called in loans in fear of the deteriorating economic condition of the country and its currency position; in **1930** there was the failure of the banking empire of Rogers Caldwell, and then of the New York based Bank of the United States, amongst many others, overloaded as they were with real estate loans; in **1974** the Franklin National Bank of New York failed after years of rampant land and currency speculation; and in **1989** there was the whole Savings and Loan farce. Each cycle happens differently, but the underlying cause is the same.

We may also have observed that each cycle involves the collapse of larger institutions with bigger and bigger numbers, affecting more and more people. Were this to happen again, two of the few financial institutions to be involved that could be bigger than the S&L numbers would be those most commonly known as Freddie Mac and Fannie Mae.

The herd mentality

More and more of today's savings are in the hands of fund managers. A fund manager's biggest fear is not performing as well as his or her peers. So they tend to be a conservative bunch, content with the same results as their fellow managers. This can lead to a bit of crowd behaviour, especially with index-type funds. They all buy at once, they all sell at once. Something to watch – if there is to be a stock market panic, it could make it worse than it might otherwise be.

The bankers

After every single land-price-induced downturn, the US government has introduced rules and regulations to make sure it won't happen again. Every upturn the banks and real estate industry find ways around these laws. Watch this time again for 'new-era' lending activities to default. The higher land price goes, the more inventive lending institutions have to become. They are of course doing no more than finding ways to increase profitability. In addition, real estate mortgages have become highly traded commodities; in the US alone up to half of all house mortgages have been securitised. In Australia this figure is around 20 per cent, but growing. Securitisation is the practice of taking a number of individual mortgages, putting them together as a group, then on-selling the grouped mortgages to another investor. This allows banks to make loans, then off-load the risk. The lending institutions don't actually care how high the land price is; they just make the loan then securitise it into the market. Rising interest rates will at some point find the weak link in this chain, which may or may not be obvious as land price turns down with the inevitable (at some future time) higher interest rates. The insiders will know, though, so reference to the appropriate charts, if any are available, will be instructive. The relevant stock market indices are a starting point, then the charts of individual banks, finance companies and mortgage brokers.

On the plus side for the bankers, nation-wide branching was finally permitted in the US in June 1997 – a long overdue move that will reduce the likelihood of isolated individual banking failures. In addition, the general banking sector is arguably better positioned this cycle to weather a land-price-induced downturn. In part this involves regulatory restrictions on how much banks are permitted to lend (create credit) on land as collateral; it is also the result of an active market for commercial and residential mortgage-backed securities. Banks are holding fewer and fewer 'whole loans' on their books these days in order to ensure strong liquidity. Time will tell. Again, higher interest rates will eventually, inevitably, expose the weak spots.

Global synchronicity

Global house prices are now more synchronised than ever before in history. This is clearly evident from research carried out by Marco Terrones at the IMF.[56] With the high and increasing levels of mortgage securitisation, problems in one country are now easily transferable to others. This too should be watched. The probability is that any downturn will be far more global in its reach this time than ever before.

Note too that the internet did not change the spatial patterns of cities. Most of the internet servers are located in larger cities. Just as the telephone did, the internet has contributed to the land value of cities.[57] The

56 *The Global House Price Boom.*
57 Tom Angiotti, 'The Real Estate Market in the United States', p.7.

economic gains of society this cycle have been prodigious. Such gains have been taken by the ever higher land price. It remains to be seen whether society, towards the end of this current cycle, is over-bidding for them.

'Left field' analysis

In all previous land-price-induced downturns, the event bringing the turn, the change in real estate buyer perception, seems to have come from way out of left field, so to speak, although in hindsight the event seemed blindingly obvious. This is as it must be, for the turn is always an event that the economy is ill prepared for – by definition, a shock to the system. Here is one thought, though: the euro. Whilst all eyes are on China (and Western banks and multi-nationals are chasing the alleged fat profits to be had) one should be watching Europe, in particular the recent entry of its newest members as they swap to the euro. If energy exporters like Russia and the Middle East start to perceive that it is in their better interests to receive 'their' oil payments in a stronger euro, rather than a weaker dollar, then the US has a major problem. No longer could it simply print dollars to pay for its oil. This is a far bigger threat to the US and its currency than a handful of manic terrorists. A turn by oil exporters to the euro could easily start a currency run. The situation is delicately poised at present. (Not to mention protected by heavy military expenditure in areas strategic to US interests.)

The world's tallest

The peak of every real estate cycle in the past, since 1837, has been sign-posted at the top with the opening of the world's tallest, biggest, widest, or most expensive; it's our most reliable indicator. This is as it must be: ever escalating land prices drive cities continually upwards and outwards. Expect huge casinos to be on the drawing boards, and other vast architectural projects (as in Dubai), the world's largest boat, the world's largest entertainment icon, or something similar in nature, built, as they are, almost entirely on credit. Then the cycle will turn.

FURTHER READING

Angiotti, Tom. 'The Real Estate Market in the United States', *Progressive Strategies*, December 1999.

Bank for International Settlements (BIS). 'Bank Failures in Mature Economies' (available online at www.bis.org/publ/bcbs_wp13.pdf).

Battellino, Ric (Assistant Governor, Financial Markets, Reserve Bank of Australia). 'Some Comments on Securitisation', a talk given to the Australian Credit Forum 2004, Sydney, July 28, 2004.

Fridson, Martin S. *It Was a Very Good Year*. John Wiley & Sons Inc., 1998.

Grant, James. *The Trouble with Prosperity: A Contrarian's Tale of Boom, Bust and Speculation*. Random House, 1996.

Herring, Richard and Susan Wachter. *Real Estate Booms and Banking Busts: An International Perspective*. University of Pennsylvania Working Paper No. 99-27, July 1999.

Partnoy, Frank. *F.I.A.S.C.O. Guns, Booze and Blood-lust: The Truth about High Finance*. Profile Books, 1998.

Pyhrr, Stephen A., Stephen E. Roulac and Waldo L. Born. 'Real Estate Cycles and Their Strategic Implications for Investors and Portfolio Managers in the Global Economy', *Journal of Real Estate Research*, Vol. 18, No. 1, 1999.

Terrones, Marco. *The Global House Price Boom*. International Monetary Fund, September 2004.

Weiss, Marc A. 'The Politics of Real Estate Cycles', *Business and Economic History*, Second Series, Vol. 20, 1991.

Periodicals:

Australian Financial Review

'Space: The final frontier for net start-ups', June 8, 2000, p.65.

'Net: The greatest real estate story ever told', March 21, 2000, p.41.

'Much Ado about Nothing', February 17, 2000, p.63.

'Some Big Holes in UK Mortgages', May 28, 2004, p.75

International Herald Tribune

'Enron Gave Bush Aides Warning of Meltdown', January 11, 2002.

'Qwest Chiefs Netted Millions', July 31, 2002, p.7.

The Nation

'The S&L Bailout: Sticking it to the taxpayers', September 4, 1989.

'Shady Customers: How S&L suspects profit from the crisis', Curtis Lang, July 30, 1990.

'The Quiet Americans', David Corn, September 10, 1990.

'Beltway Bandits', January 25, 1993.

'Big Bank Bonanza', April 4, 1994.

Time

'No End in Sight: Politicians hurl blame as the $500 billion crisis races out of sight', John Greenwald, August 13, 1990.

'Special Report: The S&L Crisis', Barbara Rudolph, February 20, 1989.

Others

FDIC Banking Review. 'The Cost of the Savings and Loan Crisis: Truth and consequences', Timothy Curry and Lynn Shibut, Vol. 13, No. 2, December 2000.

Fortune. 'S&Ls: Where did all those billions go?' September 10, 1990.
Insight on the News. 'Savings and Loan Bailout: The bills keep coming', June 7, 1999.
Los Angeles Times. 'Accounting Firm to Pay Record Fine over S&L Failures', Robert Rosenblatt, November 24, 1992.
The Economist. 'The Power of WorldCom's Puff', July 20, 2002, p.58.
The Economist. 'The Great Telecoms Crash', July 20, 2002, p.11.
The Weekend Australian. 'How to Buy with Others' Money, March 11-12, 2006, Business, p.39.
Wall Street Journal. 'Wrong Numbers: Telecom debt debacle could lead to losses of historic proportions', May 11, 2001, p.A1.

Asian Crisis:
Asian Currency Crisis. Report, Economic Indicator Services, October 31, 1997.
Australian Financial Review
'New Strategies Devised to Prop up Economies in Crisis', June 19, 1995, p.4.
'Experts Missed Signals of Economic Collapse in Thailand', September 20-21, 1997, p.11.
'Fraud or Flawed: Culprits sought in Thai Bank Fiasco', March 5, 1998.
'Warning of Food Crisis in Indonesia', April 2, 1998, p.12.
'Asian Crisis Could Derail US', May 23, 1998.
'Black Picture of Bad Loans Emerges', March 5, 1999
'Thailand's Tallest Hotel Stays Aloof from Slump', October 29, 1999, p.62
'Wong Kwan Seeks His New Genesis', June 26, 2001, p.56.
Harrison, Fred. 'The Losses of Nations'.
Insolvency Law and Practice in Asia, Queensland University of Technology, 1998. Quoted also in 'Don't Talk Gloom, it Might be a Prophecy', *Business Review Weekly*, August 10, 1998.
Jones, Frederic J. *The Chaos Makers: The Butterfly and the Cusp: A Study of Economic Catastrophes*. Othila Press Ltd, 1997. (Includes an introductory chapter by Fred Harrison, 'The Dreamers and the Deceived'.)

Russian bond default:
Australian Financial Review. 'Banks Blinded by Hedge Fund,' February 1, 1999, p.26.

PART III

THE FUTURE

There is no new thing under the sun, but that we simply resurrect the old ones. 'How do I forecast future cycles?' you may ask. In order to forecast future cycles, the most important thing is to begin right, for if we have the right beginning, we will get the right ending.

W.D. Gann., *Tunnel Through the Air*, p.78.

15

Knowledge We Gained Along the Way

Land is virtually indestructible, the oldest and most enduring source of wealth. Yet much of it is constantly changing in its nature of usage. And it is the impact of this conversion that frequently enhances its value and triggers the biggest profits reaped by real estate developers.

Dana L. Thomas, *Lords of the Land,* p.209

The key investment finding

HISTORY REVEALS that investors who made land speculation their sole business enterprise have rarely held on to their profits; the cycle usually wiped them out in the end. Those who had real businesses, with real earnings and real cash flow, who purchased real estate with the profits but did not speculate in it, went on to make a fortune. Towards the end of each real estate cycle, investors and speculators seem to lose sight of this crucial observation – if indeed it had ever been understood in the first place – that the best real estate is bought at a price that does not have its future use value already capitalised into it. Attentive study of the growing needs of an expanding city – population growth and the probable expansion of highways, public transport, airports and infrastructure in general – is required. Only then can one avoid buying where the full value of these improvements has not already been added to the price, especially at real estate cycle peaks.

As regards government-granted licences in general, the story of Henry Miller is instructive. Miller did not do what everyone else was doing at the time: he did not dig for gold. (How many gold diggers died fabulously wealthy?) Miller mined for water – better still, the rights to water, which the community, represented by its government, happily gave away. There's much in the adage that it's better to sell shovels to miners than to dig for gold. Invest, as everyone else is, in the next sure thing and you will end up like everyone else – which is mostly poor. Building wealth takes time and hard work, preferably in some sort of business – but it is much better if the business has control of a government-granted licence. As Rupert

Murdoch once pointed out:

> Because capitalists are always trying to stab each other in the back, free markets do not lead to monopolies ... Monopolies can only exist when government supports them. John Bonython Lecture, Australia, October 20, 1994

The largest government-supported licence is the right to own property, which, more importantly, includes the right to collect the rent so generated.

Every 18 years

THE UNITED STATES National Bureau of Economic Research (NBER) lists the years when the US has suffered an economic contraction, using data going back to 1857:

> 2001/2, **1991**, 1982, 1980, **1974**, 1970, 1961, 1958, **1954**, 1949, 1937, **1932**, 1927, 1924, 1921, 1919, **1914**, 1907, 1904, 1900, 1897, **1893**, 1891, 1888, 1884, 1879, **1873**, 1866, 1861, **1857**, 1847, **1836/7**, 1825, **1819**.

It defines 'economic contraction' not as two successive quarters of negative economic growth but by a defined set of economic indicators determined by them.[1]

For the period prior to 1857, I have myself listed those years which saw obvious downturns, as revealed in the literature of the time. If data were available it would probably reveal one or two more contractions.

At first reading the list seems confusing, random even. Clearly, however, some of the recessions proved deeper, longer lasting and more memorable than others. Dates in bold type show the real estate or, more correctly, land price cycle.

This, as we have discovered, is to do with speculation in government-granted licences and privileges, the largest of which is land value – facilitated by the banks through the process of fractional reserve banking. This process is purely man-made; it is not a natural phenomenon and is very definitely not ordained by any higher power – a topic taken up in the examination of Ricardo's Law of Rent (the next chapter).

US historians consider the first real 'industrial' recession to have been in 1819 – hence that is where we picked up the trail of our research. This was, as it happened, 18 years after the federal government's official 'enclosure' – the first selling-off of its real estate that began on May 10, 1800.

It was in the 1930s that Homer Hoyt, then a postgraduate student at the University of Chicago, conducted his research into trends in Chicago land values over the surprisingly long period of one hundred years. His thesis,

1 The Business Cycle Dating Committee of the NBER has a mandate to decide when recessions start and finish. It considers US gross domestic product (in real terms) as the best single measure of economic activity, but takes into account a selection of other measures, including personal income, employment levels, industrial production and retail sales. See www.nber.org

published in 1933 as *One Hundred Years of Land Values in Chicago*, claimed the discovery of a regular cycle averaging 18 years for the city of Chicago, which he considered representative of the nation as a whole. At the same time, though independently, Roy Wenzlick, from St Louis, assembling data from more than 120 other US cities, also revealed an average 18-year real estate cycle. In his 1936 best-seller, *The Coming Boom in Real Estate and What to Do About It*, Wenzlick accurately predicted a recovery in the US property market after the Great Depression, and a continued 18-year cycle (a forecast few could believe at the time). Wenzlick's book is testament to the speculative forces driving the cycle that have not changed to this day.

Hoyt went on to update his material, which Fred Harrison included in his insightful *The Power in the Land*,[2] Harrison adding the US building cycle peaks he had himself researched:

US land value peak	US building cycle peak	US recession
1818	—	1819
1836	1836	1837
1854	1856	1857
1872	1871	1873
1890	1892	1893
—	1916	1918
1925	1927	1929

Harrison then updated this further, to 1983:

—	War interrupted	1955 land rent bottoms
1973	—	1974
1989[3]		1991[3]

Extrapolating from here, it is not unreasonable to expect the next real-estate-led recession towards the end of the next decade, 2009/10.[4]

There is one peak in land values missing: the decade of the 1910s. Harrison attributes this to the looming war, disturbing 'the benign psychological outlook which is necessary for speculation.'[5] Hoyt observed, significantly, that for Chicago at least memories of the 1893 depression were strong, and lingered throughout the first decade of the new century. Enough to have caused a permanent shift in investment patterns for those concerned? Speculation on my part, but certainly possible. We know that such a shift in behaviour was seen in investors who went

2 Shepheard-Walwyn, 1983, p.64, Table 5:1.
3 At the time these were forecasts.
4 This section, 'Every 18 Years', was written for EIS subscribers in 1999, explained in classes held shortly after that time, and then progressively updated via emails as the real estate cycle unfolded. It is not something that was written just yesterday (the emails updating the forecast to 2010 can be viewed at www.businesscycles.biz/past forecasts).
5 p.64.

through the Great Depression of the 1930s: they developed a lifelong addiction to saving cash.

Observe in the table that each peak in land values was reached *12 to 24 (perhaps even as long as 36) months before* the recession. In other words, the downturn in land values has on each occasion preceded the decline in general economic activity. Our own examination of federal government land sales up to 1924 (the complete chart is on page vii) confirms the extensive research in Harrison's Table 5:1.[6] I am confident that data for the current real estate cycle into 2010, when it becomes available, will confirm this remarkably consistent pattern.

Observe also that the peaks in the building cycle usually *follow the peaks in land value but precede the recession*. Once land costs too much, activity in the construction industry, house building in particular, is curtailed, dampening activity over the wider economy. This is how the land price downturn transmits itself to the wider economy.[7]

For whatever reason, this activity has generated a reliable 18-year-average cycle in the US since the land rent was first enclosed.[8] Indeed, ***the cycle is resulting directly from the enclosure***.

This fact the reader will find of enormous value in accurately forecasting future economic activity: that the real estate cycle results directly from the enclosure of the economic rent so generated. Understand this and a whole new panorama opens up. It will help you identify where the economy is at any particular time in the real estate cycle. Each cycle will manifest differently, of course, the repetition could never be exactly the same; but, as the historical chapters have shown, the similarities have been astounding. As rents recover, banks create credit against increasing land value; this leads to a boom, real estate speculation goes 'over the top'; then comes a big bust and recession, first in housing and related sectors, then in the general economy.

To forecast business cycles, and especially the real estate cycle, one should measure construction activity, sure – but, more importantly, land value. It is here, particularly for the US, that one comes up against a dearth of any meaningful statistics. No US economist takes the time to accurately measure land value and interpret its significance for the economy. One reason is that all economists today will argue that land is part of capital, and therefore not something to be measured separately. Do not fall into this blinding misapprehension. What is happening with land value is the key to forecasting.[9]

6 See also Newman, *The Building Industry and Building Cycles*. Newman lists the US building peaks (data from 1875 to 1933, Statistical Appendix, Table IX, p.63) as 1892, 1916 (June) and 1925 (November) – a further confirming source for the data in Harrison.

7 Harrison, p.65.

8 Discussed further in Chapter 17, 'Why 18 Years?'

9 The US may finally be seeing some intelligent statistics in this matter. See, for example, the recently released November 2006 paper by Morris A. Davis and Jonathan Heathcote, 'The Price and Quantity of Residential Land in the United States (www.9.georgetown.edu/faculty/jhha/land-final.pdf).

We have described the past US real estate cycles as: 1800-1819, to 1837, to 1857, to 1873, to 1893, to 1914 (war interrupted), to 1932 (war interrupted again), then 1955 to 1974, to 1992, and to 2010 (forecast).[10] We saw that the give-away of the public domain, and the attendant speculation, peaked in 1818, 1836, 1854, 1869, 1888, 1908 and 1926; building activity peaked after that in approximately 1944. There was little real estate speculation during the Second World War, but, once the distortions of war were past, real estate speculation peaked in the very early 1970s, again in 1987 (if the S&L figures are anything to go by), and yet again in 2006. Eighteen years has proved a remarkably consistent pattern.

The Banks

IT IS THE CREDIT created by banks that fuels the real estate cycle. This is the result of the fractional reserve system of banking (as outlined in Chapter 3, 'Mad Cash Disease'). Only through this prodigious credit creation can the price of land be driven to such great heights – and then collapse.

> Bankers own the earth; take it away from them, but leave them with the power to create credit, and with the stroke of a pen they will create enough money to buy it back again ... If you want to be slaves of the bankers, and pay the cost of your own slavery, then let the banks create money.
>
> Lord Stamp[11]

Such is the system we have today. It behoves us to use it to our best advantage. As noted by a few of the more savvy real estate players over the years, the best way to make a million is to borrow it and let someone else pay off the interest.

Credit growth fuels bank profitability, so banks are always on the lookout for ways to increase this growth. Always try to observe how and when this takes place in the property cycle. A reading of history reveals that each real estate recession brought new rules and regulations to the banking industry, designed to stop problems and abuses, and in each upturn new ways were found to flout the rules and add to profitability. The rules introduced after each recession to try to fix banking problems are necessary only because society permits the private capture of the public value that is land rent – discussed further in the next chapter. New banking rules that do not address this fundamental issue simply will not work. Though well intentioned, they will make future cyclical volatility even more

10 I disagree slightly with the dating in Harrison's Table 5:1 of the 1918 recession, for reasons that I explain in my chapter on the 1932 cycle, but this is immaterial in the wider context of our discussions. So far, only world war has been able to exert enough pressure within the US to upset the 18-year rhythm; barring another world conflict, one can reasonably expect this cycle to continue into 2010 and beyond. Given that the underlying reasons for the cycle are unlikely to change soon, the US can expect another bout of wild real estate speculation as we go into the 2020s, leading to a further land-price-induced recession (much like 2009/10 is going to be), into 2030.

11 Lord Josiah Charles Stamp (1880-1941), 1st Baron Stamp of Shortlands, and Bank of England director 1928 to 1941, in a public speech at Central Hall, Westminster, England, 1937.

pronounced. This is happening now with the creation of 'moral hazard': if banks know that ultimately the government will come to their rescue, or they underwrite deposits through insurance, why be prudent in lending?

We have also learnt that in each cycle the turning point will be marked by the collapse, or near collapse, of a major bank. This has always been the result of the bank's having placed itself at the mercy of expensive funding in its quest for growth – exposed in the end by rising interest rates. Without a change to the driving forces of credit, created and backed by the government-granted licence that is land value, the real estate cycle, and the banking practices within it, will continue. Only the numbers will get bigger.

The repetition of history

BY 2007 no one under the age of 40 anywhere in the English-speaking world had any direct investment experience of a land-price-induced downturn. They have seen house – in reality land – prices go in only one direction: up. They remember only the downturn of 2002, which, since it involved the stock market only, was fairly easy for the Fed to reverse: it simply lowered interest rates. The next downturn will be different. It will be land-price induced. Lower interest rates will not solve the problem in the short term. This is because the problem will involve banks and their large loan write-offs, necessitating the rebuilding of their capital base. Because of the value of the loans to be written off, the process of recovery will take years, not months. During this phase, a contraction of bank credit is certain, and land prices will fall. Average price falls in the past have been around 20 to 30 per cent from the peak.

> On the upside (recovery and expansion phases), the cycle usually goes up faster and higher than is anticipated by market participants. The market produces 'overpriced' real estate. For example, values in Texas cities in the mid-1980s rose 25% to 50% higher than were expected; unfortunately, market participants acted as if the trend would continue forever. On the downside (contraction and recession phases), the cycle usually goes down faster and lower than is expected. This results in 'underpriced' real estate. During the down cycle in Texas (1987-1991) it was common to see values of commercial real estate values drop by 60 to 80 percent from previous highs. Office properties that sold for $100 to $120 per square foot in 1985 were sold for $25 to $35 per square foot in 1992. Apartment buildings that sold for $25,000 to $30,000 per unit in 1985 were sold for $7,000 to $10,000 per unit in 1991. Zoned office land that sold in 1985 for $25 to $30 per building square foot (with approved site development permits) sold for only $4 to $5 per square foot in 1992-1993.
>
> Stephen A. Phyrr, Stepeh E. Roulac and Waldo L. Born, *Real Estate Cycles and Their Strategic Implications for Investors and Portfolio Managers in the Global Economy*, 1999

The same can be said for every past real estate cycle. A similar scenario can be expected for the current one.

The herd

> Land values, as distinguished from land prices, grow almost exactly as population increases, for they are determined by the economic returns in rents when improved, while real estate prices are not determined by intrinsic values, but largely by sentiment, so that prices and values do not necessarily, in fact, rarely mean the same thing. In 1889 everybody thought real estate prices would never stop going up, while now they are just as firmly convinced that they will never stop going down … Hoyt, p.223

AT THE EXTREMES, the herd is *always* wrong. One should not underestimate its capacity for stupidity.

In 1970 and '71, at the height of the land speculation in the US for that cycle, the federal Office of Interstate Land Sales Registration (OILSR) funded TV advertisements warning about land swindles in an invented town they named 'Rainbow City'. Within weeks the OILSR began receiving letters asking how to go about buying lots in the town.

Most of us are mindful of the last crisis – the one we can remember – like generals fighting the previous war. This is probably the last thing we should be worried about. It is one reason why the real estate cycle is so hard to understand. The slowdown in the middle of the 18-year cycle confuses us so that, by the end of the full cycle, few investors have any actual investment experience of a *land-price*-induced downturn – a downturn which will be much nastier than the mid-cycle slow-down.

Economic and social circumstances also manifest differently, of course, though importantly the driving force behind them remains the same. For example, interest rates are now far lower than in the previous two land-price-induced downturns of 1989 and 1974. Then rates were on the upswing. In 2009 we will have to be far more in debt for there to be the same leverage effect – which is of course exactly what is happening. Lower interest rates but record debt levels (all to afford land price) in the years after 2005 will mark the end of this real estate cycle. Investors, speculators and house-buyers with little equity who buy in at the end of the cycle will be wiped out by the downturn – as always.

War is a lucrative business

WAR IS a lucrative business. There has grown up a well-connected vested interest in maintaining it. Whoever said the price of freedom is eternal vigilance is certainly correct. Tomorrow's wealthy businessman or politician was often yesterday's war financier.

Robert Morris and William Duer made a fortune as arms suppliers to the US revolution. Bankers like J.P. Morgan and Jay Cooke made a killing supplying weapons to armies or selling bonds to a gullible public during the Civil War. Du Pont and other family-based firms amassed an even greater fortune supplying both sides with military hardware during the

First World War. Military suppliers grew fat and rich out of Vietnam, just as Bechtel and Halliburton will do from Iraq.

The effect of war on the economy is highly expansionary; it almost always involves a huge expansion of credit. Today it is exceptionally easy to finance. Fractional reserve banking encourages the State to make, or manufacture, war.

> War has always been the occasion of a great – and usually permanent – acceleration and intensification of State power of society. War is the great excuse for mobilizing all the energies and resources of the nation, in the name of patriotic rhetoric, under the aegis and dictation of the state apparatus. It is in war that the state really comes into its own: swelling in power, in number, in pride, in absolute dominion over the economy and society. Society becomes a herd, seeking to kill its alleged enemies, rooting out and suppressing all dissent from the official war effort, happily betraying truth for the supposed public interest. Society becomes an armed camp, with the values and the morals … of an 'army on the march'.
>
> Murray N. Rothbard, *For a New Liberty: the Libertarian Manifesto*, 1989

One does not need to be as libertarian as Murray Rothbard to see this. Smedley D. Butler, America's most decorated war veteran, went on to write an anti-war classic, *War is a Racket*:

> War is a racket. It always has been … Only a small inside group knows what it is all about. It is conducted for the benefit of the very few, at the expense of the very many.

Observers of history are familiar with the war story.

> The first panacea for a mismanaged nation is inflation of the currency; the second is war. Both bring a temporary prosperity; both bring a permanent ruin. But both are the refuge of political and economic opportunists.
>
> Ernest Hemingway, 'Notes on the Next War', *Esquire*, September 1935

On government and politicians

YOU'VE ALL seen 'The Weakest Link' – a number of contestants answer questions and at the end of each round someone is voted off. Usually the dullest contestant is thrown out – in the beginning. But ever noticed what tends to happen when there are fewer contestants remaining? The person voted off is then usually the one who is the biggest threat to the others. Therein lies the fundamental flaw of a centrally governed democracy. Leaders of political parties are *never* the intellectually brightest or best for the community. They are the smartest politically. Often they are beholden to some vested interest. Usually they are willing to sacrifice idealism to political power for themselves.

Most politicians are on someone's payroll. The best book on the subject is Phil Grant's *Wonderful Wealth Machine*, which exposes the ruse for what it is: the give-away of rental licences. Policy can only ever be framed for the benefit of the licence-holder, never for the voting public. So 'state power is a much coveted prize in capitalist circles'.[12]

> … the State throughout history has been essentially an organization of a segment of the population that forsakes peaceful economic activity to constitute itself as a ruling class. This class makes its living parasitically by establishing a permanent hegemonic or 'political' relationship between itself and the productive members of the population. This political relationship permits the rulers to subsist on the tribute or taxes routinely and 'legally' expropriated from the income and wealth of the producing class. The latter class is composed of the 'subjects' or, in the case of democratic states, the 'taxpayers', who earn their living through the peaceful 'economic means' of production and voluntary exchange. In contrast, constituents of the ruling class may be thought of as 'tax-consumers' who earn their living through the coercive 'political means' of taxation and the sale of monopoly privileges.
>
> Joseph T. Salerno, introduction to Rothbard's *A History of Money and Banking in the United States*

> The capitalist state will operate in the long term interests of capitalists independent of their direct participation in the policy making process or mobilization of resources. Central to this objective relation under capitalism, the state must promote capital accumulation because its own survival depends on tax revenues derived from successful profit making activity, as well as political stability that is contingent upon economic growth.
>
> K. Calavita, R. Tillman and H.N. Pontell, 'The Savings and Loan Debacle: Financial Crime and the State', *Review of Sociology*, Vol. 23, 1997

In the coming downturn we can be certain that everything possible will be done by the State to stop the land price collapse, including, ultimately, a state bailout of the worst affected banks. In the land of the free, this is socialism run riot. It is also the State offering continued protection to the licence holder.

What we need to know as investors is that the system of government-granted licences/monopoly capitalism is spreading. Witness, for example, recent World Bank initiatives to ease the burden on poorer nations whereby debt-strapped countries may qualify for partial debt relief. The relief comes with conditions. To get a recent loan, Ghana had to allow private-sector ownership in water distribution.[13] Of far more significance, in this cycle from 1991 we have seen Russia adopt legislation privatising its land resource. Most of the former communist regimes are doing the same, with China about to follow, perhaps by 2010. This will commit such nations to the monopoly capitalist system and ensure land booms and busts well into the 21st century and beyond. Humans will no doubt take the system into outer space should real estate opportunities open up on other planets

12 Mike Davis, *Under the Perfect Sun*, p.9.
13 *New Internationalist*, August 2001.

or nearby asteroids. (Expect private ownership of the asteroids' mineral wealth to be claimed by the 'discoverer' and 'protected' by the military.)

Captain Kirk of the starship *Enterprise* once suggested that by his time (in the 23rd century) human-kind had long since banished poverty from the planet. This just isn't possible so long as the rent of government-granted licences is permitted to capitalise into a tradable commodity, collectable only by those who have the 'licence'.

Napoleon's lesson in selling

NAPOLEON SOLD 757 million acres of dirt to the US in 1803, the so-called Louisiana Purchase, for the then unheard of sum of $15m – roughly 3 cents per acre. Napoleon used the money to wage war: for recurrent expenditure. The US used the land rent to create lasting wealth. Need one say more? Few ever learn the lessons of history. Assets should be used to create further income to build further assets, never to accumulate further liabilities. Most Lotto winners do the opposite, spending their winnings on all manner of consumption and high living.

Napoleon himself was later heard to lament: 'America is a fortunate country. She grows by the follies of our European nations.'[14] No longer, however. The Republican administration in 2008 has not learned much from history, in particular what Napoleon had to say about finance. History dictates that the consequences will be keenly felt within the US once the next land-price-induced recession really gets underway. Substantial real estate bargains will be available at this time in 2010 for those with the cash resources at hand.

14 Quoted in Shosuke Sato, *History of the Land Question in the United States*, Johns Hopkins University, Studies in Historical and Political Science, p.129.

16

Why the Repeat?

Ricardo's Law of Rent: The Government-granted Licence

Every improvement in the circumstances of the society tends either directly or indirectly to raise the real rent of land, to increase the real wealth of the landlord, his power of purchasing the labour, or the produce of the labour of other people.

Adam Smith, *The Theory of Moral Sentiments*[1]

The meek shall inherit the earth, but not its mineral rights.

J. Paul Getty

THE REAL ESTATE CYCLE is all about the rent, the economic rent – the one big-ticket item the political world refuses to acknowledge, and few investors make any attempt to understand. The economic rent was highlighted first by English economist David Ricardo (1772-1823), a key figure in the development of economic theory.

Ricardo spent only the last fifteen years of his life as an economist, and then only because of a chance reading of Adam Smith's *The Wealth of Nations*. This prompted Ricardo's first contribution to economic thought in 1810, when he wrote that the inflation England was then experiencing was a direct result of the Bank of England's excessive printing of bank notes. Readers today would recognise that as something to do with the quantity theory of money, or monetarism. It gained Ricardo a degree of notoriety amongst fellow economists.

In 1815 Ricardo turned his attention to the Corn Laws. In *Essay on the Influence of a Low Price of Corn on the Profits of Stock* he articulated what came to be one of the fundamental laws of economics, the Law of Diminishing Returns, pointing out that, as additional resources are combined and added together with production on a fixed resource, additional output will diminish.

Ricardo opposed the Corn Laws themselves as being protectionist. He tore apart the existing belief in their benefits by explaining the idea of

1 1759, Liberty Classics, 1969, p.275.

comparative costs, what we would now call 'comparative advantage'. Today this theory is the foundation stone of ideas about free trade between nations. No economist worth his salt would argue against the obvious fact, uncovered by Ricardo, that any country that chooses to trade its own products for products it can get from another nation at lower cost will immediately be better off as a result. Ricardo's theory was proved correct beyond any doubt in the years after Britain finally abolished its Corn Laws.

But it is for his Theory of Rent that David Ricardo is most famous. Simply put, Ricardo said that the economic rent is not a cost of production. He defined 'rent' as the difference between the costs of production from different acreages of land. Investors today may not know much about it, but those living at the fringes of society quickly learn about its practical application. In London some years back, one enterprising duo, John Bird and Gordon Roddick, hit upon an idea to put the homeless back to work. They published *The Big Issue* for those on the streets to sell, thus providing a regular income that wasn't welfare.

The idea worked and was copied in other cities, including San Francisco, but sellers were quick to notice that those who stood on busy street-corners (say, the corner of Market and New Montgomery) sold more magazines for the same application of labour than those at quieter sites. Fights broke out for control over the best location. Soon, sellers were prepared to bid for these best locations, or defend theirs with violence. This value, that arises independently of labour, is what Ricardo was first to identify as a 'surplus', the economic rent. Real estate investors know it today as locational value.

Australia's early politicians knew all about this phenomenon. They too were having fights – about where to establish the capital of the new federation of Australian states. Neither Sydney nor Melbourne would consent to the other becoming the capital. For a while after 1901 the two cities agreed to rotate the responsibilities and take turns seating the elected parliamentarians to govern the country until a new capital could be built somewhere in between.

The elected leaders were well aware of what an announcement (or fore-knowledge of such an announcement) would have on land value in the chosen region as land speculators piled in for a quick profit from the rapidly appreciating locational value, or economic rent. To defeat them, Australia's first Prime Minister, Edmund Barton, declared that:

> So far as the law of the land allows, land within the federal area will not be sold. Its ownership will be retained in the Commonwealth. The land will be let for considerable terms but with periodical re-appraisement so that the revenues thus obtained will assist the cost of creating the Commonwealth Capital. More than that, we shall take care to put no fancy prices on land. We shall not play into the hands of the speculators …
>
> *Sydney Morning Herald*, January 18, 1901

An annual rent of not less than 5 per cent of the unimproved value of the land, as assessed by an appropriate authority, was eventually prescribed for all persons who wanted to live and work in the new capital, payable quarterly in advance. The unimproved value of the land was to be re-appraised at the expiration of twenty years, and thereafter at ten-year intervals. With such a simple and elegant idea, Australia went on to build the city of Canberra, truly one of the world's most spacious and amenable of capital cities.

So, if you decided to move to Canberra and the site you intended to own was appraised as worth $1,000, you paid rent to the commonwealth of $50 per year. The site was yours, to do with what you wanted: you owned it with clear title, subject to the lease; you just had to pay the economic rent for the privilege. The politicians knew what they were doing. Collecting the worth of the site yearly in advance meant that the rent of the site could not capitalise into a tradable commodity. There would be no price in which to speculate.

The price of the site, therefore, is zero.

But, although the price is zero, this does not destroy the site's use value, or worth.

This has some astounding ramifications. To live in Canberra, one did not need to take out a mortgage to afford the site. (This upset the banks.) Canberra sites could never be hoarded or kept out of use in expectation of future gains: the holding cost of doing so (because you owed the land rent to the commonwealth) was too high. Credit could not be created upon the capitalised land rent. There wasn't any.

No capitalised rent, no real estate cycle.

No capitalised rent, no need for the vast amount of fractional reserve banking required to buy it.

Had past US federal government politicians been a bit more enlightened, and not had so many fingers in the rent trough, US history could have been fundamentally different, and far more peaceful. The founding fathers of the US constitution could have chosen to collect the rents, rather than giving them away or parcelling them out in the beginning (mostly to themselves). The American railroads might have been better built, and profitable from the start, instead of soaking up bond monies and real estate. In 1877 Haggin and Tevis could never have acquired title to approximately 150 square miles of California real estate to the exclusion of everybody else. Neither could Henry Miller have appropriated his one million acres, with full rights to the water of the Kern River. Such a disastrous downturn as the Great Depression could never have happened. And, in the 1980s, the selling of land back and forth by Texan real estate developer Danny Faulkner and friends, so that the land appeared to be increasing in value, justifying ever-larger loans for the hundreds of apartment projects developers were building along Interstate 30, would never have been thought of (see Appendix 9).

A few daring US pioneers did know about Ricardo's Theory of Rent, and sought to put it into practice in the creation of several towns and cities, including Fairhope (Alabama), Free Acres (New Jersey) and Arden (Delaware). Each was reasonably successful in its own way, after what were at the time some very unusual experiments in the sharing of locational value in ways other than allowing the rent to capitalise into a tradable price. The state of Alaska developed this approach to share its oil rents fairly among all its citizens, distributing the surplus each and every year to *all* its people by way of a citizen's dividend.[2] It is what should have happened in Iraq.

The macroeconomic effects of such an approach were tested in Denmark between 1957 and 1960.[3] In the elections of May 1957 three parties came together, the Justice Party, the (labour) Social Democrats and the (liberal) Radicals, with a view to, amongst other things, implementing free trade and the collection of the economic rent for government revenue, in lieu of other taxes. They were elected on this platform and duly passed legislation to carry out the reforms. The effect in reducing land speculation was immediate. Inflation levels went virtually to zero because the purchasing power of individuals was now only obtainable through production. The balance between production and purchasing power resulted in stable prices. Unemployment dived; so did the rate of interest; and there were no new taxes levied in the period. So pronounced were the economic effects that, in the *New York Times* of October 2, 1960, under the headline 'Big Lesson from a Small Nation', Henry Steele Commager suggested that other nations had something to learn from what was happening there.

But the Danish opposition didn't take the improvements lying down and, in the elections of 1960, used the largest amount of money ever (donated by conservatives and property owning associations) to overthrow the triumvirate of upstarts. The power of vested interests. It has been downhill for the small nation ever since, and back to boom bust.

The ownership of land in all Western economies, and in more and more countries around the world, is permissible only through title. It is in reality a government-conferred privilege – a government-granted licence. There are other types of government-created licences – for example a banking licence, the right to own a cab, a casino or a broadcasting station – but it is the right to own land that manifests by far the largest capitalised

2 The 2007 dividend paid by the State of Alaska to every citizen was $1,654. Such an idea is nothing new and can be traced back to Thomas Paine's essay 'Agrarian Justice' (for more information see www.en.wikipedia.org/wiki/citizens_dividend).

3 Information sourced from a paper delivered by Knud Tholstrup, Member of the Danish Parliament, within the Justice Party, 1946-1958, 'How Denmark Stopped Inflation', delivered to the Board of Governors Annual Meeting, Copenhagen, September 21-5, 1970; and from the journal *Progress*, magazine of Prosper Australia, July 1970.

rental. If any government attempts to collect it, you can be sure the owners will soon identify themselves.

The Law of Rent has stood the test of time. In addition to enlightening the rest of the world through his writings, David Ricardo put his knowledge to great personal use and retired immensely rich (with an estate valued in excess of $100 m in today's dollars, from highly successful stock and real estate market investments).[4]

It is thanks to Ricardo's Law of Rent that today's economists realise that agricultural support schemes do not assist farm production but simply add to the wealth of the landowner. Economists will also explain to anyone who wants to listen that the restriction on the number of medallions for New York cabs does not benefit cab drivers' wages; it is the owner of the medallion (a government-granted licence) to whom the benefit capitalises.[5]

Few, however, are listening. Which is why the knowledge contained in this chapter is so valuable to investors. The real estate cycle could not manifest without the ability of the economic rent to capitalise into a tradable privilege. Once the cycle is created then, unless something is done to stop that rent from being freely traded as a price, the cycle will repeat. The only questions left are: Why 18 years? and, Can we identify, in advance, the cyclical turning points?

FURTHER READING

Brennan, Frank. *Canberra in Crisis: A History of Land Tenure and Leasehold Administration*. Dalton Publishing, 1971.

Brittan, Samuel. 'A tax idea that cannot be buried', *Financial Times*, April 15, 2005.

Commager, Henry Steele. 'Big lesson from a small nation; Denmark – an orderly land, and a prosperous one – has qualities, and American finds, that bear examination by other countries', *New York Times*, October 2, 1960.

Fairhope Single Tax Corporation. *A History of the Fairhope Single Tax Corporation*. Fairhope, Alabama.

Geonomy Society. *Where a Tax Reform has Worked: 28 Case Studies* (available at www.progress.org/geonomy/geono05.php).

Samuelson, Paul A., K. Hancock and R. Wallace. *Economics (Australian Edition): An Introductory Analysis*. The chapter on the taxation of land surplus, p.595 in particular, where Samuelson states (and eloquently illustrates): 'Pure land rent is in the nature of a "surplus" which can be taxed without affecting production incentives.'

Silagi, Michael. 'Land Reform in Kiaochow, China', *American Journal of Economics and Sociology*, Vol. 43, No. 2, April 1984. (Translated by Susan N. Faulkner.)

4 *Concise Encyclopaedia of Economics*, www.econlib.org/library/Enc/bios/Ricardo.html

5 And with the creation of the licence there comes immediately into existence a vested interest dedicated to preserving it.

17
Why 18 Years?

> ***There exist in our minds preconceptions about the economic process that are much more dangerous to the cumulative growth of our knowledge and the scientific character of our analytic endeavours because they seem beyond our control in a sense in which value judgements and special pleadings are not ... We shall call them ideologies.***
>
> Joseph Schumpeter[1]

WHY 18 YEARS? This is a tough one.

We have discovered that, if the economic rent could not be capitalised, there would not be a real estate cycle, or at least not one with such violent boom/busts. (There would still be slight seasonal variations, and structural building and population issues from time to time.) But why should the cycle we have, have averaged out to be 18 years? Since the land price low of 1955, after the Second World War, they have been exactly 18 years in duration.

Perhaps the answer is to be found in the historical long-run rate of interest – which is 5 per cent. In fact the key number in the real estate cycle may well be 14, not 18: 14 years just happens to be the time in which a sum of money, at 5 per cent compound interest, is doubled.

The sleuthing for a possible explanation of the length of the cycle was done by Fred Harrison in his book *Boom Bus*t (Chapters 2 and 5 in particular). The history goes back to the English 'Terminating Societies'. During the Industrial Revolution, when people were shifting into the newly developing industrial centres, those without capital (the vast majority) had great difficulty affording a house. Back then there were no banks and credit institutions such as we are accustomed to today. How might this problem of affordability be solved?

The answer was found in a Birmingham pub in the late 18th century. The ale drinkers decided one day to band together, pool their savings and buy their way into the housing market. It was agreed that each member of the group was to be levied 10s a month. In the group so formed lots were drawn to decide which person would have his house built first.

1 *Essays on Entrepreneurs, Ideologies, Innovations, Business Cycles and the Evolution of Capitalism*, Transaction Press, 1989, p.274.

Obviously the group member who drew the first lot would not yet have saved up enough money to pay for the construction of his house. How could the other members of the group be certain that he would continue to contribute his levy until all the remainder of the group had houses too? The answer was to execute a mortgage over the property until the full amount had been collected.

> In this way, the financial contributions were equalised in value and everybody received a house. The interest rate of 5% determined the timetable – it took 14 years to raise enough cash for everyone to secure a home.
>
> Harrison, *Boom Bust*, p.31

By the fourteenth year, all members had a home and the club could be disbanded.

These were the Terminating Societies, the forerunner of what became known in the UK as Building Societies and in the US as Savings and Loans institutions. The first advertisements for such groups appeared in 1778, and they continued well into the 19th century. The Halifax Building Society in the UK was launched in 1853 and offered shares at £120, payable at 10s a lunar month at 5 per cent interest. This would render a share fully paid up in 13 years and 7 months. The Temperance Permanent Building Society followed in 1854, also with shares at £120 and a house to be built for every member at a cost not exceeding £80.[2]

Harrison goes on to give a profile of how he sees the 18-year real estate cycle, which he illustrated diagrammatically in *Boom Bust* as Figure 5:1 and which he has kindly allowed me to reproduce here (Graph 17.1).

Graph 17.1: Profile of the 18-Year Real Estate Cycle

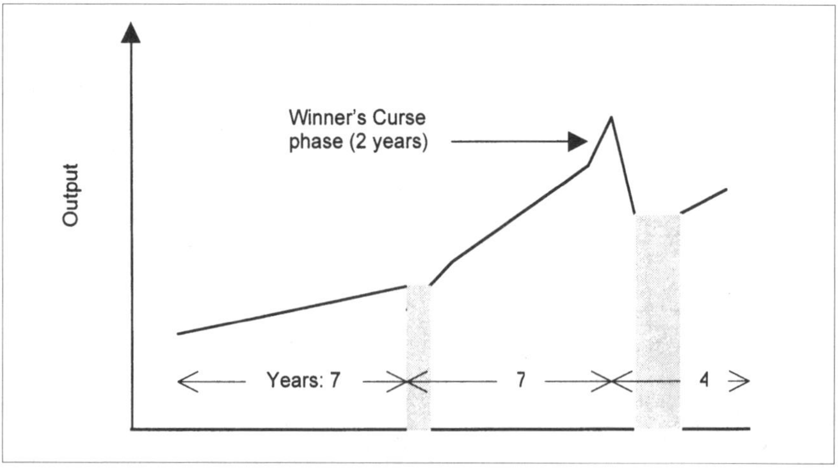

Source: Fred Harrison, *Boom Bust*, p.87.

2 Harrison, p.32.

Particular emphasis may currently be placed on the 'winner's curse' phase of the cycle. It is usual for a majority of the *mortgaged* real estate buyers in this phase of the cycle to end up with negative equity in their house once the cycle finally turns down. The US will again see this phenomenon as the cycle progresses further into 2008 and beyond.

Since the land price low in the US in 1955, this profile of the cycle by Harrison has proved remarkably resilient. 'After 1955, the first bust in listed real estate stocks came on May 28, 1962,' [3] which is, as it happens, 7 years after the land price low. (The May and June 1962 slowdown was discussed in Chapter 12.) We know, too, that the cycle went on to peak a little over 7 years later in the very early 1970s, and then the US experienced its 1973/4 property crash.

Table 17.1: Real Estate Stock Price Index[4]
1965 = 10

Year	High	Low
1965	11.22	9.05
1966	12.35	9.00
1967	23.62	10.67
1968	45.23	20.85
1969	**52.12**	37.09
1970	43.81	24.14
1971	43.29	32.98
1972	47.48	31.96
1973	36.69	13.20
1974	16.41	**6.01**
1975	14.86	8.27
1976	16.15	11.33

Recovery followed the 1974 recession, leading to growth, stalling in 1981/2, about 7 years later; then the cycle peaked in the late 1980s, with a winner's curse phase clearly evident at that time. The US again saw a mid-cycle recession some 7 years into the current cycle, yet another winner's curse phase almost 7 years after that, and without doubt another property low coming soon. Curious isn't it?

> In the building industries of the 18th and 19th centuries, production would last for as long as it took for people to buy the land and pay for their homes to be built. The duration of this process was 14 years. This period was determined by the cost of borrowing money ... Harrison, p.87

The financial arithmetic in the house-building cycle, related to the long-term historical interest rate average of 5 per cent, seems to be dictating a 14-year construction cycle, divided into two distinct phases of about 7

3 Alan Rabinowitz, *The Real Estate Gamble*, p.179.
4 Data from Rabinowitz, Table 4, p.169.

years each – something worth watching for in future cycles. Harrison notes that the two 7-year phases match the average period that UK property owners at least live in their homes before selling and moving. The same can be said of Australia. It is also the time it takes in the UK to deliver new commercial property to market, from conception through to delivery.[5]

In the land market, it is worth noting that the time frame of land speculators fits into the 18-year real estate cycle scenario. The most exhaustive study ever conducted into the reasons for ownership of land on the urban fringe of American cities (some 700 owners of such land at the edge of six metropolitan areas were interviewed between 1977 and 1979) found that the change in ownership from farmer to investor/speculator to developer begins some 15 years before the land is put to urban use.[6] Similar time frames were found in a study of vacant sites in South Wales: '64 per cent of the sites were held idle for 15 years or over, with the most popular period of vacancy being 15 to 19 years.'[7]

Theoretically, there was no reason why more Terminating Societies could not have been started up smoothly once others had fulfilled their purpose. The building of the houses should rightly have been related to both the purchasing power of individuals and population growth. The reason this didn't (and still doesn't) happen is to do with the enclosure of the economic rent (the locational value the sellers of *The Big Issue* came to see so quickly) which is permitted to capitalise into a tradable privilege – and, worse still, commercial banks creating credit backed by this price. Where land is enclosed, the price of land and the creation of credit upon it will eventually far outstrip the ability of wage earners to pay for it. Hence we get the real estate cycle – the cyclical termination of building activity followed then by a disruptive land-price-led slump. About every 18 years so far, since the rental enclosures began after 1800.

5 Harrison, p.56.
6 H.J. Brown, R.S. Phillips and N.A. Roberts, *Land into Cities*, Lincoln Institute of Land Policy, Cambridge, Mass., 1980.
7 Harrison, p.67.

18

The Reliability of the Real Estate Cycle Repeating

Some Graphic Evidence

> ***By 2007, Britain and most of the other industrially advanced economies will be in the throes of frenzied activity in the land market to equal what happened in 1988/89. Land prices will be near their 18-year peak, driven by an exponential growth rate, on the verge of collapse …***
>
> Frederic J. Jones and Fred Harrison, *The Chaos Makers*, 1997

REAL ESTATE CYCLES have been with us for more than two hundred years now. They have repeated in times of inflation or deflation, whether the US economy was experiencing high interest rates or low, with trade barriers or with free trade, with government subsidies, high taxes, low taxes, or even no taxes at all. The only constant element in all the cycles has been a so-called 'collective land monopoly'.

The term 'collective land monopoly' refers to the capitalization of the rental value of land into a tradable commodity (the enclosure of the rent), the rights to which are bought and sold in a free market sanctioned (indeed authorised and protected) by government legislation. Whilst this factor remains unchanged, all the trade cycles, but especially the real estate cycle, must repeat. Only the timing remains in question.

We can place this into some degree of perspective, allowing us to believe that the current US real estate cycle will repeat, as have all others, by studying the evidence in Professor Frederic Jones's *The Chaos Makers: The Butterfly and the Cusp, A Study of Economic Catastrophes.* The book draws upon statistics from Chicago, Japan, Australia, the UK and Denmark, in different eras, to reveal how the capitalising of land rent fed the real estate cycle in each of these locations.

Chicago

THE CHART for the city of Chicago (Graph 18.1) is based on Professor Jones's figures[1] illustrating the economy of Chicago at the end of the 19th century, when it was still a frontier town free from any government regulation save protection of the property right itself. It measures the ratio between annual gross land values and contemporary trade figures, the trade figures in this instance being substituted for the Gross National Product (GNP) used in the other illustrations. (The phenomenal real estate booms and busts in the city of Chicago have been covered in Chapters 5 to 13.)

Graph 18.1: Chicago Land Value
as a % of total trade

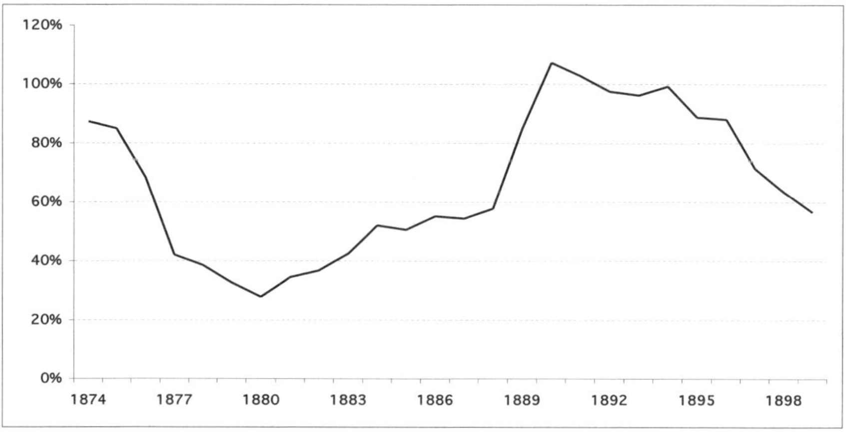

Most economic commentators cite political management of the economy as one of the prime reasons for the cycle, but the figures for Chicago reveal that there is more to it than that. Very little government management of the economy took place during the early growth of Chicago, yet the city saw some of the world's most intense real estate speculation.

As the Chicago figures highlight, and as noted by Professor Jones himself, 'recessions occur naturally in the capitalist system whether governmental steps are taken to prevent them or not.[2] He goes on to say that the swings highlighted by the figures

> appear to be in some way closely linked to the varying ratios that land values assume over GNP. In effect these ratios implicitly highlight the true periodic swings in trends of investment between land and the entrepreneurial spheres of any given economy.
>
> Jones, p.42

1 Table 1, p.72.
2 Jones, p.42.

We examine this measurement in more detail in Chapter 20 – it helps us to time the cycle.

Japan

COMPARE THE CHART of Chicago to Japan (Graph 18.2). Japan is an opposing case study, very different from that of free-trade Chicago.

> The Japanese data reflects a highly protectionist economy; but despite governmental intervention on a large scale in the post-war period, especially in the area of protective tariffs and public health directives levied against foreign goods, booms and slumps are still in evidence … This recent recession [of 1991] marks the really prolonged and damaging Japanese slump of the 1990s. It demonstrates that while protectionism can put off the evil day of collapse for a time, it cannot prevent it ultimately from taking a heavy toll …
>
> Jones, p.45

As the Japanese soon discovered, their land-price-induced slump went so far as to threaten the viability of the banking system itself, which 'had to be bailed out by the government because a dramatic fall in land values used as collateral for loans … undermined their reserves.[3]

Graph 18.2: Japan Land Value as a % of GNE

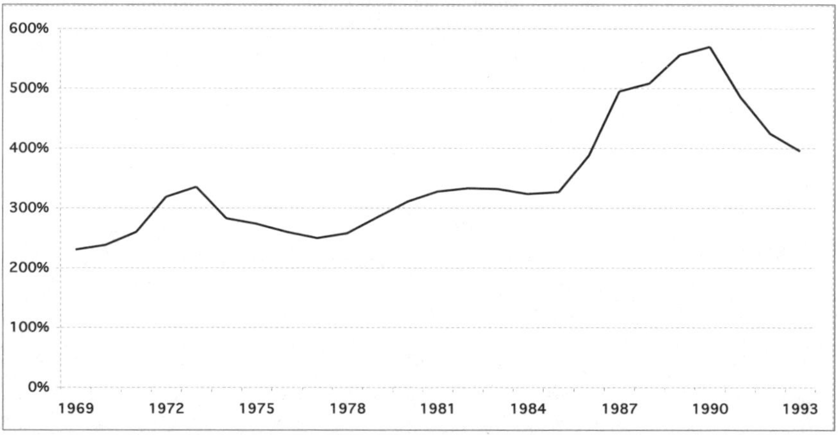

A not unfamiliar scenario, of course, and something playing out yet again in the US economy, exactly as it has in the past. The size of the credit problem in 2007, once again related to bank loans on land value, came as a big shock to regulators and the market in general. It is, however, history repeating.

3 Jones, p.46.

Australia

THE CHART of the Australian economy offers another perspective on the pattern of real estate boom and bust. This is, in part, a consequence of the Australian government's distinctive and unorthodox forms of land intervention from the 1970s onwards.

> The pattern appearing in statistics from Australia is perhaps exceptional for a western type of economy. Interventionist actions such as those, for instance, of the Melbourne authorities, who ran a state land-banking scheme with negative real interest rates and also imposed a steady reduction in the rate of taxation on land values, may partly be responsible for the unexpected support of land prices in that country during the mid seventies. The result was, as in the case of Japan, several [booms] followed by a somewhat precipitous decline. Once again [Australia's] figures reveal that persistent governmental or state attempts to manipulate the economy eventually failed to prevent the reappearance of a deep [slump] over the longer term, since the final slump figuring in the statistics is by any standards a sharp one. Such a dramatic downturn in the nineties appears to mark a process of normalisation, partly rectifying the cumulative imbalances of the interventionist periods of the past.
>
> Jones, p.84

The process of 'normalisation' will now take place in the US into 2010.

Graph 18.3: Australia Land Value as a % of GNP

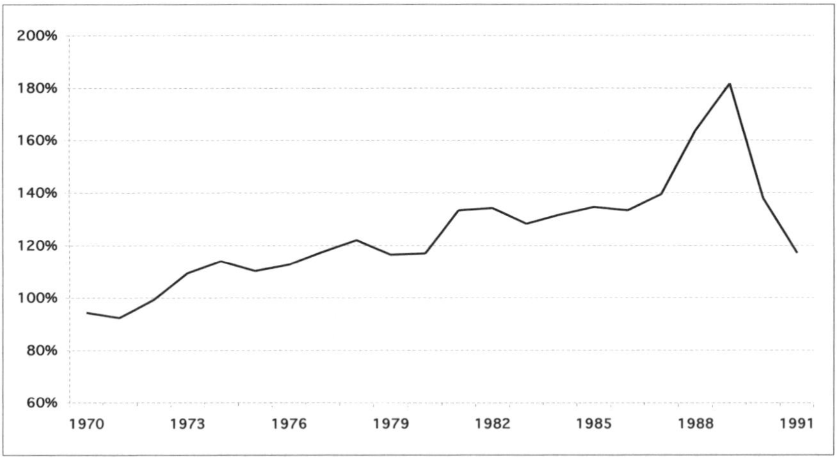

There is a warning in Australia's figures for all Western governments currently attempting to support property prices in the first decade of the 21st century. They will simply make the eventual slump, the final reckoning, worse and more prolonged. How deep it must be will depend upon how much speculation was permitted and how high land value gets as a percentage of the nation's GNP. Bank lending for real estate, and interest rates themselves, will also be factors. In Australia government support of land values is an endemic feature easily seen on Australia's stock market: a disproportionate number of the largest listed companies are banks, finance companies and gaming operators, all dependent upon government-granted licences and effectively non-producers that do not create any real wealth, merely acting to redistribute it. This is often the case in a resource-rich country. Massive government support for land price occurs in the US as well, and is a growing phenomenon worldwide.

The United Kingdom

THE UK IS NOT immune to the cycle of boom and bust; indeed, it is probably where the regular real estate cycle originated.

> The trends of the UK economy presented here can only be provisional … because British statistics do not separate land values from property values, except in the case of agriculture and – partly – in housing, and so the figures have had to be calculated by introducing a bold series of assumptions about the respective values of land and the buildings constructed on it. In this regard house prices have been regarded as representing within themselves a land component of about 30% and warehouses the same, factories and offices have both been rated at 40%, and shops on a significantly higher level of 60% … these are clearly by no means ideal assumptions …
>
> Jones, p.48

Graph 18.4: UK Land Value as a % of GNP

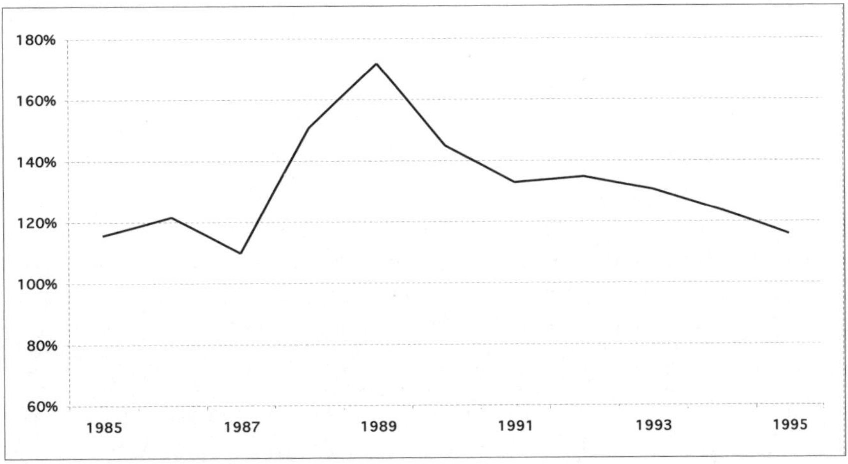

The same boom and bust cycle appears, however, as became obvious to UK investors in 2007. Back in 2002, when these charts were put together for subscriber use, it was noted that

> the real estate market in England, London especially, is once again heating up, so you know what that means; just add 18 years to 1991 for the next severe recession scenario, top of the boom, then bust.
>
> EIS note to subscribers, 2002

We cannot do a similar calculation for the US, as useful as this would be in providing an early warning signal of an overheating of the US real estate market, because no one bothers to collect land value statistics at a national level. The country measures everything else, just not the worth of its land.

Denmark

THE STATISTICS for Denmark are more moderate (Graph 18.5). Denmark has a history of levying taxes on land rents, which acts to moderate speculation – as the chart clearly shows. In the late 1950s the newly elected Danish government – the Justice Party – was actually elected to power on a platform of land taxes. Such taxes on rent were, however, not heavy enough to deter speculators.[4] Consequently, Denmark still reveals the roughly 18-year cycle of boom and bust.[5]

Graph 18.5: Denmark Land Value as a % of GNP

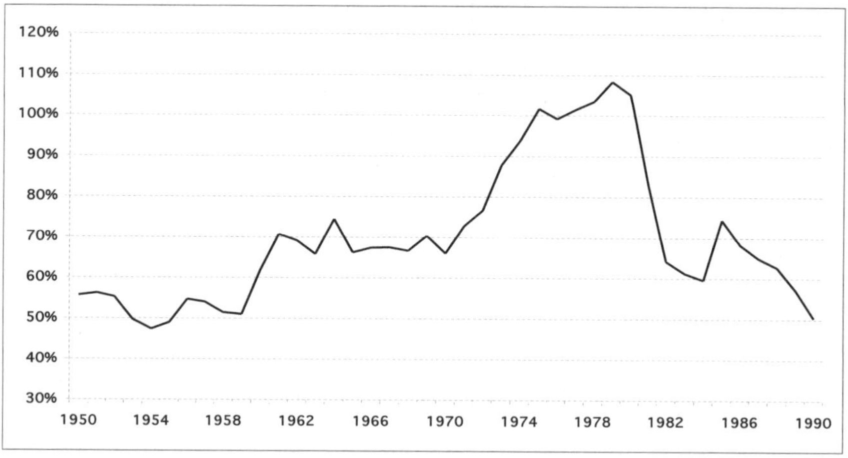

4 Evidence from surviving Justice Party followers, several of whom the author has had the great privilege of meeting, suggests that the levying of the land tax actually had the unforeseen effect of inducing such a swing away from land speculation, to other more productive enterprises and activities, that the rent of many sites went up (due to increased demand for use by the new entrepreneurs), meaning that land prices went up too, despite the land tax. This was confusing to voters, many of whom had been told that land taxes would bring land prices down to more affordable levels. It shows what could be achieved if land rents were not permitted to capitalise in the first place but were collected on behalf of all citizens. (It reveals, too, just how underutilised many sites are.) The Justice Party was soundly defeated by conservative interests at the next election and the land tax laws were immediately repealed.

5 Interesting, too, that Denmark saw a land boom, then a peak, 18 years after the events of 1960 and the repeal of the land tax laws.

WHAT WE HAVE seen in this chapter is five very different economies, in varying periods of history, all of which allowed the capitalisation of land rent into a tradable commodity. In each case the result was a real estate boom followed by a significant economic contraction. We can feel confident that the property cycle is with us still because the underlying cause for it has not changed. Government intervention in the markets does not create, and cannot suppress, the real estate cycle.

It is likely, as more countries join the land monopoly way of life (Russia, China, India …), that the cycle can only strengthen and synchronise. The destabilising influence of bank-created credit used for land speculation was again highlighted in the South East Asian land-price-led downturn that began in 1996 and crystallised with a currency run in Thailand in July 1997. This, and its effects on the United States, was discussed in Chapter 14.

Is it clear therefore

> … that an identical underlying process of instability is as detectable in the highly protected market of Japan as in the more laissez-faire markets of Europe, and even in the apparent middle course adopted by Australia. Most significantly of all, slumps were present in the almost totally free-trade economy of Chicago in the [19th] century … Jones, p.48

This is as the charts have revealed. The seemingly mysterious shrinkage of consumer demand at the end of each real estate boom – something no economist or academic has ever been able to explain satisfactorily – is nothing more than the result of a switch in economic behaviour away from productive investment activity and into speculation in land values. Of course this is not how the rest of the world describes it: these days it is referred to as 'housing' or 'commercial investment' activity. In reality it is an increased money supply (credit from a bank) chasing rising land prices.

As the 'investment boom' continues into the final years of the cycle, reserve bankers the world over start to fret about inflation; governments of all persuasions voice concerns about a 'wages breakout'. Readers will know better now. Land price is the thing to keep one's eye on. This can be seen in the chart of house, land price, earnings and building costs for the UK from 1983 to 2006 (Graph 18.6 on the next page). As US land price figures are not available, we are forced to use a proxy. To see the huge uptrend in UK earnings, a magnifying glass would be helpful. We can be certain US figures would show something similar.

It is, as Professor Jones points out:

> The ensuing relatively uncontrollable series of fluctuations is … halted momentarily at the bottom of slumps, [only] after the speculative land bubble bursts and lower land prices allow the weight of investment capital to move away from speculation in real estate and return to the financing of

> profitable investment projects. It is highly significant in this regard that land values always rise disproportionately at the height of booms and only fall sharply just before the upturn in the cycle. Jones, p.40

This is an important clue as to how to use the real estate cycle for our financial benefit. Buy at the end of a slump, sell into the peak some 14 years later.

Graph 18.6: House Price, Land Price, Earnings and Building Costs UK, 1983-2006

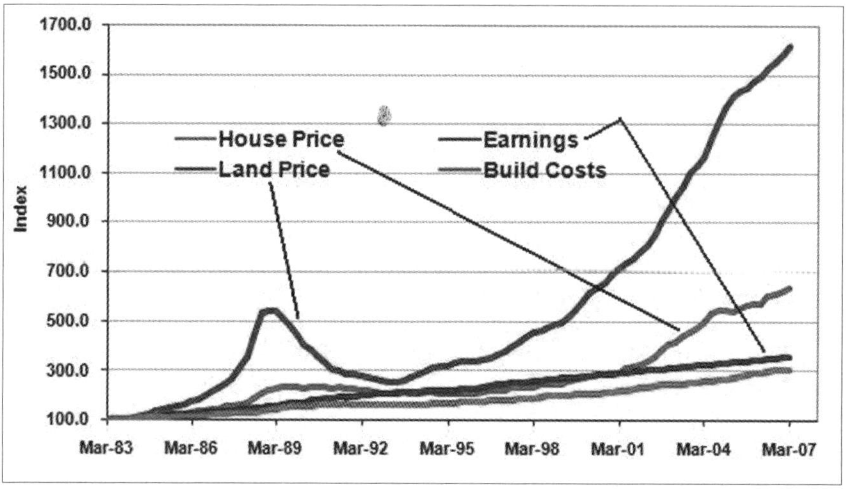

FURTHER READING

Harrison, Fred. *The Power in the Land.* Shepheard-Walwyn, 1983.

Jones, Frederic J. and Fred Harrison. *The Chaos Makers: The Butterfly and the Cusp, A Study of Economic Catastrophes*, Othila Press Ltd, 1997.

19

What Time Is It?

The Cyclical Turning Points

Here is the moral of all human tales,
'Tis but the same rehearsal of the past;
First freedom and then glory; when that fails,
Wealth, vice, corruption, barbarism at last,
And history, with all her volumes vast,
Hath but one page. Byron, *Childe Harold*

IN THIS CHAPTER we analyse the real estate cycle from three different perspectives: a theoretical overview of the cycle is presented first, then some historical data to help guide us through the actual events of past cycles (so we might learn to foresee more easily the next one), and finally something visual in the shape of a 18-year real estate clock that was put together for subscriber use a few years ago. (It has tracked the current 2010 cycle very well.)

A theoretical overview

IF, IN ANY economy, the value of government-granted licences and privileges (especially land) are permitted by law to capitalise into tradable commodities, then the flow of events within the economy will become inevitable. Such events will follow each other in a cyclical way and repeat generally, as follows.

At the bottom of the cycle, cheaper land and lower interest rates will allow production to expand, particularly after business confidence begins to return. Demand for land will increase as a result of the expansion in economic activity. Land, however, is in fixed supply. If we were to consider it a commodity (which it is not) it would be the only commodity the supply of which cannot be increased to match increasing demand. Land prices will rise. A price rise of any other commodity would eventually attract more supply, ultimately lowering prices. Not so with land. As land prices rise, owners will hold out for yet further price rises. The higher the price, the more it is hoarded.

Demand for land increases. Being fixed in supply, prices rise, and land becomes 'scarcer'. A more noticeable shift in investment activity will begin, away from industry and commerce and into land speculation. (More visibly in what is built on the land, though in reality it is the land price which is increasing, not the value of the buildings.) Interest rates will have bottomed out; then they start rising. The percentage rises are more important than the actual figures themselves. Wider forces such as the Kondratieff Wave,[1] and lower forces like the decade cycle play a part here; so too the banks and their fractional reserve system of credit creation.

Higher rent charges, and the increased cost of borrowing for working or investment capital, begin to squeeze the productive sectors of the economy. Higher returns in the property sector are seen by all now. Speculation will intensify. A mid-cycle slowdown is likely at this point – the decade cycle in operation. Do not confuse this with the longer and more deadly real estate cycle. Bank collapses involving real estate lending are usually not involved at this point, though the stock market may see reversals, especially if businesses have been built on other natural resources involving the issue of a government-granted licence.

The one area where business can cut costs is wages. Pressure builds to exercise wage restraint, most noticeably in the second half of the cycle. Governments agree, supported as they are by vested interest groups and the owners of the government-granted licences. Unions, seeing nothing but escalating living costs, push for wage increases to cover them. At this point it is easy to confuse the symptoms of the economic illness – higher interest rates, increasing unemployment, government intervention etc – with the cause, which they are not. The real cause is the speculation that takes place in a price that is not produced – land value.

It is very important to note that the land market is not subject to economic competition, as is the entrepreneur. Therefore the normal pricing signals won't act to make real estate speculators see their excesses. Property owners simply continue to press for ever higher rents from their tenants.

The point will arrive when the productive sectors of the economy can no longer afford the rent. A downturn is then imminent and inevitable. Its severity will be determined not only by the height and intensity of the boom, but also by the extent to which banks have become involved in lending upon land value. A bank collapse will usually mark the turn of the

1 Named after Nikolai Kondratieff (1892-1938?), a Russian economist working for the Agricultural Academy and Business Research Institute in Moscow, who undertook empirical analysis of wholesale commodity prices and production data for coal, pig iron, lead and other commodities. His research appeared to indicate the existence of 50 to 60 year cycles of crisis, recovery, prosperity and then stagnation in capitalist economies. His thesis, however, was deemed by his communist superiors to be 'potentially subversive' since he said that capitalism seemed to have some sort of self-correcting mechanism to push itself out of each long-wave crisis. Kondratieff was sent to a Siberian labour camp, where he is reported to have died in solitary confinement. His thesis, *The Long Wave in Economic Life*, was posthumously translated into English in the 1930s and unleashed an intense debate, which is ongoing. More information can be found on the EIS website.

cycle. Other events, however, like the oil crisis of 1974, almost always take place simultaneously – since economic activity is frenetic at the peak – to disguise the turn. Nevertheless, it soon becomes obvious to all that a downturn is taking place, for which absolutely everything else will take the blame except the real culprit, the privatisation of the rent.

This movement of capital back and forth between the productive and speculative sectors of the economy is best illustrated by the ratio of land values to GDP – the EIS land price barometer, highlighted in the next chapter.

The real estate cycle as applied to the United States has measured on average 18 to 20 years, trough to trough, since 1800. Only two world wars have been strong enough to distort this rhythm.

The flow of the cycle

TAKING THE BOTTOM of our cycle as the beginning, the trough of the average 18-year cycle will bottom out as credit conditions ease. The first to trough will be the stock market; once it does so, it will quickly price in the assured easier credit conditions to follow.

This can be picked up early in the stock market when continued bad economic news brings higher lows in the market, not lower lows. (See, for example, Graph 4.3, page 89, for the 1842 lows, Graph 6.1, page 108, further illustrating the 1842 lows and then the higher lows of the early 1860s after the 1857 panic, Graph 8.2, page 168, and Graph 9.3, page 192). Stock market recovery has been quicker these days than several cycles ago as Reserve Banks worldwide have found alternative strategies to ensure formerly mortgaged and foreclosed real estate does not flood the market all at once; they are also far quicker to instigate reflation strategies such as emergency interest rate cuts.[2]

Available credit is the key. To understand the economy, it is usually suggested that one should follow the money, but why does the money flow where it flows? It follows the rent mostly, the biggest gain for the least amount of effort. The slope of the yield curve helps identify the improving economic conditions; at an economic trough the curve will be normal, but steeply sloped.

Residential real estate will recover first from the downturn. This is not something that occurred only in this current cycle, after 1991. Roy Wenzlick had already noted the phenomenon in 1947:

> Historically, office building construction has always taken place toward the tail end of the big real estate booms of the past. In the first part of a real estate boom the great activity is always in residential properties. Only after the boom has continued over a period of years do space stringencies develop

2 A much more in-depth analysis of this phenomenon was done for subscribers some years ago and is worth a review. The analysis can be found here: www.businesscycles.biz/subscriber/theflow.htm

> in the office building field, with rapidly rising rents. Even then leases delay the rise. By the time that net income becomes high in relationship to construction costs, the boom is near its end.
>
> *The Real Estate Analyst*, Vol. XVI, No. 53, November 29, 1947, p.443

Real estate cycles since then have unfolded in exactly the manner Wenzlick describes. Residential prices recover first, then commercial prices.

A feature of the recovery process in the past was the US federal government's finding new ways to give away its acquired lands. After land became fully enclosed, banks developed ways to offload the risk and pass on their foreclosed real estate without greatly depressing prices.

Four or five years in, nervous recovery gives way to confidence among buyers. Soon a boom is back. By this time banks are aggressively seeking borrowers with whom to do business. Credit growth surges.

Economist Milton Friedman made a study of money and credit, publishing the details in *A Monetary History of the United States, 1867-1960*.[3] The way Friedman chose to break up his credit history into phases is interesting: 1867-1879, 1879-1897, 1897-1914 and 1914-1933. The dates should be familiar. Friedman's data clearly shows the growth and then contraction of credit over the life of the real estate cycle. Credit growth has proceeded in waves.

Eight to ten years in, a mid-cycle slowdown develops. It does not involve real estate, so land prices usually continue to rise – especially these days when interest rates are lowered as a deliberate strategy to foster growth at any price.

After that the public will turn en masse to investing in real estate. It never goes down, they will be told. Stories will surface of the huge returns some investors have made, attracting even more opportunists. In the past this has been described as 'greengrocers and servant girls' taking to land speculation; by 1929 the expression was 'bootblacks and waiters', in the late 1980s 'house painters and office girls'. Perhaps next time we should watch for professional athletes and actors expressing their 'faith' in the market and offering all manner of advice.

Eleven to twelve years in, competition to erect 'tallest' buildings starts in earnest, a sure sign that credit is easy to get: commercial skyscrapers are mostly built with other people's money. Site owners start to complain that their property tax bills are 'destroying' business. Ostentatious displays of wealth are lauded. Everyone aspires to being one of the nouveau riche. Travel programmes and real estate shows will have long since replaced the sit-coms that dominated the airwaves when economic times were at their most severe.

The illusion of wealth is all-pervasive – reinforced as the US stock market crosses the old highs of the previous decade cycle. In all past 18-year real estate cycles for which there is data, the stock market has

3 His charts can be seeen at www.businesscycles.biz/subscriber/theflow.htm

done this – taken out the tops made in the prior decade before the mid-cycle slowdown. It happened again in 2006 (take another look at the stock market charts). Below the surface, however, the economy will be under increasing stress, built as it is upon credit. A bank's profit is geared to its lending, so a bank will always seek to be 'fully loaned-up', as Murray Rothbard pointed out, 'to expand as much as is legally possible up to the limits imposed by the legal reserve ratio.'[4]

Until, that is, a banker's fear overtakes his greed.

Into the very final years of the cycle, the point at which things will most likely appear rosiest (watch for authorities congratulating themselves on how well they are 'managing' things), an event will take place to raise doubts in the minds of investors. The event may be trivial, it may or may not be credit-related, but it is enough to prompt a few people to cash in. Then another event will create a real crisis in confidence. This time it will need to be of a financial nature. It takes everybody by surprise because it shows the economy for what it is: heavily mired in debt. The rush for liquidity will not be far behind.

Significantly, land price must also have climbed high enough to threaten the banking sector's loan book built upon this value. For the real estate cycle, land price is the indicator to watch, bearing in mind that ***the peak in land values is reached 12 to 24 – even perhaps as long as 36 – months before a recession.*** This history teaches us.

The crisis at the end *always* comes in an environment of rising interest rates. This can be seen in Graph 6.2, page 109, for the 1857 cycle (the data is scarcer the further back one looks), Graph 8.2, page 168, for the 1873 cycle, Graph 9.5, page 194, for the 1893 cycle, and in Graph 10.1, page 199. Graph 20.4, page 372, reveals what happened since 1950.

Businesses that expanded exponentially on debt will be the first to fail. The banks most exposed to real estate are the first to reveal 'problem' loans. In this regard the Fed is part of the problem, not the solution. In 1974, for example, the Fed actively encouraged banks to expand their international lending activities (the Franklin bank trauma); in the 1980s action by Fed President Volcker worsened the problem of the thrifts. The thing to watch in a bank, going into the end of the real estate cycle, is a heavy reliance on short-term borrowings to finance long-term loans, a situation that can persist only whilst land prices are going up.

There have always in the past been tell-tale signs, going into the peak, that the economy was experiencing credit stress. Easy to see in hindsight, but let us see if history gives us some clues about what to look for at this most important time in the cycle. Below are listed events in each cycle that revealed the stresses. Because of the lack of understanding of economics today, these events are usually cited as the cause of the following downturn, but if you have studied the works of David Ricardo, Henry

4 *A History of Money and Banking in the United States: The Colonial Era to World War II*, p.143.

George or Ludwig von Mises you will know this is not actually correct. Such events only bring a downturn because so much credit was created in the first place to finance the purchase of government-granted licences, the largest of which is land value. The banking system is the linchpin. Money will become tighter in the final years of the cycle. The credit tightening is most dangerous when asset prices have been permitted to rise to unaffordable levels.

The collapse of a financial institution takes on extreme importance if (1) we are approaching the end years of the cycle, and (2) extensive credit growth has financed a large rise in asset prices, especially land value.

1991 downturn
December 1988. The Savings and Loans banking crisis. A whole series of increasingly serious banking failures were brought into full view after the government could no longer suppress the information following the 1988 elections. Land prices had been rocketing in the years prior to this. Lending to the real estate sector stalled in 1988.

1974 downturn
October 1973. The collapse of US National Bank of San Diego, the largest bank failure in forty years. The bank was owned by C. Arnholt Smith, Richard Nixon's chief campaign organiser, fundraiser and close friend, a very large real estate speculator in Southern California. Land prices had seen a sustained increase in the very early 1970s.

1955
There was no cycle to speak of, the economy being war affected. There had been no real land price gains; the Great Depression and the war were still very much in the minds of most people.

1932 downturn
November 1930. The collapse of the banking empire of Rogers Caldwell, heavily invested in real estate. Only after this banking failure did the downturn, and subsequent depression, begin. In October 1930 the stock market had broken below its 1929 crash low (a mid-point of the 1920s run-up) and it was realised that further bad news was on its way. The 1930s US depression was brought on by collapsing real estate values (after sustained increases throughout the 1920s), placing great stress on the banking system that the Fed did little to alleviate. The Great Depression was *not* caused by the stock market collapse. Real estate had seen wild speculation until 1926/7, after which prices had stopped rising.

1914
The downturn was cut short by the First World War. There had been little land speculation in the lead-up to these years, at least not in the manner of previous cycles, though land prices did rise steadily. Ironically, the

world's new tallest building, the Woolworth building, (opened in 1911), was built solely with cash and occupied by its owner.

1893 downturn

November 20, 1890. The collapse of Barings Bank, the Queen's own banker, in London. Two weeks before, on November 7, the Bank of England had lifted its discount rate from 5 to 6 per cent. In the US Decker, Howell and Company failed on November 11 after sharp declines in the stock market, though markets had already been declining for most of the year. The Decker failure also involved the Bank of North America. US markets recovered from this shock after good grain harvests in 1891 (a buoyancy in which the rest of the world did not participate). Credit difficulties were obvious by February 20, 1893, however, when the Philadelphia and Reading Railroad company collapsed after struggling to meet its bond payments. The US market went on to panic on May 4, 1893, exactly 180 weeks from the 1890 events. There had been substantial land speculation in the lead-up to these events.

1873 downturn

September 8-17, 1873. Data gets harder to find, even harder to analyse, the further back we look. It is clear that railroad companies were struggling in the lead-up to this month, though this may not have been obvious to an outside observer. The market – or at least the weight of general opinion expressed in the index price – knew, however: the rails index had been slowly declining since its peak in May 1871. There had been substantial land speculation prior to all these events, especially through listed railroad companies.

1857 downturn

August 24, 1857. The failure of the Ohio Life Insurance and Trust Company (a bank), a Cincinnati operation with its New York office one of the most respected banks in that city. There was a panic in October. Massive land speculation resulting from easy credit policies had occurred after 1852.

1837 downturn

July 11, 1836. President Jackson's infamous specie circular enforced payment for federal lands in silver or gold only (bank notes had up until that time been acceptable). The circular coincided with the failure of several banks in London. Substantial land speculation had been taking place using the easy credit (bank-note issue) provided by the growing number of banks in the new territories. There was panic in May 1837.

1819 downturn

Prior to the 1819 panic, a premium for specie had emerged, and in March 1818 for Spanish dollars in particular – the major circulating medium of the time.[5] This indicated that public confidence in bank notes was deteriorating. In December 1818 and January 1819 the price of cotton halved, eventually flowing through to the land used to grow the crop – a price upon which banks had been happily creating prodigious quantities of credit. Banks started collapsing as a result.

Into 2010

As we progress well into the first decade of the 21st century, land prices (or, as experienced by most individuals, house prices) have been skyrocketing. And the banks have been throwing credit at us. Stock markets are hitting new highs worldwide on the back of feverish merger and acquisition activity financed by credit and margin loans. Interest rates are no longer at historically low levels and have been rising. Federal Reserve bankers are worried about the threat of inflation. The last years of the 18-year cycle are approaching. Sound familiar? Significantly land price is at a level from which it could easily collapse if confidence is shattered by events.

In the lead-up to the final few years of every cycle one should observe which credit-creation institutions are significantly increasing their risk profile and exposure to real estate lending. The bankers' own bank, the Bank for International Settlements (BIS), itself noted in its study of banking failures:

> … the widespread banking crises that involved credit risk were remarkably similar. A period of financial deregulation resulted in rapid growth in lending, particularly in real estate related lending, rapidly rising real estate prices encourage more lending, abetted by lax regulatory systems in many cases. When economic recessions occurred, inflated real estate prices collapsed, leading directly to the failures. *Bank Failures in Mature Economies*, BIS, 2004

The end to the current cycle, whenever it comes, will not be different from last time.

At the real estate cycle peak, as almost always in the past, the US administration is preoccupied with other issues. This tends to focus the public mind on those issues so that it misses the subtle signs of impending trouble. It really has all been said before:

> Every great crisis reveals the excessive speculations of many houses which no one before suspected. Walter Bagehot explaining banking in the early 1800s

> At any time there exists an inventory of undiscovered embezzlement in – or more precisely not in – the country's businesses and banks. This inventory – it should perhaps be called the bezzle – amounts at any moment to many millions of dollars. John Kenneth Galbraith, *The Great Crash of 1929*

It was the lowering of interest rates that brought on the credit growth and rise in asset speculation; it is the inevitable rise in interest rates that

5 Murray N. Rothbard, *Panic of 1819*, p.11.

will put the entire system into stress. The inevitable land price collapse will complete the job and wipe out those at the end most highly leveraged.

As investors it is crucial for us to understand that there is absolutely nothing the Fed or any government can do to stop this process if the economic rent is permitted to capitalise into a tradable privilege. Under such a system all the players are endogenous to the system; none can act outside it.

Clock time

WHAT FOOLS everyone is the difference between the usual credit-related 'investment' or decade cycle, which runs about 8 to 11 years, and the longer 18-year land-price-led cycle. To see the difference, a better clock was needed. Most investors are familiar with the investment cycle, pictured here (Figure 19.1). It was first published in the London *Evening Standard* in 1937, and was apparently based on a study of trade cycles going back a century or more.[6]

The 18-year real estate clock, Figure 19.2, page 360, removes the confusion between cycles. The cycle from 1991 progressed as predicted: the clock proved a reliable guide as the cycle unfolded. As you study the clock, a few notes will prove beneficial.

Figure 19.1: The Decade Clock

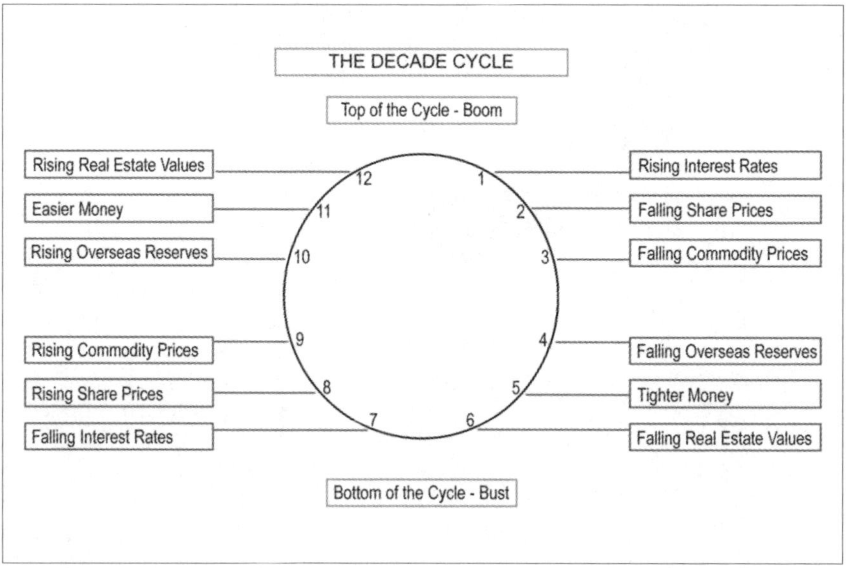

6 The EIS website describes the hours of the investment clock in much greater detail: www.businesscycles.biz/business.htm

Figure 19.2: The 18-Year Real Estate Clock

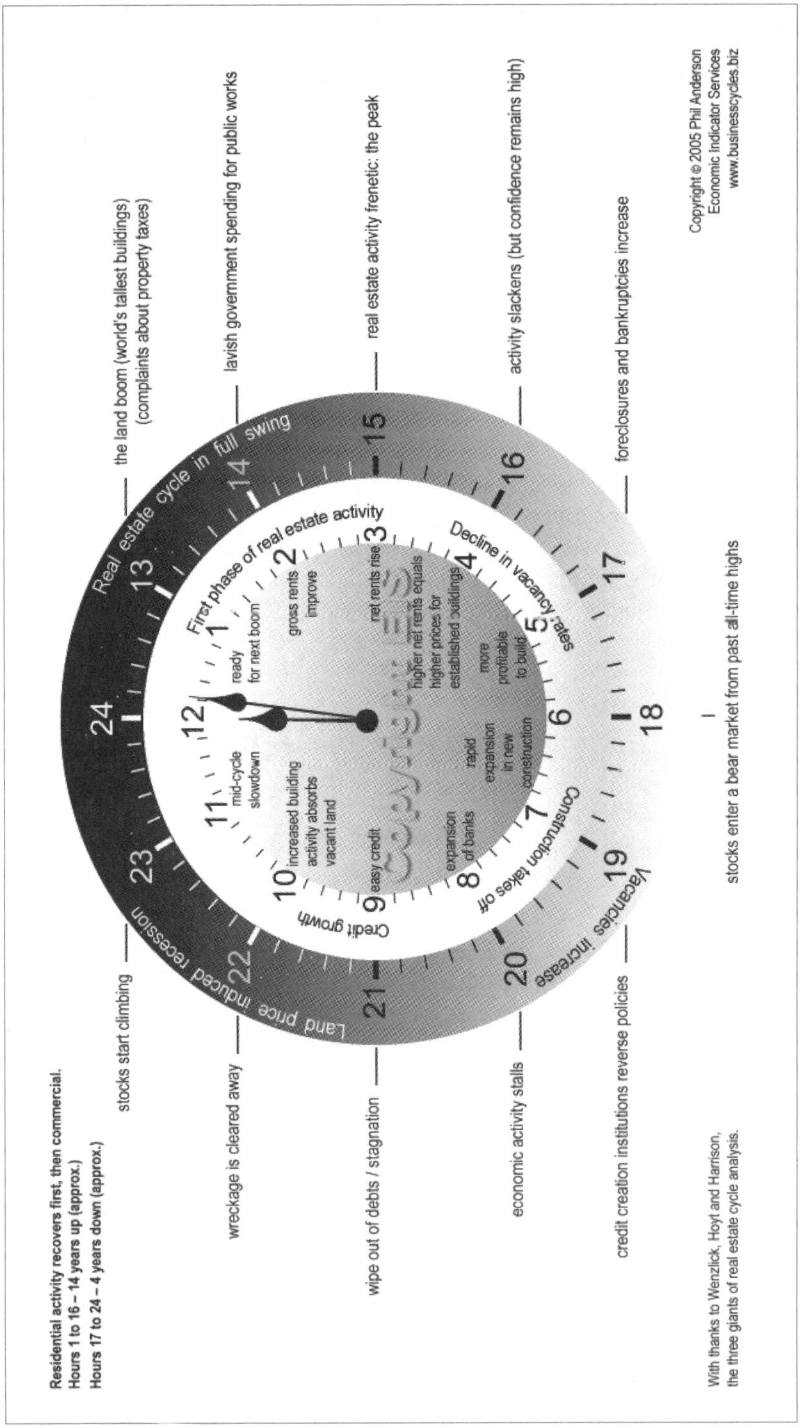

- The cycle is a long one and much happens in between. Most people will not be able to apply what they have learned from one cycle to corresponding conditions in the next. An investor's own experience must be supplemented with historical knowledge.
- The clock is a working guide and should not be taken too literally. The stages described at each o'clock can and do merge into one another, or can take place simultaneously. Common sense must be applied.
- Real estate is not like other commodities: demand and supply laws do not apply in the same way. A shortage of housing in one city cannot be filled from an over-supply in another. New houses would have to be built. Local influences apply as real estate is fixed in location.
- If the final extreme stages of the cycle can be identified, it is then wise to do the opposite of the crowd; the herd is always wrong at these extremes. You can be sure that at the peak, 15.00 hours, the public will long ago have stopped buying on the basis of earnings and yield (if they ever knew how to do that in the first place) and be buying only to 'flip' the property for a quick sale. Few get out before the end with all their profits intact. Likewise at the low, at 23.00, few have the cash resources left to take advantage of all the bargains on offer.

The movement of property over the course of the cycle would seem to be erratic – random even. Keep the 18-year clock handy as the next cycle unfolds; it will prove to you this is not the case. As prosperity returns after the slump, brought about perhaps by increasing population or, more likely, improved production techniques and technological innovation which lower costs, vacancies will decline. As they do, rents will increase. A rental increase implies an increase in capital value. This will invite building activity, lifting prosperity, and the new boom will begin to feed off its own activity. Take the time to ride the cycle and it will bring real estate riches to you for little effort. Run counter-clockwise to this cycle and you will lose your investment shirt.

20
Help with Telling the Time

Some Indicators:

- **The land price barometer**
- **The Cantillon Effect**
- **The price of copper**
- **The yield curve**

> ***... since land values tend to follow a major rise of building activity, they contribute to the profitability of building transactions and thus become a cumulative factor in such a boom. Excessive land values, reached after the boom has continued for some time, are eventually found to have no counterpart in increased earnings, and therefore contribute to the break of the building boom; and since land prices are slow to move downward, they tend to increase the severity of the decline in building activity.***
>
> William H. Newman, 'The Building Industry and Building Cycles', *Studies in Business Administration*, Vol. V, No. 4, The School of Business, University of Chicago, July 1935

THIS CHAPTER is concerned with finding ways to forecast the 18-year real estate cycle, and a more scientific way of knowing where we are in the cycle. In this chapter we are not concerned with short-term monthly or even half-yearly movements of the economy, we want to know what can guide us through the 18 years or so from trough to trough. Are there useful and reliable indicators as we progress through the cycle?

The land price barometer

LAND PRICE is a function of its rent, capitalised at the prevailing interest rate. Other things being equal, land price averages 14 to 17 times its annual rental value. But, as we know, things are rarely equal.

Land has a peculiar trait: it has no cost of production. Its value comes from the presence and activity of the community, which will manifest as a locational value: the price. If an area becomes popular the land price will rise without the owner of the site needing to exert any personal effort to make it happen.[1]

Rent is a naturally occurring value that will arise, indeed must arise, wherever community exists. This was highlighted in Chapter 16, where we rediscovered Ricardo's Law of Rent, a law largely overlooked these days but knowledge of which will prove immensely useful to investors in the next cycle.

The land price barometer is designed to compare a nation's land price to its Gross Domestic Product. This helps identify where a nation's investment is going – either

- into land price, a non-produced item, or
- into goods and services, a far more productive use of limited resources.

The US neglects to calculate its land value, so for the sake of this exercise the nation of Australia is used as a proxy. The economic link between the US and Australia is well accepted (some Australians would argue that Australia has been the 51st State of the Union for years), and since 1893 at least Australia's boom-bust scenario has mirrored that of the US. Australia is one of only very few nations that keeps track of the value of its land resource, data for which we have managed to source back to 1911.

Graph 20.1: Land Price Barometer, Australia
land price/GDP

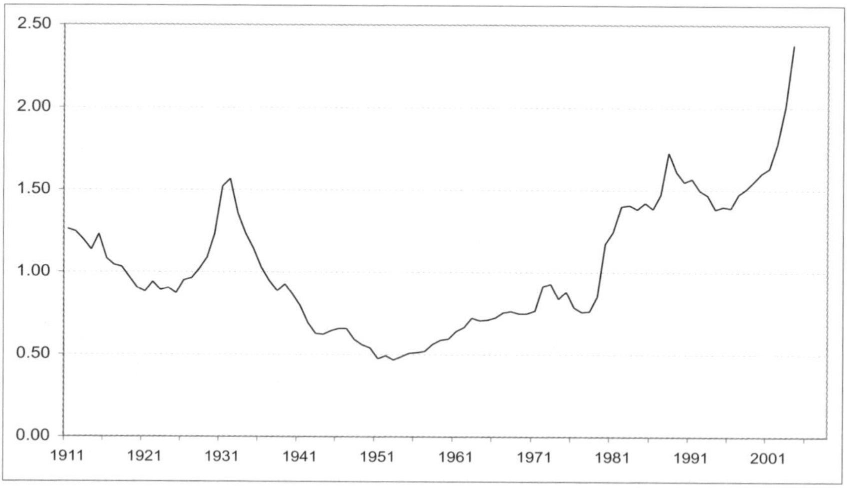

Source: Economic Indicator Services. (Assistance from the Land Values Research Group gratefully acknowledged.)

1 Large rises in house prices are celebrated within the community as a good thing. The price of the building does not rise substantially: it is the locational value – the land price – that brings about the increase. An unsustainable rise in locational value does not just signal a recession ahead, *it is actually the cause*. The celebration of large rises in land value by politicians and the public is misguided. Unless you happen to own this increase in value.

The land price barometer for Australia (land price divided by GDP) is shown as Graph 20.1.

A strong rise in the barometer is a clear signal of too much land speculation. Such events have in the past always been followed by a decline in economic activity, then recession. Changes in the indicator can therefore be a useful guide to the possibilities of recession in the years ahead.

It should be noted that it is not the recession that damages an economy; the damage arises from the precursor: an unsustainable rise in land price. In every past Australian cycle, the strongest rise in land price has taken place towards the end of the 18-year real estate cycle. Our research into US cycles found the same, especially in Chicago. The current cycle into 2010 is not proving an exception. The higher the intensity of land speculation, the greater the eventual bust.

Tall buildings and what they indicate: the Cantillon Effect

> Not everything longer than it is wide is a phallic symbol.
>
> Sigmund Freud, talking this time about his cigar

IN THE VERY early 1800s, a Manhattan carpenter named Lozier came to the startling conclusion that the city in which he lived was dangerously lopsided, having too many buildings on its lower end. If any more went up, he warned, the island would sink into the Hudson River. To head off this calamity, Lozier suggested to the city's mayor that a chunk of Manhattan's northern end be hacked off, towed down the Hudson and attached to the southern tip. This would redistribute the island's weight.[2] Impressed with Lozier's ingenuity, the mayor commissioned him to commence work at once, handing over wads of cash from the City Treasury.

To help him with his plan Lozier advertised for workers. More than five hundred showed up, braving the winter cold to wait for the boss.

But, as you may have guessed, our carpenter boss was long gone, taking with him the city's money.

Over the years New York City has had its fair share of real estate swindles. Another one was suspected when a fifty-metre-high 'superstructure' was started on a six-and-a-half-metre plot of Broadway land in the spring of 1887. The owner, a Manhattan realtor named John L. Stearns, actually owned the neighbouring plot as well, off lower Broadway in New Street. The front plot, facing Broadway, had become so hemmed in that Stearns had found it unsaleable except at a give-away price.

2 The question visitors to the Empire State Building (dubbed the Empty State Building after the Great Depression because it was vacant above the 60th floor) ask most often is whether the weight of the building (over 360,000 tons) is forcing Manhattan to sink lower into the water. Another oft-asked question is whether it could blow over! The Empire State sways little more than an inch at the top in gale-force winds. The building also survived an Army B-25 plane accidentally crashing into the 78th and 79th floors, killing 13 and injuring 26.

Frustrated, he approached Bradford Lee Gilbert, a nearby architect, for a way out. The solution, Bradford recalled in his reminiscences, was to build an iron bridge truss, and stand it on its end – a solution that took him a full six months to conceive and design, he said later. The real structure of the building would start several stories above the curb, and the height would maximise occupancy and rentals.

Satisfied as to the design's safety, and once negotiations with the New York Building Department had been completed (the structure was so different, no law was present on the books under which the department could approve its commencement), Gilbert was ready to begin building. New Yorkers were aghast at the notion that a building in the city would tower above their sidewalk to a height of 160 feet. Newspapers ridiculed the proposed structure as 'idiotic'; fellow architects pronounced it unsafe; building experts said it would blow over in the wind. A fellow engineer and friend begged Gilbert to abandon the idea, pointing out that if the building really did fall over his legal bill would ruin him. Lawyers confirmed the likelihood.

Stearns himself began to have second thoughts. Gilbert knew better. He pointed out that the way the building was structured, with wind bracings from top to bottom, the harder the wind blew, the safer the building would be. It was a scientific certainty. To put the matter to rest Gilbert requested the top two floors for his own offices.

Building began, attracting crowds of onlookers. On one particular Sunday, when the wind was really howling, Gilbert went to inspect his project. A huge crowd had gathered in anticipation of the inevitable collapse. Gilbert asked the foreman for a plumb line and began ascending one of the ladders.

> When Gilbert reached the thirteenth story, the wind was blowing so fiercely he was unable to stand upright. He got on his knees and began to crawl along the scaffolding. He dropped the plumb line, lowering it to the ground. There wasn't the slightest vibration; the building stood steady as a rock. Exhilarated, Gilbert straightened up, waving exultantly to the crowd.
>
> Dana L. Thomas. *Lords of the Land*, p.250

Suddenly a gust of wind caught him and carried him right out towards the end of the scaffolding. 'It is in emergencies like this that a man prays, if he ever prays,' Gilbert recalled afterwards. As he hurtled towards the end of the platform, a rope swinging in the wind from an upright beam of the tower swept within his reach. Gilbert grabbed it firmly, went down on his knees and crawled slowly back to the ladder …

The world's first skyscraper, built of skeletal steel, was born. So ingenious was the design, utilising a small space of land as never before, that it brought the owner of the building $90,000 a year more in rentals than would otherwise have been possible. A mania for tall buildings quickly developed, a phenomenon that continues to this day.

This phenomenon may be called the Cantillon Effect. Richard Cantillon (1680-1734), an Irish banker, was the first economist to suggest that a change in the supply of money and credit will affect the economy by changing prices. Cantillon recognised that an increase in the availability of credit will result in economic expansion, but that ultimately this will be overdone as prices rise and imports increase. His work pre-dates that of Adam Smith and is just as important, if not more so.

The world's tallest buildings have a consistent habit of being completed right at the top of the real estate cycle (since Gilbert's first tower, there has not been an exception), producing for us – at least so far – *the* most reliable indicator of an approaching peak.

Completion of the world's tallest buildings

Year completed	Name of building
1830s	Astor House, New York
1850s	Produce Exchange, Studio Building, New York
Early 1870s	Haight House, Stuyvesant Apartments, New York Drexel Building, Block Apartments, New York
Early 1890s	Masonic Temple, Chicago Manhattan Building, Marquette, Chicago Old Waldorf, Cable Building, Downing Building, New York
1907/8	Singer Building
1909	Metropolitan Life
1910	Hearst Building, Chicago
1913	Woolworth Building
1929	40 Wall Street (Bank of Manhattan Building) New Waldorf Astoria
1930	Chrysler Building
1931	Empire State Building
1972/3	World Trade Centre
1974	Sears Tower, Chicago
1989	Zarro's Arrow 445 metre tower planned by Gold Coast (Australia) developer Pat Zarro, unveiled in the late 1980s but never built – developer went bust) John Minuzzo's 107-story Tower, Brisbane, Australia (never built – developer went bust) (Both were designed as taller than Sears Tower)
1997	Petronas Tower, Malaysia
Into 2010	Herron Tower, Bishopsgate, London Shard of Glass (yet to be built), London U2 Tower, Dublin 101-story Shanghai Tower, Shanghai, China The Burj, Dubai Chicago Spire, Chicago (to be the world's tallest residential building)

Because skyscrapers are generally speculative projects, built by developers with other people's money, they will be built only when credit conditions are easing, or at their easiest, and when developers are most flush with funds. Hence the link with credit and Richard Cantillon.[3]

As an indicator, the Cantillon Effect should only be considered in conjunction with the 18-year real estate cycle. For example, the taller the building is on the drawing board, the easier it is to procure bank credit. Reference should also be made to the 18-year real estate clock.

The construction of the Singer Building in 1907 did not mark the height of that year's panic because the normal 18-year real estate cycle had not yet run its full course from the downturn of 1893. The opening of the Woolworth Building in 1913 was right on cue, just over 18 years from the previous real-estate-led downturn. However, the war intervened to stave off the collapse or lengthen the cycle, the only event so far that has been able to change the 18-year cycle. Significantly, if not ironically, the Woolworth Building was not built with bank credit.[4]

We can expect the next land-price-led downturn in 2009/10. It is interesting to observe just how many 'world's tallest' buildings are due for completion at that time, and the intensity of the competition and the owners' egos involved. It is likely that most of these buildings will open as many parts of the world, especially the US, are in, or about to go into, recession – the hangover after partying on too much easy money.

Tall buildings are a visible reminder of easy credit conditions. Although the skyscraper is considered an art form, its construction is essentially a business. The builder is constrained by the economics of the time and by how much profit can be generated. Most books about skyscrapers do point this out. 'Architecture simply doesn't count … With pitifully few exceptions in the past, New York skyscrapers have never reached for anything but money.'[5] Writers on architecture also point out more frequently than do economists that it is easy financing that underlies all building booms: '… all skyscrapers – even corporate showcases – can be viewed as real estate ventures, either as income-generating properties or as long term investments in high-value urban land.'[6]

Which is why the Cantillon Effect will continue to work. 'The history of speculative bubbles in construction is paralleled by a history of big increases in debt financing whether it is generated by endogenous factors, gold flows, central banks … or bank regulators.'[7] Skyscrapers are real

3 A few charts and images to highlight the effectiveness of tall buildings as a forecaster of land price peaks in the past can be found on the EIS website. For more, see: www.businesscycles.biz/businesscantillon1.htm

4 The architect Cass Gilbert described his 1913 Woolworth Building as 'A machine for making the land pay' (quoted in *Financial Times*, August 4, 2007). This tall building was financed entirely with cash.

5 Ada Louise Huxtable, *The Tall Building Artistically Reconsidered: The Search for a Skyscraper Style.*

6 Carol Willis, *Form Follows Finance: Skyscrapers and Skylines in New York and Chicago*, p.146.

7 Mark Thornton, 'Skyscrapers and Business Cycles', *Quarterly Journal of Austrian Economics* 8 (1), pp.51-74.

estate ventures. Land price goes higher the longer we proceed into the real estate cycle and the more available credit becomes. As the land price rises, taller buildings are required to offset the cost of building a square meter of lettable space. 'Becausc escalating land prices drive up the number of stories needed to spread the cost of a lot, the tallest buildings generally appear at the end of a boom cycle.'[8]

Canning Fok, CEO at Hutchisons, one of Hong Kong's richest companies, said much the same to *Fortune* magazine:[9] 'The more the plot of land costs, the taller the building must be to get your money back.' Given the nature of human speculative behaviour, the completion of the current crop of 'world's tallest' buildings is highly likely to mark the peak and turn of the next downturn.[10]

Of course the Cantillon Effect, like other indicators, should not be studied in isolation. The appearance of tallest buildings should be linked to what the yield curve and the land price barometer are also telling us. Towards the end of this decade, if, as the world's tallest buildings open for business, the yield curve is close to or goes negative and the land price index is way out of proportion, we have a very high probability of a peak in the real estate cycle, with a downturn to follow. As builders begin work on the roof of the world's tallest, we could look for a double top: the top of the tower *and* of the real estate market.

The price of copper

COULD THE PRICE of copper be considered an indicator of economic health, as related to the real estate cycle?

Copper is used extensively in many essential items we take for granted. In just Australian coinage alone, the 5 to 50 cent pieces are 75 per cent copper; the $1 and $2 coins 92 per cent. Copper also has key industrial uses: a motor vehicle uses on average 35kg of copper; a Boeing 747 1.8 tonnes. Computer circuit boards and wiring contain the stuff; so do mobile phones, iPods, air-conditioners and TV sets.[11] Copper is also a key product in the building of houses: each new American house contains on average 90kg of the metal.

On the copper charts the 18-year real-estate-led recession dates have been marked as vertical black lines (Graphs 20.2 and 20.3). Copper prices in all instances have spiked into the last years of each real estate cycle. (The other influence on price would appear to be war.) The huge spike in the price of copper in 2006 came into the peak of yet another US housing boom.

8 Willis, p.166,
9 January 8, 2001.
10 The indicator does not have to be 'tallest', either. Look also for the world's biggest Ferris wheel or largest boat – anything particularly speculative in nature which requires a good dose of credit to get started. Perhaps we could have named the Cantillon Effect the 'mine's bigger than yours' syndrome.
11 *The Age*, April 9, 2006.

Graph 20.2: Copper Prices
1870-1970

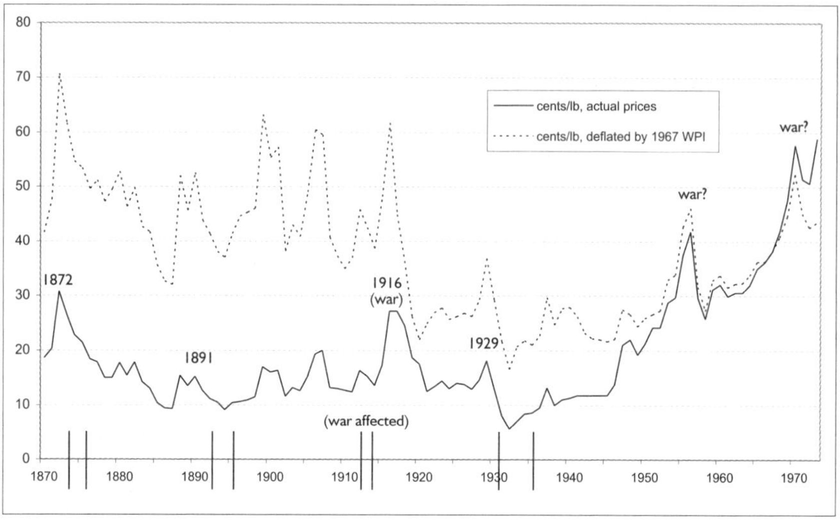

Source: Manthy, Robert S., *Natural Resource Commodities – A Century of Statistics*, Johns Hopkins University Press, 1978.

Graph 20.3: Copper Prices
1968-2007

The yield curve

THE YIELD CURVE is an excellent predictor of recessions if you know your real estate cycle history. First, an explanation of what the yield curve is. In the following interest rate curve examples, long-dated rates are 10 years or more, short-dated are 90 days to 2 years, very short 30 days or less.

Normally short-term interest rates (bills) are below long-term interest rates (bonds). This is taken as normal because the longer one's money is invested, the greater is the risk to one's savings. As the yield to maturity lengthens, the interest rate will rise – or, as economists would say, the slope of the curve measuring the yield to maturity should slope gently upwards. There are, however, different shades of normal.

Normal, steep-sloped curve

When the difference between long and very short-term interest rates is quite wide, the curve is said to be normal but steeply sloped. Two things are usually happening: (1) the Fed is cutting interest rates, and (2) long-term bond-holders are of the opinion that the economy is likely to grow strongly in the immediate future. A steeply sloped yield curve is most often seen just after the end of economic recession, once confidence has returned to the market.

Such conditions existed in 2003, 1993, 1983, 1976, possibly in 1971, and in 1962. These years are clearly visible in the chart of interest rates, the 10-year bond matched against the federal funds rate (Graph 20.4).

A steep curve is a reliable bet for increased economic expansion in the year or two following. The historical chapters describe this more fully, and the reasons for it, especially the first couple of pages of Chapter 14, 'Life, Liberty and the Pursuit of a Mortgage', which describe events after the 1989 downturn.

Normal, flat yield curve

This is a situation where long-term bond rates are the same, or nearly the same, as their shorter-term counterparts. The flattening curve generally signals slowing – or slower – economic growth ahead, as in 1997, 1987, 1978 and 1966. What will happen after the curve flattens is not so easy to determine. This is where knowledge of the real estate cycle is crucial. This is what this book and no other can teach you.

The inverted yield curve

This is when shorter-term interest rates rise above the level of the long bond. Rates invert – the opposite of the normal state of affairs.[12]

All recessions since 1960 have been preceded by an inverted yield curve, brought about most often by a sustained increase in the federal funds rate. Such inversions just prior to each recession stand out in the accompanying chart. Since 1800 or so all downturns have been preceded by an increase in interest rates, often quite a sharp spike, as described in the historical chapters.

12 A seeming paradox: bond holders are accepting lower interest rates than short-term investors even though they are tying up their money for longer. They will do this if they think interest rates will go down in the future. They are not often wrong.

Some observations

However, since 1913, for recession to occur after tightening by the Fed and the inversion of the curve, the tightening should see *both* long- and short-term interest rate levels rise prior to the inversion. This confirms that the Fed is tightening to lower inflation by slowing growth and that bondholders agree that inflation levels are expected to rise in the near future – a rise they attempt to price in by demanding higher interest rates to cover the risk.

Graph 20.4: US Interest Rates
10-year bonds and Fed funds rate, 1953-2007

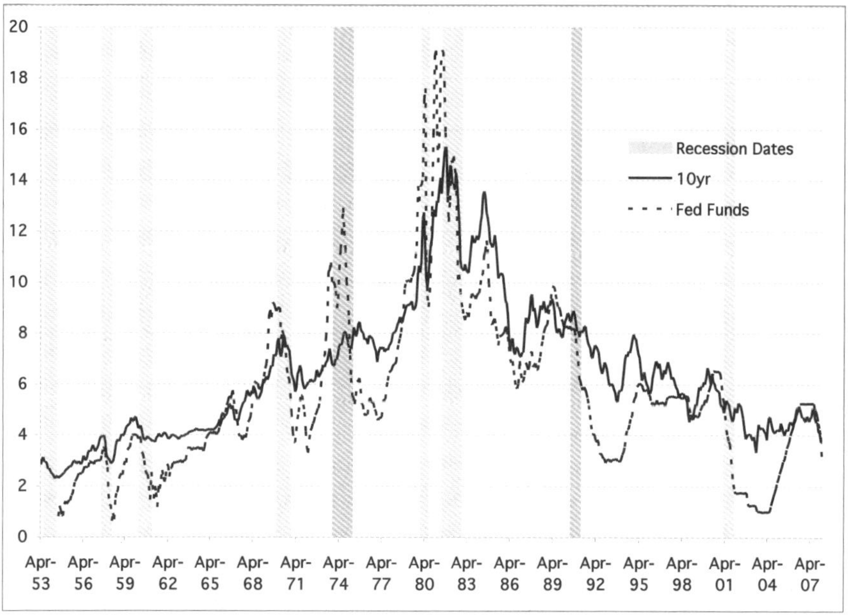

Source: US Federal Reserve.

The curve has to flatten before inverting, but not every flattening leads to an inversion. It is helpful to know where the economy is positioned in relation to the real estate cycle. Every real estate cycle downturn so far has been preceded by a flattening of the yield curve, then an inversion. There has never been a land-price-induced downturn without such an inversion. Rising inflation levels are usually the culprit, not to mention intense real estate speculation (amongst other things) in the final years of the cycle. Speculation is always at its most intense at the peak of the cycle.

Observe how real estate prices did not collapse despite the prodigious increase in short-term interest rates in 1980/1, and despite the substantial drop in GDP and the manufacturing slump that accompanied it. A real-estate-led recession will always be more calamitous, so *any yield curve inversion into the final years of the 18-year cycle must be treated with the utmost respect.* This is the key to understanding the importance of the yield curve: combine it with your new-found knowledge of the 18-year cycle.

In past real estate (and indeed normal decade) cycles, few investors have noticed the inversion. Investors are too busy speculating. Business looks good and credit is widely available. But, as we have seen, the fractional reserve banking system is built on quicksand and such conditions sow the seeds of its own demise.

There is, however, no correlation between a yield curve inversion and the depth or severity of the recession or depression that follows. The depth of a recession depends upon the intensity of real estate and other asset speculation that went on beforehand.

For the current real estate cycle, even though interest rates are at historically low levels, corresponding debt levels have increased to historically high proportions (to make the land price affordable, mostly). So it may not require a yield curve inversion at high interest rates, or indeed much of an interest rate inversion, to move the economy into recession.

Keep in mind where we are in the real estate cycle when the inversion is taking place. An inversion late in the cycle signals lower real estate prices to follow.

FURTHER READING

Arturo Estrello and Frederic S. Mishkin. 'The Yield Curve as a Predictor of US Recessions', *Current Issues in Economic and Finance*, Federal Reserve Bank of New York, June 1996.

Galbraith, John Kenneth, Edward R. Dewey and Edwin F. Dakin. *Cycles: The Science of Prediction.* Henry Holt & Co, 1947.

Grant, James. *The Trouble with Prosperity: A Contrarian's Tale of Boom, Bust and Speculation.* Random House, 1996.

Huxtable, Ada Louise. *The Tall Building Artistically Reconsidered: The Search for a Skyscraper Style.* Berkeley University of California Press, 1992.

Thomas, Dana L. *Lords of the Land: The Triumph and Scandals of America's Real Estate Barons from Early Times to the Present.* G.P. Putnam's Son's, New York, 1977.

Thornton, Mark. 'Skyscrapers and Business Cycles', *Quarterly Journal of Austrian Economics* 8 (1), Spring, 2005, pp.51-74.

Willis, Carol, *Form Follows Finance: Skyscrapers and Skylines in New York and Chicago.* Princeton Architectural Press.

Leithner Letter (www.leithner.com.au/newsletter/issue34.htm).

'Developers Bicker over Tall Storeys', *Herald Sun*, Melbourne, Australia, January 12, 2005, p.34.
'Hutchison Sells Out for Now', *Fortune*, January 8, 2001.

NOTE 1

It is said that land price cannot be measured. This is claimed by some economists, yet the Inland Revenue Directorate of Denmark does not have this problem: it's been able to predict that country's land value to within 1 per cent of market value for years. Australian local governments have, for decades, also successfully valued land exclusive of improvements. A rough land value of your own property is not hard to work out. Recall the price you paid for your own home (house and land), then have a look at the price it's insured for, which should be the cost of rebuilding your house, after a fire for example. Should the house burn down, the land would still be there, unchanged in value (or perhaps increased if the house was a run-down eyesore). Subtracting the insured value from the purchase price gives, roughly, your land value. The price you paid for your home has two easily measurable components, the cost to build it and the locational advantage of living there.

NOTE 2

Recession dates in the US are determined by the National Bureau of Economic Research (NBER), which may not necessarily infer two quarters of negative growth as usually defined by economists. For further details about this determination, see the NBER website.

21
They Say It Can't Be Done

His study,* The Coming Boom in Real Estate, *published in 1936 and reprinted in the* Reader's Digest, *was such an accurate forecast that it was reprinted 25 years later without changing a single word.

Greater Portland Commerce, January 1970, p.19

HISTORY REPEATED. Roy Wenzlick knew it would, much as he might have wished it otherwise. Wenzlick ran an appraisal business, valuing real estate for banks, insurance companies and other interested parties. But his files, now in the Western Historical Manuscript Collection at the University of St Louis, Missouri, reveal that Wenzlick's great passion was economic forecasting. Wenzlick went on to publish the *Real Estate Analyst* from the early 1930s right up until his retirement in 1974. It was the only national statistical forecasting service on real estate when it started.

Wenzlick was able to offer an accurate forecast in his book, *The Coming Boom in Real Estate and What to Do About It* (1936), because he had studied history, in particular the history of each real estate cycle. He'd seen the common outcome that chasing the capitalised rent creates.

One of Wenzlick's outstanding indicators was his measure of voluntary real estate transfers (not to be confused with selling price): he studied the relationship between the number of voluntary transfers in the principal metropolitan areas of the United States and the number of families living in these areas. A cursory glance at Wenzlick's 1936 chart from his book,[1] shows the booms in real estate activity – 1872, 1890, 1906 and the 1920s – and the lows – 1878, 1900, 1918 and 1933.

Wenzlick's 1936 book was based in part on this information, though there was a lot more to his research than just the transfer figures. In the book he forecast further boom times for real estate, with a peak in activity between 1943 and 1946. He was exactly right. This was a big call at the time. The book also pointed out the reasons why a cyclical recovery in rents, real estate values and building construction would develop, when it would do so and through what stages it would pass.

1 Available at www.businesscycles.biz/subscriber/1936book.pdf

After the Second World War, Wenzlick's services were in great demand. He continued to attract a good deal of attention by forecasting in 1948 that real estate activity would return to normal levels by 1950 and hit a low point in 1955. As we know now, the low point in land price arrived in 1955 exactly; however real estate activity continued to climb. Wenzlick did not know then, though he had worked it out by the late 1950s, that his real estate transfers index was no longer a reliable indicator for the post-war years. He later noted:

> … the general explanation for the downward drift in the transfer figures on practically all cities is that most of these cities are now building more apartments and larger commercial and industrial buildings, and as a result the transfers are generally far larger in dollars, but fewer in number.

Another important factor noted by Wenzlick was a change in the structure of the house mortgage after the war – to one of a level monthly payment amortising over the life of the loan. This decreased the number of distress sales in economic downturns, helping to limit their severity.[2]

Wenzlick clearly suspected a problem with his index earlier than he actually said so. In a 1953 speech he reported:

> 'I am afraid that in the United States we are going to go back to an inflationary policy. I do not believe there is any chance of a collapse, similar to the [19]30s … Regardless of what the administration might want, I believe that Congress is going to insist on every possible aid to business … I believe the next big real estate boom in the United States is going to peak sometime in the middle or late 60s. I believe the selling price of real estate at that time will be considerably higher than the selling price at the present time.'
>
> Quoted in *Skyscraper Management*, May 1954

Exactly right of course. Wenzlick knew his history. In 1954 the US had well and truly abandoned the gold standard and was able to print its dollar bills without restriction – the Fed has increasingly continued to do so (more now, in this decade, than ever before). Future administrations have been left to pay off the debt – incurred more often than not to pay for war – in an inflated currency. This made Wenzlick's inflation forecast easy.

It is Homer Hoyt, however, who is described as the father of the 18-year real estate cycle, having apparently been the first author to identify it in the early 1930s, though it is possible that Wenzlick was first. Certainly Wenzlick went on to make far better forecasts using his own data

2 Perhaps Wenzlick should have gone on to measure just land price, though this is not easy in the US. The best he could say on the issue was that 'the real estate cycle was so firmly and definitely established in our earlier history and in the history of many foreign countries that it may be that this cycle is still continuing on a basis similar to the cycle of the past, but that the means of measuring it have changed so that it is practically impossible to determine whether the cycle has completely disappeared or is merely hidden by the change in the type of figures' (from the author's own notes at the Manuscript Collection). Wenzlick was well aware of what the increasing availability of credit was doing to real estate activity too, in this developing era of easy finance.

out of St Louis. Hoyt went on to suggest that the cycle he documented so well was probably by then redundant, belonging only to newly developing cities, and even then would not likely recur on a national scale. This despite all the evidence to the contrary that he had accumulated. It was the opposite of what Wenzlick went on to say.

Regardless, the lack of a 1955 recession fooled just about everybody. No one delved deeper to explain the actual cause of the property cycle, despite the fact that writers like Ricardo and George had already put forward a sound thesis. My study of the Wenzlick material at the University of Missouri suggests that Wenzlick was aware of the cause but did not actively pursue this line of thought in his *Real Estate Analyst* publications.

Hoyt's research,[3] covered extensively in the historical chapters, does tend to add weight to my thesis that, towards the end of the 18-year real estate cycle, land values peak first, then construction activity. By the time the general economy is about to tip into recession land values are already well down from their previous peak levels. This will continue to repeat whilst the economic rent remains 'enclosed'.

Clarence D. Long also wrote extensively about real estate cycles in the US.[4] He describes four cycles between the end of the Civil War and the late 1930s: a trough after the panic of 1873; peaks in the 1880s and early 1890s; a panic in 1893/4; recovery through the recession to a high around the time of the First World War; a trough in 1918; and a 1920s boom (starting slowly out of the recession of 1920), ending in the trough of 1933/4. Long's work

> reflected the idea that long cycles averaged about 18 years, but he wrote at length on the difficulty of explaining why such cycles existed. Population changes did not seem to have an influence, although he felt that wars might. He was forced to cast out the impact of physical deterioration, since the product lasted so much longer than the cycle, leading him to suggest that there was a psychological life to buildings. In any case, the 'economic life' of a building was an intangible, possibly related to the exhaustion of book depreciation and to the consequent release of income in business firms, but although much of the stock was not formally depreciated, the non-residential sector seemed to have a shorter cycle than the residential sector. The role of the investment community was obscure in the real estate processes he described, but he was convinced that long cycles had a more profound impact on investment in construction than did short cycles.
>
> Alan Rabinowitz, *The Real Estate Gamble*

US author Fred Foldvary has had no trouble explaining why such cycles exist and has put together a rather neat synthesis of competing theories that he calls his geo-Austrian explanation. It makes for intriguing reading. The predictive power of Foldvary's thesis should not be underestimated: having laid out the thesis in 1997, Foldvary used it to predict,

3 Fig. 99, p.411 in particular, reproduced here as Graph 11.2, page 216.
4 *Building Cycles and the Theory of Investment*, Princeton University Press, 1940.

a full ten years before it happened, that the next US real estate bust would occur in 2008.[5]

The best analysis, though, has been done by Fred Harrison. Harrison's original book, *The Power in the Land* (1983), clearly explains the origins of the real estate cycle and was prescient in forecasting the subsequent 1991 real estate bust. It is essential reading. Harrison continued to forecast the cycle and in 1997 wrote of the UK economy:

> By 2007 Britain and most of the other industrially advanced economies will be in the throes of frenzied activity in the land market equal to what happened in 1988/9. Land prices will be near their 18-year peak, driven by an exponential growth rate, on the verge of collapse …
>
> *The Chaos Makers*, Vindex in association with the Land Policy Council, 1997

Harrison put it all together for his 2005 *Boom Bust* and in this book showed how and why the UK real estate market would peak at the end of 2007.

Few believe that the economy can be so predictable. They say it can't be done. But this is only because so few go to the trouble of arming themselves with a workable thesis as to how the economy actually works. This thesis is Ricardo's Law of Rent. Be warned, though. If you truly come to understand why the Law of Rent works, you will also come to see the flipside: why such knowledge cannot be admitted by the elite. To do so would bring into question their source of power and control, and explain the method of dismantling it.

ESSENTIAL READING

Foldvary, Fred. 'The Business Cycle: A Georgist-Austrian Synthesis', *American Journal of Economics and Sociology*, Vol. 56, No.4, October 1997.

Hudson, Michael. *The New Road to Serfdom: An Illustrated Guide to the Coming Real Estate Collapse.* Harpers, May 2005, available here: www.harpers.org/archive/2006/05/0081029

5 *American Journal of Economics and Sociology*, 1997 (some of Foldvary's work can also be seen at www.foldvary.net/works/geoaus.html and www.foldvary.net/works/rebc.html).

22

The Secret Life of Real Estate and Banking

The Secrets

If a tax were imposed equal to the annual value of real property ex its improvement, so that it would now have no net earnings and hence no capital value of its own, progress would be orderly and its fruits would be equitably shared.

John Kenneth Galbraith, winner, Presidential Medal of Freedom, 1946 and 2000 (quoted in *The Affluent Society*)

... pure land rent is in the nature of a 'surplus' which can be taxed heavily without distorting production incentives or efficiency ...

Paul Samuelson, Nobel Laureate in Economics, 1970, explaining Ricardo's Law of Rent[1]

There is a sense in which all taxes are antagonistic to free enterprise. And yet we need taxes ... So the question is, which are the least bad taxes? In my opinion, the least bad tax is the property tax on the unimproved value of land ...

Milton Friedman, Nobel Laureate in Economics, 1976. (Interview in the *Times Herald*, Norristown, PA, December 1, 1978)

THE SEVEN SECRETS of real estate and banking are:

Secret One: Understand the economic structure

To do this, a thorough working knowledge of Ricardo's Law of Rent is required. The majority of economists today teach that land is merely a part of capital. As a result, Ricardo's Law of Rent has been relegated to an historical footnote, rarely discussed in today's economic literature. In actual fact, land produces a (ground) rent, independent of the return to labour and the return to capital. This rent can be taxed away without affecting the economic potential of society. Understand that, and your investment knowledge takes a quantum leap forward. There can be no doubt this extra

1 For the whole quote, see Paul A. Samuelson *et al*, *Economics*, 2nd Australian edn, Chapter 27, 'Factor Prices and the Theory of Rent', p.623.

knowledge gave the above-quoted economists their stupendous advantage over other, lesser known economists – Galbraith in particular.

Absolutely everything that happens in society flows from this (ground) rent – the unimproved value of the land, or rental value. How a society allows this rental value to manifest determines how that society develops. Wherever the rental value is capitalised, a real estate cycle – a boom then a bust – *will* develop. The *ONLY* way the real estate cycle can be stopped is by taxing away the unimproved value of the land.

Secret Two: Ownership of the rental value is obtainable only via a government-granted licence

It is protected by the State, and endorsed and accepted by general community agreement. Long-term ownership of this licence is the most secure way to accumulate wealth with the least amount of effort. For what should by now be obvious reasons, this is why the ruling elite will never permit the taxing of the rent. Further real estate cycles – booms, then busts – are therefore absolutely certain.

Secret Three: Where the rental value is permitted to capitalise, economic history *will* repeat, but never in an obvious fashion

Suffice it to say, if history did repeat exactly everyone would see it and undertake action to avoid it, or to take advantage of it, thereby cancelling out the repeat. So things can never repeat exactly the same way. Nevertheless, though one cannot forecast the next real estate cycle down to particular specifics, the 18-year real estate clock will prove a reliable guide to the process of repetition, underpinned as it is by Ricardo's Law of Rent. When you see, say, the 8 o'clock action on the clock, the expansion of banks, you can be absolutely certain that an expansion of credit is at hand, leading into easy credit at 9 o'clock. Next time you see a real estate mogul stand up and proclaim the everlasting, eternal nature of the one-way direction of real estate prices – upwards – you will know that 15:00 is approaching. He'll likely be aged under 42. (And yes it will be a 'he'.)

It is worth noting that the introduction of new technology will not alter the real estate cycle, nor will it affect the timing. In 2005 Fed chairman Alan Greenspan spoke knowingly of how all the recent new technology was improving credit standards. At the Fed's fourth Annual Community Affairs Research Conference (April 8, 2005), Greenspan told the assembled audience:

> As has every segment of our economy, the financial services sector has been dramatically transformed by technology. Technological advancements have significantly altered the delivery and processing of nearly every consumer financial transaction, from the most basic to the most complex. For example, information processing technology has enabled creditors to achieve significant efficiencies in collecting and assimilating the data necessary to evaluate risk and make corresponding decisions about credit pricing.

It may have enabled efficiencies but, as we have subsequently seen, it didn't change the outcome. The same could have been said every cycle, especially about what happened with the banking innovations of the 1920s (page 228).

Secret Four: Few investment experts understand the real estate cycle – in particular they have absolutely no knowledge of its *cause* – so listening to their advice would be financial suicide

The 18-year real estate clock is your best guide. This highlights the importance of understanding the structure of today's economy, which is built on the capitalisation of the rental value (of the unimproved value of the land) into a tradable commodity, supported by the banks' credit-creation processes. As just one example of the complete uselessness of other economic forecasts, the Fed in May of 2007 forecast that the developing housing slump would not bring the then six-year economic expansion to a halt. This is similar to what Dr Greenspan said in January 1991 (see the quotes in Chapter 14, 'Life, Liberty and the Pursuit of a Mortgage', page 291) and to what Fed chairman Arthur Burns was saying in the early 1970s, and it was also the general Fed belief in late 1929. The Fed does not study causes, which is what the material in this book is all about. Know the cause and you can easily forecast the result.

Similarly, do not believe all the prevailing literature about markets being random. They are not.[2] Ignore the sceptics. History will repeat whilst we continue to permit the enclosure of the rent into a tradable commodity and then, further, allow banks to create credit on this capitalised rental value. This also means that you do not have to spend time coming to grips with all the peripheral indicators within the economy: deficit levels, consumer spending, wages growth and the like. Such indicators will do nothing but confuse you as to the turning of the real estate cycle. The 18-year real estate clock will tell you what is coming next in the cycle, and if the next move on the clock isn't obvious yet, then it is probably still to occur.

Secret Five: The best long-term path to profit (or avoidance of a loss) is to identify the economic turning points – the real estate extremes in other words

At such extremes, do the opposite of the crowd. Such extremes do not happen in a period of months; they take years to develop. Here are a few pointers to maximise profits:

- Protect your capital. Never buy real estate in the winner's curse phase of the cycle (Chapter 17, 'Why 18 Years?', page 340). Doing so at that time is a certain way of ending up with negative equity in the property for years afterwards, if you survive the downturn.

2 The academic belief that history is useless to study began in earnest in 1957 with the publication of Karl Popper's *The Poverty of Historicism*.

- Do not try to pick the top of the real estate market. Selling into the 13th or 14th year, assuming you wish to sell, is adequate. The absolute peak of the market probably cannot be ascertained until it has passed, so why try? The 18-year real estate clock will tell you well enough how the economy is placed.
- Never buy in a falling market at the end of the cycle. Real estate downturns that have taken place each 18 years or so have lasted years, not months. This latest downturn will be no different.

One of the best ways to take advantage of the peak of the real estate cycle is through the stock market.[3] It is commonly said that the stock market goes up by the stairs but down by the elevator. Finance and real estate stocks have always been great 'shorts' at the end of a real estate cycle. Note though, such stocks will be well on the way down before most real estate players realise a land-price-led recession is on the way. History shows – for the repeats are crystal clear – that banking concerns that have built up the largest exposure to real estate and are financing this exposure by 'borrowing short to lend long' will provide the best 'short' or 'put option' strategies. As a further clue, such banks at the time of the next real estate downturn will probably be run by upwardly mobile executives under the age of 42, with little knowledge of history and no memory of the previous *land-price-led* downturn.

The stock market is also an effective guide to the bottoming of the real estate market out of recession and the start of the new 18-year cycle.[4] For long-term holding and maximum gain, once the stock market has bottomed is the best time to buy real estate, but it is of course usually the hardest time to obtain credit.

Secret Six: Understand the credit creation process

Banks do not lend money, they create credit – out of thin air. The critical thing to understand is this: the process itself is actually desirable. It is the lifeblood of any economy and is always needed by business. Fractional reserve banking is overwhelmingly beneficial to society. The process is compromised only by credit created on the enclosed rental value of the land. Banks own the earth not because they create credit but because we permit them to mortgage it. No capitalised rent, no need for the vast amount of fractional reserve banking required to buy it, as noted in Chapter 16, page 336. Banks could then be run like any other business, and rise or fall depending on their ability to lend astutely. This is something very, very few persons actually understand. The violence of the boom, then bust, of the real estate cycle begins here.

3 For real estate investors, knowledge of the stock market, and the chart-reading methods of W.D. Gann, is highly recommended – perhaps a topic for another book.
4 See Chapter 19, 'What Time Is It?', the section on the flow of the cycle.

This is not a conspiracy, and certainly not a banking conspiracy of any sort. It's just the way the system is, because so few people are willing to look for any alternative – although there is one. Given the system, therefore, it behoves investors to borrow as much of this created credit as possible, secure as much rental value as possible with it, and then have someone else work to pay off the interest expense. Just don't begin the process into the peak of a real estate cycle.

Secret Seven: Who owns the well?

Societies today are classed by economists as capitalist, communist, socialist or a mixture of all three. They are nothing of the sort. Each is built on differing degrees of enclosure of the land value into a tradable privilege. To see things this way is a paradigm shift for most people, but it does produce a better investor. It is individual effort to maximise the enclosure value that brings the maximum investment return, but also moves the cycle along its path.

WHICH BRINGS US BACK full circle to Dr Jung's artesian well (page vi) – where, actually, Dr Jung failed to see the whole picture. The well does in fact need to be owned, and fenced, and an admission charged. When this is done, a rental value will arise quite naturally – it is exactly what society needs, and should have. It is society's only hope of ever sharing the well's resources in a just manner, and the only way environmentally poor practices will ever be stopped. The determining factor is what society chooses to do with the rental value so generated. Allow it to be privatised, to be traded and to have credit created upon it, and we get the results we see all around us in the world today, complete with our boom/bust real estate cycle. Good for the owners of the well.

Collect the rental value so that the rental value cannot capitalise into a *price* (i.e. no net earnings), and a whole new panorama of possibilities opens up for society. The water would indeed flow without effort, or limit. Good for everyone.

For example, in the downturn into 2010, governments around the world will be taking strenuous action to stop land (house) prices from declining. All sorts of remedies will be proposed: mortgage relief, debtor relief, shared equity schemes, government building more 'affordable' homes, tax handouts, stamp duty offsets and reductions, bank bailouts, printing money – anything so long as that damned land price stops collapsing. These schemes are necessary only because land price was permitted to capitalise in the first place.

Society does not need land price in order to function. In fact it would function far better without it. 'Progress would be orderly and its fruits would be equitably shared.' Even the Fed itself, as an institution, is only required because a land *price* exists. See this, given the present system we have inherited, and one's ability to use the system is magnified many times. This book has shown you why.

Good luck with your new-found real estate cycle knowledge.

APPENDIX I

The Panic of 1907

What the newspapers were saying ...

EBULLIENCE AT the top:

> There is not a single note of pessimism to be found in all the statements made by the leading merchants. Their reports show that business conditions are in a strong position. *Wall Street Journal*, September 26, 1907

The turn to fear:

> There was never a time in the country's history when our industrial affairs were in such a tangle, and were going down hill as rapidly as they are today. *Wall Street Journal*, March 9, 1908

Blame the government:

> There can be no return to prosperity until Roosevelt is retired to private life. *Wall Street Journal*, April 11 1908

> The panic was the result of the Republican incapacity to act. *Boston Evening Transcript*, December 2, 1907

Blame anything except the speculation in government-granted licences and privileges:

> Wall Street, the most colossal, crooked, merciless and dangerous institution in all history. *Wall Street Journal*, March 23, 1908

> Luxury is unquestionably one of the great causes of the present panic and depression, as it is invariably one of the great causes of all panics and depressions. *Wall Street Journal*, February 25, 1908

> Panics are the result of overextensions and abuse of the credit system. *Wall Street Journal*, February 28, 1908

> The depression in insurance; the depression in Wall Street, the impaired public confidence in securities; are the work primarily of the men who have mismanaged corporations. *Wall Street Journal*, October 7, 1907

> Extravagant living by those who have made money easily during prosperous times; and the efforts of others to live on an equal scale, were cited as

leading causes for the present financial difficulties by Wm. H Colvin of the Chicago Stock Exchange.

New York Globe and Commercial Advertiser, November 16, 1907

I think if we should analyse the cause of most financial panics we should find that they were caused by the failure of American women to spend their money wisely and well.

New York Globe and Commercial Advertiser, January 29, 1908, quoting Ida Tarbell

APPENDIX 2

Rogers Caldwell (1930 Cycle)

Rogers Caldwell dominated southern financial circles in the 1920s to the point that he was often called the 'J.P. Morgan of the South'. In a career that spanned only 20 years, he built a financial empire that collapsed abruptly in November 1930, shaking the foundations of Tennessee's economy and government. *The Tennessee Encyclopedia of History and Culture* website, 2002

Gawd, this ain't a business. Who told you this was a business? This is a Hindu rope trick. Duckfoot Blake, explaining the bond business after a question from new company recruit and former college football star Jerry Calhoun, in the Robert Penn Warren novel *At Heaven's Gate*

ROGERS C. CALDWELL founded his business Caldwell & Company in September 1917 with a view to marketing bonds – in particular, southern municipal bonds. The son of James E. Caldwell, an already prominent Nashville banker, Rogers C. had seen a niche making such bonds available to investors. After World War I there was a dramatic upsurge in businessmen seeking finance for construction and investment. Though the south had historically been regarded as risky because of its previously high default rate, the lack of competition in this area gave the young Caldwell an early advantage in benefiting from the investment surge.

Caldwell specialised in surety bonds for county and municipal construction projects. The capital from bond sales handled by his company was a major impetus for the southern states to build schools and highways, and carry out various extensive improvements. This activity brought Caldwell into close contact with state government authorities.

Caldwell's expansion really got underway with the founding, in 1919, of The Bank of Tennessee. This bank 'functioned solely as a depository for funds raised through the company's bond sales. These funds earned no interest for the bond issuer and were dispersed only when construction projects required.'[1] In other words, if the state of Tennessee wanted to finance some infrastructure, it raised the funds via a bond issue, some of which a bank like Caldwell's would handle; the proceeds would then sit in the bank awaiting disbursement. If Caldwell had the contract to build what the state wanted to finance, then the bonds would be paid out to one of Caldwell's building companies. The potential for such capital sitting in the bank had not gone unnoticed by the new banker. He was quick to

1 *Tennessee Encyclopedia.*

exploit it to his advantage. The deposits provided him with a considerable amount of investment capital.

During the 1920s Caldwell expanded into numerous other fields, buying up not only other banks but also insurance companies, department stores, resource companies (especially oil), textile mills and even a baseball franchise. Crucially, he also expanded his business interests and bond operations into real estate by helping underwrite the construction costs of office buildings, hotels and apartment blocks. Business grew and by 1925 Caldwell had opened fourteen branch offices.

Around this time he entered into business dealings with one Luke Lea, a major player in Tennessee politics and a firm believer in building up the state's infrastructure. Together they purchased an interest in another bank, the Holston National, and two newspapers, the *Memphis Commercial Appeal* and the *Knoxville Journal*; Lea already owned the *Nashville Tennessean*. Using Lea's political influence, Caldwell was able to supply road asphalt (under the trade name Kyrock) to the state without going through the usual tender process. The extent of Lea's influence within banking circles is revealed by Lea's subsequent election to the board of the Federal Reserve Bank of Atlanta.

Lea made extensive use of the banks he now partly owned for personal loans to finance his Nashville real estate operations. The new president at the Holsten National in 1928, J. Basil Ramsay, 'proved to be an ideal bank President from the standpoint of Lea because after taking office he directed its policies to benefit Lea as much as possible.'[2]

By the late 1920s Caldwell had company men in key positions within the Tennessee State Banking Department who could tip him off about any looming state audit of his banks, and also within the Tennessee State Funding Board which was responsible for issuing state bonds. After the Tennessee gubernatorial campaign of 1928, Caldwell's company 'won a bid to sell millions in Tennessee bonds and [accordingly] the state dramatically increased its deposits in his Bank of Tennessee'.[3]

Behind the scenes, however, a less rich story was emerging. Only in 1925 did the bank's accounting department make its first successful trial balance. Up until that time accounting employees simply made the entries they thought should be made, with the department 'more or less running itself'.[4] Things did improve after 1926.

Caldwell was developing an expensive lifestyle, which included lavish entertainment, exclusive club membership, connections to many of America's rich and famous, and a developing passion for fine blooded race horses – a lifestyle he was perhaps struggling to afford and for which he was increasingly billing his company. Nevertheless, in October 1929, with his associates Mason Houghland and John Branham (a Chicago

2 John Berry McFerrin, *Caldwell and Company*, p.69.
3 Tennessee Encyclopedia.
4 McFerrin, p.33.

advertising agency owner recently relocated), Caldwell bought the 632 acre 'Fairview' for $74,000. The idea was simple: to allow a select group of millionaires access to this property for $10,000 each, and then lease or buy the eighty adjacent farms which covered an area of 28 square miles. A vast hunting preserve and sportsmen's club would be created on land bounded on three sides by water and on the fourth by a paved road that no fox was likely to cross. Despite the stock market crash two weeks later – it affected only stocks, it was reasoned, in an area where wealth was measured in land – the plan went ahead and a prospectus was produced proclaiming the benefits of this 'island of sport'.

> Every imaginable sport was either provided for or planned, including: beagling, polo, dove and quail shooting, pheasant hunting, duck shooting, horse breeding stables and programs, fishing, boating, swimming, golf privileges … tennis, restaurants … and residential accommodations

with the inaugural steeplechase and fox hunt scheduled for December 6, 1930.[5]

Alas Caldwell's debt bomb from his 1920s business expansion was ticking. In hindsight, a number of problems can easily be identified. The assets in which the bank had invested consisted of a number of slow moving securities, a number of investments in non-liquid assets of a permanent nature that proved almost impossible to sell at short notice without loss (though they may well have proved profitable in the very long run), and loans made on real estate that proved non-collectable when the market turned.

Caldwell's business remained afloat only because of the continued supply of state funds going into the Bank of Tennessee. Persistent rumours about the health of Caldwell's bank, however, forced the Tennessee state auditors to examine the bank on November 7, 1930. They declared it insolvent and in default on its state deposits. This action precipitated runs on other Caldwell banks throughout the state and Caldwell and Coy, the largest banking concern in the south, went into receivership seven days later, on November 14. Within two weeks, more than one hundred other banks across seven southern states were out of business. The collapse of Caldwell put the state of Tennessee into crisis: at least $3.4m in state funds was now missing. This was reckoned to be about 10 per cent of the budgeted expenditure for the forthcoming year, and 'virtually all the cash on hand'.[6] The first banking panic of the Great Depression had begun.

Probably the Caldwell banks should have collapsed some weeks before they actually did. Caldwell himself admitted this years later:

> 'But it was the end of October 1930, and we were afraid of what effect the bank closing would have on Governor Horton's re-election. We held out. We stayed open until the day after Horton was elected.'
>
> Quoted in McFerrin, p.xviii

5 See www.billpuryear.com for more on Fairview.
6 See www.tennesseehistory.org

In 1931 the states of Tennessee and Kentucky indicted Caldwell on several charges. He was convicted on one count of breach of trust in Tennessee, but the State Court granted his appeal. That new trial was never held, however, and he successfully avoided extradition to Kentucky. Caldwell, at the height of his power and worth an estimated $650m,[7] retired from business to live out his remaining years in his purpose-built mansion, Brentwood Hall. Built on his father's land, the house had been paid for not by Caldwell but by his bank, and was included by the bank on its list of assets in the accounts. The state finally caught up with Caldwell in 1957, when legal action by the state of Tennessee resulted in the seizure of the Brentwood property.

Caldwell's business partner Luke Lea eventually served a prison sentence in North Carolina for fraud, though he was later pardoned.

Fairview staged a second horse race in December 1931, though to declining attendance. In March 1932, with Caldwell unable to continue payments on the additional land that was being acquired, receivers were appointed.

Pulitzer Prize-winning author Robert Penn Warren is believed to have based his book *At Heaven's Gate* on the empire of Rogers Caldwell and his bond-trading house Caldwell and Coy. Said the author, 'I was living there [in Nashville] when I was 25 years old, and I was seeing those same things happen.'

FURTHER READING

The Tennessee Encyclopedia of History and Culture website, 2002.

McFerrin, John Berry. *Caldwell and Company: A Southern Financial Empire.* Vanderbilt University Press, 1969.

Warren, Robert Penn. *At Heaven's Gate.* Harcourt Brace & Co, 1943.

7 Tennessee Department of Agriculture website, www.state.tn.us

APPENDIX 3

Penn Central (1974 Cycle)

WHEN PENN CENTRAL failed in June 1970 it was the largest bankruptcy in America up to that time. There are always good reasons why a corporation fails – internal reasons largely. Often it is because the company gets into additional activities it does not understand, or ignores the one it is presently in. And, when the failing company is a large listed corporation, insiders usually know well before the public that something is amiss …

Penn Central came about as a result of a merger between two rail lines, the Pennsylvania line and the New York Central line. Talks about merging had been going on for years before the merger actually occurred in 1965. The CEO of the Pennsylvania line, Stuart Saunders, took charge of the merged entity.

In describing Saunders, Robert Sobel notes a conversation that took place between Saunders and a Pennsylvanian politician, Milton Shapp:

> 'I've been to several parties with him where he had a few drinks, and he was always talking about Litton Industries and how Litton and other conglomerates had cash coming in and were putting it to good use … He said he wanted to keep the money for real estate investments instead of putting it in the f—— railroad.' *When Giants Stumble*

Saunders lived up to his statement.

> Saunders razed Pennsylvania station in New York and created the Madison Square Garden, along with two office towers. In return for the property, Penn retained a quarter interest in the complex. And then Saunders went after the Great Southwest Corp [with interests in property], Arviva, a Florida land company, a mobile home company, and Executive Jet Aviation from which Saunders sought to start a major charter service, along with others.
>
> www.buyandhold.com

The merging of the Pennsylvania with the New York Central gave Saunders a higher profile, and enhanced borrowing power. The evolving financial techniques of the time made Saunders' quest for more and more acquisitions that much easier too. Listed companies simply issued debt for each acquisition in the commercial debt markets of the time – all to push the share price along, of course.

But, with such debt outstanding, a tightening of the credit cycle can be deadly. Added to this, rail companies were seeing their market for freight haulage and distribution erode as shippers took advantage of the growing road networks. In late 1969 and early 1970, when Penn Central had $100m in debt maturing, it realised it did not have the cash to meet it and sought to float some bonds to cover the debt. Meantime the company reported a loss, raising doubts in the market as to the worth of the bond issue. Penn Central stock fell to $15 from about $85 a year earlier.

A government bail-out was sought for the ailing Penn Central (and other rail lines also having trouble). The President approved an overall $750m package but Congress did not in the end authorise payment. The government did step in to preserve the rail service, however, splitting Penn Central into Conrail for freight service and Amtrak for passengers.

It was subsequently disclosed that the earnings of Penn Central associated corporations had in previous years been used to prop up the share price of Penn Central itself. Alan Lechner in *Street Games* noted:

> The Penn Central wasn't exactly the SEC's shining hour. Penn Central Transportation Company, the world's largest privately owned railroad company, with assets of over $6 billion, was an American institution ranking just behind hot dogs. On June 21, 1970, it collapsed. Businesses had gone bankrupt before. But Penn Central stands as a glaring example of how the great institutions, the financial institutions on which we place our reliance, will get out whilst the going is good and leave investors, even or especially those institutions' own clients, to get skewered …
>
> A lot of banks had lent money to Penn Central. A lot of banks had trust departments that were heavily invested in Penn Central stock. It is illegal to trade on inside information, but when serious trouble began to show at the railroad, you can be sure that the bankers were the first to know about it – in their role not as trust officers but as lending bankers. Ray Dirks had gotten the wind knocked out of him by the SEC when he got his customers out of Equity Funding. But what happened to Chase Manhattan Bank, Morgan Guaranty Trust, Continental Illinois National Bank and Trust, and all the others when Penn Central began to go? You bet. Their trust departments sold massive amounts of the company's stock. Put it out on the market for us investors to buy up. There had been some talk circulating in the Street about difficulties with Penn Central. Nothing serious. But these banks unloaded. As for the SEC. Once again it studied. Its conclusions: 'Although at this point serious questions exist about whether sales were made on inside information, it should be noted that proof of insider trading is always difficult. The difficulty is increased where, as here, there is some public adverse information that might explain the trade. Unless direct testimony or documents can be obtained on the use of inside information, it is difficult to sustain a charge of misuse of information.' And then the SEC added: 'Both the commercial lending departments of Morgan and Continental had inside information at the time the trust department was selling Penn Central stock, but the parties to the decision to sell deny under oath that the trust department had access to the information.

The public announcement of the Penn Central collapse marked the bottom of the market for 1970.

FURTHER READING

Daughen, Joseph R. and Peter Binzen. *The Wreck of the Penn Central*. Beard Books, 1999.

Lechter, Alan. *Street Games*. Harper & Row, 1980.

Sobel, Robert. *When Giants Stumble: Classic Business Blunders and How to Avoid Them*. Prentice Hall Press, 1999.

Trumbore, Brian (www.buyandhold.com/bh/en/education/history/2001/the_collapse_of_penn_central.html).

APPENDIX 4

C. Arnholt Smith
and the Westgate-California Corporation (1974 Cycle)

> A few years ago, political influence was wielded by Republican bosses who owned savings and loans and big law firms and tuna fleets, like C. Arnholt Smith … They shaped the downtown skyline of the day and handpicked the candidates who ran for office. *San Diego Union Tribune*, August 4, 2002

> Perhaps the swindler of the century.
> *Forbes Magazine*, 'Crime in the Suites', August 15, 1975

THE UNITED STATES National Bank of San Diego (USNB) collapsed amidst charges of fraud in October 1973. The President and chief stock holder of the bank was C. Arnholt Smith, a resident of San Diego; some held that he *was* the town of San Diego. Over the prior two decades, Conrad Arnholt Smith (he dropped the Conrad sometime on the way up) had put together interests in ship-building, hotels, tuna fishing (owning the third largest fleet in the country), taxis (including a controlling interest in a cartel that included the yellow cab franchise for most of the larger Californian cities), real estate, banking, airlines (Air California) and of course baseball – all under the umbrella of the conglomerate Westgate-California Corporation. Along the way he became the best friend of presidential aspirant Richard Nixon and, as co-campaign finance chair, raised tens of millions of dollars, including millions of his own money, for the 1968 presidential campaign.

Early on, 'I was kinda embarrassed to be in public, and couldn't handle myself very well, and I didn't like it,' Smith once admitted. But in 1955 he bought the local minor-league baseball team, the Padres, for $300,000 and found himself in the public eye. The first thing the team needed was a better baseball park, and advice was sought from appropriate professionals as to where to build the new stadium. 'I almost fell outta my shoes when they picked a ranch that we owned down in Mission Valley,' said Smith.[1]

In true baseball franchise tradition, the owner then had the city build the necessary infrastructure around it. Roads, parking lots and various amenities financed by municipal city bond issues added immensely to the value of the team franchise, and the land upon which the stadium was built.

1 See San Diego online, www.sndiegomag.com/retro/febretr3.shtml

(A Texan Governor also added to his wealth this way once, on his way to the presidential suite.) The public got used to the idea of a taxpayer-supported stadium after relentless articles in local newspapers owned by Smith's contacts and supporters.

Luck followed Smith for years. A significant share of San Diego's tourist dollar seemed to be collected by him. The ideal San Diego tourist, wrote Mike Davis,

> could 'fly in on a Smith airline (Golden West or Air California), take a Smith-owned cab to Smith's opulent Westgate Hotel, where he would eat a Smith dinner before catching a Padre night game at Westgate Stadium. Perhaps the next day, after cashing some travelers' checks at Smith's bank, the same tourist might visit Shelter Island, developed by Smith, or cross the border to bet on the ponies at Caliente Racetrack, owned by Smith protégé and business partner John Alessio. If the visitor were truly upper crust, he might even wrangle an invitation to Smith's elite Cuyamacas Club, the new inner sanctum of downtown power. *Under the Perfect Sun*, p.81

If the cash flow from these operations slowed, Smith simply went to his own bank, the USNB.

> When the cash flow from tuna couldn't keep pace with his acquisitions and deal making, Smith simply lent money to himself from his US National Bank. To conceal his transactions he created almost a hundred corporate shells registered in various states. When, on occasion, federal or state regulators came close to uncovering his machinations, Smith was ready with a gift or job offer. Thus in the late 1950s, as the *Wall Street Journal* later reported, 'three Internal Revenue Service agents were assigned to examine the books of a Smith company … he wound up hiring two of them before the examination was completed. Davis, p.81

Smith had a closer call in 1962 when a bank examiner discovered that fully 21 per cent of USNB's portfolio consisted of loans to Smith's other companies. Self-financing on this scale was of course illegal, and the examiner recommended a Justice Department investigation. Instead, Comptroller of the Currency James Saxon transferred the examiner to San Francisco and hushed up his allegations. Smith, according to *Forbes Magazine*, avoided further embarrassment over the next decade by ensuring that bank examiners were 'entertained lavishly and offered jobs. Indeed, one became a vice president of the bank.'

By 1968 Smith found himself sitting with Richard Nixon in Nixon's Waldorf Towers suite, watching his race to the White House culminate in election. Smith had personally contributed or raised over $1 m to fund it. At the pinnacle of his success, Smith, with his new – and expensive – wife, embarked upon the building of the Westgate Hotel, a hotel to be designed along the lines of the classical European 'Hotel Palace de Grand Luxe', as noted on the website of the Westgate Hotel itself.

By the time the hotel was completed in 1970 (going into the end years of the real estate cycle) it was the most expensive ever built in the US. Smith and his wife had taken time to wander all over Europe to find just the right furnishings, the best equipment and most expensive and appealing paintings. No ordinary hotel, said *Esquire* magazine, rather, 'a contemporary version of such elegant buildings as the Ritzes of Paris, Madrid and London, the Grand in Rome, the Amstel in Amsterdam and the Imperial in Vienna.'

But, whilst Smith was out spending, hostile political forces were gathering. San Diego's small-time underground press began exposing loaned funds, corrupt politicians and Mafia links. For their trouble they were harrassed by the police, fire-bombed and received death threats.

In April 1969 the prestigious and conservative *Wall Street Journal* published a piece exposing Smith's use of the capital of Westgate (a public company) and the USNB to feather his own nest at the expense of other shareholders. Specifically the *Journal* described a $650,000 profit Smith made by selling and reselling a small life insurance company from one Westgate entity to another. The *Journal* also highlighted the Republican Smith's unwavering support for Bert Betts, the Democratic California state treasurer, who used Smith's bank as an official repository of state funds.

There was also the matter of Smith's relationship with John Alessio, rumored for decades, along with his brothers, to have maintained good connections with the underworld through their book-making operations across the border in Mexico in a 'sleeping partnership' with Mexican President Miguel Aleman Valdes. After years of working together, the Alessio Corporation had merged in 1964 with Westgate-California. Alessio then served on the board of Westgate.

By March 1970 a case against the Alessios was launched by the Inland Revenue Service (IRS) and the Justice Department for unpaid taxes. The US attorney for the San Diego area, Harry Steward, was a Nixon appointee on a recommendation from Smith. The case went nowhere, as Mike Davis notes,[2] until J. Edgar Hoover, the head of the FBI, intervened, probably after a presentation from the California racing industry which was losing millions because of the Alessio operation across the border. The Alessios were eventually indicted in one of the largest tax fraud cases in US history, despite the fact that the brothers had been heavy contributors to Nixon's fund-raising.

But back to Smith. In March 1972 *Life* magazine hit the streets with the headline that the Nixon administration had seriously hampered justice in the city of San Diego, detailing 'five instances of White House interference in local criminal justice investigations involving Smith, Alessio, or their political allies'. As described by Davis,[3] *Life* also noted Smith's

2 p.95.
3 p.99.

efforts with the Nixon administration to try to have the Department of Justice cease its enquiries and stop the tax evasion investigation into the Alessio family. With the *New York Times* supporting *Life* magazine's assertions, the IRS and then the SEC began investigations. Soon shareholders of Westgate filed a suit to recover lost funds.

Said the *San Diego Reader* in 1999:

> But when Nixon began his downfall, Smith's fortunes also reversed. Protected by Nixon's cronies from the prying eyes of federal regulators, Smith, it was later revealed, had systematically looted his bank of millions of dollars by making bad loans to companies controlled by himself or his friends, many of them connected to the Mafia. The notoriously mobbed-up La Costa Resort was financed largely by money from Smith and the Central States Teamsters Union pension fund. But as Nixon's hold on power weakened in the fall of 1973, auditors finally blew the whistle. The bank, with nearly a billion dollars of deposits, collapsed in October of 1973. It was, to that date, the biggest bank failure in United States history. www.sdreader.com

All 4,600 Westgate shareholders lost their entire investment. The collapse wiped out the value of the pensions of USNB employees, the pensions being paid in USNB stock (anticipating Enron exactly thirty years later). Smith himself, the originator of the largest looting of any US public company up to that time, was handed by Judge Robert Schnake (a Nixon appointee) a fine of $30,000, to be paid at the rate of $100 a month over 25 years, without interest.

FURTHER READING

Bergman and Robach. 'C. Smith and the San Diego Connection', in Weissman, Steve, *Big Brother and the Holding Company: the World Behind Watergate*.

Davis, Mike. *Under the Perfect Sun: The San Diego Tourists Never See*. The New Press, 2003.

Life magazine article by Denny Walsh and Tom Flaherty, March 29, 1972.

APPENDIX 5

Franklin National Bank of New York (1974 Cycle)

'Luck, more than anything,' said Federal Reserve Board Chairman Arthur Burns, talking to a *Newsday* reporter in late 1974 after describing having just averted a worldwide financial panic. 'We were sitting on a volcano. People were concerned in this country, but they were really scared abroad. We can't let it happen again, because we might not be so lucky the next time.'

FRANKLIN NATIONAL BANK opened as the Franklin Square National Bank, with $50,000 in shareholder capital, in 1926. After the Second World War, with Arthur T. Roth as the new president, the bank began its growth. Roth developed new, consumer-friendly styles of banking, pioneering drive-in facilities, bank credit cards, instalment loans and longer-term mortgages. By 1950 or so Franklin was the largest bank in its area of Long Island.

In 1961, seeking further aggressive growth, Franklin's directors successfully applied for permission to establish a branch office in New York City. With the new branch adopting a liberal lending policy in pursuit of growth, Franklin's assets doubled from $1.5 bn in 1964 to $3 bn by 1969, but the earnings and quality of the loan portfolio suffered somewhat as the growth proceeded. Noted Joan Spero, author of a major study of Franklin Bank, in 1980:

> In order to establish a position and to continue its rapid growth in the highly competitive New York market, Franklin made loans to companies which had low credit ratings and which found it difficult to obtain credit from the major New York banks. Despite the lower quality of these loans, Franklin charged rates other banks were charging prime customers and required lower compensating balances than other major banks. *The Failure of the Franklin National Bank*, p.26

In the late 1960s and early 1970s, an era of aggressive bank growth, further major changes were afoot for Franklin. In July 1968, after an annual general meeting at which shareholders expressed dissatisfaction with mounting bad loan debts and a declining stock price, president Arthur Roth was ousted. In 1972 a little-known Italian financier, Michele Sindona, paid $40 m for a controlling interest in the bank. The purchase was not unrelated to what had been developing in international markets in these years, in particular the Euro-dollar and Petro-dollar markets.

These new dollar markets were allowing US banks to upscale their operations dramatically by opening foreign branches – internationalising where the money was now collecting – thereby increasing the scale of their borrowing and lending. A number of banks, Franklin included, developed into multinational corporations during these years.

> Franklin's move abroad can be explained in part by its pursuit of growth and profit. These traditional economic motives took on a special character and intensity in American banking in the 1960s. The emergence of a new generation of bankers, the growing needs of a dynamic economy, and the encouragement of the Comptroller of the Currency led to a significant change in US commercial banking. The twin goals of high earnings and rapid growth replaced the conservative emphasis on safety and asset quality; bank structure changed through mergers, acquisitions, and the creation of bank holding companies; banks expanded activities such as real estate, municipal and consumer finance, and foreign operations (which were often more risky); and these new activities were financed not by traditional sources of lendable funds such as checking and savings deposits but by the issuance of short-term liabilities such as negotiable certificates of deposit, Federal funds, and Eurodollar placements and by greater leveraging through long-term debt of the new bank holding companies. Franklin National Bank, one of the fastest growing American commercial banks in the 1960s and early 1970s, was part of this revolution in banking. Franklin's growth policy and quest for higher profits were the necessary, though not the sufficient, condition for Franklin's move abroad. Spero, p.25

In particular, the move abroad enabled such banks to circumvent regulation Q. Regulation Q, explained Spero further,

> prevent[ed] American banks from paying interest on domestic demand deposits and establish[ed] ceilings on interest rates paid on domestic time deposits of less than $100,000, but [did] not apply to deposits held in foreign branches of American banks. Thus American banks with such branches could attract demand deposits by paying interest and could use foreign branches to attract time deposits by paying higher interest rates than those allowed at home. p.45

The Fed did not disapprove of these developments; indeed its authorisation for foreign expansion was required beforehand and was seldom refused. Under Sindona, the new Franklin owner, the bank's expansion overseas and into foreign exchange operations went into overdrive.

Sindona was a shadowy character. Nobody could actually work out where he got his money. After his (and Franklin's) downfall, authorities tracked down 125 corporations in eleven countries and a good many real estate operations and foreign exchange speculation vehicles, all connected by a complex group of holding companies in the tax havens of Liechtenstein and Luxembourg. There was also his control of SGI, Societa General Immobiliere, a giant Italian real estate development company which counted the financial arm of the Vatican an important shareholder. Said Sindona himself: 'Banking is a matter of connections … I have personal connections in all important financial centres. Those who do business with Michele Sindona will do business with Franklin National.'

Importantly, and perhaps due to connections, Sindona's holding company Fasco International, and Fasco AG, were not declared bank holding companies under US law, despite what looked like a controlling interest in Franklin. This meant Sindona could avoid US regulation and surveillance, a crucial development given the burgeoning of foreign exchange operations under the new floating exchange rates. Previously banks had bought or sold foreign currency mostly for the needs of customers. Now whole new bank departments opened up to trade their own accounts under the developing and irresistible temptation to speculate in currency movements. When it mattered most, though, several things went against Franklin in the year before its demise, as the bank stepped up its currency trading.

> Over a decade of rapid growth and poor management had left Franklin with a number of domestic problems, most importantly an excessive reliance on short-term financing, a dismal earnings record, and illiquidity of its assets. Franklin National Bank was heavily dependent on short-term borrowed money. Instead of financing growth through increased bank equity capital or increased demand, savings and time deposits, Franklin National like many other banks used funds borrowed short-term from other banks or from large lenders.
>
> Spero, p.70

In other words they were relying on certificates of deposit with maturity of less than 90 days or using overnight federal funds to finance loans of several years or more. When interest rates were put up in 1973 and '74, Franklin's operating costs went up with them. (The funds rate went from about 12 per cent to 20 per cent during 1973.)

Franklin had entered into foreign exchange trading in a search for profits to compensate for losses in other areas, but exchange trading losses ultimately bankrupted the bank. In a now familiar story, poor accounting procedures, mis-posting, unrecorded contracts and trader bets the wrong way (gambling and losing) were to blame. The worse the position became, the more the traders gambled. Informed and knowledgeable domestic money market participants began to withdraw deposits from Franklin.[1] C. Arnholt Smith's bank, the US National, had already folded in October 1973, so depositors and shareholders everywhere were now alert to the fact that, yes, a US bank could indeed collapse.

Franklin collapsed on October 8, 1974, though the onset of the crisis dated back to May 8. With the collapse, Sindona's connections became apparent. He was found to have 'borrowed' \$18m from his Italian bank, Banca Unione, and \$22m from Banca Privata Finanziara, also in Italy. The money was used to buy the controlling interest in Franklin. Sindona had used \$200m of Franklin's money, without approval, to underwrite a \$1bn

1 Spero, p.86.

notes issue of another Sindona bank in Italy, all of which unravelled as the market lost confidence when Franklin failed – causing further losses of confidence and losses of deposits in all connected Italian banks.

Franklin's failure was, at the time, a huge threat to the proper functioning of the world financial system. The Fed pumped an unprecedented $1.7bn into Franklin to prevent its collapse, taking measures as it did so not to alert the public to what was going on, for fear of starting a general panic.[2]

By 1983 Sindona was a man very much in demand. There was an ongoing investigation into a helicopter attempt to free him from his US prison cell. There was also a July 1981 Italian government indictment charging him with having ordered the murder of Giorgio Ambrosoli. (Also named in that arrest warrant were his son Nino Sindona and his son-in-law Pier Sandro Magnoni.) There was a January 1982 indictment from Palermo, Sicily, in which Sindona and 65 members of the Gambino, Inzerillo and Spatola Mafia families were charged with operating a $600m per year heroin trade between Sicily and the United States. Further Sicilian indictments followed which charged Sindona with illegal possession of arms, fraud, using a false passport and violating currency regulations. More indictments were issued by the Italian government in July 1982 charging Sindona and others, including the Vatican's Massimo Spada and Luigi Mennini, with a long list of criminal offences connected with the fraudulent bankruptcy of Banca Privata Italiana.[3]

Eventually twelve Franklin employees were indicted for falsifying records. Sindona himself was indicted and convicted under US law, then extradited to Italy, where he was convicted not only of fraud but of murder as well. Michele Sindona's knowledge of his bank's illegal dealings with the Mafia, the Vatican Bank and other well connected Italian bankers would have given him much of which to be fearful. He died in prison in 1986. Some say he was poisoned, others suggest he committed suicide by swallowing cyanide.

FURTHER READING

Cornwell, Rupert. *God's Banker: The Life and Death of Roberto Calvi*. Unwin Paperbacks, 1984.

Spero, Joan. *The Failure of the Franklin National Bank: Challenge to the International Banking System*. Columbia University Press, New York, 1980.

Yallop, David A. *In God's Name*. Johnathon Cape Ltd, 1984.

2 Spero, p.148.

3 David A. Yallop, *In God's Name*, p.304.

APPENDIX 6

Walter J. Kassuba Realty and the REITs (1974 Cycle)

TO DESCRIBE what happened to Walter J. Kassuba Realty we first need to highlight the role of the new Real Estate Investment Trusts (REITs). Dana L. Thomas gives a good description of this:

> The concept behind the trusts was both sound and useful. It was … a vehicle which would allow the nation's smaller shareholders to invest in a diversified portfolio of real estate ventures while providing a substantial new source of capital for large-scale developments like urban renewal. What made the trusts especially intriguing was the role they were designed to play in periods of tight money. When the pressure is on the commercial banks to cut down their business loans, the first borrowers to feel the pinch are typically real estate builders who are the riskiest customers. When the banks withdraw, a wide-open opportunity is provided for a trust to move in and build its portfolio of construction and development loans. So thought the pundits …
>
> The trust concept became the hottest property on Wall Street. Analysts gleefully called them 'perpetual moneymaking machines'. The effect of leverage on their earnings could be amazing. For instance, if a trust were earning \$1.50 a share and its stock was selling at 20, it would go to the public market to obtain new capital cheaply and expand its lending operations. Suppose it sold a hundred thousand shares for \$2 million; it would put these funds immediately to work in construction and development loans that yielded, in a period of tight money, 14 percent, generating for the trust new earnings of \$280,000. In short, the hundred thousand shares of new capital would return \$2.80 a share, boosting overall earnings as well as book value. Then the trust would come to Wall Street for still another public stock offering at an even higher price, boost its earnings again, and so on and on. That, at least, was the theory.
>
> Not surprisingly … the potential of the trust excited the imagination and the greed of Wall Streeters. Borrowing cash at 10 percent and lending it at 14 percent, returning at least 90 percent of their tax free profits as dividends to shareholders, while the price of their stock continued to soar to increasingly higher multiples – how could an investor go wrong with that? A crowd of wheeler-dealers, outside the real estate field as well as in it, rushed headlong to set up their own trusts. 'People with no background whatsoever in the business came to me and demanded that I raise fifty million to start an REIT,' reported one leading underwriter in Wall Street. 'I asked them what they knew about real estate; and their answer was that they didn't have to

> know a damn thing about it. They could always hire a mortgage man from a bank.' Most underwriters in those euphoric days needed no further persuasion. Some of the latter got involved in promoting trusts of their own.
>
> By 1969 the trusts were by all odds the glamour equities of Wall Street. The stock of almost any new REIT that came to the market was snapped up and a cinch to climb 100 percent or more in price without scarcely a pause. A huge rash of trusts were launched on the premise that the boom in real estate – in shopping centers, commercial buildings, residential apartments – would go on indefinitely. Within a period of six years, industry volume rose from a mere $1 billion to almost $20 billion. By the early 1970s the trusts were accounting for over 20 percent of all the construction and development loans to the real estate industry. *Lords of the Land*, p.283

As the number of REITs exploded, the pressure to lend more money increased. The risks increased in direct proportion to the quality of the borrowers demanding ever more funds. Problems were building in other areas too. Sometimes a REIT not only lent money to a builder but also subsidised him for the interest payments due on the loan, often right up until the final payment when the builder had to pay back not only the interest but the principal as well. Meanwhile the REIT accounted for the loan income in its books as if it were actually receiving each monthly instalment (it was good for the share price). This became a problem since by law the REIT had to distribute 90 per cent of its income each year to shareholders to maintain its tax exempt status. So some REITs were in effect distributing profits before actually receiving them.

> With practices like this prevailing, it was inevitable that the first major downturn in real estate would bring down the REIT industry with a crash. In December 1974, the collapse of a major builder who had borrowed heavily from a number of trusts started the dominoes tumbling. Walter J. Kassuba Realty, a Florida-based corporation, which had a $550 million investment in 119 properties around the nation, including 35,000 apartment houses and a wealth of offices and shopping centers, suddenly filed for bankruptcy under Chapter XI. Caught up in the tight money squeeze, beset by shortages of materials and cost overruns, thinly capitalized and dangerously overextended, the thirty-nine year old Mr. Kassuba ran out of cash, stranding over two thousand secured and two hundred unsecured creditors, including some of the nation's biggest mortgage bankers and insurance companies. In addition to such victims as John Hancock, Connecticut Mutual Life Insurance, Northwestern Mutual Life Insurance Company, and Chase Manhattan, which was a trustee for clients who lent Kassuba money, no less than a dozen real estate investment trusts were stuck with $110 million in bad loans.
>
> Thomas, p.287

'Real estate has historically thrived on cheap money like a lighted match on Kerosene,' Thomas noted earlier. And so it is. The party turns into a hangover when the interest rate – the cost of money – is tightened. Leveraged players, like the REIT industry of the time, feel these effects first.

APPENDIX 7

US Financial Corporation
and Its Land Office Business (1974 Cycle)

> Essentially, the land developers buy huge quantities of undeveloped land in Florida, Arizona, California, and other exotic sounding sunshine states. They then turn their agents, brokers and salesmen (and sales ladies) loose on vacationers who are in a mood to speculate on land values and on those dreaming of a retirement haven at the end of the rainbow. The sales techniques might well serve as a basis for movie scenarios … the hard sell after a day's outing by plane, boat, bus, with luncheon or dinner thrown in.
>
> Abraham J. Briloff, *Unaccountable Accounting: Games Accountants Play*, p.164, describing the late 1960s and early 1970s land office business

TYPICALLY, the contract of sale for those speculating on land value called for a fairly small up-front payment to the developer; the remainder was payable over a longer term, often up to ten years, in small monthly payments. For the developer company accounting rules allowed for some interesting sleight of hand. The developer, quite legally, was permitted to count as revenue the full value of the contract of land sale in the year the contract was signed. As the 1960s progressed, a trend developed. It was seen that such accounting could produce for a company quite a lovely set of books that, when tallied for shareholders – as distinct from the tax department, where naturally the contract revenue was reported only when actually banked – presented a robust picture of a growing business.

By the end of the 1960s,

> [t]his combination of front-end loading of income and the exaggeration of the amounts being recognized, produced a most ebullient financial picture – making these companies the 'love children' of 1969. Briloff, p.163

This was not the only accounting trick available to land developers either. Land companies could, and did, claim as a deduction for tax purposes the expenses of interest or any property taxes payable on the land they were land-banking for subsequent development, though in reporting these to shareholders such expenses became 'pre-paid', qualifying them as an asset of the business, not an expense – further enhancing the year's 'profit' figure.

This is what Penn Central was doing in its chase of Great Southwest Corp, with its interests in property, gerrymandering and contriving earnings, if Briloff's case is to be believed.[1]

US Financial (USF) was doing all these things, and more. USF was a builder of homes. In its 1971 prospectus, the corporation noted:

> USF conducts a significant portion of its single-family home production as a participant in joint ventures. Typically, USF's joint venturer is an independent general contractor and developer who is familiar with local industry conditions and regulations. Such joint venturer contributes half the equity capital (which may be borrowed from USF, if secured by the pledge of collateral), his skill as general contractor and administrator of the project, and, in some instances, the land to be developed. USF typically invests the remainder of the equity capital and provides interim financing and related services. USF controls the design of construction, the rate of development, cash disbursements and accounting, and performs a wide variety of other related services. At December 31 1970, USF was a participant in 67 joint ventures.

With some joint venture accounting tricks of the time, USF was able to account for any profits using joint venture accounting rules (rather than consolidation principles), and at the same time put the risk of any failed developments back onto the joint venturer and not USF itself. A failed development could therefore avoid disclosure to shareholders. It was all done, often legally, to overstate income, inflate earnings per share and hence underwrite the stock price. The tricks unravelled towards the end of 1973 as land prices began to soften with the rising interest rates.

FURTHER READING

Briloff, Abraham J. *Unaccountable Accounting: Games Accountants Play*. Harper & Row, 1972.

1 See p.217 for the nitty gritty, which will not be further detailed here.

APPENDIX 8

Equity Funding Corporation
and the Missing $100m in Assets (1974 Cycle)

> The customers didn't exist. Their mutual fund shares didn't exist. The funded loans didn't exist. The phony customers' phony pledges of the phony fund shares to buy phony insurance ultimately became numbers on a computer tape, which then printed out phony assets for Equity Funding Corp's phony books.
>
> *The Wall Street Journal* explaining the Equity Funding Corporation to its readers, August, 1973

DESPITE 64,000 fake transactions ($2bn dollars worth), $25m in counterfeit bonds and $100m in missing assets, the Equity Funding fraud went entirely undiscovered by regulatory authorities and the auditors.

> Gordon McCormick was an insurance and mutual fund salesman. He came up with the bright idea of combining these products in a package deal for investors. First, the customer would invest in a mutual fund; second, the customer would select a life insurance program; and third, the customer would borrow against the mutual fund shares to pay each annual insurance premium. Finally, at the end of ten years, the customer would pay the principal and interest on the premium loan with any insurance cash values or by redeeming the appreciated value of the mutual fund shares. Any appreciation of the investment in excess of the amount paid would be the investor's profit.
>
> David R. Hancox, 'Could the Equity Funding Scandal Happen Again?'

Put more simply, the customer was signing up to buy shares in the fund every year, then to borrow against this value to pay yearly premiums on a life insurance policy.

McCormick was joined by Stanley Goldblum, and together the two salesmen began to grow the company; control was later taken over completely by Goldblum. As growth continued, Goldblum began an acquisition programme of other insurance companies, something that soon required more and more money. And, for the buying to be effective, it was critical to maintain Equity Funding Corp's stock price. A higher price made it easier to compensate the owners of companies being bought out. Earnings growth for Equity Funding was therefore critical.

> The fraud began in 1965, when Mr. Goldblum told the chief financial officer of Equity Funding to make fictitious entries in certain receivable and income accounts. By inflating these accounts, the earnings per share

> increased; and the stock price rose to higher-than-expected levels. Fictitious entries alone do not bring in cash; but selling policies for fictitious customers could – and did – produce cash for Equity Funding, much of it from other insurance companies.
> Hancox

The fraud involved the practice of reinsurance. Reinsurance occurs when one insurance company sells to another some of its policies for cash, and to offload part of the risk should a large payout on the policy occur.

> In a typical reinsurance deal the selling company receives $1.80 from the buyer (the re-insurer) for every $1 in policy premiums. The price takes into account the heavy first year commissions the seller has paid to obtain the policy – of course, they paid none at Equity Funding – and affords the seller a small profit. In succeeding years, the buyer may get 90 cents on every premium dollar, allowing ten cents to the seller, who handles all the policy accounts and claims. The only way the reinsurance company makes money on the policies is through the policyholders' payment of subsequent years' premiums. Since these policyholders were nonexistent, Equity Funding planned to pay for the premiums through the sale of more phony policies, or through the 'death' of fictitious policyholders.
> Hancox

The creation of these fake policies and associated fake files required a lot of work.

> As the fraud progressed, more and more employees got recruited to help … The problem with phony policies was that the company's auditors would randomly select some every now and then and ask to see the real-world files behind them. There were no files, of course, since there was no insurance. So to prop up the scam, conspirators threw late-night 'fraud parties' to create phony files. When that solution proved inadequate, conspirators set up a secret office devoted exclusively to fabricating medical records and application forms on demand. The employees at the office, known as the Maple Drive Gang, spent most of their days killing time with knitting, champagne and Quaaludes … except when the clueless auditors at the main office would ask to see files for phantom policies. That's when the Maple Drive Gang would spend a frenzied few days creating dozens of policy files – then return to their endless round of office parties.
> www.thestreet.com

At the same time as the Maple Drive Gang were spending their days knitting or in a frenzy of creation, Equity Funding Corp was writing special software to create some of the insurance policies, to save time for the gang. When the fraud was discovered the company was in the process of updating the software to 'kill off' a set number of the created policies each year without making the reinsurers overly suspicious. Half the insurance policies of Equity Funding Corp were entirely fictitious by the time the fraud was discovered.

And within Equity Funding Corp itself there was plenty going on. In addition to the fraud the company was already engaged in, management discovered in 1972 that four of its employees had banded together to embezzle company funds by registering fake deaths. Instead of being fired, three were rewarded with stock bonuses and all four were put to further work supervising fake death claims on behalf of the company.[1]

None of this was ever discovered by the auditors. For their tardiness, the court gave the audit team two-year prison terms, four years probation and two thousand hours of charity work. Goldblum, along with eighteen of the twenty-one other indicted employees, pleaded guilty to the frauds. All received prison sentences.

FURTHER READING

Hancox, David R. 'Could The Equity Funding Scandal Happen Again?' (available online at www.findarticles.com/p/articles/mi_m4153/is_n5_v54/ai_20057314).

Seidler, Lee J. *The Equity Funding Papers.* John Wiley & Sons, 1978.

'The Great Wall Street Scandal: Inside Equity Funding' (www.buyandhold.com/bh/en/education/history/2004/ray_dirks.html).

1 See www.thestreet.com/pf/stocks/brokerages/791614.html

APPENDIX 9

A Review of Some of the Thrifts
and How They were Looted (1991 Cycle)

Empire Savings and the Texas appraisal

EMPIRE S&L in Texas grew 17-fold in the two years after the 1982 deregulation of the thrift industry.[1] Later regulators at the FSLIC would allege that the officers and management at Empire, amongst them Texas real estate developer Danny Faulkner, would sell land back and forth amongst themselves or associates so that it would appear to be increasing in value. This was used to justify ever larger loans for the hundreds of apartment projects developers were building along Interstate 30, east of Dallas.

The value of one section of 117 acres increased from $5m to $47m in just a few weeks.[2] It was allegedly properly valued by local appraisers, who are supposed to know roughly what a property is worth. The acreage was then sold to investors, who naturally borrowed from Empire to fund the purchase. Faulkner and his partners would organise the land selling (called flips) over weekend brunches at Wise's Circle Grill in the Interstate-30 corridor.

> Invited guests included officials from Empire Savings and Loan, investors, appraisers, and, increasingly, politicians, who drew huge campaign contributions from the events. Properties quickly changed hands over breakfast, and millions of dollars of phony profits were made in a few hours.
>
> K. Calavita *et al*, *The Savings and Loan Debacle*, p.50

At the bottom of any effective real estate loan is an honest property appraisal, which lending institutions rely on to determine the true value of the collateral being offered for the loan. If the borrower defaults, the property value should cover the loan. Regulators reviewing the condition of Empire after it was closed down in 1985 found more than four hundred examples of faulty or fraudulent property valuations. The $60m in real estate collateral for the loans was found to be worth just $8m.

The hundreds of miles of condos built along I-30 – condominiums only, no schools or stores – did not ever fill, and rotted under the Texan sun. Empire's losses on its loan book ran to $300m.

A later report of the Texas thrift industry revealed that real estate

1 Stephen Pizzo, *Inside Job*, p.4.
2 Pizzo, p.341.

developers had entered the thrift industry en masse in the early 1980s. By 1987 they owned 20 of the 24 most deeply insolvent Texas thrifts.[3]

Land flips at State Savings of Salt Lake City

IN 1977, San Francisco loan broker J. William Oldenburg bought 363 acres of land in California for $874,000, with a downpayment of just $80,000. In 1979 an appraiser valued the land at $32.5 m. Three years later, in 1982, the same appraiser was again asked by Oldenburg to value the same 363 acres. The new value was $83.5 m. Now who in their right mind would buy the acreage at such a clearly inflated price? Oldenburg supplied the answer.

The next year, 1983, Oldenburg was given approval to buy State Savings, a thrift in Salt Lake City, for $10.5 m. A short time later the thrift paid Oldenburg $55 m for the California property.

After a series of poor loans over the next several years, State Savings failed in 1985, owing $416 m to depositors. This the federal government (through the FHLBB) was obliged to reimburse to a limit of $100,000 per depositor as the deposits were federally insured.

Oldenburg was indicted in February 1989 for fraud.

Centennial Savings, Guerneville, Northern California

IN DECEMBER 1980 the board of Centennial elected Erwin (Erv) Hansen as president. Hansen was considered a conservative banker, though he preferred not the traditional banker's clothing but sports coat and cowboy boots. A new president such as Erv, it was felt by the board, could safely steer the thrift into the fresh deregulatory waters of S&L banking. In these new waters a different style of lending started almost immediately. Local lending on houses was out. Exotic investment in almost anything else was in.

In July 1982 Centennial loaned a Dutch investor Nicholas Sandmann (an acquaintance of Hansen) $5.4 m to redevelop a thousand-acre ranch near Santa Rosa. In the new regulatory environment such a loan significantly improved the financial health of the struggling thrift – at least in the accounting sense. Just for making a loan thrifts could now, under RAP accounting rules, book 2 per cent of the loan (2.5 per cent if the loan was for real estate construction) as income, and show it as such in the accounts. In 1979, 2 per cent fees had been permitted expressly for the purpose of increasing S&Ls' reported earnings at a time when their spreads were being squeezed by rising interest rates.[4] This income is of course merely a paper profit.

Thrifts quickly learnt that they could book other fees too, such as loan origination fees. They learnt also that they could add these origination fees

3 Calavita *et al*, p.35.
4 Martin Lowy, *High Rollers*, p.81.

to the amount of the loan – the larger the loan, the more income that could be 'booked'. And, if the thrift could somehow inflate the valuation of the real estate upon which the loan was based, an even larger loan could be justified – hence more income to book – in turn allowing even better bonuses for thrift owners at the year's end.

Soon some thrifts were even adding the interest payable on the loan to the loan itself. If a borrower wanted, say, a $5 m loan, the thrift would loan him or her $5.4 m and account for the difference by putting it to a reserve, out of which the next several years worth of interest would be made as and when it was due, usually monthly. This meant that the loan would always appear 'current' on the books and not in arrears, regardless of the true state of the project or the whereabouts of the borrower.

> This bookkeeping anomaly, resulted in the most desperate thrifts making the most, the largest, and the riskiest loans in an attempt to make the S&L's financial statements look better – or to give the borrowers a couple of years getaway time.
>
> Pizzo, p.335, n.4

Centennial's Santa Rosa ranch deal ultimately ended in default and allegations of fraud. The thrift, though, continued to book all the income due on all the loans it was making, and moved further down the road in its quest for growth.

In August 1982 Hansen bought into the construction industry with the purchase of Piombo Corporation for $13 m, making Piombo's owner Sid Shah an executive at Centennial. California state had just passed its Nolan Act, allowing a state thrift to invest 100 per cent of its assets in speculative ventures like Piombo. 'The beauty is that there's going to be enough money in this for everyone,' boasted Hansen.[5]

To pay for Piombo, Centennial placed advertisements in the *Wall Street Journal* offering what were called 'insured certificates of deposit', which guaranteed that Centennial would pay interest on any depositor's money at a rate slightly higher than the prevailing rate of 10.4 per cent. Deposits flowed in. Centennial was able to grow faster and larger than might have been the case had it been forced to rely on local depositors as in the past.

To see what this might look like in practice, it is worth examining a typical, though hypothetical, thrift balance sheet. In the beginning it might have looked something like this:

Assets		**Liabilities**	
Cash	10,000	Deposits (owed to depositors)	109,000
Mortgages	100,000	Owed to other banks	2,000
Property/equipment	5,000		
Total	115,000	Total	111,000
		Net worth	4,000
		Total liabilities and net worth	115,000

5 Quoted in Pizzo, p.27.

Clearly attracting more deposits means more money is available to lend, means more fees as income, means more profit.

The thrift in this example would not become insolvent just because a few depositors decided to withdraw their money. Say, for example, $15,000 in deposits is withdrawn. Provided the thrift has $5,000 worth of mortgages it can sell for exactly what it says they are worth, there is no problem. The new balance sheet would look like this:

Assets		**Liabilities**	
Cash	nil	Deposits (owed to depositors)	94,000
Mortgages	95,000	Owed to other banks	2,000
Property/equipment	5,000		
Total	100,000	Total	96,000
		Net worth	4,000
		Total liabilities and net worth	100,000

Despite the withdrawals, the thrift's net worth has not changed. As a percentage of total assets its net worth has actually improved: net worth was 4,000/115,000; it is now 4,000/100,000. More important is the use to which the thrift has put the deposits.[6]

At Centennial Hansen lent out such deposits ostensibly to make money. The accountants had managed to have Centennial's mortgages and assets valued at roughly $400m by August 1985; they were just $49m at the beginning of 1983. Hansen and Shah came to rely heavily on incoming deposits to fund their growth plans.

However, with Centennial paying ever slightly higher interest rates on deposits in order to attract the money, it was expensive funding for the thrift. So good ideas were needed to put the money to profitable use. Real estate speculation was the thing, in the short term at least. One such loan was to Shah, who decided a fortune could be made in land and mushrooms. He took Hansen and another Centennial director into the operation. Centennial loaned the group $1.5m to acquire a large, formerly bankrupt mushroom company in Washington state, the plan being to corner 80 per cent of the West Coast market. Ultimately for Centennial it was a $4m non-performing loan.

Along the way Centennial bought and refurbished a large office building in Santa Rosa for $7m. With all the new loan business, new offices were deemed necessary.

> Everything at the new office was first class: oak, brass, etched glass, box-beamed ceilings, mirrored walls, plush carpets. There was a board room big enough to jog in with a conference table long enough to skate on. Western oil paintings graced the walls and cowboy sculptures stood on cabinets and desks. A five-foot-high solid crystal horse head dominated the conference room.
>
> Pizzo, p.35

6 How the value of the mortgages is accounted for is another question, at cost, at market, and in the end what they can actually be sold for, which will affect the accounting net worth, but we will overlook this at the moment.

It seemed only appropriate that directors should be rewarded for their efforts in growing Centennial. In 1984 it was announced that Shah and Hansen would be awarded bonuses of $818,000 each, from the $2.6m 1983 accounting (read paper) profit. There was nothing dodgy about the bonus though: that was solid cash.

As Centennial grew, so did the spending.

> Hansen, a renowned ladies' man, had made the acquaintance of a stunning young woman who fancied herself an interior decorator. He took an immediate liking to her, and the two began a relationship that would cost Centennial hundreds of thousands of dollars. When Hansen needed a decorator … he hired his young friend. Over the next few months, the two of them flew often to Los Angeles and Las Vegas, on Centennial's twin-engine Cessna, on 'buying trips' … antique desks … a gold and silver chess table with an inlaid marble top and matching gold-and-silver chessmen. Pizzo, p.36

Hansen spent $90,000 decorating his own office. Before long he had five cars for himself and his family, paid for with a Centennial cheque. The director of every Centennial subsidiary received a new Mercedes.

> It wasn't long before the spending sprees caught the attention of the public. Few knew quite what to make of them, but most people accepted the ostentatious life-styles … as one more piece of proof that the area was becoming a playground for the rich and famous … Pizzo, p.37

Hansen knew that by throwing money around he could rise to a position of importance in northern California.

A few thought the spending looked out of place. One was Stephen Pizzo himself, a journalist at the local *Russian River News*. He published pieces questioning where the money was coming from at a once local thrift. Hansen's reply was to seek out the offices of the competing local paper, simply called *The Paper*, which as it happened had money troubles. Financial support was offered. Hansen hoped this might alter the balance between the two publications.

There was more than a good press to buy. Centennial, through its directors, was an active corporate citizen when it came to local political campaigns. As for the regulators in these early days of deregulation, as on-site examinations were difficult they relied on supervision by mail, often simply requesting what was needed from Centennial's directors. If further appeasement was required, Hansen might attempt to hire them at double their former regulator salary.[7] In the same way Centennial ended up hiring seven of its former auditors, who had often sat in on board meetings anyway, helping the thrift to structure its real estate deals.

Poor lending practices cannot go on forever, though. Loans were made without proper real estate valuations and other supporting documents.

7 Pizzo, p.47.

Meanwhile on the payroll was a $48,000 European chef (to prepare meals for thrift guests in the gourmet kitchen at the office), a corporate jet costing $35,000 a month, a San Francisco penthouse and 25 company cars.

Federal regulators finally got round to properly auditing Centennial about two years later and, amidst great shock, fired all the officers and directors and quietly closed it down. $165m of federally insured deposits had vanished. Hansen, at 55, was found dead shortly thereafter from a cerebral aneurysm. The death was given special attention by the coroner due to the suspicious circumstances.[8] Sid Shah was later indicted by the federal Organised Crime Drug Enforcement Task Force for laundering drug proceeds through a complex set of property projects.[9]

Bank queues in Maryland, 1985

THE EVENTUAL 1989 S&L crisis was not without prior warning. In mid-May 1985 a crisis occurred in the state of Maryland after press allegations about insider improprieties at Baltimore Old Court Savings and Loan. Panic spread to other thrifts when it was thought that the state's private insurance fund might not have enough funds to cover losses. Depositors, reported *Time* magazine,[10] 'gathered up their lawn chairs, thermos bottles and portable radios and lined up outside the banks'. Fearful depositors withdrew $630m in two months. 'What scared everyone was that everyone else was scared of losing his or her savings.'[11]

Between 1982 and 1985, it was later discovered, Old Court's owner Jeffrey Levitt had increased the assets of the thrift from $140m to $873m through esoteric real estate deals and Wall Street securities trades, many of which were now souring. This in addition to his lavish consulting fees and insider loans.

Regulators stepped in to calm the situation and reassure nervous depositors. Old Court, found to be insolvent because of the bad loans, was later quietly sold off to a larger New York institution, as were several other insolvent Maryland S&Ls. The US is a big place, however, and one state's thrift problems did not immediately present themselves to others. The general crisis occurred only when real estate values across the country crashed at the end of the decade.

At Old Court Jeffrey Levitt and his wife Karol were found to have taken out over $2m a year in salaries. They had used Old Court to buy $500,000 worth of jewellery and a good deal of artwork, to finance gambling excursions to nearby Atlanta, to buy two beach condos, three racehorses, and an apartment in Baltimore and one in New York City. On his way to prison Levitt said simply; 'I got carried away.'[12]

8 Pizzo, p.57.
9 See Pizzo.
10 May 27, 1985.
11 *Time*, May 27, 1985.
12 Calavita *et al*, p.62.

The dentist at North American

NORTH AMERICAN Savings and Loan was founded in 1983 by Duayne Christenson, a dentist. When not pulling teeth Christenson would make real estate investments on behalf of relatives and his girlfriend.[13] Christenson, 'tired of begging for loans from straight laced thrift officers,' opened his thrift in Santa Ana, California. Married and with children, Christenson had undergone some sort of mid-life crisis and had 'taken up with a flashy real estate lady' from Oak Grove, California named Janet F. McKenzie.[14]

Soon Christenson and McKenzie began investing the thrift's deposits in real estate projects that had been grossly over-appraised and in which both were holding indirect interests. One project in particular, earlier acquired for $4m, was 'sold back and forth to artificially increase [the project's] value to $40 million', as later reported by regulators.[15]

To get around federal laws that prohibited thrifts from lending to their owners and officers, Christenson would use nominee loans and so-called straw borrowers – people who would nominally stand in place of himself for loans.

> In one typical scheme straw borrower David Morgan purchased property brokered by McKenzie's real estate company and financed by North American. [Christenson] then resold the property at an inflated value to his own holding company.
> Calavita *et al*, p.19

McKenzie's company made excellent commissions, North American booked profits from the loan fees (paper profits, not cash) and Christenson had control of yet another property loan.

In 1989 McKenzie and four others were indicted on charges of racketeering after their thrift collapsed in June 1988. A $209m reimbursement to insured depositors was necessary. As regulators went in to check the books they found evidence of 'fake certificates of deposit, forged bank confirmation letters and other cover-up materials'.[16]

Christenson himself was killed the day before regulators seized the thrift in a mysterious car crash, leaving McKenzie as sole beneficiary of a $10m life insurance policy.

Ramona and the rug man

RUG SALESMAN John L. Molinaro and partner Donald P. Mangano, owner of a construction company, were granted a charter to open Ramona Savings and Loan in April 1984. Once deposits had been garnered, Ramona made continual loans to Mangano and Sons Construction Com-

13 *Time*, June 20, 1988.
14 Pizzo, p.22.
15 Pizzo, p.22.
16 Calavita *et al*, p.19.

pany to build condominiums, the floors of which were later covered with carpets from Molinaro's store.[17]

Ramona collapsed a mere two years later, costing the regulatory authorities, the FSLIC, $70m in reimbursements. About a year after Ramona's collapse, Molinaro was apprehended leaving the US for the Cayman Islands on a dead man's passport. He later admitted that he had already deposited $3m in the First Cayman Bank. When investigators had a look, diamonds, gold and millions of dollars in cash were found.

Fast Eddy at 'Gunbelt' Savings

THIRTY-THREE-YEAR-OLD Edwin T. McBirney – 'Fast Eddy' to friends – grew Sunbelt Savings and Loan in Texas from a one-time obscure $90m S&L into one, just four years later, with $3.2bn in assets. McBirney was able to do this, as were other thrift owners, by using unlimited access to brokered deposits, which since the 1982 Garn-St Germain Act were being courteously 'packaged' in $100k lots by deposit brokers. Once the deposits were in, the money could be loaned out. For any purpose.

> 'I remember one closing we had,' said a real estate sales person, describing how they flipped land to raise its value. 'It was in the hall of an office building. The tables were lined all the way down the hall. The investors were lined up in front of the tables. The loan officers would close one sale and pass the papers to the next guy. It looked like kids registering for college. If any investor raised a question, someone would come over and tell them to leave, they were out of the deal.' Pizzo, p.207

At the end of the day's flipping, huge loans based on the inflated values created by the flip sales would be taken out on the properties.

Regulators were apparently shocked by this prevailing Texan thrift mentality. As one regulator told it:

> 'I went down there and this Texan showed me this piece of land and told me how this guy had sold it to that guy, and that guy had sold it again, until it had been sold about six times, and I said, "Oh my God, that's terrible," and he said, "Only if you're sixth."' Calavita, *et al*, p.51

Some unfortunate thrift was usually sixth.

Fast Eddy was best known for his wild and crazy parties. According to one regulator, Sunbelt (known in the industry as 'Gunbelt' in recognition of its quick-draw approach to loan deals), spent $1.3m, perhaps more, on Hallowe'en and Christmas digs in 1984 and 1985, including a $32,000 payment to Fast Eddy's wife for organising them. Sunbelt later sued McBirney for the return of sums spent on him in those two years, including $61,800 for Christmas gifts, $15,000 for accommodation, $100,000 for meals and $70,000 for limousine service.[18]

17 Pizzo, p.23.
18 Pizzo, p.206.

In 1993, according to the Department of Justice (DoJ), McBirney settled with the FDIC in the amount of $8.5 m, to be paid back at an agreed schedule, for actions committed at Sunbelt, but then soon after entered into a trust scheme designed to defraud the FDIC of its right to restitution. In 2004 the DoJ announced a 21-count indictment[19] for mail fraud, making false statements, concealing assets, and money laundering. The case is pending.

Vernon's lavish living

DON DIXON, a former real estate developer, bought into Vernon Savings and Loan by offering the previous owners $5.8 m for Vernon's outstanding shares, the money being loaned to him by his good friend of some years, Herman K. Beebe. Vernon S&L, with $82 m in assets and just $90,000 in bad loans, was reportedly one of the healthiest thrifts in the state of Texas.[20] By 1986 Vernon was to report assets of $1.3 bn. Regulators, 'who had begged entrepreneurs to step in and save the ailing thrift industry',[21] were delighted. Vernon was quickly added to their published list of 'High Performance Associations'. Vernon S&L was just another example of what American business could do when government got out of its way, said the regulators. The reality proved a little different.

Don Dixon and his wife Dana divided their time between a $1 m beach house north of San Diego and a chalet in a luxury ski resort in the Rocky Mountains. Vernon had paid $1.9 m for the Swiss-style stone chalet. Chalet owners were transported to the ski lifts in chauffeured limos serving coffee and doughnuts on the way out and champagne on the way back.

> They went on luxury vacations across Europe, including one adventure they called 'Gastronomique Fantastique', a two-week culinary tour of France coordinated by Philippe Junot, former husband of Princess Caroline of Monaco, and paid for by Vernon. Dixon purchased a 112 foot yacht for $2.6 million, with which he wooed members of Congress and regulators on extravagant boating parties. To pay for all this, Dixon set up intricate networks of subsidiary companies for the express purpose of making illegal loans to himself.
>
> Calavita, *et al*, p.25

Defending the overseas trips as a necessary part of business, Dixon later asked: 'You think it's easy eating in three star restaurants twice a day six days a week?'[22]

Regulators later pointed out that Dixon had used the thrift to take money from brokered deposits and channel it into his holding company, Dondi Financial Corporation. Once it was there,

19 An indictment is an accusation by a federal grand jury; the defendant is innocent until proven guilty.
20 Pizzo, p.191.
21 Pizzo, p.193.
22 Pizzo, p.196.

> Dixon could use federally insured deposit money to fund whatever venture he and his associates could conjure up, which usually involved adding commercial real estate to the already glutted Texas market. Calavita, *et al*, p.25

One would have thought a few warning signs of a glutted market might have been noticed by Dixon – he and a former developer partner had been busted by the 1973 property downturn – but it was not to be. Greed blinds some to the obvious. Up-front fees charged on the real estate and land loans made on over-inflated property values meant that large bonuses could be paid to thrift owners and officers. Vernon paid $22 m to its owner, Don Dixon, who was known to flip land as if it were pancakes,[23] usually over breakfast.

When Vernon was finally closed down in 1987 an unbelievable 96 per cent of its loans were found to be overdue or in default,[24] and $1.3 bn in federally insured deposits had disappeared – which the government would have to reimburse. In the end taxpayers footed the bill. Said one FSLIC attorney: 'If you know the Vernon story, you know three percent of what happened in Texas.'[25]

> 'The real tragedy in Vernon Savings,' said one of its officers, Woody Lemons, after he had done some jail time for the frauds, 'is what it did to [the town of] Vernon. So many people depended on us. We employed a lot of people and we were a big taxpayer. So it affected a lot of lives and the community as well.' Interview, *Times Record News*, January 5, 1998

Renda and the money brokers

ONCE THE THRIFTS were free to pay going rates of interest on deposits, and Congress had decided in its wisdom to insure thrift depositors up to a ceiling of $100k, the deposit brokerage business saw a marked increase in activity. One man quick to see the implications of the new deregulation was Mario Renda. Changing professions from tap-dancer to international financier to money broker, Renda set up his First United Fund (FUF) in January of 1980, complete with two members of staff. What Renda saw early was that savers could get their high return risk-free, courtesy of federal government insurance, and thrift owners could loan out the funds risk-free as well, courtesy of that same insurance. Would anybody care what was done with the money?

Renda matched the savers with the borrowers, deducting a commission for his efforts – enough commission to fund a BAC-111 80-seater jet (once leased, rumour has it, to the film set of *Wall Street* for use by Michael Douglas), a second Rolls-Royce Silver Spirit, jewellery for his wife, English silverware, Persian rugs for the office (that also had an elevated desk so that visitors had to look up at him), and, in those cold winter months,

23 J. O'Shea, *Daisy Chain*, p.76.
24 *Time*, June 25, 1990.
25 Pizzo, p.228.

a chauffeur-driven limousine kept running all day in front of the office so that the interior remained warm.

Renda had plenty of schemes going once the money started flowing. Details later came to light, through the dogged tenacity of Federal Prosecutor Mike Manning, of how Renda invented schemes to broker deposits into certain thrifts on condition that they agreed to make loans to him or any of his associates: 'linked financing' it was termed. To get around legislation limiting the amount thrifts could lend to any one borrower, Renda sent in agents – straw borrowers – who did all the paperwork and, for a fee, passed on the loan proceeds. This was not actually illegal. The first trial of the scheme was at Indian Springs State Bank (which later failed), then Renda moved on to other thrifts including Consolidated Savings, owned by Robert Ferrante (with whom Renda would occasionally vacation on FUF's 100-foot yacht *Surrenda*), Coronado S&L (a neighbour at Indian Springs), and many others.

Renda put the loans straight into Hawaiian real estate, a location where Renda's activity was making him 'an important man'.[26] Other loan proceeds, Renda later admitted, would be wired directly to his personal Swiss bank account. Loan foreclosure papers, of course, would go to the duped straw borrowers. The key to this arrangement was the deposits. By June 1982 brokered deposits into thrifts stood at $26bn, roughly a ten-fold increase from the year before. Renda brokered his share by taking out extensive advertisements in the *Wall Street Journal*.

Renda's scheming grew even while he was being investigated by regulators. He believed he had little to worry about.

> [I]n those days before everyone wised up, the FDIC and FSLIC would send in two separate teams of auditors when they seized a bank like Indian Springs. One team would only look at the deposit side of the operation and the other the loan side. The two teams of auditors never ever compared notes.
>
> Pizzo, p.108

So Renda felt the auditors would never make a connection between his FUF and the Hawaiian loans.

The investigators are not confident they will ever know the full extent of Renda's schemes – exaggerating the interest paid by thrifts, skimming cash in different ways, not declaring income to the IRS. By 1988, however, the Federal Reserve Bank did have a list of 160 banks known to have been used by Renda, a document quietly leaked to Pizzo and his co-authors. This is instructive since it reveals that key insiders at the Federal Reserve, and perhaps other law enforcers, knew far more about the goings on at thrifts than they were admitting publicly. As land price deflated further in '88 and '89, putting terminal pressure on thrifts and their non-performing real estate loans, insiders would have been well aware of the bad news about thrifts which was still not public. (This is why markets

26 Pizzo, p.98.

successfully discount future news, as proved years ago by W.D. Gann.)

What escaped the FDIC and FSLIC did not escape Federal Prosecutor Mike Manning, who eventually unmasked Renda's deposit broking activities. Renda was dragged through the courts in a long process that began in late 1987. He was found guilty on one count of conspiracy, sentenced to two years in prison and fined $100,000.

Renda's fund First United placed more brokered deposits into thrifts than any other brokerage house, including bigger ones such as Merrill Lynch. Renda would tell his employees (over a hundred of them once the firm grew) that, stupid and sheep-like as bankers were, savings and loan officials were on an even lower level of intelligence.[27] This is not quite true. It is now clear that more than a few thrift managers knew exactly what they were getting themselves into, and why.

Other thrifts and banks

Bell Savings and Loan, California

BELL S&L failed in 1985 with losses regulators estimated at $500m.[28] Amongst other causes for the failure, authorities found that one Bell executive had used some of the thrift funds to buy some rather expensive airplanes. Such loans do not usually accrue interest for the thrift. Airplanes probably lose their value quickly, and would have required monthly maintenance.

Gateway Savings, Oakland, California

Gateway thrift was put under federal control in 1986 (a move designed to forestall collapse). The thrift was found to have had 'unsafe and unsound lending practices', in the words of one examiner, since 1983.[29] These included a $150,000 loan to a borrower with no job or income to support it, almost $10m worth of real estate loans where no valuation had been made, and 53 loans worth $2.1m to board members, many of which were in arrears.

Ostensibly to avert a public panic and run on the system, deliberate government secrecy kept much of the S&L fraud just that, secret. Details of the Gateway Savings fraud examined by the regulators came to light only by accident when the California state archivist inadvertently permitted a *San Jose Mercury* news reporter, Gary Webb, to review a few boxes of confidential 1980s bank documents.

American Diversified Savings Bank, Lodi, California

Time magazine[30] reported that this thrift, under the ownership and guidance of Ranhir Sahni, a former airline pilot for Air India, had squandered

27 Calavita, *et al*, p.56.
28 *Time*, August 15, 1988.
29 *Washington Monthly*, December 1990.
30 June 20, 1988.

its assets on ventures ranging from synthetic fuel schemes to a national paging system. The cost of closing American Diversified when it eventually failed because of its loan policies was more than $1 bn.

> Sahni bought American Diversified in 1983 and quickly turned the small-town thrift into a highflier. First he stopped writing home loans entirely, then closed the teller windows, and finally shut down the storefront bank, opening up instead ninth-floor space for receiving brokered deposits and transacting his many investment schemes. Calavita *et al*, p.52

Most of the schemes involved Sahni's two wholly owned subsidiaries, American Diversified Capital and American Diversified Investment.

> In one notorious transaction, Sahni invested federally insured money in a giant windmill farm in the desert between San Bernardino and Palm Springs. Thousands of modern windmills with steel sails now sit idle in the central Californian desert. American Diversified also 'invested' in a chicken farm purportedly designed to process chicken manure into methane energy, shopping centres and condominiums, and $300 million in worthless junk bonds. It was later revealed that Sahni was a partner in all of the real estate deals and alternative energy projects his thrift invested in. Calavita *et al*, p.52

This was the fastest growing thrift in the US at the time.

Manning Savings and Loan

As the 1980s wore on, some thrifts went to great lengths to hide fraud or growing insolvency from the ever-dwindling number of regulators available to check on the health of the thrifts. US Attorney Anton R. Vakulas reported:

> In the prosecuted cases of Manning Savings and Loan, American Heritage Savings and Loan and First Suburban Bank of Maywood, when the [nominee] loans became non-performing the assets were taken back into the institution, again sold at inflated prices to straw purchases financed by the institution, in order to inflate the net worth of the bank or S&L. The clear purpose was to keep the federal regulatory agencies ... at bay by maintaining a net worth above the trigger point for forced reorganisation or liquidation. US Congress, House Committee on Government Operations, Subcommittee on Commerce, Consumer and Monetary Affairs 1987b:99-100

Golden Pacific Savings and Loan

The owners, Jay and Leif Soderling, were charged in March 1987 with loan fraud in connection with a series of land transactions that had netted them $10m.[31] They pleaded guilty and the court sentenced them to one year in prison and ordered them to pay restitution. Unbelievably, on the same page of the newspaper as the report of the Soderling Brothers' penalty was the story of a man jailed for seven years for holding a friend's parrot to ransom.

31 Pizzo, p.56.

And at other thrifts…

At one unnamed thrift regulators discovered three sets of books, two kept on different computer systems and one done manually. At another customers were often persuaded to borrow more than they actually wanted so that they might use the excess to buy default loans or now worthless (but yet to be written off in the books) pieces of real estate from the thrift, thereby removing them from the books, helping to keep the thrift looking profitable. At yet another, in Southern California, regulators found a number of appraisals on a single property that started at $2m and went right up to $175m.

Cushing First National and 'The General'

Banks were not immune to thefts and dodgy land deals. In August 1988 a federal grand jury in Oklahoma City charged James Wasson (known at the bank as 'The General' for his close-cropped hair and commanding attitude) and partner Melvin Pulliam with conspiring to embezzle $1.3m from the bank. Regulators allege the pair used confidential records of soldiers who had served in the local National Guard Unit to create phony loan applications for six loans, the proceeds of which were then put to the two men's own companies.[32]

Herman K. Beebe and the dark side

> By the end of 1981, Beebe was a man to be reckoned with. Beebe was prepared to use everything he had learned over the years about banking and newly deregulated thrifts to build potentially one of the most powerful and corrupt banking networks ever seen in the US. Pizzo, p.239

How? 'Cause that's where the money is.

Some have called the Savings and Loan scandal 'one of the worst financial disasters of the twentieth century'.[33] To others it was a premeditated conspiracy to move funds out of the country for use by the CIA.[34] The *Seattle Times* called it the 'single greatest case of fraud in the history of crime'.[35] Regardless, a lot of money went missing from the S&Ls throughout the 1980s. A lot. $20bn, $50bn, perhaps more; no one really knows exactly. And, whilst much of it disappeared in poor lending and then the deflation of land values, made worse when the real estate market tanked nation-wide after 1988, much of the money was stolen.

Some of the stealing was done by awfully dodgy figures, many, it transpired, well connected to Mafia-controlled families, the CIA, or both. You can make up your own mind after working through the extensive reading list below. What follows here is merely the briefest glimpse of some

32 *Time*, August 15, 1998.
33 Calavita, p.1.
34 Joel Bainerman, *The Crimes of a President.*
35 June 11, 1991.

of the criminal behaviour. It is not in dispute; it has been well researched and documented by many writers.

Herman K. Beebe

Beebe started his company American Motel Industries (later shortened to AMI) in 1961; it was based in Shreveport, Louisiana. AMI started investing in hotels – Holiday Inns usually – but soon diversified into banks, thrifts, nursing homes and insurance companies. Beebe's banks would require borrowers to buy their insurance from AMI. 'When Congress announced that it intended to deregulate thrifts,' writes Pizzo,[36] 'Beebe immediately saw the possibilities.' Real estate in Texas was white hot, and deregulated thrifts could make more commercial real estate loans than ever before and with fewer restrictions than ever before. 'Beebe began to diversify,' says Pizzo, 'investing in more S&Ls, and he helped his friends do the same. Word got around that anyone who needed money to get control of a thrift should see Beebe.'[37]

Trouble was, alleged federal authorities some years later, Beebe was one of his banking conglomerate's biggest customers, 'using the network of banks and thrifts to finance ventures in which he held hidden interests … Rather than exert his ownership outright, Beebe often held control behind the scenes.'[38]

As became obvious later, one of Beebe's favourite tactics was to finance friends like Don Dixon who sought ownership of various thrifts. (Dixon relied on Beebe's backing to acquire Texas-based Vernon Savings and Loan in 1982.) The Comptroller of the currency listed 55 state banks and 29 thrifts which were all at various times controlled by Beebe and his associates.[39]

Beebe was living the high life. His house in the family compound was described by the *Shreveport Times* as an 11,000 square foot, $1m Colonial mansion, with swimming pool, tennis courts and private pond, which had seven bedrooms, 24-carat gold-leaf Spanish chandeliers, a separate smoke-house and a six-car garage. A deal with a Beebe bank, or one controlled by his network, might look something like this:

> Someone who wanted a real estate development loan would be required to borrow more than he needed and to use the excess as Beebe directed (to pay off a loan that Beebe owed or that was owed to him, or to buy stock in a Beebe bank). And once the development was completed, a Beebe associate might buy it with another (over funded) loan from a Beebe controlled institution. The whole process resembled a Ponzi scheme (*that could only last as long as real estate values were climbing*). Pizzo, p.237 (emphasis added)

36 p.236.
37 p.236.
38 *Time* February 20, 1989.
39 Secret Comptroller of the currency report dated June 3, 1985, later leaked to Pizzo and published by him as Appendix A to his book.)

The S&L troubles intensified shortly after real estate values stopped climbing. The Texas energy bust and associated decline in land values crystallised the thrift crisis in that state after 1986. In reporting this Pizzo writes that the runaway real estate development craze had resulted in such a property glut that shopping centres and condos stood vacant all over town.[40] In Dallas alone almost 38 million square feet of office space (equivalent to 17 Empire State buildings) stood vacant. Perhaps as much as $10bn in reckless loans had eventually been handed out.[41]

Pizzo alleges a good many Beebe connections to high-placed senior Mafia figures, often the Godfather himself, as does fellow journalist Pete Brewton, who describes Beebe as a 'Louisiana organised crime associate'. In words reminiscent of the first chapter of Dale Carnegie's *How to Win Friends and Influence People*, where Carnegie points out how even gangsters rarely believe they have done anything wrong, Beebe stated through his lawyer, after being hounded by the IRS, FSLIC and the FDIC, that: 'The FSLIC was encouraging the thrifts to be aggressive. Herman felt he could make money, so he got in. He doesn't feel he did anything wrong.'[42]

Palmer National Bank

The Washington-based Palmer National bank was set up in 1983 by Stefan Halper, policy director for George Bush's 1980 presidential campaign, and Harvey McLean Jnr, Southern Finance Chairman for Bush on the same campaign and a former Dallas real estate developer. The seed money, $2.8m, came from Herman K. Beebe. (George Bush had been CIA Director from January 1976 to January 1977, and eventually ended up in 1980 as Reagan's running mate.)

One of the established accounts at Palmer was that of the National Endowment for the Preservation of Liberty (NEPL), eventually found to be a front organisation for Oliver North, the man who helped run the Iran/Contra arms funding deal under the nose of President Reagan and of Congress. Through Palmer money was channelled to North's Swiss bank account and, through Palmer, Carl Channell, one of the few private citizens convicted in the scandal, secured a $650,000 'loan' to purchase weapons for the Nicaraguan Contras. (Remember, bank deposits are insured so the ultimate risk lies with the federal government.)

The NEPL raised over $10m to assist the Contras. Many writers allege that the CIA used the thrift deregulation process to help pay for covert operations and other activities Congress would not or could not support (despite the fact that Republican right-wingers had majority support). After a thrift in question collapsed, 'obstacles' might miraculously appear in the way of FBI investigations.

40 p.246.
41 *Time*, February 20, 1989.
42 *Time*, February 20, 1989.

Vision Banc Savings

This is what Robert Sherrill[43] wrote about Vision Banc Savings, himself quoting the work of Pete Brewton and the *Houston Post*:

> In March 1986, Houston developer Robert Corson bought the Kleberg County [Texas] Savings and Loan for $6 million and changed the name to Vision Banc Savings. To get his thrift, Corson reportedly used a letter of recommendation from a judge who in 1988 would head George Bush's campaign in Harris County (Houston). Later, the judge said he hardly knew Corson ... Brewton claims Corson is identified in federal law enforcement records as a known money launderer and says that one former CIA operative told him that Corson frequently transported large sums of cash ... for the agency. At the time of purchase, the thrift had assets of $70 million. Four months later it was insolvent. How come? Partly, says Brewton, because of a $20 million loan to help finance a Florida land deal. Corson's thrift lost $17 million of the $20 million. Another thrift, Hill Financial Savings in Red Hill, Pennsylvania, put up $80 million to seal the land deal; it lost $40 million ... Brewton says the Pennsylvania thrift, which has since gone bankrupt, had ties to the CIA and organised crime, as did one of the men who put the land deal together, Miami Lawyer Lawrence Freeman, a convicted money launderer for drug runners.

Mario Renda

Renda's techniques used to rob the banks have in part been described above (see 'Renda and the money brokers', p.418). *The Nation*[44] succinctly described what Renda was engaged in: 'If you ... make loans to certain borrowers that I send you, I will supply the money to lend to them.' As it turned out, a decent proportion of the borrowers Renda sent to collect the loan proceeds were Mafia connected. Renda was in effect laundering Mafia money. All up, he directed deposits of about $5 bn per year into 130 thrifts, every single one of which later failed.[45]

Renda did eventually go to prison (perhaps he worked washing real laundry) but no government agency ever made any attempt to trace all the washing that his borrowers took with them, or sue to get any of it back.

Indian Springs State Bank

This is what transpired at Indian Springs State Bank, as noted by Gary W. Potter, Professor of Criminal Justice and Police Studies at Eastern Kentucky University.[46]

> The fourth largest stockholder in Indian Springs was Iranian expatriate Farhad Azima, who was also the owner of an air charter company called

43 *The Nation*, November 19, 1990.
44 November 19, 1990.
45 Jonathon Kwitny in *Village Voice*, October 20, 1992.46 Details can also be found in Bainerman, *The Crimes of a President*,.pp.279-80, and Brewton, *The Mafia, the CIA and George Bush*, pp.197-200.
46 Details can also be found in Bainerman, *The Crimes of a President*,.pp.279-80, and Brewton, *The Mafia, the CIA and George Bush*, pp.197-200.

Global International Air. The Indian Springs bank had made several unsecured loans to Global International Air, totalling $600,000 in violation of the bank's $349,000 borrower limit. In 1983 Global International filed for bankruptcy, and Indian Springs followed suit in 1984. The president of Indiana Springs was killed in 1983 in a car fire that started in the vehicle's back seat and was regarded by law enforcement officials as of suspicious origins.

Global International Air was part of Oliver North's logistical network which shipped arms for the US government on several occasions, including a shipment of 23 tons of TOW missiles to Iran by Race Aviation, another company owned by Azima. Pete Brewton, in his investigation of the Indian Springs bank collapse, was told that the FBI had not followed up on Indian Springs because the CIA informed them that Azima was 'off limits' (*Houston Post*, February 8, 1990). Similarly the assistant US Attorney handling the Indian Springs investigation was told to 'back off from a key figure in the collapse because he had ties to the CIA.'

Azima did indeed have ties to the CIA. His relationship with the agency goes back to the late 1970s when he supplied air and logistical support to EATSCO (Egyptian American Transport and Services Corporation), a company owned by former CIA agents Thomas Clines, Theodore Shackley, and Richard Secord. EATSCO was prominently involved in the activities of former CIA agent Edwin Wilson, who shipped arms illegally to Libya. Azima was also closely tied to the Republican Party. He had contributed $81,000 to the Reagan campaign.

Global International also had other unsavoury connections. In 1981, Global International made a payment to organized crime figure Anthony Russo, a convicted felon with a record that included conspiracy, bribery, and prostitution charges. Russo was the lawyer of Kansas City organized crime figures, an employee of Indian Springs, and a member of the board of Global International ... Global International's planes based in Miami were maintained by Southern Air Transport, another CIA proprietary company. According to Franck Van Geyso, an employee of Global International, pilots for Global International ferried arms into South and Central America and returned to Florida with drugs. Indian Springs also made a loan of $400,000 to Morris Shenker, owner of the Dunes Hotel in Las Vegas, former attorney for Jimmy Hoffa, and close associate of Nick Civella and other Kansas City organized crime figures. At the time the loan to Shenker was made, he, Civella, and other Kansas City mobsters were under indictment for skimming $280,000 from Las Vegas' Tropicana Casino.

The Comptroller

As the '80s roared on, the man Reagan appointed to the post of Comptroller of the Currency (the government man in charge of all the banks), was a Bush colleague, Robert L. Clarke. Jonathon Kwitny reported[47] that

47 *Village Voice*, October 20, 1992. Kwitny died in 1998 of cancer, aged 57. He was an award-winning journalist, perhaps best known for his 17 years of investigative reporting at the *Wall Street Journal*, and then for his critically acclaimed national television news programme, *The Kwitny Report*, aired on PBS.

Clarke had once helped organise a bank that laundered thrift money into an overseas account. Clarke, according to Kwitny, was also a shareholder in a bank the government found to be under the 'influence or control' of a Mob figure. The official OCC (Comptroller) site says of Robert L. Clarke:

> [A] Texas banking Attorney, [he] was named Comptroller by President Reagan. His tenure coincided with an era of extraordinary turbulence in financial institutions and the financial marketplace in the United States. Under Clarke, the agency strengthened its managerial and supervisory capabilities to deal with changes and stresses in the national banking system. Clarke led the effort to expand the national bank powers in order to better meet the competition from non bank providers of financial services. His leadership helped to reduce the costs of bank failures and to restore the safety and soundness of the national banking system.

The 1980s banking events would seem to indicate otherwise.

A Summary of Beebe and the dark side

Only a fraction of the moneys lost in the whole S&L scandal have ever been publicly accounted for. Journalist Pete Brewton at the *Houston Post* documented 22 thrifts and two banks eventually bailed out by the Bush Administration that had links with the CIA, 16 of them in Texas. Bainerman concluded that hundreds of billions of dollars was moved offshore by the CIA and others within the government by looting S&Ls, and via budget deficits and Star War myths, in an effort to fund covert operations aimed at toppling communism.[48]

But all this must not allow us to be deflected from the main game. Most of the S&L looting was done by supposedly respectable businessmen, often former real estate men, loaning other people's money – often to themselves – for pie-in-the-sky dreams. Much of it was like a pyramid scheme that could last only as long as land values kept rising. The cycle turned eventually. Falling real estate values in the late 1980s finally brought an end to the partying, after which the usual hangover lasted the usual couple of years.

Jeb Bush at Broward Federal Savings and Loan

THE 1980s Vice-President's son, Jeb Bush, had a hand in yet another thrift failure, Broward Federal Savings and Loan in Sunrise, Florida. The *Wall Street Journal* and *Washington Post* told the story.

Broward loaned \$4.5 m in February 1985 to real estate developer J. Edward Houston. The only security required was a personal guarantee from Houston. The same day he received the Broward loan, another Houston entity loaned the same dollar amount to the partnership of Jeb Bush

48 David A. Yallop's *In God's Name* suggests the Catholic Church used a number of Italian banks for the same purpose – toppling communism – by getting funds to the Polish Solidarity movement.

and Armondo Codina. With the funds they purchased a Miami building. The Houston entity required the partnership to repay the loan only if rents from the building were enough to cover the repayment.

No repayments were ever made on the loan. In 1987 J. Edward Houston defaulted on his loan from Broward Federal.

In 1991, after the thrift had collapsed with $285m owed to depositors, the FDIC sued the directors of Broward Federal for negligent lending practices, citing the Bush/Codina loan as being one example that contributed to the collapse. Eventually, in settling with Jeb Bush, the FDIC allowed the Bush/Codina partnership to keep ownership of the Miami building by repaying just $500,000 of the original $4.5m loan.

FURTHER READING

Empire Savings and the Texas appraisal

'Banking on Unreal Estate – the Appraisal Scam', *Washington Monthly*, Vol. 18, February 1986.

Calavita K., Henry Pontell and Robert Tillman. *Big Money Crime: Fraud and Politics in the Savings and Loan Crisis*. University of California Press, 1997.

Pizzo, Stephen. *Inside Job: The Looting of America's Savings and Loans*. McGraw Hill Publishing Co, 1989.

Land flips at State Savings of Salt Lake City

Pizzo, Stephen. *Inside Job: The Looting of America's Savings and Loans*. McGraw Hill Publishing Co, 1989.

San Francisco Examiner, April 1984.

Wall Street Journal, June 1984.

Centennial Savings, Guerneville, Northern California

Lowy, Martin. *High Rollers: Inside the Savings and Loan Debacle*. Praeger, 1991.

Pizzo, Stephen, *Inside Job: The Looting of America's Savings and Loans*. McGraw Hill Publishing Co, 1989.

Bank queues in Maryland, 1985

Calavita, K., Henry Pontell and Robert Tillman. *Big Money Crime: Fraud and Politics in the Savings and Loan Crisis*. University of California Press, 1997.

Koepp, Stephen. 'Another time bomb goes off', *Time*, May 27, 1985.

The dentist at North American

Calavita K., R. Tillman and H.N. Pontell. 'The Savings and Loan Debacle: Financial Crime and the State', *Annual Review of Sociology*, Vol. 23, 1997.

Pizzo, Stephen. *Inside Job: The Looting of America's Savings and Loans*. McGraw Hill Publishing Co, 1989.

'Too far gone to bring back', *Time*, June 20, 1988.

Ramona and the rug man

Pizzo, Stephen. *Inside Job: The Looting of America's Savings and Loans*. McGraw Hill Publishing Co, 1989.

Fast Eddy at 'Gunbelt' Savings

Calavita K., Henry Pontell and Robert Tillman. *Big Money Crime: Fraud and Politics in the Savings and Loan Crisis*. University of California Press, 1997.

Pizzo, Stephen. *Inside Job: The Looting of America's Savings and Loans*. McGraw Hill Publishing Co, 1989.

Vernon's lavish living

Calavita, K., Henry Pontell and Robert Tillman. *Big Money Crime: Fraud and Politics in the Savings and Loan Crisis*. University of California Press, 1997.

'Good Ole Bad Boy', *Time*, June 25, 1990.

'How to Rob Banks without a Gun', *Time*, August 15, 1988.

O'Shea J. *Daisy Chain: How Borrowed Billions Sank a Texas S&L*. Pocket Books, 1991.

Pizzo, Stephen. *Inside Job: The Looting of America's Savings and Loans*. McGraw Hill Publishing Co, 1989.

'Vernon S&L Scandal: A Memory', *Times Record News*, January 5, 1998.

Renda and the money brokers

Calavita K., Henry Pontell and Robert Tillman. *Big Money Crime: Fraud and Politics in the Savings and Loan Crisis*. University of California Press, 1997.

Pizzo, Stephen. *Inside Job: The Looting of America's Savings and Loans*. McGraw Hill Publishing Co, 1989.

Other thrifts and banks

Bock, Gordon. 'How to Rob Banks without a Gun', *Time*, August 15, 1988.

Calavita K., Henry Pontell and Robert Tillman. *Big Money Crime: Fraud and Politics in the Savings and Loan Crisis*. University of California Press, 1997.

Pizzo, Stephen. *Inside Job: The Looting of America's Savings and Loans*. McGraw Hill Publishing Co, 1989.

Simons, Teresa. 'Banking on Secrecy', *Washington Monthly*, Vol. 22, Issue 11, December 1990.

'Too far Gone to Bring Back', *Time*, June 20, 1988.

Herman K. Beebe and the dark side

Bainerman, Joel. *The Crimes of a President: New Revelations on Conspiracy and Cover-up in the Bush and Reagan Administrations*. S.P.I. Books, 1992.

Brewton, Pete. *The Mafia, the CIA and George Bush*. S.P.I. Books, 1992. (And various *Houston Post* articles.)

Calavita K., Henry Pontell and Robert Tillman. *Big Money Crime: Fraud and Politics in the Savings and Loan Crisis*. University of California Press, 1997.

Kwitny, Jonathon. 'Signs Point to Mob Involvement in Savings and Loan Mess', Editorial, *Seattle Post Intelligencer* (available at www.freerepublic.com/forum/a389b6b6e3fd7.htm).

Kwitny, Jonathon. 'The Real S&L Scandal: How Bush's Pals Broke the Banks', *Village Voice*, October 20, 1992.
'Minority Report', *The Nation*, July 9, 1990.
'Oval Office Secrets Revealed in New Book', *Filipino Reporter*, October 14, 1993 (available at Highbeam Research website, www.highbeam.com).
Pizzo, Stephen. *Inside Job: The Looting of America's Savings and Loans*. McGraw Hill Publishing Co, 1989.
Potter, Gary W. 'Organized Crime, the CIA and the Savings and Loan Scandal', Eastern Kentucky University (available at www.thirdworldtraveler.com/CIA/S&L_Scandal_CIA.html and also at www.btinternet.com/~nlpwessex/Documents/Kentuckystatecrime.htm).
Sherrill, Robert. 'The Looting Decade: S&Ls, Big Banks and Other Triumphs of Capitalism', cover story, *The Nation*, November 19, 1990.
'Thompson's Supporting Role', *The Nation*, July 21, 1997.
Yallop, David A. *In God's Name*. Johnathon Cape Ltd, 1984.
Woodbury, Richard. 'Dad Would Make a Deal with the Devil', *Time*, February 20, 1989.

Jeb Bush at Broward Federal Savings and Loan

Austin American Statesman, May 17, 1992, p.G1.
The Nation, December 11, 1990.
Wall Street Journal, August 9, 1988, p.A1.
Washington Post, October 15, 1990, p.A24.

APPENDIX 10

The Keating and Neil Bush Scams (1991 cycle)

Charlie Keating and Lincoln Savings

> Buying the bank was the best bet of all, because that's where the cash was kept.
> Michael Binstein and Charles Bowden, *Trust Me*, p.55

> 'Lending money here, buying land there, money flowing here, money flowing there, accounting rules pressed right to the edge…'
> A key legal aide to Charles Keating defending the books of Lincoln S&L[1]

> Congressmen, seldom in our experience as accountants have we encountered a more egregious example of the misapplication of generally accepted accounting principles … Lincoln was manufacturing profits by giving its money away.
> Kenneth Laventhol, an outside accountant hired by the Federal Government to investigate Lincoln Savings & Loan[2]

AS WE SAW in Chapter 13, the federal government, in an effort to overcome the S&L problems of the early 1980s, further deregulated the banking field, urging cashed-up companies to take the S&Ls over. American Continental Corporation (ACC), a builder of homes, of which Charles ('Call Me Charlie') Keating was Chairman and the largest shareholder, bought Lincoln Savings and Loan of Phoenix, Arizona, paying the $51 m with junk bonds issued through Michael Milken's Drexel Burnham. (Paying with debt, in other words.)

Normally an S&L simply took in deposits and lent them out as home loans. Charlie Keating promised, as part of the buyout agreement with the regulators, to continue this operation. The next year, however, Lincoln made only eleven home loans, four of them to ACC employees. New state banking laws were now permitting investments in virtually anything else a thrift chose. So, like many of the other thrifts, Lincoln commenced buying brokered deposits, $5 bn worth by May 1988. The incoming deposits were used to buy junk bonds and raw land (almost a billion dollars worth in Arizona alone), make trades in gold and silver and pay out $34 m in wages to family members.[3] Making loans to insiders and political mates was also a popular activity.

In one sense it doesn't matter what the deposits are used for provided it generates a profit.

1 Quoted in Binstein and Bowden, p.266.
2 Binstein and Bowden., p.369.
3 Binstein and Bowden, p.47.

> [F]or every deposit acquired by the savings and loan a place must be discovered to plant the money, a place where when harvest time comes the money has grown and is larger than the deposit plus the interest. Or Lincoln goes broke.
>
> Binstein and Bowden

That is all. In the banking business it is pretty clear cut. So began the deal-making to generate those profitable harvests. Binstein and Bowden report one of them thus:

> There are 2,700 square miles of vacant land west of Phoenix, and Charlie Keating's dream city of Estrella, at twenty-six square miles, is less than 1 percent of this land bank. It is March 31, 1987, and it is time to attend to this dream. Keating has bought the land for about $3,000 an acre, and on the last day of March he sells one thousand acres to West Continental Mortgage Investment Corporation (Wescon) for $14 million, or $14,000 an acre. Lincoln records a profit of $11.5 million on this deal. Wescon puts down $3.5 million cash and takes out a non-recourse note of $10.5 million to cover the rest of the transaction. This is a remarkable feat for Wescon since it has a net worth of $30,000 and total assets of $87,000. But of course, the deal is not as simple as it at first appears. A few days earlier, on March 25, an independent appraiser had told Lincoln that the thousand acres were worth only $8.5 million, about $5.5 million less than Wescon was happy to pay (the appraiser also noted on his report that he was assessing the land for one Ernest C. Garcia). Also on March 30, Lincoln loaned $30 million to a company owned by Ernie Garcia, and Garcia immediately drew $19.5 million of this sum as cash. That very day Garcia loaned $3.5 million to Wescon, precisely the amount of the down payment on the land in a portion of the Estrella project called Hidden Valley – which at the moment is a remote patch of desert linked to the outside world by a jeep trail. Garcia's loan to Wescon is a non-recourse note, meaning if they don't pay it off he can collect only by taking over the parcel of land in Hidden Valley. Out of this transaction Lincoln books a substantial profit of $11.1 million, and naturally, 40 percent of this amount must be sent to ACC for the escrow tax fund. Ernie Garcia himself gets the use of millions of dollars for his own ambitions. And so it goes, deal after deal, quarter after quarter.
>
> p.283

Accounting profits, note. Not cash flow.

The deals and investments continued. Lincoln bought almost $12m 'Circus Circus' company junk bonds. The thrift invested $132m in the stock of takeover target Gulf Broadcasting Corporation. Lincoln was also found to be making regular payments to its owner, ACC, ostensibly to cover federal income taxes, despite the fact that ACC did not have a tax liability to the government.

To keep the regulators off his back, Keating hired a squad of lawyers; between $4m and $9m a year was spent on them.[4] It proved money well spent. When William L. Robertson, the chief examiner at one of the

4 Binstein and Bowden, p.220.

regulating boards, sent an 18-page report to his boss asserting that Keating has acquired his S&L through misrepresentation and was investing federally insured funds in risky ventures with very few safeguards, he was removed from the auditing task and demoted.

The lawyers made further suggestions to push Keating's cause. Economists were hired to study the thrift industry and write reports on such operations and their merits. Keating hired the promising economist Alan Greenspan (soon to be appointed Fed Chairman), who charged Keating $32,000 and reported that Lincoln was a 'new, innovative and soundly-run institution that poses no foreseeable risk to the FSLIC'. Said *The Washington Monthly* later, in March 1997: 'Not long after, all the thrifts on Greenspan's [innovative and soundly-run] list failed but one, and the survivor – although Greenspan didn't seem to know it – was not a thrift.'

What Keating wanted most, however, was a monument.

> Charlie Keating leaves a trail of deals and various forms of paper. But no monument. And like many men who taste power, he eventually wants to produce something that is physical, that he can show people who do not know a bond from a bidet. He wants to build hotels. There are financial reasons – under the current tax laws governing limited partnerships such investments can be very lucrative shelters. In the current buying frenzy, they can be sold at a great profit. If a hotel is kept occupied, it becomes a cash cow as guests fling money into the till on a daily basis. And cash flow is like blood for anyone who loves to do deals. But the reason of the heart is that Charlie Keating wants a monument. Charlie Keating is going to build the finest hotel on the surface of the earth. Not a Hilton, but a place to rival and exceed the grand hotels of Europe. He is going to build it in Phoenix, Arizona. In order to do this he needs deep pockets that are not anxious about immediate returns on capital. He has, under deregulation, part of the necessary equation in Lincoln Savings and Loan. And now, as Toufic Aboukhater and his sons dine at his table, he has within reach the other piece of the equation, Middle Eastern oil money. He will need it all because before the Phoenician opens its doors on October 1, 1988, over $300 million will have vanished into its six hundred rooms. Binstein and Bowden, p.187

Note the timing. The 'finest hotel on the surface of the earth' … using someone else's money … as the real estate cycle approaches its end. The building of the hotel is worth describing, such events being a historically reliable guide to the top of the real estate market when they come towards the end of the 18-year cycle – as they usually do. Binstein and Bowden quote the words of several of the contractors:

> 'The whole thing has a seat-of-the-pants quality. When they started pouring concrete it was for a 400-room hotel, now it's a 600-room hotel. Then Charlie adds on a golf clubhouse, casitas, a health spa, an underground parking garage for 1,200 cars, a tennis complex, a pool island restaurant. The rooms go from white oak to red oak and back to white oak.' 'We had a very active owner,' one contractor confesses. 'You know that there's heart and soul in

> that building, you can look at it, everything in that building is of the utmost quality.' 'Nothing was off the rack,' the contractor continues. 'Every item that you look at in the Phoenician you'll notice has no brand names on it, no exposed fasteners with the exception of hinges on the doors. Okay, this room is fine, we'll go to the next one. I think there are fifty-six different varieties of rooms. Holiday Inn has one. Fifteen in a luxury hotel is maybe reasonable, not even that much. They went through consultants like water.'
>
> p.32

Meanwhile the Arizona real estate market was flattening, adding pressure to the cash flow and that later harvest time of profitable lending. But somehow Keating always managed to stay one step ahead of the regulators, who continually wondered how he did it. Later the supposedly secure telephone line from the examination office at Lincoln to headquarters in Los Angeles was found to have been bugged: Keating's executives had been listening in.[5]

Keating's thrift failed, and failed miserably, its vaults short at least a billion dollars. Eventually $2.5 bn was found to be missing. On January 6, 1993 the people delivered their verdict: Charles Keating, never actually listed as an employee of Lincoln on any documentation, was found guilty of racketeering and fraud.

He served just 46 months of his sentence. The conviction was overturned on appeal.

Neil Bush and Silverado Savings and Loan

> 'It was the roaring '20s. Every other car on the street was a Mercedes … there was money to burn everywhere.'
>
> Charles Hull, a banker at Denver's Colorado National Bank[6]

THE S&L crisis was not a big media issue in the 1980s; mainly the stories broke in the business sections of newspapers and magazines. The financial problems of the thrifts required some effort on the part of investigative reporters to follow: this was not part of the normal daily routine at most newspaper offices, focused as they are on getting out the next issue. And, as the decade progressed and the problems grew worse, the Bank Board and other federal regulators did their best to ensure the stories did not get out. A panicked public was most definitely not in the regulators' interests and would not look good for a government seeking re-election.

A few journalists did break the news of S&L collapses but, despite the magnitude of the money involved, the stories seemed to get lost in the fine print. Until Silverado.

The President's son, Neil Bush, was a director of Silverado Savings and Loan and this thrift collapsed in December 1998, just one month after the federal election. It owed an incredible $1.6 bn to depositors after having

5 *Washington Monthly*, March 1997.
6 Quoted in Steven Wilmsen, *Silverado: Neil Bush and the Savings & Loan Scandal*, p.19.

given out millions in loans to insiders and well connected real estate men. Suddenly the press had a poster boy, and the public had an image. Suddenly Joe Average realised he had been swindled. Even worse, it was he, the taxpayer, who the government was ordering to pay for it. Worse still, property values nation-wide were collapsing. Didn't they always go up? It looked like Neil was to blame.

Silverado had started life as Mile High Savings and Loan in 1956 and like every other S&L of the time did well following government instructions in the housing boom after World War II. Like most other thrifts, it found itself in trouble in the inflation and high interest rate environment of the 1970s. Helpfully, Mile High was taken over by Denver businessman James Metz. He renamed it Silverado, hired a new go-getting, image-conscious CEO, Michael Wise, to run it and moved the offices to a 'more suitable' downtown Denver address. Wise immediately took advantage of the new deregulation. He infused the thrift with new $100k deposits by promoting his new 'Silverado Prime', which guaranteed a higher rate of interest than any other thrift was offering. Commercial loans to much bigger real estate developers soon followed. The day Wise's thrift hit $1 bn in assets, he threw a party. A very emotional Wise handed out thousands of buttons and key chains that read, 'Thanks a billion, Jan 25, 1985'.

This is the banking world into which Neil Bush walked when he was invited by Michael Wise early in 1985 to join the board of Silverado. The advantages of having a Vice President's son (and presidential aspirant) among them was not lost on other Silverado board members.

Denver had been floating on oil for some years. The city was rich. 'Money was everywhere, and making it in great quantities was surpassed in importance only by spending it.'[7]

Steven Wilmsen writes of one oil magnate who built an 18-hole miniature golf course in his house because his daughter did not like waiting in line at the public facility down the road. Real estate developer Richard Rossmiller installed an elevator just to get him down to the wine cellar in his basement. The feeling was that Denver had finally become a real city.

> People were doing enormous second mortgages on their homes because property values were going up so fast you couldn't lose ... Bankers were lending money like crazy. We thought values would go up forever. Nobody could see an end in sight.
> Wilmsen, p.23

This was, after all, the city where oil billionaire Blake Carrington in the TV series *Dynasty* was living.

Silverado was determined not to miss out on the hay-making. Firmly encouraged by the government to lend themselves out of their inflationary troubles, the thrifts, including Silverado, proceeded to do just that.

7 Wilmsen, p.18.

> Loan officers handed out money wherever they could. They regularly invited other institutions and mortgage companies to send borrowers their way. They gave their loan forms to any mortgage company that would take them, not just in Colorado but across the country Wilmsen, p.46

Sometimes the thrift gave borrowers more money than they asked for: the fees it charged could be based on the amount of money borrowed, so the bigger the loan the bigger the fee. With a little help from those accounting rule changes, Silverado began to appear wildly profitable – on paper. Real estate developers climbed over one another to borrow money to buy vacant property or build offices, condos and strip malls. 'The demand for money was exceeded only by the rate at which real estate values climbed.'[8] Did it really matter if Silverado lent more money for a piece of dirt than it was really worth? In a year or two, even a couple of months if they were lucky, the dirt would be worth more. 'And so what if the loan went bad? Silverado could afford to chuck bad loans into a closet like used furniture; for every loan that went bad, it made ten new ones, using the fees to make up for losses on souring loans.'[9] Here was the problem that Neil Bush lacked the experience to see. Silverado, like other thrifts, was relying on high-cost borrowings (its deposits) to finance loans to people with doubtful ability to pay it back.

Within this world of borrowers and borrowings were an incestuous lot of real estate characters.

> Kenneth Good, a charming and free-wheeling huckster who had made and lost $1 million in Texas real estate by the age of 26, and was now using his high-wattage personality and borrowing power at Silverado to create his real estate empire and $10 million mansion on Cherry Hill, the largest home in Colorado. (15 bathrooms of exotic marble and wood, six kitchens, one of which was a catering kitchen with stainless-steel-edged granite counter tops, a wine cellar, guest suites with private offices in case the guests wanted to work, special plumbing throughout the house in which to pump scotch, gin or vodka direct from the wine cellar, health club, front-tennis court, racquetball court, bicycle trainers, electric massage table, saline flotation tub and marble walled male and female locker rooms to mention just a few of the attributes.)
>
> Bill Walters, an aggressive Denver developer who had built a $100 million net worth fuelled in large part by loans from Silverado and was now the chief of the city's Chamber of Commerce, and Larry Mizel, the chairman of MDC Holdings and more than 100 front companies that was using Silverado as his 'personal piggy bank'. *The Nation*, October 1, 1990

The trouble for Neil Bush was that Good ended up defaulting on $30m of his loans from Silverado, Walters on nearly $100m worth, and Mizel was trading MDC's undesirable land to Silverado in exchange for its non-performing derelict loans so that the books of both would present better.

8 Wilmsen, p.47.
9 Wilmsen, p.47.

CEO Wise, on behalf of Silverado, spared no expense in not highlighting to regulators such activities. All four were lavish in their contributions to Denver and the state's politicians, including having recently hosted a luncheon for President Reagan that had raised more than $1 m for the Party. Within weeks of Neil's appointment to the board he was voting to approve all those loans that would never be repaid. Worse, he had had prior dealings with both Walters (a friend of his dad's) and Good: they had provided the money for Neil's now floundering oil venture, JNB Exploration, which had opened for business at the tail end of the oil boom.

After 1986 the oil-driven real estate boom began to slow down; then it went bust. People stopped moving into the state. Vacancy rates climbed and property values began their long, slow deflation. It was obvious that downtown Denver had been 'seriously overbuilt'.[10] The relationship between the developers and Silverado now grew deeper and darker as both sides concocted arrangements to keep the other from collapsing. At Silverado 66 per cent of the loan portfolio was now concentrated in high-risk loans; some 22 per cent of its loans were already bad.[11] Perhaps Silverado's officers knew this, perhaps they didn't. When some of the developers who owed money came back to the thrift a year later, having paid back nothing on their first loan, Silverado would roll the whole loan over and give them more money on top to pay the new fees and next year's interest.[12]

Good and several associates 'traded two parcels of vacant land three times in six months with the value increasing each time' until they finally sold it to Silverado for a $3.2 m profit.[13] A pay-back, perhaps, for the time Good and Walters had helped Silverado increase its capital base by issuing stock to the men in exchange for real estate (the thrift then including the land in its capital on the balance sheet).

Silverado bought some land in the Arizona desert – dirt cheap – which MDC was selling. This allowed MDC to book a profit of 400 per cent on the sale. MDC had originally bought the land off Charlie Keating, or rather Keating's S&L, Lincoln Savings, which of course in turn had booked its profit. 'Completing the cycle', says Wilmsen[14] Silverado 'sold the property to a Nevada-based development firm called R.A. Holmes,' which regulators later proved was a front for Lincoln Savings.

In another deal,[15] MDC sold Rancho Acacia, several hundred acres of real estate in Southern California, to Silverado for $13.3 m. A few months later, MDC bought it back for $17 m. A few months after that MDC sold the ranch to Hamilton Homes, yet another Lincoln subsidiary, for $14.9 m. Everyone was a winner. Forbes in 1985 proclaimed MDC the nation's

10 Wilmsen, p.89.
11 Wilmsen, p.95.
12 *The Nation*, October 1, 1990.
13 Wilmsen, p.81.
14 Wilmsen, p.131.
15 Wilmsen, p.131.

fastest growing home builder. No wonder, with deals like that, and an obliging bank.

Then there was the new $2 bn airport, announced by Denver's Mayor Federico Pena in 1985. It was going to be

> the largest public works project in the nation and [would] become the busiest airport in the world … With huge open spaces, futuristic sculptures and forty-foot escalators leading to underground trains where passengers would be directed by electronic voices, the airport would make Denver the hub of the western United States, possibly the world. Wilmsen, p.136

And the land around the site – 15,000 acres – had just become the hottest development area in the country.

As luck would have it, Silverado had just, a few months before, paid an 'absurdly high $38,000 an acre'[16] for 39 acres of land that now was the most valuable plot in the whole site. MDC announced that it was holding another 877 acres nearby. Now that the news was public, Silverado, MDC and Bill Walters, amongst others, 'went crazy' buying land around the site. All $70 m worth of depositors' money was financed by Silverado.

> No sooner did [Silverado, MDC and Walters] have the property in their hands than they began buying and selling it amongst themselves, inflating the prices and making a killing each time [the] land changed hands … Thousands of acres of airport land moved in similar ways … Each time they all made money and Silverado was the piggy bank. Wilmsen, p.138

While all this was going on, Ken Good was discovered 'dating' Bill Walters' wife.

Swapping all this airport land was, of course, betting all the chips on one hand. It turned out that the airport was not a done deal. There were a number of government and voter hurdles still to be jumped before building could start. The Silverado players naturally backed pro-airport candidates at each election. 'Wise whipped his employees into a pro-airport frenzy … mounted telephone campaigns to encourage voters and volunteered to drive people to the polls …'[17]

In May 1988 the airport was finally approved – too late to save Silverado. The very next month, June 8, a Fort Worth real estate developer missed his $3 m payment on a loan from a Dallas bank, the holder of first lien on the property. Under the surprising terms of the loan, Silverado was now liable for this payment. The developer could not pay Silverado for its share of the loan ($74 m) either, so the Dallas bank foreclosed. Silverado became technically insolvent.

Silverado announced its worsening condition to the public on August 2. On August 7 the FHLBB sent $450 m to the thrift to cover deposit runs

16 Wilmsen, p.135.
17 Wilmsen, p.143.

and stave off collapse – in the middle of a presidential election campaign in which the Bush family was deeply involved.

On September 12 the FSLIC recommended Silverado be put into regulators' hands. An unexpected call to regulators from Washington said this ought to be put off for 45 days. Government work on the thrift stopped. George Bush was elected President on November 8. Silverado was seized by regulators on December 9.

In the wash-up Bill Walters defaulted on all his outstanding loans, moved to a California beach house, and filed for protection from his creditors through bankruptcy law. The airport land went back to the government. Ken Good's companies crumbled under the weight of debts and falling real estate values. The FDIC, into whose hands that \$10 m mansion had fallen, could not immediately sell the property as no one could afford to buy it. Neil Bush became the public's poster boy for all that was wrong in the thrift industry, but was in the end given the mildest possible penalty for a negligent thrift director. All up, it cost the government \$1.6 bn to repay Silverado depositors.

Finally, the Silverado board settled a \$200 m civil suit, brought against it by the FDIC, for \$49.5 m, Neil Bush handing over his own cash, most of which came from insurance claims.[18]

Asked by Congress what he might have done differently to avoid the \$1 bn-plus bill to taxpayers, Neil said: 'I wouldn't have allowed for that high a concentration of commercial real estate.'[19]

FURTHER READING

Charlie Keating and Lincoln Savings

Adams, James Ring. 'How to Win Friends and Influence Regulators: The Delayed Closing of Lincoln Savings Cost the Taxpayer \$1 Billion', *National Review*, Vol. 42, Issue 5, March 19, 1990, p.36.

Binstein, Michael and Charles Bowden. *Trust Me: Charles Keating and the Missing Billions*. Random House, New York, 1993.

Corn, David. 'People in Glass S&Ls', *The Nation*, Vol. 249, Issue 20, December 11, 1989, p.708.

Davis, L.J. 'Will Charlie Keating Ride Again?' *Washington Monthly*, Vol. 29, Issue 3, March 1997, p.28.

Fowler, Jack. 'The Keating Fizzle', *National Review*, Vol. 3, Issue 2, February 11, 1991.

Museum of American Financial History (www.financialhistory.org/fh/2002/75-1.htm).

Sherrill, Robert. 'The Looting Decade: S&Ls, Big Banks and Other Triumphs of Capitalism', cover story, *The Nation*, Vol. 251, Issue 17, November 19, 1990.

18 *Counterpunch*, 2004.
19 US Congress: House, 1990, p.132.

Simons, Teresa. 'Banking on Secrecy: With Our Banks about to Go the Way of Our S&Ls, It's Time We Made the Freedom of Information Act Cover Financial Institutions Too', *Washington Monthly*, Vol. 22, Issue 11, December 1990, p.31.

Neil Bush and Silverado Savings and Loan

'A Bank they Called Desperado', *New York Times*, July 17, 1990, p.A21.

'Hey Brother, Can You Spare a Million?', *Counterpunch*, April 3, 2004.

'Running with a Bad Crowd: How Neil Bush Let Himself Get Caught up in the $1 Billion Silverado Debacle', *The Nation*, Octonrt 1, 1990.

'Rush for Gold', *Time*, August 13, 1990.

Silverado Banking, Savings and Loan Association. Part I, *Committee on Banking, Finance and Urban Affairs*. 101st Congress, 2nd session. Washington DC: Government Publications Office.

'The Relatively Charmed Life of Neil Bush', *Washington Post*, December 28, 2003, p.D01.

Wilmsen, Steven. *Silverado: Neil Bush and the Savings and Loan Scandal*. National Press Books, 1991.

Acknowledgements

IT'S ALL Hari Seldon's fault, that psycho-historian living on Terminus City. Could the future really be forecast like that? I thought it worthy of some further study. Let the reader be the judge.

Fortunately, along the way, I ran into some wonderfully interesting individuals also keen on such a study, many of whom I must now thank. First and foremost, my continuing subscribers: too many to name, but you know who you are. Some amazingly talented people. I would particularly like to thank them for so many freely given testimonials over the years. It has been extremely gratifying to receive them. I know that this knowledge has immeasurably enriched many of you, and for yet others been a life-changing event.

Economic Indicator Services (EIS) would never have started without much help from a great mate, John Bennett. (Thanks JB.) Tough times at the start, as always. The School of Economic Science proved the soundness of the economics, particularly John Tippet, to whom I shall be forever truly grateful. The late eighties classes were nothing short of inspirational – had to be, given the timing every Friday night for three years. I found out why I am here. Can there be any better realisation? I have been working on that ever since.

The book could not have been written without the assistance of a goodly number of librarians in different parts of the world. In particular I must thank Doris and Zellie at the University of Missouri, St Louis (Thomas Jefferson Library, Western Historical Manuscript Collection) for generously allowing me free rein to study the Wenzlick material in their care.

Thanks to the Munich crew the times I was there, Jens and Gisela in particular, to Ros and the gang; Dom, Di and Jeff, and Sunday night Vietnamese where I could talk anything but the book, to Brendan and his sensational London cash-flow group, to Don in the UK for helping make London happen, to the EIS staff and codirectors, thanks awfully for the help (Dave, get your book out mate!), to Jeff Smith, Ed Dodson and Dave Giesen for some invaluable US guidance and talks, Linda for her kicks up the backside when crises of confidence threatened, and of course immediate family members, and mum and dad. With two mothers, I have been lucky in this regard.

To my publisher, Anthony Werner, I am grateful for his generous assistance in taking me through the maze that is publishing. Thanks also to those brave souls that took an interest in reviewing the manuscript and providing feedback: Bruce Kirkham, Steve Harvey, Bob Taylor, Colin Johnson and Howard Errey. I am also most grateful to Jean Desebrock for her patient editing. Writing a book is a lonely discipline that permits of little else but sitting down to write. Friends, now you know where I have been all those years. I do hope we can renew acquaintances once again very soon.

Index

ABN Amro (Netherlands) 5
Adelphia Communications 312
Agricultural Adjustment Act 249-50
Aldrich-Freeland Act 198
Allen, Frederick Lewis 230, 247
Amalgamated Copper 209-10
American Continental Corporation (ACC) 431-2
American Diversified Savings & Loan 420-1
American Home Mortgage Investment Corporation 8-9
American Motel Industries 423
Ames, Oakes 146, 148-9
Anarchists 208, 220
Asian economic flu 302-7
Australia 127, 206, 214, 220, 242, 275, 308, 310, 315, 317, 334-5, 342, 343, 346-7, 349, 364-5, 367, 369, 374

Bagehot, Walter 358
Bakunin, Michael 208
Baltimore Old Court Savings & Loan 414
Bank for Commerce and Credit International (BCCI) 287
Bank for International Settlements (BIS) 358
Bank of England 10, 35, 61, 86, 95, 110, 130, 270, 300, 333
Bank of New England (BNE) 285, 286, 301
Bank of North America 35-6, 48-9, 211, 357
Bank of Pennsylvania 122
Bank of Sandstone 102, 126
Bank of Tennessee 387-90
Bank of the United States, First (BUS) 37-43, 47, 49, 50, 51, 65, 82, 97, 100, 316
Baring Brothers Bank 184, 189, 190, 300, 357
Barnes, Peter 175-6
Barrons 248
Barton, Edmund 334
Baruch, Bernard 206
Bear Stearns 6-7, 11, 13, 17
Beebe, Herman K. 417, 422-4, 427
Beecher, Henry Ward 165
Bell Savings & Loan 420
Bennett, James Gordon 120-1
Benton, Senator Thomas Hart 76, 106
Benton (town) 151
Bentson, Lloyd 301
Berkeley, Sir William 19, 26
Bernanke, Ben 4
Bethlehem Steel 217, 230
Beverly Hills Bancorp 271
Biddle, Nicholas 78, 91, 92-3
Big Issue, The 334, 342
Billington, Ray Allen 31, 47
Billion Dollar Congress 182
Binstein, Michael & Bowden, Charles 431-4
Bland-Allison Act 178
BNP Paribas bank (France) 8
Brandeis, Louis D. 208
Brewton, Pete 424-7
Briloff, Abraham J. 404-5
Brooks, John 221, 259
Broward Federal Savings & Loan 427-8
Bryan, William Jennings 205 (n.2), 213
Buchanan, President James 103
Buffet, Warren 3, 273 (n.8)
Burr, Aaron 47-8
Bush, Jeb 427-8
Bush, Neil 286, 434-9
Bush, President George 286, 292, 294, 296, 297, 424-7
Bush, President George W. 4, 12, 14, 141, 313
Butler, Smedley D. 330

Calavita, K. *et al* 331, 409, 415-18, 421
Caldwell, Rogers 242, 316, 356, 387-90
Calomiris, Charles W. and Mason, Joseph R. 251-2
Canberra 335
Cantillon Effect 365-9

Cantillon, Richard 367, 368
Capital National Bank 188
Carlson, Mark 135
Carnegie, Andrew 166, 206
Cassel, Sir Ernest 97
Centennial Savings 410-14
Central Pacific railroad 147, 181
Centrust Savings Bank 282
Centrust Tower 287
Chambers, John 5
Chancellor, Edward 142-4, 161-2, 221
Chandler, Alfred 21-7, 43, 46, 56, 70, 91, 128, 141, 149, 162, 182-3
Chase Manhattan Bank 263, 392, 403
Chase, Salmon P. 117, 133, 153-5
Chemical National Bank of Chicago 187-8
Cheves, Langdon 56
Chicago 4, 81, 83-5, 88, 106, 113-15, 120, 122, 135, 142, 144, 150, 152, 157-60, 162-3, 171-6, 179-80, 187-9, 203-4, 206-9, 213, 216, 219-20, 226-7, 236, 237, 243-4, 246-7, 253, 255, 264, 272, 273, 309, 324-5, 343-5, 349, 365, 367, 386, 388
Christenson, Duayne 415
Citigroup 14, 311
Civil War 52, 75, 77, 97, 101, 102, 127, 133, 134, 140-2, 148, 152, 155, 157-9, 165-7, 170, 182, 183, 189, 208, 313, 329, 377
Clarke, Robert L. 426-7
Clemens, Samuel L. 146, 155
Clinton, President William Jefferson 78, 250, 301
collateralised debt obligations (CDOs) 6, 8, 17
Collins, Gail 165
Columbia National Bank 188
Columbia Savings and Loan 283, 293
Columbus, Christopher 21, 24, 174
Commager, Henry Steele 336
Continental Congress 30, 31, 33, 38
Cooke, Jay 143, 152-63, 169, 181, 316, 329
Coolidge, President Calvin 221, 228
copper price 6, 82, 209-11, 369-70
Corrigan, Gerald 291
Countrywide 4, 16-17
Cowan, David Jack 40, 41
Coxey, Jacob Sechler 12, 191
Credit Mobilier 147-9, 181
Crime of 1873 176-9
currency futures 156, 274, 305
Cushing First National 422
Davis, Dave 224
Davis, Mike 395, 396
Decker, Howell and Company 357
Denmark 336, 343, 348, 374
derivatives 4, 5, 17, 274-5, 299, 300, 305, 307
Desert Land Act 175
Dewey, Edward R. and Dakin, Edwin F. 353-4
Dice, Charles Amos 230
Dirks, Raymond L. 265, 392
Disraeli, Benjamin 228
Dixon, Don Ray 283, 417-18, 423
Dondi Finncial Corporation 417-18
Douglas, Stephen A. 146
Dow, Charles 45, 59, 91, 139-40, 161, 172
Dow Jones Index 205, 211-13, 217-18, 226, 229, 232, 233, 239, 240, 243, 252, 253, 256, 260, 261, 271, 293, 298, 299, 310, 313
Drew, Daniel 139, 141, 145, 161-2, 166
Du Pont 217, 329
Duer, William 37-42, 46, 47, 329
Duluth 152, 159, 163, 179
Durant, Thomas 146, 148

Ebbers, Bernie 311
Economic Indicator Services (EIS) xi, 5, 348, 353, 441
Efficient Market Hypothesis (EMH) 273
Ely, Bert 279
Empire Savings 409
Eno, John C. 172-3
Enron 235, 308, 310, 311, 397
Equity Funding Corporation 265, 392, 406-8
Exchange Bank of Shiawasee 126

Fannie Mae (Federal National Mortgage Association) 14, 15, 316
Faulkner, Danny 335, 409
Federal Deposit Insurance Corporation (FDIC) 15-17, 278-80, 286, 293, 294, 296, 297, 299, 309, 417, 419-20, 424, 428, 439
Federal Home Loan Bank Board (FHLBB) 279, 285, 294, 410, 438
Federal Reserve Act 198
Federal Reserve System 97, 197, 217-19, 221, 248, 255, 258
Federal Savings and Loans Insurance Corporation (FSLIC) 279, 285, 294, 409, 416, 418-20, 424, 427-8, 433, 439

First Magnus Financial Corporation 9
First Priority Bank 16
First United Fund (FUF) 418-20
Fisher, Carl 224-5
Fisher, Irving 203, 217, 228
Fiske, Jim 145-6, 166, 167
Florida 4, 15, 23, 81, 171, 181, 222-7, 249, 264, 265, 282, 391, 403, 404, 425-7
Foldvary, Fred 175, 377-8
Ford, Henry 217, 223, 248
fractional reserve banking 35, 59, 61-8, 77, 81, 98, 101, 116, 136, 200, 251, 302, 324, 327, 330, 335, 352, 373, 382
Franklin National Bank 13, 264, 271, 316, 398-401
Franklin, Benjamin 30, 43, 142
Franz Ferdinand, Archduke of Austria 215
Freddie Mac (Federal Home Loan Mortgage Corporation) 14, 15, 316
Freud, Sigmund 365
Fridson, Martin S. 213, 217, 218, 248, 256, 271, 301
Friedman, Milton 272-5, 278, 279, 354, 379

Galbraith, John Kenneth 47, 56, 61, 64-5, 116, 145, 152, 169, 177, 205, 259, 260, 262, 358, 379, 380
Gann, W.D. 161, 185, 212, 219, 232, 300, 321, 420
Garn-St Germain Depository Institutions Act 280, 416
Gates, John 146
Gateway Savings 420
Gaubert, Tom 283
George, Henry 127, 208, 355-6, 377
Gibbons, J.S. 123, 125, 131
Gilbert, Bradford Lee 366-7
Glass-Steagall Act 252
Glickman, Mike 285, 287
Glidden, Joseph 175
Golden Pacific Savings and Loan 421
Goldman Sachs 9
Gonzalez, Henry 292
Good, Kenneth 436, 438, 439
Gordon, John Steele 72, 77-8, 85, 86, 109-10, 113, 120, 145, 148, 211
Goude, William 56
Gould, Jay 145, 167
Granger movement 160, 193
Grant and Ward 172
Grant, James 291, 293, 298, 300
Grant, Phil 330
Grant, President Ulysses S. 145, 148, 164, 169, 172, 175
Great Depression 71, 86, 197, 221, 244, 251, 271, 277, 293, 299, 325-6, 335, 356, 389
Great Northern Railway 166
Green, Edwin 136, 215, 228
Green, Hetty 146
greenbacks 133, 141, 154
Greenspan, Alan 5, 269, 291, 294, 380, 381, 433

Haggin and Tevis 175-6, 335
Halifax Building Society 340
Hamilton, Alexander 32-7, 37, 39, 47, 48, 97, 125, 142
Hamilton, Charles 197, 219
Hancox, David R. 406-7
Hansen, Erwin 410-14
Haraszthy, Count Agoston 110-11
Harrison, Fred 9, 11, 222, 255, 263, 268, 270, 271, 325-7, 328 (n.10), 339-43, 378
Harrison, President Benjamin 169, 182, 184, 191
Harrison, William Peter 45, 139-40, 172
Hatry, Clarence 231-2
Heinze, F. Augustus 209-12
Hemingway, Ernest 330
Herman Schaffner & Co 188
Hill, J.J. 166
Hirtzel, Sir Arthur 219
Holiday Inn 257, 423, 434
Homestead Act 140-1, 175
Horan, James D. 243
Hoyt, Homer 3, 81, 83-4, 88, 106, 113-15, 120, 122-3, 152, 157-9, 161, 163, 171-4, 180, 187-90, 204, 206-7, 213, 216, 220-2, 226-7, 246, 253-5, 268 (Note 4), 324-5, 329, 376-7
Hull, Charles 434

IKB Deutsche Industriebank 7
IMF (International Monetary Fund) 14, 18, 302-3, 305, 313, 317
Independence of the Sea 12
Indian Springs State Bank 419, 425-6
IndyMac Bancorp 15
Insana, Ron 56, 72, 73, 105, 111, 112, 124, 272, 274-5, 285, 288
Insull, Samuel 236-7, 245

Integrated Resources 292-3
Intel 263

J.P. Morgan Chase 13
Jackson County Bank 102, 126
Jackson, President Andrew 52, 75-9, 85-6, 93, 106, 112, 140-1, 357
James, F.C. 244
Japan 262, 285, 343, 345, 346, 349
Jefferson, Thomas 32, 34-5, 47, 50, 72, 142
Jerome, Addison 146
Jerome, Leonard 121
Johnson, Paul 23-4, 28, 55, 56, 73-6, 182
Jones, Frederic J. 343-7, 349-50
Jung, Carl vi, 383

Keating, Charles 286, 287, 431-4, 437
Keep, Henry 146
Kemmerer, Edwin W. 198
Kennedy, Joe 250
Kern River 175, 335
Keynes, John Maynard 245, 254, 257-60, 270, 272, 274-5
Kimmitt, Robert J. 3
Kindleberger, Charles 91, 119, 127, 231, 246, 273
Kirk, Captain 332
KKR Financial Holdings 9
Klondike 206, 207
Knapp, Charles 296
Knickerbocker Trust Company 209, 211-12
Kredit-Anstalt bank (Austria) 7, 245
Kreuger, Ivar 235-6, 245
Kwitny, Jonathon 426-7

land price barometer 353, 364-5, 369
Lasker, Bernard J. 259
Latham, Frank B. 203
Lawrence, Joseph Stagg 203, 245-6
Laventhol, Kenneth 431
Lay, Kenneth 310-11
Lease, Mary Elizabeth 208
Leeson, Nick 184, 300
Lehman Brothers 14
Levitt, Jeffrey 414
Lewis, Michael 273-4, 278, 280-1
Lightner, Otto C. 87, 119-20
Lincoln Savings and Loan 286, 295, 431-4, 437
Lincoln, President Abraham 67, 133, 140, 141, 143-4, 152, 170 (Note)
Lindeman, J.B. 264
Livermore, Jesse 121, 209, 233
Long Term Capital Management 12, 302, 307
Long, Clarence D. 377
low documentation (low-doc) loans 315
Lozier 365
Lusitania 218

MacVeagh, Franklin 198
Madison Guaranty Savings and Loan 301
Maisel, Sherman J. 258
Manning Savings and Loan 421
Marx, Groucho 226, 233
McBirney, Edwin T. 283, 416-17
McCartney, Ernest Ray 167
McCaw, Craig 311
McGrane, Reginald Charles 75, 79-81, 84-5, 90-3, 107
McKenzie, Janet F. 415
MDC Holdings 436-9
Mellon, Andrew 221, 227, 240
Merkel, Angela 3
Merrill Lynch 11, 14, 420
Milken, Michael 275-6, 431
Miller, Henry 117-18, 323, 335
Mitchell, Charles 235
Molinaro, John L. 415-16
monetarism 272-4, 333
Monroe, President James 69, 76
Morgan, J.P. 13, 144, 146, 163, 206, 210, 212-13, 217, 219, 233, 235, 249, 311, 329, 387
Mormons 110, 151
Morris, Robert 32, 33, 35-6, 49, 329
Morse, Anthony 143, 146
Mozilo, Angelo 4, 16
Myers, Gustavus 151

Napoleon 65, 72, 332
national banking system 97, 102, 133-7, 152, 154-6, 189, 194, 197, 200, 214, 427
National Bureau of Economic Research (NBER) 324, 374 (Note 2)
National Endowment for the Preservation of Liberty (NEPL) 424
NetJ 310
New York Stock Exchange 42, 102, 112, 120, 130, 139, 162, 173, 186
Niles, Ezekiah 55, 58
Nixon, President Richard 261, 263, 264, 275, 356, 394-7

North American Savings and Loan 415
Northern Pacific railroad 152, 157, 159, 162, 163, 166, 169, 181-2, 187
Northern Rock 10, 11, 13
North, Oliver 424, 426
Noyes, A.D. 210, 211

Office of Thrift Supervision 15, 294
Ohio Life Insurance and Trust Company 105, 121-2, 128, 357
Old Court Savings and Loan 414
Oldenburg, J. William 410
OPEC (Organization of the Petroleum Exporting Countries) 262-3

Padover, Saul K. 166
Palmer National Bank 424
Palmer, Potter 158
Parker Vein Coal Company 126
Penn Central Transportation Company 261, 391-3, 404
Philadelphia and Reading Railroad 150, 185, 357
Phoenician Hotel 287-8, 433-4
Phyrr, Stephen A. *et al* 328
Pizzo, Stephen 297, 411-13, 416, 419, 422-4
Potter, Gary W. 425-6
Prins Valdemer 226
Proudhon, Pierre 208
Pullman, George 174

Rabinowitz, Alan 270, 376
Radio Corporation of America (RCA) 234
Raguet, Condy 53
Ramona Savings and Loan 415-16
Rand, Ayn 275
real estate clock xii, 11, 351, 359, 360-1, 368, 380-2
Real Estate Investment Trusts (REITs) 258, 260, 263, 265, 270, 300, 402-3
Reconstruction Finance Corporation (RFC) 248-9, 252
Renda, Mario 418-20, 425
Resolution Trust Corporation (RTC) 294-6
Rezneck, Samuel 45
Ricardo, David 53-4, 355, 377
Ricardo's Law of Rent 9, 313, 324, 333-7, 364, 378-80
Richardson, Reed 112
Riordon, J.J. 234
roaring twenties 221-2, 230, 434
Robbins, Roy 80-1, 141
Robinson, H.P. 203
Rockefeller, William 210, 211
Rogers, H.H. 210, 211
Roosevelt, President F.D. 248, 250-3, 268 (Note 3), 283, 385
Rothbard, Murray N. 28-9, 35-6, 50-4, 56, 59, 70, 82, 116, 152-6, 176, 227, 249, 252, 267-8, 330, 331, 355
Russian bond default 12, 302, 307-8

Sakolski, A.M. 80-1, 157, 166
Salerno, Joseph T. 331
Samuelson, Paul 379
Savings and Loan (S&L) scandal 276-86, 292-4, 296, 297, 299, 301, 356, 409-30, 431-40
Schabacker, Richard 230
Schumpeter, Joseph 339
Schuyler, Robert 125-6
Schwartz, Alan 13-14
Second Bank of the United States (Second BUS, SBUS) 53, 55-6, 58, 76-8, 81, 91, 93, 94, 97, 100-1, 106, 242-3, 316
Secrist, Ronald 265
Securities and Exchange Commission (SEC) 15, 17, 250, 312, 392, 397
Shah, Sid 411-14
Sharp, James Roger 77-8, 94, 108
Sherman Silver Purchase Act 178, 189, 205
Sherrill, Robert 425
Silverado Savings and Loan 280, 286, 295, 434-40
Simons, Algie Martin 35, 43, 58-9, 69
Sinclair, Upton 208
Singer Building 367, 368
Sloan, Alfred 232
Smith and Cole 57, 88-90, 108, 124
Smith, Adam 333, 367
Smith, C. Arnholt 264, 356, 394-7, 400
Smoot-Hawley Tariff 245
Sobel, Robert 82, 120, 126, 161, 210, 212, 230, 240-1, 258, 391
Soderling, Jay and Leif, 421
Sooners 182, 183
Soros, George 275
Sovereign Wealth Funds 14
Spargo, John 208
Sparks, Commissioner 182-3
Spero, Joan 398-400
Spiegel, Thomas 283, 293
Sprague, O.M.W. 184, 189, 214
Stamp, Lord Josiah Charles 61, 327

Stampp, Keneth M. 117, 119, 122, 123, 127, 128, 130, 146-7
Standard Oil 166, 208, 212, 219
State Savings (Salt Lake City) 410
Stearns, John L. 365, 366
Stiglitz, Joseph 18
Strong, George Templeton 105
Stroud, Hubert B. and Spikowski, William S. 264
structured investment vehicles (SIVs) 7, 8
Sullivan, Lawrence 245-6, 253, 268 (Note 3)
Sullivan, Mark 239
Summers, Lawrence 13
Sunbelt Savings and Loan 283, 416-17
Symmes, John Cleve 46

Tarbell, Ida 208, 386
Temperance Permanent Building Society 340
Terminating Societies 339, 340, 342
Thomas, Dana L. 111, 270, 323, 366, 402, 403
Thornburgh, Richard 296
Tobin, John W. 146
Toll Brothers 9
Tonkin Gulf 258-9
Townsend, Francis Everett 12, 251
Trump, Donald 300
Turner, Frederick Jackson 182
Tweed, William 164

Union Pacific railroad 147-8, 151, 157, 181, 187
United Copper 211
United Kingdom (UK) 7, 10-11, 12, 16, 18, 30, 56, 75, 91, 128, 206, 210, 217, 268 (Note 4), 270, 275, 315, 340, 342, 343, 349-50, 378
  Britain 11, 30, 31, 74-6, 85, 95, 110, 112, 127-8, 217, 219, 228, 334, 343, 378
  England 22, 24-6, 30, 51, 74, 100, 163, 173, 184, 225, 277, 287, 348, 333
US Financial Corporation (USF) 265, 404-5
US National Bank of San Diego (USNB) 264, 271, 356, 394-7
US Steel 206, 229, 233, 240

Vakulas, Anton R. 421
Valentine, Harold 292
Valentino, Rudolph 231
Van Buren, President Martin 85, 106
Van Vorst, Marie 208
Vanderbilt, Commodore Cornelius 139, 144, 146, 161, 167, 173, 181
Vans, The 234-5
Vernon Savings and Loan 283, 295, 417-18, 423
Villard, Henry 163
Vision Banc Savings 425
Volcker, Paul 273-4, 278, 355
von Rothschild, Baron Carl Meyer 163

Walker, Samuel H. 163
Walter J. Kassuba Realty 265, 402-3
Walter, R.H. 265
Walters, Bill 436-9
Washington, President George 27, 34, 42, 50, 72, 142
Wasson, James 422
Weber, Axel 10
Webster, Daniel 76, 93
Wenzlick, Roy 254, 325, 353-4, 375-7
Westgate-California Corporation 264, 394-7
Westgate Hotel 395
Whitney, Richard 233, 237
Wicker, Elmus 187, 188, 243-4
Wiggin, Albert 235
Wilmsen, Steven 280, 435-8
Wisconsin 80-1, 84, 117, 119, 122, 191
Woolworth building 357, 367, 368
World Bank 302, 307, 331
World's Fair 174, 179-80, 187-90, 236
Wynne, Nick 224

Yergin, Daniel 257
yield curve 6, 10, 294, 298-9, 308, 310, 314, 315, 353, 369-73
Young, Roy 203

Feedback

PHIL ANDERSON, and Economic Indicator Services (EIS), value your feedback. Tell us what you thought of the book. Anything we left out or could have better explained? Something more you would have liked to see in a book such as this?

Go to www.businesscycles.biz and simply click on the feedback form. We'd be delighted to hear from you.

Whilst there, you will find plenty of follow-up material and research. Try the FAQs for starters. The site also continues to update the information from September 7, 2008, the day I signed off on the book. No doubt there will have been a few more bank collapses since then, and further land price declines to add to the existing problems. This US (and worldwide) real estate cycle will trough 18 years after the last one back in 1992.

If you are really serious about knowing how to forecast the economy better, and wish to learn how to profit from this knowledge, you will find a subscription to the EIS service of great assistance, and fantastic value. Details are on the website (www.businesscycles.biz).

ALSO FROM SHEPHEARD-WALWYN

ISBN 978-0-85683-250-5
£30.00

ISBN 978-0-85683-241-3
£18.95

ISBN 978-0-85683-244-4
£16.95 pb

www.shepheardwalwyn.com